Essential Public Affairs for Journalists

Essential Public Affairs for Journalists

FOURTH EDITION

James Morrison

OXFORD
UNIVERSITY PRESS

Great Clarendon Street, Oxford OX2 6DP,

United Kingdom

Oxford University Press is a department of the University of Oxford.
It furthers the University's objective of excellence in research, scholarship,
and education by publishing worldwide. Oxford is a registered trade mark of
Oxford University Press in the UK and in certain other countries

First edition 2009

Second edition 2011

Third edition 2013

Impression: 1

Published in the United States of America by Oxford University Press
198 Madison Avenue, New York, NY 10016, United States of America

British Library Cataloguing in Publication Data

Data available

Library of Congress Control Number: 2014959633

ISBN 978-0-19-870875-9

Printed in Great Britain by
Ashford Colour Press Ltd, Gosport, Hampshire

For my beloved Annalise, Scarlet, Rosella, and Ivor Munro

New to this edition

- Details of the Coalition government's cuts programme and recent changes to the welfare system, education, the NHS, and local government.
- Developments in the on-going debate over Britain's future in the European Union, with fully up-to-date material on the rise of UKIP and the 2014 European Parliament elections.
- Updated with reference to the immediate aftermath of the referendum on Scottish independence.
- New key points sections at the end of each chapter, together with topical feature ideas to stimulate and inspire students to develop their own public affairs stories.

Preface—the changing face of public affairs

If a week is a long time in politics (as Harold Wilson may or may not once have said), then two years feels like an aeon. As I sat down to pen this fourth edition of *Essential Public Affairs for Journalists*, I was naive enough to think that, on this occasion, what lay ahead was little more than a light edit. Compared to the hefty rewrites necessary for the second and third editions—with some chapters requiring top-to-bottom surgery to absorb the scale of changes introduced since the previous volumes—this was certainly the case. Yet while the early legislative hyperactivity of the Lib–Con Coalition may have abated some time ago, the rollout of policy on the ground (successfully or otherwise) continues apace even now. And this was to say nothing of my 11th-hour scramble to tweak key sections to reflect the outcome—and likely consequences—of Scotland's independence referendum...

Beyond this, though, what new developments are there to report for the fourth edition—bereft of the eye-catching new initiatives and radical breaks with the post-war consensus that necessitated so many revisions for the third? Well, for starters, it is only now—two years after the biggest top-down reorganization of the National Health Service since its inception—that we can cast an eye, with some authority, over how the (not so) new structure is bedding down (if you'll pardon the pun). The same goes for the success of Michael Gove's mass rollout of academies and free schools, the implementation of the first, tentative, neighbourhood plans, and all manner of other 'Big Society'-inspired innovations, from police and crime commissioners (PCCs) to the trumpeted community rights to 'bid', 'build', and 'challenge'. Meanwhile, influenced by the rise of the United Kingdom Independence Party (UKIP), Britain's edgy relationship with the European Union (EU) continues to dominate media and political discourse (particularly on the Right) in a way that it hasn't since the heady days of John Major's 'Maastricht rebels' more than two decades ago.

This is to say nothing of the genuine political developments since last time: the privatization of Royal Mail; the post-Stafford creation of a Chief Inspector of Hospitals; Britain's long-awaited emergence from recession; the introduction of the 'bedroom tax', and the Department for Work and Pensions' stuttering new Universal Credit and disability benefit reforms; and Croatia's accession to the EU as temporary restrictions on migrants from Romania and Bulgaria were lifted. Then there is the million-dollar question of how Britain's new, supposedly tighter, system of banking regulation will play out now that the much-maligned Financial Services Authority (FSA) has finally expired.

But what of the book itself and its format? Two significant changes are worth noting on this occasion. First, mindful of the potential for a book of this kind to continue expanding in length exponentially, to make room for any and every new change in government, an executive decision was taken to slim down the volume somewhat compared to its predecessors. Although it would be a stretch to call this a leaner, meaner *EPAFJ*, it is some 15,000 words (35 pages) shorter than the last two editions—meaning that it has to work harder and faster than both. To this end, it has lost some of the (more distant) historical background, to accommodate all of the most important contemporary developments in public administration. Second, in place of the 'review questions' of old, we have endeavoured to give students of public affairs something for which many have been screaming all along: a short crib sheet, in the form of a bulleted list of 'key points', to take away from each chapter, to concentrate minds on the core facts and figures most vital to success in the Essential Public Affairs exam.

Happily, this is where the 'big' changes end, though, for this fourth edition. With the recently revised National Council for the Training of Journalists (NCTJ) programme of study now firmly in place, it has been possible to focus more closely than ever on honing the book and aligning it more precisely to the core concerns of the syllabus—while also (one hopes) retaining more than enough of use (and interest) to early-career journalists let loose in the field. Each fresh edition offers opportunities to amend and refine what has gone before, as well as to add new material (or, given the strictures of word counts, to substitute 'old' for 'new'). And, given the relative lightness of the rewrites needed for this new edition, I have had more time to tweak and improve the *existing* content than previously. So don't be surprised to find some added value woven in this time—from tips on how to 'visualize' (and make sense of) the sea of data unleashed by councils in the name of the Coalition's transparency drive, to details of just how much the Queen does salter away in her personal stash of money, the Privy Purse. Next time around, though, expect bigger changes: with a general election fast approaching and the longer-term fallout from the Scottish referendum yet to emerge, who knows what the government (whatever its complexion) will have in store for us come 2017?

JM

Praise for *Essential Public Affairs for Journalists*

An essential guide for everybody in our trade. Finding your way around public bodies and laws is to discover how much of Britain works. And his time in journalism has taught James Morrison what journalists need to know: where and how to find stories.

Kevin Maguire, Associate Editor, *The Daily Mirror*

A work of extraordinary range and ambition that brilliantly succeeds in laying bare the workings of our nation. Above all else this is a readable, useable book; the information is accessible and the analysis is snappy and fair-minded.

Justin Webb, Presenter, The Today Programme, BBC Radio 4

If this compendious volume had been at my elbow, explaining how all the bits join together as I started out in journalism, many things would be been easier to understand and write about.

Michael White, Assistant Editor and former Political Editor, *The Guardian*

Journalists need to know what they need to know. Government, at every level, and public bodies are where they will find the stories that really affect their readers, listeners, and the viewers. This is a practical guide to help cut through the bureaucracy, jargon, smoke-screens, and secrecy.

Bob Satchwell, Executive Director, Society of Editors

Acknowledgements

I would like to thank my colleagues on the NCTJ's public affairs board. Thanks, too, are due to the various other lecturers and journalists who reviewed the chapters as I wrote them, for their invariably salient advice. Special mention must go to Ron Fenney and to David Kett (the nearest that Britain has, surely, to a public affairs guru) for the huge amount of legwork that they both did before me to make sense of the tangle of legislation and 'officialese' that bedevils local and central government today. I would also like to thank the Department for Communities and Local Government (DCLG), the National Archive, and the Economic and Social Research Council (ESRC) for their prompt responses to requests for data, and their willingness for us to reproduce tables and charts (which we have credited where this is the case). Finally, thanks to the various other government departments, executive agencies, and quangos that have helped with enquiries in one way or other both in relation to this and the previous editions: HM Treasury; the Department for Work and Pensions (DWP); the Foreign and Commonwealth Office (FCO) Europe Delivery Group; the School Improvement Division of the Department for Education (DfE); the Care Quality Commission (CQC); the Department of Health (DoH); the United Nations Department of Public Information (UNSPI); the Directorate General for Budget of the European Commission (DG Budget); and the Institute of Fiscal Studies (IFS).

For permission to reproduce articles and documents in the topical feature ideas we are grateful to Wales Online (www.walesonline.co.uk), BBC News online (www.bbc.co.uk/news), The City of Edinburgh Council, Bristol City Council and Grant Thornton UK LLP, City of Bradford Metropolitan District Council, the *Yorkshire Evening Post*, the *Oxford Mail*, and Peterborough City Council. Finally, I'd like to thank the 'class of 95' on my first paper, the *North Devon Journal*—James Cornish, Mark Devane, Tahira Yaqoob, Kent Upshon, Matt Radley, and Rob Baker—for keeping my spirits up.

Every effort has been made to trace and contact copyright holders, but this has not always been possible. If notified, the publisher will undertake to rectify any errors or omissions at the earliest opportunity.

Brief contents

Detailed contents

Guide to the book's features

Each chapter in Essential *Public Affairs for Journalists* contains a selection of features to help you to navigate your way through the book and to direct you to sources of further information.

> devolution Constitutional concept of delegating a degree of power from central parliament to regional and/or local assemblies. In the UK, Scotland, Wales, and Northern Ireland were all granted devolution in 1998—with the Scottish gaining the most powers, including the right to vary income tax by up to 3 pence (later 10 pence) in
>
> 1999, every he entitled by bir of Lords, but a have since bee colleagues) ha removed under Act 1999.
>
> election deposit D candidate who

Glossary terms

Key terms are emboldened in the text and are defined in a glossary at the end of the book.

> ☰ Topical feature idea
>
> Low voter turnout has been a mounting problem in all ty recent decades. Although 2010 saw an increase, only are electors actually turned out on polling day. With the 201 your editor wants a background feature looking at the is various ways in which it might be boosted. What was tur

Topical feature ideas

Topical feature ideas at the end of chapters suggest possible sources for a story on each subject.

> ✳ Current issues
>
> ■ **The rise of UKIP and other minority parties** The Lib-
>   80-year hegemony of the 'two-party' system, and the
>   elections suggest that we are entering a new era of 'f
>   Dems and UKIP as third and fourth, respectively). De
>   in the 2011 referendum, British voters have demonst

Current issues

Current issues highlight contemporary topics that are particularly relevant to journalists and provide a starting point for further exploration.

> ▦ Key points
>
> 1. The NHS operates on the principle that it is a 'univer
>   be accessed by British residents 'free at the point of
> 2. It is funded from a combination of general taxation a
>   80:20 per cent split. At least £60 billion of its annual
>   the control of clinical commissioning groups (CCGs)

Key points

A bulleted list outlining core facts and figures most vital to success in the Essential Public Affairs exam is supplied at the end of each chapter.

Further reading

Take your learning further by using the reading lists at the end of each chapter to find more detailed information on a specific topic.

→ **Further reading**

Cooper, K. and Macfarland, C. (2012) *Clubbing Together: Communities*, London: ResPublica. **Report by 'Red To how community-based social activities, clubs, and so Society-style projects delivering public benefit.**
Hodge, M., Leach, S., and Stoker, G. (1997) *Local Governm*

In the margin, you will also find a number of icons with the following meanings:

This icon indicates discussion of an issue concerned with **devolution** in the United Kingdom. It allows you to see at a glance where devolved subjects are explored.

This icon occurs where there is discussion of public affairs **reporting in practice**.

The **Online Resource Centre** icon appears to remind you when additional or updated material can be found on the book's accompanying website: www.oxfordtextbooks.co.uk/orc/morrison4e/

Guide to the Online Resource Centre

Essential Public Affairs for Journalists is accompanied by an Online Resource Centre that features a range of helpful additional materials to augment the printed text. These resources are available free of charge and can be found online at:

www.oxfordtextbooks.co.uk/orc/morrison4e/

Regular updates
Key new developments in public affairs are succinctly summarized so that you can always keep up to date.

News feeds
Links to real articles from various news sites are provided via RSS.

Additional and updated tables

Tables with information that changes regularly can be found in an updated form online, alongside additional tables that do not appear in the book.

Topical feature ideas

Further topical feature ideas are provided to help you to consider where to find a story or to prepare for the NCTJ portfolio assessment.

Web links

Useful websites relating to the topics in each chapter are listed to allow you to find further information.

Introduction

▶ Confessions of a local council reporter

I'll always remember the name Mervyn Lane. From the moment I arrived as a naive raw recruit on the *North Devon Journal* in Barnstaple—bristling with high ideas, most of them hugely unrealistic and some more than a little 'conspiracy theorist'—Mervyn and I were destined to clash. I'd been taken on as a junior reporter without a car (or, for that matter, a driving licence) and was hired only on condition I passed my test within six months of starting. Logically enough, I was immediately posted to Bideford—the area's 'second town', some 10 miles west of the paper's Barnstaple headquarters—but still expected to soldier into head office each day, and to cover a sprawling patch of rustic terrain into the bargain.

To top it all, I was required to generate a district edition single-handedly each week, filling three pages of news and finding at least one front-page lead without fail. Bideford being Bideford, there were few obvious sources of scoops: the edgiest events tended to be an annual Easter fair, known dubiously (but all too descriptively) as 'Cow Pat Fun Day', and the occasional drugs raid on a pint-sized sink estate at East-the-Water, the town's ungrammatically named answer to Moss Side.

Unsurprisingly, it wasn't long before I was turning to the local authority for inspiration (or, more accurately, out of desperation). Little did I know how fruitful this would be. Those wintry evenings spent pinching myself awake through meetings of Torridge District Council's planning committee invariably threw up a last-minute gem that, with a bit of creative editing (and barring news of an international sheep-rustling scam), would generate enough ire to merit a splash.

From the humdrum ('Supermarket Threat to Town Centre') to the absurd ('Ships in Our Back Garden'), Torridge seldom failed to deliver the goods.

Inevitably, it was only a matter of time before I crossed swords with the venerable Mr Lane—at that time leader of the district council's ruling Liberal Democrat group, chairman of its powerful policy and resources committee, and both a Bideford town councillor and Devon county councillor to boot.

The first of our many run-ins was sparked by a front-page story I wrote about a decision to award free parking permits to all Torridge councillors and 92 senior officers (dubbed 'essential users' by the council) for use in council car parks in central Bideford whenever they were on local authority business. As controversies go, this may sound small beer—there was nothing illegal or improper about the policy—but, boy, did it upset the locals. To understand the scale of the furore among residents and businesses, a little context is needed. Parking and the wider subject of transport were perhaps the most toxic issues facing Bidefordians. For various reasons, driving was pretty much the only way most people had of gaining access to the town for shopping or tourism, thanks to a train line that was (literally) a museum piece (take a bow Dr Beeching) and an antediluvian bus service. The notoriously perilous North Devon Link Road and a winding, hazardous 'coastal route' were all that connected it to civilization (or Barnstaple, at any rate)—providing lifelines for those living in outlying villages. Yet, in central Bideford—in the words of one councillor, 'a medieval town with a twentieth-century traffic problem'—any street wide enough to admit vehicles seemed to have been daubed with double yellow lines, putting the limited parking spaces available at a premium. Hence the incendiary reaction.

My parking story was one of many to irritate Mr Lane during my 18-month tenure as Bideford district reporter. But he wasn't the only local dignitary to be the focus of embarrassing headlines on the *Journal* during this time . . .

Let's not forget George Moss, the Bideford mayor who arrived in full regalia to turn on the town's Christmas lights one November only to find that a timer switch had done so automatically several hours earlier—the moment dusk had descended. He didn't fare any better a year later, when the precautions that council engineers took to avoid a similar fiasco proved so watertight that the lights couldn't be switched on at all.

Of course, council stories don't need to emanate from committee meetings—or, for that matter, councillors. Take the example of Les Garland, a community activist from Northam—a strip of suburban housing, pockmarked with scrappy golf courses, which runs along the Torridge Estuary to the east of Bideford. Armed with little more than a tape measure, he led a one-man campaign to rid the whole of Devon of the peril of 'hazardously placed' A-boards. (To the uninitiated, A-boards are the signs one finds outside newsagents bearing misspelt headlines from papers such as the *Journal*.)

Insisting that they posed a hazard to pedestrians, by blocking pavements and tripping people up, Les set about scouring the small print of Devon County Council's highways regulations—not to mention various Acts of Parliament—in search of a clause that would back his assertion that they contravened health and safety legislation. I clearly remember a conversation with an apoplectic county councillor, who stormed into the *Journal's* Bideford office to inform me that the county could be faced with rewriting its entire highways policy, at a cost of tens of thousands of pounds, if Les were to force the issue.

Perhaps inevitably, Les had the last laugh. When I last visited North Devon, in 2003, I picked up a copy of that hallowed Bideford edition of the *Journal*. Turning to the district pages, I was greeted by a familiar visage, grinning at me over a caption about a good citizenship award he'd received for serving the local community. As I wandered down Bideford high street later that day, I couldn't help noticing that several shops still had A-boards placed perilously distant from their doorways—but the memory of Les's beaming face reminded me that, in one way or other, his dogged devotion to civic duty had paid off.

My purpose in highlighting these anecdotal examples is to illustrate a simple point: that knowledge of public affairs (and, for the rookie journalist, local government especially) *matters*. Whether it be protests by angry parents over changes to school catchment areas, demands from worried residents for 'speed bumps' to prevent accidents on dangerous roads, or controversies about New Age traveller camps, waste disposal sites, or parasitical out-of-town superstores, local newspapers are chock-full of council-related stories on a daily and weekly basis. And to identify, research, and write up these stories in a way that is comprehensible and meaningful to their readers, journalists first need to grasp the basics of how government works and the parameters within which it operates.

This book aims to make that process easier.

1

The British constitution and monarchy

▶ What is a 'constitution'?

For any state to achieve a sense of order and identity, it requires its subjects to recognize a shared set of values. Such values tend to be instilled by a system of fundamental laws and principles, and upheld by parliaments, courts, and other institutions established to maintain and reinforce them.

This notion of shared membership, of collective rights and responsibilities—as common to commercial companies and supranational organizations such as the European Union (EU) as states or governments—is known as a 'constitution'.

Constitutions come in all shapes and sizes. They can be formal or informal, long or short, absolute or merely advisory. Most significant, though, is the difference between the two broad types of constitution adopted by individual states: *written* and *unwritten*. Naturally, for any set of ideas related to one's citizenship of a state to be sustained effectively, some kind of written record must exist. Yet there is an important distinction between constitutions described as 'written' and those that are not. All constitutions of any value comprise elements written in a *literal* sense—for example laws set down in documentary form. But this does not make them 'written constitutions' per se. Written constitutions are, rather, *codified* frameworks: single manuscripts summarizing the rights, values, and responsibilities attached to 'membership' of a state.

For historical reasons, some states have adopted written constitutions while others have not. Written constitutions have tended to emerge in countries undergoing sudden transformations in their entire systems of government following political upheavals such as wars, invasions, or revolutions. This was certainly the case for two nations with which the term is perhaps most closely associated—France and the United States—both of which adopted their codified constitutions following popular uprisings against oppressive elites (the French royal family and the British government respectively).

The origins and sources of the British constitution

Britain—more accurately, the 'United Kingdom of Great Britain and Northern Ireland'—is a different case entirely. The story of the UK's constitutional evolution is of the gradual unification of disparate kingdoms under one national sovereign (monarch), followed by a long struggle for supremacy between sovereign and Christian Church, and ultimately between Crown and Parliament. More recently, the union of Britain's four component nations—England, Scotland, Wales, and Northern Ireland—narrowly avoided dissolution, after Scottish residents voted to reject independence in September 2014.

As these various power struggles have played out, at several points in history Britain has come close to adopting a formal framework specifying its citizenry's rights and responsibilities, but has yet to do so. Although documents of various kinds form a huge part of the constitutional framework governing UK citizens, there exists no single statement of principles. Therefore, in defiance of campaigns by pressure groups ranging from the Chartists of 1848 to the coalition of liberal thinkers who revived their name 140 years later with Charter 88, officially Britain's constitution remains unwritten.

As such, the British constitution has clear advantages: it is *flexible* enough to be amended or supplemented according to the will of Parliament, without any of the tortuous procedures required whenever the slightest break with tradition is sought in the United States, France, or the UK's nearest neighbour Ireland. In light of the narrowness of Scotland's 'no' vote, this flexibility is certain to be called on in coming years to allow a significant transfer of legislative powers to Britain's individual nations—and perhaps even regions. Conversely, unwritten constitutions have the disadvantage of provoking as much wrangling among lawyers, politicians, and historians as they ever circumvent, by leaving layers of ambiguity around sometimes crucial issues relating to their subjects' liberties and entitlements. Former Prime Minister Gordon Brown's controversial decision to sign the European Union's 2007 Lisbon Treaty—seen by some as a 'European constitution' in all but name—demonstrates how easily Britain can adopt significant changes to its constitutional fabric without any of the debate rendered necessary by rigid rule systems in other countries. Meanwhile, the perceived assault on individuals' civil liberties represented by the rash of anti-terror legislation following the attacks on the Twin Towers on 11 September 2001 were viewed by some human rights campaigners as examples of the dangers of failing to enshrine core principles in a solid constitutional statement.

So what are the primary sources of Britain's constitution? Its main components fall into the following five categories:

- *statute*—individual laws or 'Acts of Parliament';
- *common law*—sometimes known as 'judge-made' or 'case' law, or 'precedent';
- *conventions*—customs, traditions, and long-standing practices;

- *treatises*—historical works of legal and/or constitutional authority; and
- *treaties*—EU and other international agreements.

Statute

Magna Carta (the Great Charter), signed by King John in 1215, is often cited as the foundation stone of Britain's constitution, because it invokes the principle of **rule of law**. This embodied the inalienable right of any citizen accused of a crime to a free and fair trial before his peers and, crucially, enshrined the principle that no one—not even a reigning sovereign—was 'above the law'. Of course, the idea that the Queen could be prosecuted is (like many constitutional concepts) somewhat problematic. In practice, because criminal prosecutions are instigated in the name of the Crown, if the monarch were to be brought before a court of law, this would provoke a constitutional crisis.

Perhaps more significant even than Magna Carta was the 1689 Bill of Rights, passed in the wake of the turbulent period stemming from the execution forty years earlier of King Charles I, and the 11-year interregnum that followed under his vanquisher, Puritan 'Lord Protector' Oliver Cromwell. Although titular head of the Church of England, Charles was felt by many to be too sympathetic to Roman Catholicism, having married the Catholic Princess Henrietta Maria of France. There was also deep unease about his invocation of the loose constitutional principle (popular among medieval monarchs) of the 'Divine Right of Kings'—a notion that the sovereign's authority was unchallengeable because it derived from his or her relationship to God. In the event, the Parliamentarians vanquished Charles's Royalist supporters in the ensuing English Civil War (1642–51), ending centuries of rule under this premise.

The Bill of Rights itself arose out of the alliance between the Protestant-dominated Parliament and William of Orange, the Dutch king whom it helped to depose Charles's younger son, James II, during the 'Glorious Revolution' of 1688. Having worked in an uneasy stalemate with James's elder brother, Charles II, following his return from exile in France after Cromwell's death in 1660, Parliament used the ascension of his uncompromising sibling (a devout Catholic) as a pretext for cementing its constitutional supremacy.

To this end, it identified James's Protestant daughter, Mary, as rightful heir. Together with her husband, William, Mary effectively deposed James. In exchange for Parliament's loyalty, they permitted the passage of the Bill, which formalized for the first time the transfer of constitutional supremacy from Crown to elected Parliament. Its central tenet ratified the principle that future sovereigns could rule only *through* Parliament—rather than by telling it what to do, as before. In other words, monarchs would have to seek formal consent from members of Parliament (MPs) before passing legislation (Acts), declaring war, or invoking other sovereign powers that they had traditionally wielded.

The Bill therefore effectively ended centuries of 'royal sovereignty' and ushered in the concept of **parliamentary sovereignty**.

This core constitutional principle symbolizes the oft-cited flexibility of an unwritten constitution. The term 'sovereignty'—or **political sovereignty**—refers to the notion of an individual or institution exercising supreme control over a geographical realm/people. Parliamentary sovereignty flows from this: as well as asserting the authority of the *institution* of Parliament over British subjects, it confers on *individual* parliaments—the bodies of MPs elected at given general elections—authority to make their own laws and to repeal any passed by previous parliaments. To this extent, it prevents any one parliament being 'bound by the actions of a predecessor'.

Many constitutional experts argue that this idea is incompatible with a conventional written constitution, because if we had such a document, one parliament could theoretically use its sovereignty to repeal the Act that introduced it. Advocates of a codified document dismiss this argument as bogus, contending that many countries with written constitutions manage to maintain them alongside their own versions of parliamentary sovereignty without encountering such conflicts. One way of embedding a written constitution into a state's political fabric is to compose a web of interlocking legislation, rather than simply passing individual Acts—making it harder to repeal. Another might be to set up an independent superior court to adjudicate in constitutional disputes. Britain's Supreme Court (see Chapter 2, 'From Wakeham to the Coalition—what next for the Lords?') could conceivably fulfil this role.

In addition to formalizing the notion of parliamentary sovereignty, the Bill of Rights granted several privileges to all 'Englishmen'—with the exception (in certain cases) of Roman Catholics. Its main tenets are listed in the table entitled 'Main entitlements listed in Bill of Rights 1689', to be found on the **Online** **Resource Centre** that accompanies this book.

It also specified conditions governing the future succession of the monarchy, in light of the coronation of William and Mary over the dethroned James II:

- James's flight from England following Mary's accession was defined as an 'abdication';

- William and Mary were officially declared James's successors; and

- the throne should subsequently pass to Mary's heirs, then her sister, Princess Anne of Denmark, and her heirs, then to heirs of William by later marriage.

Finally, the Bill also introduced a further constitutional principle fundamental to the workings of today's Parliament. Often incorrectly described as a 'convention' (rather than a product of statute, which it is), this is **parliamentary privilege**. In brief, parliamentary privilege enables any MP sitting in the House of Commons or peer in the House of Lords to make accusations about individuals or companies in open debate in the chambers without fear of prosecution for defamation.

Recent years have seen several high-profile examples of parliamentary privilege being used by members to 'name and shame' private individuals in ways that would be considered defamatory (and invite legal action) if repeated outside Parliament. In 2001, for example, Peter Robinson, then deputy leader of the Democratic Unionist Party (DUP), used it to 'out' Brian Keenan and Brian Gillen as members of the Provisional Irish Republican Army (IRA) ruling Army Council.

A flipside of the legal protection afforded by parliamentary privilege is the fact that certain words and phrases are construed as 'un-parliamentary language' and therefore unacceptable if directed at fellow members in either chamber. Most notorious is the word 'liar', which is held to conflict constitutionally with the freedom given to members under parliamentary privilege to speak their minds. In November 1993, then DUP leader the Reverend Ian Paisley was famously suspended from the Commons for five days for accusing Prime Minister John Major of lying after it emerged that, despite previously insisting that the idea of negotiating with Northern Irish republicans (whom he dubbed 'terrorists') would 'turn his stomach', he'd held secret talks for more than a year with Sinn Féin, the main republican party.

More recently, Commons Speaker John Bercow has frequently berated MPs for hurling insults: in May 2012, he ordered David Cameron to apologize for dismissing Shadow Chancellor Ed Balls as a 'muttering idiot' while answering Prime Minister's Questions (see Chapter 2, 'Question Time'). Controversially, the following month he failed to reprimand Shadow Immigration Minister Chris Bryant for accusing Culture Secretary Jeremy Hunt of having 'lied' to the Commons over the extent of his contacts with senior figures at News Corporation during the run-up to a decision by Ofcom about whether it should be allowed to buy up BSkyB (see Chapter 3, 'Press'). On this occasion, Mr Bercow cited an obscure ruling to justify his leniency: namely, that Mr Bryant's language was acceptable in light of the fact that the Opposition motion being debated by MPs concerned the question of 'whether he [Hunt] breached paragraph 1.2c (giving accurate and truthful information to Parliament)... of the Ministerial Code'. In other words, the motion implicitly revolved around Mr Hunt's honesty.

Just as parliamentary privilege protects MPs and peers from being sued in court for defamatory statements made in Parliament, it also safeguards the media, to some extent, from action arising out of repeating those claims: contemporaneous reports of what is said in either chamber, as well as parliamentary committee rooms, are covered by *qualified privilege*. By way of further complicating explanations of this privilege, however, according to a literal interpretation of the Bill of Rights it also protects the press from proceedings arising from 'a report alleging wrongdoing in Parliament by an MP'. This legal argument enabled *The Guardian* to defend a libel action brought in 1996 by former Conservative minister Neil Hamilton over its allegations two years earlier that he had accepted cash from Harrods owner Mohamed Al Fayed for asking parliamentary questions designed to advance the latter's business interests. To further muddy the constitutional waters, as a sitting MP Mr Hamilton had to obtain formal permission to sue the newspaper in the first place. In the event, a new clause was inserted into the 1996 Defamation Act (section 13) enabling him to waive his right to parliamentary privilege by suing the newspaper as a private citizen (an action that, in any event, failed).

In November 2008, a row erupted about a more obscure aspect of parliamentary privilege when it emerged that the Conservatives' immigration spokesman, Damian Green, had been arrested and questioned by police over allegations that he unlawfully solicited leaks about government policy from a Home Office civil servant. Both Opposition and government MPs united in criticizing the police action. Many saw it as an abuse of the long-established constitutional right of members to conduct free and open conversations with officials in the Palace of Westminster—and a throwback to Charles I's challenge to parliamentary freedoms in the seventeenth century. Members on all sides turned their fire on then Commons Speaker Michael Martin, who, as its overall custodian, was accused of allowing officers to search Mr Green's office—potentially jeopardizing the confidentiality of sensitive information relating to his constituents.

Perhaps the most contentious attempt to use parliamentary privilege as a protection was the interpretation cited by Labour MPs Elliot Morley, Jim Devine, and David Chaytor, and Tory peer Lord Hanningfield after they were each charged with false accounting over their Commons expenses claims. They invoked Article 9 of the 1689 Bill of Rights to argue that, because any alleged wrongdoing had been committed by them while performing official duties, it was for Parliament alone to try and (if necessary) punish them. In the event, the courts dismissed their argument and all four were convicted (see Chapter 2, 'MPs, conflicts of interest, abuses of privilege—and how to avoid them').

Of Britain's other key constitutional statutes, the most historically significant are the 1701 Act of Settlement and 1706–07 Acts of Union. The former built on the newly introduced rules relating to monarchical succession in the Bill of Rights by setting out the conditions for future sovereigns, as outlined in the table entitled 'Rules governing monarchical succession in the Act of Settlement 1701', to be found on the **Online Resource Centre**. Its principal condition—that Roman Catholic heirs or those who married Catholics should be barred from inheriting the Crown—remained in place for 324 years, until the Succession to the Crown Act 2013 (see 'The succession' in this chapter).

The Acts of Union, meanwhile, were twin laws passed first in England, then Scotland, in 1706 and 1707 respectively, which formalized the overarching Treaty of Union—the agreement unifying the countries as one United Kingdom

Table 1.1 Key statutes absorbed into the UK constitution in the twentieth century

Statute	Effect
Race Relations Acts 1965, 1968, and 1976	Outlawed racial discrimination
Government of Scotland and Government of Wales Acts 1998	Paved way for national referendums to establish devolved power in Scotland and Wales
Human Rights Act (HRA) 1998	Incorporated into British law the European Convention on the Protection of Human Rights and Fundamental Freedoms (the European Convention on Human Rights, or ECHR), signed by the Council of Europe in 1950
House of Lords Act 1999	Removed all but 92 hereditary peers then remaining and created 'transitional' Lords to remain until decisive reform agreed by both Houses (see Chapter 2, 'The House of Lords Act 1999')

under a single sovereign and Parliament. Key Acts absorbed into UK law more recently include those listed in Table 1.1.

The penultimate Act listed in Table 1.1—the Human Rights Act (HRA) 1998—justifies some discussion here, given the growing contention by many lawyers, human rights campaigners, and constitutional experts that it conflicts with Britain's constitution as it previously stood. For this and other reasons, the Conservatives entered the 2010 election with a manifesto commitment to replace it with a new Bill of Rights tailored specifically to UK citizens. But their plans to repeal the HRA were put on hold after they were forced into coalition with the Liberal Democrats (committed supporters of the Act). To this day, tensions continue with the European Court of Human Rights (ECtHR)—the principal court of the Council of Europe, the body that established the European Convention on Human Rights (ECHR—see Chapter 10, 'The Council of Europe'). The Court has repeatedly demanded that Parliament abandon its long-standing opposition to allowing convicted prisoners the vote (see Chapter 4, 'The British franchise today—who can vote?'). And in October 2014 both Home Secretary Theresa May and Prime Minister David Cameron confirmed that the 2015 Tory manifesto would contain a promise to replace the HRA with a new 'British Bill of Rights'. Although it received royal assent in November 1998, the HRA came into force only in October 2000. Among its stipulations was that every future Bill put before Parliament must now include a preface confirming that the relevant secretary of state is happy that it conforms with the Convention. The main rights safeguarded by the Convention are as outlined in Table 1.2.

In addition, the UK has accepted the First and Sixth (now Thirteenth) Protocols to the ECHR, of which there are 14 altogether. The First Protocol includes additional rights for property (Article 1), education (Article 2), and free and fair elections (Article 3). The Thirteenth Protocol formally abolishes the death penalty.

Table 1.2 Articles of the European Convention on Human Rights (ECHR)

Article	Right or freedom enshrined
1	Obligation to respect human rights
2	Life
3	Protection from torture and inhuman or degrading treatment
4	Protection from slavery and forced or compulsory labour
5	Right to liberty and security of person
6	Right to a fair trial
7	Protection from retrospective criminalization of acts or omissions
8	Protection of private and family life
9	Freedom of thought, conscience, and religion
10	Freedom of expression
11	Freedom of association and assembly
12	Right to marry and found a family
13	Freedom from discrimination
14	Prohibition of discrimination
15	Derogations
16	Exemption for political activities of aliens
17	Prohibition of abuse of rights
18	Limitations on permitted restrictions of rights

Although the HRA has, in theory, strengthened the ability of ordinary people to challenge the actions of governments, public bodies, and private companies in British and EU courts, by taking legal action through the ECtHR, there are limits to its pre-eminence, as test cases have demonstrated. By general consensus, the principle of parliamentary privilege remains unaffected by the Act. In addition, British judges—although required to take account of ECtHR judgments when making rulings in UK courts—are not permitted simply to override extant parliamentary legislation that appears to contravene the Convention.

Further, the following formal qualifications exist in relation to the Act's enforcement:

- claims must be brought against offending states or public bodies 'within one year of the action about which the complaint is being made';
- some rights can theoretically be breached if not 'in accordance with the laws of the country' that is a signatory; and
- breaches are tolerated 'in the interests of national security, public safety, or the country's economic well-being; for the prevention of crime and disorder, the protection of health or morals, or to protect the freedom and rights of others'.

In Britain, the HRA has arguably been breached repeatedly by successive home secretaries. The Anti-terrorism, Crime, and Security Act 2001 allowed the detention and deportation without trial of people suspected of terrorist links, and then Prime Minister Tony Blair repeatedly threatened to amend the Act to prevent judges blocking further crackdowns—particularly on the activities of extremist Islamic preachers, following the 2005 London bombings.

In Scotland, the Act came into force in 1998—two years ahead of England. By November 1999, the High Court had already declared unlawful the appointment of 129 temporary sheriffs (judges in the Scottish criminal courts) because they had been hired by the Lord Advocate, the member of the Scottish Executive responsible for prosecutions—a clear conflict with one of the constitution's fundamental guiding principles, the separation of powers.

Besides the showpiece constitutional Acts listed in Table 1.1, several others have contained key clauses with serious implications for the workings of the British constitution. Among these are the myriad Parliament Acts passed before the Second World War (see Chapter 2, 'What is the point of the Lords?'). Perhaps the single most significant constitutional reform introduced by any of these was the stipulation, in the Parliament Act 1911, that general elections must be held *a maximum of five years after the previous Parliament was convened* (in other words, a little over five years after the previous polling day). Until then, parliaments could theoretically last up to seven years, under the terms of the Septennial Act 1715. It would be another century, however, before 'fixed-term parliaments' were introduced, by the Coalition (see Chapter 4, 'The British franchise today—who can vote?').

Common Law

For several centuries before the emergence of parliamentary democracy, many English laws were decided by judges, on a case-by-case basis. When this system began emerging in the eleventh and twelfth centuries, judicial decisions were often taken ad hoc and locally, leading to wide disparities between one area and another—both in terms of what was (and wasn't) perceived a criminal offence, and the range and severity of punishments applied when laws were broken.

In 1166, the first Plantagenet king, Henry II, began institutionalizing a unified national framework of common law derived from 'case law' or 'precedent'—in essence, what he regarded as the more reasoned judgments made in individual local hearings over previous decades. This new framework—which came to apply throughout England and Wales, although not Scotland—elevated some local laws to national status, eliminated arbitrary or eccentric rulings, and established a great enduring constitutional right of citizens charged with criminal offences: a jury system, enshrining defendants' entitlement to be tried by 'twelve good men and true' from among their fellow citizens. To ensure that these practices were implemented consistently and fairly nationwide, Henry appointed judges at his own central court and sent them around the country to adjudicate on local disputes.

Many statutes that were passed—and constitutional conventions that evolved—subsequently were rooted in common law. Even now, common law is still occasionally 'created': judges often have to make rulings based on interpretations of ambiguously worded Acts, or conflicts between domestic and international laws. Such 'test cases' are, in their way, common law hearings.

Conventions

Another feature of Britain's unwritten constitution is its incorporation of all manner of idiosyncratic, quaint, and occasionally absurd traditions and customs. These well-worn practices have become accepted as part of the constitutional framework through little more than endless repetition.

Many key conventions operating in Parliament and government today are discussed in detail elsewhere in this book. These include the doctrines of collective responsibility and individual ministerial responsibility (Chapter 3, 'Collective responsibility, ministerial responsibility, and the Ministerial Code'), and the tradition that sovereigns accept Parliament's will by rubber-stamping legislation with the royal assent (Chapter 2, 'The passage of a Bill'). More amusing conventions include the fact that the Speaker in the Lords (until recently, the Lord Chancellor, but now an elected Lord Speaker) sits on a woolsack and wears a wig. The annual State Opening of Parliament by the monarch is heralded by a procession led by a ceremonial officer known as 'The Gentleman Usher of the Black Rod'. It is the task of Black Rod—as he is commonly known—to lead MPs ('strangers') from Commons to Lords to hear the Queen's Speech. On arriving at the Commons to summon MPs, he has the door slammed in his face and is forced to gain entry by rapping on it three times with (what else?) a black rod. This ritual derives from a famous confrontation between Parliament and the sovereign in 1642, when King Charles I tried to arrest five MPs in what the Commons regarded as a breach of parliamentary privilege. Within Parliament today, a form of light 'class warfare' between the chambers remains: MPs refer to the Lords only as 'another place'.

Treatises (works of legal authority)

Just as judges often have to disentangle contradictory elements of Britain's unwritten constitution when ruling on cases, so too are constitutional historians, philosophers, and political scientists forever arguing about it.

Of the myriad books and theses written about the UK constitution down the centuries, a handful have become so revered that they now qualify as constitutional documents in their own right. Some are considered so indispensable that they are effectively used as 'handbooks' by everyone from the Speaker of the

House of Commons to High Court barristers and judges. Many of today's new laws and court judgments are framed in reference to the wisdom imparted in such tomes, the most celebrated of which are listed in the table entitled 'Seminal British constitutional treatises', to be found on the **Online Resource Centre**.

Treaties

Over recent decades, Britain has signed many international treaties. Only a handful of these are 'constitutional' (legally binding). Most—such as the 1945 Charter of the United Nations and the North Atlantic Treaty, which established the North Atlantic Treaty Organization (NATO) in 1949 (see Chapter 10, 'Life after the Cold War—Britain's ongoing role in NATO')—are little more than membership agreements and, as such, could theoretically be 'opted out of'.

However, some—like the ECHR—have effectively been incorporated into Britain's constitution and would require legislation to 'remove' the obligations that they impose on it. There has also been considerable debate about the growing powers of the EU (see Chapter 9), which Britain joined (amid some controversy) in 1973, when it was still known as the 'European Economic Community' (EEC). Recent treaties—notably the 2007 Lisbon Treaty—have solidified the relationship between member states and the EU's governing institutions, leading 'Eurosceptics' to claim that Britain has signed up to an 'EU constitution' by the back door and is now part of a 'European superstate' governed from Brussels, rather than an independent sovereign nation.

The separation of powers in the UK

Perhaps the most fundamental guiding principle underlying the British constitution is the **separation of powers**. Based on the theories of French political thinker Baron de Montesquieu (1689–1755), the *Trias Politica* is a notional model that splits the state into three branches:

- the 'executive' (the government);
- the 'legislature' (Parliament); and
- the 'judiciary' (the courts).

The idea is that, to avoid arbitrary or dictatorial government, a constitutional framework is needed that does not confer too much power on one or more individuals. In theory, if the executive is wholly 'separated' from the legislature, and in turn the judiciary, each acts as a 'check and balance' on the other.

Montesquieu purportedly formulated his theory based on the workings of the UK system, although Britain's democracy arguably adheres far less strictly to this model than many established since. In practice, numerous overlaps have emerged over time between the roles, powers, and even membership of the key institutions charged with preserving the separation of powers. These include that:

- constitutionally, the reigning monarch (as 'head of state') is titular head of all three branches of the constitution;

- for centuries, until the post was reformed in 2007, the Lord Chancellor was a member of all three institutions, as Speaker of the Lords (legislature), 'manager' of the legal profession (judiciary), and a Cabinet minister (executive);

- most ministers, including the prime minister, are members of both government (executive) and Parliament (legislature); and

- before the independent Supreme Court was established in October 2009, the Law Lords collectively constituted Britain's highest court of appeal (judiciary), as well as being voting peers (legislature).

Such constitutional overlaps are not confined to Britain. Many other parliamentary democracies—particularly those directly modelled on that of the UK, as in many Commonwealth countries—display a similar fusion of powers, rather than the 'separation' to which they aspire. Constitutional historians increasingly distinguish between countries that practise 'presidential government' and those characterized by 'parliamentary government'. In the former (including the United States, France, South Africa, and Australia), separation is felt to be both more practised and practicable than in countries like Britain, where the most senior politician (prime minister) is today drawn from the ranks of ordinary MPs and represents a constituency in the same way as his or her peers.

In Britain, executive decisions are taken primarily by prime ministers and ministers, before being presented for approval to Parliament (where they also tend to be present, as voting MPs and peers). In the United States and other states, in contrast, the most senior elected politician is the president—who, in the absence of a monarch, is also head of state. Crucially, unlike in Britain and other parliamentary states, presidents are usually elected on different timetables from those of their national parliaments. Separation of powers in the United States is more pronounced than in Britain because Congress (the Senate and House of Representatives—the US equivalent of Britain's Parliament) is largely elected on a different date, in a different manner, from the president. More crucially, the president (unlike Britain's prime minister) is not a member of either House; so while he or she may present policies to Congress for approval, he or she does not lead or participate in ensuing parliamentary debates in the way that prime ministers do in the Commons.

Another feature of the separation of powers enjoyed by presidential states is the fact that, historically, they tend to develop more genuinely independent judicial systems than prime ministerial ones. The United States has long had a Supreme Court that (theoretically) is entirely separate from the political process. Notwithstanding controversies over the president's ability to nominate judges to replace those who retire (President Bush was castigated in 2005 for choosing Harriet Miers, his former adviser, who later withdrew her candidacy), this system is felt to be more appropriate than one in which judges straddle the divide between legislature and judiciary by serving in both a legal and law-making capacity. To this end, Jack Straw, as inaugural Secretary of State for Justice (and de facto Lord Chancellor), removed the Law Lords from Parliament in 2009, to sit in the then new Supreme Court.

▌ The monarchy

Britain's reigning sovereign is head of a 'constitutional' monarchy. This means that while he or she remains head of state, with the notional prerogative to govern and to take major constitutional decisions, in practice he or she does not. Unlike in presidential countries, Britain's head of state is a figurehead with little real power; instead, day-to-day decisions regarding domestic and foreign policy are left to Her Majesty's government (see Chapter 3).

Authority invested in successive prime ministers to appoint their ministers, devise and draft legislation, and decide whether to take Britain to war is derived from another key constitutional principle: the **royal prerogative**. This is the body of customary privileges and powers historically acquired by reigning monarchs (predominantly in the Middle Ages). Today, most 'prerogative powers' derived from this principle are exercised not by the Crown itself, but by Parliament.

The origins of the modern British monarchy

The present monarchy is also descended from several powerful families with roots outside the UK. However, Queen Elizabeth II reputedly traces her ancestral line directly to King Egbert—the ruler who united England under one throne in AD 829. The position that she occupies is that of Britain's longest standing secular institution (its only interruption being the aforementioned interregnum).

Although short-lived, this 'English Revolution' marked a break with the past that changed the monarchy's role forever. Beforehand, the prevailing rationale for the sovereign's existence derived from the 'Divine Right of Kings'. By propagating the idea that they should not be answerable to 'man-made' institutions, European medieval monarchs sought to reign with minimal outside interference—their authority challenged only by the Church. Henry VIII's inability to obtain permission from the Pope to divorce his first wife, Catherine of

Aragon, exemplified this. Parliaments were generally regarded as tools to enable kings and queens to raise taxes, pass edicts, and declare wars with impunity.

In England, all this changed after Charles I's execution. While his eldest son, Charles II, ultimately succeeded him following Cromwell's death, the concept that any monarch had a divine right to rule unchallenged had by then been all but rescinded. Through a succession of landmark constitutional statutes—principally the Bill of Rights and Act of Settlement—a newly liberated Parliament stamped its authority on the state and (in all but name) the monarch.

The role of the monarchy today

In *The English Constitution*, Bagehot (1826–77) argued that it was incumbent on monarchs to embody the following qualities:

❝ The right to be consulted, the right to encourage, the right to warn. ❞

Specifically, the role and powers of the monarch are best explained by splitting them into two broad *actual* and *notional*.

Actual prerogative powers—those exercised by the monarch

Despite huge upheavals in recent centuries, the sovereign still holds the following constitutional offices:

- head of state;
- head of the executive, legislature, and judiciary;
- commander-in-chief of the Armed Forces;
- supreme governor of the established Church of England;
- head of the Commonwealth (and head of state of 15 of its 53 members); and
- the authority from which the Royal Mint derives its licence to coin and print money in the monarch's image.

So much for the official titles, though: what do monarchs actually *do*? More specifically, which prerogative powers do they still personally exercise in an age when governments take most key political decisions?

The core roles and duties of the monarch—many largely ceremonial—include:

- reading Her Majesty's Most Gracious Speech or 'Gracious Address'— known as the **Queen's Speech**—at the annual State Opening of Parliament (historically in October or November, but generally held in May or June under the Coalition) or after a general election;
- governing the Church of England;

- 'creating' peers and conferring knighthoods and honours;
- meeting the prime minister weekly (usually on Tuesdays) to discuss Cabinet business and to offer advice on affairs of state;
- entertaining visiting heads of state at Buckingham Palace;
- touring other nations on official state visits as Britain's premier overseas ambassador;
- chairing meetings of the Privy Council (a body of advisers made up of members of current and previous Cabinets, plus other distinguished individuals, which issues Royal Charters and Orders in Council—see Chapter 2, 'Secondary legislation'); and
- attending 'Trooping the Colour' (the monarch's annual birthday parade, led by regiments of HM Armed Forces).

Although this list of 'powers' may appear feeble in the scheme of things, there is anecdotal evidence to suggest that recent monarchs have discharged their duties rigorously. In her first audience with then newly elected Labour Prime Minister Harold Wilson in 1964, Queen Elizabeth II famously wrong-footed him by expressing interest in proposals for a 'new town' near Bletchley—something about which he knew nothing, having not yet read his Cabinet papers. In his 1976 resignation speech, Wilson joked about the episode, advising his successors to 'do their homework' before meeting the Queen.

As well as retaining some prerogative powers, the sovereign has traditionally been called on to fulfil a unifying role as a national figurehead at times of crisis. The late HM Queen Elizabeth the Queen Mother toured bomb sites in London's East End to provide comfort to dispossessed families during the Blitz, while the Queen's annual televised Christmas Day address is designed as much to 'sum up' the past year and look to that ahead on the whole nation's behalf as to update her subjects on her own regal affairs. Such is the onus placed on the sovereign to 'speak for Britain' at times of tragedy or disaster that the Queen's initial silence following the death of Diana, Princess of Wales, and her lover, Dodi Fayed, in a Paris car crash in 1997 became a cause célèbre among her critics—allegedly prompting newly elected premier Mr Blair to appeal to her to issue a tribute to her daughter-in-law.

In terms of public profile, the reigning monarch must retain the appearance of political neutrality at all times—in particular, standing 'above' *party* politics. However, in recent times, concerns have been raised that her heir, the Prince of Wales, has repeatedly expressed his personal political views to government ministers. At time of writing, *The Guardian* was campaigning for the release of letters from the Prince to various government ministers whom he allegedly lobbied for changes in government policy (see Chapter 20, 'The Queen and Royal Household'), while in May 2014 he sparked a diplomatic row with Russia after reportedly comparing the country's president, Vladimir

Putin, to Adolf Hitler in a private discussion (leaked to the media) with a woman who fled the Nazis.

Although she has generally been scrupulous about avoiding such scrapes, the Queen herself was embroiled in controversy after delivering the June 2014 Queen's Speech. Labour formally complained to the head of the Civil Service that the speech contained Conservative Party slogans, including the phrase 'long-term plan' repeatedly used by ministers to promote their economic strategy. This echoed a similar complaint by Mr Cameron about Gordon Brown's final Queen's Speech, in 2009, which he had dismissed as a 'Labour press release on Palace parchment'.

Notional prerogative powers—those deferred to government

Most sovereign powers are exercised 'on the advice of ministers', meaning that it is they—and the prime minister mostly—who actually take decisions. In practice, then, it is the monarch who offers 'advice' to prime ministers, rather than the reverse, and premiers who discharge the following functions:

- dissolving and summoning Parliament—calling elections and forming new parliaments after elections;
- giving royal assent (the final 'rubberstamp' of approval) to Bills passed by Parliament;
- appointing ministers and other senior public officials, including judges, diplomats, governors, military officers, police chief constables, and Church of England bishops and archbishops;
- devising the legislative agenda for each parliamentary session (year of Parliament) and *writing* the Queen's Speech, which outlines that agenda and is read out by the sovereign at the State Opening of Parliament;
- declaring war and peace;
- proroguing Parliament—that is, suspending its activities over holiday periods, such as the summer recess. and annual Christmas and Easter breaks; and
- drawing up lists of nominations—in consultation with Opposition party leaders—for peerages, knighthoods, and other honours to be confirmed by the sovereign in the New Year Honours List and Queen's Birthday Honours List.

In addition, the monarch occasionally issues 'royal pardons'—formally known as 'royal prerogatives of mercy'—to convicted criminals. This tends to happen either when convicts are pardoned in light of new evidence or (rarer still) when their actions are deemed to merit their early release from jail. Unlike all other sovereign powers exercised by the government on the monarch's behalf, pardons are issued on the advice not of the prime minister, but of the Justice

Secretary (in England and Wales), Scottish First Minister (Scotland), or Northern Ireland Secretary (Northern Ireland), following the introduction of devolution. A recent example of a royal pardon was the posthumous forgiveness offered to families of all British soldiers executed for cowardice during the Second World War.

How the monarchy is funded

For 40 years before the 2012–13 tax year, the income of the reigning monarch and his or her immediate family—the 'Royal Household'—derived from the following:

- the Civil List;
- grants-in-aid;
- the Privy Purse; and
- personal income.

However, the Sovereign Grant Act 2011 introduced a rationalized funding regime, which has seen the first two sources of sovereign income (both funded by the taxpayer) supplanted by a single annual payment: the **sovereign grant**.

From old to new—finances in transition

Often invoked by those who favour abolishing the monarchy as shorthand for the Royal Family as a whole, the Civil List originated in the Bill of Rights. With William and Mary's accession, Parliament voted to pay the Royal Household £600,000 to aid it in 'civil government'. The List in its more recent form was established in 1760, during George III's reign. In return for the king surrendering to Parliament his 'hereditary revenues'—income generated by the Crown Lands (estates owned previously by the monarch)—MPs agreed a fixed annual income for the Royal Household. In practice, this exchange has reaped huge dividends for Parliament: in 2012–13, the income generated for the Treasury by the Crown Lands (as administered by the Crown Estate Commissioners) was around £250 million, compared to £31 million paid to the monarch in sovereign grant.

In 2001, the List itself was fixed at £7.9 million a year for the Queen until at least 2011, with her husband, the Duke of Edinburgh (Prince Philip), receiving a separate £359,000 annuity. In a deal struck with then Chancellor Mr Brown, the Queen agreed to finance increases in her outgoings from a 'reserve fund' worth up to £30million, accumulated over the previous decade. In return, her and Prince Philip's 'fixed' incomes would rise by 7.5 per cent a year to keep abreast of inflation (which, at 3 per cent in 2001, was less than half as high). As a result, by the end of 2009–10, the List had swelled to £14.2 million. Like many households, though, the royals emerged from the recession less solvent than beforehand: when the 2009–10 Buckingham Palace accounts were published in July 2010, they revealed that the Queen had supplemented the official Civil List pot by a record £6.5 million during that year, reducing her reserve fund to £15.2 million. Even before replacing the old funding system with the sovereign grant, Coalition Chancellor George Osborne made the Royal Family's taxpayer-funded income subject to the same scrutiny as government departments, amending the Civil List Audit Act 1816 to hand auditing powers to the National Audit Office and the influential Public Accounts Committee of MPs. And in his subsequent Comprehensive Spending Review (CSR) (see Chapter 7, 'Managing national debt'), he revealed that the Queen had agreed to a two-year freeze in her grant funding, in 2011–12 and 2012–13, necessitating a 14 per cent reduction in the Royal Household's spending.

In the last few years before it was abolished, the List funded the following expenses for the royal couple:

- the salaries of the retinue of 645 servants, butlers, and other Royal Household employees (70 per cent); and
- the costs of royal garden parties (attended by 48,000 people each year) and hospitality during state visits (30 per cent).

In addition, several parliamentary allowances were issued annually to individual Royal Family members, including the Duke of York (Prince Andrew) and the Princess Royal (Princess Anne), under the Civil List Acts. These generally amounted to £2.5 million extra, although from April 1993 the Queen refunded £1.5 million to Parliament in practice, using her personal pot of money, the Privy Purse (see next section). The remaining £1 million was retained as income for the Duke of Edinburgh and, until her death in 2002, the Queen Mother. All other senior royals performing official duties received annuities from the Privy Purse rather than the Civil List.

Perhaps surprisingly, one of few key Royal Household members who did not benefit from these annuities was Prince Charles, who, as Duke of Cornwall, earns substantial income from his sprawling 130,000-acre Duchy of Cornwall estate. Originally bestowed on the Black Prince in 1337, the Duchy extends over 23 counties. According to the Prince of Wales and Duchess of Cornwall's Annual Review 2014 (available online at www.princeofwales.gov.uk), in 2013–14 it generated income of £21.68 million (including departmental subsidies and the portion of the sovereign grant spent on the couple's main residence, St James's Palace). This was a year-on-year increase of £1.48 million, or 6.8 per cent.

While the Civil List covered the Royal Household's day-to-day living costs, the other customary pot of taxpayers' money, grants-in-aid, maintained the 'occupied royal palaces'—those, including Buckingham Palace, Kensington Palace, and Windsor Castle, in which Royal Family members still lived—and its personal transport—that is, the Royal Air Force (RAF) aircraft of the No. 32 (The Royal) Squadron, the Royal Train, and numerous chartered and scheduled flights used by senior royals for official visits. These were awarded by the Department of Culture, Media, and Sport (DCMS) and the Department for Transport (DfT), respectively.

In recent years, disclosures of the Royal Family's travels in the preceding 12 months have attracted heavy media attention. Its 2013–14 accounts, published in July 2014, were no exception. A last-minute charter flight for Prince Charles to the funeral of former South African leader Nelson Mandela cost taxpayers £246,160, while his and his wife's overseas tour of Sri Lanka and India during a 2013 Commonwealth heads of government meeting cost £433,020—including £82,607 spent by his staff on scheduled flights for 'reconnaissance' and 'advance visits'. Prince Andrew—nicknamed 'Airmiles Andy'—also raised eyebrows, by chartering a £14,692 flight from Farnborough to Scotland to visit the Royal Highland Fusiliers, before attending the Golf Open Championship at Muirfield.

Despite such examples, an ongoing public backlash against royal transport costs has encouraged the Royal Household to reduce its overall travel spending significantly, reducing it from from £6.5 million in 2008–09 to £3.9 million in 2009–10. Although it bounced back to £6.1 million in 2011–12, the 2013–14 outlay was back down to £4.2 million—£0.3 million less than the previous year.

The remaining grants-in-aid budget, as was (typically one tenth of the total), was spent on royal 'communications': letters, telephone bills, and other correspondences—including invitations to those fabled garden parties.

The new sovereign grant was initially set at 15 per cent of the net revenue generated each year by the Crown Estates—and, as such, amounted to £36.1 million in 2013–14, with a projected rise to £37.9 million the following year. The more generous annual settlements are designed to enable the Queen to finance future repairs to her palaces without the need for further public subsidy. An early example of this was the £4.5 million renovation of the Kensington Palace apartment used by the Duke and Duchess of Cambridge revealed in her 2013–14 accounts. The parliamentary annuities that the Queen used to receive (and reimburse) for family members have also now ceased. If there is money left from the sovereign grant in a given year, this is paid into a reserve fund overseen by the Royal Trustees (up to a maximum value of half of the grant awarded). Conversely, if the Queen requires more money one year, she can dip into this fund to meet any unforeseen expenditure.

The Privy Purse

Dating back to 1399, the Privy Purse derives from income generated by the Duchy of Lancaster—a huge expanse of land covering 19,268 acres and the sole surviving Crown estate still 'owned' by the monarch. It is kept under lock and key by her personal accountant, and administered by the Chancellor of the Duchy of Lancaster—usually a senior Cabinet minister—and the Keeper of the

Privy Purse (currently Sir Alan Reid). The most recent Duchy of Lancaster accounts show that, in 2013, the Privy Purse's net income was £12.5 million (down from £13.3 million four years earlier), while the estate's value rose to £428.3 million (£322 million in 2009).

Personal income

Senior Royal Family members, despite deriving significant income from the state, are free to generate earnings like anyone else—provided they pay income tax on these. Personal incomes earned by individual members include the military salaries drawn by Prince Charles, who served for a time in the Royal Navy, Prince Andrew, who saw action during the Falklands War, and Prince Harry, currently a captain in the Household Cavalry (Blues and Royals). Other examples include income earned by Prince Charles's Duchy of Cornwall from rent and sales of its produce—including his 'Duchy Originals' biscuits. His youngest brother, Prince Edward, Duke of Wessex, once owned a film and television company (Ardent Productions).

More sporadic sources of income might include everything from share dividends to windfalls from betting on the races (the Queen Mother famously liked a flutter).

Taxation and the monarchy

Like everyone else, the Queen has always paid indirect taxes—value added tax (VAT) and other tariffs levied on consumer goods and services. She also voluntarily pays Council Tax. It was not until 1993, however, that she agreed to pay income tax—prompted by a public backlash over the revelation that much of the £60 million cost of repairing Windsor Castle after a devastating 1992 fire was funded by taxpayers, despite the fact they already heavily subsidized her household.

The monarch and certain immediate family members do, however, still enjoy substantial tax breaks not granted to her subjects. While the Privy Purse pays tax and the Queen's personal estate incurs inheritance tax, the sovereign grant is untaxed, and so is any transfer of property 'from sovereign to sovereign' (between the Queen and her successor).

The succession

As in other European nation states, the monarchy has, for centuries, passed from father to son in Britain, through a process known as 'eldest male primogeniture'. When a male line (going through the eldest son) is exhausted, the crown passes to the eldest male sibling of its originator, and only after his male line ends will it ever reach a woman. Under this system, Prince Charles would inherit the throne from his mother and, after his death, it would pass to his eldest son, William, and then to *his* son, George. If William were to also have a daughter, the crown might eventually reach her—but only after any other son (and his line) had first inherited it. It would finally pass to William's younger brother, Harry, only after first going through each of the former's offspring.

This was the route that the Crown *would* have taken after the death of the present Queen. However, in a radical constitutional departure, the Coalition dispensed with centuries of tradition by passing the Succession to the Crown Act 2013, which ends the eldest male primogeniture principle with effect from the succession of Prince William. Had the first child of the Duke and Duchess of Cambridge been a girl, she would automatically have succeeded to the throne following William's death, rather than losing out to a younger brother. Before confirming the change, ministers formally obtained approval from the 15 other Commonwealth countries reigned over by the Queen, but all approved the move at a 2011 summit. In a further significant change, the Bill of Rights, Act of Settlement, and Royal Marriages Act 1772 have all been amended to allow future sovereigns to marry Roman Catholics without forfeiting their titles. The legal obligation of every descendant of George II to seek the monarch's permission before getting married has also been limited to the six family members closest to the Crown.

Monarchy versus presidency—which way forward?

Although Britain has had a monarchy for some 1,500 years, today it is one of the few 'developed' nations to retain one—let alone boast an extended Royal Family, funded largely by taxpayers. Unsurprisingly, recent years have witnessed growing calls for it to be replaced by an elected head of state. These have been fuelled by a succession of controversies surrounding the Royal Household, in particular that relating to Prince Charles's divorce from Diana, Princess of Wales, and revelations about his long-standing relationship with Camilla Parker-Bowles (now his second wife and Duchess of Cornwall). Further succour was given to those arguing for Britain's hereditary figurehead to be replaced by an elected one by the Australian electorate's narrow decision to retain the Queen as Australia's head of state in November 1999.

The argument for an elected head of state is self-explanatory: in a modern democracy (so the republican case goes), it is surely only right that the state's ultimate ambassador—the individual who publicly represents its interests on the global stage—should seek a 'mandate' from his or her subjects. But what are the arguments for retaining a monarch? Opinions differ among constitutional historians about the institution's merits, but an oft-cited argument favouring the hereditary principle is that it produces heads of state capable of maintaining an objective, independent-minded *distance* from the day-to-day workings of the political process—rather than being hidebound by the narrow, short-term thinking that constrains politicians reliant on the votes of a fickle electorate. In addition, the presence of Queen Elizabeth II through 60 years of changing governments and shifting political priorities has provided, some argue, a degree of continuity absent from presidential states.

▌ Devolution—from union to government in the nations

Most of this chapter has focused on outlining the process by which the modern British state came into being, and the rules, customs, and laws that have evolved to determine the balance of powers between Parliament, monarchy, and citizens.

The UK is a 'representative democracy'—a state that exercises its power through democratically elected representatives (MPs in the House of Commons). There are two main types of democracy: *federal* and *unitary*. In federal democracies, countries are divided into separate political units, each with considerable autonomy over its own affairs. The United States is an example of a federal democracy: major foreign and domestic policy decisions are taken by the national government (president and Congress), but many day-to-day matters are decided on a state-by-state basis. The most oft-cited example of **federalism** in action relates to the way in which different states punish felons convicted of serious crimes such as murder and rape: while 14 US states favour custodial sentences, the remaining 36 still practise capital punishment.

Britain, by contrast, has long been a unitary democracy. Since the passage of the 1706–07 Acts of Union, most power has resided with its central government and Parliament. But while its constitutional story since the late medieval period has mostly been one of the gradual unification and consolidation at the centre, in recent decades this has been compromised by gradual decentralization, with power shifting incrementally closer to the people from whom it derives. This trend is likely to be consolidated following Scotland's independence referendum, with Britain potentially moving towards a federal structure.

The story of the emergence of local government—elected councils, funded by local taxpayers, which run local services—is told in Chapter 11. But, at a higher level than the strictly 'local', there now exists in Scotland, Wales, and Northern Ireland a further tier of government to which significant powers have been devolved by Westminster. This statutory transfer of power from central government to the separate nations that make up the UK alongside England is known as **devolution**.

Before proceeding further, there is an important distinction between devolution and **independence**. Although the parties most enthusiastically embracing devolution in Scotland, Wales, and Northern Ireland tend to be 'nationalist' ones—that is, those that would ultimately like to break away from Britain to become independent states—devolved power does not amount to independence. Neither does it inevitably follow that, having gained devolution, a country will one day become independent. Indeed, a principal argument used by Labour to justify devolution was that, in granting it, the party was safeguarding the union, by permitting a limited degree of autonomy that made practical sense and would answer many frustrations voiced by otherwise loyal British subjects in those countries. Conversely, advocates of independence have argued that, in the long term, it makes little sense for national assemblies in Scotland or Wales, which take most of their own day-to-day decisions, to remain Westminster's vassals, making fuller self-government of one kind or another a logical next step. To this end, barely an hour after the Scottish referendum result was announced, Prime Minister David Cameron confirmed plans to set Britain on a more federal course, as part of a 'devolution revolution'—with Scotland rapidly gaining significant additional devolved powers, to be outlined in draft legislation as early as January 2015, and Wales, Northern Ireland, and even England also gaining greater autonomy over their own distinctive internal affairs (see also 'The West Lothian Question' in this chapter).

The unification of Great Britain

Like much of Britain's constitutional heritage, the concept of devolution originated in the Middle Ages, when Wales and Scotland first began demanding the right to govern themselves independently of the English sovereign. Of the two countries, Wales has the longest formal association with England. The main stages in its moves towards incorporation into the UK are outlined in the table entitled 'Timeline for the incorporation of Wales into the UK', to be found on the **Online Resource Centre**.

Scotland's progress towards integration in the UK was more complex—in part because it had never been formally absorbed into the Roman Empire. It took centuries of conflict during the medieval period for it to succumb finally to the authority of the English Crown. A timeline showing this is outlined in the table entitled 'Timeline for the incorporation of Scotland into the UK', to be found on the **Online Resource Centre**.

Northern Ireland's incorporation was still more problematic, encompassing as it did its split from Southern Ireland (Eire). The early stages of the process are outlined in the table entitled 'Timeline for the incorporation of Northern Ireland into the UK', to be found on the **Online Resource Centre**.

The path to Scottish devolution

Of the three UK countries besides England, Scotland has the most extensive powers, following enabling legislation passed to formalize devolution in 1998.

Table 1.3 Timeline for the introduction of devolution in Scotland

Date	Event
1973	Royal Commission on Constitution recommends devolution to Edward Heath's Conservatives
1978	Re-elected Labour government passes Scotland Act, allowing referendum on Scottish self-government: 40 per cent of Scottish electorate must vote for devolution for it to be granted
March 1979	Devolution put on hold because, although 52 per cent of those who voted supported it, this was equivalent to only 32 per cent of total electorate
July 1997	Newly re-elected Labour government publishes Scotland's Parliament White Paper advocating devolution
11 September 1997	New referendum attracts 60 per cent turnout, with 74 per cent of voters backing devolution and 64 per cent voting 'Yes' to second question, backing Scottish Parliament's having tax-varying powers
1998	Government of Scotland Act passed, conferring devolution
12 May 1999	Queen opens new Scottish Parliament after its remit confirmed by consultative steering group
7 September 2004	Grand opening of £420 million purpose-built Scottish Parliament at Holyrood, by foot of Edinburgh's Royal Mile
18 September 2014	Scottish electorate votes in referendum to remain in UK and Alex Salmond resigns as First Minister and leader of the Scottish National Party (SNP)

In part, this reflects the fact that, for complex historical reasons, the country has long had certain devolved functions—notably a distinct legal system. More significantly, however, it is a legacy of growing calls north of the border, after 18 years of Conservative rule at Westminster, for greater autonomy from a national Parliament that seemed increasingly remote (both politically and geographically) from Scottish interests.

The path to Scottish devolution began in the 1960s, when the then Labour government established a Royal Commission to examine the arguments for some form of 'home rule'. The sequence of events leading to devolution—and later agreement to extend the scope of the Scottish Parliament's devolved powers—is outlined in Table 1.3.

Unlike Wales and Northern Ireland, where devolved powers have so far been limited, the Scottish Parliament has considerable authority; only foreign affairs, defence, social security, and overall tax policy have been outside its remit—and these powers will soon be further enhanced. Immediately after the 2014 referendum, Mr Cameron confirmed that welfare and taxation were likely to be devolved to Scotland in coming months (see 'The West Lothian Question' in this chapter), acknowledging the significant support expressed for full-blown independence. Since its inception, the Scottish Parliament's powers have included determining its own education, health, environment, and transport policy, and being able to 'vary'—raise or lower—income tax by up to 3 pence in the pound (the so-called 'Tartan Tax' option). The Scotland Act 2012 conferred more extensive tax-varying powers on it (up to 10 pence in the pound) and a distinctive 'Scottish rate' of income tax was due to come into effect in April 2016, with replacements for stamp duty and landfill tax introduced a year earlier.

The Scottish independence campaign—and its outcome

Although Parliament's approval is technically required for independence to be granted, demands for a breakaway Scottish government became a clamour when Alex Salmond, bullish and charismatic then leader of the Scottish Nationalist Party (SNP), was elected his country's First Minister in May 2007—eradicating Labour's majority share of the vote in Scotland for the first time in 50 years. The clamour grew even more acute when, four years on, his party achieved an outright majority.

Mr Salmond's repeated pledges to hold a referendum were addressed in part by a draft Bill published in February 2010, outlining proposals for two separate ballots of Scottish voters. The first would ask if they supported the Scottish Parliament being granted more devolved autonomy, with two alternative models proposed: one—dubbed 'devolution max', or 'devo max'—involving the handover of all remaining Westminster powers to Holyrood (apart from defence policy, foreign affairs, and financial regulation); the other envisaging a more limited extension of devolution, along the lines of changes suggested in June 2009 by Sir Kenneth Calman (including that 10 pence should be top-sliced from the basic and higher rates of income tax in Scotland, with the Scottish Parliament left to decide whether to make up the shortfall by levying its own top-up tax). Mr Salmond also proposed to ask voters, in a second ballot, if they wanted Holyrood's powers extended to full-blooded independence. But, even under these plans, the Queen would have remained Scotland's head of state and the country would have sought to stay in the European Union (although the European Commission would later make clear that it could not do so without formally 'reapplying' as an independent state). Mr Salmond's speech garnered a mixed reception, with critics stressing that the near-collapse of both Halifax Bank of Scotland (HBOS) and Royal Bank of Scotland (RBS) during the 2008–09 financial crisis, and their subsequent bailouts by HM Treasury (see Chapter 7, 'The global banking crisis and its fallout'), had underlined the importance of the economic security provided by the union.

Unbowed, Mr Salmond renewed his calls for independence in January 2012 when, challenged by Mr Cameron to 'put up or shut up', he published a Consultation Paper setting out a detailed timetable for achieving his goal—including the desired wording of his referendum 'question'. Stating that he intended to hold the crucial vote in autumn 2014, he revived the notion of putting more than one scenario to the Scottish people, including a 'devo max' option. The main item on the ballot paper, however, would be an 'in or out' question, worded as follows:

> Do you agree that Scotland should be an independent country?

Buoyed by opinion polls suggesting that seven out of ten Scots wanted to preserve the union, Mr Cameron argued that the referendum should concern itself solely with gauging support for full-blown independence. After intense negotiations, Mr Salmond finally agreed a deal in October 2012 to put a single 'yes or no' question to the Scottish people. His preferred wording was also amended, after the **Electoral Commission**—the body responsible for ensuring that elections and referendums are conducted fairly—argued that it could be seen as a 'leading' question. The final wording was as follows:

> Should Scotland be an independent country?

In return for dropping his demand for a second, 'devo max', question, Mr Salmond secured the Coalition's promise that the outcome of the vote would be binding, under an obscure constitutional instrument known as 'Section 30'— that is, if the Scots opted to leave Britain, formal independence would be granted. In the event, they voted by a margin of 44.7 to 55.3 per cent against independence on 18 September 2014, and Mr Salmond resigned hours later— paving the way for his equally fiery deputy, Nicola Sturgeon, to succeed him as SNP leader and First Minister.

In the run-up to the vote, it had become clear that, whatever its outcome, the referendum would have major ramifications for the future of Britain's system of government. With opinion polls suggesting the gap between support for the 'yes' and 'no' camps was dramatically narrowing in the closing weeks of the campaign, Mr Cameron's insistence on a simple 'yes or no' question came to be viewed as a tactical error: by depriving the Scots of a compromise 'devo max' option, he appeared to have made the prospect of a 'yes' vote more likely. In what the media—and Mr Salmond—portrayed as a panic reaction, the pro-union 'Better Together' campaign sanctioned an offer by former Labour premier Mr Brown of a sweeping extension of Scottish devolution, comparable to the 'home rule' settlement once sought by nationalists in pre-partition Ireland. This was swiftly followed by a joint statement of support from all of the main party leaders—dubbed 'the vow' in a famous front-page splash on the *Daily Record*—which led to Mr Cameron's pledge to confer further powers on Holyrood. One other development that looked certain to have implications for future voting across the UK was that, unlike in any previous election, 16- and 17-year-olds were allowed to take part. Labour has committed to implementing this change for other elections if returned to power in 2015 (see Chapter 4, 'The future of voting').

The 'West Lothian Question'

The growing assertiveness of devolved assemblies, and ongoing enhancements of their powers, has raised significant constitutional issues. None is more explosive than the 'West Lothian Question': the argument that it is unfair for MPs representing Scottish (or indeed Welsh and Northern Irish) constituencies to continue voting on matters that affect only England, while English members have no say over issues particular to the devolved nations. Although devolution was introduced only in 1998, this quandary was first raised in debate in the Commons by Labour backbencher Tam Dalyell in the 1970s. It was dubbed the 'West Lothian Question' by then Tory MP Enoch Powell after the name of Dalyell's constituency.

Under devolution, Westminster governments have bolstered shaky Commons majorities in votes on controversial legislation with the help of Scottish, Welsh, and/or Northern Irish MPs—including, in some cases, those who did not support the same policies being applied in their own countries (see Chapter 6, 'The end of the post-war consensus and the birth of NHS markets').

Today, debate over the West Lothian Question rages louder than ever. Within an hour of the Scottish referendum result, Mr Cameron addressed it directly outside Downing Street—stating that, at a time when Scotland was about to acquire new devolved powers, the 'question' of 'English votes for English laws' required a 'decisive answer'. In this spirit, he announced that not only Wales and Northern Ireland, but also England, would be given more direct legislative control over their own affairs, on the same timescale as Scotland. Lord Smith of Kelvin was appointed to draft further Scottish devolution plans, while Leader of the House of Commons William Hague would chair a new cabinet committee devoted to ironing out the practicalities of giving English MPs exclusive jurisdiction over English-only matters.

The next stage of Britain's putative new democratic settlement is unlikely to maintain the backing of a cross-party Westminster consensus (as the fight to preserve the union did)—not least because finally 'answering' the West Lothian Question presents a particular dilemma for Labour. As the party tends to rely for Commons majorities on the 40-plus Labour MPs customarily elected in Scotland, the introduction of new rules allowing only English members to vote on English matters raises the prospect that future Labour governments might be prevented from passing radical domestic legislation. To do so, the party would also need to muster a majority of MPs in England—a feat several Labour governments (notably Wilson's 1964 and 1974 administrations) failed to manage. Fears about such an eventuality were heightened in November 2014, with publication of the Smith Commission report, which recommended that Scotland be given full control of its own income tax and VAT rates—and allowed to keep all the money it raised to spend as it chose. Such enhanced devolution might lead to Scottish MPs being barred from voting on the overall UK Budget, increasing the likelihood that a minority Labour government (or one with a

Table 1.4 Timeline for the introduction of devolution in Wales

Date	Event
July 1997	White Paper entitled A Voice for Wales outlines proposals for Welsh devolution
18 September 1997	Referendum attracts low turnout of around 50 per cent, but 50.3 per cent approve devolution
1998	Government of Wales Act passed to lay out framework
1999	National Assembly for Wales (Transfer of Functions) Order introduced, providing a legal and constitutional framework
6 May 1999	First election for National Assembly for Wales
12 May 1999	National Assembly for Wales meets for first time
1 March 2006	Queen officially opens new, purpose-built £67million Welsh Assembly building in Cardiff

small majority) might struggle to pass its Finance Bills —an outcome which would almost certainly bring down the administration.

The path to Welsh devolution

Welsh devolution was introduced as outlined in Table 1.4.

The rocky road to Northern Irish devolution

As a result of the fallout from 'The Troubles', the devolution process in Northern Ireland has been more drawn out, with various parties unable to agree a workable framework for devolved government until, finally, a landmark agreement was signed in 2007. With the ruling DUP accepting that the IRA had decommissioned its weapons, the Northern Ireland Assembly was restored.

The saga that led to the granting of meaningful devolution to Northern Ireland lasted decades, so it would be impractical to list every twist and turn here, but the most significant events are outlined in Table 1.5.

Ironically, the *level* of power devolved to the province has, so far, been much more limited than that of Scotland or Wales. As in Wales, before it gained greater autonomy over health and education policy, Northern Ireland has largely been restricted to:

- determining budgetary priorities in education, health, etc.;
- funding, directing, and appointing managers of its National Health Service (NHS) bodies;
- administering any EU structural funds; and
- determining the content of its version of the National Curriculum in schools.

Table 1.5 Timeline for the introduction of devolution in Northern Ireland

Date	Event
1968	Civil Rights Movement starts in Ulster between Protestants and Catholics (dawn of 'The Troubles')
1972	Most notorious explosion of violence in history of The Troubles—'Bloody Sunday'—occurs in Londonderry, culminating at Catholic ghetto the Bogside
1972	Northern Ireland constitution, prime minister, and Parliament suspended for year owing to escalating violence
November 1985	Anglo-Irish Agreement ('Hillsborough Agreement') signed by Britain and Ireland, recognizing that constitutional change can occur only with agreement of population through referendum
November 1992	Inconclusive end to talks flowing from Anglo-Irish Agreement
December 1993	UK Prime Minister Major and Irish Taoiseach Albert Reynolds issue Joint Declaration from 10 Downing Street ('The Downing Street Declaration'), stipulating that future participation in discussions about government of Northern Ireland should be restricted to parties committed to 'exclusively peaceful means'
August 1994	IRA announces 'complete cessation of military operations'; Combined Loyalist Military Command confirms own ceasefire
February 1995	British and Irish governments launch proposals for new democratic institutions
February 1996	Docklands bomb ends IRA ceasefire
June 1996	Former US Senator George Mitchell convenes Northern Ireland Forum, outlining six 'Mitchell Principles' for peace process; Sinn Féin excluded until IRA formally readopts ceasefire; two further IRA blasts follow, in Manchester and County Antrim
July 1997	Sinn Féin president Gerry Adams and vice-president Martin McGuinness elected Westminster MPs, and IRA resumes its ceasefire; International Commission on Decommissioning set up under Canadian general John de Chastelain to oversee process
September 1997	Sinn Féin signs up to Mitchell Principles and multiparty talks start at Stormont; after switching to Lancaster House, London, deadline of 9 April 1998 set for agreement
10 April 1998	'Good Friday Agreement' (Belfast Agreement) enables dual referendums on devolution in Northern and Southern Ireland; constitutionally, way is paved by Northern Ireland (Elections) Act 1998 and nineteenth Amendment to Irish Constitution (renouncing Eire's claim on the north)
22 May 1998	Referendum of all Ireland produces 94 per cent backing for devolution in Eire and 71 per cent 'Yes' vote in Northern Ireland
25 June 1998	First elections for Northern Ireland Assembly see Ulster Unionist Party (UUP) gaining most seats (28), with Social Democratic and Labour Party second (24)
1 July 1998	New Assembly meets for first time, with Lord Alderdice as Presiding Officer and David Trimble, UUP leader, First Minister Designate; at least three nationalists and three designated unionists to be included in government under devolution deal known as 'd'Hondt procedure' (after Belgian Victor d'Hondt); each party allocated seats on 'largest average' basis relating to number of votes it receives

(*continued*)

Table 1.5 (*continued*)

Date	Event
15 August 1998	Twenty-nine people die in Omagh bomb planted by 'Real IRA' splinter group
1 December 1999	Direct rule of Northern Ireland from Westminster ends with Queen's signing of Northern Ireland Act 1998
2 December 1999	Anglo-Irish Agreement replaced by British-Irish Agreement, formally creating North–South Ministerial Council and British–Irish Ministerial Council envisaged in Good Friday Agreement; on same day, Irish Parliament replaces Arts 2 and 3 of Irish Constitution—formally abandoning Eire's historic claim to Northern Ireland
11 February 2000	Assembly suspended owing to disagreement about pace of weapons decommissioning; prolonged period of intermittent direct rule resumes
December 2003	Assembly elections give largest number of seats (30) to DUP, followed by UUUP (27), Sinn Féin (24), and SDLP (18)
March 2007	After further elections in Northern Ireland and power-sharing talks, agreement finally struck to restore devolution
April 2007	Loyalist Volunteer Force follows IRA's declaration of 'final cessation of hostilities' in August 2005 by announcing that it is winding up
May 2007	Power-sharing resumes in Assembly

However, in a highly significant and symbolic development recognizing the unique historical and geographical factors distinguishing Northern Ireland from Scotland and Wales, April 2010 saw the devolution of policing and justice powers. Defying trenchant opposition from the Ulster Unionists, the ruling DUP–Sinn Féin coalition won sufficient cross-community approval to drive the process to its next, decisive stage: the appointment of a Justice Minister.

A month later, another watershed was reached, with the long-awaited publication of the final report of an official inquiry set up by Mr Blair into 'Bloody Sunday'—after 12 years of hearings, costing £200 million. The 5,000-page report concluded that when, on 30 January 1972, British paratroopers fired on a civil rights march in Londonderry, killing 13 civilians, none of the dead had been armed, the paras had shot first and without warning, and some had lied about their actions. In a Commons statement, Mr Cameron apologized to the bereaved families on behalf of the UK government, describing the shootings as 'unjustified and unjustifiable'.

Devolution in England—time for a revival?

Leaving aside the wider issue of England's 'national' autonomy (see 'The West Lothian Question' in this chapter), the introduction of devolution in Scotland, Wales, and Northern Ireland has led to periodic demands for major English *regions* outside London to be given similar powers to run their own affairs.

Tentative moves towards embryonic English regional devolution actually emerged under the Tories, when Mr Major set up regional offices manned by civil servants seconded from the main Whitehall departments. The role of these nine 'Government Offices of the Regions', however, was largely administrative and there were no moves toward any form of elected regional *government*.

When Labour returned to power in 1997, steps were taken to introduce elected English regional authorities by then Deputy Prime Minister John Prescott's short-lived 'super-ministry': the Department for the Environment, Transport, and the Regions (DETR). Each region—East Midlands, East of England, North East, North West, South East, South West, West Midlands, and Yorkshire and Humber—was given an unelected *regional chamber*, intended to pave the way for elected assemblies. After a lengthy, but (many argued) poorly publicized, consultation process, the DETR instigated referendums to be held simultaneously in each of the eight regions in November 2004. But the North East Regional Assembly was the only one to hold its vote (a postal-only ballot) and, by decisively rejecting the idea (by 78 to 22 per cent), it appeared to kick regional devolution into touch for the foreseeable future.

One outcome of the Scottish referendum has, however, been revived calls for greater English autonomy. The favoured 'solution' of some, such as former Tory Cabinet minister John Redwood, is to give England its own national parliament and, potentially, government and First Minister (see Chapter 3, 'The Scottish Government/Executive')—whether that involves timetabling specific days at Westminster on which only English MPs may sit, or establishing a separate devolved chamber, perhaps based outside London, like those at Holyrood, Cardiff, and Stormont. Also on the table is a far wider, and deeper, extension of the devolution principle, to reintroduce the idea of *regional* (or even *city*) government, potentially with levels of autonomy more commensurate with federalism than mere devolution.

☰ Topical feature idea

According to data published by polling organization Survation in April 2014, 65 per cent of British adults believe that 'too much of England is run from London' and that more powers should be devolved to either local government, regional partnerships, or other bodies. With Labour leader Ed Miliband pledging to introduce 'the biggest economic devolution of power to England's great towns and cities in a hundred years' if he is elected in May 2015 and Coalition Chancellor George Osborne devolving new powers to Greater Manchester and other northern centres, what do people think in your area about the prospect of regional, or more local, devolution? Find out what powers people would like to control. If the area were to come under a regional assembly, where would it likely be based?

✳ Current issues

- **Further devolution across Britain** Having failed to secure independence, Alex Salmond resigned as its first minister and SNP leader—but not before demanding the swift introduction of additional ('devo max') powers, as promised by leaders of the 'Better Together' campaign in the run-up to the referendum, including full control over taxation and social security benefits. Mr Cameron pledged that Wales, Northern Ireland, and even England are also to gain more autonomy, on the same timetable.

- **Fixed-term parliaments** The Coalition has introduced fixed-term parliaments to prevent future prime ministers 'cutting and running' at times when it suits their own political fortunes, rather than the country's interests. Five-year fixed-term parliaments will begin on Thursday 7 May 2015, but it remains to be seen whether Labour will keep them if returned to office.

- **Introduction of the sovereign grant** The Coalition has reformed royal funding, bundling the Civil List and grants-in-aid together into a single sovereign grant. The new regime rationalizes the existing set-up, but is beginning to generate even more taxpayer-funded income for the Queen than the previous arrangements.

▦ Key points

1. Britain has a flexible, 'unwritten' constitution that derives from a number of sources—principally statute, common law, works of legal authority, and convention.

2. The British constitution is underpinned by two key principles: the *rule of law* stipulates no individual is 'above the law', while the *separation of powers* ensures that executive/government, legislature/Parliament, and judiciary/courts act as 'checks and balances' on each other. Members of Parliament are part of the legislature and their role includes approving or rejecting legislation.

3. Britain has a constitutional monarchy. The reigning sovereign is head of state, commander-in-chief of the Armed Forces, and supreme-governor of the Church of England, but most of his or her prerogative powers are exercised in practice by government and prime minister.

4. The monarchy today has two principal sources of funding: the *sovereign grant*, an annual payment to the Queen and the Duke of Edinburgh; and the *Privy Purse*, a personal income derived from the income of the Duchy of Lancaster estate.

5. Scotland, Wales, and Northern Ireland have been granted differing levels of devolution: the ability to govern their own affairs in relation to a wide range of policy areas, such as health and education. Scotland also has growing power over its taxation rates.

→ Further reading

Bogdanor, V. (2009) *The New British Constitution*, Oxford: Hart Publishing. **Insightful critique of New Labour's constitutional reform and how it fits into Britain's established constitutional framework.**

Jowell, J. and Oliver, D. (2011) *The Changing Constitution*, 7th edn, Oxford: Oxford University Press, **Seventh edition of essay collection focusing on recent developments in the British constitution, incorporating evaluation of the Coalition's reform programme.**

Leyland, P. (2013) *Constitution of the United Kingdom: A Contextual Analysis*, 2nd edn, Oxford: Hart Publishing. **Fully updated new edition of acclaimed analysis of the historical and cultural context of the British constitution, taking account of developments since the 2010 election.**

Loughlin, M. (2013) *The British Constitution: A Very Short Introduction*, Oxford: Oxford University Press. **Concise, punchy, and up-to-the-minute introduction to all aspects of the UK's evolving constitution.**

Olechnowicz, A. (2007) *The Monarchy and the British Nation, 1780 to the Present*, Cambridge: Cambridge University Press. **Informative cultural history of Britain's relationship with its monarchy down the ages.**

Turpin, C. and Tomkins, A. (2011) *British Government and the Constitution: Text and Materials*, 7th edn, Cambridge: Cambridge University Press. **Fully updated guide to the impact of the UK constitution on day-to-day government, replete with extracts from case law and parliamentary documents.**

ⓦ Online Resource Centre

www.oxfordtextbooks.co.uk/orc/Morrison4e/
Visit the Online Resource Centre that accompanies this book for web links and regular updates.

2

Parliamentary democracy in the UK

▌ The origins of the British Parliament

As explained in Chapter 1, the reins of power in Britain no longer lie with the sovereign, but with the Houses of Parliament and, specifically, **members of Parliament (MPs)** elected to its primary legislative chamber: the House of Commons.

But what are the origins of today's 'bicameral legislature'—a Parliament comprising twin chambers, each with its own distinct constitutional role? How does it discharge its functions and hold ministers accountable for their use of the prerogative powers vested in them by the Crown? And what are the implications for Parliament of devolution in the provinces?

Britain's Parliament, famously dubbed the 'mother of parliaments' by nineteenth-century social reformer John Bright, is rooted in successive institutions that emerged in the medieval period—initially to bolster, but ultimately to counteract, the power of monarchy. The most significant of these originated in Norman times, in the era of root-and-branch constitutional upheaval that also witnessed the publication, in 1086, of the Domesday Book—England's first great population census. To provide mechanisms through which the sovereign could tax and rule his subjects, a succession of bodies was established. These included the *Magnum Concilium* and *Curia Regis*—early forerunners of Parliament—and the **Privy Council**, a conclave of the sovereign's personal confidantes, at which meetings they continue to officiate. For more detailed explanations of the roles of these bodies, see the table entitled 'The role and composition of forerunners of the Houses of Parliament', to be found on the **Online Resource Centre** that accompanies this book.

Parliament today

Parliament long ago took precedence over the sovereign in the day-to-day exercise of constitutional power. By the fourteenth century, monarchs were already being forced to recognize that the earls and barons on whom they depended to maintain their authority had, for that reason, to be consulted on major affairs. It was during this tumultuous century that kings reluctantly came to accept the need to gain consent from their landed supporters to levy taxes and, in ensuing decades, a newly assertive Parliament of 'Commoners' secured the right to play an active part in converting royal petitions (Bills) into statutes (Acts).

Then, in the seventeenth century, came the English Civil War and with it the sequence of decisive breaks with tradition outlined in Chapter 1. While these began the process of ushering in a new order, it would be another 200 years or more before most people were granted a true stake in parliamentary democracy through the vote.

These developments are discussed in Chapter 4, which explores the British electoral system. But what exactly is this Parliament—this great organ of government and citizenship—in which UK citizens are expected to invest such faith? This chapter explores two key aspects of Britain's parliamentary democracy: the nature and composition of the various institutions of Parliament; and the roles, duties, and responsibilities that its members discharge on the country's behalf.

Hansard

Before examining the workings of Parliament, it is worth pausing to consider how its practices are recorded. Since 1909, all debates, votes, and other proceedings have been painstakingly transcribed for a sprawling record known as **Hansard**. Excepting the words of serving prime ministers, Hansard is not verbatim—'repetitions, redundancies, and obvious errors' are omitted—but it is the nearest we have to a definitive account of Parliament's business.

Although Hansard has been published by Parliament itself for only a century or so, it has existed far longer. As early as 1771, a printer named Miller was hauled before the Lord Mayor of London for producing illicit reports of parliamentary debates, while radical free speech campaigners John Wilkes and William Cobbett fought for the right to publish their own versions. The first detailed parliamentary reports appeared from 1803 in Cobbett's *Political Register*, courtesy of one Thomas Curson 'TC' Hansard—the printer after whom the 'official' record was named. Today, Hansard is one of the most reliable sources of news stories for political journalists at both local and national levels, providing full details not only of contemporaneously reported debates, but also of written parliamentary questions and answers, early day motions (EDMs—see Table 2.3), and petitions. Like live debates, it carries qualified privilege and can be accessed electronically (online at **www.publications.parliament.uk/pa/cm/cmhansrd.htm**). A more critical overview of individual voting records of MPs and peers can be found at **www.theyworkforyou.com**.

▌ The House of Commons

The linchpin of modern constitutional government in Britain is the 'lower house': the House of Commons. It currently comprises 650 MPs, each representing a **constituency**, or 'seat' (electoral district), averaging 65,000 inhabitants. In practice, wide disparities exist between some relatively underpopulated rural seats and others covering built-up areas. To this end, the Conservatives had hoped to cut the number of MPs to 600 by the time of the 2015 election and to redraw constituency boundaries to 'equalize' the sizes of populations covered by each one. However, their Liberal Democrat Coalition partners withdrew their backing for these proposals in response to the Tories' failure to support Deputy Prime Minister Nick Clegg's plans for House of Lords reform (see 'The House of Lords' in this chapter).

Unlike many other parliaments, the Commons chamber is ranged along two sets of opposing benches, presided over by its chairperson, the **Speaker**. To the right of the Speaker's chair are the government benches, while on the left are those occupied by 'Her Majesty's Loyal Opposition' (the Opposition)—generally the second biggest party after a general election. All MPs not allied to the governing party (or parties) sit along this side.

The Commons' adversarial layout mirrors the 'two-party politics' that (barring occasional interludes) has characterized Britain's parliamentary scene for centuries. Since the later medieval period, debate has been divided broadly along conservative versus radical/reformist lines with, at various times, Royalists ranged against Parliamentarians, landowning Whigs battling an upwardly mobile, entrepreneurial breed of Tories during the Industrial Revolution, and, latterly, Liberal, then Labour, MPs championing the rights of the 'common man' against the forces of a more establishment 'big C' Conservatism.

In modern times, two-party politics has continued to prevail, largely as a result of the inequities of the electoral system. As we will see in Chapter 4 ('How the British electoral system works'), the 'first past the post' (FPTP) voting process sees only candidates who win a *relative majority* of votes cast in their constituencies—that is, more than any of their rivals—elected to the Commons; all votes cast for anyone else are effectively 'wasted'. As a result, the electoral process favours parties that can muster sufficient concentrations of support in enough constituencies to win the number of seats needed to form a government—so discriminating against minority interests and independent candidates.

Table 2.1 Annual House of Commons timetable

Date	Event
May/June	State Opening of Parliament
May (one week over spring bank holiday)	Whit recess
July–September (two months)	Summer recess
September/October (three weeks)	Party conference season
October/November	Prorogation
December–January (for four weeks)	Christmas recess
February (one week)	Half-term recess
March/April (two weeks)	Easter recess

Table 2.2 Weekly House of Commons timetable

Day	Time of sitting
Monday	2.30–10.30 p.m.
Tuesday	2.30–10.30 p.m.
Wednesday	11.30 a.m.–7.30 p.m.
Thursday	10.30 a.m.–6.30 p.m.
Friday (13 days a year for private members' business, including private members' Bills)	9.30 a.m.–3.00 p.m.

While Commons debates are chaired by the Speaker, its business timetable is set by a Cabinet minister: the **Leader of the House**. The typical Commons year is outlined in Table 2.1, while its usual weekly sittings are set out in Table 2.2.

The role of a member of Parliament (MP) in relation to constituents

As of 1 April 2014, ordinary MPs each receive salaries of £67,060—the result of a second successive annual rise of just 1 per cent. These below-inflation increases have deliberately been set by the Independent Parliamentary Standards Authority (IPSA) to reflect the capped pay rises among public-sector workers imposed by the Coalition's austerity drive (see Chapter 7, 'Managing national debt'), and continuing public resentment over the parliamentary expenses scandal (see 'MPs, conflicts of interest, abuses of privilege—and how to avoid them' in this chapter). However, in a controversial move condemned by the leaders of all three main parties (although opposed in a Commons vote by only 40 of their colleagues), IPSA announced in December 2013 that MPs' salaries would rise by £7,000 in 2015—to £74,000 a year—making up for the previous years of restraint. Thereafter, they are expected to increase annually in line with average earnings. Not that MPs had been entirely short-changed under the previous regime: in addition to their salaries, they retain generous personal allowances enabling them to employ their own secretaries and/or researchers.

At any time, the serving government numbers between 80 and 100-odd MPs. All other MPs—save Opposition 'shadow ministers'—are known as 'backbench MPs', or **backbenchers**. Once elected, it is the duty of every MP—whether back-bencher or frontbencher—to represent the concerns and interests of *all* of their constituents, regardless of individual voters' political affiliations. Following the parliamentary expenses scandal (see 'MPs, conflicts of interest, abuses of privilege—and how to avoid them' in this chapter), the Coalition pledged to introduce a new power for constituents to 'recall' MPs found guilty of 'serious wrongdoing'—potentially forcing them to fight to retain their seats in by-elections. A Recall of MPs Bill was duly included in the last Queen's Speech before the 2015 election, but many of those campaigning for the changes argued that it fell well short of the Coalition's original promise. Under its proposals, constituents would be empowered to sack any MP sentenced to up to 12 months in prison, provided that one in ten of them signed a petition to this effect within eight weeks of the Commons ruling that he or she faced possible recall. This would theoretically rectify the 'anomaly' under which only MPs serving sentences of a year or more are automatically expelled from Parliament. However, campaigners, including Tory backbencher Zac Goldsmith, branded the Bill 'meaningless', because it contained a clause stipulating that any final decision to sack an MP and trigger a by-election would rest with a committee of fellow MPs.

Members discharge their constituency duties in the following ways:

- holding weekly 'surgeries' for constituents;
- writing to departmental ministers to try to resolve grievances voiced by constituents;
- asking written or oral questions in the Commons at Question Time—both 'Prime Minister's Questions' on a Wednesday and other regular slots, during which senior ministers answer for their departments;
- canvassing support among fellow MPs for early day motions (EDMs)—formal parliamentary records expressing strong views on issues dear to them;
- requesting leave from the Speaker for adjournment debates, urgent debates, or debates on e-petitions;
- introducing private members' Bills (PMBs)—a form of primary legislation that, if passed, would change the law of the land (see 'Private members' Bills' in this chapter); and
- coordinating e-petitions on behalf of constituents and/or the wider public interest.

The main forms of debate that may be tabled or promoted by backbenchers are explained in Table 2.3, but certain of their roles justify more detailed explanation.

Table 2.3 Types of Commons debate that may be tabled or promoted by backbenchers

Name	How it works	Example
Early day motion (EDM)	'Paper' record of strong view expressed by number of MPs. Rarely results in actual 'motion' (vote) or wins sufficient signatures to warrant full debate (for which at least half of sitting MPs must support motion), but, as part of official Commons record, has official status greater than minor procedures. Often gives journalists stories—and can, over time, influence government. Most importantly, enables backbenchers to highlight issues of personal concern, gauging colleagues' support for more definite attempts to initiate change through PMBs (see 'Private members' Bills' in this chapter)	Most significant EDM of recent times was tabled by then Opposition leader Margaret Thatcher in 1979, censuring Jim Callaghan's ailing Labour government. Callaghan's administration had been unstable since the collapse of the 'Lib–Lab Pact' negotiated with David Steel's Liberal Party the previous August, and Mrs Thatcher's motion precipitated a 'vote of no confidence' that brought it down. What followed for Labour, on 4 May 1979, was election loss to Tories. Other EDMs have included an influential motion signed by 412 of 646 MPs, days after the 2005 election, calling for a Climate Change Bill, which followed in 2006. Only three other EDMs had ever received more than 400 signatures.
Adjournment debate	Half-hour debate on motion that 'this House do now adjourn', held either in Commons or neighbouring Westminster Hall at end of day's business. Presents opportunity for a backbencher to raise issue of concern to /her constituents—and to 'summon' a minister to respond. As with EDMs, adjournment debates rarely result in votes, other than when debate raises a nationally significant issue over which strong disagreement exists	Conservative Prime Minister Neville Chamberlain, signatory to the Munich Agreement with Nazi Germany, was brought down by a motion flowing from adjournment debate: while the government won the vote—effectively a motion of confidence in his leadership following Hitler's breach of agreement by invading Poland—he resigned and was replaced by Winston Churchill.

Urgent debate	A backbencher may apply to the Speaker for urgent debate 'on a specific and important matter that should have urgent consideration' under Standing Order No. 24. In practice, far more MPs apply than are granted debates and the Speaker allows only one or two per session. If granted, debate takes place within 24 hours.	Recent urgent debates have included one called by Prime Minister David Cameron in August 2013 to determine whether Britain should back military action against the government of Syria, amid claims that it had used chemical weapons on its civilians.
e-petition debate	The Coalition introduced e-petitions to boost public engagement with Parliament. Anyone can start e-petitions by setting them up online at http://epetitions.direct.gov.uk. If it receives 100,000 or more signatories, e-petition is referred to the Backbench Business Committee for consideration for full Commons debate on one of 35 days each session. Campaigning backbenchers increasingly help to coordinate e-petitions to win parliamentary time for debates on pet issues.	Several parliamentary debates have been prompted by e-petitions, with grass-roots campaign groups such as 38 Degrees and Avaaz leading calls for MPs to debate issues ranging from the 'Robin Hood Tax' on the big banks to electoral reform. Labour used the justification of an e-petition attracting 170,000 backers in support of urgent debate on the Coalition's NHS reforms to table a last-minute attempt to halt them in March 2012—weeks after ministers blocked an e-petition debate on the same issue, arguing that it had already been debated in Commons. Backers of an e-petition demanding reinstatement of the death penalty (coordinated by political blogger Guido Fawkes via his order-order.com website) failed to secure debate after attracting just 26,000 signatories.

Surgeries

Also known as 'clinics', these weekly drop-in sessions may be attended by constituents wishing to voice concerns. They are normally held on Fridays (when little parliamentary business is timetabled), or Saturdays in the case of MPs whose constituencies are distant from London. Although many MPs hold surgeries in their constituency offices, today they frequently take place in more informal surroundings, such as church halls, community centres, and even pubs.

Question Time

An opportunity to quiz senior departmental ministers directly about their policy decisions and the day-to-day workings of their ministries, **Question Time** is held for at least one hour a day whenever the Commons is sitting. On Mondays and Tuesdays, it takes place between 2.30 p.m. and 3.30 p.m.; on Wednesdays, from 11.30 a.m. to 12p.m.; on Thursdays, from 10.30 a.m. to 12.30 p.m. (the two-hour slot on this day is intended to make up for the fact Parliament rarely sits on Fridays).

Each department takes turns to answer questions from the Commons floor on a fortnightly rota. In addition to these *departmental* question times, the prime minister answers questions on Wednesday lunchtimes, between 12 noon and 12.30 p.m. Between its introduction in 1961 and Mr Blair's election in 1997, 'Prime Minister's Questions' (or PMQs) occupied a twice-weekly 15-minute slot: on Tuesdays and Thursdays, between 3.00 p.m. and 3.15 p.m. Mr Blair's decision to combine the two into a single session was widely criticized as a high-handed presidential-style gesture calculated to limit opportunities for Parliament (and his own party) to scrutinize him publicly.

Nonetheless, the bumper Wednesday PMQs slot—which, since 1989, has been televised live on BBC2—remains a knockabout media highlight of the weekly Commons timetable.

Questions posed at departmental question times tend to be for verbal ('oral') responses. They are answered by ministers according to a rota called the 'Order of Oral Questions'. Prime Minister's Questions, in contrast, take one of two forms: oral or written (officially 'questions for a written answer').

Posed, as they are, in front of television cameras, oral questions attract most media attention—often for their 'Punch and Judy' nature rather than their substance. Because PMQs can be heavily oversubscribed, MPs keen to ask questions are advised to give the Speaker three days' advance notice of their intentions, to ensure that their names appear sufficiently early on the order paper for them to be called in the allotted time. Giving such notice does *not* mean that MPs must specify the *exact wording* of their questions at that stage; merely that they let it be known that they wish to ask them.

Prime Minister's Questions follow several curious conventions. The first question is always one asking the prime minister about the other engagements he/she has scheduled for that day. This will usually be immediately tailed by a 'follow-up' question tabled by whichever MP posed the initial procedural one. This is the *real* question and, while the prime minister may have prior notice of the subject to which it relates, he or she rarely knows exactly how it will be phrased. The prime minister's hope is that he or she has been adequately briefed by civil servants on the issue concerned to be able to ad lib a convincing answer (or to sidestep it effectively). When, later in the session, premiers refer, before taking a question, to 'the reply I gave some moments ago', they are alluding to the fact that the MP about to question them has used the same procedural nicety about their engagements to get his or her name on the order paper.

Despite being the most talked-about parliamentary activity, PMQs is often criticized by serious-minded observers for being superficial and insincere, and playing to the cameras. And it is not only the prime minister and his or her would-be replacement on the Opposition frontbenches who are accused of this: the most derided questions are often those asked by jobbing backbenchers using the session as an opportunity either to curry favour with the media in their own constituencies (and by extension their electorates) by focusing on extraordinarily specific local issues, or to massage ministers' egos in the hope of gaining promotion.

In general, MPs genuinely seeking to hold ministers to account for their actions and to influence decision-making on behalf of their constituents will pose *written questions* (which, as well as being 'put on paper' themselves, are intended for written answers). This enables them to be forensic—seeking more detailed replies than are likely to be delivered during the theatrical point-scoring exercise that PMQs often resembles. Although ministers invariably try to put a positive gloss on their policies—and the luxury of being able to map out a considered written answer gives them ample scope to do so—they are under a constitutional obligation to reply to these questions thoroughly and accurately. From a journalistic viewpoint, while snappy oral sound bites may generate easy headlines, stories that emerge from skilfully worded written questions can be more newsworthy in the long run.

An alternative is to table 'urgent questions'. These are on issues that have suddenly come to light and do not require MPs to give the usual three days' notice. In recent times, this device has increasingly been used by shadow ministers, as well as backbenchers, to hold ministers to account: since entering Opposition in 2010, Labour has tabled numerous urgent questions, grilling the Coalition on everything from its controversial reforms of welfare and the NHS, to the UK economy's loss of its 'triple-A' credit rating.

None of this should downplay the importance of straightforward oral questions—PMQs in particular. As a weekly barometer of how the political wind is swaying, there is nothing to rival it. While ordinary backbenchers may ask just one question, the Leader of the Opposition is allowed to pose six supplementaries and that of the second largest opposing party (normally the Liberal

Democrats), two. In May 2010, Mr Clegg forfeited his right to ask questions for the duration of the Coalition government that he formed with Conservative leader David Cameron. Indeed, as deputy prime minister, Mr Clegg has since stood in at the despatch box for Mr Cameron whenever he has been abroad.

Prime Minister's Questions have long generated lively exchanges between serving prime ministers and the pretenders who would dethrone them—and are said to make or break party leaders. Despite a shaky start, Mr Blair became an adept Question Time operator in his decade in power. Nonetheless, on stepping down in summer 2007, he confessed that he had always privately dreaded the weekly ordeal. While there was criticism of Mr Brown's testy, stilted performances at PMQs (despite his experience of 10 years as Chancellor of the Exchequer), Mr Cameron represented something of a return, at least initially, to the breezier style of Mr Blair.

The role of an MP in relation to Parliament and party

The primary duty of care of an MP lies, constitutionally, with his or her constituents. In addition, MPs have a responsibility to Parliament, and the British people generally, to participate in debate and to scrutinize the workings of the executive (government and Cabinet). A chief way in which they discharge this responsibility is through the committee system—a key 'check and balance' built into the workings of the legislature to ensure the transparency and accountability of government.

In practice, however, the nature of Britain's party system means that these constitutional responsibilities can conflict with the pressure under which most MPs come to support and defend the official policies of their parties. This instilled 'party loyalty'—increasingly enforced by a strict whip system—is known as 'toeing the party line'. This archaic expression refers to the clearly delineated lines drawn along the length of the Commons in front of each set of benches, behind which members on either side are required to stand while debating. It relates to the principle that opposing MPs should be made to stand sufficiently far apart to ensure that if they were to draw their swords in the heat of debate, they could hold their arms fully outstretched without their weapons clashing.

Parliamentary scrutiny and the committee system

Most backbenchers—and peers, who have an equivalent system in the Lords— are members of at least one committee. Each comprises a minimum of 11 members, one of whom is elected to chair. The proportion of committees chaired by MPs or peers drawn from one party or other has customarily reflected the distribution of Commons seats. Between May 1997 and May 2010, therefore, Labour had proportionately more chairpersons than all other parties put together, reflecting its majority, while the same is currently true of the Tories.

Although committees have become more 'fluid' in the forms that they have taken recently—a Committee against Anti-Semitism was formed in 2005—they can generally be divided into three types:

- select committees;
- general committees (including public and private Bill committees, and grand committees); and
- joint committees.

Select committees

The most frequently publicized type, **select committees** scrutinize the workings of individual government departments and Parliament itself, and as such are permanent (at least until the department to which they relate is renamed or disbanded). At present, there are 38 select committees, covering a mix of departmental matters, interdepartmental policy issues, and internal parliamentary and wider constitutional matters. This latter category includes the Backbench Business Committee, which decides how the (limited) time allotted to backbenchers is divided up, and a European Scrutiny Committee, charged with assessing the legal and/or political importance of newly issued European Union (EU) documents. Departmental committees include the Education Committee—which scrutinizes the Department for Education (DfE)—and the Culture, Media, and Sport Select Committee. There is also a Commons Liaison Committee (established by Mr Blair), comprising the chairpersons of all other select committees, to which prime ministers submit themselves for questioning on government policy twice a year.

Select committees have powers to summon MPs, senior civil servants, and other public officials as witnesses, and to publish reports on their findings, which are delivered to the Commons, printed, and placed on the Parliament website. However dissembling their responses might be, governments have only 60 days in which to reply formally to committees' published recommendations. One of the most explosive hearings of recent times occurred on 15 July 2003, when late weapons inspector David Kelly was grilled by the Foreign Affairs Select Committee amid the controversy over a dossier compiled by the Blair government to justify its case for war against Saddam Hussein's Iraq. Members subjected Dr Kelly to intensive questioning about whether he was the source of a report by BBC defence correspondent Andrew Gilligan for Radio 4's *Today* programme, which claimed that senior intelligence sources were concerned that ministers had 'sexed up' the dossier by exaggerating the likelihood that Saddam's forces could unleash weapons of mass destruction (WMDs) within 45 minutes of being ordered to do so. Dr Kelly was found dead in a wood near his Gloucestershire home two days later.

Because they are permanent, the composition of select committees has become increasingly contentious, in light of their customary inbuilt bias towards governing parties. During the Thatcher and early Blair years, Parliament was often criticized for failing to hold ministers adequately to account, and committees in particular often seemed neutered—not least because premiers had a habit of using their party whips to parachute favoured placemen and women into chairperson roles. It was against this backdrop (and the general loss of public trust in MPs sparked by the expenses controversy) that the Commons Parliamentary Reform Select Committee recommended in 2010 that all future chairpersons should be formally elected by fellow MPs. The Coalition implemented this recommendation, introducing elections by alternative vote (AV—see Chapter 4, 'Proportional representation (PR) and other voting systems') for most chairs and extending the scope of elections further, to cover all members of such committees. Henceforth, committee seats allotted to each party proportionally would be filled by MPs elected by their fellow party members.

General (including public and private Bill) committees

The other most influential type of committee is the **general committee**—an overarching category embracing public Bill committees, private Bill committees, and grand committees. Most numerous are the first of these (previously known as 'standing committees'). The role of **public Bill committees** is to scrutinize, comment on, amend, and/or refer back to the Commons for further consideration Bills in the process of becoming Acts. Unlike the standing committees of old, they have enhanced powers, including the ability to summon expert witnesses and officials from outside Parliament to give evidence.

Because the work of public and **private Bill committees** can take weeks or months, governments sometimes try to bypass them by rushing through legislation that they deem urgent. If agreed by the Speaker, in such cases the Commons itself takes on the role of such a committee, as a 'Committee of the Whole House'—an approach that the Lords uses more routinely for its own committee stages. This crucial stage in the passage of a Bill is explored in more detail in the section entitled 'The passage of a Bill'.

Most **grand committees** are concerned with debating the impact of legislation on specific geographical nations and regions. There is, for example, a grand committee for the East Midlands and another for Scotland. Grand committees also exist for delegated legislation, European documents, and the House of Lords—which uses them for committee stages not taken on the floor of the House.

Joint committees

So-called because they are composed of both MPs and peers, joint committees include the Joint Committee on House of Lords Reform, formed in 2002 to consider a range of alternative options for the composition of the 'Upper House' in the wake of the as-yet-incomplete Lords reforms (see 'The House of Lords' in this chapter). Since 1894, there has been a joint committee devoted to assisting the swift passage of laws designed to rationalize the number of Acts on the statute book (the record of all parliamentary legislation in place at any one time). These 'consolidation Bills', normally introduced in the Lords rather than the Commons, seek to combine disparate Acts on the same or similar subjects into single statutes.

Into the twenty-first century—juggling parliamentary and constituency work

A significant development approved in October 2011 was the use of Twitter in the Commons. After the House Procedure Committee recommended that portable electronic devices be permitted in the main chamber, MPs voted 206 to 63 against a motion to block use of the social media web service, defying warnings by opponents, including Lib Dem Deputy Leader Simon Hughes, that this could lead to tweeting members appearing 'disconnected' from debates in which they were meant to be participating.

In theory, using Twitter (and indeed SMS text messaging and email) via mobile smartphones could prove revolutionary, enabling MPs to juggle parliamentary duties with answering constituents' queries and receiving feedback. In practice, questions remain about whether most members are up to such multitasking. Even as the Commons voted in favour of tweeting (provided that it was done silently), the *Huffington Post* ran a news feature revealing that MPs who tweeted most frequently and/or had the greatest number of followers tended to be those with the poorest parliamentary attendance. Meanwhile, in July 2012, members of the Commons Treasury Committee were widely criticized in the media for tweeting while they were supposed to be concentrating on questioning former Barclays chief executive Bob Diamond over the Libor-rigging scandal (see Chapter 7, 'Short-selling, interest rate "fixes", and wider questions about banking')—prompting some members of the public to tweet back urging them to get on with the job in hand.

Party loyalty and the whip system

As noted earlier, British MPs tend to be affiliated to political parties. There have been notable exceptions, such as Martin Bell, the one-time BBC foreign correspondent who overturned disgraced former Conservative minister Neil Hamilton's huge majority in Tatton in 1997, standing as an independent candidate on an 'anti-sleaze' ticket. But, mostly, the nature of Britain's electoral system tends to guarantee candidates backed by party machines—particularly those representing the three main ones—the best chances of election. More recently, the 2010 election saw Caroline Lucas elected as Britain's first Green Party MP in Brighton Pavilion, while in March 2012 former Labour backbencher George Galloway trounced his old party in a dramatic by-election win for Respect in Bradford West. As the sole members for their parties, Ms Lucas and Mr Galloway are arguably independent MPs in all but name. Following the defection of two Tory MPs, Douglas Carswell and Mark Reckless, to the United Kingdom Independence Party (UKIP), and their successful defence of their seats in two subsequent by-elections, a new 'minority' force entered the Commons just months before the 2015 election.

Party membership is a double-edged sword. Being selected as a candidate for a major party grants an individual access to a huge support network, including significant financial backing in election campaigns. Independents, in contrast, must largely fund themselves. But being a partisan MP also comes at a price. Parties in Britain have traditionally been 'broad churches' representing people united by common ideals, but who may hold a variety of shades of opinion on specific issues. In recent times, however, party leaders (particularly serving prime ministers) have been criticized for stifling dissent in their ranks by using the whip system to force their MPs to back official lines when voting.

There are three broad definitions of the term **whip**:

- whips;
- party whip; and
- three-line whips.

Whips are individuals (MPs or peers) charged with 'whipping into line' back-benchers when a debate or vote that the leadership regards as important is pending. It is the job of whips, led by a chief whip, to persuade MPs whose views are known to differ from those of their leadership' to attend debates and to vote with their party at the appropriate time.

Whips have frequently been accused of cajoling or bullying MPs into doing their leaders' bidding. When John Major was struggling to pass the Maastricht Treaty into British law in May 1992 following a backbench rebellion by Eurosceptic Tories (see Chapter 9, 'Towards an EU "superstate"?'), ailing loyalists—including one who had just had brain surgery—were taxied to the Commons to act as 'lobby fodder' for the government. The media dubbed this the 'stretcher vote'. Under New Labour, whips would notoriously bombard MPs with pager alerts urging them to turn up and vote along party lines, and to stay 'on message' when speaking publicly.

Mr Blair's prolonged honeymoon with his backbenchers after his 1997 election victory ended abruptly in his second term, when he faced a succession of knife-edge votes, despite retaining a large Commons majority. He squeezed through some of his more controversial reforms, such as foundation hospitals and university top-up fees, by wafer-thin margins. In his third term, he actually lost the vote to extend the length of time for which terrorist suspects may be questioned by police without charge from 14 to 90 days, in spite of rigorous arm-twisting by then Labour Chief Whip Jacqui Smith.

In addition to being fixers, the whips also play a more 'constructive' role. Crucially, they act as unofficial personnel officers for the party leadership—talent-spotting potential future ministers and frontbench spokespeople, and providing important lines of communication between leader and party.

The term 'party whip' effectively refers to an MP or peer's 'membership' of his or her parliamentary party. Like any such affiliation, this can be withdrawn if he or she breaks the 'rules' attached to membership. Mr Major temporarily withdrew the whip from the 22 'Maastricht rebels'—including future party leader Iain Duncan Smith—as a punishment for their disloyalty. Mr Galloway, as Labour MP for Glasgow Kelvin, had the whip removed in October 2003 following his repeated public attacks on Mr Blair over the invasion of Iraq. The same fate befell several Labour backbenchers prosecuted for bogus allowance claims in the fallout from the 2009 expenses scandal, while in 2012 another Labour backbencher, Eric Joyce, was expelled from the party after assaulting four fellow MPs in the Commons Strangers' Bar—an incident leading to his subsequent conviction.

Votes judged to be of the highest importance are highlighted—and underlined three times—in a weekly circular, *The Whip*, sent to MPs and peers. These votes are known as 'three-line whips', and attendance and voting along party lines is regarded by party leaders as mandatory. There are two lower levels of voting:

- 'one-line whips' (or 'free votes') tend to be called on 'matters of conscience'—non-party political issues, such as fox hunting or euthanasia; and

- 'two-line whips', under which MPs are told that they 'must attend' unless they have made legitimate arrangements to be absent under the *pairing* system.

Pairing is a traditional parliamentary convention allowing one MP sitting on one side of the House to miss a vote on which he or she would have voted one way if an MP with opposing views on the opposite side of the chamber also misses the vote—each missing vote 'cancelling the other out'. Although regarded as acceptable, leaders would obviously prefer all of their MPs to attend and vote with their party, regardless of whether members on the other side are absent, to increase the leader's chances of winning votes. In turn, certain 'tribal' members—notably the late former Labour MP Tony Benn—have refused on principle to participate in pairing.

For a number of years, Labour called a halt to pairing—in retaliation for a 1996 incident in which, while Mr Major's government was in power, three

Conservative MPs cheated by each pairing up with members from both major Opposition parties (thereby cancelling out six, rather than three, votes). Despite reviving the convention more recently, the party remains guarded about when, and how often, to use it. In December 2010, Mr Miliband sparked a row with the Coalition by refusing to pair one of his own MPs with then Environment Secretary Chris Huhne to allow him to miss a crucial vote on the proposed tripling of undergraduate tuition fees while he attended a United Nations climate change summit in Mexico.

Three-line whips have long been used as the ultimate call to arms (and disciplinary device) by party leaders—so much so that the term has passed into popular vernacular to denote engagements at which attendance is compulsory. But, as with collective responsibility (see Chapter 3, 'Collective responsibility'), the Coalition agreed early on to compromise established practice in areas of principled disagreement between the parties, in the interests of preserving the overall alliance. For example, the official 'Coalition agreement' included provision for a three-line whip to force through the Referendum Bill, which paved the way for the 2011 public vote on electoral reform (although Tories were permitted to campaign *against* changing the voting system when the referendum came).

MPs, conflicts of interest, abuses of privilege—and how to avoid them

Recent years have seen MPs accused of compromising their responsibilities to their constituents and Parliament by affiliating themselves to 'outside interests' other than those to which they have constitutional obligations. To promote greater openness about such interests—and avoid charges of corruption or deceit about their motives—since 1974 they have been expected to declare any gifts or income received over and above their parliamentary salaries on a **register of members' financial interests** (formerly the 'register of members' interests').

The idea that MPs might have financial or non-pecuniary interests in organizations other than the Commons is hardly new. Eighteenth- and nineteenth-century MPs were often industrialists, agriculturalists, and/or landlords first and foremost, and elected representatives second—their decision to stand in the first place motivated as much by commercial self-interest as by concern to improve the lot of their fellow man. Conversely, when the Labour Party was formed, one of its aims was to get working-class candidates elected to the Commons, to counter the long-standing dominance of the middle and upper classes. To enable people from poorer backgrounds to fight elections, the trade union movement (one of several bodies that united to form the party) offered to 'sponsor' them—a traditional source of funding that continued for more than a century, but recently switched from MPs themselves to their constituencies. Even Mr Blair—one of his party's most determined 'modernizers'—was sponsored by the (now defunct) Transport and General Workers' Union (TGWU, later T&G) for much of his time as an MP, while the constituencies of some 102 of Mr Miliband's MPs receive funding from its successor, the Unite union.

While Labour has long been accused of being in the unions' pockets, similar charges have been levelled at the Conservatives in relation to big business. When Kenneth Clarke, a former Tory Health Secretary and Chancellor, retired (temporarily) to the back benches in 1997, after losing a leadership contest to William Hague, he took on several company directorships as well as the chairmanship of British American Tobacco (BAT). But the outside interests of some of his erstwhile frontbench colleagues were more controversial still. Jonathan Aitken, Minister for Defence Procurement in Mr Major's government, notoriously signed a 'gagging order' during the 'Iraqi Supergun' affair, preventing it being disclosed that a British arms company of which he was a non-executive director, BMARC, had sold weapons to Saddam's regime. Another major lobbying saga under Mr Major erupted over 'cash for questions': in October 1994, Trade Minister Neil Hamilton and a colleague, Tim Smith, were accused in *The Guardian* of receiving money in brown paper envelopes from Harrods owner Mohamed Al Fayed in exchange for asking parliamentary questions on his behalf—a clear breach of Commons rules. Both were forced to resign, and although Hamilton was granted immunity from parliamentary privilege to sue both the paper and Al Fayed, he was unsuccessful.

Following the Hamilton debacle and a series of personal scandals involving other ministers, Mr Major established a new Committee on Standards in Public Life under distinguished judge Lord Nolan. After six months' deliberation, the Nolan Committee published *Seven Principles of Public Life* (see Table 2.4), to which it stated MPs and other senior public officials should in future adhere.

If 'cash for questions' marked a low point for Mr Major, its fallout was nothing compared to that from the MPs' expenses scandal that erupted under Gordon Brown. What began as a trickle of minor revelations about the questionable claims of a handful of MPs—exposed by requests under the Freedom of Information Act 2000 (FoI) from journalists Ben Leapman, Jon Ungoed-Thomas, and Heather Brooke—had, by May 2009, become a flood, with the release of unexpurgated details of the accounts of hundreds of MPs in a flurry of front-page scoops by *The Daily Telegraph*.

An early casualty of the furore was Conservative backbencher Derek Conway, who had the whip withdrawn by Mr Cameron after it emerged that he had used his parliamentary allowance to pay his younger son, Freddie, £40,000 and his eldest, Henry, £32,000 for purportedly working as his researchers. The scandal centred less on their being employed by their father—it soon emerged that such nepotism was commonplace at Westminster—than on whether they actually carried out the duties, of which no records were kept. The three main

Table 2.4 Nolan's *Seven Principles of Public Life*

Principle	Meaning
Selflessness	Duty to act solely in terms of public interest (i.e. not for financial gain for himself/herself, his/her family, or friends)
Integrity	Duty not to sustain any financial obligation to outside individuals or organizations that might seek to influence him/her in performance of his/her duties
Objectivity	Principle that appointment to his/her position be based purely on merit
Accountability	Duty to be accountable for his/her actions to public and to submit him/herself to 'whatever scrutiny is appropriate' to his/her office
Openness	Duty to be open about his/her actions and decisions in office
Honesty	Duty to declare any private interests relating to his/her public duties and to take steps to resolve any conflicts of interest
Leadership	Duty to promote all principles by leadership and example

parties swiftly ordered their MPs to declare any relatives whom they were employing, the nature of their engagement, and details of their remuneration.

The ensuing controversy led to further disclosures about Parliament's arcane allowances regime. It transpired that many MPs—including then Speaker Michael Martin—were claiming up to £22,000 a year to help with mortgage repayments on second homes (those in their constituencies), despite the fact that some had long since repaid the loans. Scenting blood, the media was soon chasing every shred of information about the obscure rules governing MPs' expenses. An early twist in the saga came when it emerged that MPs claiming £250 or less on expenses were not even required to submit receipts to the authority then in charge, the Commons Fees Office (formally titled the 'Operations Directorate of the House of Commons Department of Resources'). Although Mr Brown immediately slashed the minimum receipted claim to £25, this change came into effect only in June 2009—by which time the saga had moved on. That March, details were released under FoI requests of a so-called 'John Lewis list' of perks for which MPs were eligible in relation to second homes: MPs could claim (at taxpayers' expense) for furnishing the properties—including around £10,000 for a new kitchen, £300 for air-conditioning units, and £750 apiece for television sets.

Two months later, the High Court ruled that a request for full disclosure of MPs' expenses, made some two years earlier under FoI, should be granted. Under intense media pressure, the custodian of this information, Mr Martin, reluctantly agreed to publish a receipt-by-receipt breakdown—in so doing, revealing that Mr Brown had claimed £4,471 to modernize his kitchen in 2005, with Mr Blair reimbursed £10,600 for one at his former constituency home in Sedgefield. Only weeks after these disclosures, husband-and-wife Tory MPs Nicholas and Ann Winterton were found guilty by Parliamentary Commissioner John Lyon of breaching rules introduced two years earlier to stop MPs reclaiming rent on properties owned by family members. Having paid off the mortgage on their £700,000 London flat in the early 1990s, the couple had placed it in a family trust to avoid inheritance tax. But since 2002 they had occupied it again as tenants, paying the trust £21,600 a year out of a Commons entitlement known as the 'additional costs allowance' (ACA)—a subsidy of up to £24,000 a year to help MPs who needed second homes because of the distance between their constituencies and Parliament. It soon emerged that 'abuse' of the ACA by MPs was widespread—with many members deliberately 'flipping' the houses and flats they designated as second homes to claim help with the cost of furnishing/refurbishing more than one residence. Among the serving and shadow ministers exposed for misusing the ACA were then Communities Secretary Hazel Blears, Transport Secretary Geoff Hoon, and future Coalition minister Michael Gove. Some members had even added value to properties at taxpayers' expense before selling them—avoiding capital gains tax (see Chapter 7, 'Fiscal policy and taxation') by designating them 'first' homes.

But 'home-flipping' turned out to be only part of the picture. Under intense pressure from its critics, the government finally relented and ordered full details of all MPs' expense receipts going back to April 2004 to be published on 1 July that year, but two months before its (heavily redacted) disclosure was published, *The Telegraph* unleashed the first of numerous sensational instalments revealing the extent of abuse of the allowance system—after obtaining a leaked disc containing data on all 646 serving MPs from former SAS officer John Wick. For weeks, the news was dominated by unravelling details of the sometimes lavish, more often trivial, and occasionally downright bizarre expenses claimed by MPs and peers. Among the most outlandish were the purchase of a £1,645 'duck island' by Conservative MP Peter Viggers, the £2,115 reimbursement to ex-minister Douglas Hogg for the cost of cleaning his moat, and a rejected claim made by then Home Secretary Jacqui Smith (apparently unwittingly) for a £67 Virgin Media bill that included two pornographic pay-per-view films ordered by her husband. She eventually resigned (officially for family reasons) ahead of the 2009 European elections, but after losing her seat in the 2010 Westminster poll conceded that one of her reasons for quitting had actually been her elevation to the status of 'poster girl' of the expenses scandal.

Inevitably, ministers had to act—and act decisively. In the end, Mr Brown's response to the scandal was threefold:

- commissioning Sir Christopher Kelly, chairman of the Committee on Standards in Public Life, to examine the existing expenses regime and to recommend reform;

- establishing IPSA to assume responsibility for policing the expenses system from the existing in-house Commons authorities, the Members' Estimate Committee and Fees Office; and

- ensuring that questionable second-home expenses claimed since 2004 were repaid by MPs in full, by authorizing retired permanent secretary Sir Thomas Legg to conduct a backdated audit—invoicing anyone whom he judged to be in breach of existing rules.

Sir Christopher's report, published in October 2009, contained several recommendations, all of which Mr Brown accepted. The most significant were:

- scrapping the ACA following an 'appropriate' transitional period;
- banning MPs from employing members of their families within five years;
- ending the generous 'resettlement grants' to which retiring MPs had been entitled, which had been worth up to a year's salary (around £65,000) depending on the members' age and length of service—the first £30,000 being tax-free, with all members now entitled to no more than eight weeks' pay; and
- transferring responsibility to IPSA for determining both MPs' expenses, and their salaries and pensions.

Not all MPs 'outed' for excessive or inappropriate claims took their punishments meekly. When, in February 2010, Sir Thomas issued individual letters demanding repayment from 390 MPs (who had collectively 'over-claimed' £1.3 million), some said that they did not have enough money available, while others criticized the 'injustice' of applying a new set of rules to claims made in good faith under old ones. By the time his final report was published—exposing a 'culture of deference' at the Fees Office—70 MPs had lodged appeals against his demands (at least nine winning them). In the end, the most substantial repayments that Sir Thomas requested included £42,458 from then Communities Minister Barbara Follett and £24,878 from Liam Fox, later to serve for a time as Mr Cameron's Defence Secretary.

More unedifying still was the prosecution for false accounting of five Labour MPs—former Fisheries Minister Elliot Morley, David Chaytor, Jim Devine, Eric Illsley, and Margaret Moran—and Conservative peers Lord Hanningfield and Lord Taylor. All but one of these parliamentarians were subsequently convicted (Ms Moran was judged unfit to stand trial owing to depression)—but not before Messrs Morley, Chaytor, and Devine had tried to invoke the constitutional protection of parliamentary privilege (see Chapter 1, 'Statute'), arguing that allowing a law court to try them would breach the principle of the separation of powers between judiciary and legislature.

Their efforts to avoid a high-profile trial were short-lived, however: in June 2010, Mr Justice Saunders ruled that there was no 'logical, practical, or moral justification' for their immunity. Expenses scandals have not been confined to Westminster. At time of writing, police were investigating claims made in a BBC Spotlight programme about dubious claims by Northern Irish MLAs from Sinn Fein and the DUP.

The Parliamentary Commissioner for Standards

To reinforce his determination to stamp out the perceived culture of 'sleaze' among certain party members, Mr Major had a formal code of conduct for MPs drawn up and appointed Sir Gordon Downey as first **Parliamentary Commissioner for Standards** in 1995. The Commissioner's job is to oversee the register of interests, summoning and holding to account any member felt to have breached the code. The current Commissioner is Kathryn Hudson, who assumed the role on 1 January 2013. To ensure that the Commissioner is correctly discharging his or her duties, a further layer of oversight exists, in the guise of the Committee on Standards and Privileges. Not to be confused with the Committee on Standards in Public Life, this is composed of sitting MPs and has the same membership as the House of Commons Commission (see 'The role of the Commons Speaker' in this chapter). A separate Lords Commissioner for Standards (currently Paul Kernaghan) oversees probity in the Upper House. Among his recent investigations was a probe into the accommodation expenses of Conservative co-chairman Baroness Warsi, after she referred herself to him in June 2012 amid allegations that she had claimed her allowance while staying with a friend, rent-free, in 2008. She was subsequently cleared of expenses irregularities, but found to have breached the Lords' code of conduct for failing to register properly a property with it.

The Independent Parliamentary Standards Authority (IPSA)

Established in Mr Brown's last year in power, the **Independent Parliamentary Standards Authority (IPSA)** was charged not only with drawing up a new allowances system, but also with setting and reviewing MPs' salaries and pensions. Although it began developing a firm 'scheme' of changes to the old expenses system in 2009, it took until after the 2010 election to implement it. While it was substantially the same as the recommendations made by Sir Christopher, finer details included:

- replacing MPs' ability to claim second-home expenses with an entitlement to help with rented accommodation costs, widening the definition of 'London area' hitherto used by MPs claiming accommodation expenses on the grounds that their constituencies were too far from Westminster for them to commute (members are now no longer to be eligible for help with overnight stays if any part of their constituency was within 20 miles of Parliament, or when a commute from any part of their constituency to Westminster was possible within 60 minutes by public transport at peak times); and

- limiting expenditure for any train journey to the cost of a standard-class (rather than first-class) open ticket.

▌ The House of Lords

Before describing the means by which Parliament passes legislation, it is necessary to look at the nature and composition of the second chamber: the House of Lords. Since the passage of the House of Lords Act 1999, which Labour introduced to start the process of reforming or replacing this institution, it has been in a state of prolonged limbo—and currently remains a 'transitional House', despite a recent attempt by Mr Clegg to revive the reform agenda (see next section).

What is the point of the Lords?

Even among parliamentarians who dispute the Lords' current make-up there is widespread support for the principle that the main law-making chamber in a bicameral legislature should be held accountable by a second. The ongoing arguments over whether the Lords should be reformed or abolished are less about any real desire to scrap the Upper House altogether than a growing recognition that, in a modern democracy, a second chamber composed primarily of political appointees and members by birthright is fundamentally anachronistic.

As long ago as the early twentieth century, the Lords had begun to seem outmoded to many. But it was Herbert Asquith's Chancellor, David Lloyd George, who brought the case for reform to a head when his 1909 'People's Budget', which sought to raise taxes to fund social reform, was rejected by the disproportionately Conservative Lords. Following his 1910 election victory, Asquith sought to prevent the Lords ever again rejecting legislation outright and, backed by a threat from George V to force through reform by creating sufficient Liberal peers to overcome its inbuilt Tory majority, Asquith succeeded in passing the Parliament Act 1911. This replaced the Lords' power of veto with a right merely to *delay* Bills—and for a maximum of two calendar years (or three parliamentary sessions). Subsequently, the Lords voluntarily ceded further powers in recognition of the unequivocal mandate for change following Labour's landslide 1945 election victory. In a constitutional tweak that became known as the 'Salisbury convention', or 'Salisbury doctrine', then Tory leader in the Lords Viscount Cranborne (later Lord Salisbury) agreed that the Upper House should not oppose the second or third readings of legislation promised in a governing party's election manifesto.

The Lords' delaying period was further truncated by the Parliament Act 1949 to two sessions over 13 months. Any attempt to delay further, in defiance of the Commons' will, has since seen governments 'invoke the Parliament Act(s)'. The Lords' repeated attempts to thwart Labour's hunting ban during Mr Blair's second term were defeated in this way.

Since Asquith's run-in with the Lords, little decisive action was taken until the House of Lords Act 1999, which banned all but a handful of hereditary peers from continuing to sit in the House. Its long-term aim was to replace the heredi-tary principle with some form of membership entitlement based on individuals' contribution to society through public service or other major achievement.

The Lords' composition prior to 1999 was as follows.

1. The **Lords Spiritual**—26 peers, comprising:

   (a) the Archbishops of Canterbury and York;

   (b) the Bishops of London, Durham, and Winchester; and

   (c) the 21 next most senior Church of England diocesan bishops.

2. The Lords Temporal—1,263 peers, comprising:

   (a) all 759 *hereditary peers* of England, Scotland, Great Britain, and the UK (not including Northern Ireland);

   (b) the *Lords of Appeal in Ordinary (the Law Lords)*—27 peers 'created' by successive governments under the Appellate Jurisdiction Act 1876 to help the Lords to fulfil its role as the UK's final court of appeal; and

   (c) 477 others with **life peerages** created in **honours lists** under the terms of the Life Peerages Act 1958.

Hereditary peers have been permitted to disclaim their peerages so that they may stand as MPs since Benn persuaded Harold Macmillan's Conservative government to change the law through the Peerage Act 1963, after inheriting the title Viscount Stansgate from his father while sitting in the Commons.

Following Mr Benn's lead, Tory MP Quintin Hogg (later Lord Hailsham) dis-claimed his family seat to fight a by-election—ironically, in his father's old con-stituency of St Marylebone. But, most peculiarly, in 1963 Lord Home performed a double-flip by giving up an inherited title that had earlier forced him to resign a Commons seat to return to the Lower House as prime minister. His action—prompted by his election to replace Macmillan as Conservative leader—had the unique consequence of creating a two-week interval between his 'resigna-tion' as a peer and re-election as an MP, during which time Britain's prime minister was a member of neither the Commons nor the Lords.

The House of Lords Act 1999

The 1999 Act contained five key clauses designed to pave the way for an—at least partially—elected second chamber. After a series of run-ins between Mr Blair, his own backbenchers, the Tories, and the Lords itself, however, it was decided to move towards reform gradually by setting up a 'transitional' chamber that would initially do little more than remove the automatic member-ship rights of all but 92 hereditary peers. In the meantime, the question of what the final composition of a new Upper House should be was handed to a Royal Commission headed by former Tory minister Lord Wakeham.

Of the 92 hereditary peers permitted to remain in the House during the transition period, 90 were elected—but by their fellow peers, not by the public. The aim was to retain individuals with a history of making valuable contributions to debates, rather than the many who seldom attended proceedings. Since 2002, whenever elected hereditary peers have died, their places have been taken not by their heirs, but by other hereditaries drawn from the pool of those initially debarred from the Lords in 1999. By-elections, conducted using the alternative vote (AV) system (see Chapter 4, 'Proportional representation (PR) and other voting systems'), must be held within three months of the peers' deaths. The only peers eligible to vote at such times are other serving hereditary members drawn from the same party grouping—or, in the case of cross-bench peers, fellow cross-benchers. At time of writing, the most recent 'new arrival' was the cross-bench (non-affiliated) peer Lord Cromwell, who was elected to replace Lord Moran following the latter's death on 14 February 2014.

As well as the 90 lords with **elected hereditary peerages**, however, a further two hereditary peers have remained *ex officio* members since 1999, based on their ceremonial significance to the chamber. These are the Earl Marshal, the Duke of Norfolk, and Lord Great Chamberlain, the Marquess of Cholmondeley. In addition, 10 new life peerages were controversially created when the Act was passed to enable several hereditary peers *not* elected to remain. These included former Tory Leader of the House Lord Cranborne, ex-Foreign Secretary Lord Carrington, and the Earl of Longford. The process by which the transitional House was set up was brokered as a compromise amendment to the Bill by Lord Weatherill, a former Commons Speaker.

After the internal election following passage of the 'Weatherill Amendment', the composition of the Lords was as follows:

- 26 Lords Spiritual; and

- 598 Lords Temporal, comprising 27 Law Lords, two non-elected hereditary peers, 90 elected hereditary peers, and 477 life peers.

Since then, life peers have continued to be appointed at a prodigious rate and the balance of power between parties has fluctuated, with Labour finally reaching the symbolic tipping point at which it had as many peers as the Tories and Lib Dems put together in 2009—12 years after regaining power. Shortly after entering coalition, Mr Cameron and Mr Clegg unveiled plans to create up to 172 new party-affiliated peers between them to ensure the uninterrupted passage of their Bills through the Lords—a move condemned by Labour MP Chris Bryant, a former Deputy Leader of the Commons, as 'the single largest simultaneous act of political patronage probably since Charles II came to the throne in 1660'. As of August 2014, the Tories and Lib Dems boasted 319 peers between them (220 and 99 respectively) to Labour's 218.

In practice, although the Lords' political composition tends broadly to mirror that of the Commons, members drawn from the governing party (or parties) often behave in a more independent-minded way than their ministerial 'masters' would like. The Coalition weathered a string of embarrassing defeats at peers' hands over its controversial Health and Social Care and Welfare Reform Bills—some spearheaded by prominent Tories and Lib Dems. Following months of horse-trading with rebel Lib Dem peers led by veteran former minister Baroness Williams, then Health Secretary Andrew Lansley finally dragged his Bill onto the statute book in 2012, but only after several attempts by those still wary of the legislation to frustrate it with eleventh-hour amendments (see Chapter 6, 'The Health and Social Care Act 2012 and the reinvention of the NHS'). And former Tory ministers Lords Mackay, Mawhinney, and Newton were among government peers who tried to thwart aspects of the Welfare Reform Bill, which suffered more than half a dozen defeats in the Lords. In the end, this Bill reached the statute book only with the help of an obscure procedural rule designed to limit 'parliamentary ping-pong' between Commons and Lords. 'Financial privilege' rules allow governments to overturn amendments tabled in the Lords to public Bills that are intended to 'make significant changes to public expenditure' and/or 'affect national or local taxation or National Insurance [NI]' (see Chapter 8, 'The basis of the "welfare state"'). Given that the Bill introduced the biggest shake-up of the welfare state since its inception—and related directly to NI-funded benefits—it was judged to pass this test.

Lords with no declared party affiliation are known as 'cross-benchers'. Appropriately, they sit on benches ranged in short rows across the width of the House, with the government benches to their left and the Opposition to their right. Although independent of party ties, cross-benchers often flex their political muscles. During the choppy passage of the NHS reforms, persistent opposition to the Bill came from then cross-bencher Lord Owen, ex-leader of the Social Democratic Party (SDP), which was set up by a splinter group that abandoned the Labour Party over its drift to the left in 1981. So opposed was Lord Owen to the Coalition's NHS policies that, following Mr Miliband's reform of Labour's links with the unions (see Chapter 5, 'The structure and constitution of the modern Labour Party'), he publicly announced his renewed support for the party—informing the convener of the cross-benchers that he would henceforth sit as an 'Independent Social Democrat'.

From Wakeham to the Coalition—what next for the Lords?

What, then, of the post-1999 plans for Lords reform? Lord Wakeham's 2000 report, *A House for the Future*, made several recommendations, subsequently crystallized in a 2001 House of Lords White Paper. This advocated a neutered version of his proposals, including the removal of all remaining hereditary peers, the retention of existing life peers 'transitionally', and the eventual capping of Lords membership at about 600. The one concrete development that happened almost immediately was the establishment of an independent **House**

of Lords Appointments Commission to ensure that while transitional arrangements remained, life peerages would be awarded principally on merit, rather than by political patronage. The Commission's main role was to vet individuals nominated by party leaders for any sign of rewards for favours—a power that it memorably used to block three of Mr Blair's nominees in 2005 (see Chapter 5, '"Lobbygate", "Cash for honours", and other recent funding scandals'). But it is also allowed to propose its own peers, focusing on non-partisan individuals with 'a record of significant achievement' in their 'chosen way of life'. To date, 51 'people's peers' have been appointed, ranging from Baroness Howe of Idlicote (wife of former Tory minister Geoffrey, now Lord, Howe) to disability rights activist Baroness Chapman.

During his remaining years in office, Mr Blair slowly edged away from advocating a partially elected chamber toward a fully appointed one—in defiance of an all-party motion in March 1999 demanding that it be entirely elected. Although he would cite in his defence well-rehearsed Conservative arguments—including the potential challenge that an elected Lords might pose to Commons supremacy—the Tories branded his alternative an attempt to shore up his power base by appointing 'Tony's Cronies'. Unhappy memories were evoked of the 'Lavender List', a notorious string of honours for trusted allies that another Labour prime minister, Harold Wilson, had patronized on his retirement in 1976.

The 'settled' view of MPs now appears to favour a largely or fully elected second chamber.

By the time Labour entered the 2010 election, after two further White Papers published by Leader of the Commons, then Lord Chancellor Jack Straw, it had finally committed itself to full elections as part of a wider package of constitutional reform, including a referendum on replacing Britain's FPTP electoral system with AV. With the Lib Dems advocating similar changes, Mr Clegg persuaded Mr Cameron to endorse a commitment to push for a new 'Senate', to be wholly or largely elected using proportional representation (see Chapter 4, 'Proportional representation (PR) and other voting systems'). A further White Paper, accompanied by a draft Bill, followed in 2011, reviving Mr Straw's idea of an 80:20 split between elected and appointed members, but proposing to cap membership at 300 (later revised to 450), with all but 90 peers elected, on non-renewable 15-year terms, and an initial poll to coincide with the 2015 general election. However, despite defying a 91-strong rebellion by Tory backbenchers to nominally reach the second reading, Mr Clegg's Bill was formally abandoned in August 2012, after Mr Cameron informed him that he could not secure sufficient support from his MPs to take it further.

The Bill's fate was ultimately sealed by an unholy alliance of Conservatives and what Mr Clegg branded an 'opportunistic' Labour Party, intent on exploiting the situation to promote cracks in the Coalition. Labour's leadership had indicated support for the legislation in principle (although it had argued for a national referendum first), but before voting 'yes' to the second reading, it forced ministers into dropping a proposed 'programme motion' to limit scrutiny at that stage to 10 days—a vote that the government would certainly have lost. In a final twist, though, Mr Clegg exacted his revenge on the Tories—by instructing his fellow Lib Dems to oppose Conservative proposals for changes to Commons constituency boundaries when they came to a vote (see Chapter 4, 'How the British electoral system works'). Although Mr Clegg made it clear that he felt the Conservatives had reneged on their half of the Coalition agreement by withholding support for Lords reform, his official reason for opposing the boundary proposals was that, in the *absence* of changes to the second chamber, reducing the number of elected MPs risked undermining the Commons' authority.

Since then, determined campaigners have continued to insist that the cause of Lords reform is still not lost—with former Liberal leader Lord Steel steering his long-cherished House of Lords (Amendment) Bill through the Lords in March 2012. This private member's Bill (see 'Private members' Bills' in this chapter) proposed new rules removing the patronage of party leaders in creating future life peers, in favour of purely merit-based decisions by a statutory appointments commission, removal of any members sentenced to more than a year in prison for serious crimes, and scrapping of future by-elections to replace deceased hereditary peers (a move that would, over time, have 'abolished' the remaining elected hereditary members as the 90 incumbents died). In reality, until such time as the Bill is picked up and pushed through the Commons by another government, it is hard to see it being implemented.

The one significant further reform between 1999 and 2012 to affect the Lords was the creation in the Constitutional Reform Act 2005 of a US-style Supreme Court—formally known as the **Supreme Court of the United Kingdom**. To reinforce the principle of separation of powers in practice, then Lord Chancellor Mr Straw divested the Lords of its judicial function, transferred its status as Britain's highest court of justice to the Supreme Court, and installed 12 of the then 27 Law Lords as inaugural Justices of the Supreme Court. The Court began work on 1 October 2009. For the duration of their service as Justices, its members' ability to sit in the Lords was curtailed, although they are entitled to return to the chamber on retirement (assuming that it still exists). Future appointees will not be given seats in the Lords. Although the new Supreme Court is the ultimate bastion of English, Northern Irish, and Scottish law, and has taken over adjudicating devolutionary matters from the Judicial Committee of the Privy Council, Scotland retains its own supreme court in criminal matters: the High Court of Justiciary.

Types of legislation

As Britain's legislature, the primary purpose of Parliament is to legislate. So how does it do this and what forms can legislation take?

British legislation is divided into two broad types: primary and secondary. Primary legislation is the umbrella term for all Bills that pass through Parliament and (when successful) receive royal assent, becoming Acts. It is also known as 'enabling legislation', in that Acts must be passed to 'enable' the government and Parliament to issue the various rules, regulations, and instructions needed to implement changes in law on the ground.

Primary legislation

The four main categories of primary Bill are as follows:

- public Bills;
- private Bills;
- hybrid Bills; and
- private members' Bills.

Public, private, and hybrid Bills

Public, private, and hybrid Bills all have one thing in common: they are initiated by the government. This, though, is where the similarities end. Whereas **public Bills** change 'the law of the land', **private Bills** seek only to affect specific individuals or organizations—for example companies or local authorities. Whichever category they fall into, these government Bills are almost always preceded by draft versions, known as **Green Papers** and **White Papers** (see 'The passage of a Bill' in this chapter).

Briefly, the majority of new laws that gain media attention are public Bills. The Academies Bill 2010 (which controversially paved the way for free schools), the Health and Social Care Bill, and the numerous 'anti-terror' Bills of recent years all are (or were) public Bills affecting the entire population of England, if not Britain. Private Bills, in contrast, are usually introduced at the request of specific individuals or bodies, either to exempt them from a law otherwise affecting the whole country or to grant them other discrete privileges. The **Highways Agency**—the **executive agency** of the Department for Transport (DfT) responsible for building and maintaining major trunk roads, 'A' roads, and motorways (see Chapter 19, 'The roles of the Secretary of State and Highway Agency')—has often been granted private Bills enabling it to extend, or introduce, roads in new areas. Hybrid Bills are a mix of the other two. Like public Bills, they affect the whole population, but resemble private Bills in that they impinge on some people more than others. Examples of hybrid Bills include the one enabling work to begin on London's Crossrail project, which affects some residents of the country (those living along the link) more than others.

Private Members' Bills (PMBs)

Private members' Bills (PMBs) warrant a separate category because, unlike all of the above types of legislation, they are introduced not by governments, but

Table 2.5 Three ways of introducing private members' Bills (PMBs)

Method	Procedure
PMB Fridays	Early in each parliamentary session, MPs enter a 'ballot' for opportunity to introduce their own Bill on one of 13 'PMB Fridays'. On these days, PMBs take precedence over government/Opposition business. First 20 names drawn in the ballot may introduce their Bills. Six or seven at top of list are likely to be discussed in detail in the Commons.
The 10-minute rule	Members may instead use the '10-minute rule' (officially, Standing Order No. 23), on most Tuesdays and Wednesdays at the start of public business. They make a 10-minute speech outlining their proposals, provided that they have 10 other members' support. An opponent may make a 10-minute speech in reply.
Presentation Bills	Members may introduce a presentation Bill (under Standing Order No. 57). This draws limited attention to an issue of concern to the MP because—unlike the other two methods—it does not allow MP to make a speech outlining the details of the Bill.

by backbenchers. Private members' Bills may be introduced in one of the three ways listed in Table 2.5.

The primary purpose of **10-minute rule** Bills is to enable MPs to raise issues that they deem important—rather than actually to get their measures onto the statute book. In practice, MPs usually struggle to persuade their parties, or governments, to allocate sufficient parliamentary time to take their Bills further.

To qualify to introduce a 10-minute rule Bill, an MP must be 'the first member through the door' to the Public Bill Office on the Tuesday or Wednesday 15 working days before the date on which they wish to present it. Their Bill must have a proposer and seconder, and the written backing of 10 colleagues.

Many significant issues have been raised through PMBs. In 1997, after initial indications that he would receive government time, Labour backbencher Michael Foster introduced a PMB proposing a ban on hunting with dogs (a measure in his party's manifesto). He later withdrew it when it became clear that ministers were not going to accord it sufficient priority to see it through all of the necessary stages in the face of mounting opposition from Conservatives and the Lords.

There have, however, been one or two celebrated cases in which governments have cleared the parliamentary timetable to smooth the path for PMBs with widespread popular support. The most famous of these was former Liberal leader Mr Steel's Abortion Bill 1967, which legalized terminations of unwanted pregnancies for the first time in Britain, albeit only up to 24 weeks after conception. Touching on an issue of huge public concern at the time, it was allotted ample time for full debate and scrutiny, and duly passed.

Secondary legislation

It has increasingly been the convention for primary legislation to cover only the fundamental *principles* underpinning a change in the law. In contrast, **secondary**

Table 2.6 Main types of secondary legislation

Name	Definition	Example
Statutory instrument	Rules, regulations, and guidelines issued by ministers to flesh out newly passed Acts and implement on ground Although no further Act is required to implement measures, they still require Parliament's formal agreement 'Parent' Act usually specifies whether affirmative or negative agreement is required (the former meaning that the statutory instrument will not come into play unless Parliament formally approves a resolution; the latter, that it will automatically do so if, after 40 days, no motion passed objecting to it)	Complex instructions issued by the Department for Culture, Media, and Sport (DCMS) to give local authorities and police responsibility for issuing liquor and public entertainment licences under the Licensing Act 2003 (which took so long to come into force that '24-hour drinking' was introduced in pubs only in November 2005—two years after royal assent)
By-law	Localized laws passed on approval of the relevant minister, the scope of which is enshrined in an existing Act	City-centre street-drinking bans introduced by councils in problem areas
Order in Council	Submitted by ministers for approval by the sovereign at a meeting of the Privy Council Draft normally agreed by Parliament before being submitted by ministers	Used to introduce much delegated anti-terror legislation relating to Northern Ireland in the 1960s and 1970s

legislation—or **delegated legislation**, or 'subordinate' legislation—refers to powers 'flowing from' Acts themselves, and rules, regulations, and guidelines drawn up to implement them. For primary legislation to be put into practice, ministers need the authority to introduce the measures it contains on the ground. This authority is exercised through 'delegated' legislative powers, the main types of which are listed in Table 2.6.

◗ The passage of a Bill

Before it can be formally introduced in Parliament, the detail of prospective government legislation is publicly aired in two early draft forms: a Green Paper and White Paper. The former is a sketchy consultation document outlining the *broad spirit* of a proposed Bill. It is open to significant redefinition depending on the response it elicits from the public and other interested parties. The latter is a more crystallized outline of a proposed law—again issued for consultation purposes—that normally prefigures a Bill to be introduced in the next session.

Bills can be introduced in either Commons or Lords, although they are normally instigated in the former. The process is outlined in Table 2.7.

Table 2.7 The passage of a Bill

Stage	Process
First reading	Reading out of new Bill's title in Commons. In practice, this can take several minutes, because full titles tend to sum up the substance of the proposals and can be lengthy.
Second reading	General principles of Bill read out, debated, and voted on for first timeThis normally happens in 'an afternoon' between 4 p.m. and 10 p.m. (barring a brief experiment, when late Leader of the House Robin Cook introduced a 'family-friendly' parliamentary timetable). The second reading can run over several days if a Bill has major implications.
Committee stage	Public or private Bill committee undertakes detailed consideration of main clauses in Bill. Sometimes, this stage occurs in the Commons itself, sitting as Committee of the Whole House (normally when a treaty is being ratified or a Bill needs to be passed urgently—e.g. New Labour's anti-terror legislation). This also happens automatically following the annual Budget Speech, when aspects of the Finance Act flowing from it are fast-tracked.
Report stage	Committee's recommendations referred to Commons in written report and further amendments can follow before Bill proceeds to third reading. This stage often involves late sittings.
Third reading	Bill reviewed and debated in final intended form. At this stage, all opportunities for the Commons to amend it have passed (although the Lords can still do so).
Bill now referred to Lords (or 'another place'), through which it follows a similar sequence as that through the Commons, but this time with a committee stage usually taken on the floor of the House.	
House of Lords and the Lords' report to the Commons	Amendments made by the Lords must be agreed by the Commons before it can proceed to the statute book. Should there be significant differences of opinion between them (e.g. over fox-hunting legislation during Mr Blair's tenure), a joint committee is usually set up to resolve them. Under successive Parliament Acts, Lords cannot delay money Bills and can delay others only by 13 months.
Royal assent	Final seal of approval, turning Bill into Act, is notionally still given by monarch, but the last time this formally happened was in 1854. It is conferred in Norman French, *La Reine le Veult*, and has not been refused since 1707, when Queen Anne declined to grant it for a Bill to settle militia in Scotland. Sentence preceding every Act reads: 'Be it enacted by the Queen's Most Excellent Majesty, by and with the advice and consent of the Lords Spiritual and Temporal, and Commons, in this Parliament assembled, and by authority of the same, as follows . . .'

Speeding up the legislative process

The legislative process can be very involved, and MPs of all parties are adept at delaying Bills to which they object. Traditionally, they conspired to do so by making excessively long speeches to frustrate governments' attempts to get through the various stages through which a Bill must pass to become law. Such 'filibustering' was at times used sufficiently obstructively to delay indefinitely, or even to 'kill off', prospective Acts. If a Bill were delayed by time-wasters long enough for a government to be voted out of office, this might well spell its end, because the Opposition waiting to take over would be unlikely to resurrect it. Similarly, 'wrecking amendments' have often been made by the Lords towards the end of a parliament in an effort to 'time out' a Bill, in the hope that the next government will abandon it. Traditionally, Bills that fail to reach royal assent before the end of a parliamentary session have had to start the whole legislative process again the following year. However, since October 2004, it has been possible for the Commons to pass 'carry-over motions', allowing Bills that would otherwise have timed out in one session to continue their passage from the same stage in the succeeding one.

The term 'filibustering' was first coined in reference to pro-independence Irish MPs in the nineteenth century, who, in an effort to force the Westminster government to hand over 'home rule' for Ireland, would deliberately hold up Bills on other issues. Today, filibustering and other forms of time-wasting, repetition, and drawn-out debate can be countered in one of the four ways outlined in the table entitled 'Devices used to speed up debate in the Commons', to be found on the **Online Resource Centre** that accompanies this book.

▌ The role of the Commons Speaker

The most important officer of the Commons, the Speaker, chairs its business. He or she presides over votes and debates, intervenes to restore 'order' when members become rowdy, and chooses which member should be next to speak when confronted by MPs waving their order papers to 'catch the Speaker's eye'. The Speaker is always drawn from the ranks of MPs, but, on taking office, discards his or her previous party allegiance for the duration of his or her period in post.

The Speaker's main roles today are:

- controlling debates, including deciding when those on specific subjects should end and be voted on, and suspending or adjourning sittings that get out of hand (for example debate over the Hutton Report into the death of Dr Kelly—see 'Select committees' in this chapter—was suspended after protesters invaded the Commons public gallery, and similar action was taken during two other protests in the House: in May 2004, when activists from Fathers4Justice, a pressure group campaigning for equal access rights to children for separated fathers, threw a missile containing purple powder from the guests' gallery at Mr Blair, and that September, when pro-hunt protestors led by Otis Ferry, son of singer Bryan Ferry, invaded the chamber);

- ordering MPs who break Commons rules to leave the chamber (for example Mr Galloway was barred from the Commons for 18 days in July 2007 for failing to declare his links to the United Nations' 'Oil for Food' programme—a charitable appeal allegedly part-funded by a supporter involved in the sale of oil under Saddam Hussein);

- certifying some Bills as 'money Bills' to give them swift approval;

- signing warrants to send members to jail for contempt of the House;

- chairing the House of Commons Commission—a body that administers the procedures of the Commons; and

- chairing the Speaker's Committee on the Electoral Commission, which recommends appointments to the board of the Commission (see Chapter 5, 'Party funding now and in the future').

Traditionally, the Speaker (the first of whom, Peter de Montfort, was appointed Parlour of the Commons in 1258) is chosen by an election of MPs called by the 'Father of the House'—the backbench MP with the longest unbroken membership of the Commons. For nearly forty years it has also been customary for the two main political parties to alternate in providing Speakers, but when the post became vacant in October 2000 after Betty (now Baroness) Boothroyd's retirement, backbenchers grew so annoyed by the government's insistence that this tradition be upheld that they defied it by voting in another Labour MP, Mr Martin, instead of Mr Blair's preferred candidate, former Tory minister Sir George Young.

In the event, Mr Martin's tenure was most notable for the ignominy of his premature departure. A series of perceived errors of judgement began in November 2008, with his mishandling of the Damian Green affair (see Chapter 1, 'Statute'). More damaging still were revelations that he had claimed £20,000 of taxpayers' money to pay City law firm Carter Ruck to defend him against negative press stories, and subsequent disclosures that his wife had been reimbursed by taxpayers for £4,000 in taxi fares incurred on a series of shopping trips to buy food and refreshment for receptions, and that refurbishments to the couple's official residence, the Speaker's House, had cost £1.7 million. The final straw, though, was Mr Martin's faltering response to the wave of revelations about MPs' expenses claims (see 'MPs, conflicts of interest, abuses of privilege—and how to avoid them' in this chapter). After appearing to do too little too late—by proposing only a prolonged sequence of meetings between party leaders and other internal Commons bodies to decide how best to reform the system, rather than any larger-scale changes—on 12 May 2009, following a decisive no-confidence vote, Mr Martin became the first Speaker to be forced out of office since Sir John Trevor in 1695.

With Mr Martin's successor, the Commons reverted to its customary pendulum swing from Labour to Conservatives: in a hotly contested election that marked a break from the 'coronations' of past Speakers, John Bercow beat several hopefuls, including fellow Tories Ann Widdecombe and Sir George Young, and former Labour Foreign Secretary Margaret Beckett. He was reconfirmed in office after the 2010 election.

Although the Speaker officially presides over the Commons, recent events have acted as a timely reminder of the presence of a further, more shadowy, figure, whose constitutional role is also to oversee debate in the chamber—on behalf of a very particular vested interest. The 'City Remembrancer'—who has a chair reserved for him or her behind the Speaker's 'throne'—occupies an obscure office of state dating back to 1571. His or her task is to act as a channel of information between, on the one hand, the City of London Corporation and its chief dignitary, the Lord Mayor of London (see Chapter 11, 'The evolution of local government in London'), and, on the other, Parliament and sovereign. Critics view this arcane post as a sinister manifestation of the grip that Britain's financial sector has long exercised over the seat of British democracy—a concern sharpened in the wake of the 2007–08 banking collapse (see Chapter 7, 'The global banking crisis and its fallout') and, in February 2012, the eviction by Corporation authorities of a camp set up by supporters of anti-capitalist protest movement Occupy from the area surrounding St Paul's Cathedral.

▌ The changing role of the Lord Chancellor

Officially the 'Lord High Chancellor of Great Britain', this ancient post—dating back at least to the 1066 Norman Conquest—has undergone significant changes over recent years. The Lord Chancellor is the second most senior of the 'Great Officers of State of the UK'—the highest ranking being the Lord High Steward (a post generally kept vacant, except during coronations). As explained in Chapter 1 ('The separation of powers in the UK'), the Lord Chancellor was, for centuries, a bastion of all three branches of the British constitution, being head of the judiciary, Speaker of the Lords (legislature), and, as Cabinet minister responsible for what until recently was known as the 'Lord Chancellor's Department', a member of the executive.

Even today, the Lord Chancellor still retains many ancient ceremonial roles. As 'Custodian of The Great Seal of the Realm', or 'The Great Seal of the United Kingdom', he or she can authorize the reigning sovereign's documents (most notably the royal assent) on his or her behalf—saving the monarch from having to sign each one personally. The Lord Chancellor also remains a minister.

Since 2003, however, post-holders have ceased to retain quite the authority enjoyed by their predecessors (to the annoyance of the Lords, which sought initially to prevent Mr Blair denuding these powers). In a notoriously botched

Cabinet reshuffle, Mr Blair replaced outgoing Lord Chancellor Derry Irvine with Lord Falconer of Thoroton. In doing so, he sought to rename the post 'Secretary of State for Constitutional Affairs'—effectively *abolishing* a constitutional role that had existed since the Middle Ages.

Mr Blair was forced to step back from scrapping the post outright, and although he did abolish the Lord Chancellor's Department, Lord Falconer retained the dual titles of Constitutional Affairs Secretary and Lord Chancellor throughout his four years in office. Further changes, however, occurred after the 2005 election, when the Constitutional Affairs Act 2005 handed responsibility for running the judiciary to the Lord Chief Justice and created a new post of **Lord Speaker**—elected by his or her fellow peers using the AV (see Chapter 4, 'Proportional representation (PR) and other voting systems')—to assume the Lord Chancellor's role as chair of the Lords. The inaugural Lord Speaker, Baroness Hayman, was confirmed in office on 4 July 2006 and succeeded by former Convenor of the Crossbench Peers Baroness D'Souza in 2011.

During Mr Brown's first reshuffle, the Department for Constitutional Affairs was renamed the Ministry of Justice (MoJ). More significantly, Lord Falconer's successor, Mr Straw, became the first Lord Chancellor since the sixteenth century to not be a lord at all, but an MP. This 'new tradition' has continued under the Coalition, with first Mr Clarke, then Chris Grayling, succeeding Mr Straw as Lord Chancellor and Secretary of State for Justice.

▌ The Opposition

The party with the most Commons seats besides the governing one forms the Opposition. In recognition of its official status, the Leader of the Opposition, Opposition Chief Whip, and Opposition Deputy Chief Whip each receive allowances on top of their normal parliamentary ones to aid with their responsibilities.

The Opposition is charged with:

- holding the government to account by appointing a 'Shadow Cabinet' covering the main departmental briefs;
- contributing to the legislative process by proposing amendments; and
- setting out its policies as an alternative government using designated 'Opposition Days', on which it, rather than the government, dictates the flow of Commons business. (In each session, there are 20 Opposition Days: 17 customarily go to the largest Opposition party and three to the second largest.)

▶ Devolution in practice—parliaments in the provinces

The first chapter laid out Britain's overall constitutional framework, while introducing the concept of devolution and how it was applied in the UK's con stituent countries outside England. This section explains how devolution works in practice through the aegis of new chambers created to implement it.

The Scottish Parliament

Comprising 129 **members of the Scottish Parliament (MSPs)**, the **Scottish Parliament** is a 'unicameral' legislature—meaning that it has only one House.

During the initial transition stage flowing from its establishment in 1998, some inaugural MSPs were permitted to hold 'dual mandates'—that is, to remain MPs as well. This swiftly changed, however, when they assumed their place as MSPs full time and by-elections were held to find replacements for their previous Commons constituencies. Similar arrangements currently exist in the Northern Ireland Assembly, following restoration of devolved government in that province, although they were due to end with the 2015 Assembly elections.

Members of the Scottish Parliament are elected using the additional member system (AMS) form of proportional representation (see Chapter 4, 'Proportional representation (PR) and other voting systems'), with 73 voted in via the UK's traditional FPTP system and the remaining 56 from a regional list designed to more fairly allocate seats to each party nationally. Each elector has two votes: one for his or her constituency; the other for a political party, the names of which appear on the list.

Members originally met in a temporary chamber at Edinburgh's Church of Scotland Assembly Hall on The Mound. This was belatedly replaced by a purpose-built Parliament in Holyrood, at the foot of the Royal Mile, in 2004. One MSP is elected 'Presiding Officer' (equivalent to the Commons Speaker), supported by two deputies. Parliament is elected for fixed terms lasting four years from its election date, with each year constituting a parliamentary session, which is further split into 'sitting days' and 'recess periods'. On sitting days, Parliament tries to finish its business at 5.30 p.m., except on Fridays, which tend to end at 12.30 p.m.

Members can raise issues by:

- asking oral questions during parliamentary sittings;
- submitting written questions; and
- giving notice of, or moving, a motion.

Scottish parliamentary committees

Unlike at Westminster, much of the Scottish Parliament's work is performed by its 18 committees—a system intended to make it easier for individual members to hold ministers to account. Committees comprise between 5 and 15 MSPs, and are chaired by 'conveners'. Meetings take place in public and can be held anywhere in Scotland. This is meant to provide more direct access to the democratic process for ordinary people. One committee member is appointed as 'reporter' and MSPs may participate in meetings of committees of which they are not members (although they cannot vote).

Committees are charged with examining:

- policy, administration, and financial arrangements of the Scottish Government or Scottish Executive (see Chapter 3, 'The Scottish Government/ Executive');
- proposed legislation in the Scottish and Westminster Parliaments; and
- the application of EU and international laws or conventions in Scotland.

The role and responsibilities of the Scottish Parliament

Until the September 2014 independence referendum, the Scottish Parliament was responsible only for domestic issues specifically relevant to Scotland, but not Britain as a whole. Roles retained by the Commons included:

- foreign and defence policy;
- most economic policy;
- social security; and
- medical ethics.

In the run-up to the narrow 'no' vote, however, the main Westminster parties—alarmed at the prospect of defeat—promised a series of major concessions to Scotland, akin to a twenty-first-century version of 'home rule' (see Chapter 1, 'The path to Scottish devolution'). Among the policy areas now almost certain to be devolved to the Scottish Parliament as part of a 'devo max'- style deal in coming months is control over the country's benefits system and a much greater say in economic policy—including the ability to raise income tax either to whatever level it pleases or by 15 pence in the pound (depending on whether the Conservatives or Labour, respectively, win the 2015 general election). At time of writing, Scotland also appeared to have been guaranteed indefinite continuation of the population-based 'Barnett Formula' (see Chapter 7, 'Public spending outside England—the Barnett Formula'), under which spending per head north of the border in 2014–15 was £1,623 (or 19 per cent) higher per annum than anywhere else in Britain. This was despite protestations by its architect, former Labour Chief Secretary to the Treasury Lord Barnett, that it should be scrapped in the interests of fairness. In addition, the Scottish Parliament will henceforth be able to decide for itself how much should be spent on the NHS in Scotland—rather than (as at present) having overall cuts to its health budget imposed on it from Whitehall.

The legislative process in Scotland

The four main types of Bill that can be introduced into the Scottish Parliament are:

- *executive*—introduced by a minister;
- *committee*—introduced by the convener (chair) of a committee;
- *member's*—introduced by individual MSPs, like private members' Bills at Westminster, with the support of 11 fellow members; and
- *private*—introduced by private individuals or promoters.

When introduced in the Scottish Parliament, Bills must be accompanied by the documents listed in the table entitled 'The documents required to accompany different types of Scottish Bill' that can be found on the **Online Resource Centre**. To become law, they must pass through the four stages outlined in Table 2.8, in a streamlined version of the Westminster process.

Table 2.8 Passage of a Bill through the Scottish Parliament

Stage	Process
Stage one	Examination of the Bill's general principles, normally handled by a specialist lead committee
Stage two	Detailed, line-by-line examination of the Bill, either by lead committee, another committee, or whole Parliament; amendments made and debated
Stage three	Final consideration of the Bill by full Parliament; amendments debated and Parliament decides whether to pass the Bill; more than a quarter of all MSPs must vote on an issue either way for it to pass
Final stage	Parliament decides whether to approve the Bill when referred back to full House; then automatically submitted by the Presiding Officer for royal assent. (There is no Lords stage.)

The National Assembly for Wales

The Cardiff-based **National Assembly for Wales** has 60 members: 40 elected for constituencies; and 20, on the basis of four for each of five larger regions. As in Scotland (and very shortly Northern Ireland), these **Assembly members (AMs)** are no longer permitted to sit simultaneously as Westminster MPs. The Assembly is elected every four years, although, under the Wales Bill currently before Parliament, it is expected to switch to five-year cycles from its next elections in 2016—in part to avoid clashes with future UK-wide general elections.

Each Welsh elector has two votes: one for a constituency member and the other for one from the relevant regional list. The Secretary of State for Wales retains a degree of responsibility for the province and, unlike in Scotland, the Assembly has, to date, only been able to vary income tax according to a 'lock-step' process, under which a change to one band must be applied to all others. The Secretary of State for Wales is charged with ensuring that devolution works effectively, by chairing a joint ministerial committee between Westminster and Cardiff.

The Assembly's responsibilities originally covered only the following:

- determining budgetary priorities;
- funding, directing, and appointing managers of NHS bodies in Wales;
- administering EU structural funds aimed at Wales; and
- determining the content of the National Curriculum in Wales.

Although it remains a poor relation of the Scottish Parliament in terms of remit, the Assembly gained notable new legislative powers through the Government of Wales Act 2006. This introduced the 'Measure of the National Assembly for Wales' (known as the 'Assembly Measure')—a form of second-tier primary legislation that allows the Welsh Assembly Government to enact statutory instruments in relation to 20 'fields' and 'matters' over which it has devolved authority. Assembly Measures can be proposed by any AM, including backbenchers, and must be scrutinized by committees, debated in plenary session, and approved in votes before adoption. Importantly, the 2006 Act also broadened the Assembly's powers to cover a wider range of areas (devolution of which had to first be approved through a form of Order in Council, known as a 'Legislative Competence Order', or LCO):

- agriculture, fisheries, forestry, and rural development;
- ancient monuments and historic buildings;
- culture;
- economic development;
- education and training;
- environment;
- fire and rescue services and promotion of fire safety;
- food;
- health and health services;
- highways and transport;
- housing;
- local government;

- public administration;
- social welfare;
- sport and recreation;
- tourism;
- town and country planning;
- water and flood defence;
- Welsh language; and
- the Assembly itself.

In July 2010, a commission set up by the Welsh Assembly Government recommended that Wales be given similar tax-varying powers to those of Scotland and a Wales Bill currently before Parliament is due to grant the Welsh Assembly the same power to set its own income tax rates, free from the 'lock-step'—subject to prior approval in a national referendum. In an earlier referendum, held on 3 March 2011, Welsh people voted 63.5 to 36.5 per cent to grant the Assembly powers to pass its own laws—known as 'Acts of the Assembly'—on all matters in the 20 'subject areas' over which it already has authority. Following Scotland's independence referendum, moreover, both Wales and Northern Ireland are almost certain to be offered additional powers, as yet unspecified at time of writing.

The law-making process in Wales

The Welsh legislative procedure resembles that of Scotland. It too is overseen by a presiding officer and his or her deputy, elected by other AMs. Again, executive functions are wielded by a First Minister at the head of a devolved government. This was initially called the Welsh Executive, but is now referred to as the **Welsh Assembly Government**.

The Assembly meets in public plenary session in Cardiff, and business is directed by the presiding officer through a business secretary and business committee. Each session allows at least 15 minutes for oral questions of the First Minister and, every four weeks, similar sessions for each departmental minister. In addition, any AM can propose a motion once a week, before the conclusion of plenary business, and there are two forms of committee to consider matters in plenary session: 'subject committees', and 'regional committees' covering specific areas of the country.

Today's Acts are passed by the Assembly in a four-stage process almost identical to that used in Scotland. In addition, some subordinate legislation (statutory instruments) introduced by ministers must now be formally approved by AMs in plenary session—a process known as the 'affirmative procedure'. Alternatively, it can be challenged by the Assembly, using a 'negative procedure', if an AM successfully tables a 'motion to annul' before a specified deadline that is upheld by a vote in the chamber.

The Northern Ireland Assembly

It was only in 2007 that devolved government at the **Northern Ireland Assembly** in Stormont finally came about, with the signing of a landmark power-sharing agreement between the two biggest parties—the late Ian Paisley's Democratic Unionist Party (DUP) and Gerry Adams's Sinn Féin—following fresh elections. In April 2008, Dr Paisley (a stalwart of Northern Irish politics for more than four decades) retired as First Minister and DUP leader, to be replaced by East Belfast MP Peter Robinson (who subsequently lost his Westminster seat, but continued as head of the Assembly). At time of writing, former Sinn Féin chief negotiator Martin McGuinness remained Deputy First Minister.

Areas of responsibility retained over Northern Ireland by Westminster

The Secretary of State for Northern Ireland remains responsible for:

- international relations;
- defence; and
- taxation.

Several Whitehall agencies remain responsible for overseeing specific areas, including the Northern Ireland Prison Service, Compensation Agency, and Forensic Agency of Northern Ireland. Policing and justice powers were devolved in April 2010 (see Chapter 1, 'The rocky road to Northern Irish devolution'). The Northern Ireland Prison Service is overseen by a recently reconstituted Northern Ireland Policing Board, with members drawn from all of the main political parties.

The legislative process in Northern Ireland

The Northern Ireland Assembly is home to 108 elected representatives, known as **members of the Legislative Assembly (MLAs)**. The nature and titles of its senior politicians and officers, and the nature of its legislative process, are virtually identical to those in Wales.

≣ Topical feature idea

Since 2010, ordinary citizens—and local MPs representing them—have been able to engage in a more 'direct' form of democracy than was previously possible, by launching e-petitions. Anyone who mobilizes at least 100,000 signatories to back an online petition supporting their cause can press the Commons Backbench Business Committee to timetable a full debate on that issue in the chamber. The advent of online activist movements such as Avaaz, Unlock Democracy, change.org, and 38 Degrees has made it easier for individuals and small community groups to mobilize support for e-petitions. But, in practice, petitions are usually 'presented' to the committee by backbench MPs representing particular constituencies or with personal interests in a campaign. Have there been any successful e-petitions mounted in your area? Are any current or pending? Why not set up your own e-petition as an experiment to see how much support can be rallied for a campaign on a local issue?

✳ Current issues

- **Reassertion of Parliament's scrutiny function** Since the introduction of elected select committees in 2010, backbench MPs have had a new lease of life—revelling in their increased legitimacy as scrutinizers of government policy. Among the more combative committee chairpersons have been Keith Vaz, chairman of the Home Affairs Committee, and Margaret Hodge, who chairs the Public Accounts Committee.

- **Continuing disaffection with MPs** According to numerous opinion polls, the parliamentary expenses scandal has left a lasting legacy of distrust towards British MPs. In 2014, concern about the Commons 'gravy train' erupted again, as IPSA prepared to award them a £7,000 one-off pay rise, with further increases in line with average earnings in future years.

- **New tax powers for Wales** Having already gained incremental increases in its autonomy, with the introduction of first 'Assembly Measures' then 'Acts', the Welsh Assembly is due to be granted the ability to set its own income tax rate, subject to the approval of a national referendum. From 2016, Assembly terms are due to be extended from four to five years.

▦ Key points

1. Britain's Parliament is a 'bicameral' legislature, comprising a primary legislative chamber, the House of Commons, and a secondary chamber tasked with revising legislation (the House of Lords). Scotland has a devolved Scottish Parliament, and Wales and Northern Ireland their own assemblies.

2. There are 650 MPs, each representing geographical areas known as 'constituencies', on average covering 65,000 people. Scotland has 129 MSPs; Wales, 60 AMs; Northern Ireland, 108 MLAs.

3. The principal duty of an MP is to represent the interests of his or her constituents, by tabling questions in Parliament, lobbying ministers, and holding weekly constituency surgeries. Members are also expected to vote with their parties in Parliament and to sit on committees tasked with holding government to account.

4. The House of Lords currently comprises a mix of 92 hereditary peers (90 elected by other peers), an ever-growing number of life peers appointed on merit, and 26 'Lords Spiritual' (the most senior Church of England bishops).

5. Bills in Parliament go through a series of key stages, starting with the first and second readings, followed by a committee and report stage, a third reading, and

consideration by the Lords. They become Acts of Parliament only after receiving royal assent. Each devolved assembly follows a similar sequence, but without the Lords stage.

→ Further reading

Jones, B. (2010) *Dictionary of British Politics*, 2nd edn, Manchester: Manchester University Press. **Thorough, accessible A–Z of terms and recent developments in British politics.**

Jones, B., and Norton, P. (2013) *Politics UK*, 8th edn, London: Longman. **Full-colour edition of established core text giving comprehensive overview of structure and workings of British political system up to 2005.**

Norton, P. (2013) *Parliament in British Politics*, 2nd edn, Basingstoke: Palgrave Macmillan. **Thoughtful evaluation of changing significance of British Parliament in light of recent constitutional developments, such as devolution and partial reform of the Lords.**

Rogers, R. and Walters, R. (2006) *How Parliament Works*, 6th edn, London: Longman. **Sixth edition of indispensable layman's guide to often complex, sometimes archaic, workings of British Parliament.**

Online Resource Centre

www.oxfordtextbooks.co.uk/orc/Morrison4e/
Visit the Online Resource Centre that accompanies this book for web links and regular updates.

3

Prime minister, Cabinet, and government

This chapter focuses on the make-up and workings of the executive branch of the UK constitution—the government—and particularly the role of the inner circle of ministers known as the **Cabinet**, and its titular head, the prime minister.

▶ The origins of the role of prime minister

Compared to ancient posts like that of Lord Chancellor, the role of **prime minister (PM)** emerged surprisingly recently, and owes its origins to historical accident. When German-born George I succeeded to the British throne in 1714, he could speak little English. Traditionally, the Cabinet had always been chaired by the monarch, but with the newly crowned king unable to speak the language of UK government a practical need arose for a senior minister to perform this duty in his place. Thus was born the post that became that of de facto head of government in Britain—or 'prime' minister. After some debate, the honour of assuming this role was handed to Sir Robert Walpole, then 'First Lord of the Treasury' (in effect, the Lord High Treasurer or official head of HM Treasury—the department responsible for raising taxes to finance government policy). His previous duties were generally assumed from this date by the Lord High Commissioners of the Treasury.

Despite assuming the day-to-day role of prime minister, however, Walpole retained his official Cabinet title, as did his successors for nearly a century. In fact, although the term 'prime minister' was used informally within government from 1714 onwards and started appearing on government documents in the 1860s, under Benjamin Disraeli, it was coined publicly only during the term of short-lived Liberal premier Sir Henry Campbell-Bannerman (1905–08).

Given the disproportionate power wielded by the PM, since the position arose it has been constitutionally contentious. Before its introduction, all ministers were regarded as equals, with shared responsibility for governing Britain. The emergence of a Cabinet chairperson from within its own ranks made an immediate mockery of this idea, by implicitly elevating him or her to a level *more equal* than others. This somewhat contradictory position spawned a Latin phrase associated with PMs ever since: *primus inter pares* ('first among equals'). Prime ministers are 'equal' to their Cabinet colleagues—and indeed all members of the House of Commons—in that as elected members of Parliament (MPs)—the last peer to be PM was Lord Salisbury, who left office in 1902—they must be voted in to represent constituencies and can be removed by local people if they become unpopular. To this extent, the PM is an ordinary MP like any other. In contrast, he or she is 'first among' those notional 'equals' by dint not only of being a senior government minister, but also of presiding over Cabinet meetings.

Monarchs have seldom even attended Cabinet meetings since the premier took on the chairman role. However, in December 2012, the Queen was invited to sit in on Cabinet for the first time since the reign of Queen Victoria, as a one-off gesture to mark her Diamond Jubilee.

The role of prime minister today

Today, there are many established conventions surrounding the office of prime minister, almost all introduced since Walpole's day. The PM tends to be leader of the party that wins the most seats in the Commons at a general election. To this extent, although British voters theoretically turn out to elect their local MPs on polling day (and, indirectly, a national government), the emphasis of elections is inherently 'presidential'. Everyone knows that if X party gets in, Y leader will become PM. Historically, premiers have always hailed from one of the two biggest parliamentary parties at any one time. In the twentieth century, five PMs were Labour and 12 Conservatives. The Tories' dominance of the office until recently saw them regarded as the 'natural party of government'.

Although many prerogative powers exercised on the sovereign's behalf are discharged collectively by Cabinet (at least notionally), the PM is customarily the only minister ever granted private audiences with the monarch. Incoming premiers first meet the Queen when they visit her at Buckingham Palace to be offered the post formally after their election. This behind-the-scenes ritual is known as the 'kissing of the hands'. (Reportedly, Tony Blair did actually kiss the Queen's hands, although this has not generally been practised for generations.)

The PM's official London residence is at 10 Downing Street and he or she also has use of a sprawling country estate at Chequers in the Chilterns. Like many conventions, such rules are there to be bent when circumstances dictate: when Mr Blair came to power, he swapped domestic quarters with his Chancellor,

Gordon Brown, whose official residence was Number 11, where there is more living space. At the time, Mr Blair had a growing family of three children, while Mr Brown was living alone.

By far the most important convention relating to the PM, however, is the fact that whoever holds the office has the authority to exercise, on the sovereign's behalf, most powers entrusted to him or her by royal prerogative.

The principal prerogative powers discharged by the premier are to:

- appoint fellow ministers of the Crown;
- chair Cabinet weekly meetings;
- appoint members of Cabinet committees;
- keep the sovereign informed of government business on a weekly basis;
- declare war and peace;
- recommend passage of government Bills to royal assent;
- recommend **dissolution** of Parliament for general elections;
- recommend **prorogation** of Parliament for summer recess and other holidays;
- draw up his or her party's manifesto at elections and write the Queen's Speech—the annual announcement of proposed government legislation;
- recommend for sovereign's approval appointees to senior clergy positions, including the Church of England bishops and deans;
- recommend the appointment of senior judges;
- recommend appointees for senior positions in public corporations, including the British Broadcasting Corporation (BBC);
- recommend prospective recipients of honours and peerages in the Queen's Birthday Honours List and New Year Honours List; and
- answer for his or her government's policies and actions at Prime Minister's Questions (PMQs).

The PM is also Minister for the Civil Service. The 'department' that he or she oversees in this capacity is the Cabinet Office (effectively the 'Ministry for the Civil Service') and, until recently, his or her **permanent secretary** (the most senior civil servant) was the Cabinet Secretary. On the retirement of then incumbent Sir Gus O'Donnell, in 2011, a decision was taken to split his previous role three ways: replacing him with not only a new Cabinet Secretary, but also a permanent secretary to the Cabinet Office and a formal Head of the Home Civil Service. But a further, more radical, reform was to come—and one emblematic of the Conservatives' wider agenda to shake up the policymaking process and inject a spirit of entrepreneurship into Whitehall. Alongside his dramatic July 2014 Cabinet reshuffle, Mr Cameron introduced a new chief executive role at the top of the Civil Service, the first holder of which was expected to be recruited from the business community. He or she was to report directly to Cabinet Secretary Sir Jeremy Heywood, who resumed the secondary role of heading up the service traditionally held by his predecessors until the retiring Sir Bob Kerslake had been handed that role, as a part-time position, in 2011.

Towards 'elective dictatorship'—are prime ministers now too presidential?

Britain's premier may not be its head of state, but to many outside observers he or she often appears so. No monarch has had the temerity to challenge the passage of a government Bill since Queen Anne more than 300 years ago. And the notion that sovereigns would defy the electorate's will to block appointments of PMs whose policies they opposed is the stuff of establishment conspiracy theories.

Perhaps unsurprisingly, power has been known to go to some PMs' heads. As long ago as 1976, Quintin Hogg—who, as Lord Hailsham, twice served as Conservative Lord Chancellor—used his Richard Dimbleby Lecture to criticize the 'elective dictatorship' of British governments. His argument was that successive PMs had accrued substantial additional power beyond that vested in them constitutionally and were increasingly using their parliamentary colleagues to steamroller policies through Parliament. Moreover, he argued, those same policies were often decided upon behind closed doors—long before being debated in Parliament. At best, this backstage policymaking would take place around the Cabinet table, among premiers and their ministerial colleagues; at worst, it might be dreamed up informally between the PM and an inner circle of trusted confidantes, not all necessarily ministers. This mode of governing is often referred to as 'prime ministerial government'—or, recently, 'sofa government'—as opposed to the more collective and traditional 'Cabinet government'.

Indeed, it was often said that 1960s and 1970s governments were prone to striking deals in 'smoke-filled rooms', with business leaders, trade union bosses, and other interest groups having a direct and unofficial input into policymaking. In the case of Labour governments, the phrase 'beer and sandwiches' was coined to refer to the cosy chats that Harold Wilson and James Callaghan reportedly had with the union leaders who helped to bankroll the party prior to announcing new wage and industrial policies.

But these tactics—increasingly common to all governing parties—are far from the only examples of perceived presidential behaviour by modern PMs. Occasional slips of the tongue by pressurized premiers have spoken volumes about their apparent sense of superiority. In 1989, Margaret Thatcher notoriously greeted news that her son Mark's wife had given birth with the 'royal 'we', telling the waiting media: 'We are a grandmother.'

Mr Blair—of all recent PMs, the one most frequently described as presidential—was also prone to such lapses during his later years in office. In a March 2006 interview with chat show host Michael Parkinson, it was put to him that his job brought with it a huge amount of responsibility, in light of his status as Britain's commander-in-chief. Mr Blair failed to challenge this assertion, despite the fact that, constitutionally, this office rests with the Queen. In the same interview, he intimated that God had guided his actions over Iraq—echoing words used by President George W. Bush several years earlier.

So much for the sound bites, though: in what ways do PMs *act* high-handedly? Examples of such presidential actions can broadly be grouped under four headings:

- bypassing or downgrading the Cabinet's role in devising policy;
- announcing policies to the media before informing Parliament or the Cabinet;
- ignoring popular opinion and protest; and
- grandstanding on the international stage.

Bypassing or downgrading the Cabinet's role in devising policy

Prime ministers chair meetings of Cabinet. It is here that policies are traditionally thrashed out, before being announced to the press and public. In recent decades, however, there has been a tendency for premiers to downgrade the Cabinet's role in policymaking—or even to bypass it entirely, instead seeking advice from select coteries of trusted friends known as 'kitchen Cabinets'.

'Kitchen Cabinets' have taken various forms, often closely reflecting the particular personalities of individual PMs. An early manifestation of a kitchen Cabinet was Conservative PM Ted Heath's Central Policy Review Staff (CPRS), a group of advisers within the Cabinet Office (see 'The Cabinet Office and Cabinet committees' in this chapter) entrusted with streamlining the formulation of government policy across departments. The formation of the CPRS had been recommended by the Fulton Committee, established by Mr Wilson in 1966 to review the workings of the Civil Service. The Committee had also suggested a separate 'policy unit' be formed to coordinate long-term planning in each ministry and, when Wilson returned to power in 1974, he acted on this suggestion by forming the Downing Street Policy Unit (effectively his own kitchen Cabinet), chaired by Sir Bernard Donoughue.

Indeed, Mr Wilson (more than any earlier PM) had a reputation for valuing the views of personal friends over those of Cabinet colleagues. His private secretary, Marcia Williams, was seen to exert an at times powerful influence on his managerial decisions. This fashion for consulting close allies—elected or otherwise—before presenting ideas to Cabinet (let alone Parliament) was also favoured by Mrs Thatcher, whose closest aides included her press secretary,

Sir Bernard Ingham, and private secretary, former businessman Charles Powell—intriguingly, the brother of Mr Blair's loyal Downing Street chief of staff, Jonathan Powell.

More recently, kitchen Cabinets have become increasingly associated with the machinations of 'special advisers' and, in particular, the **spin doctors** whom ministers employ to put a positive gloss on government policy. This development will be discussed more fully later, but it is worth considering here in relation to one particular casualty of the 'sofa government' favoured by Mr Blair: Cabinet decision-making. As with his weekly meetings with the Queen, when the Iraq War was in full swing Mr Blair downgraded formal Cabinet meetings to such an extent that deliberations that traditionally took several hours were often reduced to 30 minutes or less. In addition, he left many detailed policy debates, customarily held in full Cabinet, to Cabinet committees—appointing his most loyal colleagues to chair those hearings to reduce the likelihood of his own ideas being disputed. It was for this and other 'undemocratic' tendencies that former Cabinet minister Clare Short later publicly dubbed Mr Blair a 'control freak'. Mr Cameron largely abandoned 'sofa government'—to such an extent that, from time to time, allies have advised him to exercise more control over senior civil servants to ensure that the Conservatives' policy priorities are steered through without obstruction. By contrast, some senior Tory ministers, such as former Education Secretary Michael Gove, have periodically been accused of allowing senior advisers to brief against their Liberal Democrat colleagues colleagues and that party's agenda. In March 2014, Mr Gove's outspoken former adviser, Dominic Cummings, became embroiled in a full-blown public row with Lib Dem leader Nick Clegg over what he dismissed as the latter's 'chaotic' and un-costed plan to introduce free school meals for infant school pupils from that September.

Mrs Thatcher and Mr Blair were also repeatedly accused of bypassing or downgrading Parliament's role in the legislative process. By using the party whip system to coerce MPs and peers to back the party line, Mr Blair was frequently accused of abusing his large Commons majority to 'steamroller' through policies unpopular with the public (and his own backbenchers). Examples include various anti-terror measures introduced following the attacks on the Twin Towers in New York and the 7 July 2005 bombings in London—many rushed through in a matter of days, with committee stages taking place on the Commons floor. In October 2011, Mr Cameron used a three-line whip to stifle a backbench revolt by Conservative MPs demanding a referendum on Britain's European Union (EU) membership. Despite this, the resulting rebellion remained the single biggest over Europe since the Second World War, with 81 backbenchers defying the party whip to support it. Nine months later, 91 Tory MPs broke ranks to vote down Lib Dem proposals for Lords reform (see Chapter 2, 'From Wakeham to the Coalition—what next for the Lords?'), while almost exactly a year after the 2011 EU rebellion by his backbenchers

Mr Cameron suffered a Commons defeat over his proposal to argue for a freeze, rather than real-terms cut, in the Union's budget.

Announcing policies to media before Parliament or Cabinet

Briefing the media (or sympathetic sections of it) on policy proposals before formally announcing them to Parliament and public has become a much criticized trend under recent administrations. Indeed, in some instances under Mr Blair, ministers close to the PM spoon-fed policy details to favoured journalists before even the Cabinet (let alone Commons) had deliberated them. Arrangements for the briefings invariably involved spin doctors and/or special advisers—principally Mr Blair's official spokesman and long-time director of communications, Alastair Campbell, and/or Mr Powell.

The most widely used forms of 'off-the-record' briefings are explained in the table entitled 'Types of media briefing used by ministers and special advisers', to be found on the **Online Resource Centre** that accompanies this book.

An infamous example of serious policy proposals being released to the press prior to full Cabinet discussion occurred in 2002, when then Health Secretary and close Blair ally Alan Milburn gave *The Times* a detailed explanation of his 'Ten-Year Plan for the National Health Service' (see Chapter 6, 'From patients to consumers—the "marketization" of the NHS'). Mr Cameron's government has repeatedly been accused of similar leaks: George Osborne's 2012 'omnishambles Budget' was as notorious for the fact that little of substance was left for the Chancellor to announce in his statement as for the perceived political folly of measures it introduced (see Chapter 7, 'The Finance Act').

Ignoring popular opinion or protest

During his first term, Mr Blair frequently consulted opinion pollsters and focus groups before taking radical policy decisions. His critics (many within his own party) argued that this was, at best, a waste of the mandate he had achieved by winning such a large majority in the 1997 election and, at worst, a betrayal of Labour's manifesto pledges.

In his second term, Mr Blair developed a tendency to do precisely the opposite—becoming increasingly bold in his political judgements. The most notorious example of this was his pursuit of the case for war with Iraq, citing supposed evidence that Saddam Hussein was stockpiling weapons of mass destruction (WMDs). Defying huge opposition in the country—articulated by the biggest peacetime demonstration in Britain's history, when some 500,000 protestors converged on Trafalgar Square just days before the war—he persuaded a reluctant Commons to vote for invasion.

Mr Blair's appetite for defying public opposition echoed that of Mrs Thatcher's. The policy that most clearly demonstrated her stubbornness in the teeth of huge public opposition would ultimately—like the Iraq War for

Mr Blair—hasten her downfall. Introducing the deeply unpopular Community Charge (see Chapter 12, 'Local taxation and the evolution of the Council Tax') to replace the age-old rates system provoked some of the largest-scale protests in British history. Mrs Thatcher remained resolute, however, and only when John Major succeeded her the following year was the tax abandoned.

Grandstanding on the international stage

As Britain's de facto head of state, the PM has the biggest global profile of any UK politician. Nonetheless, some premiers take to the role of international statesperson more than others. Liberal William Gladstone and Tory Benjamin Disraeli were the nineteenth century's most accomplished and successful British premiers, but it was the latter—famous, like Mrs Thatcher and Mr Blair, for his interventionist foreign policy—who impressed most on the international stage. Of twentieth-century PMs, Winston Churchill was widely regarded as the greatest statesman, principally because of the leadership he gave to Europe during the Second World War.

Recent examples of 'presidential-style' grandstanding at a global level have included Mrs Thatcher's decisive handling of the Falklands War and high-profile White House 'love-ins' with US President Ronald Reagan. Her implacable opposition to communism and her determined negotiation of various British opt-outs from EU legislation also helped to maintain her high international profile.

Mr Blair, meanwhile, waged four wars during his decade in Downing Street—pursuing a proactive defence policy known as 'liberal interventionism'. During his first term, he helped to launch two military campaigns: the North Atlantic Treaty Organization (NATO) intervention over alleged 'ethnic cleansing' of Albanians by Slobodan Milošović's Serbs in Kosovo, and a decisive move to halt civil war in the former British colony of Sierra Leone. In his second, he became forever wedded in the public eye to George Bush's US administration by pledging to 'stand shoulder to shoulder' with him following the 11 September terrorist attacks, and actively supporting the invasions of Afghanistan and Iraq.

Earlier, Mr Blair had stamped his international profile with 'missions' to tackle poverty in Africa, to forge peace in Northern Ireland, and to promote a decisive 'two-state solution' to the long-running stand-off between Israel and Palestine in the Middle East. His involvement in brokering the latter saw him rewarded after stepping down as PM with a new diplomatic role as Middle East peace envoy for 'the Quartet'—a loose international consortium representing the EU, United Nations, United States, and Russia. In many ways, Mr Cameron has continued this interventionist 'tradition'—drawing international praise for his Commons statement following publication of the long-awaited 'Bloody Sunday' report, making repeated high-profile visits to China and

India to promote British business interests, and playing a leading role in pushing for military action against Muammar Gaddafi in Libya and (unsuccessfully) Bashar Al-Assad in Syria (see Chapter 10, 'The Foreign and Commonwealth Office (FCO)').

Holding the prime minister to account

Given the degree of power accrued by PMs, what mechanisms exist to hold them to account? As we know, monarchs have long since lost their inclination (if not constitutional 'right') to challenge premiers. Notwithstanding Queen Elizabeth II's predilection for wrong-footing Wilson and her reputedly frosty relationship with Mrs Thatcher, there has been little evidence in modern times of reigning monarchs displaying any appetite for confrontation. Nonetheless, there remain significant means by which the actions of PMs can be influenced, if not directly controlled. These can be divided into four areas:

- public;
- press;
- Parliament; and
- party.

Public

The primary means of holding premiers accountable returns to that first principle: that they are ultimately MPs like any other and must stand for re-election in their constituencies come polling day. Their parties are similarly dependent on mandates for their Commons majorities: if enough of their MPs lose their constituencies' support, other parties will secure more seats to supplant them in government.

Mr Major's resounding defeat in 1997 by 'New Labour' was the clearest example in recent times of an ailing administration being unceremoniously ejected by a determined electorate. Not only did the Tories suffer a landslide defeat, but also many senior MPs—including future political pundit Michael Portillo—lost their seats. Although Mr Major escaped this ignominy, it has been known for PMs in some countries to lose their own constituency seats, as well as their parliamentary majorities. Australian premier John Howard lost his parliamentary seat in that country's 2007 election, after more than a decade in power, while Northern Ireland First Minister Peter Robinson suffered a similar fate in the 2010 UK general election (see Chapter 2, 'The Northern Ireland Assembly').

Prime ministers are also accountable in other ways. It has long been the practice for local authority, European, and by-elections to be treated as anti-government 'protest votes'—giving PM's a 'bloody nose'. Other voters prefer to withhold their support from governing parties that they might still back at general elections by abstaining altogether. There was significant anecdotal evidence that protest votes rose under New Labour, especially among traditional party voters disillusioned by the Iraq invasion. The combined effect of protest votes and abstentions, on one side, and renewed determination to harness support, on the other, can lead to situations like that witnessed in the 2007 and 2008 local elections, both of which were 'won' by the then resurgent Conservatives.

Other forms of public pressure that can be put on PMs include demonstrations (such as the Stop the War Coalition marches over Iraq and that of the Countryside Alliance over hunting), industrial action by public sector employees, and rejections of key policies in national **referendums**. Although British governments rarely put individual questions to the public vote—preferring to invoke the constitutional principle of parliamentary sovereignty, which leaves decisions to Parliament between elections—both Messrs Blair and Brown were accused of purposely avoiding referendums on the EU's 2007 Lisbon Treaty for fear of losing (see Chapter 9, 'Britain's twisty path to EU membership').

Press

If there is one thing guaranteed to send a PM scurrying in pursuit of populist policy ideas to regain public support, it is a run of negative tabloid headlines.

In recent years, the national press—particularly the biggest-selling daily papers, *The Sun* and *Daily Mail*—has arguably wielded disproportionate influence on successive governments' actions. Mrs Thatcher's hat trick of election victories was attributed, in part, to the support of 'white van' or 'Essex' man—terms denoting a new breed of aspirational working-class voter weary of the class warfare espoused by old-school Labour politicians, and attracted by the entrepreneurial doctrines of share and home ownership ushered in by Thatcherite ideology. Although formerly a red-blooded Labour paper (the *Daily Herald*), under Rupert Murdoch *The Sun* came to epitomize this new spirit of aspiration, while the high moral tone of the *Mail* appealed to more 'traditional' Conservatives.

Throughout the 1980s, *The Sun*, under bullish editor Kelvin Mackenzie, remained a staunch advocate of Thatcherism, using many memorable front-page headlines to bolster support for her resolutely patriotic brand of politics. Its most controversial splashes included its celebration of the sinking of the Argentine warship *General Belgrano* with the headline 'Gotcha!' and one aggressively urging voters to support Mr Major rather than Labour leader Neil Kinnock in the 1992 election. After years of supporting the Conservatives, though, Britain's biggest-selling paper switched horses in the run-up to the 1997 election, backing Mr Blair (before eventually returning to the Tories on the morning after Mr Brown's speech to the 2009 Labour Party Conference).

Although this was strenuously denied by both Mr Blair and Mr Brown, the liberalization of UK media ownership laws enabling Mr Murdoch to buy a stake in ITV was rumoured to have come as a result of his behind-the-scenes lobbying. Mr Cameron also faced serious questions over his perceived closeness to the Murdoch empire following his decision, while in Opposition, to hire former *News of the World* editor Andy Coulson as his personal spokesman shortly after the latter's 2007 resignation over a (then incipient) scandal about the practice of reporters at the Sunday paper 'hacking' into their contacts' mobile phone messages. Although Mr Coulson quit his Downing Street post in February 2011 (amid growing allegations about his collusion in a cover-up at his old paper), the uncomfortably close relations between the Murdoch press and Mr Cameron's Tories was laid bare in detail during a series of hearings at the public inquiry convened in 2011 by Lord Justice Leveson to examine the culture and practices of the British media following further phone-hacking revelations. Among the nuggets to emerge were anecdotes about Mr Cameron's cosy chat with then News International chairman James Murdoch in a Mayfair club, during which he learned that the paper's sister title, *The Sun*, was reverting to supporting the Conservatives, and furious phone exchanges between the company's chief executive, Rebekah Brooks, Labour's serving premier, Mr Brown, and his First Secretary, Lord Mandelson, which followed the paper's formal switch of loyalties later in 2009.

More controversial still were questions that emerged about the extent of unofficial Coalition endorsement of News Corporation's attempt to purchase the 61 per cent of shares that it did not yet own in UK-based satellite television broadcaster BSkyB. In his evidence to the inquiry, Murdoch junior disclosed a slew of email exchanges between Adam Smith (a special adviser to then Culture Secretary Jeremy Hunt) and News Corp lobbyist Frederic Michel, which appeared to reflect the minister's implied support for the bid. At a later hearing, Mr Smith revealed a memo sent to Mr Cameron by Mr Hunt, in which he apparently urged the PM to back the takeover. The note was sent on 19 November 2010—a month before Mr Cameron appointed Mr Hunt to succeed Business Secretary Vince Cable in determining the outcome of the BSkyB bid, following the latter's indiscreet confession to two undercover reporters from *The Daily Telegraph* that he had 'declared war' on Mr Murdoch.

Set alongside the latter's recollection of chatting to Mr Cameron about the takeover plans over Christmas dinner at Mrs Brooks's Cotswolds home and the regular text messages sent to the latter by the PM (signed off with a familiar 'DC'), an impression emerged of unprecedented levels of intimacy between Britain's most powerful media company and the holder of its highest political office.

While it has long been commonplace for newspapers to take partisan stands, in Britain broadcasters are bound by a strict code of impartiality upheld by the Office of Communications (Ofcom—see Chapter 7, 'Communications') and, in the case of the licence-funded BBC, the BBC Trust.

Parliament

Prime ministers are held to account by Parliament in various ways, the most demonstrable being Prime Minister's Questions (PMQs)—the Wednesday lunchtime half-hour session in which the PM is quizzed about his or her actions (see Chapter 2, 'Question Time').

Most MPs also sit on committees. On select committees, they examine the workings of individual government departments—and, indirectly, the Cabinet. General committees, meanwhile, scrutinize prospective legislation, the bulk of which will have originated in the in-trays of the PM and his or her most senior ministerial colleagues. Prime ministers also now subject themselves to twice-yearly scrutiny by the Commons Liaison Committee.

Members of Parliament can also use a variety of other parliamentary procedures outlined in the last chapter to influence or criticize PMs. But perhaps the single most powerful way in which MPs—and, to a lesser extent, peers—conspire to embarrass serving PMs is by voting down their policies in Parliament. Because most governments tend to have working Commons majorities and can usually marshal sufficient support from loyalists, historically government legislation is rarely defeated. Occasionally, however, PMs have found themselves so out of step with their parliamentary parties that (whatever their nominal majorities) they have struggled to get their proposals passed.

Party

When Parliament conspires to censure PMs, to derail their legislative programmes, or otherwise to undermine their authority, it usually succeeds only with the complicity of government backbenchers so dismayed at their leader's direction that they are prepared to vote against it en masse. During Mr Blair's second and third terms, backbench rebellions became so frequent at times that Labour MPs were increasingly described as the 'unofficial Opposition'—particularly when the *real* Opposition (the Tories) were still under the stuttering leaderships of William Hague, Iain Duncan Smith, and Michael Howard.

The most serious form that backbench rebellions can take is a 'motion of no confidence' (also known as 'vote of no confidence', or 'censure motion'). This is when a device such as an early day motion (EDM) is put before the Commons—customarily by the Leader of the Opposition—inviting MPs to pass a motion (vote) expressing loss of 'confidence' in the serving PM. If he or she loses, this normally means that even his or her own MPs have withdrawn their support and an election must therefore be called.

The election that brought an end to Callaghan's Labour government in May 1979 was ultimately precipitated by a confidence vote tabled by Opposition leader Mrs Thatcher. Because Callaghan had been leading a minority government following the collapse of a fragile deal with the Liberal Party (the 'Lib–Lab Pact'), he was increasingly reliant on support from the Ulster Unionists and Scottish Nationalists. When his government refused to implement a proposed Scotland Act to introduce devolution (a referendum had backed it, but on only a relatively low turnout), the nationalists tabled a confidence motion, which Mrs Thatcher swiftly emulated.

Prime ministers in desperate straits have even been known to call their own confidence votes to instil discipline in their party ranks and to force through unpopular legislation. In 1993, Mr Major tabled a 'back me or sack me' motion to force the hand of the 'Maastricht rebels' (see Chapter 9, 'Towards an EU "superstate"?'). In the event, he won—not least because most rebels represented marginal seats and could easily have lost them to other candidates or parties in the event of an election.

Traditionally, confidence motions require only *simple majorities* of MPs' votes—50 per cent of those cast, plus one—to bring down a government. So it was with alarm that some constitutional experts and politicians initially greeted the Coalition's proposals in May 2010 to introduce not only five-year fixed-term parliaments (see Chapter 4, 'The British franchise today—who can vote?'), but also a new rule preventing elections being called mid-term unless 55 per cent of MPs voted in favour of dissolution. Critics argued that the proposed '55 per cent rule' could be used to insure Mr Cameron against the possibility of his coalition partners pulling the plug on it prematurely (between them, the Lib Dems, Labour, and all minority parties would have mustered only 53 per cent of Commons votes if the former were to switch loyalties).

They also complained that it would render the confidence procedure redundant. Although a government could theoretically still be defeated by such a vote, the backing of a further 5 per cent of MPs would be needed to force an election—potentially leaving a 'defeated' administration limping on like a 'zombie'. In the Coalition's defence, then Leader of the House Sir George Young argued that its opponents were missing the point: rather than enabling PMs to prolong their tenures against Parliament's wishes, the new rule would instead liberate the Commons by equipping it with a mechanism to demand dissolution without formality of a confidence vote. Nevertheless, when Mr Clegg confirmed the final proposals in a Commons statement two months later, he announced that the 55 per cent rule was being dropped and elections would instead continue to be triggered by a no confidence vote alone. However, in performing his U-turn, he introduced a new lifeline for struggling minority governments—granting them a two-week breathing space after losing confidence votes to try to form alternative administrations and stay in power. At the same time, the Commons would still have the ability to prompt dissolution by a straight vote, although only if two-thirds of MPs (as opposed to the mooted 55 per cent) were to approve it. The proposed new power echoed one previously adopted by the Scottish Parliament.

There are, of course, various other ways in which governing parties can hold their leaders to account—and even depose them. Once a week, when Labour is in government, leaders subject themselves to a lengthy meeting of the **Parliamentary Labour Party (PLP)**—a body representing all Labour MPs. Although Mr Blair was given a famously easy ride for his first few years in power, after the Iraq debacle PLP meetings became increasingly strained, with the PM fielding harder questions and occasional heckling.

Conservatives have an even more ferocious means of grilling (and removing) their leaders. The **1922 Committee** is a body made up of all Tory MPs. Actually formed in 1923 (its name refers to the 1922 election), this has an 18-strong executive committee charged with overseeing the election of new leaders At times, it has replaced existing ones. As the 'voice' of Tory MPs, the 1922 Committee is seen to represent the collective 'mood' of the parliamentary party. If it passes a vote of no confidence, it is normally only a matter of time before the leader jumps (assuming that he or she is not pushed).

The 1922 Committee is examined in more detail in Chapter 5. But it is relevant here to the unseating of a particular Tory premier: Mrs Thatcher. Her downfall was effectively instigated by her former Cabinet colleague, Michael Heseltine, who challenged her for the party leadership in November 1990. Although she won the first round of voting, she did so by too small a margin to seal the contest. To do so she had to secure an *absolute majority*—more than half—of all Tory MPs and achieve 15 per cent more votes than her nearest rival—a target she narrowly missed. Despite initially announcing her intention to continue into a second round, in the interim Mrs Thatcher was visited by a deputation of backbenchers who persuaded her that she had lost her MPs' backing. After taking counsel from fellow ministers, she withdrew her candidacy—paving the way for Mr Major's election.

▌ Cabinet versus government—what's the difference?

Despite clear moves towards more presidential—or 'prime ministerial'—forms of government, constitutionally the role of Cabinet remains of paramount importance in the exercise of elected power in Britain. So what exactly *is* the 'Cabinet', and how does it differ from and relate to the 'government'?

The Cabinet is a 'subset' of the government. While governments comprise *all* ministers appointed by the PM, Cabinets comprise only the most senior. Governments and Cabinets have varied wildly in size from one administration to another, with some favouring a more compact, rationalized approach and others a more all-embracing one.

As explained in Chapter 2, governments can number anything between 80 and 100-plus ministers. In October 2011, the Coalition was criticized by the

Commons Public Administration Committee for hitting record highs—with 119 ministers and 46 ministerial aides on the government's payroll. Historically, the average Cabinet size has been 20. Yet, for much of the Second World War, Winston Churchill ran a Cabinet numbering 68 ministers, while in 1922 Andrew Bonar Law formed a peacetime Cabinet of only 16. In contrast, Labour PMs have tended to appoint larger Cabinets— as a bulwark, in part, against what the party long saw as the intransigence of senior civil servants against implementing radical reform. Mr Wilson had one Cabinet comprising 24 members and Mr Blair, 26. Mr Brown, meanwhile, appointed an enlarged 'hybrid' first Cabinet, effectively numbering 29—before expanding it still further, to 34 (including 'occasional' members such as Olympics Minister Tessa Jowell). Its numbers were boosted, in part, by Mr Brown's decision to create a new Department of Energy and Climate Change (DECC), and to reinstate two distinct offices for Defence and Scotland, in response to criticisms from military chiefs and the devolved Scottish Government respectively of his earlier decision to combine the two under one minister. Despite the overall size of its government, the Coalition Cabinet has generally numbered around 23 ministers.

Cabinet ministers have, until recently, always been either MPs or peers. Although some critics and constitutional historians regard the idea of peers being entrusted with ministerial briefs as contentious, there have been many high-profile examples of such appointments, including Lord Young of Graffham (Trade and Industry Secretary under Mrs Thatcher, and appointed by Mr Cameron to lead a review of health and safety laws) and Lord Adonis (first Education Minister, then Transport Secretary, in Blair's and Brown's administrations). Today, the appointment of peers to senior positions (if not that of PM) barely raises an eyebrow.

Mr Brown took the PM's discretion to choose ministers from outside the Commons to a new level, with his declaration on entering office that he wanted a 'government of all the talents'. This assertion (an extension of the 'big tent' politics for which Mr Blair was often criticized by Labour traditionalists) saw several individuals from outside his party appointed to senior advisory positions in government. Baron Jones of Birmingham, former director-general of the Confederation of British Industry (CBI), was appointed a minister at the then Department of Business, Enterprise, and Regulatory Reform (BERR)— despite publicly declining to join the Labour Party. Sir Mark Malloch Brown, former UN Deputy Secretary-General and neither a peer nor an MP, was appointed Minister for Africa, Asia, and the UN. Mr Brown also dispensed with another Cabinet tradition: for the first time since 1963, he switched his Cabinet meetings from Thursdays to Tuesdays.

Most Cabinet ministers have the title **secretary of state**, rather than **minister of state**, denoting their seniority. This normally means that they head up a major spending department, such as health, and often have several junior ministers answerable to them. The choice of ministerial posts included in the Cabinet can vary greatly, depending on the political priorities of the day. Until Mr Blair's 1997 election victory, overseas aid/development was treated as a relatively minor ministerial area and was the responsibility of a non-Cabinet Foreign Office minister. When Labour was re-elected, the post's incumbent was promoted to 'International Development Secretary', with his or her own dedicated ministry.

In addition to obvious senior departmental posts, the Cabinet traditionally contains one or two honorary ones awarded to loyal lieutenants of the prime minister whom he or she wants to keep close at hand, but for more general duties than overseeing specific portfolios. One such post is that of 'Chancellor of the Duchy of Lancaster'—a sinecure deriving from an office once involved in the daily management of the sovereign's one significant surviving estate following the handover of the Crown Lands to the state (see Chapter 1, 'The Privy Purse'). When veteran Labour MP Jack Cunningham was appointed to this post in 1998, the media dubbed him variously 'Cabinet enforcer' and 'Cabinet fixer' because his brief was taking charge of coordinating the government's message in its dealings with press and public. Another such post is that of 'Minister without Portfolio'—an office briefly assumed after the 1997 election by Mr Blair's close ally Peter Mandelson (who made two subsequent returns to Cabinet). In forming his coalition, meanwhile, Mr Cameron dispensed with convention by appointing the Lib Dem leader, Nick Clegg, deputy prime minister without allocating him a departmental brief. Following an extensive reshuffle designed to line up a younger, more diverse body of ministers in the run-up to the 2015 election campaign, as of 15 July 2014 the composition of the Cabinet was as listed in Table 3.1.

So much for the Cabinet: what of the government as a whole? Its size can also vary, but in modern times it is customary for it to number up to 100 ministers. The most junior ministerial post is that of **parliamentary under-secretary**, ranking beneath both ministers and secretaries of state. Also included are government whips and any MP appointed a **parliamentary private secretary (PPS).** These are junior posts ascribed to ambitious MPs who aspire to ministerial office. They serve as points of contact or liaison in Parliament (or, as some would have it, 'spies') for serving ministers and are informally connected to their departments. The PM tends to have two PPSs.

Ministerial salaries

In recognition of their responsibilities, ministers who are MPs receive substantially higher salaries than backbenchers. Precise levels of ministerial salaries can vary widely, depending on their seniority and the complexity of their jobs. As of the 2008–09 tax year, then Prime Minister Gordon Brown and his ministers declined their automatic annual 1.5 per cent salary increases in a gesture

Table 3.1 The composition of the UK Cabinet (July 2014)

Title	Name
Prime Minister/First Lord of the Treasury/Minister for the Civil Service	David Cameron
Deputy Prime Minister/Lord President of the Council	Nick Clegg
Chancellor of the Exchequer	George Osborne
Secretary of State for Foreign and Commonwealth Affairs (Foreign Secretary)/First Secretary of State	Phillip Hammond
Secretary of State for Justice/Lord Chancellor	Chris Grayling
Secretary of State for the Home Department (Home Secretary)	Theresa May
Secretary of State for Defence	Michael Fallon
Secretary of State for Health	Jeremy Hunt
Secretary of State for Energy and Climate Change	Edward Davey
Secretary of State for the Environment, Food, and Rural Affairs	Liz Truss
Secretary of State for International Development	Justine Greening
Secretary of State for Business, Innovation, and Skills	Vince Cable
Secretary of State for Work and Pensions	Iain Duncan Smith
Secretary of State for Transport	Patrick McLoughlin
Secretary of State for Communities and Local Government/Minister of State for Faith and Communities	Eric Pickles
Secretary of State for Education/Minister for Women and Equalities	Nicky Morgan
Secretary of State for Culture, Olympics, Media, and Sport	Sajid Javid
Secretary of State for Northern Ireland	Theresa Villiers
Secretary of State for Wales	Stephen Crabb
Secretary of State for Scotland	Alistair Carmichael
Chief Secretary to the Treasury	Danny Alexander
Leader of the House of Commons, First Secretary of State	William Hague
The following senior ministers are also allowed to attend Cabinet:	
Chief Whip and Parliamentary Secretary to the Treasury	Michael Gove
Minister for Universities and Science Minister of State for Cabinet Office (Cities and Constitution)	Greg Clark
Attorney General	Jeremy Wright
Solicitor General	Robert Buckland
Minister for the Cabinet Office/Paymaster General	Francis Maude
Leader of the House of Lords/Chancellor of the Duchy of Lancaster	Baroness Stowell
Minister for Business, Enterprise, and Energy	Matthew Hancock
Minister without Portfolio	Grant Shapps
Minister of State for the Cabinet Office, with responsibility for policy/Lord Privy Seal	Oliver Letwin
Minister of State for Cabinet Office/Minister of State for Schools	David Laws
Minister for Employment and Disabilities	Esther McVey

NOTE: A regularly updated version of this table can be found on the **Online Resource Centre** of solidarity with public sector workers, whose pay rises were being limited because of (in his words) the 'economic uncertainty' of the times. This initially meant that Mr Brown was paid £132,923 on top of his basic MP salary of £64,766 (a total income of £198,661—several thousand less than his entitlement), but soon after he left office in May 2010 it emerged that, for the previous year, he had quietly taken a further cut—bringing his salary nearer the level of ordinary senior ministers (£150,000). For the two years prior to Labour's electoral defeat, Cabinet ministers and the government chief whip had each earned £145,492 in total. During his first week in power, Mr Cameron went further—cutting salaries of those around the top table by 5 per cent in absolute terms and freezing them at those levels for the rest of the parliament. In so doing, he brought his own political earnings down to £142,500, those of Cabinet ministers to £134,565, and pay for ministers of state outside Cabinet from £100,568 under Labour to £98,740.

Although peers are not yet paid, those occupying government positions do receive parliamentary remuneration. Cabinet ministers drawn from the Lords receive £101,038, while ministers of state get £78,891. Until 2007, the highest-paid minister of all was not the PM, but the Lord Chancellor, who earned the princely sum of £232,900. But both Coalition incumbents thus far, Kenneth Clarke and Chris Grayling, and their immediate predecessor, Jack Straw, are MPs, and have therefore drawn £145,492 and £134,565 respectively.

Substantial salaries are also paid to senior Opposition frontbenchers, although at a lower level than those of their government counterparts. The leader of the Opposition currently earns £139,355 a year.

Collective responsibility, ministerial responsibility, and the ministerial code

The actions of ministers, especially those in Cabinet, are governed by two constitutional conventions—collective responsibility and individual ministerial responsibility—and an increasingly strict statutory 'rule book', the Ministerial Code.

Collective responsibility

Cabinet ministers are expected to endorse publicly the actions of governments of which they are members, even if they privately disagree with them. This **collective responsibility** doctrine rests on the assumption that individual ministers broadly support the policy programme adopted by their government, but may occasionally disagree with specific proposals. It has therefore long been the custom for ministers to bite their tongues. On many notable occasions, however, individuals have found themselves increasingly out of step with the views of their Cabinet colleagues over time and have ultimately resigned—freeing themselves to speak out.

In 1986, then Defence Secretary Michael Heseltine quit the Cabinet over the proposed merger of Westland, Britain's last surviving helicopter manufacturer, with US company Sikorsky. He stormed out of Cabinet in full view of waiting television cameras, exasperated with what he saw as Mrs Thatcher's dictatorial decision-making style. In 2003, the late Robin Cook, then Leader of the House, resigned from government in protest at the invasion of Iraq. He was followed, some time later, by International Development Secretary Clare Short, who blamed the country's chaotic reconstruction following Saddam's defeat for her decision. John Denham, reappointed to the Cabinet under Mr Brown, resigned from a junior post over Iraq. More recently, in July 2012, ministerial aide Conor Burns quit his Coalition government post, and fellow Tory Angie Bray was sacked, over their opposition to Lords reform.

Very occasionally, collective responsibility has been waived by PMs to encourage frank and open debate about serious constitutional matters. In a risky, but ultimately shrewd, tactical manoeuvre, in 1975 Labour PM Wilson temporarily suspended it during the run-up to a national referendum on Britain's continued membership of the European Community (which he subsequently won). Recognizing the divisions it might otherwise open up in his own Cabinet, he allowed ministers strongly opposed to the policy to campaign for a 'no' vote. Among the Eurosceptics was left-winger Tony Benn, who argued that the 'Common Market' (as it was widely known) would destroy British jobs by preventing Britain using customs duties (protectionism) to inflate the price of imports of manufactured goods, in the interests of persuading people to 'buy British'. Asked about his similarly tolerant policy towards troublesome colleagues, US President Lyndon B. Johnson once remarked of FBI director J. Edgar Hoover:

> It's probably better to have him inside the tent pissing out than outside the tent pissing in.

In the early days of the Coalition, there were signs that Messrs Cameron and Clegg were looking to mimic Mr Wilson's tactic in relation to policies over which there remained clear divisions between their parties. To win the latter's support, the Conservatives agreed to let Lib Dem frontbenchers 'continue to make the case for' alternative policies in areas such as the proposed renewal of Britain's Trident nuclear programme, while Tory ministers were allowed to campaign against the introduction of the alternative vote (AV—see Chapter 4, 'Proportional representation (PR) and other voting systems') prior to the May 2011 referendum on electoral reform. But while the Coalition agreement allowed for limited open Cabinet 'dissent' in specified areas, Lib Dem MPs (both front and back bench) were generally bound by an undertaking not to vote *against* policy proposals, but only to abstain. Nonetheless, the tradition of collective responsibility has continued to show strain as the Coalition's term of office has wound on, with Business Secretary Vince Cable in particular often voicing open disagreement with the Treasury (and, by inference, his Lib Dem colleague Danny Alexander) over various aspects of economic policy.

Individual ministerial responsibility

The other major convention relating to ministers' work is that of **individual ministerial responsibility**. This is the doctrine that should a serious error or scandal occur 'on the watch' of a departmental minister, he or she should do the honourable thing and resign. Lord Carrington, for example, stepped down as Foreign Secretary over the Argentine invasion of the Falkland Islands in 1982.

In contrast, recent history is littered with examples of significant departmental errors for which ministers have been reluctant to take the blame. The fiasco over Britain's sudden withdrawal from the European exchange rate mechanism (ERM) in 1992 would, on many other occasions, have seen the immediate departure of the Chancellor of the Exchequer—the minister in charge of the economy. In fact, then Chancellor Norman Lamont stayed on for several months before belatedly being sacked by Mr Major.

Culture Secretary Mr Hunt doggedly defied calls for his scalp following the Leveson Inquiry's revelations about email exchanges between his special adviser and a senior News Corp lobbyist focusing on the company's bid to take over BSkyB—an example of ministerial responsibility that some critics, including outspoken Culture, Media, and Sport Select Committee member Tom Watson, argued was also a breach of the Ministerial Code (see 'The Ministerial Code' in this chapter).

Those who have 'fallen on their swords' recently include Liam Fox, who was forced to resign as Defence Secretary in October 2011 following revelations that he had allowed his former best man, Adam Werritty, to accompany him on official overseas visits and to attend sensitive meetings that might have aided the latter's business interests. Mr Werritty, a freelance corporate lobbyist who had not received Ministry of Defence security clearance, had exacerbated the situation by handing out business cards falsely claiming to be an adviser to Dr Fox. In practice, ministers are often sacked before they have a chance to quit. The premier's ability to remove colleagues unceremoniously dates back to a convention initiated by William Pitt in the early nineteenth century and perfected by his Tory successor, Harold Macmillan, when, on Friday 13 July 1962, he sacked seven ministers: the notorious 'Night of the Long Knives'. Sackings almost always precipitate 'Cabinet reshuffles', during which other ministers are moved from one job to another to fill gaps created by their colleagues' removal.

The Ministerial Code

The most recent redraft of the **Ministerial Code** was agreed by the then newly formed Coalition government in May 2010. Its opening line sets the tone of the document, stating:

❝ Ministers of the Crown are expected to behave in a way that upholds the highest standards of propriety. ❞

The implication is clear: while Lord Nolan's *Seven Principles of Public Life* (see Table 2.4) are intended to encourage responsible behaviour by parliamentarians, the bar is raised higher for members of Her Majesty's government. To this end, the Code lays out the following 10 additional principles governing ministerial conduct:

(a) The principle of collective responsibility, except when explicitly set aside, applies to all ministers.

(b) Ministers have a duty to Parliament to account, and be held to account, for policies, decisions, and actions of their departments and agencies.

(c) Ministers must give accurate and truthful information to Parliament, correcting inadvertent errors at the earliest opportunity. Those who knowingly mislead Parliament should offer their resignations.

(d) Ministers should be as open as possible with Parliament and public, refusing to provide information only when disclosure would not be in the public interest, which should be decided in accordance with relevant statutes and the Freedom of Information Act 2000.

(e) Ministers should require civil servants who give evidence before parliamentary committees on their behalf and under their direction to be as helpful as possible in providing accurate, truthful, and full information in accordance with the duties and responsibilities of civil servants as set out in the Civil Service Code.

(f) Ministers must ensure no conflict arises, or appears to arise, between their public duties and private interests.

(g) Ministers should not accept any gift or hospitality which might, or might reasonably appear to, compromise their judgement or place them under an improper obligation.

(h) Ministers in the Commons must keep separate their roles as minister and constituency member.

(i) Ministers must not use government resources for party political purposes.

(j) Ministers must uphold the political impartiality of the civil service and not ask civil servants to act in any way which would conflict with the Civil Service Code as set out in the Constitutional Reform and Governance Act 2010.

The Code stipulates that it is the PM's personal responsibility to refer alleged breaches to an independent adviser on ministerial interests (at time of writing, Sir Alex Allan), which Mr Cameron did in June 2012 in relation to the expenses claims of then Conservative Party co-chairman Baroness Warsi (see Chapter 2, 'The Parliamentary Commissioner for Standards'). It also describes at length the array of duties that accompany ministerial office—ranging from the obligation to chair departmental board meetings to responsibility for the conduct of appointees, including special advisers. It was in relation to this latter point that Mr Hunt faced calls for his resignation over the Murdoch emails affair. Even more important, perhaps, than their responsibility for their staff's conduct is ministers' obligation to ensure that no conflicts of interest arise—or 'could reasonably be perceived to arise'—between their ministerial positions and private interests, 'financial or otherwise'. To this end, a formal list of ministers' interests is now published online, and regularly updated, as an additional level of transparency beyond the register of members' financial interests to which all MPs are subject. Among the interests declared by Mr Cameron on the list as of October 2013 were his vice-presidency of the National Society for Epilepsy, presidency of the Lords and Commons Tennis Club, and honorary membership of Ellesborough Golf Club. Both Mr Cameron and Mr Clegg also declared relevant roles held by their wives, including Samantha Cameron's post as creative consultant of upmarket Bond Street stationers Smythson, and Miriam Clegg's as both a partner at international law firm Dechert and independent adviser to Spanish construction company Acciona.

The Cabinet Office and Cabinet committees

The Cabinet Office is effectively the 'Civil Service of the Cabinet'—the administrative staff and machinery that organizes its meetings and business on a day-to-day basis. It comprises a Cabinet Secretariat, responsible for recording Cabinet minutes, and the Office of Public Service, which oversees overall government business. It is headed by the Cabinet Secretary.

In turn, the Secretariat is made up of six separate departmental secretariats:

- the Economic and Domestic Affairs Secretariat;
- the Defence and Overseas Affairs Secretariat;
- the European Secretariat;
- the Constitution Secretariat;
- the Central Secretariat; and
- the Intelligence Support Secretariat.

In addition, **Cabinet committees** are increasingly formed to deal with the finer points of policymaking. They tend to be chaired by ministers whose personal views are close to those of the PM. Under the Coalition, many of the nine full cabinet committees and their 16 subcommittees have been chaired by the so-called 'quartet' of most senior ministers: Mr Cameron, Mr Clegg, Mr Osborne, and Mr Alexander. There are several types of Cabinet committee, as outlined in the table entitled 'Types of cabinet committee' to be found on the **Online** **Resource Centre**.

▶ The Civil Service

If ministers are the government's 'architects'—brainstorming and formulating policies in Cabinet—civil servants are its construction workers, responsible for putting together the building blocks that transform their ideas into reality. The 'Civil Service' is the collective term for the administrative structure that carries out the work of government departments and the numerous agencies that implement policy.

Dating back to the secretariats that first emerged, piecemeal, in the eighteenth century, the Civil Service has become the one constant of UK government. The fact that government continues uninterrupted even after governing parties change at elections (and indeed while the country is without MPs—although not ministers—during election campaigns) is a tribute to the continuity guaranteed by the professionals responsible for 'keeping things running'. This continuity role has rarely been more starkly apparent than during the five days between the May 2010 election and the formation of the Coalition, when caretaker PM Mr Brown agreed to give both other main parties access to then Cabinet Secretary Sir Gus and other high-level mandarins as they drafted their prospective deal. He also revealed the existence of a working document that he had asked Sir Gus (jokingly nicknamed 'GOD' by colleagues) to produce in the run-up to the election clarifying the constitutional position of sitting premiers and Opposition leaders in a hung Parliament.

The foundations of today's Civil Service were laid in the Northcote–Trevelyan Report 1854, which stipulated that:

- all appointments should be made on *merit*; and
- there should be *fair and open competition* for advertised posts.

Efforts were quickly made to establish a professional structure for the Civil Service and successive governments have made this progressively more rigorous. Senior civil servants—or 'mandarins'—are recruited by independent Civil Service Commissioners through the Civil Service Board. Some recruits rise to senior ranks swiftly, via the Fast Stream development programme, which admits around 300 graduates a year.

Altogether, Her Majesty's Civil Service comprises around 500,000 officials working across anything up to 60 departments and 100 associated bodies—primarily executive agencies (see 'Executive agencies' in this chapter)—based principally at Whitehall and Millbank, a stone's throw from Parliament. Each department is headed by a permanent secretary. As with lower-ranking civil servants, they are employed because of their expertise in the particular areas overseen by their departments. Not to be confused with secretaries of state, they often have long records of service to their departments, given that they are permanent Crown employees and, as such, will remain in post irrespective of changes of government. Although they come into close daily contact with ministers and often advise them on policy, as paid officials, permanent secretaries are expected to be politically neutral.

Political neutrality in practice

Although the 'political neutrality' doctrine is sacrosanct in the Civil Service, controversies have sometimes arisen over civil servants who have acted in a politically motivated way. The machinations of Sir Humphrey Appleby—the odious permanent secretary for the Ministry for Administrative Affairs in the classic 1980s BBC1 sitcoms *Yes, Minister* and *Yes, Prime Minister*—were inspired by real-life Whitehall shenanigans. More radical governments, from Clement Attlee's Labour to the Coalition, have also characterized civil servants as small-c conservative. But perhaps the most significant Civil Service scandal of modern times occurred in 1985, when Clive Ponting, a civil servant in the Ministry of Defence, was tried under the Official Secrets Act 1911 for passing classified details to an unauthorized person about the sinking during the Falklands War of the Argentine ship the *General Belgrano*—allegedly while it was both retreating and outside the 'exclusion zone' declared by the British government around the islands. Although Ponting (who later became a successful writer) was acquitted of breaching section 2 of the Act, the case prompted then Cabinet Secretary Sir Robin Butler to issue the following 'Note'—as an addendum to the Civil Service code of conduct:

> ❝ The determination of policy is the responsibility of the minister ... When, having been given all the relevant information and advice, the minister has taken the decision, it is the duty of civil servants loyally to carry out that decision ... Civil servants are under an obligation to keep the confidences to which they become privy in the course of their official duties. ❞

Following the Ponting affair and a series of smaller-scale 'leaks' by similarly ethically motivated 'whistle-blowers', new stipulations were drawn up to clarify the *levels* of political neutrality expected of civil servants on different rungs of the professional ladder. While civil servants of all ranks were expected to remain politically impartial in the workplace, it was decided that the extent to which they had to be entirely neutral *outside* it would depend on their seniority (see the table entitled 'Levels of political impartiality in the Civil Service', on the **Online Resource Centre**). In addition to the expectation of political neutrality, the most senior civil servants—notably permanent secretaries—and all those involved in dealing with the press or giving ministers policy advice on a regular basis are also politically restricted—that is, barred from participating in any direct political activity outside their day jobs, unless they first resign. This extends from election canvassing and leafleting, to standing as candidates in any election themselves, be they local, national, or European.

Despite these safeguards, apparently politically motivated policy leaks have continued. The Home Office was embroiled in controversy after a series of leaks to then Opposition MP Damian Green led to the police searching his office (see Chapter 1, 'Statute') in November 2008, and months later a disc containing details of MPs' expenses claims was leaked to *The Daily Telegraph* (see Chapter 2, 'MPs, conflicts of interest, abuses of privilege, and how to avoid them').

In running their departments on a day-to-day basis, civil servants are expected to abide by the 'three Es': 'economy, efficiency, and effectiveness'. This maxim has been underlined by two key milestones: the Efficiency Strategy published in 1979 by Sir Derek (now Lord) Rayner; and the 1982 Financial Management Initiative, which sought to provide departmental managers with 'a clear view' of the responsibilities of their individual ministries.

Civil Service accountability

Several recent government initiatives have attempted to give the Civil Service a better name by making it appear leaner and meaner. In 1991, Mr Major launched a 'Citizen's Charter' calling for a 'revolution in public services', while 11 years later New Labour extended the scope of 'Charter Mark' services to cover purely 'back office', as opposed to 'public-facing', departmental divisions.

Executive agencies

The work of the Civil Service is so all-consuming that governments have often tried to rationalize departments, breaking them down into smaller, more manageable units. These units—effectively *subsets* of their parent departments—focus exclusively on *delivering*, rather than *formulating*, policy. Today most are known as 'executive agencies'.

Initially established in 1988 by Mrs Thatcher—who sought to abandon what she saw as an over-centralized, monolithic structure—these smaller-scale, breakaway bodies were designed to resemble commercial companies rather than traditional organs of government. As such, they were each given chief executives, who presided over boards of directors—a radical departure from the bureaucratic way in which the Civil Service had previously been run. Unlike commercial companies, agencies had no shareholders (and therefore no profit motive) and were staffed by civil servants seconded from their parent departments. But as time went on, their managers were increasingly drafted in from industry, rather than graduating from the Service itself (the theory being that importing talent from the private sector would increase efficiency). This approach would ultimately have a sweeping impact across the public sector that continues to be felt today, with everything from local NHS trusts to further education colleges adopting a 'chief executive and board' model.

Initially, there were only a handful of executive agencies, the first of which, the Vehicle Inspectorate—now the Vehicle and Operator Services Agency (VOSA)—was established in August 1988. Their number mushroomed under Labour, which ended up with 130 in total—90-plus reporting to government departments at Whitehall, with the remainder answering to the three devolved administrations in Scotland, Wales, and Northern Ireland. While some smaller spending departments have only one or two agencies beneath them, bigger ones such as the Home Office and Department for Work and Pensions (DWP) allocate much of their day-to-day work to agencies. The single biggest agency, in terms of staffing and budget, is **Jobcentre Plus**, which employs 100,000 people and spends £4 billion a year of taxpayers' money. With 36, the Ministry of Defence (MoD) has the most.

One criticism of executive agencies is that they are used by ministers to absolve themselves from individual ministerial responsibility. By devolving power to 'breakaway' sections of their departments, they might disclaim personal liability for their mistakes. This arguably happened in November 2007 when Chancellor Alistair Darling refused to accept culpability for the loss of two unencrypted computer discs containing the names, addresses, birthdates, National Insurance (NI) numbers, and bank details of 25 million families by HM Revenue and Customs (HMRC), an executive agency of HM Treasury (see Chapter 7, 'HM Revenue and Customs').

Quangos

Long before executive agencies existed, there were already a large number of taxpayer-funded organizations carrying out work delegated by government departments. But, historically, these non-departmental public bodies (NDPBs) tended to be staffed not by seconded departmental civil servants, but their own employees, which they recruited as discrete entities, notionally independent of government. Over time, an umbrella term has evolved for these bodies: 'quasi-autonomous non-governmental organizations', or **quangos**.

Quangos are often confused with executive agencies—and it is easy to see why. Like agencies, they have their own management boards—although these are headed by honorary chairpersons, rather than salaried chief executives.

They also control significant, largely taxpayer-funded, budgets. But this is where the similarities end. As the term implies, quangos are 'semi-independent' of government and, for that reason, are tasked with overseeing areas of practical policy at an arm's length from ministers. They also have the freedom to be more outspoken than agencies: Culture Secretaries have often had to weather the barbs of chairpersons of Arts Council England (ACE), for instance, over cuts to regional theatres and museums.

Perhaps unsurprisingly, quangos are frequently condemned by the media for lacking accountability. Whereas agencies are at least answerable to ministers who can be ejected at elections, quangos have always been more autonomous. Yet, like agencies, they receive most of their funding from taxpayers—through the aegis of related departments.

Lack of accountability is one criticism levelled at quangos; another is nepotism. How can we be certain that board members appointed by ministers will be genuinely chosen on merit? The now disbanded BBC Board of Governors—charged with holding the Corporation to account for its public service broadcasting responsibilities—was a quango in all but name, and Mr Blair was criticized for choosing Labour donor Gavyn Davies as its chairman in 2000.

Sustained criticism of the 'quangocracy' has led to several recent moves to address the nepotism question. In 2000, the government introduced an Appointments Commission to propose chairpersons and non-executive directors (NEDs) of NHS bodies, including hospitals, primary care trusts, and strategic health authorities (see Chapter 6). It also has powers to vet appointees to other local, regional, and national quangos. These appointments are themselves regulated by an Office of the Commissioner for Public Appointments (OCPA).

In July 1996, a democratic audit identified 6,224 executive and advisory quangos, run by 66,000–73,500 people and responsible for spending £60.4 billion. On entering power, Mr Blair vowed to scrap 'unaccountable quangos' and Mr Brown spoke of a 'bonfire of the quangos'. But in August 2007 Cabinet Office figures revealed that quangos had spent £167.5 billion the previous year. The Coalition revived the 'bonfire' concept, with Cabinet Office Minister Francis Maude promising to cull some 192 and merge 118 others in October 2010. While few can have lamented the passing of obscure bodies such as the Zoos Forum or the Government Hospitality Advisory Committee on the Purchase of Wines, there was widespread criticism of the decision to scrap the UK Film Council, which had co-funded numerous globally successful British-made movies, including that year's big Oscar winner, *The King's Speech*, while the government's pledge to replace the Audit Commission—the national quango responsible for auditing council accounts—with a patchwork of private contractors was seen by some as an example of free market ideology trumping transparency (see Chapter 14, 'From "Beacon Councils" to the National Indicator Set—the growth of performance data'). In practice, the

Coalition has acted much like previous governments: liberally chopping quangos in some areas, while introducing new ones elsewhere. According to a widely reported exchange between Mr Cameron and Labour leader Ed Miliband during PMQs on 29 June 2011, the Coalition's health reforms were destined to see the number of NHS quangos alone more than triple—from 163 to 521.

Taskforces and tsars

A new form of non-elected body created by New Labour, particularly during its first term, the number of taskforces in place by 2000 was already 44. They were generally set up to deal with short-term issues of public concern and were headed by senior public figures dubbed 'tsars' (effectively, hired trouble-shooters). Examples include the Rough Sleepers' Unit, led by 'Homelessness Tsar' Louise Casey, which set out to tackle street homelessness, and a short-lived drugs taskforce run by 'Drugs Tsar' Keith Hellawell. Although the term 'taskforce' is seldom heard today, Mr Cameron has continued the trend for 'tsars', allowing the term to be used to denote advisory roles given to former Labour MPs Alan Milburn and Lord Hutton (as 'Social Mobility Tsar' and 'Pensions Tsar', respectively), current Labour MP Frank Field ('Poverty Tsar'), and Will Hutton, ex-editor of *The Observer* ('Fair Pay Tsar').

Think tanks, the private sector, and the future of public policymaking

Even policymaking—long the preserve of Whitehall mandarins and their underlings—is now on the verge of being outsourced to the private sector. In May 2012, then new Cabinet Secretary Sir Jeremy floated the 'perfectly legitimate' idea of contracting private companies to devise future ministerial initiatives. In so doing, he appeared to be advocating a move that, critics argued, could open up the highly sensitive area of policy formulation to commercial conflicts of interest, dilute the institutional memory of the Civil Service itself, and relegate highly knowledgeable and experienced officials to the status of mere administrators. Within weeks, Mr Maude had published even more radical proposals, including allowing ministers to appoint future permanent secretaries, rather than relying on the Civil Service's own promotional structure—an idea that immediately revived concerns about the 'politicization' of policy delivery.

Spin doctors and special advisers

Under the Ministerial Code, each Cabinet minister may employ up to two special advisers—colloquially known as 'SPADs'—while other government ministers permitted to attend Cabinet meetings may appoint one. The total number of special advisers, in particular spin doctors, has multiplied in recent years. By the end of Mr Major's reign they had increased to 38, but under Mr Blair there were consistently as many as 74 at the highest level. At its peak, the advisers' salary bill topped £3.6 million, but their number has since declined.

Unlike civil servants, special advisers are normally *party*, rather than government, appointees. This was the case with most Downing Street big-hitters of the Blair years, including Mr Campbell and Mr Powell. Sometimes, however, the edges are more blurred: Sir Bernard Ingham began as a civil servant, before switching to the Conservatives' payroll while Mrs Thatcher was PM. When a party is in opposition, it pays for its advisers, but once in government, they (like civil servants) are usually paid from public funds.

Under Mr Blair, some special advisers became bywords for cold-hearted calculation. Jo Moore, an adviser at the Department of Transport, Local Government, and the Regions (DTLR), resigned in February 2002 following a series of controversies about her management style, and in particular the publication of an explosive email she sent on 11 September the previous year—the

date of the terrorist attacks on the Twin Towers—describing it as a 'very good day' to 'bury' bad news.

Mr Blair's reliance on advice from spin doctors and party appointees over senior civil servants frequently saw him accused of 'politicizing' the Civil Service. One of his first actions was to pass an executive order allowing senior advisers like Mr Campbell and Mr Powell to issue orders to civil servants. Mr Brown revoked this, symbolically, within hours of replacing him at Number 10, but cynics dismissed even this gesture as spin, in light of recent statistics indicating that the number of government special advisers, spin doctors, and press/marketing staff continued to climb during his tenure. A Whitehall audit found that 68 additional advisers were employed by ministers during 2007 and all were still in post six months after Mr Brown took office. The overall number of press office staff (many civil servants, but nonetheless employed to put a positive gloss on government policy) had risen to 3,250. Between 1997 and 2007, Labour increased the annual cost of 'government PR' (public relations) to £338 million—with a £15 million rise in 2007 alone.

In July 2001, the Labour government finally published a Code of Conduct for Special Advisers. It defined them as 'temporary civil servants', who did not necessarily have to be appointed 'on merit', but were nonetheless expected to comply with the Civil Service Code and could not use 'official resources', such as stationery, for party-political purposes. If they wished to campaign on behalf of their ministers during the lead-up to an election, they must first resign from their posts in recognition of their political affiliation. Mr Campbell did this in 2005.

The Parliamentary Ombudsman

Despite its title, the **Parliamentary Commissioner for Administration** (part of a wider regulatory body known as the **Parliamentary and Health Service Ombudsman**) investigates public complaints not about Parliament itself, but about government departments and other public bodies, including quangos. The basis of an individual's complaint must be that he or she has suffered an injustice owing to maladministration arising from delay, faulty procedures, errors, unfairness, and/or bias. Complaints against judges, police officers, and councils are investigated by separate bodies.

The Ombudsman is sometimes derided as 'a watchdog without teeth', because even though it can recommend that departments or bodies should 'remedy' mistakes, its maladministration rulings cannot be *enforced*.

Since devolution, there have been separate ombudsmen for Scotland and Wales.

▌ Devolved government—executive decision-making in the regions

Chapter 1 and 2 laid out, first, the manner in which devolution unfolded in Britain and the forms of government subsequently settled on in each of the three countries outside England. There follows now a brief overview of the manner in which government is constituted in those countries.

The Scottish Government/Executive

Just as the legislative process prevailing in Scotland is distinct from those in Wales and Northern Ireland, so too is its executive framework. Scotland now boasts its own **Scottish Government**, headed by a First Minister (the country's prime minister in all but name). More fully formed than its cousins in Cardiff and Stormont, the Scottish Government has its own Cabinet, which meets on Tuesday mornings at Bute House in Edinburgh's Charlotte Square (the First Minister's official residence). The administration itself is based at St Andrew's House, with its own secretariat, and has two subcommittees: a Cabinet subcommittee on legislation, and an emergency room Cabinet subcommittee.

The Welsh Assembly Government

Like its Scottish equivalent, the Welsh Assembly was formally known as an 'executive', rather than 'government' per se. It too is led by a First Minister (currently Labour leader Carwyn Jones). After the 2007 Welsh Assembly election, Labour entered a coalition with the Welsh nationalist party, Plaid Cymru, under the banner 'One Wales', but since May 2011, when it scored its biggest victory since devolution began, it has governed alone.

The Northern Ireland Executive

The 'power-sharing executive' in Northern Ireland, also lead by a First Minister, has been a coalition since its inception and began functioning properly only following the conclusion of a substantive peace agreement in spring 2007. Since May 2011, it has remained a coalition of the two biggest parties: the Democratic Unionist Party (DUP) and Sinn Féin.

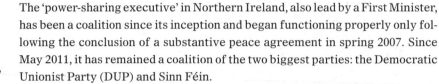

☷ Topical feature idea

You work on a local evening newspaper. With the 2015 general election fast approaching and opinion polls suggesting that it could lead to a change of government, your editor wants you to write a feature explaining the roles of the prime minister and how the prerogative powers that he or she exercises on the Queen's behalf impact on your readers' lives on a daily basis. Who would you contact, and how would you approach researching and writing up this piece—bearing in mind that you need to make your feature as relevant to a local audience as possible?

✳ Current issues

- **The later stages of coalition government** At time of writing, Conservative and Lib Dem backbenchers were becoming increasingly combative over policy compromises agreed by their leaders, and tensions had spread to the top table, with some Tory ministers said to have sanctioned briefings by their special advisers against Lib Dem colleagues and their policies, and vice versa.

- **The future of coalition government and collective responsibility** Despite being in coalition, the Conservatives and Lib Dems continue to fight council and European elections on different manifestos, and campaigned against each other in the 2011 alternative vote referendum. With recent opinion polls signalling the likelihood of another hung Parliament in 2015, coalition governments—and a relaxed collective responsibility principle—might be here to stay.

- **The contraction of the Civil Service** The Coalition has frozen Civil Service recruitment indefinitely. Although portrayed as stasis rather than a cut in civil servants, critics argue that it means job losses, because those retiring go unreplaced. With

Labour pledging to respect the Coalition's short-term spending limits if it wins power again in 2015 and to move towards a Budget surplus, any boost to Civil Service numbers seems unlikely.

⸬ Key points

1. Most prerogative powers are exercised on the sovereign's behalf by the government, in particular the prime minister (First Lord of the Treasury).

2. The government is the collective name for the ministers of the Crown who oversee departments of state. The most senior ministers, chaired by the prime minister, sit in Cabinet.

3. Government ministers must abide by two key constitutional principles: collective responsibility and individual ministerial responsibility. The first is the convention that all ministers should publicly support government policy, whatever their private misgivings. The second requires them to resign for major mistakes made by their ministries.

4. Civil servants are the paid officials employed to implement government policy and to administer departments on a day-to-day basis. They are expected to be politically neutral.

5. The most senior departmental ministers are known as secretaries of state. Top departmental civil servants are permanent secretaries. They are politically restricted—that is, barred from political campaigning or standing in elections.

→ Further reading

Budge, I., Crewe, I., McKay, D., and Newton, K. (2007) *The New British Politics*, 4th edn, London: Longman. **Fourth edition of acclaimed critical introduction to British politics at the dawn of the twenty-first century, updated to cover Brown's administration.**

Burnham, J. and Pyper, R. (2008) *Britain's Modernised Civil Service*, Basingstoke: Palgrave Macmillan. **Thorough examination of recent Civil Service developments, incorporating analysis of the impact of changes introduced by the Thatcher, Major, Blair, and Brown governments.**

Campbell, A. (2012) *The Burden of Power: Countdown to Iraq—The Alastair Campbell Diaries 4*, London: Hutchinson. **Candid, if 'on message', fourth volume of personal diaries by Tony Blair's chief spin doctor, charting the turbulent period between the terrorist attacks of 11 September 2001 and 'the British/US 2003 invasion of Iraq.**

Crossman, R. (1979) *The Crossman Diaries: Selections from the Diaries of a Cabinet Minister, 1964–1970*, London: Book Club Associates. **Widely regarded as among the most incisive and revealing political diaries written by a British minister, these** highlights are edited by one of Britain's foremost contemporary political biographers.

Mullin, C. (2010) *View from the Foothills*, London: Profile Books. **Witty, warts-and-all account of the follies and foibles of the Blair government by a former junior minister. Best read as a counterpoint or companion piece to the more positive spin in Campbell's diaries.**

 Online Resource Centre

www.oxfordtextbooks.co.uk/orc/Morrison4e/

Visit the Online Resource Centre that accompanies this book for web links and regular updates.

4

The electoral system

The legitimacy of Britain's legislature—and the executive drawn from it—today derives from more than mere historical precedent. It stems from the principle of liberal democracy and the system of democratic elections that is the bedrock of modern UK government.

▌ The origins of the British franchise

British social reformers were demanding the vote for centuries before it was granted. For John Lilburne's Levellers, who propelled Oliver Cromwell to power, the English Civil War was about far more than a tussle for constitutional supremacy between Parliament and Crown: parliamentary sovereignty meant nothing if it was not exercised by ordinary people. For this to happen, he argued, all 'free-born Englishmen' must be given a direct say in how Parliament was run: in short, a vote.

Lilburne's arguments would echo down the centuries before being answered, even in part—through the writings of Thomas Paine, the marches of the nineteenth-century Chartists, the speeches of the Labour Party's firebrand first member of Parliament (MP), James Keir Hardie, and the campaigns of the suffragettes. But it was another century before every adult (regardless of class or gender) was granted a say in the running of Britain's affairs. The slow extension of voting rights is charted in the table entitled 'Acts of Parliament that extended the UK franchise' on the **Online Resource Centre** that accompanies this book.

While the primary significance of these Acts was to extend voting entitlements to more people, the most radical went further. To ensure that parliamentary democracy operates fairly and equitably, successive governments have introduced further incremental reforms.

The 'Great Reform Act 1832' owes its place in history less to a wholesale extension of the franchise than to its abolition of 'rotten boroughs'—by that point a shameful hangover from medieval times. The term 'rotten borough' was used to refer to areas in which constituency boundaries ought to have been altered to reflect dwindling population numbers, but had not—with the result that, in some areas, the number of voters was so minimal that it was possible for candidates to win seats by literally bribing the whole electorate. In 1831, the year before the Act was passed, the constituency of Old Sarum in Wiltshire had just three houses and 11 registered voters. Gatton, in Surrey, had 23 houses, but only seven voters. As a result, rotten boroughs had become a byword for corruption, with some constituencies effectively being bought and sold, and others passed from father to son like inheritances. Before being awarded a peerage (and eventually becoming prime minister) Arthur Wellesley, Duke of Wellington, once served as MP for the rotten borough of Trim, County Meath. Rotten boroughs were memorably satirized in the BBC1 sitcom *Blackadder the Third,* in which a dog won the fictitious seat of 'Dunny-on-the-Wold'.

Another significant reform was the abolition of 'plural voting'. This was the tradition allowing individuals who owned properties in two or more areas—or those attending university in one area when their family home was elsewhere—to have a multiple say in an election's outcome, by voting in each constituency. This practice (not to be confused with that, still common today, allowing individuals in these positions to choose in which constituency they would like to vote) was ended by the Representation of the People Act 1948.

The British franchise today—who can vote?

Elections to the House of Commons are known as **general elections**. For convoluted historical reasons, polling days tend to be on Thursdays and have traditionally taken place up to five years to the day after the previous Parliament was assembled following a poll (between the Septennial Act 1715 and the Parliament Act 1911, the electoral terms had been as long as seven years). Prime ministers' ability to call elections at times that suited them—often quitting while ahead in the polls, rather than seeing through policies that might be for the good of the country, if not their own approval ratings—was, however, highly contentious. As a result, the Coalition passed the Fixed-term Parliaments Act 2011 to introduce new, immovable, five-year terms, commencing with the next election, on Thursday 7 May 2015. But this decision, too, proved controversial, with some critics suggesting that it was being used as a device to prolong the life of the Coalition beyond the more usual four-year terms of most parliaments.

As the name implies, at general elections all sitting MPs formally resign to contest their seats. This means that elections are held simultaneously in all 650 Commons constituencies and a new Parliament is normally summoned by the sovereign as soon as all votes are counted and seats allocated. After the 2010 election, the distribution of Commons seats was as outlined in the table entitled 'The distribution of seats in the House of Commons following the May 2010 election' on the **Online Resource Centre**.

This result left Britain facing its first hung Parliament since February 1974. Under these circumstances, it typically takes several days for new governments to be finalized. The Lib–Con 'Coalition agreement' was signed only on Tuesday 11 May—five days after polls closed.

Whereas, in local and European elections, the franchise has gradually been extended to include European Union (EU) citizens resident in Britain, voting is more restricted in general elections. Currently, it is open to British, Irish, and Commonwealth citizens normally resident in the UK, subject to their:

- names being on the electoral register for constituencies in which they live; and

- being over the age of 18 on election day (although they may enter their names on the electoral register from age 17).

Despite these broad qualification criteria, the following individuals are barred from voting:

- peers entitled to sit in the Lords;

- foreign nationals (including citizens of other EU states);

- patients detained under mental health legislation for crimes;

- people detained in prison (other than those awaiting trial); and

- people convicted during the preceding five years of 'corrupt' or 'illegal' election practices'.

General election voting rules also have the following quirks.

- Members of the Armed Forces and Crown servants of British embassies, the Diplomatic Service, and the British Council employed overseas (and their partners or other family members) may vote in constituencies 'where they would normally live'.

- UK citizens living abroad ('ex-pats') for fewer than 15 years can make annual declarations allowing their names to be included in registers for constituencies 'where they were living before they went abroad'. They can vote by proxy—appointing friends or relatives to vote on their behalf—at any Westminster, Scottish Parliament, Welsh Assembly, and European Parliament (but not local) election.

- Holidaymakers are allowed 'absent votes' under the Representation of the People Act 1985—provided that electoral registration officers are 'satisfied that the applicant's circumstances on the date of the poll will be or are likely to be such that he cannot reasonably be expected to vote in person'.

- Although there is nothing stopping monarchs and their heirs from voting in theory, they have refrained from doing so in practice, because this would be seen as unconstitutional.

Registers of electors are compiled by local electoral registration officers and filling them in is compulsory—although, unlike in countries such as Australia, voting is *not*. Many people technically broke the law when charged the Community Charge ('Poll Tax')—a head tax payable by each individual, rather than household (see Chapter 12, 'Local taxation and the evolution of the Council Tax')—by deliberately leaving forms blank to avoid being billed.

The Representation of the People Act 2000 has changed the way in which registration takes place as follows.

- Before the Act, electors were registered wherever they were living on 10 October each year. Although an annual canvass is still conducted (on 15 October), a rolling registration system now exists, enabling electors to register at new addresses at the beginning of any month.

- Draft registers are open for inspection until 1 December. Registers cannot be altered (except after a formal appeal) once the final registration date has passed.

New Labour also liberalized some pre-existing voting disqualifications, while remaining strict about others. Until recently, many people detained in hospitals under mental health legislation were barred from voting, on the grounds that they were not of 'sound mind'. This is no longer the case (unless they are convicted criminals). Homeless people were also enfranchised formally for the first time under the 2000 Act. People with no permanent address may now vote subject to a 'declaration of local connection'. Following repeated appeals by convicted prisoners against their prohibition from voting under the European Convention on Human Rights, Coalition ministers have been forced to consider amending the law to allow some categories of inmate to vote—despite Mr Cameron's protestation that the thought of doing so made him feel 'physically sick'. At time of writing, however, this matter remained unresolved.

Although its stance was more liberal than those of previous governments in some respects, Labour tightened up certain qualifications. The Representation of the People Act 1989 made it easier for ex-pats to vote in general elections—allowing them to do so up to 20 years after emigrating. At the time, this was viewed by critics of the then Conservative government as a manoeuvre designed to boost its vote (the assumption being that many people retiring abroad were likely to be wealthy Tory supporters). After the 2001 election, Labour reduced this entitlement period to 15 years.

▶ General elections and candidacy—who can stand?

Any citizen of Britain, the Irish Republic, or a Commonwealth country resident in Britain and over the age of 18 on the day he or she is nominated (until June 2007, the age qualification was 21) has been able to stand for election—provided that he or she is not disqualified because he or she is:

- a peer retained in the House of Lords;
- an undischarged bankrupt subject to a bankruptcy restriction order under the Enterprise Act 2002 in England and Wales (because he or she has acted dishonestly or in an otherwise 'blameworthy' way), adjudged bankrupt in Northern Ireland, or someone whose estate has been sequestered in Scotland;
- a mental patient detained for criminal activities;
- someone sentenced to or currently serving more than one year's imprisonment;
- someone found personally guilty of *corrupt* election practices during the preceding 10 years (if in the same constituency) or the last five years (if a different one);
- someone found personally guilty of *illegal* election practices in the last seven years (if in his or her constituency) or five years (elsewhere); or
- a holder of the offices listed in the House of Commons Disqualification Act 1975—that is:
  - a holder of a **politically restricted post** in the Civil Service (see Chapter 3, 'Political neutrality in practice');
  - a member of the regular Armed Forces or the Ulster Defence Regiment;
  - a serving police officer;
  - a holder of judicial office; or
  - a member of a specified commissions—for example the Equality and Human Rights Commission (EHRC), the Independent Police Complaints Commission (IPCC), and the Lands Tribunal.

Some disqualifications are more liberal than others. While convicted prisoners have long been denied the vote in general elections, they may stand as candidates—provided that they are serving 12 months or less. This 'loophole' was once even more open-minded: Provisional Irish Republican Army (IRA) member Bobby Sands was imprisoned for 14 years for possessing firearms in 1977, yet managed to get himself elected as MP for Fermanagh and South Tyrone in April 1981, after standing on a so-called 'Anti-H Block/Armagh Political Prisoner' ticket. He was on hunger strike at the time, however, and died several weeks later. After his death, Margaret Thatcher's government hastily passed the Representation of the People Act 1981, which introduced the current 'maximum 12-month sentence' qualification for serving prisoners with parliamentary ambitions. The swiftness with which it did so stopped any of Sands' fellow hunger strikers replacing him.

How the British electoral system works

The system used to elect MPs is colloquially known as 'first past the post' (FPTP)—or, more technically, *plurality voting*. This means that, in each constituency, the candidate receiving most votes—a relative majority—is elected. Similarly, the political party gaining the most Commons seats once all constituency votes are counted nationally normally forms the government. Historically, one party has tended to win an *overall majority* nationally—more seats than all other parties and independent MPs put together (or a majority 'over all'). More rarely, one party emerges with only a handful more seats than its nearest rival—allowing it to form only a *minority* administration (as Labour did temporarily in February 1974) or to forge a coalition with another party/parties. Such a result is known as a **hung Parliament**.

Britain's most recent hung Parliament followed the 2010 election, when no single party won an overall majority, but the Conservatives secured 307 Commons seats, Labour, 258, and the Lib Dems, 57. With Lib Dem leader Nick Clegg holding the balance of power—despite a disappointing election-night result, which saw his party make a net loss of five seats—he was invited into swift negotiations with David Cameron's Tories. After five days of furtive deal-making (which, at one point, saw Mr Clegg holding parallel talks with Labour), the Lib Dems agreed to join a Conservative-led government—marking the start of the UK's first formal coalition since the Second World War. Unlike the fragile 'Lib–Lab Pact', which saw David Steel's then Liberal Party prop up James Callaghan's Labour government for 15 months between 1977 and 1978, the 2010 arrangement saw Lib Dem frontbenchers enter Cabinet in senior positions, with their leader anointed deputy prime minister.

The British electoral system has long been controversial, because of the frequent imbalance between numbers of votes cast for particular parties and the shares of seats into which these translate. Because only first-placed candidates in each constituency are elected, all other votes cast (often tens of thousands) are 'wasted'. For many years, it has been only the Conservatives and Labour who have stood realistic chances of forming governments on their own, because in order to win sufficient seats parties have to rely on *concentrations* of support. Traditional heartlands—for the Tories, the affluent south-east; for Labour, the north and Scotland—tend to swing the pendulum between them.

General elections have also produced governments with numbers of seats vastly outstripping their shares of the vote. The 2005 poll saw Labour win well over half the available seats, despite gaining only 35 per cent of the vote (equivalent to 21 per cent of registered voters, given the low turnout on the day). And the inbuilt Labour bias under FPTP was underlined still further when, in 2010, the Tories won 36 per cent of the votes, compared to Labour's 29 per cent and the Lib Dems' 23 per cent, but were 19 seats short of the winning post. Detailed analysis of the 2005 results had found that the average Labour MP needed only 26,858 votes to be re-elected at that time, whereas Tories required 44,241 and Lib Dems 98,484.

Hardly surprising that, in a move presented as an attempt to rectify this imbalance (and cutting the cost of Parliament to taxpayers), Mr Cameron hoped to reduce the number of MPs to 600 and make constituency populations more equal from 2015. However, this plan floundered in 2012, when Mr Clegg withdrew the Lib Dems' support for it in protest at the Tories' refusal to back his proposals for House of Lords reform (see Chapter 2, 'The House of Commons').

Few dispute, however, that some reform is needed. An example of the wild disparities in the sizes of UK electorates in 2010 was the fact that the Isle of Wight (a Tory stronghold) boasted 110,000 voters, while a populace of 22,000 was sufficient to return a Scottish Nationalist Party (SNP) MP in the Western Isles. If Mr Cameron's planned changes had occurred, the Isle of Wight would have been split into two constituencies—each covering some 50,000 electors. While still embracing twice as many people as the Western Isles, each seat would nonetheless have been well below the customary 65,000-voter average.

Some election results have been notoriously unfair. In February 1974, incumbent Prime Minister Ted Heath's Tories won 225,789 more votes than Labour, but secured four fewer seats. Heath's attempts to strike a survival deal with then Liberal leader Jeremy Thorpe failed, largely resulting from the Conservatives' unwillingness to countenance electoral reform. Within days, Wilson took office, consolidating his victory that October by securing a small working majority of three and 1 million more votes than the Tories, but this did little to defuse the initial sense of injustice. It has not always been this way around, though: in 1951, Labour Prime Minister Clement Attlee was beaten by Winston Churchill's Tories, who won 26 more seats despite polling 250,000 fewer votes. Labour had polled a total of 13,948,385 votes—a colossal 48.8 per cent share and, at that point, the most votes ever cast for a single political party in British history. The huge combined Labour–Tory vote share in 1951 (amounting to nearly 97 per cent) was down to two principal factors: a (by today's standards) stratospheric turnout of 82.6 per cent, and the extreme weakness, by this stage, of a residual Liberal Party (led by Clement Davies), which could barely muster 730,000 supporters. An oft-cited curiosity is that it was another party struggling to cling to power (in its case, successfully) that managed the highest ever popular vote to date: against the backdrop of the highest national turnout in 18 years (77.67 per cent), in May 1992 John Major's Conservatives won just under 14.1 million votes. It was a combination of the complexities of electoral arithmetic and the fact that, by then, the Liberal Democrats were polling 22 times as many votes as Davies's Liberals (nearly 6 million) that prevented them achieving more than a slender Commons majority of 21. Five years later, on a significantly lower turnout (71.2 per cent), Labour would achieve the biggest post-war landslide victory—a majority of 179—on a little over 13.5 million votes (half a million fewer than Mr Major had achieved in 1992). As ever, it was a combination of factors—not least the uneven distribution of votes around the country and the fact that the Commons had gained eight seats since 1992 (up from 651 to 659)—that worked in the victor's favour.

Tactical Voting

In recent elections, it has become increasingly common for electors in certain constituencies to vote *strategically*—backing candidates other than those they most want to see elected, in the hope of blocking those they like least. This method of casting votes—rejecting one's 'sincere preference' in favour of a compromise candidate who is more likely to win—is known as **tactical voting**.

An oft-cited example of this is when voters who strongly identify with Labour, but live in constituencies in which the sitting MPs are Conservative, vote Lib Dem instead. If, at the previous election, the Labour candidates had come third—behind not only the Tories, but also Lib Dems—on this basis votes for Labour would be considered 'wasted'. So, with the Lib Dems better placed to beat the Tories, the Labour supporter might be better voting tactically—backing his or her 'least worst option' over the one that he or she most favours.

Examples of MPs elected by tactical voting abound. Lib Dem Mark Oaten's decisive 1997 victory in the Winchester by-election prompted by an electoral petition from Tory Gerry Malone (see 'Voting procedure on the day—the role of the returning officer' in this chapter) is believed to have been secured by a wholesale tactical switch by Labour supporters to the Lib Dems. Indeed, by 1997, the Conservatives had become so unpopular, after 18 years in power, that widespread tactical voting was used to boot them out. In 2001, singer Billy Bragg organized a national campaign to prevent the Tories winning seats by getting fellow opponents of the party to 'trade' their tactical votes with electors living elsewhere in Britain. A Lib Dem voter living in a Labour/Tory marginal constituency, for example, might 'vote by remote' for his or her preferred party in a distant Lib Dem/Tory marginal—trading his or her own constituency vote with a Labour supporter whose home was in that area.

▶ The election process

The sequence of events leading to a general election is outlined in Table 4.1.

Each candidate must put down a £500 **election deposit**, which is returned provided that he or she receives at least 5 per cent of votes cast in the relevant constituency. The deposit was introduced in 1918 to discourage 'frivolous' candidates—and, cynics suggest, to boost the Treasury's coffers (it made £800,000 from forfeited deposits in 2001).

Voting procedure on the day—the role of the returning officer

Local administration of voting in general elections is tightly regulated. After polling closes, it culminates in an election-night 'count' at a chosen venue—normally a large council building somewhere near the constituency's geographical centre—overseen by a **returning officer**. In practice, the returning officer's role tends to be discharged by a senior officer in the local authority containing, coterminous with, or neighbouring the constituency—often its chief executive. But in theory it is the responsibility of the council's chairperson or mayor, except in

Table 4.1 The general election process

Event	Condition
Election date announced	Elections must be called at least 17 working days before polling.
Nominations for candidates—until recently, prospective parliamentary candidates (PPCs)—entered	Nomination process closes at 12 p.m. on 19th day before election (excluding Sundays and Bank Holidays).
Application for postal ballots closes	All applications for **postal votes** must be made by 5 p.m. on 11th working day before poll.
Checking that nomination meets basic conditions for eligibility and registration	Each candidate must have his/her nomination proposed and seconded by two 'subscribing' local electors and signed by eight 'assenting' electors. Nominations include a brief description of candidate on ballot paper (six words, including name and political affiliation). Candidates are not always backed by parties (i.e. can be 'independent'). Each is allowed to post one 'election communication' to registered voters.
Disqualification of invalid nominations	Returning officers (see 'Voting procedure on the day—the role of the returning officer' in this chapter) may reject nomination papers deemed 'out of order' on polling day.

'county constituencies' (rural ones), in which the role now falls to 'acting returning officers' (electoral registration officers employed by nearby district councils). Electoral procedure on the day is outlined in Table 4.2.

Should results be especially close and it is felt that disallowed ballot papers might have produced a different result if included, dissatisfied candidates can apply to the High Court for an 'election petition' against the returning officer. This happened in 1997 when Mr Malone lost his Winchester seat by just two votes to Mr Oaten—the closest result since 1945. Mr Malone's petition succeeded, but when the election was rerun that November, he lost by a 21,566-vote landslide (proving that nobody likes a bad loser!). The by-election result is almost certain to have been nearer the electorate's original wishes than the knife-edge outcome of the general election poll, given that, on that earlier occasion, many voters had been confused by the candidacy of Richard Huggett, who listed himself on the official ballot paper as 'Liberal Democrat Top Choice for Parliament' (forcing Mr Oaten to have the words 'Liberal Democrat Leader

Table 4.2 The electoral process on polling day

Event	Conditions
Polling stations open at 7 a.m. and close at 10 p.m.	Registered electors not choosing to vote by post, email, or proxy may do so at stations based at schools, community centres, pubs, and supermarkets. Ballot papers issued to voters at polling stations by election staff (with official marks impressed at this stage).
Absent votes may be cast in advance	Those who cannot reasonably be expected to vote in person (e.g. are on holiday) can apply for 'absent votes', while people unable to vote because of disability, nature of their work, or fact that they have moved constituency since electoral roll was last updated can apply for 'indefinite absent votes'. Anyone entitled to absent vote can either vote by post or proxy. Postal ballot papers cannot be sent to addresses outside the UK.
Secrecy of ballot preserved—no interference with ballot boxes	Ballot boxes sealed at close of poll, before being taken to counting place to be counted.
Official count starts after close of poll—only valid papers counted	Count supervised by returning officer—observed by candidates, agents, media, and small number of 'scrutineers'. Any 'spoilt' ballot papers—e.g. those defaced or with crosses beside more than one name—disallowed.
Deadline for voting—including receipt of postal votes	All votes must have been cast and postal ballot papers received, by 10 p.m. on polling day.
Recount if result too close to call	If winner's victory is marginal, candidates can demand recount (occasionally, more than one—until returning officer decides result is clear). In dead heat, returning officer required by law to settle victory by intervening directly. He/she will normally either toss coin or ask neck-and-neck candidates to write their names on slips of paper and draw winner from hat (sortition).

Paddy Ashdown' written beside his name). Mr Huggett stood again in the ensuing by-election—under the label 'Literal Democrat'—but the adverse publicity
generated by his first campaign undermined his vote. The use of such deliberately confusing labels was subsequently banned by the Registration of Political
Parties Act 1998, which established the Electoral Commission (see 'The role of
the Electoral Commission' in this chapter).

On the exceptionally rare occasions on which an election results in a dead
heat—with multiple recounts confirming that two candidates have received
exactly the same number of votes—it can fall to the returning officer to supervise the most primitive possible way of deciding the contest: asking the joint
winners to draw lots. Most recently, 'sortition' (the name coined for the process
in ancient Athens) was used in the 2011 local elections to determine political
control of Bury. On this occasion, Joanne Columbine drew the longest straw to
clinch the borough council for Labour from the Tories.

Disputes over close-run contests are not the only thing that can cause headaches on election night. Occasionally, more serious administrative problems
occur. Besides being the first election for 36 years to produce a hung Parliament,
the 2010 poll was notable for widespread controversy over the number of electors unable to vote because of localized organizational hiccups. As early results
were announced on the evening of 6 May, live reports about registered voters
being denied their rights began flooding in from areas as disparate as Hackney,
Liverpool, and Newcastle-upon-Tyne. Some had spent hours queuing, only to be
locked out of polling stations when clocks struck 10 p.m. In Sheffield Hallam
(Mr Clegg's constituency), the returning officer blamed a last-minute influx of
students without polling cards for delays resulting in a number of people being
denied votes. A swift investigation by the Electoral Commission found that
1,200 voters were barred from voting. The Commission's initial recommendation was for a wholesale modernization of the voting process—which to date
has relied largely on paper, rather than computerized, records. The 2010 election also saw a significant increase in postal voting—one of the main devices
used by recent governments to boost otherwise dwindling turnouts (see 'The
future of voting' in this chapter). In some areas, the number of people voting
by post soared by as much as 60 per cent, but with this increase in apparent
electoral engagement came a wave of allegations that supporters of one party
or other were abusing it to fraudulently bolster their favoured candidates. In
Oxfordshire, 667 postal ballot packs vanished a week before the election, by
error or design, while some 50 separate investigations into alleged fraud were
under way on the eve of polling. Notoriously, however, it can take years for
police to bring successful prosecutions. It was not until September 2010—four
months after that year's election—that two former councillors and three other
men were jailed for an unsuccessful attempt at the 2005 poll to use fraudulent
postal votes to swing the marginal seat of Bradford West behind then Tory
candidate Haroon Rashid.

In addition to their procedural arrangements, election days witness curious conventions. Most notable is the 'blackout period' or 'election silence' that sets in on polling day itself, when most parties traditionally abide by a gentlemen's agreement to cease active campaigning to allow electors the opportunity to reflect before casting their votes. For the broadcast media, if not newspapers, Ofcom rules stipulate that they must not broadcast any material that might be judged capable of influencing voters while polls are still open.

Limits on election spending

Election spending is closely controlled by the Electoral Commission to stop any candidate or party 'buying' a significant advantage over his or her, or its, competitors. Each candidate must appoint an election agent with a constituency-based office. The maximum sum that candidates may spend campaigning in their seats is fixed by law. At time of writing, it was just under £7,150, plus 5 pence per voter in urban ('borough') constituencies and 7 pence in rural ('county') ones. At a national level, however, parties may also spend £30,000 fielding each candidate.

In addition, 'recognized third parties' may separately spend money campaigning in support of (or against) a candidate—up to £500 apiece. They are, however, permitted to spend considerably more supporting a party as a whole. **UNISON** is registered as a 'recognized third-party' supporter of Labour. This allows it to spend up to £793,500 in England, £108,000 in Scotland, £60,000 in Wales, and (if appropriate) £27,000 in Northern Ireland on the party's behalf at a general election. Other organizations or individuals wishing to campaign on behalf of political parties (rather than individual candidates), but 'unregistered', are legally limited to spending £10,000 in England or £5,000 in the other UK countries.

In referendums, meanwhile, 'permitted participants'—those registered to campaign for 'yes' or 'no' votes—may spend up to £500,000 on a UK-wide poll, but only £10,000 may be spent by anyone *not* so permitted. The Commission may 'designate' specific permitted participants to campaign for a 'yes' or 'no' vote to ensure order. Such bodies may claim up to £600,000 to finance their campaigns and spend up to £5 million.

▶ Before the event—how constituency boundaries are decided

There are currently 650 Commons constituencies in England, Wales, Scotland, and Northern Ireland. Historically, the number has fluctuated 'naturally' in line with population changes—aside from periods during which governments have consciously shaken up the system to distribute electors more fairly. Variations in population not only have an impact on the number of constituencies, however, but also influence the size and shape of seats. In some cases, constituencies with falling populations cease to exist or are merged with neighbouring ones, while large localized increases in population can lead to the introduction of additional seats or existing ones being split.

Regular reviews of parliamentary electoral boundaries occur on an 8–12-year cycle, to ensure that they keep pace with demographic fluctuations. The task of conducting these reviews falls to the **Boundary Commission for England** and three others, covering England, Scotland, Wales, and Northern Ireland. These are also responsible for periodically reviewing the boundaries of constituencies for the devolved assemblies. Under the Political Parties, Elections, and Referendums Act 2000, Labour had planned to transfer the Commissions' duties to the Electoral Commission. However, the Local Democracy, Economic Development, and Construction Act 2009 repealed this prospective change, and there are now no plans for the Boundary Commissions to cede their boundary-drawing functions. The next boundary reviews for parliamentary constituencies are due to be published by 2018.

Boundary changes have always been controversial. Abolishing constituencies, creating new ones, and subdividing or merging them can have a significant impact on the ability of particular parties to win seats at subsequent elections. Although Commissions are meant to be non-partisan, successive governments have been accused of influencing their decisions, to ensure that proposed changes are favourable to their own parties at election time. That said, New Labour's last boundary review was widely interpreted as a boost to the Tories, particularly given the eventual outcome of the 2010 election. Confirmed by the English and Welsh Commissions in April 2007, with new boundaries for Assembly member (AM) constituencies in place for the National Assembly of Wales elections in May that year, it proved controversial in Labour heartlands, because all four new constituencies were in the south. The Conservatives' abortive attempt to cut the number of constituencies to 650 would also have created a number of new southern seats.

The role of the Electoral Commission

Having been divested of its status as boundary-setting authority—a responsibility it also lost in relation to local elections under the 2009 Act—the Electoral Commission nonetheless retains the following responsibilities:

- registering political parties (and preventing their names being used by others);
- ensuring that people understand and follow rules on party and election finance;

- setting standards for running elections and reporting on their implementation;
- ensuring that people understand the importance of registering to vote and how to do so; and
- making sure that candidates fund their election campaigns legally and transparently.

In addition to overseeing election-related funding, the Commission also polices party finance as a whole, by vetting how parties raise money and declare donations (see Chapter 5, 'Party funding now and in the future').

How parties select candidates

Just as different political parties have their own membership policies, they also have preferences about how to select the candidates they field at elections. The workings of Britain's main political parties, and the internal structures and procedures distinguishing one from the other, are the subject of Chapter 5, but it is worth considering here significant trends and developments in candidate selection procedures.

The Conservative Party

Historically, the Conservatives have favoured a centralized selection procedure, with lists of 'approved candidates' compiled by Conservative Campaign Headquarters. This initially involves staff from the party's Candidates' Department sifting through applicants' CVs and letters, and inviting a selection to attend a 'candidates' weekend', at which they face aptitude tests to ascertain their suitability. A central list is then drawn up and distributed to local Conservative constituency associations, which advertise vacancies for prospective local candidates as and when they arise (sitting MPs wishing to run again are normally automatically reselected, as in the other main parties). After several public meetings, at which between three and five competing applicants have the chance to prove their mettle in debates with rivals, a vote is held among party members on which individual should be adopted to fight the seat.

Mr Cameron's tenure as party leader has seen contradictory moves towards greater centralization, on the one hand, and localization, on the other. A controversial early move was his drawing up of an 'A-list' of aspiring Tory MPs prior to the 2010 election, including the likes of 'chick-lit' author Louise Bagshawe (now Louise Mensch) and Zac Goldsmith, editor of the *Ecologist* magazine and son of late Tory defector Sir James Goldsmith (whose Referendum Party had stood against Europhile Tory MPs in the 1997 election). Both were elected, although Ms Mensch has since quit Parliament. But Mr Cameron has also pioneered 'open primaries' modelled on the US voting system. These give everyone on the electoral register in a constituency a chance to vote on which prospective candidate should stand for the Conservatives at an election—irrespective of whether they are Tory members (or even supporters).

The Labour Party

Labour's selection process has traditionally been more democratic than that of the Conservatives. Under Mr Blair, however, it became increasingly centralized and, given moves by the Tories to encourage greater public involvement in their internal party procedures, Labour can no longer so easily claim to be more transparent.

Up to 31 January 2001, constituency Labour parties (equivalent to the Tories' constituency associations) and affiliated organizations, including unions, could each nominate up to two candidates from lists approved by local party leaderships. The general councils of Constituency Labour Party (CLP) branches then circulated shortlists among local party members, and they voted either by postal ballot or at 'hustings'—public meetings involving debates between the rival candidates (as described above in relation to '**The Conservative Party**').

Mr Blair introduced a streamlined version after 31 January 2001. To speed up initial vetting procedures, future candidate lists would be centrally approved by the party's 'ruling' National Executive Committee (NEC). Constituency Labour Party branches needing new candidates would be presented with these lists and asked to vote for one of the approved names. Mr Blair's critics saw this as a clear attempt to weed out left-wing candidates and impose a more Blairite agenda on the party's grass roots.

An earlier example of the centralizing tendency among recent Labour leaders was the party's adoption of all-women shortlists for parliamentary candidates in 1993. Positive discrimination was brought in to increase the number of women MPs, to reflect better the gender balance in the British population (which is 51 per cent female). In 1996, Labour's stand was judged unlawful, in a case brought under the Sex Discrimination Act 1975, but once in power the party introduced the Sex Discrimination (Election Candidates) Act 2002, which guaranteed the legality of all-women shortlists until 2015. In the run-up to the May 2010 election, Mr Cameron became a convert to all-women shortlists and Labour continues to use them in many areas. Nonetheless, the policy still has its critics—notably some groups representing ethnic minorities, who argue that white women may get selected in some areas known for their racial diversity at the expense of strong potential minority candidates who happen to be men.

The Liberal Democrat Party

Although they often claim to be more democratic than their rivals, the Lib Dems use a similarly centralized selection system. A list of approved names is drawn up centrally. Constituencies looking for new candidates must first advertise in *Liberal Democrat News*, the party's main publication, and individuals whose names are on that list may apply for vacancies. A selection committee then interviews them and a shortlist is put before local party members.

Quirks of the electoral system

Parliamentary candidates may stand, and even be elected, in more than one constituency. If returned in both, they must immediately decide which constituency they would like to represent and 'stand down' from the other. The seat forgone will pass to the second-choice candidate in that constituency. This follows rules set out in Erskine May (see Chapter 1, 'Treatises') and laid down in House of Commons procedures.

Candidates may withdraw their nominations, provided that they do so in writing (with one witness attesting) by noon on the 16th day before polling. This throws up the intriguing possibility that an individual might one day be elected to Parliament, despite having decided against standing at the last minute.

Since 1935, elections have generally been held on Thursdays for curious historical reasons. As the traditional Christian day of worship, Sundays are out, and weekends, as a whole, are seen to present too many leisure options to ensure that voters will discipline themselves to vote. Mondays have the highest employee absence record of any working day—making it difficult to be sure of a solid turnout—while Tuesdays and Wednesdays are the main working days (providing few opportunities for people to escape the workplace to vote). As the traditional market day in many towns and cities, Thursday is traditionally favoured. In addition, holding elections before a weekend is seen to have advantages if there is a change of government, because new administrations have Saturday and Sunday to prepare themselves to start work properly the following week.

The British electoral system produces a clear divide between 'marginal constituencies' (or 'marginals') and 'safe seats'. In marginals—key battlegrounds on election day—incumbent MPs have small majorities (in some cases, having won only a handful more votes than their nearest rivals at the previous election), so their seats are considered vulnerable and key targets for competitors. Candidates concentrate their energies on attracting the support of 'swing voters': individuals with no firm historical loyalty to one party. Safe seats, in contrast, are those in which sitting MPs have large majorities that (barring huge upsets) they are unlikely to lose. These tend to be located in party political heartlands—traditionally, the north for Labour and Home Counties for the Tories. Such seats would require huge 'swings' (switches of support from one candidate or party to another) to change hands.

Other than local and European elections, one of the biggest litmus tests of British public opinion is the by-election—a vote in a single constituency to replace a sitting MP who has either retired, been deselected (see Chapter 5, 'The deselection process'), or died between elections. Under Mr Major, by-elections frequently produced bruising results for the Tories. By 2008, it was Labour's turn to suffer. Over a three-month period, the party sustained several humiliating defeats, including two in previously safe seats: the Crewe and Nantwich constituency of veteran backbencher Gwyneth Dunwoody, whose 7,000–strong majority was overturned by the Conservatives in their first by-election victory over Labour for 30 years, and Glasgow East, a dyed-in-the-wool Labour seat on Mr Brown's doorstep, which the Scottish Nationalists snatched on a 22.5 per cent swing (although Labour regained it at the 2010 election). More recent by-elections have seen significant swings to UKIP, with two seats falling to the party in late 2014.

▶ Proportional representation (PR) and other voting systems

Such are the inequities of the British electoral system that pro-democracy campaigners have long argued for its replacement by one that more accurately reflects the distribution of votes between rival candidates or parties. Pressure groups such as the Electoral Reform Society and Charter 88 (recently incorpo-rated into Unlock Democracy) advocate **proportional representation (PR)**—an umbrella term referring to various alternative models that they judge fairer (see Table 4.3). Such a switch has, for many years, been official policy for the Lib Dems, who have long suffered more than other parties under FPTP, owing to the wide geographical dispersal of their vote.

It has often been observed that, given the two main parties' vested interest in retaining the old system, the Lib Dems would need to achieve power to intro-duce it—but that, paradoxically, this is unlikely to happen without it. However, the eventual outcome of the 2010 election forced the Tories to agree to a referen-dum on whether to adopt PR. As a result, on 5 May 2011 (a year after the Coalition's formation), the public was given its say on whether FPTP should be abandoned—though not in favour of the single transferable vote (STV) (the complex, if more proportional, system preferred by Lib Dems), but the alternative vote (AV). This system, used in Australia (and, interestingly, in most elections for the chairpersons of Commons select committees—see Chapter 2, 'Select committees'), requires electors in each constituency to mark candidates in order of preference. Depending on how the system is implemented, a candidate will be elected if he or she wins either a 'simple majority' (50 per cent plus one of all votes cast) or one that is 'absolute' (50 per cent plus one of all eligible voters). If (as commonly happens) no one reaches this based on first preferences

Table 4.3 Different types of proportional representation (PR) and how they work

Name	How it works	Where used
Single transferable vote (STV)	System favoured by Liberal Democrats; STV states have multi-member constituencies, so voters are more likely to end up represented by the party they support	Irish Dáil
		Scottish local authorities
		Northern Ireland Assembly
	Electors mark candidates in order of preference and, once one achieves a predetermined quota (e.g. one-fifth of votes cast if five seats available), he/she is elected. Second choices listed on all 'surplus' papers naming that candidate as 'first choice' are then treated as first choices and distributed accordingly among remaining candidates.	Local and European elections in Northern Ireland
	Means by which some ballot papers designated 'surplus' varies: in some countries, 'surplus' papers are selected randomly from all those with initial winning candidate as first choice, while elsewhere papers are accorded primacy on 'first come, first served' basis (those submitted later become 'surplus').	
	Process of reallocating second choices, third choices, etc., as 'first choices' continues until required number of candidates are elected.	
Party list systems	Seats allocated to parties in direct proportion to their vote share. Candidates chosen by voters from lists supplied by their parties—meaning that they can theoretically opt for someone with local connection to area, even if 'constituency link' preserved by UK elections is more remote.	European elections in most member states
		Regional and national parliamentary elections in European states, including Sweden and Netherlands
	In 'open' list systems, they vote for both party and individual: parties supply candidate lists; electors choose ones they want; party then allocates seats it wins to named candidates, according to those expressed preferences.	Israel's Knesset
	In 'closed' list systems, parties have already decided which candidates they wish to take seats, if they win enough votes.	
	Britain, like all other EU states, already uses a party list system to elect members of the European Parliament (MEPs). In 2004, European Parliament elections UK Independence Party used the closed list system to ensure that BBC talk show presenter and ex-Labour MP Robert Kilroy-Silk was elected.	

Table 4.3 (*continued*)

Name	How it works	Where used
Alternative vote (AV) or preferential voting	Similar to STV, except only one MP elected per constituency—meaning that extent to which election's outcome pleases most voters is limited—but it is still widely seen as producing more accurate reflections of voters' preferences than FPTP. If one candidate has simple majority after count—more than half votes cast—he/she is immediately elected. Otherwise, candidate with fewest 'first choice' votes is struck out and 'second choices' on all papers putting them top redistributed among others as if first choices. Process continues until one candidate has more than half the votes cast.	Australia's House of Representatives
Supplementary vote (SV)	Modified version of AV If no candidate initially obtains absolute majority—more than half eligible voters—all but top two eliminated and their 'second choices' reallocated to produce winner.	English mayoral elections, including that for London Mayor
Additional member system (AMS)	Hybrid of different systems: some candidates elected in single-member constituencies (normally using FPTP) and second—'additional'—votes used to top up from regional lists, introducing measure of 'proportionality' between votes and parties. As with party list system, lists can be open or closed.	Elections for Scottish Parliament, Welsh Assembly, and London Assembly Parliaments in Germany, Italy, Mexico, New Zealand, and Venezuela

alone, the lowest-placed candidate's name is struck off the ballot paper and his or her second preferences redistributed among the remaining contenders as if first choices. This process continues until one candidate finally has a majority. In the event, after a lacklustre 'yes' campaign, and amid fearsome opposition from a much better funded and organized 'no' lobby, the Lib Dems and their supporters (including Labour leader Ed Miliband) lost the AV referendum— and with it, perhaps, a once-in-a-generation chance to improve Britain's increasingly outmoded-looking electoral system. On a nationwide turnout of just 42.2 per cent—ironically, a symbol of the disengagement with parliamentary politics that reformers had hoped to rectify—the 'no' vote triumphed by 68 to 32 per cent.

Nonetheless, the referendum was significant in two respects: it was the first such public vote to be held across the whole UK since Britons were asked if they wanted to remain in the then European Community (now the EU) in 1975,

Table 4.4 Pros and cons of PR

For	Against
Governments elected under FPTP often win majority of seats despite securing only minority of votes.	PR produces more coalition governments. These can be less decisive or coordinated in policymaking. Extremist parties (e.g. France's Front National) can sometimes hold balance of power because their support is vital to enable mainstream ones to form governments.
Many votes wasted under FPTP because numerous electors denied representation by MPs of same persuasion; PR produces overall results that better reflect distribution of votes cast.	Voters under PR are less able to hold a particular government responsible for actions by booting it out.
Alternating government between Left and Right can bring abrupt changes of policy direction—leading to lack of long-term continuity.	Some PR systems break constituency link between individual voters and MPs—a cornerstone of Britain's democracy.
FPTP denies voice in Parliament to minority parties with significant support in country, but no elected MPs.	PR can lead to frequent elections and big policy compromises, because many coalitions are unstable. Firmer leadership or action is sometimes needed.

and it marked the belated revival of a review of the electoral system that had originally commenced under Tony Blair, in December 1997. Chaired by the late Lord Jenkins, a Lib Dem peer and former Labour Chancellor, this proposed either a hybrid system modelled on that to be used in Scotland and Wales or a new system called 'alternative vote plus' (AV+). This would have involved 80–85 per cent of MPs continuing to be elected on a constituency basis, with the rest voted in via a 'top-up process', using electors' second votes to better reflect the electorate's overall preferences. Although Lord Jenkins never lived to see his advice acted upon, after the 2010 election several senior Labour politicians, including outgoing Home Secretary Alan Johnson and Welsh Secretary Peter Hain, indicated their approval for an AV+ model.

Key arguments used by advocates and opponents of the introduction of PR in the UK are outlined in Table 4.4.

▌ Elections under devolution

The devolved chambers in Scotland, Wales, and Northern Ireland have, up to now, been elected on set timetables every four years—electoral cycles bearing closer resemblance to those of local authorities than those the Commons. As of 2016, the Welsh Assembly is due to revert to a five-year cycle, like that recently adopted at Westminster (see 'The British franchise today—who can vote?' in this chapter). Unlike Parliament, none of them uses FPTP; each has adopted a voting system incorporating elements of PR.

In Northern Ireland, the single transferable vote (STV) is now used, in line with the system used in Southern Ireland since 1919. Both Scotland and Wales have adopted the 'additional member' system (see Table 4.3).

▌The future of voting

Since 2001, electoral turnout has been consistently lower than at any time since the Second World War, although it rose by nearly 4 per cent in 2010—from 61.3 to 65.1 per cent—in the midst of a period of political and economic upheaval following the recession and the MPs' expenses scandal. This has prompted an ongoing debate about voter disengagement—whether resulting from the widespread perception that the policies of the mainstream parties are increasingly indistinguishable, or the perception that politicians say one thing in their manifestos and do another once elected. Others point to the increasing prominence of 'career politicians'—Oxbridge-educated academics who start out as bag-carrying political researchers before working their way up through the ranks of think tanks and party policy units themselves, and ultimately securing safe seats after two or three attempts at less winnable targets. A *Guardian* survey published in June 2014 found that 54 per cent of candidates selected by Labour to contest marginal seats in the 2015 election came from such backgrounds, compared to 46 per cent for the Lib Dems and only 17 per cent for the Tories (the bulk of whose candidates hailed from the worlds of business and finance). Mr Miliband, Ed Balls, and David Cameron all read for degrees at Oxford—significantly, in philosophy, politics, and economics (PPE), a customary breeding ground for future government ministers—and started their working lives in special adviser roles, rather than what might be considered 'normal' trades or professions.

Although there remains a wide spectrum of different views on the merits and pitfalls of FPTP, there is a growing cross-party consensus that more needs to be done to encourage people to vote. One approach would be to make voting *easier*. The Representation of the People Act 2000 authorized various pilot schemes to see which worked best, including:

- electronic voting (via email, SMS text, the Internet);
- global postal voting;
- elections spread over several days or on Saturdays; and/or
- taking polling stations to the voter (that is, to supermarkets, doctors' surgeries, etc.).

Though Labour was a big advocate of postal voting, presiding over a 60 per cent rise in some areas in 2010, it continues to be seen as vulnerable to fraud. In multi-occupancy households, one resident could theoretically vote multiple times by filling in his or her housemates' forms. Indeed, elections for Birmingham City Council in 2004 exposed systematic corruption after a number of Labour Party workers were implicated in fraudulently submitting forms in support of it. At time of writing, the question of how to increase voter turnout was back on the agenda following the 2014 local and European elections—both of which inspired barely a third of the electorate to turn out. In the wake of these results and the wildly contrasting 84.6 per cent showing for Scotland's independence vote—Britain's highest ever recorded turnout—Labour confirmed plans to follow the referendum's lead by opening up voting to 16-year-olds, should it be re-elected in 2015.

Ironically, the one significant reform that *has* been introduced recently has been criticized for acting as a potential *deterrent* to voters: since summer 2014, every adult has had to proactively register himself or herself by providing proof of identity (for example date or birth and/or National Insurance number) to his or her local electoral registration officers. This individual voter registration system—ostensibly designed to combat electoral fraud—replaces the long tradition of one person in each household taking responsibility for registering all eligible voters. Critics have criticized it as a Conservative ploy to boost the party's vote, given that older people tend to be most diligent about signing the electoral roll and a disproportionate number of them vote Tory.

☰ Topical feature idea

Low voter turnout has been a mounting problem in all types of election in Britain in recent decades. Although 2010 saw an increase, only around two-thirds of registered electors actually turned out on polling day. With the 2015 election fast approaching, your editor wants a background feature looking at the issue of turnout—and the various ways in which it might be boosted. What was turnout like in your constituency in 2010? Were there any patterns among those who turned out to vote and those who did not? What do local people think about the idea of electronic voting, voting on Saturdays, or compulsory voting? Do they have any other ideas?

✳ Current issues

- **The Conservatives' and Labour's struggle for a majority** To win a Commons majority in 2015, the Conservatives must increase their voting share by at least 2 per cent (from 36.1 per cent in 2010). It is 60 years since any incumbent government increased its voting share after several years in power (Anthony Eden in May 1955—up from 48 to 49.7 per cent). But Labour's task is tough, too: no defeated party has returned to power with an overall majority after just one term in Opposition for 80 years.

- **Britain's first fixed-term parliament election** The first ever general election under a fixed-term parliament is due to take place on Thursday 7 May 2015—ending the age-old constitutional convention allowing prime ministers to 'quit while they're ahead' by dissolving Parliament mid-term.

- **Open primaries** Labour has indicated that it will use open primaries to select some parliamentary candidates in 2015. The Conservatives pioneered this experiment ahead of the 2010 poll, in seats such as Totnes, and used it to select their candidate for the ill-fated Rochester and Strood by-election that they lost to UKIP in 2014.

⠿ Key points

1. The House of Commons is elected using a first-past-the-post (FPTP) system. In each of 650 constituencies, the winner is the candidate achieving a relative majority of votes (more than anyone else).

2. Opponents of FPTP argue that it unfairly benefits parties with concentrations of support over those whose supporters are spread out geographically. This encourages people to vote for 'least worst options', rather than candidates whom they actually support (tactical voting).

3. Electoral systems that produce more equitable distributions of seats are collectively known as 'proportional representation' (PR). Forms of PR include the single transferrable vote (STV) and party lists.

4. To be eligible to vote in general elections, you must be aged at least 18 and a UK, Commonwealth, or Irish citizen living in Britain. Peers and convicted prisoners are among those barred.

5. To stand as an MP, you must be aged at least 18, a British, Commonwealth, or Irish citizen, and not disqualified for another reason—such as holding a peerage or serving a custodial sentence of 12 months or longer.

→ Further reading

Blais, A. (ed.) (2008) *To Keep or to Change First Past the Post? The Politics of Electoral Reform*, New York: Oxford University Press. **Expert analysis of the relative merits of 'first past the post' and other electoral systems, and critique of failures of the UK, United States, and other countries using FPTP to achieve reform**.

Denver, D., Carman, C., and Johns, R. (2012) *Elections and Voters in Britain*, 3rd edn, Basingstoke: Palgrave Macmillan. **Second edition of authoritative text focusing on UK voting patterns. Includes data from British Electoral Study (BES) surveys.**

Farrell, D. (2011) *Electoral Systems: A Comparative Introduction*, 2nd edn. **Illuminating comparative study of the six types of electoral system used in seventy of the world's most advanced democracies.**

Renwick, A. (2011) *A Citizen's Guide to Electoral Reform*, London: Biteback Publishing. **Expert and balanced analysis of pros and cons of various electoral systems used in Britain and other leading democracies.**

 **Online Resource Centre**

www.oxfordtextbooks.co.uk/orc/Morrison4e/
Visit the Online Resource Centre that accompanies this book for web links and regular updates.

5

Political parties, party funding, and lobbying

The 'party system' has long been a cornerstone of British democracy. It derives from a series of nineteenth- and early twentieth-century works of political science, notably *American Commonwealth* (1885) by English scholar James Bryce, and later writings by Charles Merriam and William Nisbet Chambers—all focusing on the emergence of what was then seen as a model democratic system in the United States. The notion of groups of like-minded individuals banding together to form 'parties' and campaigning collectively to win power might have been relatively new across the Atlantic, but in Britain the party was already a long-established institution, as was the country's own peculiar version of party politics: the 'two-party' (or, occasionally, 'three-party') system.

'First past the post' (FPTP) voting has always favoured candidates representing the two or three main parties. Given that British general elections produce 'winner takes all'; outcomes at constituency level—with single representatives returned in each—it has tended to be those candidates most closely identified with the concerns of each area who have been elected (historically, social reformers in the industrial north and conservatives in the wealthier south). The formation of a coherent nationwide government is possible only if a number of elected representatives agree to share power and ascribe particular responsibilities to individuals from their number. All this was conducive to the emergence of Britain's party system.

From the point at which Parliament wrested sovereignty from the monarch in 1689 up to the emergence of the Liberal Party some 170 years later, the two-party system revolved around two political groupings: Whigs and Tories. While the former are often crudely identified with the progressive tendencies later embodied by nineteenth-century Liberals and the latter, with the modern-day Conservative Party (the term 'Tory'; is still used as shorthand for 'Conservative'), in truth the distinction between the two was more nebulous.

Both were associated, to a greater or lesser degree, with the moneyed classes and aristocracy. What differences there were initially rested largely on Christian denominational grounds, with the Whigs identifying more with non-Anglican believers ('dissenters' such as the evolving Presbyterian Church in Scotland) and the Tories, the Church of England.

By the late eighteenth century, however, clearer party lines had emerged, with the ascendancy of Charles James Fox and William Pitt the Younger as Whig leader and Tory prime minister, respectively. Within a few short decades, the Whigs would be advocating the abolition of slavery, the introduction of overseas free trade, and wider voting rights.

Although the purpose of this book is to give journalists a clear understanding of Britain's present-day political framework, no explanation of the British party system would be complete without a brief summary of how today's main parties came into being.

▶ The Conservative Party—a potted history

For much of the period from the 1950s to the 1990s, the then Conservative and Unionist Party was viewed as the 'natural party of government'. Of 21 prime ministers in the twentieth century, 13 were Conservative, three Liberal, and five Labour. The Tories held power for 55 years, the Liberals for 17, and Labour, 28.

Although William Pitt the Younger is widely viewed as the first true 'Conservative' premier, he was the last of a long line of political leaders whose affiliation was rooted in that looser Tory persuasion spawned in the seventeenth century. It was only after his death, in 1812, that a cohesive Tory Party organization emerged, initially under Lord Liverpool (who, in Downing Street for 15 years, remains Britain's longest-serving prime minister). Not until a decade later, however, was the term 'Conservative' tentatively coined by his short-lived successor, George Canning.

The title 'Conservative Party' was officially adopted in 1834 by Sir Robert Peel, widely credited as its true founder, who formalized it in a paper viewed as the blueprint for its later constitution: *The Tamworth Manifesto*. Ironically, he later all but destroyed the party, over his decision to repeal the 'corn laws'—tariffs protecting the profits of British agriculturalists by artificially inflating the prices of imported foreign grain—to allay the suffering caused by the 1845–46 Irish potato famine. After being deposed, Peel formed his own faction in Parliament—the 'Peelites'—and was briefly courted by a coalition of Whigs and Radicals (later to form the Liberal Party).

The late nineteenth century was notable for the emergence of two progressive political giants in the Conservative Party: Benjamin Disraeli, who served twice as prime minister between 1868 and 1880, and his successor, Lord Salisbury. Despite his imperialistic approach to foreign policy, Disraeli marked a break with Tory tradition, extending the voting franchise and embodying a more paternalistic attitude towards the poor. He even introduced a right to peaceful picketing in industrial disputes.

Disraeli's brand of moderate conservatism foreshadowed the 'One Nation Toryism' that would characterize the policies of post-war twentieth-century premiers such as Harold Macmillan. Only with the emergence of Thatcherism—and its adherents' derogatory labelling of their ilk as 'Wets'—did the party's pendulum swing decisively back to the right, adopting a more solidly free-market approach to its handling of the economy, public services, and social welfare.

The last Conservative prime minister of the twentieth century was John Major, who served from 1990 to 1997. Today, the party is still associated with certain core Tory values—notably privatization and low taxes—and, despite early emphasis on David Cameron's distinctly One-Nation-inflected concept of 'the Big Society', has arguably given way to a repackaging of Thatcherite values such as self-help, individual responsibility, and small government, with a determined effort to accelerate the outsourcing and marketization of public services started in the 1980s.

▌ The Labour Party—a potted history

Despite long ago supplanting the Liberals (today the Liberal Democrats) as Britain's second major political force, Labour is little more than a century old. For much of the 1800s, the Liberals were the 'progressive' party—advocating what would later become core Labour values, such as social justice, voting rights, equality of opportunity, and a foreign policy founded on internationalism rather than imperialism. Only when the vote was finally extended to men on more modest incomes—ironically, a policy ushered in by both Disraeli's Tories and William Gladstone's Liberals—did rumbling calls for a parliamentary voice for the working classes, to counter the middle and upper echelons who had so far dominated, become a clamour.

Unlike the Conservatives, who emerged 'organically' from the propertied classes over a period of decades, Labour was formed through the coordinated amalgamation of several organizations founded to safeguard the interests of ordinary working people and united by a shared belief in democratic socialism. The first of these were the trades unions, which evolved out of the aftermath of the Industrial Revolution to provide protection and representation for employees in the workplace. Having failed to persuade the Liberals to sponsor sufficient working-class candidates to stand in elections in the later nineteenth century, the unions turned their attentions towards establishing their own party.

Around the turn of the century, several like-minded organizations began talking seriously about forming a new party: notably, two early think tanks, the Fabian Society and the Social Democratic Federation, and a body of aspiring parliamentary candidates and their supporters calling itself the Independent Labour Party (ILP). In 1900, at a special conference convened by the Trades Union Congress (TUC) in Farringdon, London, they collectively formed the Labour Representation Committee (LRC). With future Prime Minister James Ramsay Macdonald as secretary, the LRC began sponsoring candidates to fight the coming election. This so-called 'khaki election', which returned the Tories under Arthur Balfour that October following his perceived success in the Boer War, delivered the first two Labour members of Parliament (MPs): Richard Bell for Derby and James Keir Hardie for Merthyr Tydfil, the latter of whom would become its first leader.

Although hardly meteoric, the party's progress in Parliament was steady. The 1906 election ushered in 17 years of reforming Liberal government, but a combination of infighting and growing Labour momentum during its later years ensured that this marked the party's last term as a majority administration. Labour had gained 27 additional seats in 1906—thanks in part to a secret pact between Macdonald and Liberal Chief Whip Herbert Gladstone, designed to stop Labour and Liberal candidates cancelling out each other's votes by contesting the same seats—but by 1910 it was up to 42. In 1924, aided by the Liberals' divisions, it won 191—enough to form its first government under Macdonald.

By now, Labour was the second party. It secured its first decisive election victory in the wake of the Second World War, in 1945—a landslide win for Clement Attlee and a radical team of ministers, who introduced the National Health Service (NHS) and free state education, and consolidated earlier moves towards establishing a welfare state to provide benefits for the unemployed, low paid, and disabled. Three further periods of government followed: under Harold Wilson (1964–70); Wilson and James Callaghan (1974–79); and Tony Blair and Gordon Brown (1997–2010).

▌ The Liberal Democrat Party—a potted history

Although technically the 'youngest' of the three main parties, the Liberal Democrats—or 'Lib Dems'—are the principal successors to the Liberal Party. The Liberals were a dominant force in British politics until the erosion of their grass-roots support by Labour and internal divisions caused by bitter rivalry between last Liberal Prime Minister David Lloyd George and his predecessor, Herbert Asquith, led to their sharp decline in the late 1920s.

Between the 1920s and 1980s, the Liberals cemented their status as Britain's 'third party', with modest parliamentary gains that were never again sufficient to propel them to power in their own right, but at times gave them a toehold in government. In 1977, buffeted by rising inflation and wildcat union strikes, Callaghan kept himself in Number 10 by negotiating a 'Lib–Lab Pact' with Liberal leader David Steel. The Liberals held the balance of power for a year, but the alliance soon broke up, and Labour were brought down on a Tory-instigated confidence vote in March 1979 (see Chapter 2, Table 2.3).

In 1981, as Labour swung to the left following its election defeat, four senior moderates—former Chancellor Roy Jenkins, Foreign Secretary David Owen, Science Minister Shirley Williams, and Transport Secretary Bill Rodgers—quit to form the Social Democratic Party (SDP). By 1983, this 'Gang of Four' had recruited enough supporters to form a credible new party, joining Steel's Liberals in the SDP–Liberal Alliance. Such was the state of Britain's economy in the early 1980s that the Tories began flatlining in opinion polls—with the Alliance initially reaping the benefit, owing to infighting within Labour. At one point in 1982 it reached a poll rating of 50 per cent, with the Tories and Labour virtually neck and neck on around half that. But for the Falklands War, it is possible that the next election would have produced a hung Parliament, with the Alliance the biggest party. In the event, buoyed by victory in the South Atlantic, Mrs Thatcher increased her majority and the Alliance went on to perform modestly in 1983 and 1987, before disbanding.

In 1988, more than two-thirds of the existing Liberal and SDP members—and all of their serving MPs—regrouped to form a new party: the Liberal Democrats. Initially led jointly by Steel and Robert Maclennan (Mr Owen's successor as SDP leader), it soon elected Paddy Ashdown to replace them. He was succeeded by Charles Kennedy, Sir Menzies 'Ming' Campbell, and Nick Clegg.

▶ The structure and constitution of the modern Conservative Party

Many aspects of the internal organization of the Conservative Party remain the same today as 100 years ago. It has, however, democratized its leadership elections since the 1990s.

As with any organization, a party's lifeblood is its grass-roots membership. It is ordinary members who swell the party's coffers by paying annual subscriptions and raising funds, who troop out, unpaid, on cold winter evenings to canvass in election campaigns, and who can usually be relied on to vote loyally come polling day. In return, it is incumbent on the party's leadership to give something back to members—policies that they can support and a sense of belonging. This can come through everything from participating in fund-raising events to attending the annual party conference. Like those of Labour and the Lib Dems, the Tory conference is held at the end of the summer recess, traditionally in a large coastal town such as Brighton, Bournemouth, or Blackpool.

Notwithstanding Labour's ties with the unions, traditionally the Conservatives have had the largest individual subscribing membership of any party. However, this has declined steeply under Mr Cameron: between his election as leader in 2005 and September 2013, it nearly halved, from 253,000 to 134,000, according to the well informed blog ConservativeHome. By contrast, Labour membership had risen to overtake it, reaching 187,537 by that date (although still well short of the 400,000-strong tally boasted by Tony Blair at the height of his populari-ty). Tory members are connected to their national party through local constitu-ency associations, which began proliferating after the Reform Act 1832. Unlike the Labour Party, in which membership activities have historically been cen-trally directed, these associations initially sprouted independently. They could, however, wield considerable clout: in affluent areas, associations would recruit candidates and finance their campaigns.

Despite being gradually incorporated into the overall party structure, asso-ciations had considerable independence until 1998, when newly elected leader William Hague formalized their party status in an effort to bring to heel errant elements he controversially labelled 'out of touch' and 'racist'. To this end, he introduced the party's first codified constitutional document, *Fresh Future*. This imposed new conditions on associations, but gave them significant new rights. Their position in the modern Conservative Party's internal hierarchy—beneath its constitutional college and **Conservative Campaign Headquarters** (formerly 'Conservative Central Office')—is explained in Table 5.1, while the way in which the various components of the party's central organization fit together is shown in Table 5.2.

Table 5.1 The internal structure of the modern Conservative Party

Level	Party in the country	Party in Parliament
Top table	**Chairman of the Conservative Party** (head of Conservative Campaign Headquarters) and Conservative Party Board	Leader
Middle tier	Constitutional college, incorporating National Conservative Convention (comprising MPs, MEPs, and other senior activists)	1922 Committee
Grass roots	Constituency associations	Individual backbenchers

Table 5.2 The main components of central Conservative Party organization

Body	Role and composition
Conservative Party Board	Ultimate decision-making body, comprising 18 members, including party chairman and deputy chairman; Tories' equivalent of Labour Party's National Executive Committee (NEC)
Conservative Campaign Headquarters	Main fund-raising, campaigning, and recruitment body, which coordinates its electioneering and marketing; headed by Party chairman
Constitutional college	Body comprising representatives from all party levels, including constituency associations and rank-and-file members, with say in questions of reform and long-term policy strategy; incorporates National Conservative Convention—made up of MPs, MEPs, and senior activists
Constituency associations	Grass-roots member organizations, originally only loosely affiliated to the party, but now formally incorporated; now permitted to play significant role in selecting prospective candidates for Parliament, European Parliament, and elections for devolved assemblies

Although the Tories traditionally perform poorly in Scottish and Welsh elections, unlike Labour they still contest some seats in Northern Ireland. This is a hangover from the party's strong historical ties to the province, as evidenced by its official 'Conservative and Unionist Party' title. In July 2008, Mr Cameron and the leader of the Ulster Unionists, Sir Reg Empey, published a joint letter in *The Daily Telegraph* pledging to revive their parties' historic electoral alliance, dating back to the 1880s, which had been severed some 30 years earlier as a result of infighting.

How the Conservatives choose their leader

From the mid-1960s until 1998, Conservative leaders were always elected by their parliamentary colleagues—with no formal input from rank-and-file members. Today, only the first stage of this process is handled exclusively by MPs and peers. Once two frontrunners emerge, their names are put before ordinary members nationwide, on a 'one member, one vote' basis. The final say rests with them.

While the introduction of this huge extension of party democracy signalled then youthful Tory leader Mr Hague's seriousness about party modernization, it was not long before his fellow MPs were regretting voting for it. When Mr Hague was defeated at the 2001 election, he resigned, to be replaced by little-known Mr Duncan Smith. Although widely perceived by both colleagues in Parliament and political commentators as uncharismatic, he beat off dynamic challengers, including Kenneth Clarke and Michael Portillo, because of his solid grass-roots support. An ex-Army officer, devoted family man, practising Christian, and Eurosceptic, he chimed far more than his rivals with typical

Tory members—the average age of whom (despite Hague's reforms) was then 64. In contrast, Clarke's pro-European views and Portillo's admission of a youthful homosexual relationship did little to endear them.

Mr Duncan Smith's later removal in a confidence vote instigated by disgruntled Tory MPs paved the way for another new leader, former Home Secretary Michael Howard. Recognizing the need to ensure that the party elected leaders more in touch with the wider public in future, after losing the May 2005 election he tried to reverse Hague's reforms in his remaining months in office. His proposals were defeated, however, after failing to win the required two-thirds majority among Tory MPs and activists in the party's 1,141-strong constitutional college.

The 1922 Committee

Also known as the '1922 Backbench Committee', this comprises all Conservative MPs apart from the leader and can therefore number in the hundreds. It is often described as 'influential'—an understatement, given that it represents all elected Tory members and is therefore able to articulate the 'mood' of the parliamentary party like no other organization. Leaders ignore its views at their peril.

Far from being a talking shop, the 1922 Committee retains huge constitutional clout. It is headed by an 18-member executive committee, the chairperson of which is often referred to as the party's 'shop steward'. He or she is responsible for organizing leadership elections—not to mention votes of confidence. Such a vote can be triggered by a letter to the chairperson signed by 15 per cent of Tory MPs. The last time this happened was in 2003, when Mr Duncan Smith was deposed. The Committee also instigated the final twist of the knife that unseated Mrs Thatcher following Michael Heseltine's 1990 leadership challenge (see Chapter 3, 'Party').

The Committee meets every week when Parliament is in session and is governed by curious conventions. For its first 88 years, frontbenchers were permitted to attend its meetings only when the party was in opposition. Even then, the leader was barred—so his or her Shadow Cabinet colleagues would act as intermediaries. When in government, neither leader nor Cabinet colleagues used to be able to attend, but barely a week after forming his Coalition government Mr Cameron surprised the committee by demanding an immediate vote on whether frontbenchers should be both admitted and granted full voting rights. Arguing that the Conservatives needed to be 'one party' in Parliament, he successfully orchestrated a secret ballot and his rule change was passed by 168 votes to 118. He was later forced into a partial U-turn, agreeing to drop his call for frontbenchers to be allowed votes in committee. His initial move had provoked fierce reactions from stalwart backbenchers. Eurosceptic Bill Cash branded it 'a great tragedy' and warned that, when seen in conjunction with other constitutional changes Mr Cameron was proposing at the time (including the '55 per cent rule'—see Chapter 3, 'Party'), it smacked less of the 'new politics' that he and Mr Clegg were espousing than an 'old politics' of empire-building.

Although the 1922 Committee is by far the most powerful party subgroup, MPs and peers may join a number of other such 'clubs', depending on where their views fall on the Conservative spectrum. These associations of like-minded left- or right-wingers—or members united over particular issues, like Europe—are customarily known as 'ginger groups', although many have recently morphed into semi-professional think tanks. Among the most active today are the Bow Group, which describes itself as Britain's 'oldest centre-right think tank', and the Thatcherite group Conservative Way Forward. As befits the online age, however, the most influential of all is arguably a collaborative website—ConservativeHome—the editor of which, Tim Montgomerie, has cultivated a good relationship with both party rank-and-file and more outspoken internal critics of its leadership. An excellent source of news and gossip for political reporters (and occasional headaches for Mr Cameron), it is found online at http://conservativehome.blogs.com.

Intriguingly, in May 2012, a newly formed ginger group was to liven up the first elections for the 1922 Committee executive since the Coalition's formation. Loyalist MPs Nicholas Soames and Tracey Crouch quit the top table voluntarily in protest at the 'factional' tactics of the '301 Group'—a pro-Cameron group named after the number of Commons seats the Tories need to win an overall majority at the 2015 election—when it published a list of candidates whom it hoped would be elected to counteract the views of 'bloody rude' critics of his leadership, including Eurosceptic Bernard Jenkin.

In addition to its various ginger groups, the Conservative Party has a long tradition of support from upmarket gentlemen's associations, including the Carlton Club.

▶ The structure and constitution of the modern Labour Party

Unlike the Conservative Party, which emerged in 'top-down' fashion from one of two principal parliamentary factions that evolved in the late seventeenth and early eighteenth centuries, Labour was created in a 'bottom-up' way—as a membership-led movement formed through a coalition of establishment outsiders campaigning for greater parliamentary representation for the working classes. Its formation was therefore more 'deliberate', with several distinct groupings coalescing to establish it formally in 1900. As such, it had a codified constitution from the outset.

In addition to its individual paying membership, Labour has long boasted de facto members in the form of hundreds of thousands of workers who have historically been co-opted into its ranks through their subscriptions to unions affiliated to the party. However, in a landmark change, current leader Ed Miliband convened a special conference in March 2014 to ratify plans to replace the 'automatic affiliation' of union members with a new 'opt-in' arrangement, under which they would be offered full membership for a cut-price 'supporters' fee' of £3. The move—approved by 86.29 per cent of those who voted—was portrayed by Mr Miliband as a way of transforming Labour back into a 'mass movement', by drawing in a new wave of fully participating members, in place of ranks of passive union ones who, in many cases, were not even party supporters. Party strategists, meanwhile, hoped the change might wrong-foot ongoing claims by Labour's political opponents that it was 'in the unions' pockets'. But Labour-supporting unions were divided about the merits of the move, with some portraying it as the first step towards a comprehensive break with the party's union ties. Ahead of the vote, Paul Kenny, general secretary of the GMB, pre-emptively announced a drastic cut in the annual affiliation fee that his union paid Labour—from £1.2 million to £150,000—while, despite initially welcoming the reforms, Len McCluskey, leader of Unite, slashed its contribution by half (from £3 million to £1.5 million).

Although it has had traditional strongholds in Scotland, Wales, and northern England, Labour does not organize in Northern Ireland. Its closest equivalent there is the centre-left Social Democratic and Labour Party (SDLP).

The main constituent elements of the Labour Party today are outlined in Table 5.3. Of its leadership bodies, the most significant is the **National Executive Committee (NEC) of the Labour Party**. Its role in relation to two other organizations, the National Policy Forum (NPF) and the Labour Party Conference, is explained in Table 5.4.

Clause 4 and the birth of 'New Labour'

The most significant internal victory for Mr Blair's leadership came not in his frequent run-ins with his own backbenchers after being elected premier, but in his first year as leader, with the party still in opposition. At its 1995 Easter conference, bolstered by his rabble-rousing deputy, John Prescott (whose similarly tub-thumping speech had helped John Smith, Mr Blair's predecessor, win the 'one member, one vote' debate—see Table 5.3), Mr Blair successfully passed a motion rewording the most symbolic sentence in Labour's constitution.

'Clause 4' had been written in the context of a pre-war British society in which ownership of the country's assets and wealth was concentrated in the

Table 5.3 Member organizations of the Labour Party

Organization	Role and functions
Constituency Labour parties (CLPs)	Equivalent to Conservatives' constituency associations and 'voice' of ordinary members/activists, their influence has diminished recently, as leadership exerts greater control over selection of parliamentary candidates and other activities. They still have final say over who represents their constituencies, but must choose only from a centrally vetted list of applicants—and NEC may overrule decisions of selection panels—parachuting in favoured candidates over those chosen locally.
	Normally run by two committees: general management committee (GC) and executive committee (EC). Former comprises delegates from branch Labour parties (smaller-scale ones in individual towns), local socialist societies, Co-operative Party branches, and unions.
	Each has several elected officers, including a chair, two vice-chairs, a secretary, a treasurer, a women's officer, a youth and student officer, and a black and ethnic minority officer. Elect representatives to national policymaking bodies, including Labour Party Conference, and nominate candidates for election to the other two ruling bodies: NPF and NEC.
Affiliated trades unions	Certain unions formally affiliated to party—many 'sponsoring' individual constituencies—UNISON and Unite among them. Union members can now 'opt in' to Labour Party for £3 fee under changes being phased in over five years from March 2014.
	Affiliated unions select 12 of 32 members of NEC and elect half party conference delegates. However, until early 1990s, unions still wielded 'block vote' at conferences—allowing them to pass or kill off policy proposals, regardless of individual members' views. This led to numerous run-ins between 'moderate' leaderships and union leaders pursuing more socialist agendas. In 1993, Kinnock's successor, John Smith, replaced block vote with 'one member, one vote'.
Socialist societies	Umbrella term referring to various smaller associations instrumental in party's foundation. Like unions, they pay affiliation fees and elect one delegate between them to sit on NEC. Most famous socialist society is Fabian Society, with early members including George Bernard Shaw, H. G. Wells, and Emmeline Pankhurst (founder of British suffragette movement).
Co-operative Party	Small socialist party formed in 1881 through establishment of joint parliamentary committee to act as watchdog on activities at Westminster for under-represented working people. Has long-standing arrangement with Labour not to contest same seats separately at elections; instead, fields joint candidates under 'Labour and Co-operative Party' banner.

hands of very few individuals, and the absence of any state provision meant that provision of 'public services' such as free health care and education was almost entirely reliant on charity. As a result, its wording bore the imprint of the Marxist ideology on which the party's original values were based—focusing on the need to take into public ownership the 'means of production' (industry and agriculture) and to give workers a greater share in their fruits. The clause,

Table 5.4 The main constitutional bodies of the Labour Party

Body	Role and composition	Notes
National Executive Committee of the Labour Party (NEC)	Often described as Labour's 'ruling' National Executive Committee (NEC), meant to represent all wings at national policymaking level, taking delegates from all affiliated groupings (see Table 5.3). Has traditionally acted as counterweight to leadership, although its influence declined under Mr Blair, who formed the NPF. As of September 2012, NEC had 31 members—not counting its two ex officio ones: party leader and deputy leader. These included former EastEnders actor and MEP Michael Cashman, stalwart backbencher Dennis Skinner, and ex-London Mayor Ken Livingstone. It also enforces party discipline: in 2003, its 'constitutional committee' expelled then Labour MP George Galloway for bringing party into disrepute in speeches condemning Mr Blair's actions in Iraq.	Mr Blair's neutering of NEC followed his predecessors' run-ins over proposed policy changes, such as party's abandonment of opposition to Britain's nuclear weapons, and repeated election to its membership of vocal leadership critics, including late left-winger Tony Benn.
National Policy Forum (NPF)	Formed by Mr Blair in 1997 under 'Partnership in Power' initiative, this draws 184 members from all levels of the party. Meets two or three weekends a year to analyse proposal documents generated by six policy commissions, members of which include representatives of leadership, NEC, and NPF. Recommendations pass to conference for ratification.	Introduced officially as means of widening party democracy in Labour's ranks, but often perceived as leadership's instrument for quelling dissent.
Labour Party Conference	Unlike Conservative conference, this was traditionally less an event than a decision-making body. Presided over by general-secretary—one of Labour Party's most senior officers.	Theoretically, conference still has final say on major policy/constitutional changes. Since 1997, leadership has made clear its willingness to overrule conference decisions. Mr Blair also reduced weight of conference vote by affiliated organizations from 80 to 50 per cent (four-fifths still wielded by union members).

penned by Marxist intellectual Sidney Webb in 1917 and formally adopted by the party a year later, vowed:

❝ To secure for the workers by hand or by brain the full fruits of their industry and the most equitable distribution thereof that may be possible upon the basis of the common ownership of the means of production, distribution and exchange, and the best obtainable system of popular administration and control of each industry or service. ❞

Basing his version on a pamphlet that he had written for the Fabian Society, Mr Blair reworded it thus:

> ❝ The Labour Party is a democratic socialist party. It believes that by the strength of our common endeavour we achieve more than we achieve alone, so as to create for each of us the means to realise our true potential and for all of us a community in which power, wealth and opportunity are in the hands of the many, not the few, where the rights we enjoy reflect the duties we owe, and where we live together, freely, in a spirit of solidarity, tolerance and respect. ❞

The rewriting of Clause 4 was a defining moment in the creation of the 'New Labour' brand—a project initiated years earlier by Neil Kinnock, who had softened the party's image by replacing its Soviet-style, Red-Flag-inspired logo (and conference anthem) with the now familiar red rose motif. Mr Blair accelerated this process, as the party embraced more mainstream policies, the language and aspirations of business, and an affinity for media management—or 'spin'—designed to improve its public image after years in the political wilderness. Soon terms such as 'third way', 'big tent politics', and 'triangulation' had entered the political lexicon to explain the tactics that Mr Blair and his apparatchiks used to neutralize opponents, by bringing together people from different shades of 'liberal' opinion in a new coalition against what he would describe in a later conference speech as the 'forces of conservatism'.

How Labour chooses its leader

Labour's leadership election procedure has trodden a long, slow road towards democratization over recent decades—although it began this process well in advance of more recent Tory moves to involve ordinary party members. From 1922 to 1981, leaders were elected solely by the party's MPs. Annual contests were held at the party conference, but in practice leaders were normally re-elected unopposed, so these were formalities.

In 1981, although it was to be some years before wholesale reform of the party's constitution, Labour established an electoral college: in future, only three out of 10 votes in leadership elections would be cast by Labour MPs, with 30 per cent going to Constituency Labour Parties (CLPs) and 40 per cent to the unions. Further reform followed in 1993, when the union block vote was scrapped and weighting equalized to give each grouping a one-third share of the vote. Inequities remained, however: individuals who were members of two or more affiliated organizations—for example a union and a CLP—could vote more than once. However, this discrepancy was addressed by Mr Miliband alongside his 2014 reforms of the party's union ties: from now on, leadership elections will be conducted on a strictly 'one member, one vote' basis. Other anomalies continue to abound, though: Labour may have balked at electoral reform while in office, but it uses the alternative vote (AV) system for its leadership elections.

While the process by which Labour elects its leader may now be more democratic, the power wielded by that individual, once chosen, has also been enhanced. In July 2011, Mr Miliband persuaded his backbenchers to abandon a decades-old tradition forcing frontbenchers to stand for re-election by the rest of the party's MPs every two years whenever Labour was in opposition.

The Parliamentary Labour Party (PLP)

Like the Conservatives, Labour has a body that represents the views of rank-and-file MPs: the Parliamentary Labour Party (PLP). It too meets weekly in a room in Parliament and has a chairperson elected at the start of each parliamentary session.

Between 1921 and 1970, the chair of the PLP was the party leader. But since 1970 the two posts have been permanently split and the PLP has become (like the 1922 Committee) largely a means for backbenchers to hold leaders to account. Unlike the 1922 Committee, however, leaders have always been able to attend the PLP, even when in government. Towards the end of his premiership, Mr Blair endured increasingly hostile receptions from the PLP (although he received a standing ovation at the meeting following his resignation). Like the 1922 Committee, the PLP can instigate a confidence vote in its leadership, but in practice Labour has refrained from dumping unpopular leaders, who have generally jumped before being pushed despite murmurings of rebellion.

As well as the PLP, Labour has within it several ginger groups and is associated with various think tanks. These include three left-leaning factions: the Campaign Group, Compass, and Tribune—the last of these revived in 2005 by backbencher Clive Efford as a direct challenge to the leadership's perceived move to the right. More Blairite examples have included Progress, Demos, and the Institute of Public Policy Research (IPPR), although this last has now distanced itself from Labour. A big influence on Mr Miliband's policy ideas (at least for a time) was 'Blue Labour'—brainchild of Westminster University sociologist and Labour peer Lord Glasman. This movement rejected the neoliberal free-market economics embraced first by Thatcher then by Blair, while advocating a return to socially conservative policies on immigration and crime and the promotion of social justice through community-level, rather than 'big state', action.

▌ The structure and constitution of the Liberal Democrat Party

As the 'youngest' of Britain's major political parties, the Liberal Democrat Party also has the newest constitution. Unlike either Labour or the Conservatives, the party has a federal organization, comprising separate but conjoined parties for England, Scotland, and Wales. As of April 2014, the Lib Dems' membership was (according to the party itself) 44,000—an increase of around 2,000 on the previous year, but a long way from the 64,000 that it boasted as recently as 2010, before its popularity suffered when it entered government. Like Labour, the party encompasses several affiliated groupings, known as 'specified associated organizations' (SAOs). Each represents a particular section of its membership, such as women, ethnic minorities, lesbian, gay, bisexual, and transgender (LGBT) members, trade unionists, and youths and students.

Like Labour and the Tories, the Lib Dems have a parliamentary party to act as a voice for ordinary MPs; in fact, their federal structure means that they have three. The party also organizes in Northern Ireland, but rather than contesting elections under its own banner, it has a semi-official arrangement to support the Alliance Party of Northern Ireland.

How Liberal Democrats choose their leader

Long before Mr Miliband's Labour followed suit, the Lib Dems allowed every paid-up member an equal say in their leadership elections. The various means by which these elections may be triggered, however, range from grass-roots-led (a petition backed by at least three-quarters of local parties sent to the party's president) to decidedly 'top-down' (a no confidence vote passed by a majority of Lib Dem MPs).

In recent years, the Lib Dems have been more than willing to depose leaders with whom they grow dissatisfied. Despite leading his troops to their highest tally of Commons seats to date under the Lib Dem banner in 2005 (62), Mr Kennedy was persuaded to resign in January 2007 following his public admission of a drink problem. Less than two years later, his successor, Mr Campbell, also quit, after senior colleagues (including his deputy, Vince Cable) disclosed to journalists their concerns about his lacklustre performance in the media and during Prime Minister's Questions (PMQs). At time of writing, Mr Clegg was facing growing calls for his resignation following the party's disastrous performance in the 2014 local and European elections (see Chapter 9, 'Towards an EU "superstate"?'). First, a group of grass-roots party supporters launched an online petition entitled '#libdems4change', urging fellow members to replace him, then former Lib Dem Treasury spokesman Lord Oakeshott resigned the whip with a prediction that Mr Clegg would lead the party to 'disaster' in 2015. Lord Oakeshott—a close ally of Mr Cable—was later found to have leaked an opinion poll, published in *The Guardian* days earlier, suggesting that even Mr Clegg's own Sheffield Hallam seat was likely to be lost.

The Lib Dem ideology—left, right, or somewhere in-between?

The question of where the Lib Dems fall on the left–right political spectrum is increasingly debatable. Traditionally, like the Liberals before them, they have been seen as centrists: pro-welfare state, on the one hand, but in favour of free markets, on the other. It is this that has arguably been their great electoral asset—enabling them to appeal to Labour voters in Tory-held marginals and Conservatives in Labour ones. In recent years, however, the Lib Dems have often appeared more conventionally left-wing in their policy ideas than Labour—thanks in part to Labour's rhetorical embrace of many Thatcherite economic reforms, the encroachment of market forces into public services, and its increasingly interventionist foreign policy. For many years, the Lib Dems advocated a 50 per cent higher rate of income tax (something that Labour abandoned for some time until its introduction in April 2010 of a new 'top rate' pegged at that level for people earning £150,000 a year or more). The Lib Dems still support a local income tax to replace Council Tax, arguing that it would take more account of individuals' ability to pay.

Under Mr Clegg's immediate predecessors, the party reasserted many centre-left tendencies, particularly in relation to civil liberties and constitutional reform, but more recently there have been signs of the return of a more 'classical liberal' free market approach. In 2004, Mr Clegg, along with several fellow leading lights, including Mr Cable, contributed to *The Orange Book*, a collection of essays advocating a return to a Gladstonian, nineteenth-century vision of liberalism. The resurgence of this 'laissez-faire' philosophy appeared to be confirmed when Mr Clegg allied himself with Mr Cameron's Conservatives rather than joining Mr Brown in a 'coalition of the defeated' in 2010. The rightward shift at the top has arguably continued in government, with Lib Dem ministers publicly endorsing—and at times initiating—market reforms in public services and other 'business-friendly' policies that the party might have opposed under Mr Kennedy or Mr Campbell. As Business Secretary, Mr Cable found himself in the invidious position of having to introduce a tripling of undergraduate tuition fees from the 2012–13 academic year (like most other Lib Dem MPs, he had signed a pledge before the 2010 election stating his opposition to fees in principle). He later went on to steer through the controversial privatization of Royal Mail (see Chapter 7, 'Communications'). Meanwhile, Chief Secretary to the Treasury Danny Alexander was made personally responsible for delivering the swingeing public spending cuts announced by Tory Chancellor George Osborne, while the entire parliamentary party was whipped into supporting controversial reforms of the NHS and social security. However, Mr Clegg and colleagues have repeatedly retorted that, despite being the 'junior coalition partner', the party has succeeded in getting around three-quarters of its manifesto commitments onto the statute book—citing policies such as the repeated rises in the personal income tax allowance, designed to lift Britain's poorest workers out of tax altogether (see Chapter 7, Table 7.1).

As a testament to the unease felt by some party leading lights about their leadership's drift away from what they considered to be its founding principles, barely a week after the formal 'Coalition agreement' was signed, ex-leader Mr Kennedy—one of a long line of Liberal leaders who had nurtured the idea of an eventual 'realignment of the centre-left'—became the first 'big shot' to out himself as opposing it. (He had abstained when the parliamentary party voted to endorse it.) In an article for *The Guardian* on 15 May 2010, he expressed alarm at Mr Cameron's use of the term 'Liberal Conservative' to describe the new government in his first Downing Street press conference and warned that the Tories might try to absorb the Lib Dems in time. This had happened to sections of the party on two previous occasions: first, when Joseph Chamberlain split it over home rule for Ireland in 1886 (ending up a Liberal Unionist); and second, when a decision by Lloyd George to continue in coalition with the Conservatives after the end of the First World War sparked a prolonged period of factional infighting, resulting in the formation of various splinter groups and the Liberals' ultimate relegation to 'third party' status.

Disgruntled Lib Dems can console themselves, though, with the knowledge that they have access to an unusual constitutional mechanism enabling them to prevent their leadership steering them in political directions with which they are uncomfortable. The 'triple lock' was originally agreed by the party's conference in 1998 amid growing concern among some members about increasingly close relations between then Lib Dem leader Mr Ashdown and Labour. It is designed to come into effect whenever the leadership makes a 'substantial proposal that could affect the party's independence of political action'—for example announcing its intention to join a coalition. To secure such a deal, leaders are required first to win support from at least three-quarters of members of both the parliamentary party and the Lib Dems' Federal Executive (an elected committee of 35 senior activists, MPs, and party officials). If no such backing is obtained, a special conference must then be convened to decide the matter, mirroring the composition and voting rights of the standard annual party gathering. The triple lock was invoked for the first time on 12 May 2010, to approve the Lib Dems' entry into government.

▌ The deselection process

Once parliamentary candidates have been selected by their constituency parties or associations and elected to Parliament, they usually serve until voted out at another election or their retirement. Under certain circumstances, however, it is possible for candidates to be 'deselected'—or sacked—by either their local parties or leaderships. The process by which this can happen varies from party to party, but in general terms follows much the same pattern.

The most recent formal deselection was that of Tim Yeo, former Tory Minister and chairman of the Commons Energy and Climate Change Committee, who was removed by his local party in February 2014 for allegedly failing to devote enough time to constituency work while awaiting the outcome of an inquiry into claims that he had abused Commons lobbying rules. Mr Yeo (who was cleared by the inquiry) demanded a formal deselection vote by all members of his South Suffolk constituency association after its executive committee voted not to readopt him as a candidate in a secret ballot the previous November. In exceptional circumstances, MPs can be 'sacked' in other ways: former Immigration Minister Phil Woolas was barred from standing again for Labour after a specially convened election court stripped him of his Oldham East and Saddleworth seat for lying about his Lib Dem rival during the 2010 election campaign.

Notable examples of MPs who have avoided deselection include several Conservatives who defected to other parties in the last years of Mr Major's government. Emma Nicholson, MP for Torridge and West Devon, switched to the Lib Dems in 1995, but continued to serve her constituency (despite quitting her local Tory Party) until 1997. Fellow Tories Alan Howarth and Shaun Woodward both jumped ship to Labour, but retained their seats after the election and went on to serve as ministers.

Between general elections, deselections of MPs normally lead to by-elections—elections in their constituencies alone, with new candidates replacing them.

❙ Party funding now and in future

One endlessly debated issue surrounding the party system is funding. Because parties are intrinsic to British democracy, there has long been a vocal lobby calling for them to be financed, at least partly, by the state. At present, only Opposition parties receive state subsidies in Britain—a privilege designed to counteract the advantage that governing parties have because of resources available to governments. Introducing wholesale state funding of parties would signal a major change. Given the scale of Britain's current Budget deficit, without significantly increasing the tax burden where would 'the state' find the extra cash needed to fund parties? And if state funding were to become an entitlement for registered political parties, would it be only the larger or more mainstream ones that benefited—or could taxpayers expect some of their money to go to minority extremist organizations such as the British National Party (BNP)?

For these and other reasons, successive governments have sidestepped the issue. But, in the absence of such grants, how should parties fund their campaigns? Because membership subscriptions provide only modest, if regular, revenue streams, parties have come to rely increasingly on bequests, loans, and donations from wealthy supporters. Naturally, this has given rise to charges of inequity—if one party attracts higher donations than another, it can mount bigger campaigns—and suspicions that rich benefactors are using their money to buy levels of influence denied to everyone else.

The 1990s witnessed various controversies over party finance. During the Major years, there was growing unease about the Conservatives' use of anonymous multimillionaire donors and money originating in offshore tax havens—particularly the 'Ashcroft millions' funnelled away by the party's ex-pat treasurer, Lord Ashcroft. Labour promised to deal with these issues by limiting the ability of 'non-domiciles' ('non-doms')—individuals living or working in Britain, but registered for tax purposes in other countries—to finance parties and making the source of their donations transparent. But, within months of his election, Mr Blair was embroiled in his own controversy when Formula One boss Sir Bernie Ecclestone was identified as the source of a £1 million donation to his campaign. The fact that the racing mogul had just been granted a temporary exemption from an impending ban on tobacco sponsorship fuelled suspicions that he had bought influence.

To wrest back the moral high ground, the party returned the donation and began reforming the rules governing party funding in two ways: introducing a statutory register of all significant donations, and creating new criminal offences relating to false and late declarations. But, 11 years later, newly released papers suggested that, contrary to Mr Blair's protestations that he was a 'pretty straight kind of guy', within hours of holding a meeting with Ecclestone he was looking for ways of exempting Formula One from the sponsorship ban.

Under the Political Parties, Elections, and Referendums Act 2000, registration of donations now rests with the Electoral Commission, which, in addition to overseeing election procedures, has the responsibilities laid out in the table entitled 'Role of Electoral Commission in relation to donations and loans', to be found on the **Online Resource Centre** that accompanies this book.

Thirteen years after the 1997 election, the Ashcroft saga resurfaced in the run-up to the 2010 poll. This time, Mr Brown's former spin doctor, Charlie Whelan (by now political director of the Unite union), mounted an aggressive counter-attack in marginal constituencies that the peer was targeting. Lord Ashcroft, who was still a 'non-dom' despite having assured then Tory leader Mr Hague a decade earlier that he intended to take up UK residency (and tax liability), was accused of pumping millions into target seats before the official launch of the campaign (thereby circumventing election rules) to 'buy' votes. Two months after the election, with a Conservative once more in Downing Street, Lord Ashcroft finally relinquished his non-dom status—agreeing to pay UK tax in return for keeping his Lords seat.

By way of a postscript, figures published by the Commission in August 2010 found that overall donations made to Britain's political parties in the run-up to that year's election had been £6 million higher than before the 2005 poll—reaching a record £26.3 million. For the first time since 1997, the Conservatives trumped Labour, raising £12 million to its £11 million, although the two biggest single donations went to the latter (including £1 million from long-time supporter steel magnate Lakshmi Mittal).

▶ 'Lobbygate', 'cash for honours', and other recent funding scandals

Mr Blair's government was frequently embroiled in controversies concerning alleged lack of financial transparency, on the one hand, and underhand links with business, on the other. By the time Mr Brown succeeded him, the tension between ministers' pledge to be 'whiter than white' financially while still raising enough money to keep the Labour machine afloat had reached breaking point. Successive scandals about undeclared (or, at best, under-declared) donations and loans had forced ministers into embarrassing admissions. The political initiative was consequently handed to Mr Cameron, who demanded a £50,000 cap on all individual payments, including its main lifeline: union donations. Whatever his political instincts, Mr Brown was hardly in a position to comply, arguing instead that union contributions should be viewed as comprising a number of smaller individual donations. With 'Middle England' deserting the party in favour of the resurgent Conservatives, disclosure of Labour's annual accounts in July 2008 revealed the full extent of the party's mounting debt: £24 million was owed to various creditors, including several individual donors. Today, the two main parties remain at loggerheads over how best to reform the donation system and talks convened after the 2010 election have repeatedly broken down. One 'sop' to the Left in Mr Miliband's 2014 reforms of Labour's union links was his pledge to leave uncapped the level of donations that they could make to the party.

'Lobbygate'

Political lobbying is nothing new. The Conservatives have never been coy about their links to business, while certain Labour constituencies have long been sponsored by unions. But the emergence of specialist lobbying companies purposely set up to help individuals and interest groups to gain access to ministers, in the hope of influencing government policy, was a phenomenon not widely witnessed until the 1990s.

The involvement of one such company, Ian Greer Associates, as an alleged intermediary in the 'cash for questions' affair (see Chapter 2, 'MPs, conflicts of interest, abuses of privilege, and how to avoid them') was, for many, the first they had heard of such practices. Labour promised to halt these activities, but within a year of regaining power senior ministers—including Mr Blair's right-hand man, Peter Mandelson—were being linked to lobbying firms boasting of their ability to buy access to ministers. One such firm was Lawson Lucas Mendelsohn, run by former Labour campaign strategy adviser Neal Lawson, business intermediary Jon Mendelsohn, and Ben Lucas, one of Mr Blair's political briefers. Another, GPC Market Access, employed one of Mandelson's ex-special advisers, Derek Draper, who is alleged to have bragged to clients that he could buy them tea with Geoffrey Robinson, Labour's then Paymaster General, or dinner with Mr Blair.

'Cash for honours'

If 'Lobbygate' and the Ecclestone affair were early shots across the bows for Labour, then the various 'cash for honours' rows that followed provided the smoking gun that proved for many that the party was as guilty of succumbing to the advances of big business as the Conservatives.

By far most damaging was the 'loans for peerages' scandal exposed by *The Independent on Sunday* in October 2005. The controversy erupted in earnest the following March, when the then recently formed House of Lords Appointments Commission rejected several nominees whom Mr Blair had put forward for life peerages. It quickly emerged that each of the men had anonymously loaned Labour substantial sums of money. A loophole in the 2000 Act meant that, although all *donations* of £200-plus had to be properly declared, the same rule did not apply to loans—provided that they were taken out on normal commercial terms.

With the party in huge debt in the run-up to the 2005 election, Mr Blair and his advisers appeared to have deliberately sidestepped a law that they themselves had introduced on the pretext of wanting to make party funding more transparent, by courting loans rather than actual donations. Although the revelation that the party had gone 'cap in hand' to anonymous lenders was embarrassing enough for the government, there was no suggestion the letter of election law had been breached (even if its spirit was). What led to the subsequent criminal investigation—and the spectacle of Mr Blair becoming the first serving prime minister to be questioned by police, albeit as a witness—was the allegation, levelled by Scottish Nationalist MP Angus McNeil, that attempts had been made by some of his aides to 'sell' honours (an offence under the Sale of Peerages Act 1925).

In the ensuing months, the spotlight focused on Lord Levy, Labour's chief fundraiser (who was alleged to have asked one of the lenders, Dr Chai Patel, director of the Priory healthcare group, to change a donation into an unsecured loan for £1.5 million, to sidestep the new rules). As the controversy escalated, Lord Levy—known as 'Lord Cashpoint' in some Labour circles—briefly faced the prospect of being charged with conspiracy to pervert the course of justice, while Downing Street adviser Ruth Turner was subjected to a dawn raid by the Metropolitan Police amid rumours that she faced similar charges.

None was ultimately brought, but the year-long investigation, which ended weeks before Mr Blair left Downing Street, cast a shadow over his final year in office. To regain the political initiative at the height of the controversy, he launched an independent cross-party review of political funding. But in October 2007 the talks were suspended amid scenes of dissent between Labour and the Tories. This did not stop its recommendations being made public—including a proposal to cap individual donations, after a transitional period, at £50,000.

When the Coalition was formed, Mr Cameron described politicians' cosy relationship with lobbyists as the 'next great political scandal' awaiting the British Parliament—after then recent furores over MPs' expenses and the near-collapse of the banking system. His words came back to haunt him, with the explosion of the *News of the World* phone-hacking saga, the prosecution of Mr Cameron's close friend and fellow Old Etonian Charlie Brooks and wife Rebekah (the paper's former editor), and the suggestion of collusion between senior ministers and News International executives over the bid by the latter's parent company, News Corp, to take over BSkyB (see Chapter 3, 'Press'). A few weeks earlier, in a separate scandal, Mr Cameron had been forced to sack his party's treasurer, Peter Cruddas, after he was filmed in a 'sting' operation by *Sunday Times* journalists boasting that Tory donors could buy 'Premier League access' to the prime minister, and even influence his policymaking decisions, by giving the party £250,000.

The Coalition finally made good on its pledge to 'crack down' on lobbying with passage, in January 2014, of the Transparency of Lobbying, Non-Party Campaigning, and Trade Union Administration Act 2014, the key measures of which are:

- the introduction of a US-style statutory register of consultant lobbyists;
- registration requirements, to be enforced by a statutory registrar;
- tighter regulation of spending on political campaigns in the run-up to elections by those not registered for election or as political parties; and
- strengthened legal requirements on trades unions to keep their registered lists of members up to date.

Although the principle of registering professional lobbyists was widely embraced, the 'Gagging Bill' (as its critics dubbed it) provoked heated parliamentary exchanges in its later stages, with key clauses repeatedly blocked by the Lords. The introduction of stricter spending rules for 'third parties' close to elections was greeted as an attempt to stifle dissent by organizations such as 38 Degrees, www.opendemocracy.net, and others who had previously launched high-profile protests against the Coalition's cuts programme and other policies—concerns echoed by more established, issue-specific groups such as Friends of the Earth. Meanwhile, Labour accused the government of mounting a one-sided attack on its funding base, by explicitly applying these rules to their main donors, the unions.

☰ Topical feature idea

Despite the barriers presented by Britain's 'first past the post' (FPTP) electoral system, recent elections at all levels have witnessed growing levels of support for minority parties. Caroline Lucas became the first Green Party MP in 2010, and the United Kingdom Independent Party (UKIP) secured two seats in 2014, while both the Greens and UKIP won more votes than the Lib Dems in the 2014 local and European elections. In the Euro poll, UKIP became the first party other than Labour or the Conservatives to win a national election since before the First World War. What level of support do minority parties have in your area? How are they likely to fare in coming elections?

✳ Current issues

- **The rise of UKIP and other minority parties** The Lib–Con Coalition broke the 80-year hegemony of the 'two-party' system, and the 2014 local and European elections suggest that we are entering a new era of 'four-party politics' (with Lib Dems and UKIP as third and fourth, respectively). Despite rejecting electoral reform in the 2011 referendum, British voters have demonstrated a growing disconnect with all three main parties. The first Green MP was elected in 2010, UKIP gained two seats in 2014, while maverick George Galloway returned as Respect Party MP for Bradford West in a 2012 by-election. The Greens beat the Lib Dems into fifth place nationally in the 2015 Euro elections.

- **Reform of Labour's union links** Labour leader Ed Miliband has reformed his party's historic union links, requiring members of affiliated unions to 'opt in' to the party, rather than being automatically enrolled, as previously. Future leadership contests will also be fought on a 'one member, one vote' basis—replacing the last element of the union 'block vote'.

- **The party funding deadlock** Labour and Tories have repeatedly suspended their talks over new party funding rules since 2010, with the former recently voting to maintain unions' ability to donate to it as much as they wish.

⠿ Key points

1. Britain's democracy is characterized by a 'party system', which developed in tandem with its FPTP voting system. The three main parties are Labour, the Conservatives, and the Liberal Democrats.

2. The Conservative and Lib Dems (formerly Liberals) emerged gradually from the landed and industrialist classes, but the Labour Party was formed deliberately by an alliance of trades unions and other organizations at the start of the twentieth century, with a mandate to get more working-class men elected to Parliament.

3. The Conservatives are headed by a chairman and Conservative Party Board, and Labour, by a National Executive Committee (NEC), comprising members from every branch of the party's organization, including Parliament and unions. The Lib Dems have a federal structure, with no formal ruling body.

4. Members of Parliament in all three main parties have mechanisms to hold their leaders accountable and, in extreme cases, to depose them. The Tories have a 1922 Backbench Committee, Labour, the Parliamentary Labour Party, and the Lib Dems, their own federal equivalents in England, Scotland, and Wales.

5. Conservative constituency associations, local Labour parties, and grass-roots Lib Dems have powers to deselect their MPs if dissatisfied with their performance and to choose alternative candidates.

→ Further reading

Bale, T. (2011) *The Conservative Party: From Thatcher to Cameron*, Cambridge: Polity Press. **Updated paperback edition of new book charting the Tories' long slide into unpopularity and their 'reinvention' as an electable force under David Cameron.**

Driver, S. (2011) *Understanding British Party Politics*, Cambridge: Polity Press. **Thought-provoking, up-to-date examination of the British party system from a post-2010 perspective.**

Pugh, M. (2011) *Speak for Britain! A New History of the Labour Party*, London: Vintage. **Thoughtful, at times revisionist, history of Labour Party, from its origins to the election of Ed Miliband as leader.**

Roy, D. (2005) *Liberals: A History of the Liberal and Liberal Democratic Parties*, London: Hambledon Continuum. **Overview of the complex history of the Liberal Party and its successors, tracing the origins of liberalism, the party's twentieth-century decline, and its 1970s and 1980s resurgence.**

ⓐ Online Resource Centre

www.oxfordtextbooks.co.uk/orc/Morrison4e/
Visit the Online Resource Centre that accompanies this book for web links and regular updates.

6

The National Health Service

No institution is capable of generating as many headlines as the National Health Service (NHS).

Founded in 1948, three years into Clement Attlee's post-war Labour government, the National Health Service was designed to be exactly that: a *national* provider of high-quality medical treatment, 'free at the point of use' or 'need', to a consistent standard the length and breadth of Britain. But subsequent decades—particularly the past 30 years—have witnessed gradual fragmentation of this idealized model of socialized health care. What was once a single, monolithic health service, run directly by central government, was transformed in the 1980s and 1990s into an umbrella organization encompassing numerous connected, but increasingly autonomous, units. Much like individual companies in the commercial marketplace, most have acquired their own management boards and delegated budgets, and are expected to 'purchase' or 'commission' services from, and 'sell' them to, one another. And with the introduction of the concept of 'patient choice'—allowing people to shop around for hospital treatment like customers—they have even begun to compete for business.

Under the Coalition, market reforms initiated by Margaret Thatcher, and consolidated by John Major and New Labour, are being taken further than ever. As a result, the structure of today's NHS in England bears little resemblance to that of the original: locally based clinical commissioning groups (CCGs), led by general practitioners (GPs) and other community-based professionals, now 'commission' care for patients from NHS trusts (hospitals or mental health units, or groups of the same), with a national body, NHS England, responsible for commissioning specialist services, such as cardiac (heart) units, cancer care, and accident and emergency (A&E) units, to ensure that such provision is available in hospital settings nationwide.

This chapter explains how this complex NHS 'internal market' structure came about and how its various strands link together.

▌ The origins of the National Health Service (NHS)

Although not formally established until the National Health Service Act 1946, the NHS emerged from mounting concern about the ever-starker inequalities in personal well-being between the richest and poorest Britons. It had its roots in two key developments: the 'Beveridge Report' (of which more in a moment); and the introduction by Liberal Chancellor David Lloyd George in 1911 of a **National Insurance (NI)** scheme, which, in exchange for docking 4d a week from their wages, insured low-paid workers against sickness and unemployment.

When this modest measure was introduced, the concept of an NHS offering a comprehensive range of treatments was still a pipe dream. But, in 1941, Labour member of Parliament (MP) Arthur Greenwood, Minister without Portfolio in the wartime national government, commissioned Liberal economist William Beveridge to head up an interdepartmental committee on social insurance and allied services. Its report, published a year later, would form the blueprint not only for the NHS, but also for the all-encompassing 'welfare state' of which it became part—leading to Attlee's famous pledge, on entering Downing Street, to harness the spirit of collectivism born out of the war effort to look after the poor, sick, and vulnerable 'from the cradle to the grave' during peacetime.

The Health Minister entrusted with launching the NHS was Aneurin 'Nye' Bevan, whose vision was inspired by his memories of witnessing the suffering of steelworkers and miners in his native Tredegar, south-east Wales, as a younger man, and the work that voluntary societies and charity-funded cottage hospitals had done to care for such people. He reputedly modelled the NHS on the Tredegar Medical Aid Society, a community-run healthcare collective set up in 1874.

With no pre-existing national template for the NHS, Bevan initially had a fight on his hands persuading family doctors and consultants—previously used to dictating their own working conditions and pay—to sign up to his project. In the end, he did so by offering them generous contracts that, by his own admission, 'stuffed their mouths with gold'. When he triumphantly unveiled the new NHS at its inaugural outlet, Park Hospital in Manchester, on 5 July 1948, Bevan declared:

❝ We now have the moral leadership of the world. ❞

Although Bevan's vision of a health service for all was largely fulfilled, the economics of providing universal health care on such a scale would soon start eating away at some of its guiding principles—notably that of universal free access to treatment, regardless of ability to pay. In May 1951, buffeted by global economic turbulence and its dependence on US loans to finance its social security programme, Labour reluctantly introduced the first NHS charges: £1 for spectacles prescribed by an optician and a half-cost price for dentures. A year later, a flat rate £1 fee for visiting the dentist was introduced, along with a 1s generic prescription charge. In what was ultimately a mortal blow for Attlee, Bevan resigned from the government even before the first charges had taken effect. Among those joining him was a young Harold Wilson, a future prime minister.

How the NHS is funded

Although the proportion of Britain's gross domestic product (GDP) (see Chapter 7, 'Promoting growth and UK exports') ploughed into the NHS each year has varied wildly between governments—with Labour traditionally investing more, even if not always wisely—the general breakdown of sources from which this investment derives has remained broadly the same since the early 1950s. Around 80 per cent comes from general taxation (income tax, value added tax or VAT, duties on tobacco and alcohol) and the remaining 20 per cent from:

- an NHS element to NI contributions;
- charges to patients for drugs (prescriptions) and treatment;
- income from land sales and income-generation schemes; and
- funds raised from voluntary sources—for example local hospital appeals.

Given the current direction of health policy, this balance is likely to shift in future years, with substantially more coming from income-generation.

▌ The end of the post-war consensus and the birth of NHS markets

For 40 years or more, the NHS retained largely the same structure: it was funded centrally through taxation, with ministers and civil servants filtering money down to hospitals, surgeries, and ambulance services. Of the tens of thousands of nurses, doctors, paramedics, cleaners, and catering staff working across the health service, most were on the government's payroll.

But a series of institutional reforms since the late 1980s has transformed the NHS into a different organization entirely. Nowadays, most family doctors—or GPs—are self-employed; many specialists work as freelance locums, moving from hospital to hospital (and public to private sector) as demand arises; and junior doctors, nurses, and care workers are increasingly hired through private agencies, rather than as full-time NHS employees. Catering, cleaning, and security workers are routinely supplied by outside contractors, and even treatment itself is increasingly contracted out to external and/or commercial providers.

So how and why did this dramatic turnabout in the day-to-day running of the NHS arise, and who is responsible for running the modern-day health service?

It is impossible to understand the shape of the NHS today without first examining the emergence of the 'internal market'. As long ago as 1973, the National Health Service Reorganization Act, spearheaded by then Conservative Health and Social Security Secretary Keith Joseph (an architect of 'Thatcherism'), aimed to shake up the NHS by introducing a more efficient management structure, with 'generalist' managers joining existing clinical experts on hospital boards and incentives to generate revenue by letting out unused wards to private providers. These themes were revisited a decade later when, alarmed at the escalating cost of NHS treatment and wage bills, another Tory Health Secretary, Norman Fowler, commissioned then deputy chairman and managing director of Sainsbury's Sir Roy Griffiths to chair an inquiry into improving NHS efficiency by cutting running costs and using resources more economically.

His resulting report made two key recommendations:

- *General managers* should be introduced to run existing district health authorities (DHAs)—essentially, the administrative presence in each area of the then Department of Health and Social Security (DHSS), and responsible for directing funding to local hospitals and surgeries. These would supplant the previous 'management by consensus' philosophy (under which medical practitioners had managed themselves), which Griffiths felt led to mere crisis management.

- There should be a greater focus on *community-based* health care—with GPs, dentists, and other primary care providers given control of their own budgets, and freedom to commission services on their patients' behalf without going through ministers (or even their health authorities). The aim was to make the allocation of finite NHS funds more efficient by replacing the 'one size fits all' approach to funding GP surgeries with targeted allocations tailored to individual patients' needs.

Amid Labour charges that they were primarily motivated by saving money (and privatizing the NHS by stealth), the Tories initially took only tentative steps towards implementing the report. But a series of subsequent White Papers paved the way for an 'internal market' that was, if anything, more far-reaching.

The Act that finally established this internal market (and defined this term for the first time) flowed from a further NHS review announced by Mrs Thatcher in 1988. At about the same time, she split the mammoth DHSS in two, in recognition of its burgeoning workload, creating the Department of Social Security (DSS) to run the benefits system and a separate Department of Health (DoH).

The National Health Service and Community Care Act 1990 implemented two White Papers: *Caring for People* and *Working for Patients*. It ushered in a phased reorganization with the following key features.

- Hospitals, mental health units, ambulance services, and other NHS patient care providers became **NHS trusts**—with their own management boards, incorporating both practitioners (consultants/other senior clinical staff) and general managers charged with improving efficiency.

- GPs were offered the opportunity to become 'fund-holders'—'opting out' of district health authority control to control their own budgets.

- GP fund-holding practices, DHAs, and family health service authorities (FHSAs) were redefined as 'purchasers' of NHS care on their patients' behalf. While GPs would now focus on *primary care*—providing 'first port of call' treatments such as diagnoses and vaccinations, and purchasing X-rays, tests, and small operations for their patients, when needed—FHSAs would buy in other community-based services, with DHAs 'purchasing' acute hospital services such as A&E facilities.

- NHS trusts were defined as service 'providers'.

In theory, the new internal market would operate as illustrated in Figure 6.1.

Figure 6.1 How the Conservatives' NHS internal market was structured

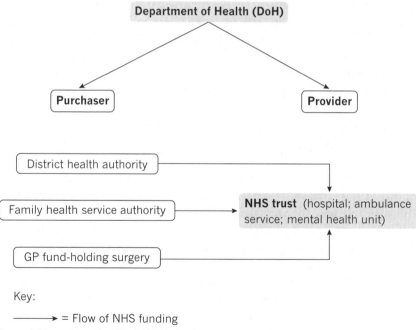

Key:

———▶ = Flow of NHS funding

Source: Article courtesy of the BMA—British Medical Association.
BMA, (2014), Commissioning structure [ONLINE]. Available at: http://bma.org.uk/commissioning [Accessed 01 October 14]

In practice, implementation was hardly smooth. As independent contractors, GPs had to *want* to be integrated into the new structure. While some relished the freedom to control their own budgets, others were alarmed at the increased workload and the risk of making unwise spending decisions—only to face tricky dilemmas should unforeseen needs arise during a financial year. Only family practices with more than 5,000 patients in England and Northern Ireland (4,000 in Wales and Scotland) were allowed to apply for fund-holder status. By the time Labour came to power in 1997, 3,500 practices and 15,000 GPs—fewer than half the estimated 40,000 practising across Britain—had signed up. By mid-1996, more than 520 trusts were in place, but mergers had reduced this tally to 450 by 1999.

The internal market was also criticized for placing too much emphasis on management and recruiting high-salaried senior staff, armed with clipboards and flow charts, rather than front-line workers such as nurses. Managers were increasingly headhunted from the private sector—reflecting the Conservatives' belief that those with business expertise would be better at running complex organizations than medical practitioners. This trend has continued to this day, with chief executives of most NHS trust boards earning six-figure salaries; figures released in September 2013 showed that nearly 50 senior managers in NHS England alone were earning more than the prime minister—with the then NHS England chief executive, Sir David Nicholson, pocketing £211,214. Only with his successor, Simon Stevens, in May 2014, did this trend finally begin to wane, after Stevens took a voluntary 10 per cent pay cut in an effort to lead by example.

The (initially short-lived) introduction of fund-holding GP surgeries—the key plank of the Tories' internal market ideal—remains an important innovation, because it would ultimately shape the party's approach to further reforming the NHS after its return to power in 2010 (see 'The Health and Social Care Act 2012 and the reinvention of the NHS' in this chapter).

The emergence of the 'postcode lottery' and treatment rationing

Despite disagreements over the wisdom of introducing an internal market, by the early 1990s there was a widespread consensus that the original 'top-down' NHS model needed to be adapted to the changing needs of a society on the cusp of a new century—not least because of widening disparities between different areas in terms of average income, age, healthcare needs, and other demographic factors. Nonetheless, the decision to grant increased autonomy to DHAs and individual GPs would have one unintended consequence: the steady emergence of significant variations in the level or nature of treatment available to people with the same conditions living in different areas. This increasing trend—which led many to question whether the NHS could any longer be described as a 'national' health service—became known as the **postcode lottery**.

An early cause célèbre for those opposing delegation of funding decisions to local level was the case of beta interferon—an expensive drug that, according to some experts, dramatically decreases the number of relapses suffered by people with multiple sclerosis. In the early 1990s, it emerged that many DHAs were refusing to fund beta interferon on the NHS—arguing that the £10,000-a-year cost per patient would be better spent on other treatments, such as physiotherapy. Its supporters claimed that prescribing the medicine early could save the NHS money in the long run, by delaying the need for residential or palliative care. Another commonly cited example of the postcode lottery is the differential availability of fertility treatment for childless couples, in particular *in vitro* fertilization (IVF)—the process by which egg cells are fertilized outside a woman's womb before being transferred back to stimulate pregnancy.

Despite Labour's early attempt to end the postcode lottery by establishing national service frameworks (NSFs) to harmonize provision of essential health services nationwide (see 'New Labour's restructuring of the NHS' in this chapter), wide disparities remain. In November 2005, it emerged that Ipswich Hospital NHS Trust and several Suffolk primary care trusts (PCTs) were rationing hip and knee replacement operations by refusing to offer them to obese patients, other than in exceptional circumstances. Dr Brian Keeble, director of public health for Ipswich PCT, justified the decision by telling the press it was for patients' own good, because overweight people 'do worse after operations' and hip replacements might fail. But critics of the move condemned it as discrimination against patients whose conditions were judged to be self-inflicted.

The postcode lottery is now such a political issue that ministers have increasingly been drawn into disputes over individual cases of patients denied treatment. So potentially damaging had the issue become by June 2008 that then Health Secretary Alan Johnson pledged to ban PCTs from denying patients costly treatments approved by the National Institute for Health and Care Excellence (NICE—see 'New Labour's restructuring of the NHS' in this chapter). Despite this, inequities remain, and some fear that real-terms budget cuts, combined with the Coalition's introduction of wholesale GP commissioning, could see widening disparities emerge in primary health provision from area to area. In June 2012, a Freedom of Information Act request by *GP Magazine* revealed that nine out of 10 NHS trusts were rationing certain operations—including tonsillectomies and cataract surgery (by 89 and 66 per cent of trusts respectively). While ministers maintained that rationing on grounds of cost (as opposed to clinical judgement) was unacceptable, David Stout, deputy chief executive of the NHS Confederation, which represents PCTs, argued that restrictions were justified in some cases, because of the 'considerable financial pressures and scarce resources' engendered by the Coalition's deficit-reduction programme (see Chapter 7, 'Managing national debt').

NHS waiting lists and the origins of Blair's health reforms

More politically explosive still in the 1990s was the unfolding 'waiting list' crisis inherited by Labour in 1997. By then, 1.3 million people were waiting for operations or other inpatient treatments, with 'guaranteed maximum waits' from initial GP referral to actual treatment of 18 months. In the final months of Mr Major's government, tabloids were filled with stories about elderly and vulnerable patients falling seriously ill, or even dying, while awaiting surgery. Equally alarming were numerous stories printed about the lengthy queues and overcrowding that people were enduring in A&E units.

Such was the public outcry that one of Tony Blair's central election pledges was to cut waiting lists by 100,000 by releasing £100 million from 'NHS red tape'. Despite a sluggish start, by November 2004 official figures indicated that waiting lists had hit a 17-year low: although 857,000 people were still listed, this was down 300,000 on 1997. Perhaps more importantly for the individuals concerned, waiting *times* had fallen, with only 19 patients waiting longer than a year for treatment and 122, more than nine months. However, within weeks of becoming Health Secretary in May 2010, Mr Lansley signalled an end to 'target culture' (a long-standing bête noire of the Conservatives) by scrapping England's 18-week appointment 'guarantee', together with the stipulation that all NHS patients should be seen by GPs within 48 hours of requesting appointments.

New Labour's restructuring of the NHS

The success of Mr Blair's blizzard of NHS reforms was mixed. Significant achievements in some areas—bolstered by unprecedented public investment—were marred by inconsistent, even contradictory, policymaking in others.

Labour had inherited a health service widely seen as crisis-stricken. After an initial period of caution, during which the new government stuck to spending limits imposed by the Tories, then Chancellor of the Exchequer Gordon Brown announced a huge increase in NHS funding—lifting it above the average annual investment of other European countries in health care. In 1997, the proportion of Britain's GDP spent annually on the NHS was 6.7 per cent, but in his 2002 Budget Mr Brown used his first tax rise (a 1 per cent NI increase) to boost it to 7.4 per cent a year. By 2010, health spending was equivalent to 9.7 per cent of GDP, but even before the Coalition announced its multibillion-pound savings programme the influential King's Fund charity predicted that, by 2016–17, it would fall back to 7.9 per cent as a result of public spending cuts—wiping out all real terms increases since 2000.

Mr Blair quickly decided that pouring more money into the NHS was not enough. To ensure that this investment was spent wisely, like Mrs Thatcher before him, he set about restructuring the health service. Having promised to dismantle the 'wasteful' internal market in opposition (and initially doing so under his first Health Secretary, Frank Dobson), he began introducing a new form of localized management and budgetary control seen by many as his own version of the Tory model.

New Labour's version of the internal market originated in the Health Act 1999 and the White Paper preceding it, *The New NHS: Modern and Dependable*. Its main emphasis was on the primacy of community-based health care—steering patients, wherever possible, away from hospital, and giving GPs and other primary care providers the money and autonomy to offer a wider range of treatments through their practices.

The resulting reforms initially appeared modest. In place of fund-holding, which was effectively fostering 'competition' between GP surgeries, Mr Blair introduced greater cooperation between practices, by establishing primary care groups (PCGs). These collaborative bodies brought together GPs, community nurses, and other related practitioners in each local area to promote closer liaison and, ultimately, more coordinated use of NHS resources. The idea was that, as PCGs grew in confidence and evolved, more responsibilities would be delegated to them. In the end, like fund-holding GP practices, they also assumed control of their own budgets, establishing NHS trust-style boards to take financial decisions for them.

By 2002, the bones of the following NHS structure were established.

- *Primary care trusts* (PCTs)—local administrative organizations covering populations of 100,000 or more—replaced PCGs. Like fund-holding practices, PCTs bought clinical services from NHS trusts on behalf of patients—except that, rather than calling this 'purchasing', Labour dubbed it 'commissioning'. They took control of 80 per cent of the overall NHS budget and virtually all local commissioning. But it was only a matter of time before health policy would return full circle, with the Coalition's pledge to abolish PCTs and hand commissioning powers directly to GPs (see 'The Health and Social Care Act 2012 and the reinvention of the NHS' in this chapter).

- After initially being replaced by 96 health authorities (HAs), DHAs gave way to much more arm's-length administrative bodies, *strategic health authorities* (SHAs), of which there were initially 28 (later 10).

- NHS trusts continued to be classed as service 'providers', but with the prospect of gaining greater financial autonomy if they performed well in 'league tables'. Ultimately, many were granted 'self-governing' status, as **foundation trusts**—a form of autonomy now available to *all* NHS trusts by the Coalition.

- County councils and unitary authorities established *local involvement networks* (LINks) to act as the voices of service users. Run directly by local

Figure 6.2 Labour's version of the internal market

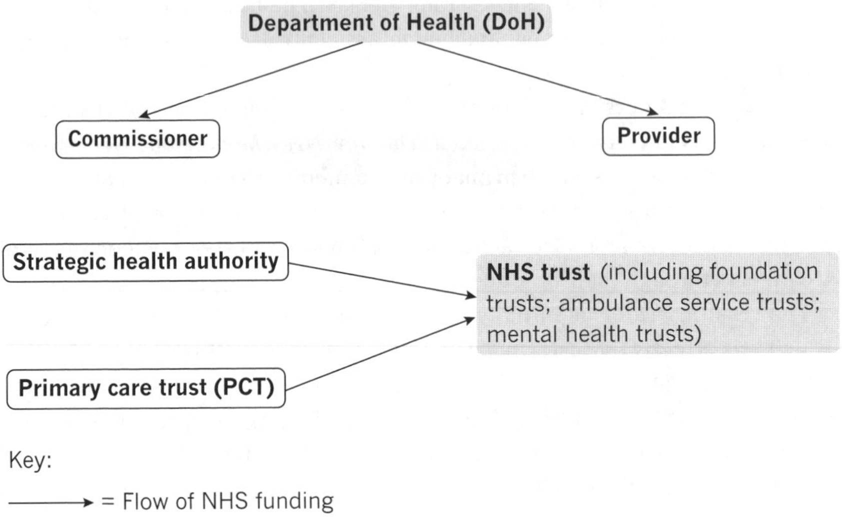

Key:

──────▶ = Flow of NHS funding

taxpayers, LINks could demand specific changes to health and social care in their areas. They replaced a prior Labour invention, patients' forums, which had been staffed by volunteers from local communities.

Labour's revamped internal market therefore works as outlined in Figure 6.2.

After this initial restructure, the NHS was rationalized more than once. On 1 October 2006, the number of PCTs was halved, from 303 to 151. The mergers enabling this to happen were intended to produce efficiency savings by preventing duplication between trusts in neighbouring areas with broadly similar needs. By the time the Coalition scrapped PCTs, many covered populations of up to 600,000. The number of trusts had also been reduced (partly owing to closures and mergers). Prior to the Coalition's reorganization, there were 168 acute trusts and 73 mental health trusts, covering 1,600 hospitals and specialist care centres. As the population covered by each SHA increased, meanwhile, its level of direct involvement in patient care dwindled. In October 2011, SHAs were merged to form four regional 'clusters' tasked with managing the NHS locally. These were abolished in April 2013.

In addition to its structural reforms, Labour strengthened the hand of the Health Secretary, giving him or her power to set nationwide targets or care standards in priority areas, to which all SHAs, PCTs, and NHS trusts must adhere. These **national service frameworks (NSFs)**, established in 1998, were 'long-term strategies' designed to provide consistency of care across Britain. In effect, they amounted to a prospectus, similar to the National Curriculum used to enforce uniformity of school teaching in core subjects. By the time Labour left office, there were NSFs and strategies covering 10 high-priority conditions—ranging from cancer to coronary heart disease and diabetes.

These are outlined in the table entitled 'NHS national service frameworks and strategies', to be found on the **Online Resource Centre** that accompanies this book. The number of NSFs and strategies was reduced to nine by the Coalition in early 2012, and at time of writing they were under review.

Although nominally retained, a closer look at the small print of the revised NSFs and strategies bears witness to greater emphasis on 'patient choice'—with individuals encouraged to take informed decisions from a range of options presented to them by professionals about how best to manage their own care. This more individualized approach (an extension of ideas road-tested by both Major and Blair governments) arguably undermines one original purpose of NSFs: to impose a degree of 'uniformity' on NHS provision across England. Supporters of the new approach would counter that it has never been the purpose of NSF to dictate a one-size-fits-all approach to treating patients with the same conditions; rather, they would argue, it is their job to establish a consistent menu of treatment *options* across the country—an idea not incompatible with allowing each patient to choose options best suited to him or her.

Nonetheless, the pursuit of greater standardization of health care was a central thread of other Labour initiatives, including the early introduction of 'health action zones' (HAZs) in deprived areas—a short-lived initiative used to address 'health inequalities' between rich and poor districts by targeting additional resources at communities with high rates of unemployment, poverty, and poor housing—followed, in 1999, by formation of the National Institute of Clinical Excellence, later renamed the National Institute of Health and Clinical Excellence, and eventually the **National Institute of Health and Care Excellence (NICE)**. Initially designated a 'special health authority', but made a non-departmental body (quango) by the Coalition in 2013, NICE approves drugs and treatments for NHS use, promotes improved public health, and ensures that consistent, high-quality health care (and social care—see Chapter 18, 'Regulating social care') is available across England and Wales, by:

- offering guidance on the prevention of illness to NHS workers, councils, and the wider public/voluntary sectors;
- advising government on whether new and existing treatments, medicines, and procedures should become/remain available on the NHS; and
- advising ministers and public on the most appropriate treatment for individuals with specific ailments and diseases.

The decisions of NICE are frequently controversial. Campaigners representing people with specific conditions have accused it of penny-pinching when failing to endorse new drugs or recommending others be abandoned (in a 2001 preliminary ruling, it determined that beta interferon should no longer be available on the NHS). Sometimes, however, its interventions are welcomed: in June 2006, it issued draft guidance to PCTs recommending that then recently licensed drug Herceptin® be used for treating early-stage breast cancer. Its decision followed the case of Barbara Clark, a 49-year-old nurse who persuaded Somerset Coast PCT to finance the £20,000-a-year drug by threatening it with litigation in the European Court of Human Rights (ECtHR).

Until Coalition Health Secretary Jeremy Hunt readopted a more interventionist approach to health policy (see 'The Stafford Hospital scandal and the new regulation revolution'), the DoH's other key roles were, for long years, reduced to providing little more than strategic direction, with service delivery largely delegated to local and regional bodies.

From patients to consumers—the 'marketization' of the NHS

The blueprint for taking Thatcher and Major's NHS reforms to their logical conclusion, and much that has followed under the Coalition, came with publication of New Labour's *Ten-Year NHS Plan* in 2000. Pledging to 'give the people of Britain a health service fit for the twenty-first century', modernizing Health Secretary Alan Milburn launched NHS 'taskforces' to promote market concepts such as 'choice' and 'competition'. At carefully choreographed intervals between early 2001 and 2003, he risked the ire of many medical practitioners (and Labour traditionalists) by outlining the radical plans listed in the table entitled 'Key reforms flowing from *Ten-Year NHS Plan*', to be found on the

 Online Resource Centre.

Mr Milburn's introduction of a 'Concordat' allowing patients to be treated in private hospitals and clinics to speed up waiting times proved deeply unpopular with some long-serving party loyalists, for whom the idea of *any* private involvement in the NHS (direct or indirect) was heresy.

It was not long before ministers stood accused of privatizing the NHS by the back door. But Mr Blair was unapologetic, arguing that it was ends, not means, that mattered and that if using a spare BUPA ward meant that frail pensioners had to wait 18 months less for hip replacements, they were unlikely to be fussed about outdated ideological objections. Yet the media was quick to highlight the

incongruous spectacle of NHS patients being flown overseas for surgery that ought to be available locally.

Vocal critics of this shake-up included Mr Dobson, who accused his party's leadership of 'following a Tory consensus'. He argued that, by naming and shaming 'failing' hospitals in league tables and allowing 'successful' ones (foundation trusts) to offer inflated salaries for the most qualified and experienced staff, Labour risked creating a 'two-tier health service'. High-performing trusts would inevitably become yet more successful and gain even greater freedoms, while those at the bottom would continue spiralling downhill— devoid of reputation, resources, or autonomy to improve their performance. Moreover, 'patient choice' was a sham: given the option of surgery at poor-performing hospitals or better ones elsewhere, few patients would surely choose the former, making 'choice' illusory. And like the most popular schools, the best-performing hospitals ultimately had finite capacity—leaving them oversubscribed and struggling to cope with demand.

For Labour opponents of the changes, the final insult came at the hands of their fellow backbenchers, on a glacial November evening in 2003. With the help of a handful of Scottish MPs—many personally opposed to having foundation hospitals imposed in Scotland, where members of the Scottish Parliament (MSPs) rejected them—Mr Blair scored his lowest Commons victory to date, squeezing the Health and Social Care Bill through by 17 votes.

As for the devolved nations, the overall structure of the NHS in Scotland today bears a strong resemblance to how it looked nationwide before Mrs Thatcher. Meanwhile, in Wales, the internal market was abandoned in time for the NHS's 60th birthday in 2008—returning to an old-style model that saw funding channelled directly from the DoH down to trusts and *health boards* (the Welsh equivalent of SHAs).

Nonetheless, by the time of the 2010 election, a broad consensus existed between the three main parties supporting moves to grant all English-based NHS trusts foundation status—giving staff and patients increasingly hands-on involvement in their running. Today's foundation trusts, overseen by independent regulator **Monitor**, have been likened by advocates to mutuals or cooperatives. Staff and public can become 'members', earning the right to elect their boards or even to stand themselves. Once on boards, they have a direct say in the appointment and dismissal of the trust chairpersons and non-executive directors, and can veto their choices of chief executive.

The Health and Social Care Act 2012 and the reinvention of the NHS

If Mr Blair's repeated restructuring of the NHS was controversial, the biggest earthquake was yet to come. Despite earlier declaring a 'moratorium' on any further 'top-down' reform of the health service, two months after entering office Mr Lansley unveiled a root-and-branch reform package unlike anything seen before. In a throwback to Mr Major's abortive fund-holding policies, he announced the abolition of PCTs and the handover of their commissioning role to GPs. Unlike fund-holding practices (which managed their finances individually), the new breed of GP commissioners would form local 'consortia'—later dubbed **clinical commissioning groups (CCGs)**—to purchase services collaboratively. But this time GPs would be *forced* to participate, rather than able to decide for themselves whether to 'opt in' (as with fund-holding)—a curious element of compulsion amid a raft of other proposals predicated on the principle of choice. More controversial still, potentially, was Mr Lansley's pledge to create 'the largest social enterprise sector in the world' by encouraging foundation trusts to effectively break out of the NHS superstructure—becoming not-for-profit companies with the ability to generate their own revenue by charging paying customers for private treatment, as well as providing traditional health care free at the point of delivery. The flipside of these freedoms was that, like commercial firms, hospitals mismanaging their finances could go bust. Moreover, the complex and costly transformation began at the same time as the NHS was ordered to find £20 billion in administrative savings—as a quid pro quo for Chancellor George Osborne's guarantee in his June 2010 'emergency Budget' (see Chapter 7, 'Managing national debt') that real-terms increases in health spending would continue until 2014.

Fears about the danger of NHS trusts being left to fend for themselves appeared to be borne out when, in June 2012, South London Healthcare, formed through the merger of three smaller trusts in 2009, was formally put into administration by Mr Lansley and warned that it faced being dissolved or losing key services after accumulating a £69 million debt. Although Labour warned that it was an early casualty of the new-look, deconstructed NHS, ironically the root of this trust's problems lay in the cost of servicing crippling private finance initiative (PFI) contracts for facilities built under the previous government (see Chapter 7, 'Private finance initiatives (PFIs) and public–private partnerships (PPPs)'). Tellingly, ministers warned that 22 other trusts were facing similar problems.

One accusation levelled at Mr Lansley was that his reforms effectively handed between £60 billion and £80 billion of NHS funds over to private contractors—with no PCTs or SHAs left to police them. He countered that GPs' decisions would be scrutinized by a new regulator, **Healthwatch**, with local offshoots based on the extant LINks bodies and beefed-up versions of the health service scrutiny committees established by Labour (see 'The Stafford Hospital scandal and the new regulation revolution'). To oversee commissioning of specialist services—and primary care itself—he introduced a new quango, now called **NHS England**, to act as a hub of the new-look healthcare market.

As for that market, the Bill's most contentious inclusion initially was a clause that smacked to many of an attempt to transform the NHS into a US-style insurance-based system. Under the new model of marketized health care, NHS trusts would be forced to compete for business with 'any willing provider' from the private or voluntary sectors—raising the prospect of multinational companies reaping huge profits off the backs of British taxpayers by 'cherry-picking' simple procedures conducive to economies of scale and leaving NHS hospitals to handle more complex cases.

So seismic was the proposed overhaul that, in August 2010, healthcare union UNISON (concerned about its members' job security) launched legal action in protest at the speed and scale of NHS reform. It argued that the public consultation ministers had instigated was a 'sham': within 24 hours of Mr Lansley unveiling his White Paper, NHS chief executive Sir David Nicholson had written to all English trusts urging them to start implementing changes 'immediately'. But respected health charity the King's Fund warned that while GPs were best placed to judge the needs of patients, many had little inclination (or ability) to become accountants. Sure enough, fears that the new consortia might end up paying for the costly expertise of commercial consultancy firms appeared to be vindicated when in January 2011—two years before the reforms were rolled out—GP magazine *Pulse* analysed 10 of the first 52 'pathfinder' CCGs set up by the government to road-test the new commissioning structure. Six had already signed contracts with private firms, including KPMG, or were about to do so. The alternative, critics argued, would be for CCGs effectively to reinvent PCTs by hiring in-house managers, administrators, and finance directors. In a further criticism of the direction of government policy, the British Medical Association (BMA), the professional body representing doctors, warned that giving GPs direct control of their own budgets (and associated tough spending decisions) risked fostering distrust between them and patients with strong ideas about their own medical needs.

The unprecedented scale of opposition to the reforms—the normally restrained Royal College of Nursing (RCN) passed a 'no confidence' vote in Mr Lansley and loyalist Liberal Democrat peer Baroness Williams led a revolt at her party's 2011 spring conference—persuaded ministers to introduce a six-week 'pause' in the Bill's passage while a specially convened panel of independent experts, the NHS Future Forum, investigated ways of introducing additional regulatory safeguards to allay critics' fears. Among the recommendations that Mr Lansley accepted to mollify opponents was to modify a clause in the original Bill requiring Monitor to 'promote competition' within the NHS—which some suggested would open the health service up to EU competition law. Instead, the Bill was amended to emphasize the need to 'promote integration' between different healthcare bodies and the treatments they offered, in the interests of increasing 'citizens' rights' and 'improving quality'. The Health Secretary's 'duty to provide' a comprehensive NHS was also reinstated—or, as ministers would have it, re-emphasized—to reassure critics that fragmentation of old structures did not amount to wholesale privatization and deregulation.

In the end, after withstanding several defeats in the Lords, knife-edge Commons debates, and more than 100 amendments from ministers alone, the Health and Social Care Bill finally received royal assent in March 2012—14 months after first presented to Parliament and 19 months after publication of the White Paper that spawned it. The structural reforms that survived its turbulent passage were as follows.

- Clinical commissioning groups (CCGs) replaced PCTs in April 2013. Unlike in the original Bill, the groups—numbering 211 at time of writing—are not solely GP-led, but collaborations between doctors and other community-based professionals, including nurses.

- NHS England was given responsibility for commissioning primary care itself and ensuring that specialist services are maintained at national and regional levels. It convenes *clinical senates* to provide medical advice on commissioning plans and *clinical networks* to advise on local service integration.

- Councils have replaced SHAs as the main bodies promoting health improvement and shaping overall NHS provision in their areas. Their role in quality assurance has been extended to cover all health providers in their areas—including those from the private or voluntary sectors— and councils have also assumed devolved powers to scrutinize public health services. Scrutiny powers are either exercised by councils' exist- ing health service scrutiny committees or 'suitable' alternative arrange- ments approved by ministers.

- **Health and well-being boards** were formed by all 130 'upper-tier' English councils (counties and unitaries) to bring together all commissioners of health and social care in each area, along with local representatives of Healthwatch, to promote integrated approaches to improving health. Boards were to include elected local councillors.

- Secondary care has been offered by 'any *qualified* [as opposed to willing] provider', embracing competition between public, private, and third sectors.

- The Care Quality Commission (CQC—see Chapter 18, 'Regulating social care') is responsible for regulating standards of health and social care across *all* providers, while Monitor issues (and withdraws) licences to registered health providers, including private companies and charities. It also promotes 'efficiency', setting prices for NHS treatment and ensur- ing that any competition works in 'patients' interests'. To prevent NHS providers from being undercut by commercial rivals, competition must be based on 'quality'—not price.

- **Public Health England (PHE)**, a new executive agency of the DoH, pro- motes healthier lifestyles and funds £4 billion worth of public health ini- tiatives across England. Public health services are now commissioned by councils from ring-fenced budgets (see Chapter 12, 'Types of revenue grant') or the NHS at local level, using PHE finance.

The DoH also created several other quangos, many themselves introduced only at various amendment stages. While Monitor's role overseeing foundation trusts has been retained for now, this will be only 'temporarily', while an NHS Trust Development Authority completes the process of converting all remain- ing trusts to foundation status. Another body, Health Education England, over- sees the training of future NHS professionals. Figure 6.3 gives a visual description of the new internal commissioning structure.

Barely two years after the new NHS structure was introduced, there are already signs that some 'privatization' fears are being borne out. Even as the

Figure 6.3 How the Coalition's new 'internal–external' NHS market is structured

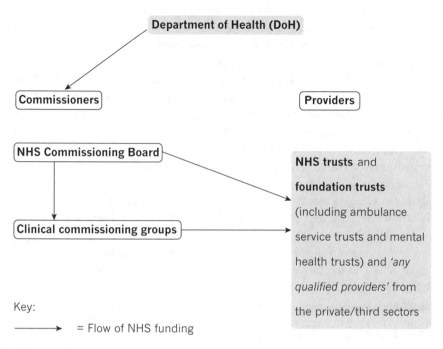

Department of Health (DoH)

Commissioners

Providers

NHS Commissioning Board

Clinical commissioning groups

NHS trusts and **foundation trusts** (including ambulance service trusts and mental health trusts) and '*any qualified providers*' from the private/third sectors

Key:

⟶ = Flow of NHS funding

Bill battled its way through its final stages, *The Guardian* and *The Independent* reported that struggling NHS hospitals were already being quietly 'taken over' by private companies. In September 2011, the former used requests under the Freedom of Information Act (see Chapter 20) to reveal how top-level talks were already under way between the DoH, the NHS, McKinsey, and private German healthcare chain Helios about 'potential opportunities in London'. The first 'public–private partnership' (PPP) contract actually signed in relation to day-to-day management of an NHS hospital was the deal completed by Circle Partnership and Hinchingbrooke Hospital, Huntingdon—coincidentally, Mr Major's former constituency—in February 2012. Under this arrangement, Circle was tasked with introducing savings to turn around the trust's £40 million debt, in return for which it would keep the first £2 million of any 'profit' generated by the hospital, a quarter of all subsequent surpluses between £2 million and £6 million, and a third of those between £6 million and £10 million. Other high-profile private companies have since profited from the NHS—for example Virgin Care, an offshoot of Sir Richard Branson's multibillion-pound business empire, is part-way through a £500 million contract to run community health services in Surrey for five years.

Meanwhile, the Coalition's decision to raise the cap on how much of their incomes foundation trusts may generate by treating private patients to 49 per cent has also met stiff opposition. Shadow ministers and union leaders have accused the government of subsidizing the private sector with taxpayers' money and running the risk of increasing NHS waiting lists by prioritizing more lucrative fee-paying customers. Labour has repeatedly pledged to repeal key sections of the Act if it returns to power in 2015.

The Faculty of Public Health, the professional body that monitors standards of care provided by public health specialists, has also issued repeated warnings about the dangers of marketizing the NHS—arguing that tying hospital funding to the number of procedures they perform will incentivize them (and rival private and charitable providers) to treat patients needlessly to raise profits. The organization's vice-president, John Middleton, argued that it would become increasingly difficult for patients with long-term conditions to receive 'joined-up care', because this would require separate organizations to collaborate—and Monitor and/or EU competition authorities might see this as 'anti-competitive' behaviour. A market-based NHS, he added, would disadvantage less educated and/or pushy patients—increasing the likelihood of further child abuse cases like those of Victoria Climbié and Peter Connelly (see Chapter 18, 'The 2004 Act and the "Every Child Matters" agenda') going unnoticed until too late, by ending the tradition of designated professionals having supervisory roles over individual cases.

The Stafford Hospital scandal and the new regulation revolution

The first sign of Mr Hunt stamping a distinctive mark on the NHS came in February 2013, following a damning report into institutionalized neglect and high mortality rates at Stafford Hospital between 2005 and 2008. The inquiry, led by Robert Francis QC, found that hundreds of patients (by some estimates, 400–1,200) had been allowed to die unnecessarily because of a hospital culture obsessed with chasing tick-box targets at the expense of providing high-quality care. Among the lurid revelations to emerge from this and an earlier investigation by the then Healthcare Commission was that some patients had been left for hours in their own urine and forced to drink water out of vases because they could not attract staff's attention. Ironically (as is so often the case in such circumstances), the resulting Francis Report made 290 recommendations for 'fundamental change'—each with the potential to lead to further box-ticking, if implemented on the ground by managers and front-line staff—the main ones being:

- the merger of care regulation into a single body;
- a new code of conduct for senior managers, who would be disqualified if they were to fail to adhere to it; and

- an increased focus in staff recruitment on care and compassion, with a new 'aptitude test' to be completed by all recruits and regular checks introduced on doctors' competence.

Significantly, Mr Francis also condemned repeated NHS reorganizations as 'remote' and 'counterproductive'—a pointed aside at Mr Lansley's reforms on the eve of their rollout.

Mr Cameron's immediate response to the Francis Report was to apologize to affected families and announce a further five investigations of hospital trusts: in Colchester, Tameside, Blackpool, Basildon and Thurrock, and East Lancashire. For his part, Mr Hunt—although at pains to avoid the 'elephant trap' of introducing yet more NHS regulation by formally implementing all of the Francis recommendations—has introduced a major shakeup of the routine hospital inspections regime, headed by a new Chief Inspector of Hospitals modelled on the equivalents for schools and prisons. The first appointee to this post (described by Mr Hunt as *primus inter pares* among NHS regulators) was leading cancer specialist Professor Sir Mike Richards, who wasted little time in sending a warning shot across the bows of NHS trusts by announcing that, like Ofsted (see Chapter 15, 'Monitoring school standards and the great "parent choice" debate'), he would be holding both 'unannounced' and 'announced' inspections, and placing hospitals in need of drastic improvement into 'special measures', like failing schools (see Chapter 15, Table 15.5). His new regime was initially introduced across 18 hospital trusts—six regarded as 'high risk', six 'low risk', and the remainder 'mixed'—and is in the process of being rolled out nationwide. In July 2014, moreover, he announced that his new, tougher, CQC was drawing up plans for a similar special measures regime to bring to heel underperforming GP practices.

The Chief Inspector has effectively become the new, overarching head of the main existing regulator, the CQC—formed from the merger of the Healthcare Commission and Commission for Social Care Inspection (CSCI) in April 2008, when health and social care were finally brought under the same regulatory framework. The CQC is charged with promoting ongoing improvements in the health service and reviewing complaints by service users unhappy with the local resolution of their cases. Individuals must, however, have gone through a formal NHS complaints procedure—starting with the trust or other body about which they are complaining—before their cases can be referred to this quango. It is authorized to issue trusts with fines, fixed penalties, and enforcement notices for breaking the terms of their registrations. It can even withdraw NHS licences from acute hospitals that persistently fail cleanliness inspections.

In Scotland, the CQC's role is assumed by the Scottish Commission for the Regulation of Care (SCRC, or Care Commission); in Wales, by Healthcare Inspectorate Wales (HIW); and in Northern Ireland, by the Regulation and Quality Improvement Authority (RQIA).

The performance of local NHS services is further monitored by **health service scrutiny committees** set up by county councils and unitary authorities (see Chapter 11). These comprise around 15 members, including chairpersons and vice-chairpersons. Membership is drawn not only from these authorities, but also from local districts or boroughs and relevant voluntary organizations, including Age Concern, the National Society for the Prevention of Cruelty to Children (NSPCC), and the National Association for Mental Health (Mind).

Introducing a new inspection regime is symbolic of Mr Hunt's distinctive approach to running the DoH, which has seen him adopt the role of glorified 'patient's advocate'—often openly castigating the NHS for its failings, as if from the position of detached observer, rather than championing and defending it in the vein popularized by previous Health Secretaries. In March 2014, he unveiled yet another element of his drive to improve hospital performance, by asking NHS trust managers to join a 'Sign up to Safety' campaign to halve the risk of patients suffering 'avoidable harm', such as medication errors, bedsores, and blood clots, by 2016–17. Three months later, he launched a new 'patient safety' section on the existing NHS Choices website, www.nhs.uk, on which the public can check levels of clinical competence at their local hospitals and compare them to those elsewhere. This came as figures revealed that, despite the furore over failings at Stafford Hospital, one in five trusts were still failing to own up and/or adequately respond to breaches of patient safety.

Hospital closures, deficits, and the perils of market-centred thinking in the NHS

At time of writing, the question of finance had once more returned to haunt the NHS—with cracks starting to show on the ground in England, in the face of real-terms spending cuts, and trouble brewing for the Welsh Assembly as it dropped any pretence of a 'ring-fence' in Wales. As newspaper headlines reverted to a familiar refrain about lengthening waiting times in A&E, closing maternity units, and front-line staff shortages, Mr Hunt introduced into the Care Act 2014 a highly controversial amendment known as 'Clause 119'. In brief, this gives the Health Secretary and **trust special administrators** appointed to act for him or her executive powers to close or downgrade A&E departments, maternity units, and other hospital services within 40 days, and with little public consultation, if neighbouring trusts are suffering financially. Mr Hunt inserted the clause after the High Court ruled in October 2013 that he had acted beyond his powers by intervening to downgrade the A&E and maternity units at Lewisham Hospital, south-east London, to save the next-door trust, South London Healthcare, from bankruptcy.

Although Clause 119 made it onto the statute book, it provoked storms of protest from an unlikely alliance of Tory backbenchers, Labour, and campaign group 38 Degrees. While, in one sense, it arguably represents the extreme end of what can transpire when a 'market-centred' approach to running the NHS fails—with financially struggling trusts creating a negative knock-on effect that sends ripples through other parts of the health service—in another it exemplifies precisely the kind of direct state intervention that Conservative governments have eschewed for decades. By interfering with the NHS internal market, rather than allowing 'failing' trusts to fail (and, potentially, close), Mr Hunt was sending out the message that a similar fate could befall any trust, however 'successful', should its neighbours be ailing.

The difficulties of forcing NHS trusts to adapt to market thinking—and the hard reality that, like individual businesses, they must balance their books to survive—is hardly new. In 2006, then Health Secretary Patricia Hewitt responded to an escalating deficit crisis in some areas by giving debt-ridden trusts permission to borrow money from 'better performing' ones with financial surpluses. That said, the deficit problem is clearly worsening: figures published in June 2014 showed that one in three acute NHS trusts was in debt by 2013–14, compared to one in 10 at the time of the 2010 election.

More recently, the Coalition has added to the likelihood of trusts building up debts by forcing hospitals that readmit patients within 30 days of discharging them for related complaints to carry out additional treatment at their own expense. Defending these penalties when he introduced them in 2010, Mr Lansley cited statistics showing that hospitals had become overzealous in discharging patients to alleviate 'bed-blocking' (see Chapter 18, 'Care homes, nursing homes, and the rise of the private sector'). As a result, between 1998–99 and 2007–08, emergency readmissions in England had risen from 359,719 to 546,354.

Deficit reduction was also the motivation for Lib Dem and Tory manifesto promises to cut wasteful spending on consultants, managers, and IT projects. Once in office, however, the Coalition quickly reneged on a related pledge: its undertaking to scrap the Summary Care Record (SCR) database, commissioned by Labour to store all electronic patient records centrally so that they can be accessed by NHS professionals working anywhere in England. The database—which patients must 'opt out' of if they want their details kept private—began rolling out in April 2010 and, by June 2014, more than half of all patients in England had their own summary care records. However, Coalition plans to extend the growing database further, by setting up a single centralized medical record system—and allowing access not only to NHS staff, but also to private companies and voluntary organizations involved in patient care—ran aground in February 2014 after privacy campaigners and consumer groups complained that it could compromise individuals' confidentiality. The new system—which people can 'opt out' of—was shelved for six months, until September that year, but debate was likely to intensify when it returned to the agenda.

▎ Complaining about NHS treatment

Prior to appealing to the CQC (see 'The Stafford Hospital scandal and the new regulation revolution'), anyone dissatisfied with his or her NHS care may make a formal complaint, initially at local level, and his or her case may be referred to one of four ombudsmen—one each for England, Scotland, Wales, and Northern Ireland. In England, complaints are handled by the Parliamentary and Health Service Ombudsman; in Wales, the Public Services Ombudsman for Wales; in Scotland, the Scottish Public Services Ombudsman; and in Northern Ireland, the Northern Ireland Ombudsman.

Each ombudsman produces an annual report for consideration by its national assembly or parliament, and handles complaints in relation to:

- failure in NHS service standards;
- failure to provide a service 'to which a person is entitled';
- maladministration by an NHS body; and
- failure in the exercise of clinical judgement by hospitals or GPs.

Complaints are handled according to the sequence outlined in the table entitled 'The complaints process to the Health Service Commissioner (Health Service Ombudsman)', to be found on the **Online Resource Centre**.

▎ NHS changes under devolution

Handing day-to-day NHS management to the devolved administrations in Scotland, Wales, and Northern Ireland was always likely to create disparities in how the health service was administered in different areas. Aside from major structural contrasts—for example the continued absence of foundation trusts in Scotland—the past few years have seen clear 'inequalities' emerge between the nations, arising from political decisions taken by individual legislatures. In April 2007, the National Assembly for Wales became the first devolved chamber to scrap prescription charges, having previously halved them. The Northern Ireland Assembly followed suit in April 2010 and the Scottish Parliament, a year later. As yet, English patients (other than children, pregnant and new mothers, and some benefit claimants) still pay. Moreover, further differentials are likely to emerge in the wake of Scotland's independence referendum—not least because, in the dying days of the campaign, Westminster's political leaders agreed to hand the Scottish Parliament enhanced devolved powers in the event of a 'no' vote, while specifically guaranteeing its future autonomy over how much is spent on the NHS north of the border.

Marginally less controversial have been the decisions by all three devolved administrations to abandon parking charges at NHS hospitals—a move that former Labour Health Minister Ben Bradshaw refused to adopt in England, arguing that many trusts needed the revenue generated to subsidize patient care.

☰ Topical feature idea

The following is an extract from an article taken from *WalesOnline*, 1 August 2013. It centres on the refusal of Welsh Health Minister Mark Drakeford to launch a public inquiry into an emerging crisis at Cardiff's University Hospital of Wales cardiac unit. He was responding to a Royal College of Surgeons report revealing that waiting times for heart surgery were so long that many patients were dying while queuing for operations. How would you develop this news story into a background feature? Who would you approach for interviews and what would you ask them?

Extract from an article published by *WalesOnline* , 1 August 2013

No public inquiry at crisis-hit University Hospital of Wales, says Health Minister Mark Drakeford

Julia McWatt

Julia McWatt

WalesOnline

1 August 2013

Web link: **www.walesonline.co.uk/news/wales-news/no-public-inquiry-crisis-hit-university-5391403**

A public inquiry into the circumstances surrounding the deaths of patients waiting for heart surgery in Wales' biggest hospital would pose a 'significant risk' to the work being done to address the concerns, Health Minister Mark Drakeford has warned.

Calls were made for a full inquiry following a damning report by the Royal College of Surgeons (RCS) which highlighted the impact of long waiting lists for cardiac surgery at Cardiff's University Hospital of Wales.

The report branded services at the hospital as 'dangerous' and of 'poor quality' and said patients were 'dying regularly' while waiting for heart surgery.

Members of the College's professional affairs board in Wales also said more than 2,000 non-emergency operations had been cancelled or not been scheduled because of a lack of beds in the first three months of 2013.

The College warned that this delay was leading to serious consequences for patients.

Its report said: 'This has resulted in increasing waiting lists such that patients are clearly coming to harm.

'In cardiac surgery we heard that patients are regularly dying on the waiting list from their cardiac pathology, mostly valvular disease.'

Following the report, Cardiff and Vale chief executive Adam Cairns admitted the health board could 'do better', although he said action had already been taken to ring-fence hospital beds and invest in the hospital's emergency unit.

Shadow Minister for Health Darren Millar said: 'When surgeons label departments in a hospital "dangerous", the time has come to act.

'Labour ministers can no longer dismiss fears and an independent inquiry into standards of care is the only way forward.

[...]

'Confidence is at rock bottom and it is more than clear that an inquiry is needed to address concerns.'

But Prof Drakeford said he believed that a public inquiry was unnecessary and that it would hamper the efforts being made to address the situation.

✳ Current issues

- **Increased waiting-times in accident and emergency (A&E)** Controversy is mounting about the length of time patients are being forced to wait on trolleys for emergency treatment—an echo of the last Conservative-run government. Health Secretary Mr Hunt argues that this is a legacy of New Labour's botched renegotiation of GP contracts, which allowed them to stop providing out-of-hours primary care—forcing more people to go to A&E.

- **NHS tops world league of health services** Britain has the best quality health care in the world, according to a study by the Commonwealth Fund published in June 2014—despite spending less per head of population on health (£2,008) than all but one other country examined by researchers (New Zealand).

- **New charges for NHS access for overseas migrants** Amid increasingly heated debate about access to health care and social security benefits granted to migrants from the European Union and elsewhere, the Immigration Act 2014 changed the definition of 'ordinary residency' in Britain (the usual qualification for free health care and a status for which people can apply only after five years in Britain).The new definition excludes all those without 'indefinite leave to remain'—meaning that foreign students, workers, and their family members will have to pay additional fees prior to entry to guarantee themselves free treatment. The Home Secretary also has new powers to charge extra 'NHS access' fees for temporary migrants intending to stay for between six months and five years.

⸬ Key points

1. The NHS operates on the principle that it is a 'universal' health service, which can be accessed by British residents 'free at the point of use'.

2. It is funded from a combination of general taxation and National Insurance, in an 80:20 per cent split. At least £60 billion of its annual £100 billion budget is under the control of clinical commissioning groups (CCGs).

3. These CCGs comprise GPs and other primary care professionals. They 'commission' secondary care from NHS trusts (hospitals, ambulance services, etc.) and 'any qualified provider' from the private or voluntary sectors. NHS England commissions specialist and A&E units.

4. The NHS internal market is regulated by Monitor, but the quality of health and social care provided by CCGs, NHS trusts, and other providers is regulated by the Care Quality Commission (CQC).

5. The NHS is structured differently in Scotland, where there are no foundation (fully autonomous) trusts. In Wales, the structure has reverted to a pre-internal-market model.

→ Further reading

Ham, C. (2009) *Health Policy in Britain: The Politics and Organisation of The National Health Service*, 6th edn, Basingstoke: Palgrave Macmillan. **Sixth edition of the leading text on the history of NHS, including updates on Labour's reforms and developments in Scotland, Wales, and Northern Ireland.**

Klein, R. (2013) *The New Politics of the NHS: From Creation to Reinvention*, 7th edn, Abingdon: Radcliffe Publishing. **Comprehensive overview of the evolution of the health service, encompassing recent market reforms.**

Leys, C. and Player, S. (2011) *The Plot Against the NHS*, Perth: Merlin Press. **Provocative interrogation of the political agenda underlying the Coalition's reform plans for the NHS, envisaging an emergence of a US-style insurance-based health system.**

Pollock, A. M. (2006) *NHS plc: The Privatisation of Our Health Care*, London: Verso Books. **Thoughtful critique of the growing involvement of the private sector in running the NHS by professor of health policy and health services research at University College London.**

⊕ Online Resource Centre

www.oxfordtextbooks.co.uk/orc/Morrison4e/
Visit the Online Resource Centre that accompanies this book for web links and regular updates.

7

The Treasury, industry, and the utilities

During the 1992 US presidential election race, James Carville, campaign strategist for then aspiring Democratic nominee Bill Clinton, coined a phrase that would go down in political folklore. Identifying the issue he judged most crucial to persuading the electorate to back a candidate, he replied: 'The economy, stupid.' So it is, arguably, in Britain. Although political historians have observed that UK voters do not always switch horses at times of economic crisis (the deep recession of the early 1990s saw John Major return the Conservatives to power, albeit with a drastically reduced majority), perceived economic competence has proved the making of certain prime ministers (Margaret Thatcher, Tony Blair) and mismanagement, the downfall of others (Ted Heath, James Callaghan).

This chapter explores the work of the two principal government departments charged with overseeing Britain's economy: HM Treasury and the Department for Business, Innovation, and Skills (BIS). It also examines the remit and composition of the main non-departmental bodies charged with managing specific areas of economic performance, such as the Bank of England's Monetary Policy Committee (MPC) and the recently established Office for Budget Responsibility (OBR).

▌ The role of the Treasury and Chancellor of the Exchequer

If the prime minister can be said to have a true 'number two', it is not the 'Deputy PM' of the day, but the Chancellor of the Exchequer. Charged with controlling the government's purse strings, the Chancellor is indisputably the most powerful minister in Cabinet beside the premier. Government would grind to a halt were it not for taxes and loans, and it is the Chancellor's job to raise this money. Even the name of the department he or she heads—the Treasury—testifies to his or her authority. Not for nothing is the prime minister's own official title 'First Lord of the Treasury'.

The Chancellor has the following key responsibilities:

- overseeing government public spending commitments by managing fiscal policy—raising or lowering taxation and investing it in public services (schools, hospitals, roads);
- managing national debt—the level of borrowing needed to top up tax revenues to finance government spending programmes;
- promoting economic growth at home and encouraging exports; and
- controlling domestic inflation (rises in the cost of living) and unemployment.

In recognition of the huge responsibility that comes with the post, he or she is assisted by one of the largest ministerial teams of any Whitehall department. Unlike most ministries, the Treasury boasts at least three secretaries of state in addition to the Chancellor: the Chief Secretary to the Treasury, the Financial Secretary to the Treasury, and the Economic Secretary to the Treasury.

Fiscal policy and taxation

One of the principal means by which British governments traditionally attempt to control the economy is through 'tax and spend' tactics—or *fiscal policy*. Based on the writings of Liberal economist John Maynard Keynes, this involves raising or lowering taxation to influence consumer behaviour (and to improve the health of the government's finances). A 'Keynesian' approach might see the Chancellor raise income tax rates, for example, in so doing cutting individuals' take-home pay and, by extension, spending power. In theory, this should have the knock-on effect of reducing demand for goods and services, thereby curbing inflation. Increasing taxes also boosts government revenue for spending on schools, hospitals, etc., reducing the need for the Chancellor to *borrow* money (which would increase the UK's Budget deficit and, over time, 'national debt').

Until the 1980s, there was a broad post-war consensus in favour of managing the economy through fiscal policy—although, on balance, this approach tended to be favoured more by Labour than Conservative governments. Labour's enthusiasm arose largely out of its traditional emphasis on taxation as an instrument for redistributing income from higher to lower earners through 'transfer payments', or benefits (see Chapter 8, 'Types of benefit and their relationship to National Insurance'). From the advent of the National Health Service (NHS) onwards, Labour also gained a reputation as the 'high tax party' because of its ideological commitment to strong investment in state health care and education (which required substantial revenues). Before the Thatcher years, the party also favoured public ownership of many industries and these, too, required huge injections of money to maintain. The Conservatives, in contrast, have traditionally been the party of tax cuts or breaks (particularly for business)—favouring a 'supply side' approach to running the economy that leaves more money in individuals' pockets in the hope of boosting growth through private, rather than public, expenditure. The theory is that keeping taxes as low as possible for everyone, including the rich, ultimately has a beneficial 'trickle down' effect on the wider economy and, by extension, lower-income households.

There are two broad forms of taxation: **direct taxes** and **indirect taxes**. Direct taxes are 'up front'—explicitly taken from individuals or businesses as deductions from their basic earnings. The main types are outlined in Table 7.1.

The fact that direct taxation is charged at different rates, according to individuals' or companies' incomes, means that it is often referred to as 'progressive'. By taking into account people's ability to pay, it is seen as fairer than flat-rate charges—such as water bills or television licences—which cost everyone the same, regardless of their earnings. This has not stopped some campaigners arguing for a more once-size-fits-all approach, however. And in light of recent debates about the perceived need to simplify Britain's hideously complex 'tax code' (the rulebook governing how much each individual is charged, based on their precise financial circumstances), the notion of combining income tax with National Insurance (NI) has been revived in Conservative circles, with Coalition Chancellor George Osborne rumoured to be considering this at time of writing. Meanwhile, the United Kingdom Independence Party (UKIP) has gone on record as favouring a flat combined income tax/NI rate of 31 per cent for everyone earning £11,500 or more.

In contrast to direct taxes, indirect ones are often described as 'regressive'. Unlike income or corporation taxes, they are built into the prices of goods and services that consumers buy (including basic utilities such as gas and electricity). Because these 'pay as you spend' charges—often described as 'hidden', or 'stealth', taxes—are levied at universal rates, they take no account of individuals' ability to pay. The most familiar—value added tax (VAT), tobacco and alcohol duties, and fuel duty—are set out in Table 7.2.

The British tax system has long been notoriously complex. For this reason, Mr Osborne established a new Office for Tax Simplification in July 2010 to rationalize the 11,000-page Exchequer Code that he had inherited—ending what he described as the 'spaghetti bowl' of UK tax law. Meanwhile, in an effort to crack down on tax evasion and avoidance—together estimated to cost Britain £14 billion a year—Mr Osborne's Lib Dem deputy, Chief Secretary to the Treasury Danny Alexander, announced at his party's 2010 conference that he would be scrutinizing the accounts of everyone earning £150,000 or more, aiming to recoup at least half of these lost fiscal receipts. Since then, the issue of 'tax-dodging' has

Table 7.1 Types of direct taxation in the UK—and how they work

Tax	How administered	Rates (2013–14)	Notes
Income tax	Pay-as-you-earn (PAYE) contributions deducted from workers' gross salaries by employers, or retrospective 'self-assessment' payments to HM Revenue and Customs (HMRC) by self-employed	Personal allowance for those aged under 65: £10,000 since 2014–15 Personal allowance for those aged 65–74: £10,500 Personal allowance for those aged 75 and over: £10,660 Standard rate: 20% (20p in £1) Higher rate: 40% (40p in £1) Additional rate for those earning £150,000 or more: 45% (45p in £1)	'Personal allowance' (the amount a person can earn before paying tax) has risen incrementally each year under the Coalition, with all those earning less than £10,000 a year taken out of tax altogether (a Lib Dem manifesto pledge) by 2014–15. Level at which 40% higher rate kicks in has been lowered incrementally, year by year, and had reached £31,866 by 2014–15. Additional rate lowered from 50% (50p in £1) in April 2013.
Corporation tax	Paid by companies on their profits—an 'income tax for companies'	Small profits rate: 20% (20p in £1) since April 2011 Main rate: 21% (21p in £1) from April 2014—down from 26% (26p in £1) when Coalition formed	Main rate expected to fall by a further 1% because Coalition opted to cut by 1% every year for four years beginning April 2011. Main rate applies to companies with profits of £300,000 or higher in given tax year. Small profits rate has fallen incrementally from high of 22% in 2009 (when 100% relief for small businesses on any capital investment up to £50,000 and 175% tax credit to encourage research and development also introduced). Small profits rate applies to companies generating profits up to £300,000.
Capital gains tax (CGT)	Paid by owners of financial assets, property, and other items, such as expensive jewellery or sports cars, sold for personal gain	Entrepreneurs' rate: 10% (10p in £1) on first £5m made during lifetime General rate: 18% (18p in £1) Higher taxpayers' rate: 28% (28p in £1)	Debates rages about CGT, in light of mammoth profits made by 'private equity' investors—wealthy speculators who club together to buy underperforming companies, improve their fortunes, and sell them for profit. Amid mounting

(continued)

Table 7.1 *(continued)*

Tax	How administered	Rates (2013–14)	Notes
			criticism of this sector (some directors were reputedly pay less tax than their cleaners), Labour introduced an 18% flat rate for CGT for anyone whose gains exceeded £1m (albeit with a 10% 'entrepreneurs' rate' for gains of less than £1m).
			Before George Osborne's first Budget, there was speculation that CGT might rise to 40 or 50%, but it finally settled at 28%—and only for higher-rate taxpayers. At same time, entrepreneurs' rate was extended to apply to first £5m of individual's lifetime gains.
Inheritance tax (IHT)	'Death duty' paid on value of estates (including financial assets, property, and other valuable items) handed down from deceased to friends/ family members by executors of their wills	Legacies of over £325,000: 40% (40p in £1)—or 36% (36p in £1) for those leaving 10% or more of net estates to charity—since April 2012	Until recently, IHT was charged at 40% on all estates worth £300,000 or more, but mounting controversy over this low threshold (average house prices were near that level by 2007) prompted Labour to introduce 'exempt transfers' for individuals who leave estates to a spouse, civil partner, or charity. In effect, this means that recipients may use both their own and their deceased partners' allowances—doubling their thresholds to £650,000. Labour was widely criticized for 'stealing' Conservative policy, and Tories entered the 2010 election pledging to raise the threshold to £1m (although Lib Dems blocked this).

NOTE: A regularly updated version of this table can be found on the **Online Resource Centre** that accompanies this book.

Table 7.2 Types of indirect taxation in the UK—and how they work

Name	How administered	Rates (2014–15)	Notes
Value added tax (VAT)	'Hidden tax' embedded in retail prices of consumer goods	20% (20p in £1)	Reduced rate of 5% for essential items, such as domestic fuel and power, while food, children's clothes, books, newspapers and magazines, and some disability equipment are exempt.
			During 'credit crunch', Labour cut rate for 13 months from 17.5% (17.5p in £1) to 15% (15p in £1).
			Coalition raised it in January 2011 to 20% (20p in £1).
Tobacco products duty and alcohol excise duties	Embedded in retail prices of items subject to excise duty	Cigarettes: 16.5% of the retail price of a packet of 20, plus £184.10 per 1,000 as of March 2014	Always controversial among smokers and drinkers, these are higher in Britain than elsewhere in the European Union (EU). Duties on alcohol products range widely from one to another. Mr Osborne froze tobacco and most alcohol duties in the June 2010 Budget, but in the March 2014 Budget it was announced that tobacco duty would rise annually by minimum of 2% above retail price index (RPI) inflation to end of next Parliament.
		General beer duty: £18.74 per hectolitre percentage (hect %) of alcohol, plus £8.62 per hect % for lower strength (1.2–2.8%) and £5.29 per hect % for high strength (over 7.5%)	
		Still cider and perry: £39.66 per 100 litres (1.2–7.5%) and £59.52 per 100l (7.5–8.5%)	
		Sparkling cider/perry: £39.66 (1.2–5.5%) and £264.61 (5.5–8.5%)	
		Wine: £84.21 per 100l (1.2–4%), £115.80 (4–5.5%), £273.31 (5.5–15%), and £364.37 (15–22%)	
		Sparkling wine: £264.41 per 100l (5.5–8.5%) and £350.07 (8.5–15%)	
		Spirits: £28.22 per 1l of pure alcohol	

(continued)

Table 7.2 *(continued)*

Name	How administered	Rates (2014–15)	Notes
Fuel duty	Additional tax added to VAT on motor fuel	Unleaded petrol, diesel, biodiesel, and bioethanol: 58p in £1 per litre since 23 March 2011	Petrol duties have also proved controversial in light of the increasing underlying price of fuel caused by an ongoing global peak oil crisis. In 2000, Mr Brown angered farmers and long-distance hauliers by raising fuel duty—and introducing an automatic annual rise known as the 'fuel tax escalator'—at a time of already rising petrol prices. In its last Budget, Labour announced that it was phasing in a proposed 'all-in-one-go' rise of nearly 3p a litre in three stages—in April 2010, October 2010, and December 2011—but in his June 2010 Budget, Mr Osborne announced no further rise in fuel duty (although motorists were still hit by an increase in VAT). He later cut duty by 1p in £1 in his March 2011 Budget and scrapped the escalator, with rises planned for January and September 2013 later cancelled.

 NOTE: A regularly updated version of this table can be found on the **Online Resource Centre**.

moved up the political agenda—following campaigns by groups such as UK Uncut and 38 Degrees highlighting the fact that the annual cost to the Exchequer of those at the top of the pile who abuse the tax system is anything up to 38 times as much as that of 'benefit fraud' (see Chapter 8, 'Jobseeker's Allowance (JSA)').

Major public spending announcements have historically been reserved for the Budget (see 'The Budget Speech' in this chapter), but in 1997 Mr Brown introduced an innovation designed to set out publicly his spending plans for three years at a time. Although keen to create the appearance of greater financial transparency, he also sought to encourage individual spending departments dependent on Treasury handouts to plan in a long-term way, rather than from year to year as previously. Spending reviews have generally been held on a three-yearly cycle ever since, with less frequent (but more far-reaching) **Comprehensive Spending Reviews (CSRs)** occurring so far on only three occasions (in 1998, 2007, and 2010).

Managing national debt

National debt—sometimes referred to as 'public', 'government', or 'sovereign' debt (see Chapter 9, 'The eurozone "sovereign debt crisis"')—is the total of all credit owed at any one time by every level of government (or government-owned institution) in a given state. Other than raising taxes, the principal way in which governments finance public spending is through borrowing. On a month-by-month basis, Chancellors run a **public sector net cash requirement** (**PSNCR**). Formerly the 'public sector borrowing requirement' (PSBR), this is effectively the difference between the total that ministers intend to spend on public services in a year and the amount available through taxation. To avoid unpopular tax rises or spending cuts, governments have historically favoured loans as a means of financing costly public expenditure. Usually, these are raised by selling bonds (known as 'gilt-edged securities', or 'gilts') to the public. These are effectively government 'IOUs', which are considered safe investments and yield steady interest payments—though far less lucrative ones than those yielded by many riskier stocks and shares. By borrowing from investors to maintain or increase spending, governments often run up short-term 'debts'—much like individuals using their bank overdrafts or credit cards. Overspends of this kind within a given financial year are known as 'annual deficits'.

Since a more 'monetarist' approach to running the economy was adopted in the 1980s (see 'The Bank of England's role in monetary policy' in this chapter), successive governments have made a virtue of trying to 'balance the books' within overall *economic cycles* (periods, usually of a few years, during which economies 'naturally' fluctuate between bouts of expansion and contraction) by reining in taxation and controlling spending. But the impact of the 2008 global financial collapse, ensuing recessions, and the 'eurozone' sovereign debt crisis changed this. In 2009–10, the last tax year before the 2010 election, government borrowing reached a peacetime record of £163.4 billion—*excluding* the cost of aid to the banking sector.

The principal debate in Britain since the Coalition came to power has centred on the state of the country's 'structural', rather than 'cyclical', deficit. The latter phenomenon—a familiar concept in most market economies—is the periodic budgetary overspend that most governments incur during periods of short-term economic turbulence (such as recessions). The former is deeper-rooted. It results from what the *Financial Times* describes as a 'fundamental imbalance in a government's receipts and expenditure, as opposed to one-off or short-term factors'. In other words, a structural deficit tends to emerge after a prolonged period during which governments have consistently spent more money than they raised through taxes and/or selling off assets—forcing them to borrow more (often at high commercial interest rates) to make up the difference.

When the Coalition took office, its ministers claimed that the 'black hole' in Britain's public finances—and the true size of its structural deficit—was even worse than previously feared. In his last Budget, Labour Chancellor Alistair Darling said that this overspend (estimated at around £77 billion of Britain's overall £167 billion deficit) had peaked at 8.4 per cent of gross domestic product (GDP) during 2009–10, and would fall to 2.5 per cent by 2014–15 on the back of a phased programme of £73 billion in spending cuts and tax rises. He repeated an earlier Labour pledge to halve the country's overall deficit within four years.

But neither Mr Darling's figures nor the speed of his response to Britain's debt crisis impressed the Conservatives. Delivering his own 'emergency' Budget barely two months later, Mr Osborne unveiled a swingeing package of austerity measures—principally a squeeze on social security benefits (see Chapter 8) and annual spending cuts of £40 billion by 2015, *in addition to* the billions earmarked by Labour. In so doing, he put departments other than those with previously ring-fenced front-line budgets on notice that their funding would fall by up to a quarter (later asking ministers to 'model' cuts of up to 40 per cent). By 2015–16, Mr Osborne predicted, the structural *current* deficit—the part of the structural deficit used to fund public sector running costs such as wages and maintenance, rather than capital investment—would enter a modest surplus, allowing him to start addressing Britain's overall national debt. Based on his Budget, the OBR predicted that this debt would peak at £70.3 billion in 2013–14—compared to the £74.9 billion anticipated for 2014–15 under Labour's plans. He was later forced to revise his timetable for eradicating the deficit, principally blaming the eurozone sovereign debt crisis for delaying it until at least 2017—two years after the 2015 election.

The fallout from Mr Osborne's rhetoric was significant. Given his repeated public pronouncement that 'we are all in this together', his contention that his Budget had been 'fair'—by, for example, raising the personal income tax allowance to £7,475, thus taking 900,000 low-paid workers out of tax altogether—was questioned as early as August 2010, when the independent Institute for Fiscal Studies (IFS) published an in-depth analysis of its likely impact on different income groups up to and including 2014. Branding the Budget 'clearly regressive', it claimed that the poorest tenth of households stood to lose 5 per cent of their incomes because of its measures, while non-pensioner households without children in the richest tenth would sacrifice less than 1 per cent. The IFS analysis—reflected in a similar assessment four months later when Mr Osborne slashed welfare further in his October CSR—prompted an unusual intervention by the director general of the Equality and Human Rights Commission, Neil Kingham, who publicly reminded ministers of their obligation under the Equality Act 2010 (passed months before Labour left office) to 'have due regard', before announcing Budget measures, to their likely impact on the disabled and other 'vulnerable groups'. He warned that the Commission might need to take 'enforcement action' if the Treasury could not prove that it had properly assessed the likely long-term fallout of the Budget against 'equality impact assessments'. Although no longer required by law, these are still observed by many public authorities prior to implementing new policy. The CSR itself went on to slash some £81 billion from public expenditure—the biggest cut by a

British government since the 1970s—and the Treasury itself estimated that nearly 500,000 public sector jobs would be lost as a result.

During acute economic crises, it has sometimes been necessary for governments to approach global financial institutions. In the mid-1970s, Mr Callaghan's Chancellor, Denis Healey, borrowed money from the International Monetary Fund (IMF)—a crisis bank that Britain had co-founded in the wake of the Second World War (see Chapter 10, 'The International Monetary Fund (IMF)')—to stabilize the economy as it was buffeted by stagflation (simultaneous rises in inflation and unemployment). The IMF agreed only on condition that the government made substantial public spending cuts to save money. Documents released by the National Archive in December 2006 under the '30-Year Rule' (see Chapter 20, 'Other sources of information—accessing historical records')—a convention stipulating that all but the most sensitive government papers should be made public 30 years after being written (a gift for journalists!)—revealed that Britain nearly had to scrap its nuclear deterrent simply to balance the books.

More recently, it emerged that the huge injections of extra funding into health and education under New Labour were financed largely by borrowing—meaning that even before it was forced into considering a multibillion-pound bailout for the banks, the government was accumulating a mounting structural deficit. According to figures released in 2008, having initially dropped sharply after the party returned to power in 1997, national debt more than doubled between 2001–02 and 2007–08, leaping from £315.5 billion to £650 billion. It rose by £100 billion in a single stroke when the government bailed out the Northern Rock bank to save its customers' deposits and restore confidence in the financial sector following its near-collapse in 2007. Northern Rock—which had overstretched itself by making high-risk home loans to customers who had no guaranteed means of repaying them—initially made an emergency plea for support to the Bank of England (reflecting trends in the US 'sub-prime market'—see 'The global banking crisis and its fallout' in this chapter). It was eventually nationalized as a 'temporary measure', after months of talks to find a private buyer failed, but in January 2012 Mr Osborne sold it to Virgin Money, for a mere £747 million—barely half the £1.4 billion that Labour had spent taking it into public ownership.

By the time Northern Rock was nationalized, the bill for propping it up had topped £100 billion (equivalent to the total annual spend on the NHS), and repaying Britain's national debt was costing taxpayers £31 billion a year in interest alone—marginally less than the country's defence budget. In July 2008, Mr Darling conceded that he was reviewing Mr Brown's fiscal 'Golden Rule': the principle, adhered to for a decade or more, that government should borrow only for *investment*, rather than *current spending*. In a swift move designed to signify that ministers had learned lessons from the Northern Rock debacle, in September 2008 Mr Darling nationalized the assets of another bank, Bradford & Bingley, to avert its collapse. While some critics immediately accused him and Mr Brown of again using taxpayers' money to secure irresponsible loans made by a reckless bank at the height of the credit boom, they were widely praised for some innovations, including the creation of a new Financial Services Compensation Scheme (FSCS). This effectively forced the banking sector as a whole to absorb Bradford & Bingley's losses, while still guaranteeing protection to those with savings up to an initial £31,700 (later to rise incrementally to £85,000 per investor per institution).

Towards the end of its 13-year rule, Labour reverted even more overtly to a Keynesian approach to buoying up the economy. As the recession bit, it committed itself to a 'fiscal stimulus' designed to limit job losses by boosting growth through strategic tax cuts (including a short-term cut in VAT—see Table 7.2) and increased public investment. The idea was that, by bringing forward capital projects originally earmarked for future years, the sharp decline in activity in the by then free-falling housing and small business sectors could be offset by the state directly keeping people in employment. Figures published by the Office for National Statistics (ONS) in July 2010 suggested that it might indeed have been the fiscal stimulus that hauled the British economy out of recession (growth reached 1.2 per cent in the second quarter).

At the height of the downturn, Labour also launched discrete initiatives to help those hit hardest. These included a Homeowner Mortgage Support Scheme, to give short-term financial aid to those with mortgages of up to £400,000 and savings of £16,000 or less who had lost their jobs, but expected to find work soon. Its aim was to avoid a repeat of the 1980s and 1990s recessions, during which home repossessions had soared. By 2010, there were indications that its impact had been positive: according to the Council of Mortgage Lenders (CML), while 46,000 homes were repossessed in 2009, this was only 61 per cent of the 75,500 seized by banks and building societies in 1991.

To stimulate a recovery in property and small business, the government began using its stake in the part-nationalized banks to nudge them into lending more money (at affordable rates) to consumers and struggling companies. An Asset Protection Scheme was also introduced to insure major British banks against potential losses caused by previous 'toxic debt' (see 'The global banking crisis and its fallout' in this chapter). At the same time, in a move unseen for decades, the Bank of England opted to use its own device to encourage more lending, pumping liquidity into the system by increasing the supply of sterling by boosting its own bank balance electronically: a process known as **quantitative easing (QE)**.

Briefly, QE involves central banks purchasing bonds or equities from retail banks, in so doing increasing the prices of those assets and reducing the interest rates payable on them. The effect of this (at least theoretically) is to help to 'recapitalize' banks, lowering overall interest rates in the economy and passing on these cheaper borrowing costs to ordinary customers, including individuals and businesses seeking loans for investment (by extension, boosting employment). In light of Britain's stalling recovery and subsequent slip back into recession, QE continued under the Coalition, but at time of writing it remained unclear how effective it had been, with some economists arguing that it had done little more than enable banks to shore up their own finances without passing on the benefits. Others predicted that QE could have the long-term effect of increasing inflation by leading to another consumer boom like those of the late 1980s and 2000s—concerns sharpened when the UK finally began emerging from recession in a sustained way in the last quarter of 2012, on the back of rising spending and a resurgent housing market.

Another recent tactic used by the Coalition to help small businesses secure the finance that they need to expand is 'credit easing'—the practice of the Treasury lending money, via banks, to companies with turnovers of up to £50 million at cut-price interest rates designed to lessen repayment costs. Mr Osborne initially released £5 billion of taxpayers' money over a six-month period at a rate 1 per cent below that commonly available commercially, with another £15 billion following over the ensuing 18 months. Participating banks included Royal Bank of Scotland (RBS), Lloyds, Barclays, Santander, and new specialist lender Aldermore.

Bond markets, borrowing costs, and the tyranny of 'credit ratings'

Just as individuals and companies have to be deemed 'creditworthy' to qualify for loans from financial institutions, so too do governments. An enduring principle underpinning the Coalition's fiscal squeeze has been its conviction that Britain must stand firm in its resolve to rebalance the nation's books—and that only by doing so will it reassure the all-important bond markets (pension funds, venture capitalists, and other institutional or individual investors) that 'UK plc' remains a safe haven for their money.

In addition, today's Chancellors are mindful of the ominous influence on the markets of *credit rating agencies*, the pronouncements of which can have the power of life and death over a state's long-term financial health. For some time, the three main agencies—Standard & Poor's, Fitch Ratings, and Moody's—continued to award Britain the maximum gold-starred 'triple-A' rating, ensuring that the interest rates the country was charged for borrowing remained low. However, in April 2013, Fitch caused a wobble in the markets by becoming the first agency to downgrade Britain's rating since 1978—reducing it to AA+ days after the IMF issued a pessimistic outlook for UK economic growth and warned Mr Osborne that he might need a 'plan B' to get it going. Ironically, a year later, with the long-awaited recovery gaining momentum, the IMF would warn of precisely the opposite risk to the economy—arguing that low productivity, combined with over-inflated house prices, could leave consumers more exposed to sudden income cuts and interest rate rises.

The Office for Budget Responsibility (OBR)

In a symbolic move intended to take responsibility for making medium- to longer-term economic forecasts out of the hands of politically motivated Chancellors, Mr Osborne introduced the **Office for Budget Responsibility (OBR)** in 2010. While the OBR gave a broad thumbs-up to the cutbacks and tax changes that he introduced to tackle Britain's deficit in his maiden Budget, one of its earliest pronouncements was remarkably positive about the economic competence of his predecessor. Although it revised down Mr Darling's predicted growth rates of 3 per cent or more from 2011 onwards (instead predicting fluctuations between 2.6 and 2.8 per cent), it revealed that surprisingly buoyant tax receipts in early 2010—boosted by the introduction of a (since abandoned) 50p top income tax rate—meant that government borrowing over the following five years was likely to be £22 billion less than he had warned. More directly embarrassing for the Coalition was the OBR's prediction in June 2010 that, by 2015, around 1.2 million fewer people would be employed across the public and private sectors (although ministers emphasized other figures suggesting that this could be offset by new job creation).

Controlling inflation and unemployment

When **inflation** is rising, unemployment tends to be low, and vice versa. Only usually at major crisis points—such as the 1930s Depression or late 1970s oil crash—do both rise noticeably at the same time. This is known as 'stagflation'.

The reasons for this trade-off relate to basic 'supply and demand' economics. When the prices of goods and services rise, this tends to mean one of two things: either demand for them is high ('demand-pull inflation') or the cost of producing them is rising ('cost-push inflation'). Demand-pull inflation comes about when shops and manufacturers find they can get away with charging more for goods and services, because rising disposable incomes mean that people are willing and able to pay. Cost-push inflation results from increasing production costs, often (but not always) resulting from mounting wage bills—in other words, more workers have been taken on to produce and deliver those goods and services, and/or their salaries have risen.

At times when demand for goods is falling, the first casualties tend to be workers employed to produce them. Employers lay off staff to cut running costs and enable them to stay in business on a more manageable scale, reducing prices to attract more custom if necessary. When such redundancies become more widespread, overall unemployment rises. And, of course, at times of high unemployment, people have less money to spend on goods and services—so prices will have to fall further if consumer demand is to be sustained.

Therefore rising unemployment tends to lead to falling inflation. A knock-on effect of this is a reduction in economic **growth**—the expansion of the economy through rising demand for goods and services, and increased private sector investment, job creation, and exports. Theoretically, growth is a virtuous circle: more jobs should mean more people with money to buy things, more companies manufacturing goods, and higher employment. In practice, the promotion of free trade has meant that many products British people buy today are cheap imports from the Far East and elsewhere—which means their purchase no longer necessarily leads to industrial expansion and job creation in Britain.

Given the tensile nature of this relationship between inflation and unemployment—referred to by economists as the 'inflation–unemployment see-saw'—governments find it difficult to keep a grip on both for very long. When Labour was elected in 1997, Mr Brown pledged to end 'boom and bust' by doing just this—words that returned to haunt him years later. Despite the fact that Britain proceeded to enjoy a further decade of sustained growth under his stewardship, two years after he became prime minister the economy slumped into its first recession for nearly 20 years.

The Bank of England's role in monetary policy

If fiscal policy was the favoured approach to keeping Britain's economy afloat in the 1950s and 1960s, 'monetary policy' has been the vogue since the 1980s. Widely credited as the 'invention' of free market US economist Milton Friedman (a hero of Mrs Thatcher's), the contrasting approach to economic management favoured by monetarism involves **interest rates**—the cost of borrowing money—being used to direct consumer behaviour and control inflation. The theory is that if rates rise, people will be more likely to *save* (banks and building societies should be offering them profitable returns for their investment) and less likely to borrow or spend (credit cards and loans cost more).

In Britain, inflation is calculated monthly. The government uses two tools to measure it: the **retail price index (RPI)** and the **consumer price index (CPI)**. Both track movements in the prices of notional 'baskets' of 650-odd items bought regularly by 'typical' households—including food, clothing, and tobacco. The difference between the two is that CPI—the measure preferred by governments and the European Central Bank (see Chapter 9, 'The launch of the euro and growth of the eurozone')—*excludes* housing costs such as Council Tax and mortgage rates, while 'core CPI' (also often quoted) omits day-to-day expenses, including food and energy bills. Both place more emphasis on goods that people buy only occasionally—for example DVD players and other electronic products. Given that routine purchases such as food and utilities are the costs that most burden households, critics view CPI as highly misleading. Nonetheless, the use of these statistics enabled Labour to maintain low rates of both 'headline' (CPI) and 'underlying' inflation (CPI adjusted to exclude volatile items, such as tax rises) on the whole, even when the RPI figures cited by the Opposition and some economists rose.

Until 1997, responsibility for reviewing interest rates monthly rested with the Chancellor. Within days of taking that job, however, Mr Brown made the **Bank of England** independent—handing it the task of controlling inflation on his behalf. Decisions about interest rates have since rested with the **Monetary Policy Committee (MPC)**, composed of nine members, including the bank's chief economist, and chaired by its governor. The government sets an inflation target—currently 2 per cent—and if this is missed by more than one CPI percentage point, the governor must write to the Chancellor explaining why and setting out the action that the MPC intends to take to lower it. In April 2007, Mervyn King became the first incumbent to have to do this, when headline inflation hit 3.1 per cent. For several years, until May 2012, when inflation finally fell back to 3 per cent for the first time in nine quarters, this was a monthly ritual.

The quest for full employment

Successive Chancellors, particularly Labour ones, have dreamed of the holy grail of 'full employment'—an ideal state in which everyone capable of work can find a sustainable job—and in April 2014 Mr Osborne surprised many by committing himself to this goal. In practice, though, it remains elusive.

At certain times, unemployment has reached levels that have been politically damaging for governments. In the early 1980s, Mrs Thatcher's mass closure of coal pits, steelworks, and shipyards in northern England, Wales, and Scotland, combined with her crackdown on trades union power (see 'The government's role in industrial relations' in this chapter), saw the national jobless total rise to between 3 and 4 million. While Labour largely maintained a much lower official unemployment rate—using a combination of 'carrot' and 'stick' policies, such as tax credits and its 'New Deal' to entice people off benefits and back to work—nationwide unemployment still hovered above 1.5 million, even before the recession pushed it nearer 2.5 million. Moreover, there has been huge criticism of the increasing 'casualization' of Britain's working environment, with many new jobs created since the early 1990s taking the form of part-time and/or short-term contracts devoid of the entitlements (for example pensions, holiday pay) available to full-time, permanent staff.

Despite remaining stubbornly high for the first three years of the Coalition—not least because thousands of public sector jobs were axed as a result of austerity cuts—officially, unemployment has since fallen. Although it had topped 2.65 million by April 2012, from that point it began to drop. By March 2014, the headline rate was down to 2.2 million—a five-year low and 133,000 down on the previous three months. However, the number of 16–24-year-olds out of work remains a cause for particular concern: while significantly lower than the symbolic 1 million mark—which it had reached for the first time in 2011—the youth unemployment rate remained alarmingly high, at 868,000.

Promoting growth and UK exports

If one word strikes terror into the hearts of prime ministers and Chancellors it is **recession**—the term denoting two successive economic quarters (three-month periods) in which the economy 'shrinks'. Such bouts of negative growth generally lead to less money being borrowed and spent by consumers, lower sales and profits for businesses, reduced production, and redundancies. Britain has lived through three recent recessions: in the early 1980s, early 1990s, and from April 2008 to December 2009. A further period of stalling or negative growth, in 2012, was for many months recorded as a slip into a second post-crash recession (dubbed a 'double-dip'), but in June 2013 revised figures from the ONS showed the economy was actually flat, rather than falling, in the first three months of that year. By 2014, annual growth had bounced back to 2.9 per cent, making Britain's the fastest growing major economy.

In light of the consequences of recessions (rising unemployment, and falling consumer spending and business investment), it is little wonder that governments are so obsessed with achieving growth. Indeed, a report published in June 2014 in the *British Journal of Psychiatry* suggested that the scale of the most recent recession was so great, and detrimental to so many individuals and families, that up to 10,000 people committed suicide across Europe and North America because of its negative effect on their lives. Two engines are traditionally used to achieve growth: boosting employment and, by extension, domestic demand; and developing overseas export markets for products manufactured at home. In theory, each should lead to wealth creation.

This chapter has already examined the inflation–unemployment conundrum and how British governments try to boost the economy by juggling these 'twin evils'. But how do they promote Britain's exports abroad—and measure their success or failure in doing so? Taking the latter question first, there are two measures:

- the **balance of trade**—the annual difference in value between the total of all goods and services bought by British residents from overseas (imports) and all UK-made products sold abroad (exports), which encompasses 'visible' items (physical goods, such as food, clothes, and televisions) and 'invisible' ones (virtual goods, including legal and financial services); and

- the **balance of payments**—the difference in value between the total of *all* payments flowing between Britain and other countries, including financial transfers and debt payments to foreigners, which means that the measure is therefore a 'subset' of the balance of payments.

If, in a given financial year, Britain purchases more foreign imports than it exports overseas, its current account (the balance between money coming into the country and going out) is in *deficit*. If it sells more abroad than it buys in, it is in *surplus*—a much healthier economic state.

Recent decades—particularly since Britain joined the European Union (EU) (see Chapter 9)—have seen it importing disproportionate quantities of cheap foreign clothing, toys, electrical items, and motor vehicles. The slow decline of indigenous industries such as shipbuilding and coalmining, meanwhile, has seen the country's economic output switch to services including telecommunications, information technology (IT), and finance. As a result, while Britain has historically had a significant balance of trade deficit in visible items, its service sector has often generated a surplus.

In addition to the balances of trade and payments, there are two other 'litmus tests' of economic growth:

- **gross domestic product (GDP)**—the market value of all goods and services produced within Britain annually, regardless of which country derives income from them (sometimes referred to as 'national output'); and
- **gross national product (GNP)**—the market value of all goods and services produced by British-owned companies, labour, and property each year, irrespective of where those assets are based (sometimes referred to as 'national income').

It has become customary for governments to cite favourable GDP as evidence of strong economic performance. In reality, however, while high GDP should reduce unemployment (a foreign-owned company on UK soil is as likely to create jobs and consumer spending as a British one), this is only part of the picture. Most income generated by foreign-owned companies flows back to the countries in which they are headquartered, limiting the longer-term benefits to the British economy brought by overseas businesses that locate here. Therefore GNP may often give a truer indication of levels of wealth generation for 'UK plc': the numerous British-based banks and telecoms firms that have recently outsourced call centres to the Far East, where labour costs are cheaper, may do little to help Britain's employment figures, but much of their income returns to the Treasury.

The Budget process

The highlight of the Treasury's calendar is the **Budget**. This used to take place in autumn, but is now held each spring. In addition, Mr Brown introduced an annual Pre-Budget Report (PBR, also known as the 'Pre-Budget' or 'Autumn Statement'), which has since been delivered each October or November. This was initially intended simply to set the scene for prospective tax and spending plans to be announced in the Budget, acting as a 'health check' on the performance of Britain's economy over the preceding 12 months. More recently, it has become almost as much of a media event as the Budget itself—with Chancellors making increasingly firm policy announcements and using these as opportunities to test public opinion on changes that they are considering.

The Budget itself has two elements: the Budget Speech/Statement and the Finance Act.

The Budget Speech

The Budget Speech is designed to:

- forecast short- to medium-term movements in the economy (one to three years) and review its performance in the preceding 12 months;
- announce rises or cuts in direct and indirect taxation and public spending, and prioritize particular areas over others (for example health, education, defence);
- announce new taxes, tax breaks, and/or benefits to finance investment or help low-income groups (for example tax credits, cold weather payments for the elderly); and
- give the Chancellor a platform for political grandstanding—allowing him or her to boast about the country's economic performance.

The Speech—which regularly runs for around an hour—is immediately followed by a similarly lengthy retort from the Leader of the Opposition (the Shadow Chancellor has his or her chance the following evening on national television) and a debate in the Commons. More than 150 years after the event, William Gladstone holds the dubious honour of having delivered the longest ever continuous Budget Speech: his 1853 address lasted four hours and 45 minutes.

The Finance Act

For measures announced in the Budget to be implemented, the Commons must legislate. Unlike most laws, however, the Bill needed to deliver the proposals is given swift passage and substantially passed on the same day as the Speech. Dubbed the 'Finance Bill', it is automatically designated a 'money Bill' by the Speaker—enabling it to bypass the usual stages that Bills must negotiate before receiving royal assent (see Chapter 2, Table 2.7). The initial 'stages' are effectively gone through in one go, with the Speech itself treated as the first reading. The Commons must pass individual resolutions to approve each specific tax or duty change within 10 sitting days, but, under the Collection of Taxes Act 1968, minor changes can be agreed immediately—enabling government business to continue in the interim. A second reading must be heard within 30 days, but the committee stage may be split, with more important resolutions heard by a committee of the whole house and remaining ones considered by a standing committee of 30–40 members of Parliament (MPs). Following this, the third reading will be steamrollered through, usually on the second day of the report stage.

Since the confrontation between the Commons and House of Lords over Lloyd George's 1909 'People's Budget' (see Chapter 2, 'What is the point of the Lords?'), there has been no Lords stage to the Finance Bill. Nonetheless, even today there is scope for Budgets to fall at a late hurdle. The row over Labour's abolition of the 10p starting rate of income tax so raised the hackles of backbench rebels led by former Welfare Minister Frank Field that, before announcing a compensation package for low earners penalized by the change, it looked as if Mr Darling's first Budget (in 2008) might be defeated, forcing his resignation. In the event, he staved off this prospect by issuing an 'emergency Budget' designed to compensate the losers—some of whom stood to be £230 a year worse off. If Mr Darling's 2008 Budget proved a political minefield, so did Mr Osborne's third. Over a period of three months or more after his March 2012 Commons speech, several provisions in the accompanying Finance Bill unravelled—with ministers performing a succession of U-turns over controversial measures ranging from a tabloid-christened 'granny tax' (proposed cuts to the personal tax allowance for those aged over 65), to a 'pasty tax' on hot takeaway snacks. The slew of policy reversals led to the Budget memorably being dubbed an 'omnishambles' by Labour leader Ed Miliband—a reference to a term coined by fictional spin doctor Malcolm Tucker in BBC sitcom *The Thick of It*.

Public spending outside England—the Barnett Formula

To ensure that Scotland, Wales, and Northern Ireland benefit fairly from central government tax revenues, public spending is allocated on a per capita basis across Britain, using a system called the 'Barnett Formula'. In theory, the formula—devised in the late 1970s by then Labour Chief Secretary to the Treasury Joel (the late Lord) Barnett—ensures that the amount given to each country corresponds to its population size (and, by definition, the extent to which its inhabitants contribute to taxes).

In practice, the formula remains controversial: successive recalculations have disproportionately benefited Scotland and the distribution of funding has moved increasingly out of step with levels of economic need in different parts of Britain. Resentment between Scotland and England, in particular, has escalated since devolution was introduced in 1998, because not only has Holyrood continued to do disproportionately well out of taxes, but also the Scottish Parliament has used its freedom to spend its share of the money, to subsidize its public sector in ways unseen elsewhere. Barnett enabled Scotland to reject university tuition fees (for the time being) and phase out NHS prescription charges—two highly controversial levies that remain in England.

The formula returned to the forefront of political debate in the aftermath of the 2014 Scottish referendum: in the final weeks of the campaign, spooked by opinion polls suggesting that independence supporters could be poised for a historic victory, Westminster's main party leaders tacitly agreed to preserve it indefinitely (much to the dismay of many English MPs, not to mention the Welsh Government).

▶ The government's role in promoting industry and commerce

For the past 30 years, British governments have taken an increasingly laissez-faire approach to 'running' the economy. The mass privatization programme of the 1980s saw a swathe of industries sold into private ownership, from motor manufacturer British Leyland to British Airways, British Steel, all major utilities (gas, electricity, water), and ultimately the railways (see 'The utilities' in this chapter). In the decades since, the mantra has been one of 'consumer choice', with successive governments promoting competition between rival private sector providers over any state monopoly. In theory, this allows people to shop around for the best deals on virtually any product—with market forces (supply and demand) ensuring their quality and competitive pricing.

In practice, however, the government continues to play an interventionist role in promoting British industry and protecting it from the worst ravages of **globalization**—the process by which national economies are becoming increasingly interdependent. Recent decisions by ministers to shore up failing banks and broker rescue packages for car manufacturers, including Nissan (which received £6.2 million from the Coalition's Regional Growth Fund for its Sunderland plant in November 2011) and Rover (the last surviving British-owned motor company until its collapse in 2005), have demonstrated this. Moreover, the free market ideal of a private sector that, left alone, will 'regulate itself' efficiently and fairly has proved elusive—forcing the state to introduce greater regulation.

The Department for Business, Innovation, and Skills (BIS)

The department responsible for promoting and regulating British industry and commerce, BIS, was known as the Department for Business, Enterprise, and Regulatory Reform (BERR) under Mr Brown. Before that, it was, variously, the Department of Trade and Industry (DTI), the Department of Trade, and the Board of Trade.

The Department's website describes it as 'the voice for business across government'. It is responsible for:

- creating conditions for business success and raising productivity in the UK economy;
- championing the interests of employees and employers;
- promoting consumer interests; and
- encouraging sustainable business development.

Although formal regulation of the business environment is delegated to various non-departmental bodies, when BERR replaced the DTI under Labour, its Secretary of State began to play a more hands-on role than previously. In January 2009, then Business Secretary Lord Mandelson tried to jump-start Britain's ailing car industry by pledging £2.3 billion in loan guarantees—including £1.3 billion from the European Investment Bank—for motor manufacturers prepared to invest in 'high technology' and green alternatives to conventional engines. BERR was proactive in enforcing regulatory judgments, too. In 2008, Lord Mandelson's predecessor, John Hutton, publicly ordered BSkyB, the satellite broadcaster part-owned by Rupert Murdoch's multinational media company News Corp, to sell more than half its shares in rival company ITV. He was endorsing a ruling by the then Competition Commission (see 'The Competition and Markets Authority' in this chapter) that the shareholding represented 'a substantial lessening of competition' in the television market.

As well as overseeing the regulatory framework, it is the Business Secretary's job to liaise regularly with the main bodies representing employees and employers: the Trades Union Congress (TUC) (see 'The government's role in industrial relations' in this chapter) and the Confederation of British Industry (CBI), respectively.

Regulatory authorities

While BIS drafts laws governing fair competition, consumer protection, and sustainable business, for years these were administered by two principal regulatory authorities: the Office of Fair Trading (OFT) and the Competition Commission. In April 2014, the two bodies were merged to form one overarching new regulator: the **Competition and Markets Authority (CMA)**.

The Competition and Markets Authority (CMA)

Established in 1973, the OFT was charged with ensuring that the 'rules' of fair play—genuine choice and competition—were applied in practice. Its founding remit was to protect both consumers and companies, shielding small businesses from anti-competitive practices by larger, more established rivals. Until 2003, it was headed by a Director General of Fair Trading (later replaced by a board and chairperson). For its part, the Competition Commission (formerly the Monopolies and Mergers Commission) was less concerned with the day-to-day market practices preoccupying the OFT than with movements in company ownership that might affect *future* competition. Although most markets are now 'deregulated'—open to full free market competition—in practice this has led to consolidations of ownership, with bigger, more profitable, companies taking over or merging with smaller ones. As a result, markets that once offered dozens of alternatives from which consumers could choose are increasingly dominated by a handful of providers—and sometimes only one or two. High-profile interventions to prevent the emergence of 'monopolies'—defined as the point at which one company secures more than a 25 per cent market share in a particular market—included the Commission's decision to approve supermarket chain Morrisons' takeover of rival Safeway in 2003 only on condition that it first sold 53 stores in areas in which local competition might otherwise suffer.

The remits of both the Commission and OFT have now been assumed by the Competition and Markets Authority (CMA), which vets prospective mergers or takeovers and polices companies' competitive behaviour on a daily basis.

With a mission statement to 'promote competition for the benefit of consumers, both within and outside the UK', the CMA's duties are to:

- investigate mergers that could restrict competition;
- conduct market studies and investigations where there may be competition and consumer problems;
- investigate where there may be breaches of UK/EU prohibitions against anti-competitive agreements and abuses of dominant positions;
- bring criminal proceedings against individuals who commit cartel offences;
- enforce consumer protection legislation to tackle practices and market conditions that make it difficult for consumers to exercise choice;
- cooperate with other regulators and encourage them to use their competition powers; and
- consider regulatory references and appeals.

To take some recent examples of alleged market abuses, supermarket chains have repeatedly been accused of unfair trading in relation to the prices that they pay their suppliers. Both Tesco and Asda have been accused of offering below-cost-price payment to producers in developing countries for everything from bananas to coffee, while British farmers have complained of similar treatment in relation to their meat and dairy products. The appalling press generated by such controversies has prompted retailers to embrace 'fair trade' goods and to invest millions in corporate social responsibility (CSR) programmes.

Of course, it is not only other businesses that are hurt by such restrictive practices; it is often consumers who suffer most. In December 2007, following an OFT investigation, Asda and Sainsbury's admitted having conspired to fix the price of milk. The supermarkets charged inflated prices for the product—despite offering farmers minimal payment—and British consumers were left £270 million out of pocket.

It was in the spirit of acting as a 'consumer champion' that the CMA mounted one of its first high-profile market interventions, in July 2014, recommending a full-scale competition inquiry into the provision of current and business accounts by the high-street banking sector.

Regulating the financial markets

In 1997, a separate regulator was set up to oversee the financial services sector—banks, building societies, and insurance companies—assuming responsibilities previously held by the Bank of England. But the effectiveness of this body, the Financial Services Authority (FSA), was called into question following its failure to act on the banking sector's increasingly cavalier mortgage lending policies prior to the collapse of Northern Rock and wider banking crisis (see 'The global banking crisis and its fallout' in this chapter). Following Labour's multibillion-pound bailout of the banks—and the soaring structural deficit that resulted—the party was condemned for adopting such 'light touch' financial regulation. Another criticism concerned the 'tripartite' nature of the regulatory regime that it had introduced—effectively splitting responsibilities for policing banking between the FSA, the Bank of England, and HM Treasury, and creating confusion over which should intervene and when. In truth, introducing the FSA had slightly tightened the regulatory framework, compared to the laissez-faire regime ushered in by Margaret Thatcher's 'Big Bang' deregulation of the City on 27 October 1986. Nonetheless, it has fallen to the Coalition to toughen up banking regulation for the future, by dividing the FSA's responsibilities between three new authorities. These bodies, which together replaced the FSA as of 1 April 2013, are:

- the **Financial Conduct Authority (FCA)**, which polices the overall conduct of every financial company authorized to provide services to the public and maintains the overall integrity of UK money markets;

- the **Prudential Regulatory Authority (PRA)**, a subsidiary of the Bank of England set up to prevent financial companies—from banks and building societies, to insurers and brokers—taking imprudent risks with their investors' money; and

- the **Financial Policy Committee (FPC)**, another new division of the Bank of England, modelled in composition on the MPC. Charged with identifying potential financial and macroeconomic risks to the stability of Britain's economy and, where possible, taking pre-emptive action to avert them, it started work a year earlier than the other two, in March 2012.

Types of company

There are three main types of UK corporate structure:

- the limited liability company (Ltd);
- the private limited company; and
- the public limited company (plc).

The principal differences between the three are explained in Table 7.3.

The role of the London Stock Exchange (LSE)

Shares in plcs are traded on global stock markets, one of the biggest being the London Stock Exchange (LSE). Established in 1760, when 150 brokers expelled from the Royal Exchange for rowdiness formed a spontaneous share-trading club at Jonathan's Coffee House, it registered as a private limited company in 1986, and finally as a plc in 2000. Like all plcs, the LSE is susceptible to potential takeover. In 2004, it became the first stock market to be targeted by a prospective purchaser when it faced an £822 million hostile bid from little-known Swedish company the OM Group, a technology manufacturer that runs the Swedish Stock Exchange. Four years later, the LSE's shareholders rejected a £1.35 billion offer by its German rival, Deutsche Börse.

Table 7.3 Types of UK company

Type of company	Definition
Limited liability companies (Ltds)	Common form of small and medium-sized enterprise (SME) (small business). Introduced to provide security for individuals who would otherwise shoulder the whole risk associated with running own businesses, it provides statutory guarantees not enjoyed by larger companies. Limited companies—including theatres, charities, and voluntary trusts—allocate 'liability' (risk) to investors only to the value of a nominal sum (usually £1) agreed when they initially sign company's 'original memorandum' and 'articles of association'.
Private limited companies	Again, usually SMEs, these cannot issue shares to public. Liability of individual investors for shortfalls/debts is limited to the nominal value of shares with which they are initially issued.
Public limited companies (plcs)	Have at least two shareholders and may offer shares to public. Owners 'float' them and they are listed on London Stock Exchange (LSE). Shareholders usually receive annual 'loyalty payments' (dividends) and can vote on certain aspects of company policy/strategic direction. Enterprise and Regulatory Reform Bill 2012 gave shareholders in UK-quoted companies 'binding rights' to reject executive pay deals, following grass-roots rebellions against boards of banks and other firms in 2012. Plcs must have issued shares to a value of £50,000 before being allowed to trade. Larger plcs are often referred to as 'blue-chip' companies (those generally considered 'reliable' investments), and include BP and Marks and Spencer.

Today, the LSE has regional bases in Belfast, Birmingham, Glasgow, Leeds, and Manchester. Some 2,600 UK and overseas companies are listed on it at any time, and shares are traded electronically via a computerized system called 'CREST'. Minute-by-minute movements in share prices of listed companies are tracked by a series of nine indices, collectively known as the 'Financial Times Stock Exchange' ('FTSE', or 'Footsie'). Most famous is the **FT100 Share Index**, which lists the 100 highest-valued companies in order of value and monitors movements in their share prices. The FT All-Share Index, meanwhile, lists all companies on the stock market, again in order.

Numerous factors can impact on company share prices. Mergers and take-overs—or the mere prospect of them—can send prices soaring or crashing, according to the market's assessment of how favourable such outcomes are for a firm's commercial fortunes. Shares in iconic high-street companies such as Tesco and Marks and Spencer (M&S), meanwhile, are notoriously prone to fluc-tuations, depending on the movements of senior personnel, and the state of their sales and profits—particularly at Christmas.

Often, companies' share prices suffer because of factors beyond their con-trol. Amid growing suspicions among share traders that the 1980s stock market bubble was about to burst, 'Black Monday' on 1 October 1987 saw the biggest one-day crash in history. Within the month, LSE shares alone had plummeted by 26.4 per cent.

As well as the LSE, London also boasts an Alternative Investment Market (AIM), launched in 1995, on which shares in smaller developing companies, ethical traders, and/or those whose value has fallen so low that they have decid-ed to 'delist' from the FTSE are traded. Sometimes, the trend goes in reverse: when The Body Shop™ was acquired by French cosmetics giant L'Oréal in 2006, it moved from the AIM to FTSE.

The global banking crisis and its fallout

After years of unsustainable growth in the mortgage sector and the credit mar-ket as a whole, autumn 2008 witnessed the biggest global financial meltdown since the 1929 Wall Street Crash and the ensuing Great Depression. Eighteen months after the term 'sub-prime' had first seeped into the mainstream media—referring to 'toxic' loans made by US banks to people with limited means and poor credit records, many of whom subsequently defaulted—major financial institutions from Europe to the Far East were brought to their knees by the knock-on effects of these and similar practices elsewhere. In the end, the posi-tion of household-name banks, from Merrill Lynch to Barclays, became so per-ilous that governments in Britain, the United States, and mainland Europe were forced into doing what the long-standing 'neoliberal' consensus would previ-ously have deemed unthinkable: pouring vast sums of money into the sector to shore up savings and pensions, and to keep the institutions afloat. But even this was not enough and, before long, Mr Brown's government was leading the way by going a stage further—taking controlling stakes in several major high-street banks. After decades of runaway privatization and deregulation, the term 'nationalization' re-entered the political lexicon.

The escalating financial crisis came to a head in late September 2008 when, within a week, investment bank Lehman Brothers filed for bankruptcy, Merrill Lynch was taken over by the Bank of America, and the US Federal Reserve Bank (the US equivalent of the Bank of England) announced a US $85 billion rescue package and effective nationalization of the country's biggest insurance firm, AIG. Within a fortnight, an even bigger collapse occurred, when Washington Mutual—the largest US mortgage lender—was shut down by regulators and sold to JPMorgan Chase. To prevent other financial giants facing a similar fate, the White House administration was left battling to force a $700 billion rescue package for the country's entire banking sector through a Congress furious at the conduct of reckless bankers.

In Britain, even more dramatic state interventions followed. Barely a week after Lloyds TSB stepped in to announce a buyout of Halifax Bank of Scotland (HBOS), one of biggest mortgage lenders, ministers nationalized the bulk of Bradford & Bingley's assets, while selling off its branches and savings operation to Spanish bank Santander. The Treasury then moved to guarantee all deposits in UK banks of up to an initial £31,700, to prevent a 'run on the banks'— that is, the mass withdrawal of savings by panicked investors worried about losing their money if institutions were to collapse.

Then, on 8 October, amid feverish rumours and jittery fluctuations on the stock market, Messrs Brown and Darling announced details of a £500 billion bailout for the UK's banking sector, which would see up to eight high-street banks and building societies part-nationalized in a last-ditch attempt to persuade institutions to resume lending to each other and—more importantly for the 'real economy'—their customers. While only Lloyds TSB, HBOS, and RBS (shares in which had plummeted) initially accepted the government's offer— other major banks such as Barclays opting to raise capital on the open market—the price paid by these institutions for their cut of the 'final' £37 billion Treasury share offer was significant. First, the FSA ordered the government to acquire both 'preference shares' (which give shareholders priority in receiving dividends, but no voting rights) and 'ordinary' ones (allowing ministers a direct say in running the companies). Second, it emerged that the government would be appointing its own directors to the banks' boards and that no bonuses would be paid to senior staff for at least the first year. This latter measure went some way towards allaying mounting public outrage at the scale of the 'bonus culture' fostered during the boom years, with directors often pocketing multi-million-pound perks irrespective of how well their companies were performing. The government replaced several leading bankers at the helm of semi-nationalized institutions, including RBS chief executive Sir Fred 'the

Shred' Goodwin, whose nickname derived from his reputation as a ruthless cost-cutter (and whose knighthood was rescinded in 2012). Royal Bank of Scotland was 60 per cent nationalized, while the state took a 41 per cent stake in Lloyds TSB and HBOS.

In the same tumultuous week, Mr Brown entered a public row with Iceland after several of its leading banks collapsed like dominoes, and it emerged that dozens of British councils, charities, universities, and other bodies had substantial sums invested in them. When Iceland's Prime Minister Geir Haarde announced that he was guaranteeing the safety of all Icelanders' deposits, but not those of Britons, Mr Brown risked international condemnation by using anti-terror legislation to freeze the £7 billion in assets held in Britain by Landsbanki, the country's national bank, to recoup some of the costs (see also Chapter 12, 'The annual budget timetable at local level').

The aftermath of the banking crisis, and its ongoing impact on Britain's public finances, saw Opposition politicians and media commentators pour scorn on City traders and demand firm action to ensure that there could be no repeat of the reckless practices that led to the near-collapse of so many institutions. Vocal critics included future Lib Dem Business Secretary Vince Cable, who ridiculed what he saw as Mr Darling's ineffectual response—a call for international action to impose strict new trading conditions on the banking sector and a one-off 50 per cent tax on bonuses of £25,000-plus that was levied only in April 2010 (although it raised £2.3 billion). However, once in office, the Coalition wavered in its professed determination to make the sector pay for its past errors: Mr Osborne initially imposed only a modest levy on the banks, based on their overall balance sheets rather than individuals' bonuses. Since then, debate has raged over how best to deter future rogue practices and ensure that the big banks saved by taxpayer-funded bailouts make fair reparations for wrongdoing. Agreement has been even slower coming over the various proposals for some form of levy on banking transactions, or a 'Robin Hood Tax'. The EU came close to adopting a Union-wide financial transaction tax (FTT), modelled on an idea first proposed by Nobel Laureate James Tobin. Its sister plan for a European Fiscal Compact (see Chapter 9, 'The eurozone "sovereign debt crisis"')—approved by all member states but Britain and the Czech Republic in March 2012—has required signatory countries to commit to maintaining national budget surpluses or balanced accounts since 1 January 2013. Mr Cameron's rationale for opting out of this deal remains that it could have a disproportionate impact on the City. While Labour has failed to commit to signing up if it returns to power, the party has repeatedly stated that it would make Britain's own bankers' tax an annual levy—using its proceeds to finance a new compulsory jobs guarantee scheme for young unemployed people.

In 2013, Mr Cable finally went some way to implementing the Lib Dems' pre-election pledge to 'break up' bigger banks into separate retail and investment arms, to stop ordinary customers ever again being exposed to the perils of high-stakes risk-taking. Following publication of a report by an Independent Commission on Banking (ICB), headed by economist Sir John Vickers, and a Treasury White Paper setting out concrete proposals for restructuring the sector, the Banking Reform Act 2013 enshrined in law three key principles relating to the future structure and governance of banking:

- that high-street banks were to be kept separate from investment banks;
- that, in the event of a bank's 'failure', its investors, rather than taxpayers, would be responsible for bailing it out; and
- that the first compensation paid out to anyone in such circumstances would be full refunds of savers' deposits.

Short-selling, interest-rate 'fixes', and wider questions about banking

Another scandal that emerged at the height of the financial crisis was the widespread practice of 'short-selling'. This shady form of stock market speculation involves seasoned speculators gambling on the fortunes of ailing companies by 'borrowing' from third parties shares in those that they expect to fall in value, selling them on, and then buying them back after their price has plummeted, before returning them to their original owner for a profit. The FSA introduced a short-term ban on this practice at the height of the banking crisis and it was later unilaterally outlawed in Germany. But in June 2012, under pressure from City-based lobbyists, UK ministers filed a lawsuit to the European Court of Justice (ECJ) challenging EU plans to empower the European Securities and Markets Authority (ESMA) to ban short-selling across the Union.

Just when the spectre of 'casino banking' finally seemed to have been banished, a major new scandal erupted. This time, the initial culprit identified was Barclays, which in June 2012 was fined £291 million by the FSA and US Department of Justice for repeatedly lying about the twin interest rates that it paid to borrow money from other institutions: the so-called London Interbank Offered Rate (Libor) and the Euro Interbank Offered Rate (Euribor). The investigation found that, from 2005, individual traders working for Barclays Capital repeatedly lied for personal gain, by claiming that rates were higher than they actually were, while at the height of the 2008 crisis their managers ordered them to make out that the bank was paying *less* than it was (a tactic known as 'low-balling'), to improve its balance sheets and reduce the rates that it was charged elsewhere. It appeared to many that Barclays had deliberately misrepresented its borrowing rates to avert its collapse and/or nationalization by the then Labour government. The scandal claimed the scalp of, among others, Barclays' chief executive Bob Diamond, although he denied any knowledge of or involvement in the Libor deceptions. The Libor scandal continues to rumble, though, with Britain's Serious Fraud Office (SFO) charging three former Barclays traders (all US-based) with conspiracy to defraud in April 2014. At time of writing, a trial date had yet to be set.

Two separate government inquiries were subsequently launched into rate-fixing: the first, by the FCA, into the operation of Libor; and the second, a parliamentary probe by MPs and peers fronted by Andrew Tyrie, chairman of the Treasury Committee. And, in June 2014, the SFO entered the fray, hinting that it might follow its US counterpart by launching a full criminal inquiry, based on initial findings by an international team set up in 2012 to probe up to 20 other institutions potentially involved in fixing Libor rates. Meanwhile, in June 2012, yet another dubious banking practice was exposed, with the FSA announcing that it had reached settlements with Barclays, HSBC, Lloyds, and RBS over its demands for 'redress' for their 'serious failings' in mis-selling specialist insurance to companies seeking to protect themselves against rising interest rates. Then, two years later, a further scandal broke, when it emerged that 15 leading banks were being investigated over allegations that their employees had been involved in rigging prices on the foreign exchange market (Forex), on which banks buy and sell currencies to each other. It was alleged that traders from rival institutions had colluded to set benchmark exchange rates at 4 p.m. each day, rather than operating independently in a competitive market. In November 2014, six banks were fined a total of £2.6 billion by the British and US regulators for the actions of rogue currency dealers on their payrolls.

On a more positive note, the Coalition has proceeded with plans for a **Green Investment Bank** originally announced in Mr Darling's last Budget. Labour envisaged the bank—to be backed by £2 billion in combined public and private sector cash—as an engine for investment in green energy projects and high-speed rail links. Based in Edinburgh and backed by an initial capitalization fund of £3 billion, the bank opened for business in November 2012. Its stated mission is to invest in environmentally sustainable infrastructure projects—addressing private sector market failures, and achieving a so-called 'double bottom line' that will both innovate in green technologies and generate profits.

▮ The government's role in industrial relations

In the 1960s and 1970s, when many industries were still state-owned, battles between government and trades unions over wages policy, working conditions, and their ability to take industrial action when relations broke down were frequently in the news. After years of struggle between unions and employers, and growing infighting in the Labour movement, tensions exploded during the 1978–79 'Winter of Discontent'—a prolonged period of wildcat action (sudden walk-outs) during which, at one point, even funerary workers joined the mêlée.

Hand in hand with its mass privatization programme, Mrs Thatcher's government introduced swingeing clampdowns on the rights of workers to take industrial action. Legal barriers were introduced to block strikes, while the new generation of private sector employers with which unions were now confronted no longer even had to 'recognize' their existence—let alone formally negotiate with them over job cuts or changing working practices. Mrs Thatcher also ended:

- 'the closed shop'—a rule forcing employees in certain trades or industries to join specific unions; and
- 'secondary picketing'—the ability of workers in trades *related* to others in dispute with their employers to take 'sympathy action'.

Although both the above remain illegal, when Labour returned to power in 1997 certain workers' rights were restored. Many of these—the right to sick pay, paid leave, and a maximum number of weekly working hours—were guaranteed under the European Social Chapter, signed by Mr Blair in 1998 (see Chapter 9, 'Towards an EU "super-state"?'). The new government also introduced a **national minimum wage (NMW)**, and extended some rights previously the preserve of full-time permanent employees to those on part-time and temporary contracts. Despite these early moves, it took nearly 13 years before a more thoroughgoing equalization of the rights of temporary or agency workers and those with full-time contracts was introduced, in the Agency Workers Regulations, which were finally adopted by Britain shortly before the 2010 election. Derived from the EU's Agency Workers Directive, this came into force across the Union on 1 October 2011 and was formally (if grudgingly) introduced by the Coalition on Christmas Eve that year. Its principal achievement was to give temporary and agency employees the same rights as permanent staff after 12 weeks' continuous employment.

The role of unions

As discussed in Chapter 5 ('**The Labour Party—a potted history**'), the unions initially emerged in the eighteenth and nineteenth centuries. They were formed to provide representation for the large groups of workers recruited by the owners of Britain's emerging manufacturing industries. In time, dismayed by the lack of attention paid to their cause by politicians, they began seeking their own stake in power and, to that end, joined with other bodies to form the Labour Party—to which many remain formally affiliated to this day (see Chapter 5, Table 5.3).

Although most workers' rights are enshrined in British and/or EU law, unions have historically adhered to a self-help approach to representing their members' interests known as 'voluntarism'—a tradition that shies away from seeking legal intervention in workplace disputes, in favour of group negotiation known as 'free collective bargaining'. In material terms, unions' principal aims are to:

- negotiate and protect a fair wage for given trades and professions;
- negotiate fair working conditions—hours, holiday entitlement, sick pay, and compensation for work-related injuries or illnesses; and
- provide members with training, educational and social opportunities, and a 'fighting fund' for living costs during prolonged industrial disputes.

In addition, unions offer legal and financial support in the event of disputes between individual employees and their employers. Unions have historically achieved many favourable settlements for aggrieved workers unfairly dismissed from their jobs, or bullied or harassed by colleagues or bosses. Sometimes, this is done on an out-of-court basis, but on other occasions unions represent workers at employment tribunals.

Over the past 30 years, the number of unions has declined by a third, with many pooling their resources to strengthen their voice at the negotiating table. The most recent amalgamation was that of the Transport and General Workers' Union (TGWU) and Amicus, Britain's biggest technical union, which merged to form Unite in 2007. As in the Labour Party, the senior officer of a trade union is usually called the 'general secretary', and (again like Labour) it usually has an elected national executive committee that debates changes of policy; beneath that, it will have regional and district organizations. It will also have branches, often based in individual workplaces, and houses, chapels, or shop stewards' committees, which act as focal points for negotiations between employees and employers.

The 'big three' British unions as of 2014 are set out in the table entitled 'Britain's "big three" trade unions', to be found on the **Online Resource Centre**.

Most unions are affiliated to a single representative body, the Trades Union Congress (TUC), which holds an annual conference like those organized by the main political parties to rally opinion from members and ratify changes in policy. The serving Labour leader is traditionally invited to give its keynote speech.

The TUC dates back to 1868 and its membership currently consists of 54 unions, representing around 6 million people (equivalent to eight out of 10 union members). It has eight regional councils in England and one for Wales. Scotland has its own equivalent body: the Scottish Trades Union Congress (STUC).

Union recognition—and what it is worth

For unions to be able to negotiate with employers about working practices, pay, and conditions, they need to be formally 'recognized' by employers. After years of having their rights diluted, unions were given a new impetus to recruit in the

Employment Relations Act 1999, which introduced a statutory process through which they could demand recognition on meeting specific criteria.

If claims for recognition cannot be satisfied bilaterally between a union and relevant employers, it may apply for help from a central arbitration committee (CAC), which assigns a three-person panel to each case. There are two main ways in which a union may achieve recognition—regardless of whether this is desired by the employers disputing it:

- *without* a ballot—a union is entitled to *automatic* recognition if *more than 50 per cent* of its 'bargaining unit' (all employees entitled to join it) have done so; or

- *with* a ballot—if *at least 40 per cent* of the bargaining unit vote in favour of recognition in a ballot and this number amounts to a majority of those who vote (a worker in a bargaining unit does not need to have joined a union to vote).

Ironically, one of the most notorious industries for union recognition is journalism. There have been many cases in which the managers of larger regional newspapers and some nationals (including Express Newspapers, and Independent News and Media) have fought to prevent it. Prior to the 1999 Act, some regional newspaper groups disingenuously argued that, to achieve recognition, the unions representing their journalists would need to obtain the support of 40 per cent of their *overall* workforces—including advertising and sales staff, etc.—rather than simply the writers and subeditors who constituted the bargaining unit.

From the mid-1980s to late 1990s, unions were restricted from taking strike action, in the sense that any withdrawal of their labour over a dispute constituted a breach of contract. Theoretically, this entitled bosses either to sack striking workers or to sue them for damages and loss of business. However, the 1999 Act entitles 'recognized' unions to be consulted formally over changes in working terms and practices for employees whom they represent—for example the movement of a British-based call centre to the Far East or a proposed organizational merger. It also gives unions immunity from prosecution for industrial action, provided that:

- the action is 'wholly or mainly in contemplation or furtherance of a trade dispute between workers and their employer' (that is, not secondary picketing); and

- the union goes through the correct ballot procedures beforehand—a secret postal ballot, followed by a letter giving the employer seven days' notice of the intended action and details of the ballot result.

Some restrictions remain, however. In addition to being barred from secondary action, unions must keep picket lines to negotiated levels to avoid intimidating colleagues not taking part. This latter clause was inserted to avoid the kinds of harassment to which 'strike-breaking' coalminers and other workers were allegedly subjected in the 1980s by picketers.

Following a coordinated strike of more than 1 million public sector workers on 10 July 2014—the latest in a succession of strikes protesting against the Coalition's imposition of wage freezes and job cuts—Prime Minister David Cameron confirmed that the 2015 Conservative manifesto would include commitments to ban unions from striking unless at least half their membership turned out to vote one way or the other, while explicitly stopping single ballots from sanctioning rolling 'programmes' of strikes, as had happened on this occasion. The vote authorizing the walkout of the National Union of Teachers (NUT) had been won on a 27 per cent turnout—back in 2012. Responding to the plans, union leaders argued that, in practice, they would have the effect of making legal strikes all but impossible if enacted. They also retorted that if the legitimacy of parliamentary elections were predicated on remotely similar measures, most MPs (including the prime minister) would never have won sufficient votes to be elected.

Other proposals have also angered the unions. In June 2012, Work and Pensions Secretary Iain Duncan Smith announced that, in future, low-paid workers who took part in strikes would lose the working tax credits that would normally top up their pay on the days concerned—in addition to wages that they forgo anyway as a result of taking action. Two months earlier, the Coalition said that it was planning to end decades of national wage bargaining by introducing regional pay scales to take account of variations in the cost of living from one part of England to another.

Avoiding strikes—the role of the Advisory, Conciliation, and Arbitration Service (ACAS)

On occasions on which employer–employee negotiations break down, one or other party may seek impartial help in reaching a settlement from the **Advisory, Conciliation, and Arbitration Service (ACAS)**.

This quango's role is to:

- *advise* warring parties how to avoid industrial action;
- *conciliate* in disputes when invited to do so and try to encourage parties to reach agreement peacefully;
- *arbitrate* to restart negotiations in disputes resulting in industrial action; and
- *mediate* over grievances between individual employees and their employers—notably in relation to prospective tribunal cases (concerning unfair dismissal, gender, age, or racial discrimination, etc.).

ACAS has been involved in numerous recent disputes. In July 2007, its chair was called in by ministers to report on the issues arising from a strike by Royal Mail workers over the imposition of new modernization plans and a below-inflation 2.5 per cent pay deal. In May 2005, it was approached by the National Union of Journalists (NUJ) to mediate between it and then British Broadcasting Corporation (BBC) director general Mark Thompson over his plans to slash 4,000 jobs.

More generally, as part of its drive to cut 'red tape' for business, the Coalition has also speeded up employment tribunals, while also cutting the number of cases brought before them. Under the Enterprise and Regulatory Reform Act 2013, employees may bring unfair dismissal cases against their employers only after working for them for two years (as opposed to one year previously), unless their case rests on alleged sacking because of their political opinions or affiliations. The Act also encourages parties to resolve their differences using a new 'early conciliation service', launched through ACAS from April 2014, and/or to reach compromises known as 'settlement agreements'. However, a recommendation by Tory donor Adrian Beecroft that Britain adopt a 'no fault' summary dismissal regime that would, in theory, have licensed bosses to dismiss staff with little or no notice, recompense, or legal redress was roundly rejected by Mr Cable as 'bonkers'. In a heated exchange between the two, played out in the national newspapers in May 2012, Mr Beecroft retorted that Mr Cable was a 'socialist' who, despite his job title, 'appears to do very little to support business'.

Workplace health and safety

Health and safety in the workplace is regulated by the Health and Safety at Work Act 1974, which covers the operation of work-based equipment, and various subsequent regulations and statutory instruments, including the Control of Substances Hazardous to Health (COSHH) Regulations 1999, relating to exposure to virtually all potentially dangerous substances.

Since April 2008, the job of both developing policy guidelines on workplace health and safety and enforcing these rules through inspections has fallen to the **Health and Safety Executive (HSE)**.

The HSE's day-to-day work is carried out by its Field Operations Directorate (which incorporates separate factory, agriculture, and quarries inspectorates) and regional officers of the Employment Medical Advisory Service. Its powers are set out in the table entitled 'The responsibilities of the Health and Safety Executive (HSE)', to be found on the **Online Resource Centre**.

In addition, some health and safety legislation (covering shops, offices, warehouses, restaurants, etc.) is enforced by council environmental health departments (see Chapter 19, 'Waste management and environmental health'). In its drive to reduce red tape—particularly for small businesses—the Coalition appointed former Tory Trade Secretary Lord Young to review existing legislation in June 2010. That October, he published a report, *Common Sense, Common Safety*, which recommended sweeping rationalization of the 'bureaucracy' surrounding health and safety rules. Subsequent legislative proposals have focused on a perceived need to simplify regulations to 'ease the burden on business' and to weed out 'rogue health and safety consultants'. A further review, published a year later by Professor Ragnar Lofstedt, proposed scrapping requirements for organizations with 'low-risk' workplaces to maintain qualified first-aid personnel and stripping the HSE of its role as approver of first-aid trainers. The Coalition has since adopted a 'one in, one out' policy towards introducing new health and safety rules, and—in true 'Big Society' vein— invited members of the public to report irritating and unnecessary regulations that they think should be scrapped as part of a so-called 'red tape challenge'.

▶ The utilities

A 'utility' is an organization—whether publicly or privately owned—that is responsible for maintaining and delivering reliable and affordable supplies of a commodity essential to the lives of a country's citizens. The main utilities are those charged with providing 'natural monopolies'—basic services needed to sustain a society, such as water and energy (gas and electricity). Traditionally, the railways, postal services, and telecommunications have also been grouped under the 'utilities' umbrella.

Recognizing the vital nature of water and power—and persuaded that everyone should have guaranteed, equitable access to them—the post-war Labour government nationalized all utilities in 1948. Until then, like schools and hospitals, they had been owned by an ad hoc medley of local corporations and charities, with the result that service standards varied wildly from place to place.

For 40 years, the utilities remained in the public sector. While individuals still had to pay their own rail fares and electricity bills (according to how much of any service they individually used), the industries were hugely subsidized through general taxation. Despite the fact that there was no outside competition from other suppliers to drive down prices, subsidies generally enabled utilities to keep charges at reasonable levels.

Privatization of the utilities

In the 1980s, the ethos governing the way in which state-owned utilities were perceived began to change, as free market economics infiltrated public services for the first time. Mrs Thatcher's government began a wholesale privatization, arguing that monolithic state-owned industries were inefficient, overly

Table 7.4 Arguments for and against utility privatization

For	Against
Privatization improves efficiency by introducing competition and enabling providers to woo managers with commercial expertise.	Introducing profits raises suspicions that providers' main priorities are to boost revenue and share dividends, rather than to use savings to lower prices or improve services.
It enables them to respond to consumers' wishes by reacting to supply and demand with wider choice of services—rather than assuming that the 'state knows best'.	Periods of intense competition between rival gas and electricity suppliers, and ineffective regulation, lead to consolidation under fewer companies. Old-style public monopolies are eventually replaced by *private* ones—and company boards (unlike governments) are not accountable to service users.
Privatization removes 'statist' philosophy imposed on publicly owned utilities, allowing them to cut waste and contract out ancillary services—cleaning, catering, etc.—to smaller specialist companies. Doing so cuts overheads, providing more cash for investment.	Some privatized utilities—particularly monopolies such as water companies—pass costs on to consumers, rather than bear them internally, to placate shareholders. Major infrastructural investment required by recent EU directives led to disproportionately high water bills increases, but dividends kept rising.
Privatization raises revenue for future government spending, while saving taxpayers' money by cutting the cost of maintaining infrastructure.	Privatization divests country of significant assets built up through prior investment of taxpayers' money, giving commercial companies 'something for nothing'. Former Tory Prime Minister Harold Macmillan called it 'selling off the family silver'.

bureaucratic, and offered too little 'choice'. Arguments for and against privatization are set out in Table 7.4.

The first utility privatized was British Telecom, a then state-owned telecommunications provider that was part of the then General Post Office. The British Gas Board followed two years later, with electricity changing hands in 1990 and railways, in 1993. The most recent privatization was the partial sell-off of Royal Mail, completed in October 2013. Each privatization is explored in more detail below.

Privatization was to be only the first step in Mrs Thatcher's mission to 'liberalize' Britain's utilities. Unusually for someone revered and reviled in equal measure for her radical handling of the economy, she initially moved tentatively—allowing minimal competition in privatized utilities to ensure that the transition from public to private sectors had time to bed down before being opened to the ravages of the free market. But by the early 1990s gas, electricity, and telecommunications had been totally 'deregulated', allowing various different companies to compete for business in each sector for the first time. On the railways, travellers began being referred to as 'customers' rather than 'passengers'.

The onward march of deregulation continues to this day, even in the few sectors still dominated by major public sector providers, with British governments favouring 'light touch' regulation, preferring to let market forces determine prices and services. That said, they continue to set certain minimum standards for each sector—for example BT (successor to British Telecom) is still required by the terms of its licence to maintain public telephone boxes to ensure that there is provision for people without mobile phones, particularly in isolated areas. Royal Mail, meanwhile, currently retains a 'universal service obligation' requiring it to deliver to every home and business in Britain, however remote (although, since privatization, its chief executive, Moya Greene, has repeatedly warned that this will be threatened if industry regulator Ofcom fails to stop competitors not bound by the same condition from undercutting it by cherry-picking easy services in urban areas). In addition, each industry is overseen by at least one regulator with a statutory duty to ensure that customers receive value for money and appropriate access to essential services. The overall responsibilities of regulators include:

- setting limits on price increases;
- monitoring service quality; and
- ensuring that true competition is maintained.

Over the years, however, there has been considerable criticism of these regulators—often derided as 'watchdogs without teeth' because of their perceived reluctance to interfere in how utilities are managed. In April 2008, the chair of an all-party committee on fuel poverty, Labour's John Battle, tabled a Commons motion demanding that ministers force the Office of Gas and Electricity Markets (Ofgem) to stop energy companies charging higher unit rates to poor households reliant on prepayment meters than better-off customers paying by Direct Debit.

Communications

British Telecom was privatized in 1984. Initially, only limited competition was allowed, with a single alternative provider, Mercury Communications Ltd, entering the market.

After a well-received trial, this 'duopoly' ended in 1991. Some 150 licensed telecommunications companies soon sprang up, including 125 cable and 19 regional and national public telecoms operators, although the market has since been rationalized through mergers and takeovers. Today, consumers can also choose from multiple mobile phone networks, the largest of which include Orange, O2, Vodafone, and T-Mobile, not to mention numerous Internet service providers, including BT Broadband, Virgin, and TalkTalk.

Confusingly, most telephone landlines are still provided by BT engineers, but customers are billed by the suppliers that they pay to deliver their services through those lines. A similar division, between the companies that own the physical infrastructure and those who use it, exists in most utilities.

In recognition of the growing convergence of telecommunications and broadcast media, since 2003 telecoms regulation has been regulated by the **Office of Communications (Ofcom)**, a 'super-regulator' that also oversees television, radio, and digital media services providers. As a media regulator, Ofcom is solely concerned with broadcast and digital or online platforms. At time of writing, oversight of print media had recently passed from the Press Complaints Commission (PCC) to a new **Independent Press Standards Organization (IPSO)** following the Leveson Inquiry (see Chapter 3, 'Press'). Unlike Ofcom, but like the PCC before it, and IPSO is 'self-regulatory' (as opposed to statutory), with a governing board comprising media and non-media professionals—a slight break with its precursor, which had been dominated by major figures from the newspaper industry, raising questions about its independence. IPSO's responsibility is to ensure that newspapers and magazines comply with an editors' code of practice covering everything from respect for the privacy of the bereaved to protection of confidential sources.

Previously, telecoms were policed by the now-defunct Office of Telecommunications (Oftel), while broadcasting had been overseen by several disparate regulators, including the Independent Television Commission (ITC) and the Radiocommunications Agency. The BBC occupies an unusual position, in that it has a discrete overseer to monitor its editorial independence, the BBC Trust, with taste and decency issues falling within Ofcom's remit.

Since 1 October 2011, with the abolition of Postcomm, the postal industry has been under the ambit of Ofcom. The consumer-run body Consumer Focus, which channelled complaints from public to government in relation to most utilities, has also been scrapped, with its role franchised to the charity Citizens Advice.

Ofcom's role in relation to postal services, acquired from Postcomm, is to:

- protect a universal postal service;
- license postal operators;
- introduce competition into mail services;
- regulate Royal Mail; and
- advise the government on the Post Office network.

The road to privatization for Royal Mail began in earnest with a series of interventions by Postcomm highlighting its ailing business model. In May 2008, the regulator issued a report warning that unless it was part-privatized, allowing it to raise investment on the open market, it might have to axe Saturday postal deliveries to save money. Despite already having controversially abandoned twice-daily weekday deliveries, in the year to March 2010 the company made a pre-tax loss of £262 million, which it blamed on growing competition from private providers and consumer resistance to rising first-class mail prices during the recession.

In late 2010, Mr Cable confirmed Coalition plans to privatize Royal Mail fully—a step further than Labour had ever dared, even under the pro-business Lord Mandelson, who shelved proposals for a partial sell-off in the dying months of Mr Brown's government. When the stock market flotation finally occurred, however, it proved more modest: only 70 per cent of the business was sold and shares were pegged at a cautiously low price of 266 pence apiece. Moreover, in a nod to the mutual model championed by Mr Cable for the future restructure of Royal Mail's counter service, the Post Office, 10 per cent of shares were reserved for its own employees. With ministers (for which read 'taxpayers') having already bought up Royal Mail's £9.5 billion pension deficit and its remaining £1 billion of debt written off, it was hardly surprising that investors were quick to buy up. By the time trading ended on day one, shares had already jumped by more than a third in value (to 455 pence each) and within five months they had risen to 72 per cent more than their sale price. At a time when the government was still pursuing a determined cuts programme, Labour and the unions condemned it for selling the service off 'on the cheap', while the independent National Audit Office concluded that the sell-off was 'marked by deep caution, the price of which was borne by the taxpayer'. In July 2014, the Commons Business Committee went further—arguing that the underpricing had short-changed taxpayers by as much as £1 billion.

Energy

In 1986, gas—then the preserve of the British Gas Board—was privatized. Although the newly rechristened 'British Gas' was initially a private monopoly, the industry swiftly became the first fully deregulated utility. At first, the emerging new generation of gas companies (like electricity suppliers later) were regionally based: households and businesses in south-east England, for example, were given a choice of only one alternative to British Gas, based in their regions. Today, most people can buy their gas from suppliers headquartered anywhere in Britain, or even abroad, and many companies, including British Gas, supply 'dual fuel' (both gas and electricity). Others, including high-street names such as Sainsbury's and Marks and Spencer, offer energy but subcontract the business of actually supplying it to British Gas or rivals such as Southern Electric.

As with telecoms, there is a division between supply companies that bill customers and the single firm that owns the infrastructure used to 'transport' fuel to them. Both the network of pipes for gas and the cables or pylons used to transmit electricity are owned by National Grid plc, a monopoly. Suppliers pay it for using its network.

When electricity was privatized in 1990, it was originally split into three generating companies and 12 suppliers. An example of a regional supply company was the South East Electricity Board (Seeboard), subsequently bought by French-owned company Électricité de France (EDF Energy) in 2002. Since then, the electricity supply chain has evolved into the three-stage process outlined in the table entitled 'The energy industry supply chain', to be found on the **Online Resource Centre**.

While England and Wales are governed by this system, Scottish Power plc and Scottish Hydro-Electric generate, transmit, and distribute all electricity in Scotland.

The gas and electricity utilities used to have separate regulators, but are now overseen by the **Office of Gas and Electricity Markets (Ofgem)** and the Director General of Gas and Electricity Markets. Following a number of controversies over double-digit rises in energy bills (blamed by companies on the rising price of crude oil—despite the fact that most have continued to report substantial profits), a succession of consumer watchdogs have also emerged. The first, Energywatch, was absorbed by Consumer Focus in 2008. Energy prices have become such a fraught issue in recent times that, in his 2013 party conference speech, Labour leader Ed Miliband pledged to freeze household bills if returned to office in 2015.

Water and sewerage

The most controversial utility privatization was that of water, which was sold off in 1989. Given the essential nature of clean, safe water supplies, many critics of privatization (and some supporters) saw the idea of opening it up to market competition as a step too far.

There were also practical objections. Given the peculiar difficulties of 'subdividing' the industry's infrastructure—to use an extreme illustration, splitting stretches of a reservoir between different companies—it quickly became clear that conventional competition would be impossible. To this day, water is supplied to British consumers by companies that are local monopolies—making a mockery, critics argue, of the premise of privatization.

Initially, 10 water and sewerage companies were formed. Each was given responsibility for supplying water, storing and recycling it, and treating and disposing of sewerage. Confusingly for consumers (and journalists), the industry today is regulated by not one, but three bodies, the roles of which are outlined in Table 7.5.

Industrial and commercial water users are metered nowadays, and households may be charged on the basis of Council Tax band or opt to be metered, depending on where they live. Consumers with a record of unpaid bills are often *forced* to install prepayment meters to avoid them slipping into future arrears and, in certain areas, including parts of the south east, companies have begun to roll out a compulsory meter programme with the stated aim of encouraging

Table 7.5 Regulation of the water industry

Regulator	Remit
Water Services Regulatory Authority (Ofwat)—formerly the Office of Water Regulation	Regulates industry's structure and financial transparency (examining accounts and vetting mergers/takeovers)
Drinking Water Inspectorate	Regulates quality of water supplied to consumers
Environment Agency	Monitors pollution and regulates water quality in inland, estuary, and coastal waters; also responsible for flood protection

people to cut back on their usage, while also charging them for their *actual* consumption, rather than an estimated one as previously. As in the energy industry, there has been periodic controversy about meters, with campaigners arguing that they leave poor people vulnerable: if they do not have change available at a given time, their water supply is cut off. Moreover, companies have been criticized for charging higher rates per unit to customers with meters than to those who pay by conventional bill. These and other concerns prompted the emergence of another watchdog: the **Consumer Council for Water**.

In Scotland, water effectively remains a nationalized utility. Three regional water authorities, covering the north, east, and west of the country, were merged in April 2002 to form a single state-owned company: Scottish Water. Scottish Water is overseen by the Water Industry Commission for Scotland (WICS) and its accounts are audited by Audit Scotland.

Railways

Rail privatization took a different route from that of other utilities and today, albeit by default, the industry remains a public–private partnership (PPP). In 1993, following years of negotiation with the private sector to sell franchises covering marginal and unprofitable lines, British Rail was finally privatized. It was initially fragmented under 100-plus private operators—companies that bought up engines and rolling stock to manage individual routes on renewable franchises. Meanwhile, as in the energy industry, ownership of the network (in this case, tracks, signals, and stations) was transferred from government to Railtrack—a private monopoly. Following a spate of controversies and rail disasters—including the 1999 Paddington train crash, in which 31 people died—ministers closed Railtrack in 2002, replacing it with a not-for-dividend company: **Network Rail**. The infrastructure was therefore effectively taken back into qualified public ownership.

Network Rail charges the remaining 25 operators for using its infrastructure, although in practice many operating companies run their local stations as subcontractors. Franchises are awarded by the government on the basis of a guaranteed 'minimum level of service' specific to each route, and companies tender for renewable terms of anything between seven and 20 years. The company that wins a franchise will usually be the one willing to run services with the lowest government subsidy—giving rise to concerns about underinvestment and price rises. Current franchisees include Southern, which runs the main London–Brighton line and manages stations for Network Rail along that route, and South West Trains, which is responsible for a number of services across southern England and greater London.

In some areas, two or more companies operate services in competition, but elsewhere local monopolies exist. Competition is arguably illusory in practice, because it is physically impossible for two companies to run directly competing services (after all, no two trains can use the same track between the same stations at the same time).

Huge increases in numbers of people commuting to work have put growing pressure on the rail network and fare prices have repeatedly risen well above inflation, even at times when service quality has deteriorated. Overcrowded carriages, broken-down engines, late arrivals, and cancellations—at a time when annual government subsidies to the rail network have remained significantly higher than those before privatization—make the railways an enduring ministerial headache. The Coalition's recent reduction in subsidies has led only to further dissatisfaction, as year-on-year price rises for commuters have soared well above wages, despite the fact the industry continues to receive £4 billion a year from the taxpayer.

Rail regulation is currently split between two authorities: the Office of Rail Regulation is meant to ensure that prices are fair and that there is equitable access to tracks for operators; the Department for Transport (DfT) itself is responsible for awarding and reviewing franchises, and for fining operators for repeated lateness, cancellations, and other aspects of poor performance. Beforehand, this role fell to the Strategic Rail Authority (SRA). There have been some recent signs of willingness by DfT to flex its muscles where services are poor. In 2009, then Transport Secretary Lord Adonis took the East Coast franchise back into public ownership after its then operator, National Express, ran into financial difficulties. The publicly run service has since been consistently rated the most comfortable and efficient line in Britain by consumers, but this did not stop Coalition ministers launching a determined effort to reprivatize it: in 2014, a list of three bidders was published—FirstGroup, and joint bids from Eurostar and French company Keolis, and Stagecoach and Virgin— and it was due to be sold off in 2015. At time of writing, Labour had unveiled a manifesto pledge to form a new state-owned company to compete for future franchises with private operators, while bringing rail operators and the network under the control of new regional and national public bodies, capping annual fare rises, and introducing a new legal right for passengers to be offered the cheapest available tickets for each journey.

As with the other utilities, there is also a watchdog to represent consumers: **Passenger Focus**.

▶ Private finance initiatives (PFIs) and public–private partnerships (PPPs)

As with major public building projects, the huge infrastructural investments required by utilities are often funded the **private finance initiatives (PFI)**—the system introduced by Mr Major's Conservative government in 1992, initially to pay for new prisons at a time of acute overcrowding and repeated breakouts (see Chapter 8, 'Recent and future developments in the prison system'). The classic PFI model sees a private company financing the bulk of initial capital investment (buildings and equipment), often along with some ancillary staff to man the facility, and effectively 'owning' it for years or decades afterwards. The taxpayer gradually 'buys it back' in a long-term leaseback arrangement resembling a mortgage.

Although initially sceptical, Labour embraced PFI as it moved to fund an extensive programme of new schools and hospitals, rechristening such projects **public–private partnerships (PPPs)**. Today virtually all new public capital investment is financed this way—and so too are some related to utilities. The proposed new generation of nuclear power stations approved in 2008 is likely to be largely, if not wholly, privately financed when it eventually materializes.

Table 7.6 Criticisms of PFI/PPP

Criticism	Explanation
Can generally be financed only through borrowing	Because government borrowing is better secured than that of the private sector, the interest rates faced by private investors are usually higher than those offered to states.
Companies put shareholders before public (or 'customers')	Private companies are legally obliged to earn profits for shareholders—so, whatever the short-term savings, the final costs to taxpayers might be greater than if the state had wholly financed the project.
PFI/PPP agreements are like credit card debt or 'hire purchase' agreements of 1960s	There is confusion over who 'owns' the project: hire purchase deals entail ministers using taxpayers' money to mortgage public assets on the 'never, never'.
Who is responsible if something goes wrong—private investor or taxpayer?	The closure of Railtrack increased pressure on the state to lure private sector investment by providing costly guarantees.

One big advantage of using private finance to fund capital projects is that initial outlays do not appear on the Treasury's balance sheet—meaning that they do not technically 'count' as public expenditure. In contrast to the huge start-up costs of some projects, the face values of contracts awarded to private businesses as incentives to carry out building work are relatively low. Critics argue, however, that PPPs have notable disadvantages—as outlined in Table 7.6—and recent difficulties encountered by NHS trusts in servicing their contracts testify to this. There has been mounting concern about the looming scale of public debt racked up by PFI/PPP contracts under successive governments. One NHS trust, South London Healthcare, entered administration at least partly because of its capital 'debt', and others have faced similar difficulties (see Chapter 6, 'Hospital closures, deficits, and the perils of market-centred thinking in the NHS'). Despite this, the success of the Coalition's still embryonic 'infrastructure plan' appears to rest on hybrid public–private funding arrangements resembling PFI/PPP in all but name.

≣ Topical feature idea

The following is the first half of a story that appeared on *BBC News online* on 11 June 2014. It concerned a report from the new Competition and Markets Authority (CMA) warning of a lack of competitiveness among 'payday lenders'—providers of short-term loans, often at high interest rates, to people struggling to budget between wage packets and benefit payments. How would you develop this into a lively backgrounder? How many of your readers have taken out payday loans and what are their experiences of repaying them?

Extract from an article published on BBC News online, 11 June 2014

Payday loan firms not competitive, says CMA

BBC News online

11 June 2014

Web link: **www.bbc.co.uk/news/ business-27790924**

Payday lenders lack price competition, so customers may be paying too much for their loans, regulators have said.

An investigation by the Competition and Markets Authority (CMA) has found that lack of competition could be adding £30 to £60 a year to customers' bills.

It has recommended establishing an independent price comparison website and telling lenders to make borrowing costs clearer.

A lenders' trade body has welcomed the proposals.

"If you need to take out a payday loan because money is tight, you certainly shouldn't have to pay more than is necessary," said Simon Polito, chairman of the CMA payday lending investigation group.

The average income of payday lending customers is similar to the overall population, but access to other credit options is often limited, he said.

"In some cases, those borrowers paying the extra costs are the ones who can afford it the least," said Mr Polito.

"This can particularly apply to late payment fees, which can be difficult to predict and which many customers don't anticipate."

Bids for customers

For a typical loan of £260 taken out for just over three weeks, lack of price competition could be adding £5 to £10 to the average cost of the loan.

On average, customers take out about six loans per year, so a typical customer could save between £30 and £60 in a more competitive market, the regulator found.

"Some customers may be getting a worse deal still, given that the gap between the cheapest and most expensive deals for a month-long £100 loan is more than £30," it added.

The role of companies that generate financial leads for payday lenders—sometimes through texts and emails—may also have to be more transparent, the CMA added.

"We found that 40% of new online borrowers take out their first loan with a lender via a lead generator, but the way in which these companies earn their money—by selling customer applications to the highest bidder—is often not made clear on their websites and some customers are unaware that these companies are not actually providing the loan," Mr Polito said.

[...]

Payday loans: check the costs

- Advertised monthly costs may seem low, but annual rates are significant
- Loans are quick but customer service can be poor. The Financial Ombudsman receives more than 50 complaints about payday lenders every month
- Other lenders like banks or credit unions may offer a better deal

© www.bbc.co.uk

✳ Current issues

- **The 'botched' Royal Mail privatization** Business Secretary Vince Cable privatized 70 per cent of Royal Mail in October 2013, but the way in which he managed the sale has been widely criticized, on the basis that shares leapt in value by 38 per cent on day one and have since hovered around the 600 pence mark (nearly three times their initial sale price).

- **Problems meeting the deficit reduction target** Mr Osborne originally pledged spending cuts of up to £31.9 billion a year by 2014–15, to eliminate Britain's deficit. Two years later, the timetable for clearing the deficit was delayed to 2017, and in the 2013 Autumn Statement, by a further year.

- **Insulating customers against the threat of a further bank collapse** The Financial Services Authority (FSA) has been replaced by three new financial regulators, and the Banking Reform Act 2013 has formally separated banks' high street and investment arms, and introduced greater protection for taxpayers and customers— by forcing investors to fund future bailouts and ensuring that the first thing to be rescued would be savers' deposits.

⸬ Key points

1. The ministry responsible for funding public spending through taxation and borrowing is HM Treasury, while British business interests are promoted by the Department for Business, Innovation, and Skills (BIS).

2. The senior minister who heads the Treasury, the Chancellor of the Exchequer, makes an annual Budget Statement—enshrined by the Finance Act—which raises and lowers taxes, increases or cuts public expenditure, and appraises the performance of Britain's economy.

3. Financial regulation is split four ways: the Bank of England's Monetary Policy Committee (MPC) controls inflation by raising or lowering interest rates; its Financial Policy Committee (FPC) identifies risks to the banking system; the Financial Conduct Authority (FCA) polices banks and other finance companies; and the Prudential Regulatory Authority (PPA) stops them acting irresponsibly.

4. Direct taxes are those paid 'up front' (for example income tax and corporation tax), while indirect ones are 'hidden' within prices of goods and services (for example value added tax, or VAT).

5. Utilities are organizations or companies providing those commodities or services that are considered essential to citizens' day-to-day lives. They include energy, water, and telecommunications.

→ Further reading

Colling, T. and Terry, M. (2010) *Industrial Relations: Theory and Practice (Industrial Revolutions)*, 3rd edn, Oxford: Wiley Blackwell. **Fully revised edition of acclaimed text focusing on the changing nature of worker–employer relations in Britain in the context of changing labour markets.**

Grimsey, D. and Lewis, M. (2007) *Public Private Partnerships: The Worldwide Revolution in Infrastructure Provision and Project Finance*, Cheltenham: Edward Elgar. **Illuminating overview of the growing role of private capital in public sector infra-structural investment, and the costs that this brings to public, including compara-tive examples of PPP-style projects from states outside Britain.**

Gumbrell-McCormick, R. and Hyman, R. (2013) *Trade Unions in Western Europe: Hard Times, Hard Choices*, Oxford: Oxford University Press. **Examination of the changing role and influence of trades unions in late-modern Britain and western Europe fol-lowing recent labour market transformations.**

Michie, R. C. (2001) *The London Stock Exchange: A History*, Oxford: Oxford University Press. **Acclaimed history of Britain's biggest money market—one of the largest in the world—incorporating up-to-date explanations of the LSE and how FTSE works.**

Monbiot, G. (2001) *Captive State: The Corporate Takeover of Britain*, London: Pan Books. **Critically acclaimed exposé by a leading campaigning journalist of the creeping growth in influence of commercial companies in British public affairs.**

Stiglitz, J. (2010) *Freefall: Free Markets and the Sinking of the Global Economy*, London: Penguin. **Searing critique by a leading economist of the social and economic folly that led to the 2008 global banking collapse and contemporary crisis in capitalism.**

 Online Resource Centre

www.oxfordtextbooks.co.uk/orc/Morrison4e/
Visit the Online Resource Centre that accompanies this book for web links and regular updates.

8

Social security and home affairs

The twin briefs of 'social affairs' and 'home affairs' occupy more newspaper column inches, broadcast airtime, and web pages than almost any other areas of British life. From government crackdowns on 'welfare scroungers' to controversies about immigration, prison breakouts, or gun crime, barely a week passes without several major stories generating screaming headlines.

The story of British citizenship in the modern age is one of 'carrot' and 'stick': the 'carrot' of rights, entitlements, and benefits for which UK citizens are eligible; and the 'stick' of prosecution, punishment, and ultimate imprisonment for those who 'abuse the system' by failing to meet the responsibilities expected of them.

▌ The basis of the 'welfare state'

The primary purpose of the 'welfare state' initiated by Herbert Asquith's Liberal government and solidified by Clement Attlee's Labour administration was to provide a safety net for members of society who fell on hard times, whether temporarily (through losing jobs or falling sick and being rendered unable to work) or indefinitely (because of serious injury or long-term illness). Other than in exceptional situations, life 'on the social', 'on the sick', or, in the case of unemployment, 'on the dole' was never envisaged as a permanent state of affairs for anyone; rather, it was meant to prevent those who, through no fault of their own, found themselves unable to work, earning low wages, or otherwise impoverished. The concept of 'deserving' and 'undeserving' poor, culturally hardwired since Elizabethan times, was arguably enshrined even in the mind of Beveridge.

According to eminent historian Asa Briggs, the term 'welfare state' was coined by William Temple, Archbishop of Canterbury, during the Second World

War. It is widely recognized, however, that the *practical* foundations of a prototype welfare state were laid during Lloyd George's time as, first, Chancellor of the Exchequer, then prime minister. His 1909 'People's Budget' (see Chapter 2, 'What is the point of the Lords?') introduced both old-age pensions and National Insurance (NI)—the progressive tax that remains the bedrock of the benefits system to this day. From the outset, the welfare state was to be based on both *need* and *entitlement*: the needy would be looked after, but their eligibility for this support derived from the presumption that if and when they were able to work and pay their way, they would do so. Today, more than ever, British citizens' ability to claim higher-rate benefits to help them through periods of sickness or unemployment is contingent on their making sufficient NI contributions and paying enough tax during periods of work.

Nonetheless, while a certain amount of 'responsibility' was always expected of those receiving welfare support, there has been a marked hardening of attitude under recent governments. The early 1980s saw a huge increase in unemployment as entire industries were effectively dismantled through Margaret Thatcher's radical market reforms. Few could argue at the time that the hundreds of thousands of workers made redundant were to blame for their own predicament. Yet Mrs Thatcher's ministers did not take long to invoke the image of the jobless layabout. Shortly after the Handsworth and Brixton Riots of 1981, her Employment Secretary, Norman Tebbit, told a journalist:

❝I grew up in the 1930s with an unemployed father. He did not riot. He got on his bike and looked for work, and he went on looking until he found it. ❞

Mr Tebbit's reply has gone down in British political folklore and would set the tone for future policy among not only the Conservatives, but also New Labour and the Coalition. When Tony Blair was elected in 1997, his Chancellor, Gordon Brown, initiated an ambitious plan to reduce unemployment under the 'Welfare to Work' banner. His 'New Deal for the Unemployed' (based on a model adopted in some US states) aimed to provide a wider choice of work-related opportunities for the long-term unemployed, rewarding those who undertook specified training programmes or voluntary work with initial £10 top-ups to their weekly benefits. In return for these entitlements, however, it would demand more stringent demonstrations of their efforts to find work, organizing regular interviews with 'supervisors' in the then Employment Service to monitor their rate of applications and to help them with job searches. This built on tough measures introduced under John Major's government, when high-profile crackdowns were introduced to target 'scroungers' and claimants who accepted cash-in-hand work, but failed to declare it. Under the Coalition, things have got tougher still. Today, the idea of 'contributory welfare' dominates popular discourse about benefits in a way seldom seen since before the welfare state was invented.

▌ Social welfare services today

As Figure 8.1 illustrates, the social security bill represents the single largest area of government expenditure in Britain. Defined broadly as welfare provision allocated to guarantee 'a basic standard of living for those in financial need', it accounts for more than 30 per cent of Britain's overall public spending budget and 21 per cent of its gross domestic product (GDP) (see Chapter 7, 'Promoting growth and UK exports'). Yet, contrary to the accusatory headlines of countless media stories that would have us believe that it is largely spent on work-shy 'scroungers', by far the biggest share of this £167 billion annual budget—£72.22 billion or 44 per cent—is reserved for pensions, while only £4.91 billion—3 per cent—goes on Jobseeker's Allowance (JSA) for the unemployed. Figure 8.2 gives the breakdown of social security spending by the Department for Work and Pensions (DWP) in 2011–12—the latest tax year for which firm statistics were available at time of writing.

Figure 8.1 Breakdown of public sector spending by department, 2011–12 (total £694.9 billion)

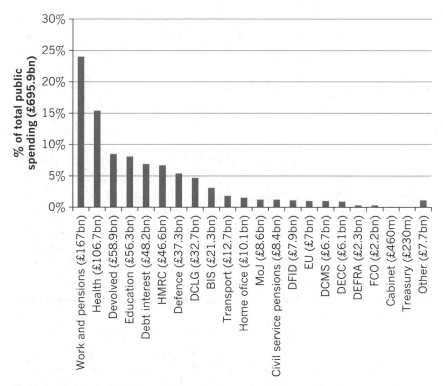

Source: Guardian Data, departmental accounts; Institute for Fiscal Studies; Public Expenditure Statistical Analysis (PESA); Office for Budget Responsibility (OBR); House of Commons Library

Figure 8.2 Breakdown of DWP spending, 2011–12 (total £166.98 billion)

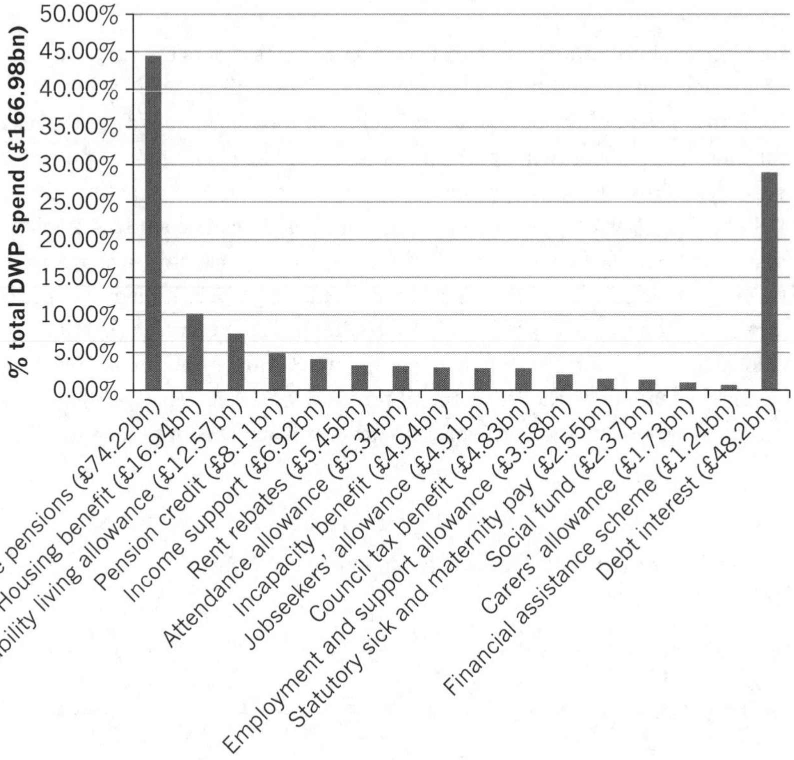

Source: Department for Work and Pensions (DWP) Annual Report and Accounts 2011–12 © Crown Copyright 2012

Over the years, social welfare services have been administered by a succession of often overlapping and sometimes conflicting departments. Today, they are split between the DWP, the Department for Education (DfE), the Department of Health (DoH), and HM Treasury—as illustrated in the table entitled 'A breakdown of the main government departments involved in social welfare', to be found on the **Online Resource Centre** that accompanies this book. At time of writing, however, it was unclear how long these arrangements would continue to apply to Scotland (not to mention Wales and Northern Ireland), as the aftermath of the 2014 independence referendum saw David Cameron promise a significant extension of existing devolution to the Scottish Parliament, explicitly including powers to determine its own social security policy.

Because the first half of this chapter is primarily focused on social security—specifically, the benefits and tax incentives introduced by governments to promote welfare and employment—it concentrates on the work of the two biggest players: the DWP and HM Treasury.

▶ The Department for Work and Pensions (DWP)

The DWP has overall responsibility for promoting employment. When Labour returned to power in 1997, its immediate concern was to tackle the emerging problem of intergenerational unemployment—the perceived rise in the number of jobless 18–25-year-olds whose parents also suffered sustained periods of unemployment. The 'New Deal' policies that followed were criticized as much for their narrow focus on these two target groups as for the stiff conditions that they imposed on those whom they were designed to help. Following the 2001 and 2005 Labour victories, the New Deal was extended to, in turn, over-25s, over-50s, lone parents, and people with disabilities.

The vast and complex benefits system over which the DWP presides is administered in practice by a range of executive agencies. Their roles are outlined in Table 8.1.

Types of benefit and their relationship to National Insurance

Although bedevilled by numerous delays and IT problems, the benefits system is currently working through the most radical shake-up since its inception, with phased introduction of the Universal Credit (UC) (see 'Rationalizing welfare— Universal Credit' in this chapter). However, even under this new regime—and certainly for those who will remain under the existing one for now—there are two broad 'categories' of UK benefit. Whether a particular payment falls into one or the other depends on the extent to which NI contributions have been made.

- **Contributory benefits** are those available to people who have paid sufficient NI contributions. These include contributions-based JSA (the

Table 8.1 Executive agencies involved in social security

Agency	Role
Jobcentre Plus	Replaced Benefits Agency (BA) in administering most state benefits, ranging from Child Benefit, maternity benefits, and widows' pensions, to Income Support, Employment and Support Allowance (ESA), Personal Independence Payments (PIPs), and Jobseeker's Allowance (JSA). Council housing departments administer Housing Benefit/Local Housing Allowance (see Chapter 18, 'Local authorities, Housing Benefit, and the Local Housing Allowance (LHA)') on its behalf.
Child Support Agency (CSA)	Assesses/collects maintenance payments for children from parents under arrangements made in family courts.
Pension Service	Helps people to navigate complex web of alternative pension options and related benefits/tax credits.

higher rate) and Employment and Support Allowance (ESA) or Incapacity Benefit.

- **Non-contributory benefits** bear no relationship to individuals' prior NI contributions. Most are 'needs-based' payments for anyone whose income falls below certain levels and/or who meets other criteria (such as disability). These include Income Support and basic JSA. Some, however, are 'universal'—for example Winter Fuel Payment, an allowance for everyone over the age of 60, irrespective of personal financial circumstances.

There are five 'classes' of NI contribution. Most working people pay Class 1, in proportion to their earnings. One oft-cited advantage of working for someone else is that for every £1 invested in the Class 1 NI 'pot' entitling people to future benefits, should they need them, a further £1 at least is contributed by their employers. By contrast, self-employed people have sole responsibility for making their NI contributions (Class 2, paid weekly, and Class 4, which are profit-based).

There are two further classes of NI: Class 1A, paid by employers operating company car/fuel schemes for their employees for private use; and Class 3, paid voluntarily by those able to afford them to safeguard future benefit eligibility. By way of a long service award, those who continue working after pensionable age no longer have to pay NI. However, their employers continue doing so on their behalf.

Different types of benefit

At present, in addition to Universal Credit (see 'Rationalizing welfare—Universal Credit' in this chapter), there remain a wide variety of distinct benefits available, depending on whether people are unemployed, disabled, or low-paid.

Jobseeker's Allowance (JSA)

Jobseeker's Allowance (JSA) is paid to adults working fewer than 16 hours a week and 'available for and actively seeking' full-time work. There are two levels: contributions-based (related to prior NI contributions); and income-based (for those who satisfy financial means tests, regardless of prior contributions). People with savings of £16,000 or more are unlikely to be eligible, while those with between £6,000 and £16,000 receive reduced payments.

As with earlier forms of unemployment benefit, JSA has been subject to periodic criticism from all sides over the criteria used to award or refuse it, not to mention its level. For decades, British governments have agonized over the benefits-related 'poverty trap'—put crudely, the fear that giving too much money to the unemployed acts as a disincentive for them to work. In taking up jobs, unemployed people instantly lose any entitlement to out-of-work benefit, and even if they continue to qualify for certain other payments—for example

Housing Benefit or Local Housing Allowance (LHA)—they will instantly be paying income tax and NI contributions out of their wages. For some, such as single parents, the option of taking up a low-paid, temporary, and/or part-time job rather than remaining on JSA often seems impractical: the cost of childcare that they would otherwise not need, combined with an immediate loss of benefits and a delay in receiving any tax credits to which they may be entitled, can make the prospect of remaining unemployed (however unpalatable) the lesser of two evils. Few would dispute that out-of-work benefits should remain lower than pay rates to encourage people to work when they find suitable jobs. But for some campaigners, including social policy think tanks such as the Joseph Rowntree Foundation, the poverty trap results less from overinflated benefits than it does from depressed wages. In the 2014–15 tax year, maximum weekly JSA rates stood at £57.35 for 18–25-year-olds and £72.40 for over-25s—hardly the stuff of which millionaires are made! Indeed, the relatively meagre level of JSA prompted an unusual intervention from the Council of Europe in January 2014, when it described the benefit as 'manifestly inadequate' and suggested that it be doubled. By contrast, for the first time since the mid-1970s, the Coalition's Benefits Uprating Bill 2013 removed the automatic annual uprating of welfare payments in line with inflation, instead pegging them to the 1 per cent cap previously imposed by ministers on public sector pay.

Labour tried to address the low wage issue by introducing Britain's first national minimum wage in 1997 (see Chapter 7, 'The government's role in industrial relations'). Yet many workers—particularly those in low-skilled jobs such as security and care work—continue to receive poverty wages that take little account of local costs of living. Concern about the poverty trap led Labour to roll out tax credits—a form of welfare payment for people on low incomes, directed to them through pay packets, rather than the traditional giro cheque-based benefits system. Such measures have, however, been tempered by continuing threats to make life harder for the minority of people whom successive governments have insinuated 'refuse' to work, despite being able to do so. In February 2008, Labour launched a major welfare 'rethink', contracting out Jobcentre-Plus-style job search advice and support services to the private sector—with companies paid for successfully finding claimants work and keeping them in those jobs for six months, backed by penalties for those who failed to attend interviews or appointments with personal supervisors.

The Coalition has taken an even tougher stance. One measure introduced has been a 'three strikes and you're out' sanctions policy for those who repeatedly refuse job offers. First-time 'offenders' today stand to lose their benefits for three months, second-timers, for six months, and third-timers, for up to three years. The extent of this refusenik problem seems to have been overstated, though. When, in 2010, BBC Home Affairs editor Mark Easton asked the DWP how many claimants had ever refused three such offers, he received the following answer: 'None.'

Coalitions ministers have also moved further and faster towards requiring unemployed people to work for their benefits, through the aegis of the over-arching 'Work Programme'—the umbrella title for a suite of schemes central to its efforts to help the young and long-term jobless to find (and retain) work.

Among its various 'conditionality-based' initiatives—inspired by the 'Workfare' system rolled out by US President Bill Clinton—are several aimed primarily at 16–24-year-olds with little prior workplace experience. Most controversial has been the self-explanatory 'Mandatory Work Activity', which requires those judged to need extra help to engage (or to re-engage) with employment to undertake unpaid four-week stints working on community projects for up to 30 hours a week. Those who fail to turn up, or to see placements through to the end, lose their benefits for three months for 'first offences' and six for the second. In June 2012, then Employment Minister Chris Grayling warned of even harsher sanctions after disclosing that nearly half of the first-wave 'jobseekers' referred for placements either failed to turn up or signed off JSA rather than undertake them. Equally unpopular with the unemployed have been new 'work experience' schemes aimed mainly at the young: although notionally voluntary, if participants leave partway through 'without good reason', they stand to lose up to two weeks' JSA.

A national backlash against these measures began in early 2012, when it emerged that Cait Reilly, a Birmingham University geology graduate, was suing the Coalition under the Human Rights Act 1998 after being forced to give up a sought-after museum placement that might have led to a professional career opportunity to undertake what she described as 'slave labour' in high-street discount chain Poundland. Amid the negative publicity that followed and a grass-roots protest mobilized by the 'Right to Work' campaign, a succession of major companies withdrew from the scheme—including Sainsbury's, Waterstones, and Superdrug. One of the few prominent surviving participants, Tesco, offered all 1,500 people on placements with it the choice of continuing on the government scheme or undertaking four-week *paid* internships, leading to guaranteed jobs if they performed well.

Similarly incendiary have been the alleged malpractices of some private companies contracted to implement the Work Programme on a payment-by-results basis. In February 2012, it emerged that four employees of A4E—a firm initially hired by Labour and the biggest recipient of DWP contracts under the Coalition—had been arrested amid allegations of fraud at its office in Slough. Following further arrests and disclosure of an internal audit showing that company bosses were alerted as early as 2009 to potential irregular or criminal activities by employees across Britain, Mr Grayling cancelled its contract to arrange Mandatory Work Activity placements in south-east England. Three months earlier, Emma Harrison, founder of A4E—which stands for 'Action for Employment'—had stepped down as both company chairwoman and the Coalition's 'Family Champion' and 'Back-to-Work Tsar'.

Even the performance of private contractors that have been honestly going about their business has failed to impress. In February 2013, the Commons Public Accounts Committee (PAC) criticized their track record after it emerged that, during the first 14 months of the government's flagship Work Programme, only 3.6 per cent of people on its books had managed to find sustainable jobs—less than a third of the number that the DWP had expected to help. In a scathing assessment, the PAC concluded that fewer people had found jobs through the scheme than would have been expected to do so of their own accord, had it not existed.

In addition to profiting from the Work Programme directly, the commercial sector also benefits from an initiative announced by Mr Cameron in August 2010 to combat welfare fraud. Defying criticism from the Information Commissioner (see Chapter 20, 'FoI appeals and the Information Commissioner'), he confirmed that private credit-rating firms—dubbed 'bounty-hunters'—would be used to snoop on the financial affairs of claimants to identify those whose spending habits suggested that they were committing fraud. Although Mr Cameron highlighted an annual cost to the public purse of £5.2 billion from fraud, official DWP and HM Revenue & Customs (HMRC) figures suggested that most of this was attributable to overpayment and paperwork errors by officials; only £1 billion was down to wilful fraud.

Income Support

Income Support is a flexible non-contributory benefit available to 16–60-year-olds on low incomes and not in full-time employment, who satisfy various other criteria (for example being single parents, full-time carers, or registered blind). As of summer 2014–15 there were two rates for single people:

- £57.35 for single 16–24-year-olds; and
- £72.40 for single people aged 25 or over.

As with other benefits, payments to couples take account of their ability to cut costs by shopping and cooking together, and paying joint utility bills. These combined payments are relatively lower as a consequence—leading critics to argue that couples are unfairly penalized by the system. The standard rate for all couples in which both partners were aged 18 or over was £112.55. Eligible single parents were entitled to £57.35 if aged 16 or 17, and £72.40 if aged 18 or over, but since 2008 incremental changes have been introduced to encourage parents to take up jobs once their children reach a certain age by withdrawing Income Support at that point. Lone parents with children aged over 12 lost their entitlements in November 2008, then those with children aged over 10 in October 2009, while from October 2010 eligibility was withdrawn from everyone with children due to reach the age of seven within the year.

As with JSA, restrictions on individuals' ability to claim Income Support apply if they have savings of £6,000 or more.

Employment and Support Allowance (ESA) and Personal Independence Payments (PIPS)

Just as there are different levels and types of JSA, so too there is more than one form of benefit for the sick and disabled. Although soon to be replaced by Universal Credit, **Employment and Support Allowance (ESA)** recently supplanted the long-standing Incapacity Benefit as the main contributions-based payment for people judged incapable of working while under State Pension age, who are one or more of the following:

- recipients of Statutory Sick Pay (SSP) through their employer that has ended, although they remain incapable of working;
- self-employed or unemployed; and/or
- former recipients of Statutory Maternity Pay (SMP) who have not gone back to work because of sickness.

Since 31 January 2011, all new applicants for out-of-work benefits related to illness or disability have been assessed for ESA. People claiming Incapacity Benefit since before that date are currently having their eligibility reviewed incrementally—a process originally due to be completed by 2014, but which has recently been delayed owing to mounting controversy over the number of people pronounced 'fit for work' who have successfully appealed against their assessments. The rate at which ESA is paid initially depends on what stage someone's application is at. During the 'assessment phase'—the first 13 weeks of claims, when decisions should be made about applicants' ability to return to work in the short, medium, or long terms—the rates for 2014–15 were:

- £57.35 for a single person under the age of 25; and
- £72.40 for a single person aged 25 or over.

Then, if assessments confirm that they have limited ability to work resulting from illness or disability, claimants will be placed in one of the following two groups and paid corresponding levels of benefit:

- the Work-Related Activity Group—claimants judged capable of under-taking structured activities designed to prepare them for returning to the workplace, for whom the benefit rate is up to £101.15; and
- the Support Group—those confirmed as being too sick or disabled to work for the foreseeable future, for whom the rate is up to £108.15.

While income-based ESA is non-taxable, a more generous rate exists for those who have made sufficient NI contributions. Claimants receiving these higher pay-ments may be liable for tax, depending on what other income, if any, they receive.

Because of its relative generosity and the sheer number of claimants (2.6 million in 2008, at an annual cost of £12 billion), Incapacity Benefit became a huge political issue towards its end. First introduced as 'Invalidity Benefit' by Edward

Heath's Conservative government, it came into its own during the Thatcher years, when the mass closure of coal pits and factories resulting from privatization and liberalized employment laws saw large numbers of out-of-work men transferred onto it. At the time, the Tories—later to lead the charge in bringing down the Incapacity Benefit bill—were accused by Labour of deliberately using the benefit as a political tool to 'massage' the true unemployment figures, while throwing many people who had previously worked all their lives onto the 'scrap-heap'. But, since the early 1990s, successive welfare ministers have made it their mission to weed out those who can work from those who genuinely cannot, by means of a series of ever-harsher tests.

In 2005, Labour announced root-and-branch reform of the rules governing Incapacity Benefit, vowing to reduce the number of recipients by 1 million. The resulting Welfare Reform Act 2007 introduced these changes and the concept of the appropriately worded 'Employment and Support Allowance'—its title denoting a new emphasis on 'supporting' people, including the majority with genuine illnesses and disabilities, to re-enter employment as soon as possible.

But the resulting regime was troubled from the start, with particular questions surrounding the conduct of the signature **work capability assessments (WCAs)** used to determine whether new applicants should be granted ESA and existing recipients allowed to continue with it. Subcontracted, controversially, to occupational health company Atos Healthcare (a branch of a French-owned information technology firm), the assessments have generally been carried out by healthcare professionals, yet last barely 30 minutes, involve no medical examination, and centre on 'tick box' questions on a computer-based form.

In May 2010, in the week during which Mr Duncan Smith first announced plans to roll out the tests to existing Incapacity Benefit claimants from 2011, a report by Citizens Advice Scotland (where the assessments were piloted) labelled them 'unfit for purpose' after finding that up to two-thirds of claimants put through them under Labour had been declared fit after their medicals—20 per cent more than anticipated. As a result, 8,000 appeals were being heard each month, with two out of five succeeding. A BBC investigation found that many general practitioners (GPs) involved in conducting the tests had strong reservations about their efficacy, particularly in relation to people with mental health problems and other less 'visible' illnesses or disabilities. And there were renewed calls for them to be scrapped in May 2012, when GPs unanimously backed a motion at the British Medical Association's annual conference condemning them as 'inadequate' and having 'little regard to the nature or complexity of the needs of long-term sick or disabled persons'. By this time, four out of 10 appeals reaching tribunals were succeeding—questioning the basis on which initial decisions were being made.

A more disturbing outcome of the new assessment regime has been the circumstantial evidence of its impact on vulnerable claimants. In June 2012, *The Guardian* revealed the existence of an internal email from senior Jobcentre Plus managers urging staff to handle 'customers' with 'utmost care and sensitivity'

to acclimatize them to 'difficult changes' to which they 'may take some time to accept and adjust'. The Black Triangle Campaign, a grass-roots group representing disabled people, had been established a year earlier, largely in response to the apparent suicide of Paul Reekie, a mentally ill man found dead beside two letters: one notifying him of a decision to cancel his Housing Benefit and the other, his Incapacity Benefit. Since then, there have been repeated claims that a number of claimants have committed suicide because of having their Incapacity Benefit/ESA cancelled, while official government statistics show that, between January and November 2011 alone, 10,600 people pronounced fit for work died from their conditions within six weeks of their claims ending. With Labour pledging to review the whole test system if returned to power, in March 2014 Atos finally surrendered its contract, announcing that it would pull out six months prematurely, in early 2015. Its decision finally to abandon the tests that it had initiated followed two years of ever-escalating poor publicity, beginning with the unedifying spectacle of disability campaigners occupying the company's London headquarters during the 2012 Paralympic Games and culminating in the government's own damning assessment of 'significant quality failures' in the standard of written reports it produced after testing claimants.

Marginally less controversial than ESA is the second principal sickness-related benefit: Disability Living Allowance (DLA), or (as it is in the process of being renamed) the **Personal Independence Payment (PIP)**. Eligibility for this non-contributory benefit is based purely on someone's verified mental or physical needs (regardless of income, savings, or ability to work). Those under 65 have traditionally been able to claim DLA if they are physically or mentally disabled. Because it covers both aspects, DLA/PIP comprises both 'care components' ('daily living components' under PIP) and 'mobility components', with some individuals qualifying for both. Nonetheless (again ahead of their transfer to Universal Credit), Coalition ministers have insisted that all new claimants undergo medical assessments since 2013. As of 2014–15, the 'enhanced' rate of PIP daily living component (the 'higher' rate of the DLA care component) was £81.30, while the PIP 'standard' rate was £54.45—the same as the 'middle' rate for those still on DLA. A lower rate still available to DLA claimants £21.55 does not exist for PIP. The comparisons between the DLA and PIP mobility components are simpler, because both have only higher and lower rates: £56.75 and £21.55, respectively.

▌ HM Revenue and Customs (HMRC)

HMRC is integral to the welfare system in two respects: it raises taxes to fund benefits; and it makes discrete payments to families, pensioners, and others on limited incomes through tax credits. The latter are designed to encourage low earners to stay in employment and others, to enter it, by rewarding them with modest 'rebates' through their pay packets. As the tax credit system has evolved, it has expanded to provide 'minimum income guarantees' (MIGs) for other vulnerable groups, including pensioners. The main types are outlined in the table entitled 'A breakdown of the main tax credits available from HMRC', to be found on the **Online Resource Centre**.

Although criticized for its complexity, the tax credit system was initially welcomed by low pay campaigners. However, in recent times, even Labour has questioned its unintended consequences, in light of research suggesting that one of its biggest effects has been to subsidize employers paying salaries at, or marginally above, the minimum wage. As the 2015 election loomed, the party was instead placing renewed emphasis on raising or enforcing the minimum wage, which research shows has steadily fallen in real-terms value, compared to prices and average earnings. It also indicated support, in principle, for a higher, 'living', wage that keeps pace with rises in household outgoings and vowed to regulate 'zero-hours contracts', under which people are employed in insecure jobs without guaranteed weekly working hours or wages.

▌ Rationalizing welfare—Universal Credit

The centrepiece of the Coalition's welfare reform programme has, from the outset, been **Universal Credit**—an 'all in one' benefit-cum-tax credit designed to combine most of the fiendishly complex array of payment types outlined above in a single one. The main aim of Universal Credit is to better incentivize unemployed claimants to enter work by supplanting an old system that effectively 'punished' people for taking up part-time or full-time work by immediately withdrawing all or most of their social security support. This sometimes left ex-claimants facing short-term 'marginal tax rates' of up to 95 per cent. In addition, those signing temporary contracts were forced to start their benefit claims from scratch if, when a contract came to an end, they found themselves back on the unemployment register. The success or failure of the new benefit will therefore rest on the ability of the computer system used to administer it to make real-time calculations of entitlement for each individual claiming it, taking account of sudden or short-term changes in his or her circumstances. It is hardly surprising, perhaps, that—as with all the best laid government plans—Universal Credit has encountered numerous delays and that the planned mass rollout in October 2013 did not materialize. In fact, by the end of September that year, only 2,150 people in the whole country were receiving it—all in the initial pilot areas of Warrington, Wigan, Oldham, and Tameside. At time of writing, a limited extension of existing pilot schemes was about to begin through other jobcentres in north-west England, with couples who would previously have been on JSA due to sign up later in 2014. In recognition of its problematic rollout, however, by June that year the government's own Major Projects Authority—an interdepartmental agency set up to coordinate large-scale initiatives—officially 'reset' the timetable for Universal Credit.

Assuming that the new benefit does eventually get on track, it is envisaged that other innovations will include online accounts, allowing most claimants to apply for and manage their claims from home, and monthly (rather than fortnightly) payments to be paid direct into their banks. Support with housing costs will also be incorporated into the benefit.

'Universal benefits' versus 'means-testing'—the future of welfare for parents and older people

In addition to some of the disability benefits outlined throughout this chapter, several other sources of support have continued to be available 'universally'—subject to recipients meeting criteria *other than* financial need. In most (but not all) cases, these tend to be payments aimed at children and the elderly.

Child Benefit has traditionally been paid to all mothers in respect of every child under the age of 18 (or 20, if still in full-time education or training). But it has long been controversial, given that high-income families arguably have little need for it, yet until recently received the same amount per child as the poor. After initially being frozen by the Coalition, since January 2013 Child Benefit has been removed from all families with at least one adult earning £60,000 or more. Parents on £50,000–£60,000 are liable to repay a portion of the Child Benefit that their household receives through tax, at a rate of 1 per cent for every £100 they earn over the lower threshold. Critics condemned the injustice of a move that enables households of two earners, each taking home £49,000, to retain their entitlements while single parents on just over that amount lose it. Yet Mr Osborne's original idea had been significantly harsher: removing it from any household in which one adult was a higher-rate taxpayer (that is, earning as little as £42,875).

That the Child Benefit debate proved such a cause célèbre had its roots in two key issues: the historical context underpinning it, and the overarching concept of 'universalism'. To begin with the former, Child Benefit—paid directly to mothers—has been seen as a means of liberating women from dependency on their husbands or partners and giving them direct control over a 'household budget' (which, in times gone by, might have been their only income). More generally, universal benefits like this have long been defended, notably by politicians on the Left, because paying them to everyone, regardless of income, gives those who do not need benefits on financial grounds a 'stake' in the welfare system—thus promoting solidarity about the importance of maintaining it. Labour also long resisted means-testing—in essence, awarding payments only to those who can prove that they are on low incomes and have minimal savings—arguing that requiring people to demonstrate their poverty was undignified and might discourage many in urgent need of financial help from claiming their entitlements.

A more pragmatic argument against means-testing is that it would be too complex and costly, given the need to reassess households repeatedly whenever their incomes fluctuated for any reason. For example, if the main 'breadwinner' were to lose his or her job, change employer, or become self-employed, this task could be onerous. Yet, ironically, such real-time adjustments are precisely the principle on which the Coalition's key welfare reform—Universal Credit—is predicated (see 'Rationalizing welfare—Universal Credit' in this chapter).

The same principle of universality currently applies to certain forms of welfare targeted at the elderly—notably, free bus passes for use on local bus services anywhere in England and Wales (for which everyone qualifies from their 60th birthdays) and the Winter Fuel Payment (which currently amounts to £200 for individuals living alone who were born on or before 5 July 1952, or £300 for those aged 80 or over in the qualifying week between 15 and 21 September 2014). As with other benefits, couples receive reduced sums (£100 and £200 each, respectively), but the poorest pensioners (those on Pension Credit, income-based JSA, or income-related ESA) receive £200 or, if over the age of 80, £300, irrespective of whether they live with another adult.

Two further universal benefits for those who meet the criteria on the basis of their family situations are Statutory Maternity Pay (SMP) and Statutory Paternity Pay (SPP). These are paid via employers to parents of recently born children. Mothers are now entitled to up to 52 weeks' maternity leave, 39 of them paid—albeit at 90 per cent of their average gross weekly earnings for the first six weeks and whichever is lowest of £138.18 a week or 90 per cent of gross earnings for the remaining 33 weeks. Fathers are eligible for two weeks' paid paternity leave, at either 90 per cent of their normal earnings or the £138.18 rate (whichever is lower)—and, since 3 April 2011, have been able to use up to six months of the maternity leave entitlement should the mother decide to return to work sooner.

Other entitlements include Statutory Sick Pay (SSP), available for up to 28 weeks to full-time employees unable to work through ill health (although the requirement to provide their employers with 'sick notes' was changed to a new emphasis on 'fit notes' in April 2010), and widows' pensions—lump sums paid to women whose husbands were below retirement age when they died. Payments begin from the date on which the husbands would have qualified for pensions had they lived.

Taken together, the sheer scope of their coverage means that universal benefits cost the Treasury billions each year. Not surprisingly, even long-time defenders of universalism are now arguing that the principle has had its day. Perhaps the most 'regressive' example of the contributory principle in action is the continued entitlement of wealthy ex-patriot Britons who retire abroad (often to sunnier climes) to Winter Fuel Payments. 'Anomalies' like this have led some observers to question whether means-testing is now necessary in the interests of fairness to those on low incomes. Other critics of universalism point out that the debate about whether to introduce means-tested benefits more widely is based on a false premise. With fewer and fewer elderly and disabled people entitled to automatic government help with social care costs (see Chapter 18, 'Community care—the limits of state provision'), because their savings or incomes are judged too high, in many areas of life means-testing already exists.

One long-standing form of welfare support that *was* targeted at those on low incomes was the one-off payment. This traditionally took one of several forms, the most common being budgeting and crisis loans—lump sums used, respectively, to smooth over gaps between pay packets or benefit payments, or to help out in the event of emergencies, such as floods or fires, or with urgent unforeseen expenses such as funeral costs. These were derived from a centrally held pot of money known as the Discretionary Social Fund. The Welfare Reform Act 2012 abolished both the Social Fund and the centrally directed loans system from April 2013, replacing them with a new £178 million annual spending pot to be devolved to councils to administer on DWP's behalf. But critics argue that this is significantly less than was previously spent nationally, and the Coalition's decision not to 'ring-fence' the money to force councils to spend it on the poor could mean that, in practice, far less is available—as hard-pressed authorities direct cash elsewhere to subsidize local services already hit by government cuts.

▌ State Pension and the great retirement debate

Although there has been much consternation in recent years about its paltry size, Britons are still automatically entitled to a state retirement pension funded out of general taxation.

Retirement ages for men and women are gradually being equalized. At time of writing, men born before 6 December 1953 were retiring at the age of 65, while women born after 5 April 1950, but before 6 December 1953, were doing so between the ages of 60 and 65. Following a review of existing retirement ages by an Independent Public Service Pensions Commission chaired by Labour peer Lord Hutton, the Pensions Act 2011 speeded up raising the retirement age for women to age 65, and this will now be phased in between April 2016 and November 2018. The Act also stipulated that:

- State Pension age for all women born on or after 6 April 1953 and all men born on or after 6 December 1953 would start rising to 66 between December 2018 and October 2020; and

- State Pension age would rise further to 67 between 2034 and 2036, and again to 68 between 2044 and 2046.

In November 2011, however, the Coalition announced plans to fast-track the rise to age 67 even sooner, bringing it forward to between 2026 and 2028. And in his March 2012 Budget, Mr Osborne went further, stating that, from that date onwards, the retirement age would be linked directly to changes in life expectancy.

The basic State Pension was one of the founding initiatives of the welfare state. Funded through NI contributions, the basic provision was supplemented in 1978 with the introduction of the State Earnings-Related Pension Scheme (SERPS), championed by the late Baroness Castle, who, as then Health and Social Security Secretary, was its main architect. SERPS—eventually replaced with the State Second Pension (S2P) by Labour itself in 2002—was seen by many as guarantee-ing a civilized degree of comfort to people in retirement because of the principle underpinning it: that pensions should keep pace with average wages.

By the late 1970s, most working people were required by their employers to contribute to second, occupational pensions (normally through their wages). Nowadays, however, pension provision in Britain is a patchwork, with many workers having neither the job security nor income to pay into a scheme beyond their state one.

Mrs Thatcher's government actively encouraged employees to opt out of SERPS and invest in potentially more lucrative (if riskier) personal pensions. In recent years, the vulnerability of some private schemes has been exposed by several major controversies—notably the mis-selling scandals that hit Royal and Sun Alliance and Standard Life, and fraudulent misuse of the Mirror Group pension fund by late newspaper tycoon Robert Maxwell.

Since the mid-1990s, the pensions issue has become increasingly toxic. As more people are living longer, radical steps will be needed to ensure that, in years to come, everyone can retire on liveable incomes. Although, in principle, individuals' entitlement to claim State Pension when they reach retirement age relates to the fact that they have part-funded their own pension (by 'paying into the pot' during their working lives), in practice the pensions of today are paid for contemporaneously by the working-age population. Given Britain's rapidly 'ageing population', no longer are there guaranteed to be enough working-age taxpayers to support the pensioners of tomorrow.

The Welfare Reform and Pensions Act 1999 paved the way for potentially radical pension changes. But ministers' attempts to move from this to a defini-tive framework for state-funded pensions stuttered for years afterwards. Following a 2006 report by Lord Turner's Pensions Commission, however, Labour proposed a radical shake-up of state pensions that would have co-opted all workers into a new national pension savings scheme from 2012 and relinked State Pension to average earnings—for the first time since SERPS was abol-ished. This move was brought forward to April 2011 in Mr Osborne's June 2010 Budget. More significantly, two radical reforms have been introduced by Coalition Pensions Minster Steve Webb. First, the Pensions Act 2011 introduced the principle of automatic enrolment ('auto-enrolment') for workers into occupational schemes, beginning on 1 October 2012. The government initially set an 'earnings trigger' forcing employers to enrol their staff in a work-based scheme automatically as soon as their salaries reached £7,475, later raising this to £10,000—in line with the PAYE personal allowance threshold (see Chapter 7, Table 7.1). Second, in the most ambitious rationalization of state pensions for generations, from 6 April 2016 all women and men born on or before 6 April 1953 and 1951 respectively will qualify for 'single-tier' pensions equivalent to the existing basic and additional State Pension combined.

Less welcome (for some) was a second piece of legislation introduced by the Coalition in the same Queen's Speech: the Public Sector Pensions Bill 2012. This has enshrined in law a requirement for state workers to retire later than previously and to pay in more to their occupational pension pots, but with lower incomes guaranteed in retirement. The Bill's confirmation followed months of acrimonious negotiations between ministers and unions, and several strikes by public servants, including teachers, doctors, and council workers, in protest at ministers' earlier imposition of tougher pension terms (see Chapter 7, 'Union recognition and what it is worth').

As of 6 April 2016, the four types of government-backed pension will be as outlined in Table 8.2.

Table 8.2 The four types of government-backed pension

Type of pension	How it works
State Pension	Contributory benefit received by those reaching State Pension age before 6 April 2016 who have made minimum of 30 years' qualifying NI contributions. Currently linked to whichever is highest of average earnings, CPI inflation, or 2.5%. Those who have not paid enough NI contributions qualify for Income Support instead.
Stakeholder pension	For those without occupational pensions (e.g. self-employed), but earning enough to save for retirement. Distinct from most pension schemes operated by banks or building societies in being cheaper and more flexible (people can move them from job to job). Government pays monthly contributions in place of employers.
Additional State Pension	Formerly 'State Second Pension' (S2P), this replaced SERPS in April 2002, providing a 'minimum income guarantee (MIG)' in retirement for some benefit claimants, including carers, by introducing NI credits for them as well as those working. Applies only to those retiring before 6 April 2016.
Single-tier pension	New single payment for people reaching State Pension age after 6 April 2016, based on 35 years' qualifying NI contributions (pro rata sums paid to others). Estimated introductory rate of £144 per week, rising annually in line with 'triple lock' (higher of inflation, average earnings, or 2.5%).

▌ Reviews and appeals under the benefits system

If claimants are dissatisfied with decisions on their eligibility for benefits, or moves to withdraw them, they may appeal. Before appealing, however, they must first go through a lengthy process, requiring them to file formal complaints with 'local decision-makers'. If dissatisfied with the outcomes of these, they may apply for 'reviews' by those decision-makers.

Finally, claimants have recourse to one last stab at 'justice': appeals handled by a branch of the Tribunals Service known as the Social Security and Child Support Tribunal (SSCS—formerly the Appeals Service). Incorporated into the Tribunals Service in 2006, this agency handles appeals about claims for all kinds of benefit, from DLA to SMP.

Once the SSCS has reached a decision, appeals can only ever be taken further on a 'point of law'. In such circumstances, they are dealt with by an independent ombudsman (either a Social Security Commissioner or Child Support Commissioner).

▌ The changing face of home affairs

Officially the 'Home Department', the Home Office was split into two in spring 2007 by Mr Blair's final Home Secretary, John Reid. He declared it 'not fit for purpose' on succeeding his predecessor, Charles Clarke, in 2006, following a succession of public embarrassments over the unwieldy department's handling of anti-terrorism and asylum policy, and a prison service creaking under the weight of too many inmates.

Mr Reid stepped down when Gordon Brown replaced Mr Blair as prime minister, but not before instigating one of the biggest shake-ups in this sprawling department's 225-year history. For some years, there had been an artificial 'Chinese Wall' between the responsibilities of the Home Office and Lord Chancellor's Department (briefly renamed the 'Department for Constitutional Affairs' in 2005) regarding crime and disorder. With the emergence of major new internal security issues in relation to the growing threat of Islamist terrorism, Mr Reid judged that the department needed to cede some criminal justice powers and to focus more effectively on the many other policy areas in its ambit.

When Mr Brown arrived in Downing Street, he replaced the Department for Constitutional Affairs with a new 'Ministry of Justice' (MoJ), headed by Jack Straw. Mr Straw became the first Lord Chancellor in 300-plus years to be a member of Parliament (MP) rather than a peer—a 'tradition' that has continued under his two Coalition successors to date, Kenneth Clarke and Chris Grayling. Reflecting his status as a 'commoner', Mr Straw was given the additional title 'Secretary of

Table 8.3 Breakdown of responsibilities of the Home Office and Ministry of Justice

Home Office	Ministry of Justice
Policing and crime prevention	Court system and sentencing policy
Security and counter-terrorism	Prisons
Human Rights Act (HRA) 1998	Probation and prevention of reoffending

State for Justice'. This better described his powers, in light of the fact that his post had lost several of the Lord Chancellor's traditional trappings—notably, his chairmanship of debate in the Lords, which went to a then newly appointed Lord Speaker (see Chapter 2, 'Conventions'). The division of responsibilities between the dual departments resulting from these reforms is now as outlined in Table 8.3.

To aid the Home Office in its new counter-terrorism responsibilities, it was given a new 'sub-department': the Office for Security and Counter-Terrorism. A National Security Board (NSB)—a weekly forum chaired by the Home Secretary—was also formed to discuss security threats when they occurred, with a National Criminal Justice Board (NCJB) promoting 'joined-up government' between the two departments responsible for different aspects of criminal justice policy (chaired jointly by the Home Secretary, Justice Secretary, and Attorney General).

The new-look Home Office

In a break with generations of male dominance in Cabinet, Mr Brown appointed Jacqui Smith Britain's first female Home Secretary in July 2007. Mr Cameron followed this example, confirming Theresa May in the same post.

Policing and crime prevention

The role of Her Majesty's Constabulary is explored in depth in Chapter 11. In examining the work of the Home Office, however, it is important to outline the extent to which English and Welsh police forces remain under the department's authority.

The Home Office funds the police and is responsible for recruitment, training, and pay. Responsibility for organizing policing on the ground, however, is delegated to local police and crime commissioners (see Chapter 11, 'Police force accountability—from authorities to commissioners'), who, in turn, appoint (and occasionally dismiss) chief constables. In practice, even today, the Home Secretary must endorse these appointments, and if there is a perception of declining confidence in either chief constables or commissioners, he or she may intervene to remove them against their wishes. In June 2001, then Home Secretary David Blunkett publicly urged Sussex Police Authority to sack local chief constable Paul Whitehouse over his handling of an inquiry into the fatal shooting by a police marksman of an unarmed alleged drug dealer, James

Ashley, in St Leonards-on-Sea three-and-a-half years earlier. Mr Whitehouse, who had promoted two of the officers involved in the incident, subsequently resigned.

The Home Secretary's traditional responsibility for overseeing policing in London, through the Metropolitan Police Commissioner, was formally handed to a newly created police authority answerable to the Greater London Authority (GLA) in 2000—and the GLA has not been afraid to use these powers. In November 2007, it passed a 'no confidence' vote in Sir Ian Blair, then Met Commissioner, following the Old Bailey's decision to convict his force for breaching health and safety legislation when anti-terror officers mistakenly shot dead Jean Charles De Menezes, an innocent Brazilian man, at Stockwell Tube station in July 2005. An inquest jury subsequently returned an open verdict into his death in December 2008—pointedly disbelieving testimony by police officers who insisted that they had shouted a warning to him before opening fire—and it was only a matter of time before Sir Ian was forced out. In October 2008, five months after Conservative Boris Johnson unseated Mr Livingstone as London Mayor, the new Mayor publicly demanded a change of leadership at the Met—leaving the Commissioner little option but to resign.

Both Labour and the Coalition have also had periodic run-ins with the police as a whole—usually over pay, recruitment, and/or pensions. In December 2007, the Metropolitan Police Federation declared itself 'at war' with Mr Brown's government over its decision to stagger a 2.5 per cent pay rise, awarding increases only when it was satisfied that crime detection and prevention targets were being met. But this was nothing compared to the glacial receptions that Mrs May repeatedly received at conferences of the Police Federation of England and Wales—the national body representing front-line officers and the police service's closest equivalent to a union. In May 2012, she was jeered and heckled while addressing its members against the backdrop of 20 per cent budget cuts, a tough new pensions settlement, and mass government-backed outsourcing of policing functions to the private sector. But two years later, she got her own back, delivering a steely speech in which she ordered the police service to reform or face enforced changes imposed 'by statute'. She also announced that the government was withdrawing state funding for the Federation with immediate effect. To place this clash in context, it came against the backdrop of a succession of high-profile embarrassments for the police— ranging from publication of a long-awaited report into South Yorkshire Police's mishandling of the 1989 Hillsborough Stadium disaster, to allegations of unlawful payments passing between News International journalists and serving officers in the Metropolitan Police. On a more 'personal' level for the Conservatives, there was lingering distrust between ministers and the Met following the bizarre 'Plebgate' row, in which former Cabinet Secretary Andrew Mitchell was forced to resign amid accusations that he had grumpily called two police officers 'plebs' after they asked him to dismount his bicycle when exiting through the gates of Downing Street on the evening of 19 December 2012. Closed-circuit television (CCTV) footage, leaked emails, and the imprisonment of one officer, PC Keith Wallis, for misconduct in public office appeared for a time to support Mr Mitchell's denials, but in November 2014 he lost a libel action against News Group Newspapers over a September 2012 article which first raised the 'plebgate' allegations. The judge in the case, Mr Justice Mitting, ruled that he probably had used 'the politically toxic word pleb'.

In policy terms, the most significant ongoing disagreement between the police and government relates to the pace and nature of reform. Although ministers initially insisted that only 'back office' police work would be franchised out to the private sector—leaving front-line policing to officers employed by the state—by March 2012 it became clear that they were minded to go further. That month, West Midlands and Surrey police forces (apparently with ministerial approval, and on behalf of all English and Welsh forces) invited bids from private companies—including the world's biggest security firm, G4S—to take over day-to-day running of a wide range of duties, including criminal investigations and detaining suspects. Earlier in the year, Lincolnshire Police had signed a £200 million contract with G4S to 'privatize' its civilian staff by transferring them to the company, which confirmed plans to build and run England's first private police station.

Within weeks, the risks of wholesale outsourcing were exposed to the harsh glare of international media attention when, a fortnight before the start of the 2012 London Olympics, G4S admitted to ministers that it could not deliver the 10,400 security guards it had been contracted to provide, owing to the 'complexity' of training and vetting so many disparate groups—from the unemployed and students looking for summer work, to individuals who had only recently left other jobs. In the ensuing political fallout, 3,500 service personnel were drafted in to boost the private security force.

Like hospitals, schools, and care homes, police forces must submit themselves to independent inspection. The body responsible, Her Majesty's Inspectorate of Constabulary (HMIC), is the oldest organization of its kind— dating back to the County and Borough Police Act 1856. Its remit covers England, Wales, and Northern Ireland—there is a separate inspectorate for Scotland—and it is headed by a Chief Inspector of Constabulary.

As with Ofsted, the Inspectorate can be outspoken. In July 2012, it warned that three regional forces—the Met, Devon and Cornwall, and Lincolnshire— were on the verge of being unable 'to provide a sufficiently efficient or effective service' because of the negative impact of budget cuts. Contrary to ministerial assurances, it estimated that there would be some 5,800 fewer front-line officers across England and Wales' 43 forces by 2015, with up to 26,600 other personnel losing their jobs.

The future of policing in the round remains a live political issue, with two rival, as yet unactioned, reviews—a government-commissioned one by former rail regulator Tom Winsor, and another, ordered by Labour from former Met Commissioner Lord Stevens—sitting in the Coalition's and Opposition's in-trays respectively at time of writing.

Security and counter-terrorism

When 52 commuters were killed in coordinated suicide bombings in central London on 7 July 2005, ministers decided that security policy must be at the heart of their future policy agenda. Ever since the attacks on New York's World Trade Center on 11 September 2001, and Britain's subsequent support for US-led military action in Afghanistan and Iraq, the country had been periodically threatened with its own atrocity—both covertly, through tip-offs gathered by intelligence services, and overtly, by the increasingly bellicose online proclamations of the late Osama bin Laden, his chief 'lieutenant', Ayman Al Zawahiri, and Abu Musab al-Zarqawi, then leader of 'Al-Qaeda in Iraq'.

Because of these threats—real and perceived—Mr Blair's government had already passed several 'anti-terror' laws long before the 7 July bombings. In fact, so proactive had it been that critics argued that, far from preventing further attacks, it might provoke them.

Of all these anti-terror policies, the most controversial and far-reaching were those relating to the detention of terrorist suspects. At the heart of the controversy was ministers' readiness to dispense with more than 800 years of due legal process by detaining people for prolonged periods without charge. Civil liberties campaigners saw moves such as the internment in Belmarsh Prison of individuals suspected of (but not immediately tried for) terror offences as a breach of the sacrosanct constitutional principle of habeas corpus—the right to a fair trial before one's peers—introduced under Magna Carta. Signed by King John in 1215 (see Chapter 1, 'Statute'), this mammoth document stipulated that:

> ❝ No free man shall be seized or imprisoned ... except by the lawful judgement of his equals or by the law of the land. ❞

The policy of detaining 'terror suspects' summarily (before trial) at Belmarsh began in late 2001, shortly after the 11 September attacks. It was not long before the government—which had opted out of the section of the Human Rights Act 1998 barring it from taking such action—faced significant challenges. As early as July 2002, the Special Immigration Appeals Commission (SIAC), a Home Office quango, ruled that four detainees imprisoned under the Anti-Terrorism, Crime, and Security Act 2001 had been unjustifiably discriminated against as foreign nationals. Although this ruling was later overturned by the Court of Appeal, worse was to come for ministers. Most significantly, in December 2004, the Law Lords ruled that continued detention of the 12 individuals still in custody was incompatible with human rights legislation.

Despite an initial show of defiance, Mr Clarke was forced to release the suspects early in 2005, replacing indefinite detention with 'control orders'—sweeping powers to confine suspects in the community using electronic tagging, curfews, and even house arrest. But these ran into trouble too. Because an order could be introduced, with little opposition, for between six and 12 months at the Home Secretary's behest, the policy again upset civil liberties campaigners. Neither was it an unqualified practical success: in May 2007, it emerged that three men allegedly plotting to kill British troops abroad, Lamine Adam, aged 26, his brother Ibrahim, aged 20, and Cerie Bullivant, aged 24, had absconded while under control orders. Later, in November 2005, Mr Blair suffered his first Commons defeat in eight years by staking his authority on a vote to increase the period of time for which police could detain terror suspects for questioning, from an existing 14-day limit to 90 days. Mr Blair—who said that senior police officers had presented a 'compelling' case for extending their detention powers—had to accept a 28-day compromise.

His successor, Mr Brown, later tried to raise this to 42 days by offering rebellious backbenchers a series of sweeteners and railroading the measure through on a three-line whip. But he and Ms Smith shelved the plans after being defeated in the Lords by a 191-vote majority. Among those resisting the measure were Mr Blair's former Attorney General, Lord Goldsmith, and Lord Falconer, ex-Lord Chancellor and one of his closest friends. Erstwhile MI5 heads Dame Eliza Manningham-Buller and Dame Stella Rimington also opposed it.

Having fought the 2010 election on pro-civil liberties platforms, the Tories and Lib Dems launched a wholesale review of anti-terrorism policies on entering government. In January 2011, they confirmed that 'Section 44' police stop-and-search powers (allowing officers to stop people without reasonable grounds for suspicion) would be sanctioned in future only with the permission of very senior officers and in circumstances in which a terrorist attack was believed imminent, while the 28-day detention period would be halved to 14 days. Ministers' recommended replacement for control orders was widely mocked, however, when it emerged that they were planning do little more than 'rebrand' them—as **terrorism prevention and investigation measures (TPims)**, lasting up to two years. Meanwhile, the ability of the authorities to impose 16-hour curfews on tagged suspects was reduced to a maximum of 10 hours—with curfews themselves redefined as **overnight residency requirements**. In July 2012, the first Tpim breach was confirmed when an alleged al-Qaeda sympathizer, identified only as 'CF', was repeatedly intercepted crossing through the Olympic Park in Stratford, east London.

Asylum, immigration, and citizenship

Another of the biggest home affairs issues of recent years has been the dual question of asylum and immigration. The term 'asylum seeker' entered the media lexicon around the time that war broke out in the Balkans in the early 1990s. The media was quick to focus on this new 'threat' to Britain's borders and, by 2002, the red-tops were filled with scare stories about impending invasions of 'asylum seekers' lured by a 'soft touch' benefits system. Their agitated prose was fuelled by the French government's initially laissez-faire attitude towards a burgeoning refugee camp at Sangatte, near Calais, from which 1,600 asylum seekers were apparently planning to sneak into southern England.

Enlargement of the European Union (EU), ultimately to 28 countries, has led to significant influxes of economic migrants from other countries—particularly those in the former Eastern Bloc—in pursuit of paid work. This, too, has been controversial, with national newspapers such as the *Daily Mail* and *Daily Express* pandering to the concerns of local communities in some areas that foreign workers were 'stealing' jobs from long-standing residents and putting pressure on already overstretched public services, such as social housing, schools, and health care. There have also been numerous headlines blaming immigrants for rises in crime. More recently, attention has switched to the supposed problem of 'benefit tourism'—specifically, migrants from poorer EU countries flocking towards Britain to exploit a 'generous' welfare system (see also Chapter 9, 'Other issues facing the EU').

In fact, according to various recent reports, migrants and immigrants have had little negative impact on either crime or demand for public services and benefits. In April 2008, the Association of Chief Police Officers (ACPO) found that offending rates in the Polish, Romanian, and Bulgarian communities (the study's focus, owing to the influx of migrants from those countries following their then recent accession to the EU) were proportionate to those in Britain's population as a whole. The same month, a joint study by the Equality and Human Rights Commission (EHRC) and Local Government Association (LGA) found little evidence that migrants were queue-jumping to obtain social housing; in fact, 60 per cent of those who had moved to Britain in the previous five years were in private rented accommodation. And, in October 2013, the European Commission found 'little evidence' that the 'main motivation' of migrants moving to Britain was the pursuit of benefits, stressing that they were more likely than native people to be in paid work. Moreover, according to the EU's statistics service, Eurostats, as of 2011 (the latest year for which figures were available) levels of UK 'social assistance' were only just above the overall EU average—and below those of Germany, France, Italy, and the eurozone countries. The highest rates were paid in Luxembourg, followed by Denmark and the Netherlands.

But not every survey paints a rosy picture of immigration: in December 2007, analysis of employment data by the Statistics Commission found that eight out of 10 new jobs created in Britain since 1997 (1.4 million out of 1.7 million) had gone to foreign-born workers. Around the same time, Ms Smith admitted as many as 11,000 non-EU nationals licensed to work in the security sector might be illegal immigrants. One had been involved in repairing Mr Blair's car; another was working as a cleaner in the Commons in February 2008. And a report by the Lords Economic Affairs Committee, published in April 2008, concluded that immigrants had had 'little or no impact' on the UK's economic well-being.

Despite widespread perceptions, asylum seekers, illegal immigrants, and economic migrants often have a far from cushy time when they arrive in Britain. In 1999, newspapers across southern England were filled with reports about the appalling housing conditions that some families endured while their applications were processed and they awaited 'dispersal' around the country. Meanwhile, an emerging black market in cheap foreign labour at the hands of unscrupulous people-traffickers has led to high-profile tragedies. In February 2004, 21 Chinese refugees were drowned in Morecambe Bay, Lancashire, while illegally working as cockle-pickers.

Sensationalism aside, Britain's population is rising fast: according to the Office for National Statistics (ONS), it soared by 8 per cent between 1971 and 2008, and had reached 63.9 million by late 2012, while the 2011 census recorded a 3.7 million increase in England and Wales alone in the previous decade (up to 56.1 million), with 55 per cent of the increase attributed to net migration. By 2029, it is expected to top 70 million. In September 2007, the ONS predicted that the number of immigrants would continue rising by up to 190,000 a year—three times higher than previous estimates—while three months later it reported that the birth rate among foreign-born women living in the UK had overtaken that of British-born mothers.

The decision by aspiring immigrants/migrants to relocate to Britain can also have a negative knock-on effect on their countries of origin. The migration of large numbers of skilled Polish workers, such as plumbers and electricians, produced as many negative newspaper headlines in Poland as in Britain. In some media, whole towns were depicted as 'drained' of their most highly trained artisans by Britain and other western European countries. Meanwhile, the backlash among some sections of the electorate over the perceived impact of inward migration on the availability of job opportunities for native Britons led to the UK imposing restrictions on incomers from the two newest member states, Bulgaria and Romania (both of which joined in January 2007), and Mr Brown's controversial pledge to work towards a guarantee of a 'British job for every British worker'.

But what do terms like 'asylum seeker' and 'illegal immigrant' actually *mean*—and what is the difference? Put simply, the term 'asylum seeker' is generally used as a synonym for 'refugee', which the 1951 United Nations (UN) Convention Relating to the Status of Refugees described as a person fleeing his or her home country because of a 'well-founded fear of being persecuted for reasons of race, religion, nationality, membership of a particular social group, or political opinion'.

The term 'asylum' is also distinct from 'immigration', because it is often used to describe a *temporary* state of affairs: an individual fleeing tyranny in his or her home country does not necessarily wish to remain permanently in

Britain. 'Immigration', in contrast, is used to describe the process of becoming a 'naturalized' UK citizen. The term 'illegal immigrant' is frequently used pejoratively by right-wing politicians and newspapers. It refers to individuals who illegally cross borders to enter a country without following official asylum procedures. Before the Sangatte camp was closed, there were several instances of refugees illicitly entering Britain through the Channel Tunnel.

Asylum policy has, since 2008, been overseen by the UK Border Agency (UKBA)—previously the Border and Immigration Agency—a Home Office agency. However, in March 2012, Mrs May split it into two following a high-profile public row with Brodie Clark, the head of its front-line arm, the UK Border Force, over the suspension of routine checks on overseas visitors with biometric passports the previous year. Briefly, Immigration Minister Damian Green had given the go-ahead for checks to be halted temporarily over Easter 2011 to cope with lengthy queues at Heathrow and other ports, but according to an inquiry published in February 2012 by John Vince, UKBA Chief Inspector, Mr Clark had unilaterally continued to waive them. Following his forced resignation, the Tories effectively revived their pre-election pledge to introduce a new dedicated border police force by announcing the formal separation of its back office and front-line functions.

The question of whether to grant asylum does not arise in the case of Irish Republic or Commonwealth citizens who had the right of abode in Britain before January 1983, or other EU citizens. It applies only marginally to nationals of the European Economic Area (EEA), a region of *potential* EU countries, which encompasses the Union itself, plus neighbouring states such as Iceland, Liechtenstein, and Norway. Residents of these countries are already allowed to work in Britain (subject to certain limitations) and, if they can support themselves, to live here. But nationals of most countries outside these areas, including many African and Asian nations, require visas before entering Britain. Some also need 'entry clearance'.

An annual cap on migrants from outside the EU was promised in the Conservatives' 2010 election manifesto and, on 19 July that year, Mrs May introduced a temporary cap on entry into the UK by non-EU citizens (of 24,100 between then and April 2011) to avoid a rush of people trying to migrate before the permanent limit came into force.

The Home Office has also introduced tough new measures to make it harder for foreigners to claim asylum. These are explained in the table entitled 'Recent rule changes covering asylum and immigration policy', available on the **Online Resource Centre**. In addition, successful applicants for British citizenship must now sign up to a number of 'responsibilities' in order to claim 'rights' that go with it—a list of conditions recently toughened by Mrs May. These are outlined in the table entitled 'Rights and responsibilities for successful immigration applicants', to be found on the **Online Resource Centre**.

The great 'Big Brother' debate

If one issue during New Labour's era exercised civil liberties campaigners more even than detention without trial it was the perceived 'Big Brother' approach that ministers took towards crime and terrorism detection and prevention. This tactic was symbolized for many by two signature Blairite policies: national identity (ID) cards and the National DNA Database (NDNAD).

Between 2009 and 2010, British citizens applying for or renewing adult passports were offered a choice between ID cards containing both their specific personal details (name, age, address, etc.) and biometric data (fingerprints, facial characteristics, irises), or new-style 'biometric passports' containing more limited information. The aim of the 'biographical footprint' held on ID cards was to enable certain accredited organizations to use it—with the cardholders' permission—to confirm their identities. Foreign nationals living and working in the UK began being issued with biometric ID cards in 2008. Although having a card was not initially compulsory, Labour sought to make it so.

Opponents of ID cards broadly fell into two camps: pragmatists and idealists. Pragmatists, such as former Conservative Shadow Home Secretary David Davis, argued that questions over the reliability of the technology used to produce the cards, combined with the fact that owning one was not initially intended to be compulsory, threatened to make the scheme ineffective. Idealists, such as campaign group Liberty, saw the cards as a dangerous next step on the road to turning Britain into a paranoid surveillance society. They also highlighted inconsistencies in the arguments that ministers used to justify the measure: when first mooted, in the aftermath of 11 September, it appeared that they were primarily intended as a weapon in the 'war on terror', but towards the end of Mr Blair's premiership he said that the government's main intention was to protect people against the growing threat of identity fraud. The ID card was abandoned by the Coalition.

Concerns about ID cards were compounded by publicity surrounding the expansion of the NDNAD—a sprawling electronic record of genetic samples taken from crime scenes and individuals held in custody. Originally established in 1995, by the end of 2009 it contained 5.9 million samples from 5.1 million people (equivalent to nearly one in 10 of the population). Since 2004, anyone penalized for an arrestable offence—even those given a simple police caution—have had their samples added to the database. In December 2006, then Home Secretary Mr Reid admitted that more than 1 million of those whose details were on the database had not even been cautioned! One reason for this anomaly was the fact that police had failed to remove the details of individuals arrested and charged, but subsequently acquitted.

To ensure that the NDNAD is not misused, it is regulated by a board comprising members of the Home Office, ACPO, Association of Police Authorities (APA), and Human Genetics Commission (HGC).

A series of high-profile convictions of serial murderers and sex attackers in early 2008 led to calls from some senior police officers for ministers to extend the database's scope to include the whole British population. But in its May 2010 Queen's Speech, the Coalition announced plans to restrict the future use and growth of the database, and also to regulate CCTV cameras, to ease existing limitations on peaceful protest, and to reduce the state's ability to monitor individuals' email and Internet records (another crime prevention measure introduced under Mr Brown). Yet full-blooded reform of the database has so far failed to materialize. In July 2011, it emerged that a Coalition commitment to remove the DNA of people subsequently deemed innocent (other than those accused of violent or sexual crimes) was being watered down; instead, police would be allowed to retain their genetic profiles in anonymized form—leaving open the option of linking these to named individuals in future.

The Coalition parties have also been accused of reneging on their declared opposition to Labour proposals to monitor individuals' Internet use. In June 2012, to the dismay of civil liberties groups and some Lib Dems, Mrs May published a draft Communications Data Bill—swiftly dubbed a 'snoopers' charter'—which, if passed, would require communications companies to store records of all UK citizens' email conversations, Internet phone calls, games, and other social networking activities for a year, and to allow police and intelligence services to access the material in pursuit of terrorists and fraudsters. At time of writing, the Bill had been mothballed indefinitely, owing to the level of public hostility that it encountered, although discussions around it resurfaced between the main parties following the 2013 murder of Private Lee Rigby by Islamist extremists on a street in Woolwich. More significantly, weeks after Mrs May had described the need for legislation to sanction greater surveillance as 'a matter of life and death' following a warning from Cressida Dick, the Met's head of specialist operations, that police were struggling to keep pace with increasingly technologically savvy terrorists, ministers provoked a fierce backlash from civil liberties groups by introducing emergency legislation ordering telecoms companies and Internet service providers to keep hold of personal communications between individuals. Its decision, sprung on the public on 10 July 2014, followed a ruling by the European Court of Justice (see Chapter 9, 'The European Court of Justice (ECJ)') that would have meant that such data need not be retained. Coalition ministers, backed by Labour's leadership, argued that private texts, emails, and social media messages that might assist counter-terrorism operations and serious criminal investigations might be junked en masse if they were to fail to act—jeopardizing public safety and potential future prosecutions. Besieged by critics, the Lib Dems (long-standing opponents of 'Big Brother' legislation) pointed to a 'sunset clause' that they had negotiated with the Conservatives, to ensure that the new Bill would expire in

2016, forcing any government seeking to retain its provisions to reintroduce it formally or to draft an alternative one.

The row about the emergency Bill came against the backdrop of mounting concern about the scale of the intelligence services' ability to monitor private electronic communications between individuals, as exposed in a series of *Guardian* articles in 2013, based on former CIA systems administrator Edward Snowden's revelations about a covert surveillance programme, codenamed 'Tempora', enabling both the US National Security Agency (NSA) and Britain's Government Communication Headquarters (GCHQ) to tap into the network of fibre-optic cables transmitting the world's phone calls, emails, and social media exchanges. Amid accusations by civil liberties groups that this represented an unethical, if not illegal, invasion of privacy, Charles Farr, director general of Britain's Office for Security and Counter-Terrorism, had admitted in June 2014 that searches on Google, Facebook, Twitter, and YouTube, and emails to and from non-British citizens abroad, were considered suitable for monitoring in counter-terrorism and other intelligence operations on the basis that they were 'external communications'.

Safeguarding human rights for British citizens

Despite Labour's predilection for vigilance, the Human Rights Act 1998 (see Chapter 1, Table 1.1) marked the beginning of a sustained championing of equality of opportunity and other basic freedoms for British citizens, which led to everything from the equalization of the age of consent for gay and hetero-sexual sex, to civil partnerships for homosexual couples. The latter right has since been extended by the Coalition, with the Same Sex Marriage Act 2013 allowing gay couples to marry for the first time.

To spearhead the government's drive to guarantee British citizens equal opportunities—regardless of age, gender, race, or disability—Labour estab-lished three new quangos on entering office in 1997, and in 2007 these were merged to form a single Commission for Equality and Human Rights, also known as the **Equality and Human Rights Commission (EHRC)**. The Commission's remit was extended to cover sexual orientation and religious beliefs, in addition to the areas overseen by the previous bodies, and it was also expected to enforce the law relating to equal opportunities and rights, to influence the development of the law and government policy, to promote good practice, and to foster better relations between communities.

The Ministry of Justice (MoJ)

Britain's criminal justice system has two core elements—the court system and the treatment of offenders—both of which are now the Justice Secretary's responsibility.

The court system and civil law

The day-to-day running of Britain's courts is overseen by an MoJ executive agency, Her Majesty's Courts Service. The Justice Secretary is personally responsible for promoting more general reforms of civil law and the legal aid system.

The government's principal legal advisers are the Attorney General and Solicitor General—both members of either Lords or Commons. In Scotland, their roles are performed by the Advocate General for Scotland (who assumed the roles previously held by the Lord Advocate and the Solicitor General for Scotland).

Subordinate to the Attorney General are the Director of Public Prosecutions (DPP), who runs the Crown Prosecution Service (CPS)—the state-owned legal service that brings prosecutions on behalf of the Crown—and the DPP for Northern Ireland, along with the Director of the Serious Fraud Office (SFO). At present, there remains an as-yet-unresolved debate about the future role of the Attorney General stemming from controversy about the perceived over-politicization of the 750-year-old post under Mr Blair. Lord Goldsmith was seen to be torn between party loyalty and legal protocol in advising ministers on the legitimacy of invading Iraq (see Chapter 10, 'The Foreign and Commonwealth Office (FCO)'), and in his later decision (subsequently overturned by the SFO) not to press charges against BAE Systems over its controversial overseas business dealings.

Criminal law

The Justice Secretary has overall responsibility for criminal law and introducing Bills to change it. This work is delegated to two principal agencies: the National Probation Service (NPS) and the **National Offender Management Service (NOMS)**.

Briefly, the NPS has traditionally supervised all individuals serving community-based sentences for criminal offences or prison terms during which they are permitted to live in the community. Historically, the NPS has overseen some 175,000 offenders a year—90 per cent male and a quarter aged 16–20. However, in June 2014, the NPS was part-privatized, with supervision of 'medium to low-risk offenders' (the overwhelming majority) transferred to 21 new area-based *community rehabilitation companies*, which replaced 35 long-standing 'probation trusts'. The remaining 30,000 'high-risk' convicts stayed the responsibility of a slimmed-down NPS. At time of writing, the PAC was warning that an absence of real competition had led to the evolution of privately owned public monopolies, in the form of companies such as G4S and Serco, which were in danger of becoming 'too big to fail'. Since 2001, the NPS has come under the Home Office's National Probation Directorate and has been supervised by an independent HM Inspectorate of Probation.

NOMS runs all 135 English and Welsh prisons—whether publicly or privately funded or owned. In Scotland, this role is retained by the Prison Service, which had it beforehand. Formed in April 2008, NOMS has a chief executive, responsible for administrative mistakes arising from its conduct. The Prison Service still exists in England and Wales—but only as one 'unit' of NOMS, with responsibility for publicly funded jails.

Recent and future developments in the prison system

NOMS employs the 50,000-plus wardens, officers, and governors who administer prisons on the ground. Since the Criminal Justice Act 1991, management of many prisons has been contracted out to private firms, as has transportation of defendants in custody to and from court.

The first four newly built prisons handed over to private managers were the Wolds (Humberside), Blakenhurst (Worcestershire), Doncaster, and Buckley Hall (Rochdale). By April 2012, there were 14 privately managed jails, run by major independent security providers including G4S Justice Services, Serco, and Sodexo Justice Services. But, given its wholesale privatization of many public services, it was perhaps unsurprising when the Coalition outlined plans to go further. In July 2011, Mr Clarke announced the biggest mass privatization of prisons in British history—putting nine jails out to tender and closing two others (the Latchmere House resettlement unit in Richmond, west London, and Brockhill Prison, Redditch) in a drive to save £4.9 million up-front from the MoJ budget and £11.4 million a year thereafter. The following March, a public spat erupted between the governor of three South Yorkshire prisons and his local probation trust after it emerged that the latter was collaborating with G4S to take over his jails. The prison expansion plans of G4S were ultimately short-lived, however: in November 2012, the company failed in a series of bids to take over additional jails and lost its existing contract to run the Wolds prison in South Yorkshire, which returned to the public sector in July 2013.

Complaints about prisons and probation services are handled by the Prisons and Probation Ombudsman for England and Wales (PPO). HM Prison Inspectorates—one for each of England, Scotland, and Wales—are charged with inspecting prisons every three years. Individual prisons and young offenders' institutions also have 'boards of visitors'—groups of locals appointed by the Home Secretary to relay complaints from prisoners in the same way as Healthwatch groups operate in the NHS (see Chapter 6, 'The Health and Social Care Act 2012 and the reinvention of the NHS').

Since the early 1990s, prisons have seldom been out of the news. Typically, stories tend to be negative, focusing on overcrowding, riots, and breakouts. To provide spare capacity, successive governments have done everything from adapting military camps to act as temporary prisons, to commissioning a 'prison ship', *HMP Weare*, moored off Portland, Dorset. During his time as a tough-talking Home Secretary in Mr Major's government, Michael Howard vowed to cut the number of community sentences and to send more people to jail, particularly violent offenders. But his famous cry of 'Prison works!' set him on a collision course with the then director general of the Prisons Service, Derek Lewis, who warned of dangerous overcrowding. In January 1995, the simmering prisons crisis came to a head during a succession of riots and breakouts, first at Everthorpe Jail, Humberside, then at Parkhurst. A damning report into the state of the system saw Mr Howard sack Mr Lewis that October—but not without facing tough questioning from Jeremy Paxman in a now legendary interview for BBC2's *Newsnight*, during which he was asked 12 times if he had 'threatened to overrule' Mr Lewis.

Overcrowding remains a serious concern today. In May 2007, the prison population reached 80,500—within a whisker of its maximum capacity. At the time, a further 300 prisoners were being held in police and court cells. Lord Falconer, then Lord Chancellor, appealed to the courts to limit their use of custodial sentences for people convicted of minor offences and it emerged that ministers were considering releasing 3,000 inmates early to free up cells for more serious offenders. To add to their blushes, Lord Phillips, the Lord Chief Justice, declared the country's jails 'full', warning that the rate of prison sentencing would soon 'outstrip the capacity of the prisons'. By the time Labour left office in May 2010, the prison population had climbed to a record high of 85,201—nearly twice the level under Mr Major.

In June 2010, the Scottish Parliament unilaterally reduced prisoner numbers north of the border, by means of a new Criminal Justice and Licensing Bill introducing a presumption against sentences of three months or less alongside a commitment to tougher community sentences. The Bill also raised the age of criminal responsibility in Scotland from eight to 12—two years higher than that in England and Wales, where Mr Brown's government had kept it at 10.

The Coalition's aim of cutting the prison population has taken longer than expected to materialize: in June 2012, it emerged that inmate numbers had actually risen by 1,500 since May 2010. Mr Clarke blamed this, in part, on a spike in jail sentences following England's August 2011 urban riots—arguing that tougher sentencing had been needed 'to restore public order' after that event, with MoJ figures showing that four out of 10 of the 1,715 convicted rioters were repeat offenders.

The rehabilitation of offenders

Convicted offenders receive sentences that are either *custodial* (detention in prison or a young offenders' institution) or *non-custodial* (for example conditional discharge, community service, probation, fines, or compensation order). The latter are supervised in England and Wales by the NPS, and in Scotland, by council-employed social workers.

Other than in the exceptional cases in which royal pardons are issued on the advice of the Justice Secretary (see Chapter 1, 'Notional prerogative powers—those deferred to government'), prisoners are generally granted early release only in recognition of 'good behaviour' in custody. This is known as **parole**. Although the application process is relatively simple, parole itself is complex, in that prisoners' eligibility depends on various factors—notably the nature and severity of their offences. Those eligible for parole may apply six months before their earliest possible release date (normally specified when they are sentenced). Files will be compiled on them and three members of the Parole Board—the body that advises the government on applications—will meet to decide whether to grant their wishes.

A swift decision may be taken for more minor offenders to allow them parole 'on licence'—under which they may be released early, subject to the condition that they do not reoffend. If they do reoffend within the remaining period of their original sentence, they may end up serving the remainder of that term after all, in addition to any further conviction period. Full Parole Board hearings tend to be called for only the most serious offenders.

As a result, in part, of concerns about prison overcrowding, parole has become all but automatic for most offenders. The Criminal Justice Act 1991 toughened the procedure. The conditions introduced to guide future decisions included the following.

- Prisoners serving between one and four years are released on licence when they have served half their sentences. Those sentenced to less than one year in jail are released halfway through their sentences without a licence.

- Inmates other than the most serious offenders (rapists and murderers) serving *four years or more* should be released on Parole Board recommendation after serving half their sentences, and normally automatically after serving two-thirds of their sentence.

- Final decisions on early release of prisoners serving *more than four, but less than seven years* should be taken by the Board.

- Prisoners sentenced to life imprisonment for certain kinds of murder—those of police officers, terrorism, and child killings—would tend automatically to serve at least 20 years. Early release of such 'mandatory life prisoners' could be authorized only by the Home Secretary in consultation with the Board and judiciary.

- Those sentenced to life for offences other than murder would normally be released by the Home Secretary after a period set by the judge at their trial. The Board would still have power, though, to order continued confinement if necessary to protect the public. Such sentences—known as 'indeterminate sentences for public protection' (IPP)—have caused headaches for recent governments. In February 2008, three Court of Appeal judges and the Lord Chief Justice ruled that the Board was not sufficiently independent of ministers to approve IPPs at their request and accused

Justice Secretary Mr Straw of acting 'unlawfully' in his prior treatment of such prisoners. Among the high-profile inmates repeatedly refused release on grounds of public safety were late Moors murderer Myra Hindley and serial killer Rose West. Peter Sutcliffe, the 'Yorkshire Ripper', was told by a High Court judge in July 2010 that he would never be released. Others, including Tracey Connelly, mother of child domestic abuse victim Peter Connelly ('Baby P'), are serving indefinite sentences (see Chapter 18, 'Care orders').

In addition to the 1991 Act, the Crime (Sentences) Act 1997 further toughened the sentencing regime by putting greater emphasis on the idea of prisoners *earning* parole—restyling them 'early release days' and introducing the idea that they could be 'gained' and 'lost'.

It also introduced:

- automatic life sentences for those convicted twice of serious sexual or violent crimes; and
- mandatory minimum prison sentences for drug dealers and serial burglars.

In opposition, the Conservatives consistently called for increased funding for additional prison places. On re-entering government, however, Mr Clarke performed an apparent volte-face, announcing a 'rehabilitation revolution' intended to cut the jail population. Pledging to 'shut the revolving door of crime and reoffending', he unveiled a new scheme analogous to that introduced by Mr Brown to find work for the long-term unemployed, under which private firms such as A4E would be paid by results for turning repeat offenders (particularly petty criminals) into 'law-abiding citizens' and prisoners would work for their keep while in jail.

Until 2006, Scottish parole policy was more lenient than those elsewhere in Britain—with prisoners serving between four and 10 years released on the Board's say-so after serving half their sentences, and only those incarcerated for more than 10 years needing the Home Secretary's consent. But under the Custodial Sentences and Weapons Act 2007 (passed by the Scottish Parliament), conditions for early release were toughened. Automatic early release without conditions for prisoners serving less than four years was replaced with a new licensing system. Anyone released early who breaches his or her licence terms is now returned to jail. In addition, sentencing judges who consider a defendant to be of particular public risk can stipulate that he or she waits longer than the usual halfway mark before qualifying for parole. The Board also has powers to increase this custodial period at a later date, should the circumstances arise. The Management of Offenders (Scotland) Act 2005, meanwhile, ended unconditional early release for sex offenders sentenced to between six months and four years, subjecting them to a new licence and supervision system.

In Northern Ireland, special circumstances apply in terrorism cases, in recognition of the unique nature of 'The Troubles'. Until 1995, terrorists sentenced to five years or more were usually paroled only after serving two-thirds of their terms, but this has since been harmonized with the rest of Britain—that is, eligibility after serving half a sentence. Terrorists convicted of another offence before the end of their original sentence must complete this before the next starts. In response to the positive progress of the Northern Ireland peace process at the time, a one-off arrangement was made allowing inmates of the Maze Prison out on licence for Christmas 1999 and New Year 2000.

☰ Topical feature idea

According to a joint report by Oxfam, Church Action on Poverty, and the Trussell Trust charity, published in June 2014, demand for emergency help from 'food banks'—services set up to provide meals and tinned goods for people living in 'food poverty'—soared by 54 per cent between 2012 and 2013. Even in affluent areas, poorer households are being forced to turn to them because of what the charities described as a perfect storm of falling or stagnant wages, benefit cuts and sanctions, and rising energy bills and food prices. Are there are any food banks operating in your area? If so, visit one and find out who is using them. What do the organizers say about the scale and nature of the demand that they are facing, and how it has changed over time?

✳ Current issues

- **The onward march of welfare reform** Despite delays in rolling out Universal Credit, the Coalition is continuing in its drive to tackle what it describes as the 'culture' of welfare, introducing a £26,000-a-year cap to the total that any single household may claim in benefits and preparing to cap the overall social security budget at no more than £119 billion a year (excluding pensions and Jobseeker's Allowance, or JSA, which is prone to short-term fluctuations caused by recessions).

- **The privatization of police, prisons, and probation service** Home Secretary Theresa May and Justice Secretary Chris Grayling have angered police, prison, and probation officers by cutting their budgets, reforming their pensions, and giving the go-ahead to outsourcing of police stations, prisons, and 21 probation services for medium-to-low-risk offenders.

- **Delays in assessment for ESA and PIPs** Work capability assessments (WCAs) for people receiving Incapacity Benefit and Employment Support Allowance (ESA) are being overhauled, but by June 2014 long delays were being reported in tests for the

Personal Independence Payments (PIPs) that have replaced Disability Living Allowance (DLA)—with some terminally ill people dying before they were assessed as being eligible for the benefit.

⠿ Key points

1. The 'welfare state' is the overarching term for the social security system administered by the Department for Work and Pensions (DWP).

2. There are two main categories of social security payment: contributory and non-contributory. Non-contributory benefits are purely needs-based, while contributory ones are awarded to people based on both qualifying criteria and prior National Insurance (NI) contributions record.

3. The Coalition's flagship welfare reform is Universal Credit—a new 'all in one' benefit set to replace JSA for the unemployed, ESA for the sick and disabled, Income Support, and various tax credits.

4. Benefits can also be divided into universal and means-tested. The former are paid to everyone who meets particular qualifying criteria, irrespective of income/wealth (for example Statutory Maternity Pay, or SMP), while the latter are available only to those on low incomes.

5. Home affairs are the responsibility of two government departments: the Home Office and Ministry of Justice (MoJ). The former is in charge of immigration and asylum policy, national security, and the police; the latter is responsible for the courts and legal system.

→ Further reading

Bartholomew, J. (2014) *The Welfare State We're In*, London: Biteback Publishing. **Openly one-sided, provocative, but intriguing critique of Britain's social security system, arguing that it has fostered a dependency culture.**

Golding, P. and Middleton. S. (1982) *Images of Welfare*, Oxford: Mark Robertson. **Classic historical overview of the evolution of welfare policy and public attitudes towards claimants, backed by authoritative analysis of media portrayals.**

Hansen, R. S. (2001) *Citizenship and Immigration in Post-war Britain: The Institutional Origins of a Multicultural Nation*, Oxford: Oxford University Press. **Accomplished evaluation of the socio-economic and cultural impact of immigration since 1945.**

Ishkanian, A. and Szreter, S. (2012) *The Big Society Debate: A New Agenda for Social Welfare?*, Cheltenham: Edward Elgar. **Bang up-to-date examination of impact of the Coalition's 'Big Society' approach to addressing social concerns of 'Broken Britain', focusing on a translation of rhetoric into Iain Duncan Smith's wide-ranging welfare reforms.**

Reiner, R. (2010) *The Politics of the Police*, 4th edn, Oxford: Oxford University Press. **Fully revised third edition of standard text on the origins, history, and present-day make-up of the British police. Includes detailed analysis of current issues, including those arising from the Macpherson Report into the Stephen Lawrence case.**

Sanders, A. (2010) *Criminal Justice*, 4th edn, London: LexisNexis UK. **Critical analysis of the British criminal justice system, focusing on all aspects of crime and punishment, including habeas corpus, the penal system, and sentencing procedures.**

Online Resource Centre

www.oxfordtextbooks.co.uk/orc/Morrison4e/
Visit the Online Resource Centre that accompanies this book for web links and regular updates.

9

The European Union

Even before the United Kingdom Independence Party (UKIP) provoked a febrile debate about Britain's 'future' in Europe, the European Union (EU) was a subject that divided politicians, public, and media into two, equally vociferous, camps. On the one side are 'Europhiles'—those who see closer economic and political integration between the EU's current 28 member states as a logical, common-sense, and desirable outcome that can only enhance mutual understanding and, ultimately, prosperity across the European continent. Then there are the 'Eurosceptics'. While some are merely critical of the EU's present composition (seeing it as overly bureaucratic and lacking accountability), others view the very concept of the Union as an anathema, arguing that it threatens individual nations' sovereignty and self-determination.

Europe generates extensive (if often ill-informed) coverage in the British press. Although EU press officers are forever complaining about how difficult it is to interest editors and reporters in writing meaningful news stories about its work, the number of column inches devoted to supposed diktats from 'Brussels' (to cite the commonly used shorthand) has steadily increased since the dramatic parliamentary scenes of the early 1990s surrounding the passage of the 'Maastricht Treaty' (see 'Britain's twisty path to EU membership' in this chapter). Furores have often verged on the farcical. In 1998, *Daily Mail* readers were greeted by near-hysterical headlines in response to the European Commission's attempt to force British chocolate manufacturers such as Cadbury to redefine their products as 'vegelate' (reflecting the high percentage of vegetable fats that they contained in comparison to cocoa butter). Then, in 2005, *The Sun* launched a 'Save our Jugs' campaign in protest at a supposed attempt by 'EU killjoys' to force busty barmaids to cover up their cleavages. The actual proposal (dropped in light of the opposition) was a draft 'Optical Radiation Directive' designed to protect workers, from builders to park-keepers, from excessive exposure to the sun. It made no mention of barmaids' breasts. A useful, often amusing, rundown of popular myths about the EU can be found online at www.the-eu-and-me.org.uk/eu-myths.

What, then, *does* EU membership mean for Britain, and how did it come about?

▶ Britain's twisty path to EU membership

The European 'Common Market' (as it was widely known in Britain until the 1970s) began slowly emerging in the post-war period, as the continent struggled to rebuild itself. But although it shared many of the same economic interests as its neighbours, for a long time Britain's attitude towards them was lukewarm. Buffered by the existence of its Commonwealth of dependent nations, on the one hand, and its emerging 'special relationship' with the United States on the other, it was reluctant to be too tied to the activities of its Continental cousins.

By 1961, however, the positive economic impact membership of the European Economic Community (EEC) appeared to be having for its member states encouraged the UK, under then Conservative Prime Minister Harold Macmillan, to apply for membership alongside Denmark, Ireland, and Norway. At the time, its application was blocked by France's then President Charles de Gaulle, who twice obstructed it (in 1963 and 1967), arguing that Britain was not sufficiently 'European' to join.

In the ensuing disagreement with fellow member states, De Gaulle precipitated one of the biggest constitutional upheavals in the history of the embryonic EU by refusing to send representatives from France to meetings of any of the three Communities from 1965 to 1966 (an affair known as the 'empty chairs crisis'). His action led, in 1966, to the Luxembourg Compromise—an informal understanding that agreements between member governments must in future be made *unanimously*, rather than by *majority vote*, as had happened before.

Following de Gaulle's resignation in 1969, negotiations began in earnest for Britain's accession to the new Community and the country was taken into it by Edward Heath's government in 1973. Ireland and Denmark joined at the same time.

Yet any hopes that accession would end years of squabbling between Britain and its European neighbours—not to mention infighting over the European Community (EC) in the UK's main political parties—were short-lived. By the time of the 1974 election, divisions were so marked within Harold Wilson's Labour Party and the country at large that he pledged to hold a referendum on the issue if returned to power. This he did, on 5 June 1975, but only after waiving the decades-old convention of collective responsibility (see Chapter 3, 'Collective responsibility, ministerial responsibility, and the Ministerial Code'), allowing members of his Cabinet who opposed his pro-European stance to campaign actively for 'no' votes. These included then Industry Secretary Tony

Benn and Employment Secretary Michael Foot, who argued that free trade between Britain and its Continental neighbours under membership of the EC was allowing cheap imports to flood high-street shops, undermining the profits of British-based manufacturers and leading to job cuts.

Despite the efforts of the 'no' lobby, Wilson got his way decisively enough to lay to rest the EC membership debate for the time being (although not forever): his 'yes' campaign clinched more than two-thirds of votes in the referendum, on a 64 per cent turnout.

Mr Wilson's triumph was pyrrhic: Britain's admission into the EU marked the beginning of what has continued to be a troubled relationship with the Union. At various points during its membership, the country has refused to toe the line—negotiating 'opt-outs' from clauses to treaties that bind most, if not all, of its peers (for example John Major's refusal to sign the Social Chapter of the 'Maastricht Treaty' and David Cameron's unwillingness to endorse the new Fiscal Compact approved by all other member states save the Czech Republic in December 2011) and struggling to win parliamentary approval for various others. In 1992, Mr Major's government was almost felled by its own back-benchers over Maastricht—an episode explored in depth later in this chapter—while more recently Tony Blair and Gordon Brown both resisted the clamour for a referendum on the 'Lisbon Treaty', a similarly controversial agreement that many Eurosceptics (and some Europhiles, such as Kenneth Clarke) argued was essentially the same document as the ill-fated 'EU Constitution' (see 'The Constitutional Treaty'). Although presently in coalition with the predominantly Europhile Liberal Democrats—whose leader, Nick Clegg, is both a former member of the European Parliament (MEP) and 'Eurocrat'—David Cameron's Conservatives remain a largely Eurosceptic party. Prior to gaining power, they formed a breakaway right-wing political grouping in the European Parliament. Since doing so, they have refused to cede any further powers to the EU without a referendum—and, in 2012, negotiated a real-terms cut in the Union's budget in line with the austerity measures that ministers were introducing domesti-cally (although, ironically, they failed to reduce Britain's contributions).

Aside from Sweden and Denmark, Britain is the only EU state to have held out against joining the euro, while its refusal to sign the Schengen Agreement (see Table 9.1) is the reason why Britons are still expected to show their nation-al passports when crossing internal EU borders—including returning to their home country—while citizens of fellow member states are not.

▶ The evolution of the European Union (EU)

So how did today's EU come about? And how was it transformed from a loose confederation of states cooperating over trade in core post-war raw materials (principally steel and coal) into a sprawling supranational alliance exercising a

Table 9.1 Chronology of evolution of the EU

Agreement	Year signed	Main provisions
Treaty of Paris	1951	Established the European Coal and Steel Community (ECSC). Membership initially limited to France, Germany, Italy, Luxembourg, Belgium, and Netherlands. Treaty initiated joint production of two materials most central to war effort (coal and steel) and fledgling European assembly, which met for first time in Strasbourg in September 1952.
Treaties of Rome	1957	Often referred to in singular, these twin treaties spawned two organizations later to coalesce—European Economic Community (EEC) and European Atomic Energy Community (EURATOM)—their joint aim being to foster trade between member nations by ending tariffs imposed by one on imports from another and removing other distortions in market, as well as:
		1. introducing Common Agricultural Policy (CAP)—encouraging free trade in agricultural products within EEC, while guaranteeing farmers' incomes in relation to competition from third-party countries through subsidies, as consolidated in 1962 by formation of European Agricultural Guidance and Guarantee Fund (EAGGF); and
		2. creating 'common market' for free movement of goods, services, and capital between member states (in practice, only free trade in goods followed until Single European Act 1986).
Merger of three European Unions	1965	In 1967, merger of ECSC, EURATOM, and EEC into single European Community (EC) came into effect, framed around four core institutions: European Commission (the EC's 'Civil Service'); European Assembly (later renamed European Parliament); European Court of Justice; and future Council of Ministers.
Launch of European Monetary System (EMS)	1979	Designed to relax exchange rates between member states, this eventually led to launch of euro.
Enlargement	1981	Greece admitted into EC.
Single European Act and further enlargement	1986	First full-scale revision of original 1957 European Treaties, defining structure of new-look EC and paving way for following extensions of community:
		1. greater economic integration;
		2. strengthened supranational institutions; and
		3. practical moves towards single European currency and linked exchange rates in form of economic and monetary union (EMU).
		In same year, Spain and Portugal entered EC.

Table 9.1 (*Continued*)

Agreement	Year signed	Main provisions
Treaty on the European Union ('Maastricht Treaty')	1992	EC formally renamed 'European Union' (EU), adding new areas of responsibility. Although signed in February 1992, had to be formally ratified by each state and passage was far from smooth in Britain (see 'The Treaty on the European Union'). It:
		1. introduced EU-wide commitment to move towards full EMU in three stages—and eventual single currency or 'common' one (native currencies retained, in parallel with EU one);
		2. established single European Union from existing communities;
		3. set up framework for potential common foreign and security policy;
		4. increased cooperation on domestic issues, particularly criminal justice;
		5. established principle of subsidiarity—system defining EU institutions as 'subsidiary to' those of individual member states and safeguarding their ability to run own internal affairs without consulting EU unless unable to achieve national objectives unilaterally; and
		6. introduced concept of 'EU citizenship'.
Corfu Treaty	1994	Allowed Austria, Finland, and Sweden to join EU in January 1995, and paved way for Norway's accession (it subsequently declined to join).
Amsterdam Treaty	1997	Arose out of 1996 Intergovernmental Conference (IGC) convened by heads of EU states. Extended rights of EU citizens in relation to:
		1. consumer protection;
		2. fight against crime and drugs; and
		3. environmental protection.
		Treaty also introduced Charter on Fundamental Workers' Rights.
		Summit had attempted to persuade member states to agree EU-wide immigration and asylum policy, but Britain, Ireland, and Denmark opted out, leaving rest to form Schengen Group, which UK declined to join at 2000 Nice Summit. Its name referred to deal known as **Schengen Agreement**—signed in two stages, in 1985 and 1990—abolishing border controls between participating nations.
Helsinki Summit	1999	This removed existing system under which notional target dates set for accession of specific countries to EU membership. From now on, any country meeting qualifying conditions would be eligible for swift entry. Entry talks quickly began with Slovakia, Malta, Lithuania, Bulgaria, Latvia, and Romania. Turkey also entered talks soon after, despite having previously been rejected in 1997.

(*continued*)

Table 9.1 (*continued*)

Agreement	Year signed	Main provisions
Agenda 2000, *For a Stronger and Wider Europe*	2000	Commission discussion document setting out blueprint for onward development of Community in twenty-first century. Many provisions intended to prevent future disagreements between members like those provoked by discussion of EMU, proposed common defence policy, and CAP. Also signalled attempt to set firm rules for acceptance of new countries. Among its stipulations were: 1. any new country wishing to join EU must meet economic and political criteria for membership and adopt *acquis communitaire*—laws and policies of EU—before being accepted (because Cyprus had just been admitted, new regulations began with 10 additional states that entered in 2004); 2. redefining CAP and 'structural funds' used to ensure equitable socio-economic infrastructure across Europe; 3. expressing then Commission's view on proposed accession to EU of countries in central and eastern Europe; and 4. proposing new budgetary framework for EU, with initial proposals for Community-wide budget 'not exceeding 1.27 per cent of EU's GNP'.
Nice Treaty	2000	'Proclaimed' EU Charter of Fundamental Rights (conflation of principles outlined in preceding European Convention on Human Rights, or ECHR, devised in 1950 by Council of Europe—see Chapter 10, 'The Council of Europe'). Charter's 53 'Articles' not legally binding, but expressed shared set of aims, including: 1. equality between men and women; 2. fair and just working conditions; 3. workers' rights to collective bargaining and industrial action; 4. public rights to access EU documents; and 5. right of elderly to life of 'dignity'. Nice Summit also aired concerns including implications of accepting 12 prospective additional members, who later joined. Consensus emerged that EU's main governing institutions would have to change over time for following reasons: 1. arrival of 12 potential new members meant they needed votes in Council of Ministers, own EU commissioners, seats in European Parliament, and judges; 2. reunification of Germany, following fall of Berlin Wall in 1990; and 3. impact of EU enlargement on asylum, immigration, and economic migration.

Table 9.1 (*Continued*)

Agreement	Year signed	Main provisions
Göteborg Summit	2001	Focused on perceived conflict between EU membership and Irish Constitution, particularly regarding province's neutrality. At around same time, Ireland narrowly voted 'no' in referendum on EU membership. Another controversy stemmed from realization of larger member states that enlargement might result in reductions in funds they received from EU.
White Paper on EU Governance	2001	Produced in response to mounting distrust of unelected EU policymaking institutions, this paved way for more democratically accountable EU by: 1. involving individual states, especially smaller ones, more openly in decisions; 2. introducing 'better policies and regulations'; 3. moving towards system of 'global governance'; and 4. 'refocusing' EU's core institutions. These ideas were underpinned by clearer list of principles that EU pledged to embody in future: 1. *openness*—encouraging its institutions to work together more; 2. *participation*—encouraging all members to take active part in decision-making; 3. *accountability*—giving clearer definitions of roles of EU institutions; 4. *effectiveness*—ensuring policies appropriate to current socio-economic climate and promptly implemented once decided upon; 5. *coherence*—making sure policies easily understood; 6. *proportionality*; and 7. *subsidiarity*—ensuring 'action' by EU in relation to member states taken only when strictly necessary.
Enlargement of the Union	2004	Czech Republic, Estonia, Hungary, Latvia, Lithuania, Poland, Slovakia, Slovenia, Malta, and Greek Cyprus joined EU.
Enlargement of the Union	2007	Romania and Bulgaria joined.
European Union Reform Treaty ('Treaty of Lisbon')	2007	Almost as contentious as 'Maastricht', this followed short-lived 'EU Constitution'—abandoned after being rejected in French and Dutch referendums. 'Lisbon Treaty' also rejected by Ireland (initially), but eventually came into force in December 2009. Its main provisions were to: 1. make Charter of Fundamental Rights legally binding; 2. extend role of directly elected European Parliament; 3. introduce permanent president of European Council in place of current 'rotating presidency' and formally recognize Council as fifth EU governing institution; and 4. give EU as a whole legal status of single entity capable of signing international treaties with other institutions or bodies.
Enlargement	2013	Croatia joined.

degree of control—often contentiously—over everything from employment rights to economic migration?

Its growth and evolution can best be charted with reference to the treaties and summits that paved the way for it to become the hugely influential entity that it is today. The most significant developments in the evolution of the EU are outlined in Table 9.1.

Of all treaties listed, the British government found it particularly difficult to ratify 'Maastricht' (see below). It was not alone: in a June 1992 national referendum, the people of Denmark rejected it. The Danish government squeaked it through 11 months later, only after negotiating 'opt-outs' from two of its key provisions: economic and monetary union (EMU), and the move towards a common European defence policy.

▍ From 'three pillars' to one EU

A key sticking point of the Maastricht Treaty for individual member states was its underlying emphasis on fostering a 'supranational' approach to major policy areas beyond the EU's traditional drive towards Europe-wide free trade. Where several countries—notably Britain, Sweden, and Denmark—wanted to limit the EU's influence to the economic sphere, the likes of France and Germany appeared willing to surrender varying degrees of national sovereignty, and were keen to roll out the Union's responsibilities to encompass everything from criminal justice and drugs policy, to defence and security.

The process of negotiating the Maastricht settlement led to the emergence of three broad areas of policy—or 'pillars': European Communities (covering economic, social, and environmental policies); Common Foreign and Security Policy (CFSP); and Police and Judicial Cooperation in Criminal Matters (PJCC). In the Lisbon Treaty (see 'The Treaty of Lisbon'), the pillars were abolished—to be replaced by a single, consolidated EU structure.

▍ The main EU institutions

Journalistically, the best EU stories invariably arise out of conflict and confrontation. Notwithstanding ongoing wrangles over the Union's future direction and scope, many contentious issues emerge from the day-to-day deliberations of the EU's five principal governing institutions:

- the European Commission;
- the European Parliament;
- the Council of the European Union (Council of Ministers);

- the European Court of Justice (ECJ); and
- the European Council.

Each institution is chaired by its own president, the methods of election or appointment of whom vary.

The European Commission

Formed in 1951 and based in Brussels, the **European Commission** is the civil service and executive of the EU rolled into one. It employs 25,000 staff working at various levels across more than 30 'departments and services'—or 'Directorates-General'.

Each Directorate-General is headed by one of 33 commissioners (at least one from each member state, appointed for a five-year period). Meetings are chaired by one of their number, elected president by the European Parliament (on the recommendation of the European Council, or Summit). The president chairs meetings of the Commission much as a prime minister sitting in Cabinet. Although the Council of Ministers, composed of representatives from each member state's government, takes final decisions on major political developments and structural changes in the EU (subject to 'emergency brake' intervention by the European Council in exceptional cases), the Commission is responsible for *initiating* policy. It does this in much the same way as national policy is originated through Cabinet government, with commissioners sitting around a table developing ideas for prospective legislation.

What makes the Commission more controversial is that none of its members is elected; rather, all are 'proposed' (nominated) by the governments of their native countries. The fact that they are chosen by democratically elected politicians arguably gives them some degree of legitimacy, but they are not directly answerable to the European citizens whose lives their proposals affect. This perceived lack of accountability was famously described in a 1980s pamphlet as a 'democratic deficit' by Liberal Democrat MEP Bill Newton Dunn.

The Commission issues its policy proposals in three broad guises: regulations, decisions, and directives. Both regulations and directives must be scrutinized by the European Parliament and Council of Ministers before they can be enacted, but this is where the similarity between them ends. Regulations are EU-wide laws similar to British primary legislation, which, once passed in Council, will automatically apply in all member states. Directives are broader 'end results' that must be achieved in each state, but it is left up to individual members to decide how to do this by, if necessary, introducing new or adapting existing national legislation. Decisions, meanwhile, are binding laws (akin to private Bills in the UK—see Chapter 2, 'Public, private, and hybrid Bills') used to impose conditions or to confer rights on individuals or authorities in a particular state—for example forcing a government department or quango to issue new guidelines to local authorities on kerb-side recycling.

Not that policies devised by the Commission are automatically a done deal: elected MEPs have ample opportunity to scrutinize and even reject them, and ultimate say-so for new regulations rests with the Council of Ministers. Moreover, although it has far greater political clout than the British Civil Service—the job of which is merely to implement government policy 'on the ground' once Parliament has approved it—the Commission also fulfils this basic administrative function. The European Parliament may, however, dismiss the Commission in exceptional circumstances—although, curiously, it is prevented from removing individual commissioners and must instead sack *all* of them. This scenario has arisen more than once in recent years. In March 1999, the Commission, under then President Jacques Santer, resigned en masse following publication of a damning report into its alleged nepotism. Although it stopped short of suggesting that any commissioner was directly involved in corrupt practices, the 144-page report, by five independent 'wise persons', singled out former French Prime Minister Edith Cresson for her 'dysfunctional' organization and favouritism in staff appointments.

Although unelected, commissioners are invariably experienced politicians or public figures who have previously served in senior positions in their home countries. Until the EU's membership expanded from 15 to 25 states in 2004, the countries with the biggest populations—Britain, Germany, France, and Italy—had two each, with smaller states having just one. Among those who served in this capacity were former Labour leader Neil Kinnock, who was Commissioner for Transport, and ex-Conservative Home Secretary Sir Leon Brittan, one-time Commissioner for External Trade Relations. Former Northern Ireland Secretary Lord Mandelson became Britain's first single Commissioner in 2004 (overseeing trade), but after being recalled to the British Cabinet in Gordon Brown's second reshuffle in October 2008 he was replaced by Baroness Ashton of Upholland. Following implementation of the Lisbon Treaty in December 2009, the Commission was dissolved and reconstituted, and Lady Ashton was elevated to the newly created role of **High Representative for Foreign Affairs and Security Policy** (and one of seven vice-presidential positions). Her swift promotion was interpreted by some in the media as a consolation prize for Britain in the wake of the EU's 'snub' to former Prime Minister Blair's designs on the first 'EU presidency'. At time of

writing, Lord Hill, the former Leader of the House of Lords, had recently succeeded her as UK commissioner, having secured a newly created brief overseeing financial stability, financial services, and capital markets.

Enduring controversy over the Commission's composition, powers, and privileges has led to repeated attempts to reform it. For many years, its mammoth expenses bill was cited as a concern for EU taxpayers, and terms such as

'Brussels bureaucrats' and 'gravy train' were frequent bedfellows in the British tabloids. This issue was somewhat addressed in the 1999 report and subsequent reforms—some instigated by Lord Kinnock, who, in his role as Commission vice-president, tried to clean up its act by establishing an internal audit service and ethics committee. But concerns about the perceived power that it wields—and the apparent dominance of certain countries in its decision-making—led to several further reforms being proposed in the 'Lisbon Treaty'. These were to have included a reduction in the number of commissioners, with only two-thirds of member states being represented at any one time from 2014 and seats distributed fairly on a rotating basis. However, Ireland's initial rejection of Lisbon in its 2008 referendum prompted the European Council to take the executive decision to retain the existing 'one member, one commissioner' system for the time being, by way of a peace offering to it and other smaller nations. The European Council's ability to do this was itself formalized by Lisbon, which gives it the right to alter the number of commissioners unilaterally at any time, subject to unanimous approval by its members.

The Commission's present composition is outlined in the table entitled 'The current composition of the European Commission', to be found on the **Online Resource Centre** that accompanies this book.

The European Parliament

Although the **European Parliament** has the appearance of a legislature, until recently it had considerably less influence on EU law-making than either Commission or Council of Ministers. Traditionally, it has tended to be *consulted* on decisions, rather than taking them itself, rather like a giant House of Commons committee, rather than a legislative assembly per se. For this reason, it was for many years caricatured as a supine talking shop. However, Maastricht gave it the ability to *reject* legislation that it dislikes, according it 'joint' legislative status with the Council of Ministers in certain areas, under a process that was known as 'co-decision'. Briefly, this works as follows: the Commission will pass a proposal for a new regulation or directive to the Parliament, which then expresses its opinion at a 'first reading'. If the Council approves of this opinion, the 'law' is passed, but if not, it will deliver its own verdict to the Parliament, together with an explanation of its thinking. The Parliament then enters a 'second reading' stage, at which it can either approve the Council's changes (in which case the law is passed), amend them, or reject the law outright. All the while, the Commission will also be giving its opinion on suggested amendments, and if it rejects any, the Council must vote to approve the amended law unanimously, rather than by a majority. If, on the other hand, a stalemate between the Parliament and Council lasts more than three months, the presidents of the two institutions may convene a conciliation committee, made up of equal numbers of MEPs and Council members, to broker a compromise.

This equal-weighted, if drawn-out, approach to law-making—renamed the 'ordinary legislative procedure' (OLP) under Lisbon—used to exist in relation to only a few areas, such as health, culture, science, sport, and some aspects of asylum policy. But Lisbon extended it to most others, including agriculture, transport, and decisions over how to allocate European structural funds. The European Parliament also has powers to legislate in relation to the smooth operation of the 'eurozone' and, crucially, veto the EU budget. And (subject to agreement with the Council of Ministers) it may take action over other aspects of economic policy: in July 2010, the Parliament passed legislation capping bankers' bonuses. Since January 2011, up-front cash bonuses have been limited to a quarter of the total (or 20 per cent for 'particularly large' bonuses), with 40–60 per cent deferred. In a move designed to deter excessive risk-taking by bankers, the rules also stipulated that at least half the total bonus should be paid as 'contingent capital'—meaning that it would be the first money to be called upon in the case of future debt or liquidity problems. On 1 January 2014, new rules were introduced to cap bonuses at no more than 100 per cent of bankers' annual salaries or twice that level if shareholders explicitly approved after being approved by the Parliament.

Despite its title, when originally christened in 1958, the European Parliament's representatives were not elected at all, but appointed, one by each member country. But, since 1979, it has been a fully elected institution. By the time of its first election, the number of representatives—today known as **members of the European Parliament (MEPs)**—had increased from 142 to 410.

The current membership numbers 751. Elections are held every five years and, prior to 1999, were conducted on a 'first past the post' (FPTP) system analogous to that used in UK general elections (see Chapter 4, 'How the British electoral system works'). The European Parliament Act 1999 changed this by introducing proportional representation (PR), generally based on the party list system. Parties are now awarded a number of seats proportional to their share of the vote.

Britain is currently divided into 12 European electoral regions (including Northern Ireland, which uses its own version of PR). Each region returns between three and 10 MEPs, depending on its population. There are 72 British MEPs altogether (down from 78 since the recent enlargements): 59 in England, six in Scotland, four in Wales, and three in Northern Ireland.

Like the Commission, the European Parliament has its own president (elected by absolute majority in a secret ballot of members for renewable terms of two-and-a-half years), and its principal base is in Brussels, where it sits for three weeks a month. For the other week, its members travel to Strasbourg in France, convening in an identical chamber.

As in Britain's Parliament, MEPs sit in political groupings reflecting their ideological affiliations, rather than regional or national delegations.

There are currently seven political groupings, although at time of writing 52 MEPs remained 'non-attached' ('non-inscrit'). The groupings sit at designated points around the 'hemispherical' (semi-circular) parliamentary chamber, according to their notional position on the Left–Right political spectrum. Communist MEPs will sit to the far left of the central seat occupied by the Parliament's president, while fascists and extreme Right parties such as France's Front National—which heads up an 'unofficial' grouping calling itself the Alliance of European National Movements (AENM)—occupy seats on the far right.

To be recognized as a legitimate grouping (and, since 2011, entitled to additional funding), an interparty alliance needs to number at least 25 MEPs from a minimum of seven member states. The current political groupings (as of May 2014) are:

- European People's Party (EPP)—221 members;
- Progressive Alliance of Socialists and Democrats (S&D)—191 members;
- Alliance of Liberals and Democrats for Europe (ALDE)—67 members;
- The Greens/European Free Alliance (Greens/EFA)—50 members;
- European Conservatives and Reformists (ECR)—70 members;
- European United Left/Nordic Green Left (EUL/NGL)—52 members; and
- Europe of Freedom and Direct Democracy (EFDD)—48 members.

While Britain's Labour Party has long been part of the socialist grouping, after much internal debate the Conservatives finally acted on a long-standing promise to pull out of the centre-right EPP after the June 2009 European elections. Mr Cameron, who had made this pledge a central plank of his 2005 campaign for the party's leadership, announced the formation of the ECR—a Eurosceptic alliance including several parties the views of which have invited disdain in the liberal media. Of these, Poland's Law and Justice Party, which draws much of its support from ultra-conservative Catholics, has been accused of homophobia, while Latvia's Fatherland and Freedom Party counts among its members a number of former recruits to Hitler's Waffen SS. The Tories' decision to quit the EPP earned it barbs from centre-right European leaders including then French President Nicolas Sarkozy and German Chancellor Angela Merkel, and it looks set to remain a point of contention in coming months and years as the EU moves to consolidate the Lisbon reforms while shoring up the embattled eurozone in the teeth of the sovereign debt crisis (see 'The eurozone "sovereign debt crisis"' in this chapter).

Administration of the Parliament's functions is overseen by yet another layer of EU bureaucracy: a 'bureau' run by the president, 14 vice-presidents, and five 'quaestors' (civil servants responsible for accounting matters directly affecting MEPs themselves). All of these officials are elected, like the president, for two-and-a-half years at a time.

The Council of Ministers

The **Council of the European Union** (or **Council of Ministers**) is the single most powerful EU institution. Comprising departmental ministers from each of the 28 member states, its precise composition varies according to the issue being debated on a given day. If the Council is debating health policy, a health minister from each member state will attend, while discussions about crime, policing, and security will involve interior ministers (in Britain's case, the Home Secretary or another Home Office minister).

The Council has 10 'configurations', reflecting the broad policy areas under its jurisdiction:

- General Affairs;
- Foreign Affairs;
- Economic and Financial Affairs;
- Justice and Home Affairs;
- Employment, Social Policy, Health, and Consumer Affairs;
- Competitiveness;
- Transport, Telecommunications, and Energy;
- Agriculture and Fisheries;
- Environment; and
- Education, Youth, and Culture.

Although policy ideas are often proactively proposed by the Commission, all but the most minor must be formally approved by the Council to make them 'law'. To this end, it is supported by a related institution, the Committee of Permanent Representatives (COREPER), comprising civil servants or ambassadors seconded from each member state (and which is itself backed by another 150 committees and working groups).

All Council meetings are chaired by a senior politician (normally the president or prime minister) from the country currently holding the rotating EU presidency. Britain last held the presidency in 2005. In view of the need for continuity emphasized by this rota, the Council has its own dedicated civil service: the General Secretariat of the Council.

Qualified majority voting (QMV)

The voting system used in the Council is complex and, as such, warrants its own section, given its importance in determining the direction of EU policy.

The unanimous approval of member states is normally required to pass major decisions with implications for the future of the EU—such as whether to admit additional countries into the Union. The annual confirmation of the EU's Budget also traditionally requires unanimity. Since Maastricht, however, an increasing number of (often significant) decisions have been agreed through a process known as **qualified majority voting (QMV).** As its name suggests, the premise of QMV is for agreement on a policy to be reached without the need for every member state to approve it—that is, on a majority basis. This majority system is 'qualified', however, in two respects, as follows.

- Member states are not accorded an equal say in the Council; rather, the number of votes allocated to each is weighted to reflect its population size, giving some countries greater clout than others.

- A simple majority system (like that which determines whether Acts are passed in the UK Parliament) has traditionally required only one more 'yes' vote than the total number of 'no' votes—but under the Nice system (due to end on 1 November 2014), approval by QMV required the backing of 74.8 per cent of weighted votes in the Council (258 out of 345), representing 62 per cent of the EU's population (on the request of a member state). The new definition of 'qualified majority', enshrined in the Lisbon Treaty, rests on a so-called 'double majority' principle. For decisions to be carried, they now require the backing of at least 55 per cent of member states (15 countries) and 65 per cent of the EU's population. At least four states must join forces to block a motion. The rationale behind this new variant of QMV is that it is 'fairer' both to larger and smaller countries—by weighting decisions to take account of both states with large populations and the sovereign voting rights of *individual* countries, no matter how small. Although this system is now firmly established, between 2014 and 31 March 2017 any member state may request that the old one be used.

Of the bigger countries, France, Britain, Germany, and Italy presently have the most votes under QMV, with 29 apiece. The least populated country, Malta, has just three. The overall breakdown of vote allocations under QMV is spelled out in the table entitled 'Allocation of voting power under qualified majority voting (QMV)', to be found on the **Online Resource Centre**.

Perhaps unsurprisingly, QMV has its critics. Some smaller states have complained of having policies imposed on them—regardless of their views—by more heavily populated ones. Eurosceptics, meanwhile, see the absence of a 'one member, one vote' system as evidence that individual countries are increasingly being subsumed within an embryonic 'European superstate', rather than treated as a confederation of independent—and equal—countries. It was partly to address these concerns that Lisbon introduced the new 'double majority' system.

The European Court of Justice (ECJ)

Established in 1952, the **European Court of Justice (ECJ)**—officially the 'Court of Justice of the European Communities'—is the EU's supreme legal institution. Unlike other bodies, it is based in Luxembourg City, but like them it has its own president (appointed by fellow judges on a renewable three-year term).

Again like the other key EU institutions, the Court comprises 28 members: one judge per member state. For practical reasons, a maximum of 13 judges will usually hear a case at any one time, sitting as a 'Grand Chamber'. The judges are assisted by nine 'advocates-general'—lawyers tasked with presenting to them impartial 'opinions' on individual cases. Judgments are made in a collegiate way and must be unanimous.

Judges are nominated by the member states from which they hail, on renewable six-year terms. Six advocates-general are nominated by the biggest EU member states—Britain, France, Germany, Italy, Spain, and Poland—with the others rotating in alphabetical order between the remaining 22. Under the Lisbon Treaty, it is now possible for 11 advocates-general to be enlisted, if the Court requests this.

The Court may be required to pass judgment in a variety of circumstances—for example if there is evidence that a member state has not implemented a treaty or directive, or if a complainant alleges that a governmental institution, non-government organization (NGO), or commercial business has in some other way broken EU law.

Areas of EU law covered include:

- free trade and the movement of goods and services in the EU single market;
- employment law and the European Social Chapter;
- competition law (cartels, monopolies, mergers, and acquisitions); and
- public sector regulation.

In practice, it is unusual for a case involving an individual or small group of individuals to go before the ECJ itself. And even when a case *is* heard by the Court, this will often be by three or five judges, rather than 13. Only in exceptional cases (such as when an EU commissioner is alleged to have seriously failed to fulfil his or her obligations) will it ever sit as a 'full court', and even then only a quorum of 15 judges—rather than the full complement of 28—is needed.

In lesser cases, hearings are convened by a junior body established in 1988 to deal with the growing number of routine complaints being generated as the EU extended its influence: the General Court (until Lisbon, the 'Court of First Instance'). Like its more illustrious counterpart, this also boasts 28 judge and a president appointed by them for renewable six-year terms. Unlike the ECJ, however, it has no advocates-general, so a judge from among its own number is sometimes nominated to fulfil this role. A 'judge-rapporteur' will also be appointed to oversee proceedings and draft a provisional judgment—to be deliberated on by the judges—after hearing representations from complainant and respondent.

The General Court's responsibilities encompass the following policy areas:

- agriculture;
- state aid;
- competition;
- commercial policy;
- regional policy;
- social policy;
- institutional law;
- trademark law; and
- transport.

It has the authority to impose various penalties, as outlined in the table entitled 'Forms of ruling that can be made by the European Court of Justice (ECJ)', to be found on the **Online Resource Centre**.

Judgments by the General Court are subject to appeals to the ECJ. In addition to the General Court, two further courts exist to deal with more specific cases: the Civil Service Tribunal, which handles complaints about maladministration by EU employees, and the Court of Auditors, which oversees its accounts.

For individual member states, the extent to which European law can be said to take precedence over national legislatures, judiciaries, and (where relevant) constitutions is a subject of intense interest and ongoing debate. In recent years, however, a series of landmark Court judgments have pointed towards a growing sense that the EU holds supreme. In 1999, Mr Blair's government faced a compensation bill of up to £100 million after the ECJ ruled that Margaret Thatcher had broken European law by passing a 1988 Act intended to ban Spanish trawlermen from using British registered boats to fish in UK waters— a practice known as 'quota-hopping'. The final judgment in this case, known as *Factortame* (after the name of one of the 100-plus Spanish fishing companies that brought the original action), came only after a decade of legal ping-pong between London and Luxembourg.

Several 'test case' rulings have focused on the scope of EU employment law—in particular, the extent to which commercial companies and other non-government organizations can be bound by it. In the 1986 case *M. H. Marshall v. Southampton and South-West Hampshire Area Health Authority*, Ms Marshall sued her employer after being dismissed from her job on reaching the then State Pension age for women (60). She argued that this contravened the 1976 Equal Treatment Directive, because men were not expected to retire before the age of 65 and the Directive created rights that could be enforced 'horizontally' between individuals. The ECJ ruled against this interpretation—stipulating that directives generally applied only 'vertically' (that is, through the aegis of the specific individuals or organizations at whom they were directed). However, there was a silver lining for Ms Marshall: because the health authority employing her was 'an organ of the state' (meaning that it was bound by the Directive on a vertical basis), she still won her case.

Some judgments have proved so momentous that new legal concepts have been named after them: in 1991, a group of Italian workers who lost their jobs when their employer became insolvent successfully sued the country's government for failing to implement the 1980 Insolvency Protection Directive, which would have guaranteed them compensation. The ECJ's ruling in favour of the workers established the principle of member states being liable for compliance with EU law by all bodies based on their soil, including private companies. This has been christened the 'Frankovich principle' (after the surname of one victor).

But not all ECJ judgments have gone the claimant's way, and some outcomes suggest a rather less clear-cut balance of power between UK courts and the EU. In the 1974 case Van Duyn v. Home Office, the ECJ found in favour of Britain after a Dutch national, Yvonne Van Duyn, sued under the Treaty of Rome for being denied entry to the country because she was a practising Scientologist. The Court ruled that member states could bar individuals on the basis of their 'personal conduct' if this conflicted with national 'public policy' objectives; the UK's public policy was to prevent the spread of Scientology. More significantly, in 1993, the German judicial system successfully asserted its supremacy over the EU in internal constitutional matters. In Brunner v. the European Union Treaty, the German Constitutional Court ruled that it was for it alone to determine whether European laws, and the powers conferred on individual Union institutions, were compatible with Germany's constitution. And, in a warning similar to Mr Cameron's recent refusal to cede any further powers to the EU without consulting the British public first, it ruled that the country would not be bound by any interpretation of the Treaty that extended the Union's overall remit (or kompetenz), or any laws subsequently adopted by the EU that increased its existing powers—unless German law decided such laws should apply.

The European Council

For many years referred to as the 'European Summit' (to avoid confusion with the Council of Ministers), the **European Council** finally gained official status as a governing institution of the EU only in the Lisbon Treaty. Composed of the heads of state or government of all 28 member states, it meets up to four times a year, usually in the Justus Lipsius Building in Brussels, headquarters of the Council of Ministers.

The Council is today chaired by a full-time, 'permanent' **president of the European Council** selected by members of the Council. The inaugural president was former Belgian Prime Minister Herman Van Rompuy, whose second two-and-a-half-year term ended on 30 August 2014, when he was replaced by Donald Tusk, former Prime Minister of Poland. Under new rules, presidents must now reflect the political composition of the European Parliament, as newly re-elected in May that year. Previously, chairmanship of the Council rotated between member states, with individual heads of government taking it in turns to hold it for six months at a time, in tandem with their parallel presidency of the Council of Ministers. While the European Council has no legislative power (unlike its near-namesake), a member state may complain formally to it if it disputes a decision taken in the Council of Ministers, under a procedure known as the 'emergency brake'. The Council may then choose to settle the matter by holding its own vote—giving it what some observers see as the ultimate veto over disputed EU policy. Since Lisbon, it has also been charged officially with mapping the EU's overall future strategic direction.

▶ The evolution of the euro

Moves towards some form of single European currency quietly fermented for decades. But what started out as the seed of an idea in the minds of European commissioners in the late 1960s took some 30 years to reach fruition. The following section focuses on the more decisive stages in the development of the euro project.

The exchange rate mechanism (ERM) debacle and 'Black Wednesday'

In an effort to curb inflation, encourage trade, and stabilize exchange rates between individual EU member states' currencies—in doing so, kick-starting the process of introducing a single currency—in 1979 the EU introduced the exchange rate mechanism (ERM). The ERM was based on the idea of fixing narrower margins between which member states' currencies would be permitted to fluctuate in value in relation to those of other members—effectively 'pegging' one country's exchange rate to another's. Before the ERM, bilateral exchange rates between EU states were based on the European currency unit (ecu), a 'virtual' European currency traded in stock markets, the value of which was equivalent to a weighted average of those of the individual EU members' currencies. As a condition of EU membership, states were required to contain fluctuations in the value of their currencies within a 2.25 per cent margin either side of their bilateral exchange rates (except Italy, which was allowed a variance of up to 6 per cent).

The Maastricht Treaty envisaged the European monetary system (EMS) moving towards full monetary union in three stages, as set out in the table entitled 'The three stages of economic and monetary union (EMU)', to be found on the **Online Resource Centre**.

Britain was characteristically slow to sign up. It finally did so in 1990, when John Major was Chancellor, but his successor, Norman Lamont, pulled out dramatically on 16 September 1992, after a panic-stricken day of stock market speculation and interest rate hikes.

'Black Wednesday'—as it came to be known—arose out of the unsustainable position in which the British currency (the pound sterling) had found itself during the months after the country signed up to the ERM. Throughout much of the 1980s, Margaret Thatcher's Chancellor Nigel Lawson had 'shadowed' the German Deutschmark when deciding whether to raise or lower interest rates to maintain sterling's value. By September 1992, this had had the effect of valuing sterling unsustainably high compared to the US dollar. Because many British exports were valued in dollars, not sterling, the UK was potentially losing significant income from overseas markets by allowing the gap between dollar and pound to widen. But with Britain pegged to the ecu in the ERM, there was limited room for the Chancellor to devalue sterling as he otherwise might have done to remedy this.

The approaching crisis reached its tipping point when US speculators, including billionaire George Soros, began frenziedly borrowing pounds and selling them for Deutschmarks in mid-September, in the belief that sterling was about to be devalued and that they could therefore profit by repaying their loans at deflated prices. This prompted Mr Lamont to raise interest rates from 10 per cent to 12 per cent on 16 September (with the promise of a further increase, to 15 per cent, later the same day), to stop sterling's value falling too far by tempting speculators to buy pounds. But, apparently disbelieving him, speculators continued selling pounds in anticipation of a slump in its value.

With sterling plummeting as a consequence, at 7 p.m. Mr Lamont withdrew Britain from the ERM—freezing temporarily interest rates at 12 per cent, rather than raising them to the promised 15 per cent. During the course of a single day, he had spent billions of pounds of foreign currency reserves propping up the pound. By the time the Conservatives lost to Labour five years later, the ultimate cost to the taxpayer of 'Black Wednesday' was £3.3 billion, according to Treasury papers released in 2005. The Tories' previous reputation for economic competence was dealt a body blow by the events of that day, from which it took years to recover.

The launch of the euro and growth of the eurozone

The **euro** (€) has existed in 'non-physical' form—that is, in the guise of travellers' cheques, electronic transfers, etc.—since 1 January 1999, but it officially came into being on 1 January 2002, when the **European Central Bank (ECB)** in Frankfurt began issuing notes and coins in the 12 EU member states that had signed up to join. At the time, there were only 15 EU states, and membership of the euro has since been extended to include six of the additional 13 countries admitted through enlargement: Malta, Cyprus, Slovenia, Estonia, Slovakia, and Latvia (the newest member, having joined on 1 January 2014). Of the 'original' 15 EU members, Britain, Sweden, and Denmark are the only three to have resisted joining. Both Swedish and Danish populations have rejected the single currency in national referendums (the latter twice), and the former has since circumvented any pressure from 'eurozone' states to make a fresh attempt to join them by failing to adhere to the 'convergence criteria' that countries are expected to meet before being accepted into the euro.

The main convergence criteria, designed to promote price stability across participating states, require an applicant to achieve the following:

- an inflation rate no more than 1.5 per cent higher than that of the three lowest-inflation member states of the EU;
- a ratio of no more than 3 per cent between annual government deficit and gross domestic product (GDP) at the end of the preceding tax year;
- a ratio of gross government debt to GDP no greater than 60 per cent at the end of the preceding tax year (although it is sometimes acceptable to approach this target);
- membership of the successor to the original ERM—'ERM II'—for at least two consecutive years without at any point simultaneously devaluing the applicant's currency; and
- nominal long-term interest rates no more than 2 per cent higher than that of the three lowest-inflation EU member states.

At time of writing, the 18 countries in the eurozone were (in alphabetical order): Austria, Belgium, Cyprus, Estonia, Finland, France, Germany, Greece, Ireland, Italy, Latvia, Luxembourg, Malta, the Netherlands, Portugal, Slovakia, Slovenia, and Spain. In addition, several European states outside the EU now using the euro—Monaco, San Marino, and Vatican City—have all signed formal agreements allowing them to issue their own euro coinage, while Andorra has a monetary agreement with the Union allowing it to do so, and aspiring EU members Kosovo and Montenegro have adopted it as their official currency, but without any formal recognition allowing them to mint coins.

Britain remains a refusenik. Mr Major's government negotiated an 'opt-out protocol' before belatedly signing Maastricht, removing any obligation on its part to move from stage two to stage three of EMU. On entering office, Mr Blair promised to hold a referendum before committing the UK to the single currency. He repeated this pledge at various points during his 10 years in power and is thought always to have been broadly supportive of the idea of joining one day. But in 1997 Mr Brown announced that, before surrendering the strength of sterling to the untested vagaries of the euro, he would need to be convinced that Britain had met 'five economic tests'. These 'tests'—actually questions to determine whether the UK economy would benefit from entry—are outlined in the table entitled 'Gordon Brown's "five economic tests" for Britain's entry into the euro', to be found on the **Online Resource Centre**.

Critics argued that these questions—which effectively kept Britain out of the euro throughout New Labour's tenure—were at best susceptible to obfuscation and at worst unanswerable. In reality, many claimed, they allowed Mr Brown to place continual delays in the way of a referendum—arguing at any point in time that one or more tests had yet to be met.

The eurozone 'sovereign debt crisis'

Because several EU member states have yet to join the single currency, the Union has often been described as a 'two-speed' Europe. Until recently, many observers argued that, whatever their preferences, a time would one day come when Britain and all other member states outside the euro would be forced to join—if only to retain their influence at the negotiating table over other issues affecting the Union.

However, tumultuous recent events in the 'eurozone' sparked by sovereign debt crises in several member states—notably the so-called 'PIGS' economies of Portugal, Ireland, Greece, and Spain—have sharpened opposition to joining within the British political establishment. Sparked, in part, by the 2008–09 banking collapse (see Chapter 7, 'The global banking crisis and its fallout'), there have been so many twists and turns in this escalating emergency that it is impossible to give a definitive account of it in a book of this kind. Nonetheless, it would be remiss not to include a broad overview of the origins of the crisis and its most immediate ramifications.

In May 2010, the euro was plunged into the biggest crisis in its history after first Greece, then several other EU states using the single currency, became the subject of intense concern over the extent of their 'sovereign debt'—the individual budget deficits that they had accumulated following the global financial meltdown and (in some cases) their previous levels of borrowing.

Trouble began in Greece, where a package of austerity measures unveiled by the government provoked a wave of wildcat public sector strikes and violent demonstrations. Financial ratings agency Standard & Poor's swiftly reduced the status of the country's government bonds to 'junk'. To contain Greece's downturn—preventing it from having a knock-on effect on the euro and, by extension, other states' economies—on 2 May the eurozone countries teamed up with the International Monetary Fund (IMF) to offer the country an unprecedented €110 billion (£93 billion) loan bailout, on condition that it imposed harsh domestic spending cuts. Within a week, though, a further massive cash injection was required to stabilize the euro. This saw Europe's finance ministers collectively approve a loans package worth £624 billion aimed at ensuring financial stability across Europe by shoring up the 16 states by that point struggling to service their debts. In one of his last actions as Labour Chancellor, Alistair Darling signed off the deal—committing Britain to providing between £9.6 billion and £13 billion to support a new £95 billion 'stabilization mechanism' designed to stop individual countries' economies collapsing.

In the ensuing weeks, governments in a succession of other eurozone states, including Spain, Portugal, and Italy, began implementing similar austerity measures. But as international money markets indicated a new wariness towards the previously unassailable euro, the crisis came closer to home, as Ireland had to accept a joint €85 billion (£71 billion) bailout by the IMF and the eurozone countries.

The following two years saw more bailouts—and further waves of painful austerity in member states forced to accept them. In unprecedented scenes, two countries paralysed by their deepening debt problems, Greece and Italy, ended up forming governments led by so-called 'technocrats'—unelected officials with extensive professional experience of working in the financial sector, but no democratic mandate. Central to the often fraught negotiations among member states—including Britain and others not in the euro—was the question of how far the country with the strongest economy, Germany, was willing to 'prop up' those in crisis to avoid collapse of the eurozone. At various stages, the idea was mooted that Greece (the state in the weakest financial position) might be forced to 'default' on its debt, or even to withdraw from the euro altogether and readopt its own currency. This would allow it to devalue in the hope of boosting export areas, such as tourism and shipping, in which it had a 'comparative advantage' (defined in economics as goods or services that a country can afford to produce at lower marginal costs than its competitors).

At the height of the sovereign debt storm, in December 2011, eurozone members led by Germany and France proposed a twin-pronged strategy for limiting the likelihood of future financial crises on the scale of that which had begun three years earlier. The first element was a new **Fiscal Compact**, which (although boycotted by Britain and the Czech Republic) now effectively allows the ECB to vet individual member states' national budget plans. Officially entitled the 'Treaty on Stability, Coordination, and Governance in the Economic and Monetary Union', the Compact requires all signatories to introduce into their domestic laws formal requirements that future governments keep their annual budgets in balance or surplus. Any state breaking this pledge will be fined 0.1 per cent of its GDP by the ECJ. The Compact was eventually ratified by 16 signatories (four more than the required 12) and came into force in those states on 1 January 2013. The second element of this eurozone 'firewall' would be the proposed EU 'financial transaction tax' (FTT), which, if implemented in the form proposed by the Commission, will now come into force on 1 January 2016 (a two-year postponement from its original intended launch date, on the same day in 2014). The FTT will see a charge of 0.1 per cent imposed against the exchange of shares and bonds, and 0.01 per cent against derivatives contracts transacted between financial institutions in all signatory states (currently 10, down from 11 originally). It was the proposal to raise some €57 billion a year through such a tax, more than the planned Compact, that prompted Mr Cameron to stage his equally celebrated and derided 'walkout' from negotiations in December 2011. He put his refusal to sign up to the FTT down to concern about the disproportionate impact that it was likely to have on the City of London and described his move as a 'veto'—although critics, including Labour, were quick to point out that it was, at best, an 'opt-out', because the treaty introducing the Compact was still certain to go ahead (as it since has). The final form of the proposed FTT was set to be decided in negotiations between signatory states due to conclude by the end of 2014.

Nearly five years down the line, the sovereign debt crisis is far from over. However, it is widely agreed that a certain amount of stability has finally returned to the eurozone. One long-term reform still favoured by some member states (but viewed cautiously by Germany) is for an additional bulwark against future financial collapse to be introduced, in the form of a eurozone-wide 'banking union' to supplement the extant financial one. This would offer centralized deposit insurance guarantees, bank regulation, and mechanisms allowing for future failing banks to be recapitalized, if necessary, from joint eurozone funds. The influential German Finance Minister Wolfgang Schauble has, however, argued that a new formal treaty would need to establish this, with appropriate safeguards included for the states contributing the most to its surety.

▌ Towards an EU 'superstate'?

Of all EU issues dividing Britain's main political parties, none is more toxic than what many perceive as the gradual shift from an EU based on mutual cooperation between sovereign nations towards a 'federal' union akin to that of the United States. By the late 1980s, the perception that many mainland European countries (particularly France and Germany) wanted to create a 'European superstate' provoked staunch resistance from Mrs Thatcher and other Eurosceptic ministers to almost any prospect of further UK involvement. Famously, during a Commons debate on charismatic European Commission President Jacques Delors' plans to accelerate further EU integration, she declared 'no, no, no'.

Although, as leader of the Opposition, Mrs Thatcher had supported the 'yes' campaign for Britain to remain in the then EEC, a decade into her premiership she saw things differently. By then, the pace of integration had accelerated, and the likes of Mr Delors and German Chancellor Helmut Kohl were championing ever-closer ties between member states, with the contents of the Maastricht Treaty a particular concern. High-profile resignations by pro-European Cabinet colleagues, such as Chancellor Nigel Lawson and Foreign Secretary Sir Geoffrey Howe, did little to dent her resolve. It was the Tories' growing internal rift over Europe as much as the Poll Tax riots that led to her being challenged for the party's leadership in 1989 by a 'stalking horse' candidate, the obscure backbencher Sir Anthony Meyer, and her ultimate downfall in her ill-fated defence against the 1990 challenge by Michael Heseltine (see Chapter 3, 'Party').

Despite producing a more mild-mannered replacement, the ensuing leadership election failed to heal party wounds. Mr Major did much to placate his Eurosceptic colleagues—in particular, negotiating British opt-outs to various clauses in Maastricht, notably the Social Chapter enshrining new rights for EU workers, including the Working Time Directive barring employers from forcing staff to work more than 48 hours a week (later signed by Mr Blair).

But such fillips to the Right could only delay an inevitable confrontation over Maastricht (which effectively *had* to be signed if Britain were to remain in the EU). By May 1992, having just secured a narrow fourth successive Tory victory, Mr Major found himself held to ransom by a hard core of Eurosceptic backbenchers, known collectively as the 'Maastricht rebels'. Only by temporarily withdrawing the whip from these MPs, building a fractious alliance with the Ulster Unionists and Democratic Unionists, and threatening his party with a further election, which it would almost certainly have lost, did he force through the European Communities (Amendment) Bill on a wafer-thin majority. Among those actively rebelling from the backbenches were bullish former Employment Secretary Lord Tebbit and a certain Mrs Thatcher. In addition to the usual suspects, such as stalwart right-wingers Bill Cash and Teddy Taylor, the rebels included no fewer than three future Coalition ministers: David Willetts, Liam Fox, and Iain Duncan Smith.

As the Tories' Eurosceptic resolve has hardened, old divisions have also resurfaced in the Labour Party. The publication in 2004 of a draft 'EU Constitution'—or Constitutional Treaty—ostensibly did little more than draw together in a single (if mammoth) document various earlier agreements, such as the 1986 Single European Act and Maastricht. But those already wary of earlier shifts towards a more centralized EU power structure saw in it a clear attempt to consolidate the Union, leading to greater federalism—a reduction in status of the sovereign governments of member states akin to the limited devolution accorded to individual US states.

Ironically, the Treaty emphasized the concept of **subsidiarity**—the antithesis of federalism, which defines member states as paramount and the EU as only a 'last port of call' should individual countries' self-determination falter. It also set out, for the first time, practical exit strategies for states keen to withdraw from the EU altogether. Nonetheless, under mounting pressure from the Tories and his own backbenchers, Mr Blair promised a referendum on the Constitution if he were to win a third term in the 2005 election (although this never materialized, on the basis that France and the Netherlands had, by then, both rejected the Treaty).

Lisbon (to all intents and purposes a rewrite of the ill-fated 'Constitution') also proved divisive. Yet, after months of pressure from his own backbenchers and a Commons debate lasting 12 days, Mr Brown formally settled the issue in February 2008 with a slim victory in support of ratifying it on a three-line whip (to the fury of Eurosceptic papers such as the *Daily Mail*, the front-page headline of which described the outcome as 'The day they betrayed British democracy'). Some 29 Labour MPs defied the party whip by backing a referendum, and it was only Mr Clegg's decision to whip Lib Dem MPs into abstaining (rather than opposing the government) that carried the day for the prime minister. In doing so, he angered some in his own ranks: three frontbenchers resigned and 15 voted for a referendum, despite his using a three-line whip to discipline them. Oddly, the Lib Dems had spent much of the previous week in Parliament demanding a referendum on Europe—but on Britain's ongoing membership of the EU, rather than the constitutional issue in particular.

While Lisbon ultimately had a smoother passage than the abortive Constitution, Britain was not the only country to have trouble ratifying it. On 13 June 2008, the only EU nation granted a referendum, the Irish, rejected it by 53.4 to 46.6 per cent (paving the way for a failed last-ditch attempt by Tory peers to delay its passage through the Lords). Facing the threat of isolation or, worse, expulsion from the EU, Ireland finally approved Lisbon in October 2009. But it was not until December that year—18 months after it had been signed in principle by EU leaders—that the Treaty finally came into force.

Today, substantial questions (and divisions) remain as to the future direction of the EU and Britain's continuing place within it. At time of writing, UKIP had recently 'won' the European parliamentary elections—coming from third place in 2010 to secure 24 seats to Labour's 20 and the Tories' 19 —and secured two parliamentary seats in by-elections prompted by Conservative defections. The growing influence of UKIP on popular debate has sparked a Eurosceptic resurgence, leading Mr Cameron to legislate for a 'referendum lock' forcing future British governments to seek the public's approval before signing any future treaties and commit to a decisive 'in or out' referendum on EU membership if returned to government in 2015. While Labour leader Ed Miliband has resisted calls from some on his own side to do likewise, he has promised to do so in the event of any further significant integration being proposed by the EU. Mr Cameron also found himself isolated in June 2014 when he defied a clear consensus among Europe's leaders and voted against the appointment of former Luxembourg Prime Minister Jean-Claude Juncker, a noted federalist, as the Commission's new president. Only one other country, Hungary, joined him in rejecting Mr Juncker's candidacy, despite earlier suggestions that Sweden, the Netherlands, and even Germany might do likewise. Mr Cameron's reluctant acceptance of the majority decision—formally ratified by MEPs three weeks later—did not come before he had fired a warning shot across the Union by stating that the anointment of a Commission president committed to (in Juncker's own words) 'ever closer' integration could leave Britain little option but to 'drift towards' the EU's exit.

▌ Other issues facing the EU

Other potentially explosive issues facing Britain's EU membership are summarized in Table 9.2.

Table 9.2 Major issues facing Britain's membership of the EU

Issue	Explanation
Common Agricultural Policy (CAP) and the British rebate	CAP takes a bigger annual chunk of EU Budget than any other area—equivalent to 44 per cent of spending each year. Mrs Thatcher negotiated a generous annual rebate for Britain from CAP and other EU subsidies in late 1980s, because Britain receives less than states more reliant on agriculture. In December 2005, Mr Blair accepted a £1bn annual cut in Britain's £3.6bn rebate following a row with French President Mr Chirac that threatened to paralyse EU Budget negotiations. Mr Blair's opponents argued that increased subsidies from richer western European countries were needed to assist then new members—particularly former Soviet countries.
Common Fisheries Policy (CFP)	Long-standing protection of fish and seafood stocks in European seas using 'quota' system for fishing rights, supposedly fairly allocated among relevant member states. In mid-1990s, there were frequent confrontations between Britain and Spain over 'quota-hopping'—alleged practice by Spanish trawlers fishing in British waters of registering boats under third country's 'flag of convenience' to enable them to exceed their country's quota. Many UK trawler-men scrapped boats because of strict quotas introduced in waters they fished.
Common Defence Policy	Concept of greater cooperation over defence formally introduced in Maastricht Treaty. In Britain, Eurosceptic Defence Secretary Michael Portillo vowed in patriotic Conservative conference speech that Britain would never surrender right to maintain independent Armed Forces. Idea of EU 'Rapid Reaction Force' designed to intervene swiftly in event of member state being threatened or invaded very much on table.

(continued)

Table 9.2 (*continued*)

Issue	Explanation
Economic migration	Expansion of EU to encompass former Eastern Bloc countries led to more economic migration from poorer to richer countries, fostered by the free movement of labour (as well as goods, services, and capital) enshrined in various treaties. Has strained community relations and public services in some areas—creating tensions between migrants and indigenous peoples. In 2007, Britain became first member state to introduce new restrictions on migrant workers from two newest EU entrants, Bulgaria and Romania (removed in 2014). Tories and Labour have both pledged to ration some NHS treatment (see Chapter 6, 'Current issues') and to curb 'benefit tourism' by barring migrants from claiming welfare for at least three months after arriving in UK or until they pay sufficient NI contributions. Outgoing EC President Jose Manuel Barroso accused them of 'scaremongering'.

▤ Topical feature idea

The topic of 'benefit tourism' by migrants from poorer EU states has provoked numerous headlines in recent months. The Tories have promised to stop incoming EU citizens claiming benefits for anything between three months and four years after entering Britain, while Labour said it would introduce a two-year ban if elected in 2015, to uphold the 'contributory principle' for access to social security. However, an October 2013 European Commission report found that, on average, EU migrants were more likely to be in jobs than natives of the countries to which they moved, while there was 'little evidence' to suggest that their 'main motivation' to move was 'benefit-related'. Your editor wants you to write a balanced background feature on this subject. To whom would you go for quotes reflecting both sides of the debate? What would you ask them? How would you find firm statistics to demonstrate the scale of migration and its impact on the benefits system in your area?

✳ Current issues

- **The rise of UKIP** Nigel Farage's anti-EU United Kingdom Independence Party (UKIP) won Britain's popular vote in the May 2014 European Parliament elections, with 27.5 per cent support and 24 seats, taking votes from both Labour (second, on 25.4 per cent) and Conservatives (third, on 23.9 per cent). Mr Farage resisted overtures to join a new grouping with Far Right parties such as Marine Le Pen's Front National—which won a quarter of the votes in France.

- **Further EU enlargement** Negotiations over Turkey's accession to the EU began seriously in 2004, but its questionable human rights record and historical tensions with other members, including Germany, have slowed progress. Kosovo is currently lobbying for entry and looks set to be accepted before Turkey.

- **Big changes at the EU top table** Following the 2014 European Parliament elections, the three main leadership roles were also scheduled to change hands before the end of the year, with the current European Council and European Commission presidents and High Representative for Foreign Affairs and Security Policy due to step aside.

⠿ Key points

1. The European Union (EU) is a community of states initially formed to promote free trade, but which has developed cooperative policies on employment rights, asylum and immigration, and security and policing. It currently comprises 28 members.

2. Eighteen EU member states share a joint currency: the euro. This is issued by the European Central Bank (ECB), based in Frankfurt.

3. There are four main governing EU institutions, each with a permanent president: the European Council; the European Commission; European Parliament; and the Council of the European Union (Council of Ministers). The last is the most powerful.

4. Membership of the Council of Ministers varies, depending on which issue is being debated (for example finance ministers attend if it is debating the economy). It votes using a system called qualified majority voting (QMV), weighted to give the biggest say to states with the largest populations.

5. Prosecutions under EU law may be brought to the European Court of Justice (ECJ), based in Strasbourg. Cases are normally held by its lower court, the General Court.

→ Further reading

Bomberg, E. and Stubb, A. (eds) (2012) *The European Union: How Does it Work?*, Oxford: Oxford University Press. **Concise introductory text focusing on demystifying key EU institutions and their sometimes arcane governing procedures.**

Geddes, A. (2013) *Britain and the European Union*, Basingstoke: Palgrave Macmillan. **Candid analysis of Britain's chequered history as a member of the EU.**

Jones, A. (2015) *Britain and the European Union*, 2nd edn, Edinburgh: Edinburgh University Press. **Invaluable introduction to EU, its history and institutions, with particular emphasis on the changing relationship between the EU and UK.**

McCormick, J. (2014) *Understanding the European Union: A Concise Introduction*, 6th edn, Basingstoke: Palgrave Macmillan. **Leading introductory text to the history, institutions, and treaties of EU. Latest edition includes a comprehensive assessment of the Lisbon Treaty and impact of EU enlargement.**

Online Resource Centre

www.oxfordtextbooks.co.uk/orc/Morrison4e/
Visit the Online Resource Centre that accompanies this book for web links and regular updates.

10

International relations

Terms like 'globalization', 'development', and 'fair trade' are increasingly familiar to the public. More than ever, Britain's fortunes are tied to those of other states, and its involvement in international affairs stretches well beyond the European Union (see Chapter 9). Until recently, the country was involved in three ongoing conflicts—in Afghanistan, Iraq, and Libya and it is currently involved in collaborative air strikes against ISIS (Islamic State of Iraq and Syria). UK-based multinationals such as Shell and BP retain oil and mineral interests across Africa, Latin America, and the Middle East. And there are even still vestiges of the once-sprawling British Empire, in the guise of Northern Ireland, the 53-nation Commonwealth, and a handful of island protectorates and dependencies, including Gibraltar, the Falklands, and Diego Garcia.

At the same time as Britain is flexing its military and economic muscle, it has become one of the biggest players in the fight to eradicate global poverty, contributing nearly £7 billion a year in overseas aid to developing countries in Africa, Asia, and South America, and leading the way at recent G8 and G20 summits for binding multilateral agreements on debt relief. The UK has also played a significant—if so far limited—role in brokering international agreements on issues ranging from climate change to human rights abuses.

▌ The Foreign and Commonwealth Office (FCO)

The Foreign and Commonwealth Office (FCO) is the government department overseeing Britain's overall foreign policy. It was formed in 1968 from the merger of the existing Foreign Office (dating from 1782) and the then separate

Commonwealth Office. At its head are several ministers, the most senior being the Foreign and Commonwealth Secretary, or 'Foreign Secretary'.

The FCO's main roles are to:

- maintain diplomatic and/or consular relations with 188 different countries;
- maintain diplomatic missions with another nine countries;
- act as Britain's main broker in drawing up international treaties, common defence policies, and economic sanctions;
- use its overseas embassies to act as local focal points for diplomatic relations between Britain and the countries concerned; and
- help to promote Britain as a trading partner with other countries through its embassies.

When Labour regained power in 1997, its newly installed Foreign Secretary, the late Robin Cook, vowed to pursue an 'ethical foreign policy', putting diplomacy and human rights campaigning ahead of narrow national interests and warfare. But, in 2001, he was replaced by Jack Straw, who had earned a reputation as a tough-talking Home Secretary in the government's first term. Within months, the FCO was dealing with the fallout from the 11 September terrorist attacks on New York. In 2006, under then Foreign Secretary Margaret Beckett (the first woman to hold the post), the FCO announced 10 new 'strategic priorities' for the next five to 10 years—an approach broadly upheld by the Coalition. These are outlined in the table entitled 'Ten-year strategic objectives of the Foreign and Commonwealth Office (FCO)', to be found on the **Online Resource Centre** that accompanies this book.

Unlike most government departments, the FCO has only one executive agency: Wilton Park International Conference Centre organizes summits on international social problems, attended by academics, business people, and other relevant professionals. There are also several independent think tanks with close links to the FCO—most famously, the Royal Institute of International Affairs, founded in 1920 and based at Chatham House, St James's Square, London (commonly known simply as 'Chatham House'). It is from Chatham House that the oft-cited 'Chatham House Rule'—beloved of (and cursed by) editors in equal measure—originates. This is a 'gentleman's agreement' allowing journalists access to candid discussions and debates held by private or public organizations in return for their agreement to respect participants' anonymity. Reporters are normally permitted to use some or all information gained from such meetings, on the strict condition that they do not attribute it to named individuals. The precise wording of the 'Chatham House Rule' is as follows:

> ❝When a meeting, or part thereof, is held under the Chatham House Rule, participants are free to use the information received, but neither the identity nor the affiliation of the speaker(s), nor that of any other participant, may be revealed. ❞

The civilized, if rather quaint, rule reflects the overall culture of the FCO, which is often criticized for its arcane procedures and maintaining a cosy 'old boy' approach to business more redolent of a Graham Greene novel than the harsh realities of twenty-first-century *Weltpolitik*. In August 2005, Andrew Mackinlay, a Labour member of the Commons Foreign Affairs Select Committee, leaked details of a report by management consultancy Collinson Grant, which suggested that it was hugely over-manned and slow to act.

Of recent controversies involving the FCO, none has been more damaging than the debacle over Iraq. There is insufficient space here to detail the circumstances leading to the US-led invasion over Saddam Hussein's alleged stockpiling of weapons of mass destruction (WMDs) or the subsequent failure to locate any such arms. It is fair to say, however, that the spectre of this conflict—not to mention the threat of terrorism, as brought home to Britain in the multiple bombings of 7 July 2005—is reflected in the wording of the FCO's current statement of 'priorities'. Its legacy has also arguably been witnessed through the recent advance of Islamist militant group ISIS through large swathes of Iraq and Syria, and its announcement in July 2014 that it had established a 'caliphate' encompassing the regions that it had annexed. Meanwhile, at time of writing, politicians and media had just learned that Sir John Chilcot's long-waited report into the sequence of events leading to Britain's decision to invade Iraq would not be published until after the May 2015 election. The latest delay to its publication—previously scheduled loosely for 'sometime' in 2014—led some critics to suggest it was being held back by political interference from senior figures who might be embarrassed by its findings. Sir John's inquiry originally started work in 2009, on the instruction of then Prime Minister Gordon Brown, with two of its most high-profile sessions featuring cross-questioning of his predecessor, Tony Blair. But in May 2014, it emerged that Britons were only ever likely to learn the 'gist' of discussions between Mr Blair and ex-US President George W Bush, in which the former was widely believed to have assured his ally that he would join in the invasion—months before publicly taking this decision or putting it to a parliamentary vote. Cabinet Secretary Sir Jeremy Heywood successfully argued that full disclosure of these records might prejudice Britain's future relations with the United States. Nonetheless, the putative Chilcot Report was still expected to criticize the former premier.

Many other recent issues faced by the FCO—and played out in the media—have also stemmed from Britain's involvement in the 'war on terror' (although this expression was pointedly dropped by the UK government, if not the United States, after Mr Blair left Downing Street). These have included Britain's belated intervention to secure the release of UK-based terrorist suspects from the US Guantanamo Bay detention camp in Cuba, from which the first four finally returned to their families in 2007—five years after being captured by the US military in Afghanistan. During Mr Brown's premiership, meanwhile, a row broke out over Foreign Secretary David Miliband's admission—contrary to previous assurances by ministers—that a British territory had been used for so-called 'extraordinary rendition' by the United States. This is the process by which suspected terrorists have been flown to third-party countries to be interrogated by agents working on behalf of the Central Intelligence Agency (CIA). Human rights organizations had criticized the process as 'torture by proxy'—arguing that, by allowing prisoners to be questioned in countries known for their strong-arm tactics, the United States had given tacit approval to interrogation practices that it banned at home. In a speech to the Commons in February 2008, Mr Miliband revealed that he had been belatedly told by then US Secretary of State Condoleezza Rice that US planes, each carrying single suspects, had stopped on the British island of Diego Garcia in the Indian Ocean.

For his part, the Coalition's first Foreign Secretary, William Hague, signalled a new, more 'clear, focused, and effective' approach to international diplomacy, emphasizing the need for Britain to be proactive in Europe and to build strong relations with emerging 'economic superpowers', such as the so-called 'BRIC' states: Brazil, the Russian Federation, India, and China. In a swipe at Labour's legacy, he argued that the UK came to be seen by some as a state that engaged with them only in the event of disaster or when it needed their support for crucial votes (an oblique reference to the elusive 'second resolution' Mr Blair had sought from the United Nations to legitimize the 2003 Iraq invasion). Somewhat incongruously, Mr Hague also accompanied Hollywood actress and campaigner Angelina Jolie on several high-profile overseas expeditions to highlight the plight of women subjected to sexual violence in war zones, convening a summit with her in London on this subject in June 2014.

However, despite having withdrawn the final combat troops from Afghanistan in 2014 and initially appearing to favour a less 'gung-ho' approach to foreign affairs than their Labour predecessors, the Coalition has periodically been accused of reverting to type. In 2011, Messrs Cameron and Hague were among the most proactive voices calling for military intervention to impose a 'no-fly zone' over Libya to prevent dictator Muammar Gaddafi's forces bombing their own people. And in August 2013 Mr Cameron recalled Parliament for a vote on possible British military intervention against Syrian despot Bashar al-Assad after grainy footage suggested that he had used chemical weapons on his own civilians (a vote Mr Cameron subsequently lost). The Coalition has also been embroiled in an on–off war of words with Argentine leader Christine Kirchner, following her decision to revive her country's claims to sovereignty over the Malvinas (to Britain, the Falklands)—a row that led the Falklanders to unilaterally stage a referendum in 2013, which (unsurprisingly) returned a 99.8 per cent majority in favour of their remaining British citizens. Meanwhile, moves to introduce closed court hearings for handling sensitive information judged to be potentially prejudicial to British national security—a throwback to the 'Big Brother' policies for which Labour was consistently berated—sparked criticism from civil liberties groups before finally being scaled back.

The Diplomatic Service

An FCO 'sub-department', the Diplomatic Service is staffed by seconded administrators, and mans the embassies and consulates through which Britain discharges its diplomatic relations with its host countries. It employs 20,000 officials and is headed not by a government minister, but by a career civil servant. Despite being a salaried official, not an elected member of Parliament (MP), this civil servant has a title similar to a certain type of minister: 'Permanent Under-Secretary of State at the FCO'.

Personnel at all levels enjoy 'diplomatic immunity'—freedom from prosecution under the laws of the countries in which they are based. They may, however, be expelled for committing offences and/or tried back in Britain.

▶ The Ministry of Defence (MoD)

Given Britain's long military operations in Iraq and Afghanistan, controversies over the treatment of service personnel at home and abroad, and periodic outbursts about these and other issues by retired senior officers, the Ministry of Defence (MoD) for some years grabbed more headlines than most government departments. When Mr Blair was elected in 1997, he made a now infamous speech declaring himself part of the 'first generation' able to 'contemplate that we may live our entire lives without going to war or sending our children to war'. Yet, by the time he left office 10 years later, he had taken Britain into four conflicts: to prevent ethnic cleansing by Serbia's Slobodan Milošević in Kosovo (1999); intervening in civil war in Sierra Leone (2000); supporting the US-led invasion of Afghanistan (2001); and 'liberating' Saddam's Iraq (2003). In addition, UK planes were heavily involved in the sustained 1998 bombing of Iraq by Bill Clinton's US administration.

Formed in 1964 from the amalgamation of four other departments—the War Office, Admiralty, Air Ministry, and Ministry of Aviation—the MoD is, despite its title, usually in the news in times of conflict. Once diplomacy has broken down and Britain has declared war on another nation, the FCO tends to fade out of the picture, giving way to the department charged with coordinating military intervention. Although its stated aim is to provide a first line of 'defence' against foreign aggressors, in practice it is more likely to see action at times when Britain is doing the attacking.

The MoD's principal roles today are outlined in the table entitled 'Principal roles of the Ministry of Defence (MoD)', to be found on the **Online Resource Centre**.

In recent years, the ministry's raison d'être has changed in light of global developments, especially the end of the Cold War and the rising terrorist threat. The recent Afghanistan occupation notwithstanding, 'conventional warfare'—involving ground troops, tanks, helicopters, planes, and ships—is becoming less common. For a time during the 1980s—before the collapse of the Berlin Wall and, in turn, the Soviet Union—the consensus was that future wars would generally be fought 'by remote', with computerized missile systems replacing traditional armaments. While nuclear strikes have yet to occur, today's field weapons are increasingly sophisticated and the number of soldiers required to fight conflicts continues to diminish as technology becomes capable of doing so. Responding to the new challenges and opportunities presented by modern warfare, Labour published two major reviews of defence expenditure: the 1998 Strategic Defence Review; and a 2003 White Paper, entitled *Delivering Security in a Changing World*.

The Coalition followed with its own 'strategic defence and security review' in October 2010—prompted as much by the swingeing departmental spending cuts ordered by George Osborne's Treasury as by any genuine desire by then Defence Secretary Liam Fox to break with Labour's policy priorities. At the time, the review sparked fury among senior military figures (and near-hysterical headlines) after it emerged that ministers would be honouring Labour's contracts for two new naval aircraft carriers—despite being unable to afford aircraft for them to carry for up to 10 years. Further opprobrium was heaped on Dr Fox, particularly in ever-patriotic *The Sun*, when he confirmed that he was scrapping orders for a new generation of both Nimrod spy planes and Harrier Jump Jets—the iconic aircraft used to devastating effect during the Falklands War (a decision reversed by his successor, Phillip Hammond). The review delayed a final decision on how, when, and whether to renew Britain's independent Trident nuclear deterrent until after the 2015 election—neatly averting a potentially incendiary row with the Lib Dems.

More worrying for service personnel was the early announcement of 42,000 redundancies in the MoD and Armed Forces, followed in July 2012 by confirmation that the British Army alone would be cut from 102,000 to 82,000 by 2020—its lowest headcount since the Napoleonic Wars and half that at the height of the Cold War. Altogether, 17 units and 36 battalions were to be scrapped, with centuries-old regimental names—the so-called 'golden thread'—perishing in the process. Critics argue that such real-terms shrinkage threatens leaving the UK incapable of ever again mounting offensives on the scale of Iraq or Afghanistan. In all, four rounds of job cuts were announced between 2011 and 2014, with 12,000 service personnel made redundant in total.

Civil Service oversight of MoD policymaking

The Chief of the Defence Staff—effectively overall permanent secretary of the Armed Forces—is supported by a Vice-Chief of the Defence Staff and the following heads of the three individual Armed Forces:

- the First Sea Lord/Chief of the Naval Staff;
- the Chief of the General Staff; and
- the Chief of the Air Staff.

Aside from the ongoing criticisms of levels of defence expenditure—the MoD's annual budget is less than the £100 billion spent by the Treasury on 'rescuing' Northern Rock from collapse (see Chapter 7, 'Managing national debt')—the ministry has weathered numerous other recent storms. At the height of the Iraq War, then Defence Secretary Geoff Hoon was accused of failing to provide adequate equipment for British troops. Years after the event, during his January 2010 appearance before the Iraq Inquiry (see 'The Foreign and Commonwealth Office' in this chapter), Mr Hoon blamed this 'scandal' on his former boss, claiming that, as Chancellor, he forced 'difficult cuts' on the MoD.

The MoD has also been castigated in the press for failing to maintain domestic quarters for personnel to a civilized standard and for selling off large amounts of military accommodation to private landlords—only to rent it back from them at inflated rates. In March 2008, it emerged that British taxpayers were paying a private housing company £29 million a year to rent 8,200 marital homes that were lying empty for lack of any Forces families to move into them.

▶ The Department for International Development (DfID)

Until 1997, humanitarian aid and investment in developing countries were the responsibility of a minister in the Foreign Office, the Minister for Overseas Development. When Mr Blair was elected, this post was incorporated into the Cabinet. When the Coalition took power, the Department for International Development (DfID) was one of very few to have a proportion of its budget (relating specifically to overseas aid) ring-fenced in the teeth of impending public spending cuts.

Today, DfID works directly with 150 developing countries—principally in Africa, parts of Asia, Latin America, and the Far East. Its annual budget is more than £4 billion and it has two headquarters: in London and Glasgow.

DfID's 'Millennium Goals' to help to eradicate child poverty, and to improve access to education and health care for women and children in developing countries, are outlined in the table entitled 'DfID's Millennium Goals', on the **Online Resource Centre**.

▌ Britain's role in the United Nations (UN)

In addition to the EU, Britain is a member of several major international organizations with differing, if sometimes overlapping, remits. Most significant is the **United Nations (UN)**—a global body set up after the Second World War with the stated aim of promoting peace, preventing future conflicts, and achieving international cooperation on economic, social, cultural, and humanitarian issues. The UN is notionally committed to solving disputes between nations by peaceful means, and when it sends troops into countries, this tends to be in a 'peacekeeping' capacity—to police borders, to protect aid routes, etc.—rather than for active hostilities.

Formally established in October 1945, the UN set out to avoid the perceived errors of its precursor, the League of Nations. The League—born out of the First World War—had imposed crippling reparations on Germany, in so doing contributing to the dire economic woes that fostered the popularity of Nazism. Initially founded by 51 states, today the UN embraces 193—with the then newly created state of South Sudan welcomed into its fold in July 2011. The most senior UN official is its Secretary-General (currently Ban Ki-Moon). UN membership is notionally open to every recognized state, but in practice individual countries are periodically excluded—or exclude themselves—in disputes over the legitimacy of their governance.

The UN is based in New York—a fact that has periodically led some member states to suggest that the US government wields a disproportionate influence on its decisions. In October 2006, Hassan Turki, deputy leader of Somalia's Islamic Courts, one of several parties wrestling for control of the war-ravaged country, declared that he did not recognize the UN—dismissing it as an 'American interest group'.

The UN Security Council (UNSC)

The term 'United Nations' was coined during the Second World War itself, when Winston Churchill and US President Franklin D. Roosevelt used it in speeches to refer to the Allies: the countries opposing Hitler. But the UN was born in earnest only after the UN Conference on International Organization, in April 1945, with a formal UN Charter signed by the majority of its founding states that October. Giving substance to Churchill's famous remark that 'history is written by the victors', of these 51 nations the five who had played arguably the biggest role in defeating Hitler (the United States, Britain, France, and the then Republic of China and Soviet Union) were awarded permanent seats on a newly formed UN Security Council (UNSC)—the body charged with allocating peace-keeping forces around the world, ratifying economic sanctions, and (in extreme cases) authorizing military action.

The UN Charter pledges to:

- investigate situations threatening international peace;
- recommend procedures for peacefully resolving disputes;
- call on other members to completely or partially interrupt economic relations and sea, air, postal, and radio communications (impose 'sanctions'), or sever diplomatic relations; and
- enforce its decisions militarily or by any means necessary.

The five permanent members of the UNSC are joined at any one time by a further 10 members, elected by the UN's 'parliament', the General Assembly, every other year. These are chosen from the remaining 187 UN countries on rotation. For the two-year periods commencing 1 January 2014 and 1 January 2015, the temporary members of the UNSC were as outlined in the tables entitled 'The temporary membership of the UN Security Council (2014–15)' and 'The temporary membership of the UN Security Council (2015–16)', available on the **Online Resource Centre**.

As a mark of its seniority, each permanent member has the right to veto prospective UN actions. It was this fact that presented the biggest stumbling block to the Anglo-American campaign to win support for invading Iraq. Both then French President Jacques Chirac and his Russian counterpart, Vladimir Putin, made it clear that they would not back any further resolution authorizing military strikes without conclusive proof that Saddam was stockpiling WMDs—the ostensible pretext for action. Their immovability blocked the passage of the 'second resolution' that the United States and UK sought, forcing them to abandon pursuing it and go it alone.

The UN General Assembly

The primary purpose of the UN's second governing body is to approve its annual budget and appoint non-permanent Security Council representatives. It also receives reports from the UN's various other subsidiary bodies and wields considerable influence over policy areas, including international aid and climate change.

Unlike the Security Council, the General Assembly gives each UN member state an equal say at meetings. It convenes for regular annual sessions, lasting from September to December, but can also be assembled for emergency meetings. It is chaired either by the serving Secretary-General or a president, elected by Assembly members on a yearly basis. Votes can be passed by a two-thirds majority of those present.

Other UN bodies and agencies

Like every major organization, national or international, the UN requires administrators. The UN Secretariat employs 8,900 staff, the majority based at its New York headquarters. Others are stationed in regional headquarters in Addis Ababa, Bangkok, Beirut, Geneva, Nairobi, Santiago, and Vienna. The Secretariat's responsibilities are divided, like those of the British Civil Service and European Commission, into separate departments overseeing discrete policy areas—ranging from the 'advancement of women' to the Office of the UN High Commissioner for Refugees.

Other significant agencies of the UN and their responsibilities are outlined in Table 10.1.

Table 10.1 Subordinate UN bodies

Body	Role and remit
International Court of Justice (ICJ)	Comprising 15 judges, elected for nine years, ICJ sits in Peace Palace in The Hague, Netherlands. It hears cases referred by member states and adjudicates between parties.
	Several countries—including United States, France, Germany, and China—have refused to be bound by rulings.
	Most famous cases include protracted trial of late Serbian dictator Slobodan Milošević on 66 charges of genocide and 'crimes against humanity', and ongoing hearings into similar charges against Bosnian Serb leaders Radovan Karadžić and Ratko Mladić.
	NOTE: Membership of Court for nine years beginning March 2007 can be found in table entitled 'The membership of the International Court of Justice (ICJ)', available on the **Online Resource Centre**.
UN Economic and Social Council (ESOCOC)	Promotes cooperation between UN states on economic and social policy; all 54 members elected by General Assembly for three-year terms. Has president, elected for one-year term from smaller and 'middle-ranking' states represented on the ESOCOC. Historically meets once a year for four weeks, in July, but since 1998 has also convened in April to liaise with finance ministers heading key committees of World Bank and International Monetary Fund (IMF). ESOCOC consults with 2,000 non-government organizations (NGOs) and oversees numerous agencies, including UNESCO, UNICEF, WHO, UNDP, ILO, and UNHCR.
UN Educational, Scientific and Cultural Organization (UNESCO)	Formed to promote cultural understanding through education, science, and arts. Comprising 193 states and six associate members, it has more members than UN itself. Based in Paris, with 30 other offices.

(continued)

Table 10.1 (*continued*)

Body	Role and remit
UN Children's Fund (UNICEF)	Formerly 'United Nations International Children's Emergency Fund', this provides urgent food and health care to children whose countries have been devastated by natural/man-made disasters. A voluntary agency, reliant for income on governments and donations.
World Health Organization (WHO)	Established on first World Health Day, in 1948, coordinates international efforts to monitor outbreaks of deadly diseases such as malaria, cholera, typhoid, and AIDS, sponsoring vaccination programmes and medical research. Among its famous pronouncements is 'Breast is Best' advice to mothers in developing countries to encourage use of breast milk to rear infants, rather than formula, which relies on clean water supplies to make it safe.
UN Development Programme (UNDP)	Executive board within Assembly, funded by voluntary donations, and world's largest source of aid for industrial and agricultural development.
International Labour Organization (ILO)	Based in Geneva, Switzerland, promotes opportunities for individuals to 'obtain decent and productive work, in conditions of freedom, equity, security, and human dignity'. Focuses increasingly on unequal plight of women in developing countries.
	Meets three times a year—in March, June, and November—and holds International Labour Conference each June.
	Boasts governing body comprising representatives from 28 governments, 14 workers' groups, and 14 employers' groups. Ten seats held permanently by United States, UK, Brazil, China, France, Germany, India, Italy, Japan, and Russian Federation; remaining ones elected by members on three-year basis.
Office of the United Nations High Commissioner for Refugees (UNHCR)/ UN Refugee Agency	Established in 1950, coordinates international efforts to protect refugees and relieve situations that might lead to indigenous peoples fleeing their countries. Employs 6,300 staff in 110 countries.

▮ Life after the Cold War—Britain's ongoing role in NATO

Founded in 1949, the **North Atlantic Treaty Organization (NATO)** is a *military* alliance, established against the backdrop of the emerging Cold War between East and West, and the ensuing nuclear arms race, to protect the security of Western powers. NATO comprises 28 member states—principally the United States, Canada, and western Europe, although since the collapse of the Soviet Union it has also embraced several former Eastern Bloc nations.

NATO's origins lay in an earlier agreement, the 1948 Treaty of Brussels, which founded the Western European Union, a smaller scale forerunner comprising only Britain, France, Belgium, the Netherlands, and Luxembourg. The decision was taken to embrace the United States and, on 4 April 1949, the North Atlantic Treaty was signed in Washington DC. At the same time as the United States and Canada, Portugal, Italy, Norway, Denmark, and Iceland were admitted. Greece and Turkey joined in 1952. West Germany had to wait longer, but it finally signed up on 9 May 1955. East Germany was effectively absorbed in 1990, following the reunification of Germany a year earlier.

Given the rapid expansion of NATO and its hostility to Stalin's growing eastern empire, it was only a matter of time before the Soviet Union retaliated. On 14 May 1955, it signed the Warsaw Treaty of Friendship, Cooperation, and Mutual Assistance—better known as the 'Warsaw Pact'. This came to encompass all Soviet countries, except Yugoslavia. But, in belated recognition of the redundancy of the Warsaw Pact following the collapse of Communism in the East, on 12 March 1999 former members Hungary, Poland, and the Czech Republic joined NATO. Bulgaria, Estonia, Latvia, Lithuania, Romania, and Slovakia followed suit in March 2004, with Albania and Croatia acceding on 1 April 2009.

NATO remains based in Brussels, but, as with the UN, this has not stopped some countries from accusing it of being in the United States' pocket.

The North Atlantic Treaty

The foundation stone of NATO was the North Atlantic Treaty. Perhaps its most defining (and oft-cited) clause is Article V, which sets down the principle of 'collective defence'. Its precise wording is as follows:

> ❝ The Parties of NATO agreed that an armed attack against one or more of them in Europe or North America shall be considered an attack against them all. Consequently they agree that, if such an armed attack occurs, each of them, in exercise of the right of individual or collective self-defence will assist the Party or Parties being attacked, individually and in concert with the other Parties, such action as it deems necessary, including the use of armed force, to restore and maintain the security of the North Atlantic area. ❞

A recent invocation of Article V came in the aftermath of the 11 September attacks on New York, when the United States argued that the terrorist strikes on the World Trade Center amounted to a military attack on the country and therefore required a joint response from NATO members. There was some dispute about whether the usual rules applied, given that precise nationalities of all of the terrorists were not immediately known—making any decision to target a specific country in retaliation problematic. Having asserted an Al-Qaeda link, the United States argued that the Taliban in Afghanistan was principally answerable, since its then leader, Mullah Omar, was believed to be harbouring leaders of the Al-Qaeda movement, including Osama bin Laden.

In the event, action in defence of the United States was authorized on 4 October 2001 (despite rowdy scenes in some meetings) and the alliance participated in two further related operations. Previous attempts to invoke Article V have, however, failed. In 1982, Margaret Thatcher's government attempted to persuade NATO to participate in response to the Argentine invasion of the Falklands, but because those islands are located thousands of miles from the UK (in the South Atlantic), the invasion was not deemed an attack on Britain.

Article V continues to be used as a political football to this day. In the weeks running up to NATO's June 2011 adoption of a new 'Policy on Cyber Defence'—intended to protect member states from the perceived threat of 'cyber-terrorism' by everyone from rogue states to nuisance hackers—General Stéphane Abrial of its Supreme Allied Command Transformation used a *New York Times* editorial to outline circumstances in which the alliance might invoke the Article against so-called 'hacktivists'. His intervention followed a series of 'security breaches' relating to senior NATO officials, including the creation of a bogus Facebook profile for its Supreme Allied Commander Europe, Admiral James Stavridis.

The North Atlantic Council (NAC)

NATO's principal governing body, the North Atlantic Council (NAC), meets twice a week (on Tuesdays and Wednesdays). Its composition varies: on some occasions, 'permanent representatives' (PermReps), salaried career diplomats from each state, meet, but when major issues are due to be debated (customarily on Wednesdays), member states usually send their foreign or defence ministers.

The most senior official in NATO, as in the UN, is its civilian Secretary-General, whose job it is to chair meetings of the NAC and to act as the alliance's public figurehead. He or she is supported by a Deputy Secretary-General. As of 1 October 2014, former Norwegian Prime Minister Jens Stoltenberg was due to take office as the latest Secretary-General.

The Military Committee

NATO's status as an alliance focusing on security- and defence-related issues means that some of its operational decisions require direct input from military personnel. To facilitate this, it has its own Military Committee, which (unlike the NAC) comprises members of the Armed Forces rather than civil servants. Each member state sends a military representative (normally chief of staff) to its meetings. The Committee has a permanent chairman and several subsets—Allied Command Europe, Allied Command Atlantic, Allied Command Channel, and Regional Planning Group (for North America)—each under 'supreme commanders'.

The NATO Parliamentary Assembly

Not actually part of NATO's official structure—but created in 1955 to complement and liaise with it—the NATO Parliamentary Assembly is a fairly informal annual convention of parliamentarians and legislators (MPs) from each member state. It meets to discuss common policy issues.

▌ The Council of Europe

Founded in 1949, the **Council of Europe** pre-dates the EU by two years (with which it and its institutions are often confused). As such, it has the distinction of being the longest-running organization dedicated to promoting European integration and cooperation. Recognized under international law, it has 47 member states (19 more than the EU to date).

Its prime purpose is to foster members' adoption of common legal standards and human rights. To this end, its most famous institution is the **European Court of Human Rights (ECtHR)** in Strasbourg, and by far its most celebrated achievement, the European Convention on Human Rights (ECHR), which the Court upholds—bringing the Council into frequent conflict with recent British governments (see Chapter 4, 'The British franchise today—who can vote?').

Moves to establish some form of European political and social confederation, of which the Council was the first expression, arose out of the anti-Nazi alliance forged in the Second World War. In a famous speech at the University of Zurich in 1946, Churchill (at the time Britain's leader of the Opposition, following his defeat by Labour in 1945) called for the formation of a 'United States of Europe', with France and Germany at its helm. Although he pointedly stopped short of suggesting that Britain should join this alliance, his coining of the term is conveniently forgotten by many of his cheerleaders on the Eurosceptic right of today's Conservative Party. In due course, the Council was established by the Treaty of London, on 5 May 1949, and a 'Statute' outlining its statement of principles signed by 10 countries: Belgium, Denmark, France, Ireland, Italy, Luxembourg, the Netherlands, Norway, Sweden, and Britain.

Article 1 of this Statute declared:

> ❝The aim of the Council of Europe is to achieve a greater unity between its members for the purpose of safeguarding and realising the ideals and principles which are their common heritage and facilitating their economic and social progress. ❞

Its overall list of aims and objectives are set out in the table entitled 'The aims and objectives of the Council of Europe', to be found on the **Online Resource Centre**.

◗ International trade and economy

Promoting peace is one key area of international cooperation in the modern world; the other is fostering free trade and financial investment between nations. Over and above the EU, UN, and Council of Europe, several key bodies were founded in the second half of the twentieth century to achieve these and related goals.

From G7/8 to G20

The **G8**—or 'Group of Eight'—is not a formal body like many others in this list, but rather a forum comprising the world's biggest industrialized nations and military superpowers. Its membership is as follows: Canada, France, Germany, Italy, Japan, the Russian Federation, the UK, and the United States. The most recent country to join was Russia. Even today, though, the group sometimes convenes in Russia's absence (as the 'Group of Seven', or G7)—and this has happened several times during the West's ongoing dispute with President Putin over his decision to annex the Crimea from Ukraine in 2014, following a referendum in the region supporting its return to Russian rule, the legitimacy of which was contested by NATO's outgoing Secretary-General, Anders Fogh Rasmussen.

The G7/8 has its origins in the seismic economic turmoil created in Europe by the 1973 oil crisis, pitting the United States, Japan, Britain, and other western European countries against Arab nations aligned to the Organization of the Petroleum Exporting Countries (OPEC). At the time, these countries were refusing to ship oil to the West in protest over its support for Israel in the Yom Kippur War. In response, the United States convened the 'Library Group'—an informal meeting of financial experts from the United States, Britain, France, Japan, and West Germany—and in 1975 then French President Valéry Giscard d'Estaing called a summit that led to the formation of a Group of Six (G6), comprising the future members of the G7 minus Canada. Canada joined the following year.

Subsequently, the G6 and its successors have held annual meetings at different locations in participating countries, under a rotating presidency. Although the group has no economic or constitutional powers per se, it is one of the most influential talking shops in global politics. At the G8 Summit in Gleneagles in July 2005, Mr Blair used his chairmanship to secure a £29 billion boost to international aid and to cancel the debt of the 18 poorest African nations. Despite criticisms from some campaigners, Sir Bob Geldof and Bono described the date of the agreement as 'a great day'.

However, since the 2008–09 global financial crisis, the G7/8 has been eclipsed in influence (and media coverage) by the **G20** ('Group of 20'), which announced in September 2009 its intention to formally supplant the G8 as the world's main economic council of wealthy nations. This expression of confidence came five months after its most significant and heavily publicized meeting to date: a conference hosted by Mr Brown in London at which, in the teeth of mass marches by everyone from climate change protestors to the Stop the War Coalition, it reached what appeared to be firm agreement on measures to stabilize the global economy. These included an international 'Financial Stability Board', a crackdown on 'tax havens', and reform of the global banking system, bringing hedge funds and private equity firms under global regulation for the first time. In practice, though, these have still not materialized in any tangible way.

The International Monetary Fund (IMF)

Like many other supranational organizations, the International Monetary Fund (IMF) was formed in response to the Second World War. It was founded in July 1944, when the representatives of 45 governments met at Bretton Woods, New Hampshire, and its remit was intrinsically economic: to restore and maintain stability in the world's financial sector, and to prevent widespread recessions by means of mechanisms including exchange-rate agreements and short-term monetary aid packages. Indeed, one of its key roles in the ensuing decades has been to provide loans to countries experiencing temporary financial blips. This money is borrowed from a pool contributed to, on a rolling basis, by member states.

The IMF today counts 188 countries among its members. All UN states, apart from North Korea, Cuba, Andorra, Monaco, Liechtenstein, and Nauru, are included. Kosovo joined in 2009 and a long excluded country, Tuvalu, acceded in June 2010, with South Sudan signing up in 2012. Its headquarters are in Washington DC—a fact that, as with the UN and NATO, has led to repeated accusations by some that it is effectively a US puppet (a similar charge is often levelled against the World Bank).

As with most banks, including the Bank of England, the IMF has a governing board. While every member state is represented on this and may vote on its resolutions, as with the EU Council of Ministers some countries wield more power than others. The extent of an individual state's say on the board is governed by its 'quota' of available votes. This relates as much to the amount of money that it has previously contributed to the IMF as to its population size. Each state also has a corresponding right in relation to how much it may borrow, should it need to, from the bank's pool of finance—entitlements known as 'special drawing rights' (SDRs).

Both Britain and the United States do relatively well from the IMF. Britain wields more than 4 per cent of the votes and the United States, nearly 17 per cent. In terms of borrowing ability, the United States has access to 42,122 million SDRs and Britain, 10,739 SDRs—compared to just 3.1 SDRs for the Pacific island of Palau. In 1976, Labour Chancellor Denis Healey had to ask the Fund for an emergency loan to enable his government to plug a huge hole in its public finances (see Chapter 7, 'Managing national debt').

The IMF has seen its fair share of controversy. Perhaps giving succour to criticisms that the United States and certain European countries wield a disproportionate influence on it, the board has in the past approved significant loans to dictatorships friendly to the West. Pinochet's Chile and Musharaf's Pakistan were both helped out, despite being boycotted by other institutions and non-government organizations (NGOs) over human rights abuses. The Fund has also been heavily criticized for imposing strict 'conditionalities' on developing countries needing its assistance. Most common is a 'structural adjustment programme' obliging a country seeking aid to privatize state-owned utilities and other industries as a prerequisite for its loan. Similarly contentious are the IMF's habits of charging high interest to countries judged at risk of defaulting and recalling loans at short notice—practices that contributed to severe financial crises in Argentina and Bolivia in the 1990s.

In May 2012, then recently appointed IMF head Christine Lagarde sparked widespread condemnation from politicians across Europe—and thousands of angry postings on her Facebook page—by using an interview with Britain's *Guardian* newspaper to criticize residents of recession-hit Greece (see Chapter 9, 'The eurozone "sovereign debt crisis"') for 'trying to escape tax', and contrasting their plight with those she judged worthy of 'more help', such as poor schoolchildren in Niger. It subsequently emerged that Ms Lagarde's £298,675 annual salary was tax-free.

The World Bank

Also based in Washington DC, the World Bank was formally established on 27 December 1945. Its remit has evolved over the decades and now principally revolves around the aforementioned 'Millennium Development Goals'. The Bank has five constituent parts, of which the following are the most powerful.

- The International Bank for Reconstruction and Development (IBRD) was originally formed to rebuild countries devastated by the Second World War, but is now primarily devoted to lending secure bonds to developing countries to relieve poverty and improve infrastructure. Its bonds are rated 'triple-A' (indicating that they are as secure as possible). This is guaranteed by the fact they are backed by member states' share capital.

- The International Development Association (IDA) provides long-term, interest-free loans to the world's 81 poorest countries for education, health care, sanitation, clean water, and environmental protection. Since its inception, it has made loans totalling nearly £80 billion (on average, £4–14 billion a year).

The World Bank, like the IMF, has encountered increasing hostility from some development charities because of the conditionalities that it requires before agreeing to assist struggling states. Some see the criteria it expects them to meet before recognizing them as stable business environments as an attempt to impose a Western-influenced neoliberal economic model on nations whose indigenous institutions and sociocultural make-up do not sit easily with it. The key factors stipulated by the Bank as necessary for promoting economic growth are listed in the table entitled 'The five key objectives of the World Bank', to be found on the **Online Resource Centre**.

The most recent row over US influence on the Bank broke in March 2005, when then President Bush nominated his erstwhile Deputy Defence Secretary, ardent 'neoconservative' Paul Wolfowitz, to its presidency. In the event, Mr Wolfowitz's inauspicious tenure ended prematurely.

The World Trade Organization (WTO)

Established on 1 January 1995, the World Trade Organization (WTO) replaced the General Agreement on Tariffs and Trade (GATT) originally signed after the Second World War to foster free trade and industrial harmony between member states. It is based in Geneva.

Although, theoretically, the WTO promotes fair trade between nations, the United States has often been accused of ignoring or bypassing its rulings: between 1993 and 2009, the UK and the EU tried to protect the Caribbean states by supporting the price of their banana exports, but the United States complained about this (in the end backed by the WTO). The United States later tried to impose tariffs on its imports of foreign steel, inflating their market price relative to domestically produced steel—a move that other UN nations denounced as protectionism—but it was quick to oppose similar treatment from China, by lodging its own complaint with the WTO.

The Organisation for Economic Co-operation and Development (OECD)

Based in Paris, the Organisation for Economic Co-operation and Development (OECD) comprises 29 industrialized member countries. It was formed in 1948 (under a different name), initially to help to implement the Marshall Plan for the reconstruction of war-ravaged Europe, but it opened its doors to non-European members in 1961.

The OECD's primary aims are to promote global free trade, together with representative democracy, and to this end (along with the G8 and World Economic Forum) its focus is the encroachment of globalization—the term denoting the increasingly interdependent nature of the global economy.

As with most supranational organizations, it has a ruling council, Secretary-General, and Secretariat (civil service).

The World Economic Forum (WEF)

The World Economic Forum (WEF) is a not-for-profit foundation based in Geneva. Its aim is to improve the distribution of economic opportunity throughout the world by fostering interaction between governments, businesses, academic institutions, and the arts. Its members meet annually at the Davos Symposium in Switzerland—an informal, but highly exclusive, summit frequently lampooned for its 'blue-sky' pontificating and culinary indulgence.

▌ End of empire—the Commonwealth and the British Council

The British Empire may have long since collapsed, but two largely benign aspects of its legacy continue, in the guises of the Commonwealth and British Council.

The Commonwealth of Nations

Today's Commonwealth comprises 53 countries—most (but not all) former British colonies. It takes its name from a remark by then Foreign Secretary Lord Rosebery, who, on visiting Adelaide in 1884, described what remained of the UK's then crumbling empire as 'the Commonwealth of nations'. The Commonwealth's current membership is outlined in the table entitled 'Current membership of the Commonwealth', to be found on the **Online Resource Centre**.

The Commonwealth's main purpose is to foster cross-cultural understanding and cooperation between developed economies and the larger number of developing nations that are also members. The broad policy areas over which it seeks to reach consensual agreement are:

- democracy;
- economics;
- education;
- gender;
- governance;
- human rights;
- law;

- treatment of small states;
- sport;
- sustainability; and
- youth.

In 1971, it formally committed itself to upholding a list of core values, by signing the Singapore Declaration (later supplemented by the 1991 Harare Declaration). These included promoting world peace, individual liberty, egalitarianism, and opposition to racism and colonialism, and eradicating poverty, disease, and economic inequality. While the Queen remains head of the Commonwealth (see Chapter 1, 'Actual prerogative powers—those exercised by the monarch'), she is now head of state of only 16 members (the 'Commonwealth realms'): Antigua and Barbuda; Australia; the Bahamas; Barbados; Belize; Canada; Grenada; Jamaica; New Zealand; Papua New Guinea; Saint Kitts and Nevis; Saint Lucia; Saint Vincent and the Grenadines; the Solomon Islands; Tuvalu; and Britain itself. Australia narrowly voted to retain her as sovereign in a 1999 referendum, while Jamaican Prime Minister Portia Simpson Miller suggested that the 'time has come' for the West Indies island to become a republic.

Other recent ructions in the Commonwealth have included South Africa's 1994 return, after a 33-year absence, following then President Mandela's election, and Pakistan's temporary expulsion in 1999, after President Musharaf's military coup. Zimbabwe withdrew voluntarily in 2003, after previously being suspended over President Robert Mugabe's dubious human rights record.

Like most other supranational organizations, the Commonwealth has its own governing and administrative institutions, as listed in the table entitled 'Commonwealth institutions and their functions', to be found on the **Online Resource Centre**.

The British Council

The British Council is a registered charity funded by a combination of an FCO grant and its income from teaching English and running British exams abroad, and managing training and development contracts. It is the UK's main agency for maintaining cordial, mutually beneficial cultural relations with other nations, and, to aid it in this regard, it has more than 200 offices and 128 teaching centres in 100-plus countries.

Among the technological, scientific, and artistic initiatives sponsored by the charity is the UK's entry to the Venice Biennale, which showcases the work of a leading contemporary visual artist every two years. In recent years, Britain has been represented by such 'Brit Art' luminaries as Chris Ofili, Gilbert and

George, and Tracey Emin. The British Council supports student exchange programmes between the UK and numerous other nations through its Central Bureau for Educational Visits and Exchanges.

Although generally perceived as a benign organization, the Council has encountered notable diplomatic difficulties. Since 1994, it has operated in Russia under an interim intergovernmental agreement focusing on the fields of education, science, and culture. But cordial relations between the charity and Russian authorities abruptly cooled when, in May 2007, Britain's government demanded the extradition by Russia of Andrei Lugovi—identified as prime suspect in the murder of Alexander Litvinenko, a former lieutenant-colonel in the Russian Federal Security Service, who was poisoned with the radioactive chemical polonium-210 while staying in London in November 2006.

Having already closed all of its branches in Russia, other than in Moscow, St Petersburg, and Ekaterinburg, the Council was ordered to shut up shop everywhere except the capital in December 2007. Justifying its actions, the Russian Foreign Ministry alleged that it was 'operating illegally' and had 'violated tax regulations, among other laws'.

☰ Topical feature idea

British combat troops have formally been withdrawn from Iraq and Afghanistan, but many are returning home to uncertain futures, in light of the Coalition's plans to make tens of thousands of service personnel redundant to save money. How many troops with links to your area have returned from the two countries and how are they adjusting to life back home? Where are they stationed now and how secure are their jobs?

✳ Current issues

- **Impending publication of the Chilcot Inquiry report** At time of writing, publication of the long-delayed Chilcot Report into the circumstances leading to Britain's decision to join the US-led invasion of Iraq remained promised for 2014. Chairman Sir John Chilcot was expected to criticize former Prime Minister Tony Blair and the weak intelligence-gathering that stoked the case for war, while refusing to disclose full transcripts of Mr Blair's conversations with former US President George W Bush ahead of the official decision to join the mission.

- **Prioritizing overseas aid spending** The Department for International Development (DfID) continues to sidestep the deep spending cuts faced by other ministries, thanks to a Conservative election pledge to ring-fence its overseas aid budget. Despite this, successive International Development Secretaries have indicated that funding might be withdrawn from states, such as India, that have traditionally received millions from Britain, in light of their increasing economic prosperity.

■ **Diplomatic standoff between the Russian Federation and Western powers over Ukraine** Relations remain frosty between Russia and the West following the former's decision to pass a law formally annexing the Crimea region of Ukraine after a popular uprising brought down the country's government, creating a temporary power vacuum prior to the election of a new administration. The European Union has since signed partnership agreements with three former Soviet states, including Ukraine.

⠿ Key points

1. International relations are overseen by three government departments: the Foreign Office (responsible for diplomacy), the Ministry of Defence (which funds the armed forces), and the Department for International Development (overseas aid).

2. The United Nations (UN) is the biggest international alliance, today numbering 193 participating states. It was set up in 1945 as a peacekeeping organization.

3. The UN's principal decision-making body is its Security Council. This has five permanent members: the United States, Britain, France, the Russian Federation, and the People's Republic of China.

4. The North Atlantic Treaty Organization (NATO) is a military alliance, initially set up by Western powers in 1949. Today, its membership numbers 28, including several former Soviet states.

5. The Commonwealth is a group of 53 independent states, most of which are former British colonies. In addition to Britain, 15 of its members retain the Queen as head of state.

→ Further reading

Baylis, J., Smith, S., and Owens, P. (2012) *The Globalization of World Politics: An Introduction to International Relations*, 6th edn, Oxford: Oxford University Press. **Updated analysis of the changing face of global relations, from a post-Cold War, post-9/11 perspective.**

Brown, C. and Ainley, K. (2009) *Understanding International Relations*, 4th edn, Basingstoke: Palgrave Macmillan. **Useful introduction to international relations and diplomacy.**

Jackson, R. and Sorensen, G. (2012) *An Introduction to International Relations: Theories and Approaches*, Oxford: Oxford University Press. **Succinct introduction to the main political theories surrounding international relations.**

Meisler, S. (2011) *United Nations: A History*, New York: Grove Press/Atlantic Monthly Press. **Comprehensive history and analysis of the evolution of the United Nations.**

Online Resource Centre

www.oxfordtextbooks.co.uk/orc/Morrison4e/
Visit the Online Resource Centre that accompanies this book for web links and regular updates.

11

The origins and structure of local government

The evolution of government in Britain can be rationalized into two phases: gradual unification beneath first a single monarch, then a centralized Parliament; followed by the incremental devolution of many powers accrued at the centre to regional and local administrations.

When the process of nation-building first began, competing kings vied with each other to extend their realms to encompass first England, then Wales, Scotland, and, in due course, Ireland. Ironically, by the time these countries were formally consolidated into a single 'United Kingdom', in the 1707 Acts of Union, the monarchy's power was already waning, and it was not long either before Parliament would begin ceding a significant amount of self-rule to 'the provinces'.

That said, the evolution of local government has been as much a bottom-up as top-down process. Medieval monarchs needed to appoint locally based courts, and created titled landowners to maintain loyalty and order among their subjects. Conversely, pressure for jurisdiction over issues as diverse as public health, road maintenance, and refuse collection to be handed to locally based individuals, guilds, and, in due course, elected councils came from artisans, manufacturers, and merchants, whose trade and enterprise depended on them. Over time, these early moves towards local government were to become increasingly sophisticated. As of May 2015, there will 418 UK local authorities (councils)—down from 433 previously. In England there are 353, in Scotland 32, and in Wales 22 (a tally that the present Labour-run Welsh Executive has pledged to cut to 12 if it wins the 2016 Welsh Assembly elections). Following tortuous negotiations, Northern Ireland's total was cut from 26 to 11 at the May 2014 local elections, though for the first year the new 'super-councils' operated in 'shadow' alongside their precursors. In England, the range of council types is particularly baffling, with many people living outside London and other metropolitan areas coming under a 'two-tier' system, in which local services are split between district or borough and county councils, while others have a single (unitary) authority. Residents of the capital and other major cities such as Birmingham, Manchester, and Sheffield, meanwhile, fall under all-purpose London and metropolitan borough councils (unitary authorities in all but name).

What follows is the story of how this peculiar framework came about.

▌ The first British local authorities

Long before the emergence of anything that could be described as a 'council'—the term by which we refer to local authorities today—it suited those at the top of British society to maintain a rudimentary 'local government'. To this end, Saxon kings set up 'shire courts' across the countryside and their Norman successors established a feudal system based on this.

By the twelfth century, with urbanization taking root, individuals and groups whose activities provided the bedrock of their local economies began to see the virtue of establishing a strengthened form of local autonomy. Their pleas were rewarded with the granting of the first 'letters patent' and 'royal charters', conferring the status of 'incorporated bodies' (self-governing entities) on first cities, then 'municipal boroughs' (smaller towns recognized as having legitimate claims to run their own commercial and legal affairs). These areas were run by nominally elected 'municipal corporations'.

Both cities and boroughs exist to this day—albeit largely in name, as their powers have been brought into line with those of other forms of council. In rural areas, however, the shire courts were short-lived and were eventually replaced by a new, solidified local regime: Justices of the Peace (JPs). The authority of JPs arose out of Acts of Parliament rather than common law and, over time, they were assisted in their work by their local 'parishes'. These bodies were effectively embryonic councils, based initially around ecclesiastical parish boundaries, but ultimately evolving into the civil parishes (see 'Parish councils, town councils, and community councils' in this chapter).

The emergence of modern local authorities

It was during the Industrial Revolution that a combination of commercial, political, and simple logistical pressures combined to promote the first true local authorities.

By the early nineteenth century, there were 800 boroughs, most governed by local majors (mayors) and councils elected exclusively from among the wealthiest merchants, industrialists, and landowners. The electorate (to the extent that it existed) was limited to other equally moneyed individuals and a handful of marginally less affluent tradesmen. Early public services—street lighting and road maintenance, for example—were delivered largely to make conditions better for commerce.

No new charters were granted in the eighteenth century, so major emerging industrial towns and cities such as Manchester and Birmingham had to make do with limited autonomy, in the form of 'improvement commissioners' approved by Parliament. In rural areas, the by then established JP/parish combination continued to hold sway. Justices and parish councils met four times a year in 'quarter sessions', which generally took place in public houses. They collected 'rates' from local households—tax based on the 'rateable' (or rental) value of land and property, which continued in one form or another until 1990—to pay for the following core officials:

- parish constables;
- surveyors of the highways; and
- overseers of the poor.

The origins of today's local government system lie in the key Acts listed in the table entitled 'Chronology of main Acts instrumental in the emergence of local government', to be found on the **Online Resource Centre** that accompanies this book.

By 1894, the following five types of local authority—which continued in more or less the same form for the best part of 80 years—were established outside London:

- county councils;
- county borough councils;
- municipal borough councils;
- urban district councils; and
- rural district councils.

▌ The rolling reorganization of local government

Since the 1970s, there have been four significant local government reorganizations:

- 1974—the introduction of a 'two-tier' structure in England and Wales;
- 1986—the abolition of metropolitan counties in major urban areas;
- 1990s onwards—the phased introduction of unitary authorities; and

- 2000 onwards—the gradual introduction of directly elected mayors in major towns and cities.

The following section examines each of these developments in detail.

Because the evolution of local government in London and Scotland followed different trajectories from the rest of Britain, they are considered separately.

The 1974 reorganization

Perhaps the largest-scale restructure of the council framework in England and Wales (excluding London), the 1974 reorganization originated with the conclusions of a Royal Commission on Local Government set up in 1965 by Richard Crossman, Minister for Housing in Harold Wilson's Labour government.

When it reported in 1969, the Commission (chaired by Lord Redcliffe-Maude) recommended that the 1,000 existing councils should be replaced by a rationalized system of 61 'local authority areas', of which 58 would be 'all-purpose'. These would effectively be unitary authorities (see 'The 1990s phased introduction of unitary authorities' in this chapter), taking responsibility for all local services. Conurbations (major urban centres where two or more towns and cities had merged to form single built-up areas), such as Greater Manchester and the West Midlands, would have their own two-tier *metropolitan* authorities, in recognition of their larger populations and community needs.

Labour lost the 1970 election and the Commission's recommendations were deemed too revolutionary by Ted Heath's incoming Conservative administration. In the event, it was not until John Major's tenure as prime minister in the 1990s that unitary authorities finally appeared. However, Heath's government recognized the need for some reform and duly instituted this in the guise of the Local Government Act 1972, which took effect in 1974. This introduced the following.

- A **two-tier structure** of counties and districts, which remained the norm until the mid-1990s and still exists in many areas. Numerous districts subsequently applied for Royal Charters, entitling them to call themselves 'borough' or 'city' councils (like the boroughs and cities of old). This move led to some districts and counties amalgamating—reducing the overall number of councils to 39 counties and 296 districts in England, with an 8:37 split in Wales.

- An alternative two-tier 'metropolitan county' structure in six pilot conurbations: West Midlands, Merseyside, Greater Manchester, West Yorkshire, South Yorkshire, and Tyne and Wear'. Each conurbation was split, for administrative purposes, into several 'metropolitan borough councils', charged with financing and running most day-to-day local services—for example rubbish collection, housing, and environmental health. Conurbations would each be overseen by single 'metropolitan county councils', in charge of services affecting their whole areas, such as strategic town and country planning, main roads linking neighbouring towns, public transport, emergency services, and civil protection. (A breakdown of the towns and cities encompassed by each is contained in the table entitled 'The composition of metropolitan county/borough areas', to be found on the **Online Resource Centre**.)

The new two-tier structure saw the end of long-standing counties such as Cumberland, Westmorland, and the three different parts of Lincolnshire, and the introduction of new ones, including Avon, Cleveland, Cumbria, Humberside, Clwyd, Dyfed, and Gwent. Some were never wholly accepted by local people and have subsequently vanished (Avon was merged with neighbouring Somerset in the post-1992 unitary settlement.) The reorganization also saw certain cities stripped of their pre-existent 'municipal borough' status. These included Nottingham, Bristol, Leicester, and Norwich—although by way of compensation they were allowed to retain the nomenclature 'city', not to mention 'lord mayors' (senior officials who perform ceremonial duties and in other towns are called simply **mayors**).

Under the rationalized two-tier structure, **district councils**, **borough councils**, and the new metropolitan borough councils were equivalent to each other, and were each given the same responsibilities—largely providing localized, 'door-to-door', services such as refuse collection. Likewise, **county councils** and metropolitan county councils became responsible for providing countywide services, with social care and education the biggest spending areas. A full breakdown of current council responsibilities is outlined in Table 11.1, and a list

Table 11.1 Breakdown of council services offered by different types of local authority

District councils, borough councils, metropolitan borough councils, and unitary authorities	County councils and unitary authorities
Environmental health (sanitation, drainage, pollution, food hygiene)	Education (schools and further education)
Development control (planning permission)	Social services (care for elderly, mentally ill, and vulnerable children)
Housing and the homeless	Highways (road-building, maintenance, and on-street parking)
Refuse collection (now incorporating waste for recycling)	Refuse disposal (landfill sites)
Car parks	Emergency planning
Council Tax and Uniform Business Rates (UBR) collection	Cultural and leisure services (libraries, museums, sports centres)
Local strategic planning	Countywide strategic planning
Licensing	Passenger transport (buses, trams)

Table 11.2 Links between local authority service areas and Whitehall departments

Service area	Department responsible
Antisocial behaviour	Home Office; Department for Communities and Local Government (DCLG)
Car parks	Department for Transport (DfT)
Children's services (schools, child protection)	Department for Education (DfE); Department of Health (DoH); DCLG
Council Tax and Uniform Business Rates (UBR) collection	DCLG; HM Treasury
Cultural and leisure services	Department of Culture, Media, and Sport (DCMS)
Further education	Department for Business, Innovation, and Skills (BIS)
Emergency planning	Department for the Environment, Food, and Rural Affairs (Defra)
Environmental health (sanitation, drainage, pollution, food hygiene, waste management)	Defra; Home Office; Ministry of Defence (MoD)
Highways (road-building and maintenance)	DfT
Housing and the homeless	DCLG
Licensing	DCMS
Passenger transport (buses, trams)	DfT
Police	Home Office
Social services (care for the elderly, mentally ill, and vulnerable children)	DoH
Town and country planning	Defra

of the central government departments at Whitehall responsible for overseeing each local authority service area is given in Table 11.2.

Northern Ireland's council reorganization took a different form, and happened at a different pace. In 1973, 26 districts emerged, but many functions were transferred from local to central government.

The 1986 reorganization

The Conservatives' 1983 election manifesto described the six metropolitan county councils that it inherited on regaining power in 1979—alongside the then Greater London Council (GLC), under the leadership of Ken Livingstone—as a 'wasteful and unnecessary tier of government'. It promised to abolish them, returning their functions to the second-tier metropolitan borough councils that still existed 'beneath' them (confusingly, redesignated as 'metropolitan *districts*' for administrative purposes).

To this end, it passed the Local Government Act 1985, which, as well as establishing metropolitan boroughs, set up new police authorities. Tyne and Wear was unusual, in that its police provision fell under the Northumbria Police Authority. Metropolitan areas also gained their own fire and civil defence and passenger transport authorities, and some acquired joint boards responsible for handling waste disposal services. This happened in Merseyside and Greater Manchester (except Wigan), although in the West Midlands, for example, joint arrangements between neighbouring boroughs were established on an ad hoc basis. In other areas, commissioning and running public transport and waste disposal services continued to fall under counties.

Other than introducing these new, service-specific types of local authority, in all other respects the effect of the 1986 changes was to replace the previous metropolitan two-tier structure with what were effectively the first unitary authorities—all-purpose councils, responsible for fulfilling the roles split in other areas between districts or boroughs and counties. Opponents of the move saw in it a clear attempt by the Conservatives to diminish metropolitan councils' authority by reducing them to lower-level administrations, on the one hand, and hiving off responsibilities formerly overseen by scrapped metropolitan counties to new bodies with limited scope, on the other. Mr Livingstone and other left-wing council leaders, including Sheffield City Council and South Yorkshire County Council's David Blunkett (a future Labour Home Secretary), saw the diluted powers as an assault on their socialist policies by a right-wing government fearful of major populated areas becoming 'states within states'. Referring to this notion explicitly at one point in the late 1980s, Sir Cyril Irvine Patnick, Tory member of Parliament (MP) for Sheffield Hallam, famously described Mr Blunkett's domain as 'the People's Republic of South Yorkshire'.

One outcome of the 2014 Scottish referendum has been an incipient revival of metropolitan-tier government—with Chancellor George Osborne taking the first step on this road by devolving £1 billion to Greater Manchester in November that year, together with sweeping powers over its own policing, transport, housing, and planning infrastructure, under a directly elected mayor (see Chapter 13, 'Local government hierarchies since the LGA 2000'). Mr Osborne had previously spoken of his desire to create a 'northern powerhouse' to rival London, encompassing Manchester, Leeds, Birmingham, and other cities (see also Chapter 1, 'Devolution in England—time for a revival?').

The 1990s introduction of unitary authorities

The most significant council restructure since 1974 began in 1992, in a phased process designed to rationalize local government across England and Wales. The aim of introducing a **unitary structure** was to improve the efficiency and transparency of local administration by reducing service duplication, slashing bureaucracy, and establishing a simplified, uniform council structure across the two countries. Unitary authorities, which to date number 56 in England,

32 in Scotland, and 22 in Wales, are defined as 'any authority which is the sole principal council for its local government area'. Meanwhile, Northern Ireland's 26 councils are 'single-tier districts' (unitary authorities in all but name).

Contrary to bold claims favouring the unitary system, critics argue that it has only added to the confusion, by creating a patchwork landscape of local government, with unitary authorities in many areas sitting directly alongside councils retaining the two-tier structure. Counties in which unitary and two-tier systems coexist are defined as having a **hybrid structure**. Examples include Lincolnshire, where Lincoln City Council (a unitary authority) sits beside Lincolnshire County Council and boroughs or districts in nearby towns such as Grantham and Gainsborough. The chronology of the phased introduction of unitary authorities is outlined in the table entitled 'Chronology of the phased introduction of unitary authorities', to be found on the **Online Resource Centre**.

In addition to hybrid counties, the unitary system produces other quirks. Several unitaries encompass entire counties—notably, the Isle of Wight, Rutland, County Durham, and Cornwall. The Isles of Scilly, meanwhile, have a unique form of council that was long treated as *sui generis* (meaning 'in a class of its own'), but is now seen as a unitary.

▶ City councils and the meaning of 'city status'

Historically, cities were synonymous with ecclesiastical seats of power and, more specifically, the presence of Church of England cathedrals and diocesan bishops. But even centuries ago this was not always the case: in the Tudor period, for instance, city status was sometimes conferred by sovereigns through letters patent (legal instruments issued by monarchs), the granting of a town's royal charter, or even, over time, accepted custom and practice.

In the nineteenth century, the Church of England actively sought to increase the number of its urban dioceses, creating more cities in the process. Not all towns designated as cities had prior royal borough status and, by the end of the 1800s, cities were springing up in places without cathedrals. Around this time, Scotland gained its first cities by letters patent and royal charter; prior to 1889, major medieval towns such as Edinburgh and Perth were often referred to by the term 'civitas' and, although the word 'city' had been coined for them by the eighteenth century, their status remained unofficial.

Today, 'city status' no longer depends on the presence of a cathedral or any significant ecclesiastical influence. Neither are cities always major population centres: with a mere 2,000 inhabitants, Britain's smallest city, St David's in Pembrokeshire, has a populace significantly smaller than most towns.

For much of the twentieth century, it was Home Secretaries' responsibility to advise monarchs on which towns should be designated cities. This happened to Lancaster in 1937, Swansea in 1969 (marking the investiture of the Prince of Wales), and Sunderland in 1992 (on the 40th anniversary of the Queen's accession to the throne). More recently, however, the rules have been bent. In December 2000, three new cities were created, in Brighton and Hove, Wolverhampton, and Inverness, as part of a 'Millennium City' competition launched by the Labour government. The Queen created a further five in 2002 to mark her Golden Jubilee: Stirling, Preston, Newport, Lisburn, and Newry. She repeated this for three more—Chelmsford, Perth, and the north Wales town of St Asaph, which boasts Britain's smallest cathedral—in the run-up to her Diamond Jubilee. This brought the overall number of cities to date to 69.

Just as the criteria used to determine whether a town qualifies for city status are nebulous, so is the degree to which becoming one has any tangible effect. A **city council**—the moniker adopted by authorities covering places with official city designation—is not a *type* of council or administration; the term is really no more than an honorary title. In terms of their functions, city councils tend to be unitary authorities (Brighton and Hove, York, and Stoke-on-Trent), metropolitan boroughs or districts (Birmingham, Wolverhampton), or simple district or borough councils.

There are some curious exceptions. Confusingly, seven English cities— Chichester, Ely, Hereford, Lichfield, Ripon, Truro, and Wells—are lowly civil parishes, in terms of their administrative status. This means that they technically fall within the remit of parish councils—the lowest tier of local government (see next section). Similarly, in three Welsh cities (Bangor, St David's, and St Asaph), the city status applies to community councils (equivalent to parish councils). In two English cities (Bath and Salisbury), meanwhile, city status is the preserve of so-called 'charter trustees'—an arcane form of local administration intended to be a temporary stopgap for towns when their borough status was removed by the Crown prior to their 'conversion' into parish councils. A full rundown of designated cities, together with details of the type of authority in each place, is listed in the table entitled 'Local authorities with city status and the types of council in each case', to be found on the **Online Resource Centre**.

▌ Parish councils, town councils, and community councils

The lowest tier of local government is represented by parish councils in England, and community councils in Wales and Scotland. Civil parish councils— not to be confused with pre-existing *ecclesiastical* parishes established by the

Church—were created under the Local Government Act 1894 to oversee social welfare and basic civic duties in villages and small towns, and to act as the 'voices' of their local communities. Historically, some parish and community councils in larger villages and small towns, meanwhile, called themselves 'town councils'. Those that still do so tend to have their own town mayors—not to be confused with the more official (if also largely ceremonial) mayors of borough and city councils, or the directly elected mayors now found in some towns and cities (see Chapter 13, 'The "directly elected mayor and cabinet" model'). Councillors take turns to spend a year as mayor, on rotation, with formal 'mayor-making ceremonies' held in town halls to mark handovers from one to another. Mayors' roles are largely ceremonial (opening church fetes, switching on Christmas lights), although they also tend to chair full council meetings.

Under the 1972 Act, all parishes with more than 150 inhabitants were compelled to establish parish councils—a stipulation that has significantly increased their number. Those with smaller populations were required only to hold **parish meetings**—regular gatherings open to all local electors. Unlike meetings held in towns and villages with formal parish councils, those convened in lesser populated parishes have statutory powers to act as de facto councils. In such circumstances, a clerk and chairman are elected to preside over business.

Today, many of the limited day-to-day powers once exercised by parish, community, and town councils are wielded by higher-level authorities. But parish councils are still allocated budgets by those authorities ('parish precepts'), which, unlike revenue raised for their own use, cannot be capped by central government. Therefore, in areas in which parishes are more proactive, precepts can be high: Thurston Parish Council, Suffolk, for example, raised its Council Tax share by 214 per cent in 2008–09. In most areas, however, the precept is usually sufficient only to rent the buildings in which it holds its monthly meetings and to fund minor local improvements, such as replacement street lights, park benches, or new goalposts for the village football pitch.

Parish councils, however, remain significant. They have a statutory right to be formally consulted by, and represented on, public inquiries into major planning applications affecting their areas. In fact, often, the first time that a reporter—and, by extension, his or her news organization—hears of a potentially controversial planning proposal will be by attending a meeting at which it is thrashed out by parish councillors. And far from being mere talking shops, there has been a resurgence recently in their muscle-flexing. Labour experimented with new models of service delivery, involving partnerships between neighbouring authorities and delegation of certain responsibilities to voluntary and lower-level statutory bodies, including short-lived 'quality parish councils' (bottom-tier authorities granted delegated responsibility for delivering some services, based on their prior efficiency in managing their previously minuscule budgets), as well as an inter-agency initiative known (while it lasted) as 'local area management'. Under the Coalition, such initiatives have given way to 'Big Society' localism ideas like those outlined in the next section.

From service 'users' to service 'owners'—the dawn of the 'Big Society'

With the Coalition came a new emphasis—part philosophical, part pragmatic—on the idea that lower-tier authorities such as parish, town, and community councils, and ultimately communities themselves, should become more involved in 'ownership', management, and/or delivery of their own services. The 'Big Society' idea was a product of the thinking of 'blue sky' policy advisers, including Mr Cameron's (now former) director of strategy, Steve Hilton, and Phillip Blond, director of centre-right think tank ResPublica and writer of an influential 2009 pamphlet entitled *Red Toryism*. 'Big Society' thinking envisages a return to a traditional, grass-roots, communitarian conservatism (in a broadly similar vein to the thinking of 'Blue Labour'—see Chapter 5, 'The Parliamentary Labour Party (PLP)'). In hard policy terms, the Coalition has introduced four 'community rights', allowing neighbourhood groups and lower-tier councils (known collectively as 'relevant bodies') to bid to take over local services that they deem to be poorly run, or physical assets that they would like to maintain themselves (see Chapter 13, 'Cameron's "Big Society"—what role for councillors and officers now?').

▶ The evolution of local government in London

London's autonomy has always been exercised in a distinct way from the rest of Britain, although at times its local government structure has resembled that of the metropolitan areas described earlier. Today, London operates under a unique two-tier system, with responsibilities for service provision split between the **Greater London Authority (GLA)**, headed by an elected mayor, and 33 second-tier councils (a system akin to the pre-1986 metropolitan county and borough structure abolished by Mrs Thatcher's government).

Of these 33 councils, 32 are London boroughs, elected in similar fashion to metropolitan boroughs, but the last is a unique entity run by an unreformed medieval-style 'old boys' network'. The City of London Corporation—officially, the 'Mayor and Commonalty and Citizens of the City of London'—is Britain's oldest surviving council. It covers the 'Square Mile' containing the capital's central financial district and, although democratically accountable like other authorities, has long attracted criticism for the anachronistic nature of its electoral processes and peculiar customs.

The City of London was the only corporation to escape the axe when the Municipal Corporations Act 1835 abolished all others. It continues to be presided over by a non-partisan administration of a kind once more widespread before the emergence of formal political parties (see Chapter 5). At its head is the Lord Mayor of London, his attendant aldermen, and a Court of Common Council, beneath which a range of committees oversee specific policy areas. Again uniquely, the Corporation was allowed to retain a system of *non-residential voting* (often termed the 'business vote') after this was abolished elsewhere in 1969. This concession was, in part, a recognition of its tiny resident population (just 7,400 as of the 2011 census).

Vocal critics of the Corporation—which many see as a self-perpetuating, privileged cabal—include Labour backbencher John McDonnell, who memorably dismissed it in 2002 as 'a group of hangers-on, who create what is known as the best dining club in the City ... a rotten borough'.

A timeline of the evolution of London local government is presented in the table entitled 'Timeline of the evolution of local government in London', to be found on the **Online Resource Centre**.

London's modern-day local government structure

As with devolution for Scotland, Wales, and Northern Ireland, Labour advocated re-establishing a single overarching authority for London long before winning the 1997 election. The 1986 abolition of the Greater London Council (GLC) was seen by some in the party as an act of war by the Conservatives. Others viewed it as an error of judgement that needed redressing for more pragmatic reasons.

In its 1997 manifesto, Labour pledged to introduce a new form of 'elected city government', topped by an EU or US-style elected mayor. A year after regaining power, the promised vote was held, and 72 per cent of London's electorate voted in favour of the proposed GLA. Twelve months later, the Greater London Authority Act 1999 formally established the new authority and, with more than a hint of déjà vu, Mr Livingstone was duly elected London Mayor in March 2000.

Although the GLA has become a model for certain other towns and cities that have since adopted elected mayors (see Chapter 13, 'The "directly elected mayor and cabinet" model'), initially its method of conducting business was unique among councils. In a manner akin to the US president's power-sharing with that country's parliament (Congress), London's mayor is elected separately to the 25-strong London Assembly with which he shares power over the GLA.

Like the US president, the mayor is responsible for proposing policy and setting out prospective annual budgets to finance services that he or she proposes to provide in coming years. The Assembly must then approve or amend these proposals, much like Congress, and its committees and subcommittees (like their Congressional equivalents) may scrutinize the mayor's actions in office and the performance of services provided by the GLA. The parallels between the London mayoral and US parliamentary systems have gone further in recent years, in light of changes to the political composition of both. Just as President Barack Obama (a Democrat) has spent much of his time in the White House fighting to get the more contentious aspects of his legislative programme through a Republican-dominated House of Representatives, Mr Livingstone had to work with Conservatives following the 2004 elections (nine members to Labour's seven), while the re-election of his successor, the Conservative Boris Johnson, in May 2012 led to a period of renewed tension between the mayor's office and a Labour-led Assembly.

The GLA is the top tier of London local government, with individual boroughs continuing to provide day-to-day services. The division between the roles of the GLA and boroughs is explained in Table 11.3; of the major roles fulfilled by the GLA, the majority are overseen by the agencies listed in Table 11.4.

Table 11.3 Breakdown of local authority responsibilities in London

Greater London Authority (GLA)	London boroughs
Transport	Schools and further education (FE)
Policing	Social services
Fire and rescue	Waste collection
Congestion charging	Highways repair and maintenance
Environmental policy	Libraries, and local leisure and cultural services (museums, theatres)
Strategic development and planning	Development control

Table 11.4 Main agencies of the Greater London Authority (GLA)

Agency	Responsibilities
Transport for London (TfL)	Manages most aspects of London's transport system, including London Underground, Docklands Light Railway, London Buses, main roads, and traffic management (incorporating the congestion charge zone)
Metropolitan Police Authority (MPA)	Oversees Metropolitan Police Service
London Fire and Emergency Planning Authority (LFEPA)	Administers London Fire Brigade and coordinates emergency planning

▌ Local government in Scotland

As with several other aspects of public affairs—notably its legal and education systems, the latter of which is explored in Chapter 15—Scotland has a different local government framework from that of the rest of Britain.

Until the 1974 reorganization, the country effectively had a single-tier system. The Local Government (Scotland) Act 1929 had replaced pre-existing parish councils with a nationwide network of district councils with significantly increased autonomy and budgets. This structure, refined by the Local Government (Scotland) Act 1947, distinguished between smaller and larger 'burghs', which were a form of local unit derived from medieval administrative boundaries. The latter—burghs with populations greater than 20,000—were handed more power.

All this changed with the Local Government (Scotland) Act 1973, which ushered in a two-tier system like that implemented in England and Wales. District councils remained, albeit with slightly refined borders and some variation in their levels of responsibility, but the newly introduced higher-tier authorities were named 'regional councils', as opposed to county councils. Three notable exceptions—the Western Isles, Shetland, and Orkney—were, however, effectively given unitary status even at this early stage, in recognition of their perceived homogeneity.

When Mr Major's government began its phased council reorganization in the early 1990s, Scotland was again treated as exceptional. In a 'big bang' approach that ministers avoided elsewhere, unitary authorities were introduced nationwide in one fell swoop. While rationalizing a patchwork system, this 'one size fits all' strategy caused controversy in some areas—not least because of the wildly varying population sizes covered by individual councils. The unitary authority for Inverclyde (an area with relatively few inhabitants) followed the same boundaries as the extant district council, while Clackmannanshire embraced the whole of that county—and Highland, a sprawling 30,650 km swathe of north-

west Scotland, encompassing chunks of the former counties of Inverness-shire, Ross and Cromarty, Caithness and Nairnshire, and the whole of Sutherland.

Today, there are 32 'council areas' covered by unitaries in place. In May 2012, a report by the Reform Scotland think tank recommended reducing the number of councils to 19, and giving them extra responsibilities by abolishing existing health and police boards, but such a change has yet to materialize.

▌ Emergency services at the local level

While ambulance services are today part of the National Health Service (NHS—see Chapter 6), with trust status akin to that accorded to hospitals, the other core emergency services are overseen by discrete local or regional authorities.

The origins of the British police force

Until the early nineteenth century, Britain had no countrywide police force; instead, it fell to town magistrates to maintain local law and order. Perhaps unsurprisingly, London was the first UK city to adopt its own police force and, in 1749, author Henry Fielding and his brother, Sir John, set up a group of semi-professional law enforcers known as 'The Bow Street Runners'. These early police officers wore civilian clothes and did not patrol the streets routinely like their modern-day equivalents, but acted to intercept criminals and bring them before the courts on the authority of local magistrates.

Shortly afterwards, an embryonic Thames Police was formed, but it was not until some 80 years later, when Sir Robert Peel was Home Secretary, that the first true constabulary was set up, in the guise of the Metropolitan Police, based at Scotland Yard. Established in 1829, and variously dubbed 'Bobbies' and 'Peelers' after their founder, the 'Met' were funded by a local tax—'the police rate'—which citizens were obliged to pay on top of the 'poor rate'. In due course, similar innovations followed in emerging borough council areas and with the introduction of new county magistrates.

Today, the UK Police Service, although notionally a nationwide organization, is divided into 39 local forces in England and four in Wales. Scotland had eight regional forces between 1967 and passage of the Police and Fire Reform (Scotland) Act 2012, when they were replaced by a single Police Service of Scotland (known as Police Scotland). Northern Ireland, too, has its own dedicated police force, dubbed the Police Service of Northern Ireland, which replaced the erstwhile Royal Ulster Constabulary (RUC) in November 2001.

Most forces in England and Wales still respect county boundaries, although there are increasing exceptions: a single force, Sussex Police, covers the twin counties of East and West Sussex, while the most south-western force is Devon and Cornwall Police. In 2006, then Home Secretary Charles Clarke proposed merging several forces (among them, the five existing ones in the East Midlands, which would be turned into a single 'super-force'), reducing the total in England and Wales to just 24, in an effort to streamline the Service and to better equip the country to fight terrorism. Although his plans were shelved, more recently individual police forces in certain regions have voluntarily entered negotiations about possible mergers. At time of writing, talks were still ongoing between the Durham and Northumbria forces.

Police force accountability—from authorities to commissioners

Other than in London, where the Metropolitan Police Authority was handed executive control over the Met by ministers in the Greater London Authority Act 1999, UK police forces all come under the overarching control of the Home Secretary (or, in Scotland, the Deputy First Minister). Until 1995, forces were regulated by police committees answerable to county councils or unitary authorities, but the Police and Magistrates' Court Act 1994 saw these replaced by a new second tier: the police authority. The change, consolidated by the Police Act 1996, reduced the involvement of councillors from relevant local authorities in favour of a mixed membership intended to represent local residents and the business community better.

Police authorities raised revenue by levying precepts (annual budget requests) on their billing authorities, which were then included explicitly in local Council Tax bills (see Chapter 12, 'Local taxation and the evolution of the Council Tax'). Their responsibilities included: maintaining effective and efficient forces for their areas (with the Home Secretary or Home Office Inspectorate empowered to 'act in default' if they failed); appointing, holding to account, and occasionally dismissing their local chief constables and assistant chief constables; and convening regular open public meetings along the lines of those held by councils, at which their members were expected to answer questions on their activities.

On 15 November 2012, all former police authority responsibilities were assumed by new US-style directly elected **police and crime commissioners (PCCs)**, in a highly contentious move condemned by some, including Sir Hugh Orde, president of the Association of Chief Police Officers (ACPO), as 'politicizing' the police. In addition, the following further duties of PCCs were set out under the Police Reform and Social Responsibility Act 2011 as:

- setting the strategic accountability and direction for policing;
- working with partners to prevent and tackle crime;
- invoking the voice of the public, the vulnerable, and victims;
- contributing to resourcing of policing response to regional and national threats; and
- ensuring value for money.

As well as the controversy flowing from the introduction of commissioners—many of whom stood for election on explicitly party-political platforms—there was considerable colour. By the time nominations closed, an eclectic array of politicians, ex-police officers, and celebrities were rumoured to be considering running for office—among them former Labour deputy leader Lord Prescott (who eventually lost the vote in Humberside), serving Mayor of Middlesbrough Ray Mallon, and Nick Ross, ex-presenter of BBC1's *Crimewatch*. Colonel Tim Collins, one of the most senior Army officers to serve in the Iraq War, began the race as Tory candidate for Kent, before pulling out in May 2012 because he could not commit to attending all of the required selection meetings. The elections, when finally held, proved contentious: amid accusations that ministers had failed to notify electors adequately to the fact a vote was even coming, let alone to explain what PCCs were, they recorded Britain's lowest ever turnouts, hovering between 10 and 20 per cent. Sixteen Conservatives, 13 Labour, and 12 independents were elected. This pattern was repeated when, in August and October 2014 respectively, by-elections to replace first the recently deceased commissioner for the West Midlands, Bob Jones, then scandal-hit South Yorkshire PCC Shaun Wright recorded turnouts of just 10.3 and 14.8 per cent in turn.

The new commissioners were established in only 41 of the existing 43 English and Welsh police force areas. The City of London (as with so many special liberties) was exempt from the arrangement on historical grounds, while the role of commissioner for the capital as a whole was automatically assumed by the Mayor of London, Mr Johnson. Since their election, PCCs have continued courting controversy—not least for their generous salaries, lack of transparency, and, in some cases, perceived low calibre. In May 2014, Ann Barnes, PCC for Kent, faced calls to resign from her £85,000-a-year post after appearing in a Channel 4 *Cutting Edge* documentary in which she was shown struggling to explain her policing strategy, bringing her dogs into her office, and writing her own job title incorrectly on a whiteboard. Ms Barnes had previously faced criticism after Paris Brown, the 17-year-old whom she had appointed as Britain's first 'youth PCC', was forced to resign over allegedly racist and homophobic tweets that she had posted between the ages of 14 and 16.

Northern Ireland's Police Service continues to be overseen by an independent Police Board.

The role of chief constables

Chief constables have always had statutory responsibilities separate from those of their governing committees, authorities, or PCCs. It is their role to deliver policy 'on the ground'. This entails appointing all officers below the rank of assistant chief constable, producing annual reports on their performance in the preceding 12 months (covering specific categories of offence, along with other areas highlighted as being of local concern, such as violent crime), and disciplining officers for misconduct.

In operational terms, it is the chief constable and his or her assistants' role to manage the force's budget, to hire and fire other officers, and to ensure that personnel are suitably allocated to maintain adequate patrols across the force area. But over the past 20 years, as both population levels and the range of policing responsibilities have increased out of proportion with rises in numbers of officers, successive governments have tried to reduce the burden of professionals' more mundane patrol duties by bolstering them with semi-trained back-up officers recruited from the local community. These include part-time volunteers known as 'special constables', or 'specials', and semi-trained policemen and women introduced by the Blair government called **police community support officers (PCSOs)**.

As at 31 March 2011, when the last definitive survey was conducted, 15,820 PCSOs were employed across England and Wales—down from a peak of 16,814 in 2009. Around a quarter were based in London, with Manchester having the second largest contingent. In November 2007, they received enhanced powers—partly in response to complaints from senior police officers that trained staff were overstretched because of increased paperwork generated by legislation designed to make stop-and-search and arrest procedures more transparent. Although they have always been entitled to paid overtime, a minimum of 21 days' annual leave, and various other benefits, PCSOs used to earn significantly less than fully trained officers. However, with starting salaries for professional police constables (PCs)—the lowest rank—reduced by £4,000 to £19,000 in 2013, to cut costs, PCSOs now earn more or less the same. In addition to PCSOs, Labour introduced another layer of partially trained, community-based officials, in the guise of 'neighbourhood wardens'. A type of glorified Neighbourhood Watch coordinator, these uniformed individuals, employed by councils or housing associations, were an initiative of the DCLG's Neighbourhood Renewal Unit. They were introduced to patrol, and be otherwise readily available, in areas with large numbers of elderly or vulnerable residents—particularly those notorious for property crime, graffiti, and anti-social behaviour. After 2005, both PCSOs and wardens began working alongside fully qualified police officers, on the one hand, and groups of volunteers, on the other, in a new breed of de facto police force called a 'neighbourhood policing team' (also known as 'safer neighbourhood teams' and 'safer, stronger community teams'). Around 3,600 were subsequently set up across England and Wales.

Today, PCSOs have considerable clout. They can issue summary fixed-penalty notices to members of the public for offences ranging from littering and cycling on footpaths, to failing to keep dogs under control. Under authority deriving from Labour's 'Respect' agenda, they may also require names and addresses from people apprehended for antisocial behaviour—for example fighting or swearing in the street. These details may subsequently be used by police or councils to apply to magistrates' courts for permission to issue individuals with summary penalties for various levels of antisocial behaviour—principally *antisocial behaviour orders* (ASBOs) until their recent replacement with several new measures by the Coalition (described later in this section). The ASBO was a civil penalty in the first instance, but individuals who breached their conditions—for example by failing to respect curfews or by remaining resident at prohibited addresses—could be prosecuted for criminal offences. The Crime and Disorder Act 1998, which introduced ASBOs, defined antisocial behaviour as conduct that:

> **❝** caused or was likely to cause alarm, harassment or distress to one or more persons not of the same household as him or herself and where an ASBO is seen as necessary to protect relevant persons from further anti-social acts by the defendant. **❞**

Towards the end of Labour's reign, the ASBO concept was extended to tackle lower-level problematic behaviour, through *acceptable behaviour contracts* (ABCs). These were agreements that young people identified as having previously acted antisocially were asked to sign, with input from their parents or guardians, pledging to change their ways and/or to make specified amends.

In addition to being able to impose orders and contracts on named individuals, both neighbourhood wardens and PCSOs were given power (like ordinary police officers) to apply to councils for *dispersal orders* to cover locations judged to be antisocial behaviour 'black spots'. Groups of two or more people alleged to be causing 'harassment, alarm, or distress' may be forcibly broken up and/or moved on from a location under such orders. Failure to comply can lead to prosecution and fines of up to £2,500.

Police can also obtain and enforce *designated public place orders* (DPPOs)—a variation on the dispersal order concept designed to clear specific streets, squares, or alleyways of drink-related antisocial behaviour. Anyone caught drinking in these locations who refuses to surrender his or her alcohol is liable for a £50 fixed penalty, or for arrest and a fine of up to £500.

Despite the widespread ridicule with which news of some ASBOs was greeted in the media (a man was banned from his own home after being given one for playing his music too loudly, while several have been imposed on grumpy pensioners for relatively minor 'offences' such as cursing at their neighbours), they proved hugely popular among law enforcement agencies and many communities blighted by unruly behaviour. According to Home Office figures, 18,566 ASBOs were issued between their introduction in April 1999 and January 2011. Embarrassingly for ministers, though, 10,380 of these were breached by their recipients at least once. Despite this, Labour used their popularity as a springboard to expand the scope of its antisocial behaviour crackdown, by increasing the range of 'misdemeanours' for which summary penalties could be issued by police and local authorities, and giving parish and community councils powers to impose them.

The Coalition has since replaced ASBOs with three principal orders, introduced by the Antisocial Behaviour, Crime, and Policing Act 2014:

- the **criminal behaviour order (CBO)**— a 'ban' on forms of antisocial behaviour, with the ability to 'force' people to undertake programmes, such as drug or alcohol rehabilitation courses, to improve their conduct;

- the **crime prevention injunction (CPI)**—a 'fast-track' ASBO for lower-level antisocial behaviour, which can be imposed more quickly (within days or hours of an 'offence' being committed) while requiring a lower standard of proof than the ASBO; and

- the **community protection notice (CPN)**—an order requiring people to do or to stop doing a specified thing, such as graffiti, dropping litter, or leaving excess refuse in their gardens or driveways.

A further proposed order—included in the original Bill as an 'injunction to prevent nuisance or annoyance' (IPNA)—had been withdrawn by the time it received royal assent, after being defeated in the House of Lords. This was

Figure 11.1 Flow chart outlining the police complaints process

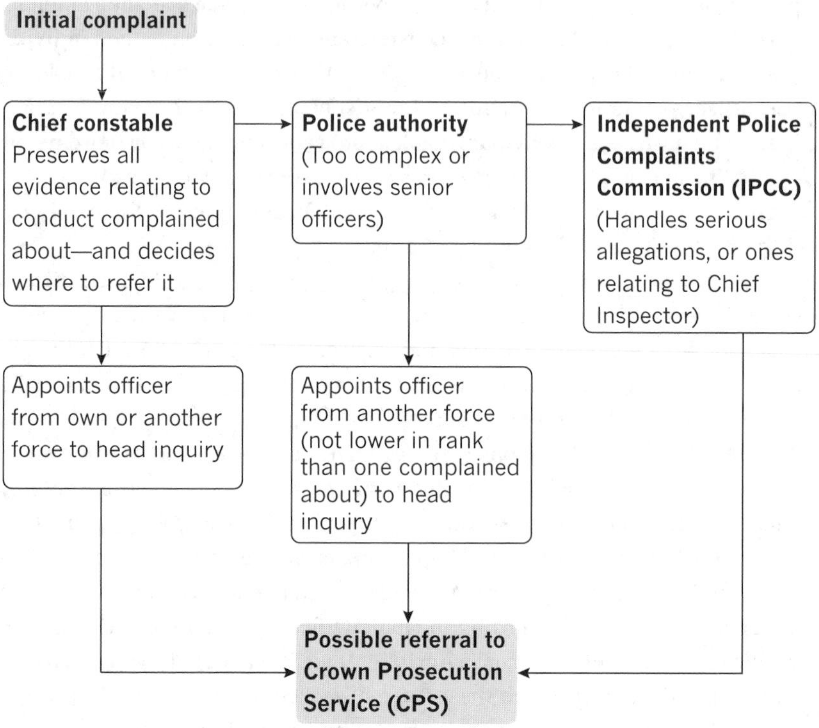

roundly lampooned in the media as something that would, theoretically, have given police a licence to penalize hawkers, buskers, screaming children, people wearing headphones, or anyone else subjectively viewed as a 'nuisance' by other members of the public.

The police complaints process

Allegations of misconduct initially follow the same process as other complaints about the local police force. This process is outlined in Figure 11.1.

All cases involving deaths in police custody or at the hands of officers in the community—for example the shooting of a suspect—are automatically passed to the **Independent Police Complaints Commission (IPCC)**. Even when matters are handled locally by the chief constable or PCC, the IPCC may intervene if dissatisfied with the choice of investigating officer. Alternatively, it will approve his or her appointment by issuing an 'appropriate statement'.

Formal disciplinary action is a matter for the local commissioner in relation to most senior officers (including chief constables), or the chief constable himself or herself with others. If a chief constable indicates that he or she is *unwilling* to take action where the IPCC has become involved, the Commission can *direct* him or her to do so. Disciplinary charges imposed on officers are heard by chief constables (unless they, or an assistant chief constable, stand accused) and punishment can include cautions, demotions, or even dismissal. There is a right of appeal from the chief constable's decision, which must go to a police disciplinary appeals tribunal. In the last resort, members of the public unhappy at how a complaint has been dealt with may apply to the courts for a private summons to prosecute the officers concerned (as attempted unsuccessfully by the family of Mr De Menezes, prior to their successful private prosecution of the Met for breaching health and safety legislation).

In recent years, there has been some controversy over the stringent 'standard of proof' required before disciplinary charges may be brought. This is illustrated by the stark contrast between the wording of the 'civil' standard—which applies in most employment-related situations—and the 'police' standard. The former is worded thus:

❝ Is it more likely than not, on the balance of probabilities, that the police officer committed the disciplinary offence? **❞**

The latter reads:

❝ Did the police officer commit the disciplinary offence, beyond all reasonable doubt? **❞**

Fire and rescue authorities

In contrast to the police (which, although divided into local forces, all fall under national police services), fire and rescue services—or 'fire brigades' as they once were—are entirely locally based. In common with the police, they are managed by separate authorities, but unlike it they do not have their own discrete body. Instead, in two-tier areas, the 'fire and rescue authorities' are usually county councils, but for fire services based in unitary and hybrid areas, 'combined' fire authorities exist. In metropolitan areas, fire services are overseen by separate fire and civil defence authorities (as in London). The history of Britain's fire services is outlined in the table entitled 'Timeline for emergence of UK fire services', to be found on the **Online Resource Centre**.

An important distinction between fire services that fall under county councils and combined fire (or fire and civil defence) authorities is that the former are supervised and managed financially by county council committees, while the latter two determine their own budgets like PCCs. They are all, however, answerable to the Secretary of State for Communities and Local Government.

It is the Communities Secretary's role to check each year the establishment schemes in place in each fire service area—that is, the level and precise nature of the provision that it makes available to local people. In law, all fire services must:

- equip and train a firefighting force;
- make arrangements for dealing with calls for help;

- gather information about local 'risk' buildings—for example high-rises, timber-framed structures, or ones housing large numbers of elderly or disabled people;
- give advice on fire protection to businesses, schools, etc.;
- ensure that local water companies maintain adequate supplies of water at pressures suitable for firefighting; and
- draw up mutually beneficial 'reinforcement schemes' with neighbouring fire services to help them to deal with major fires.

Fire services are also called on to deal with other emergencies. These 'special services' are divided into two broad categories: humanitarian (for example serious road accidents and floods), and non-humanitarian (less urgent calls, such as requests to help residents to gain access to their homes after losing their keys). Whereas firefighters would once willingly answer calls to scale trees in pursuit of errant cats, it has become increasingly commonplace for today's services to charge for such 'non-essential' operations.

Under the Fire Precautions Act 1971, various premises are now barred from operating without official fire service seals of approval in the form of fire certificates. These are issued, following inspections, by fire authorities. The types of premises affected include:

- offices;
- sports grounds;
- hotels; and
- theatres.

Other Acts passed to increase fire safety include:

- the Public Health Act 1936, which stipulated that fire escapes must be provided in buildings such as hotels and theatres; and
- the Fire Safety and Safety of Places of Sport Act 1987, which introduced tough new seating standards following the 1985 Bradford City Football Club tragedy (including a cut in attendance limits at football grounds).

Emergency planning and civil defence

The aspect of 'emergency services' provision in which councils have historically been most directly involved is contingency planning and civil defence. The notion of 'civil defence' in particular—namely, protection of citizens against enemy attack or other forms of security emergency—arose after the Second World War. As a policy, it was initiated by the post-war Labour government, but has remained largely a notional peacetime responsibility—its most tangible application being plans for a hypothetical nuclear attack expected to be updated by councils at various junctures during the Cold War. Notable exceptions included strategies employed to safeguard London's population from terrorist bombs during The Troubles and measures implemented following the Real IRA's attack on a Manchester shopping centre in 1996. In this age of increased security threats, however, it is not hard to imagine a time when renewed importance may be attached to civil defence departments.

As recently as 2004, a new Civil Contingencies Act effectively replaced the entire body of existing emergency planning legislation on the statute book. The most significant aspect of the shake-up, ordered by then Secretary of State for Transport, Local Government, and the Regions Mr Prescott, was the new requirement placed on so-called 'responder' organizations in each area to appoint a full-time **emergency planning officer** (sometimes known as a 'civil contingencies officer', 'civil protection officer', or 'resilience officer') to coordinate measures that would be implemented in the event of a civil emergency. As well as security threats, civil emergencies might include any number of natural or man-made disasters—for example floods, major fires, landslides, or nuclear accidents. Responder organizations are divided under the Act into 'Category 1' and 'Category 2'. The list of bodies in each category is outlined in the table entitled '"Responder" bodies that are required to appoint emergency planning officers', to be found on the **Online Resource Centre**.

The history of local government's involvement with civil defence began with passage of the Civil Defence Act 1948, under which the Home Secretary was empowered to direct councils to take 'appropriate measures' to ensure that their populations' civil defence requirements were met. These were further defined by the Civil Defence (Planning) Regulations 1974, which gave county councils powers to 'make plans to deal with hostile attacks' and, in certain circumstances, to prepare for war, in consultation with boroughs or districts. It was only in the 1990s, after the Cold War ended, that the term 'emergency' was explicitly redefined to cover peacetime disasters such as floods—an issue that has returned to the fore in recent times, following the devastating 2013–14 winter storms that left thousands of families isolated, without power, and, in areas such as the Somerset levels, homeless. Finally, in 2001, responsibility for civil defence shifted from the Home Secretary to a Cabinet Office coordination unit.

A further type of agency involved in preparing for civil emergencies is the recently formed 'regional resilience board'. Sometimes referred to as 'regional control and resilience boards', these are joint bodies drawing together representatives from police forces, fire authorities, and council civil defence departments to oversee overall emergency planning for entire regions. The 2004 Act also required responder organizations to form more localized versions of the regional boards—'local resilience forums' (LRFs)—based in each police area. These are expected to produce community risk registers specific to their localities, outlining particular locations, buildings, businesses, or residential areas seen to be particularly vulnerable. They are overseen at national level by a Cabinet Office executive agency: the Civil Contingencies Secretariat.

The government's much-vaunted new 'resilience' strategy for the country was prompted, in large part, by the 11 September 2001 terrorist attacks and the 2004 Madrid bombings (not to mention persistent fears of an avian flu pandemic, which have been periodically publicized by the media since 2003). But this new state of preparedness failed to prevent the 7 July 2005 attacks on London. And more embarrassing still for ministers has been the organizational chaos and buck-passing between local authorities, Environment Agency, and central government that greeted the widespread winter floods that devastated parts of Britain in 2007, 2009, and 2014.

At the top of the chain of command for emergency planning is an ad hoc government committee, codenamed 'Cobra' and headed by the prime minister, which meets in the Cabinet Office as and when necessary. (Despite its James Bond-style title, the acronym actually stands for the breathtakingly banal 'Cabinet Office Briefing Room A'.) Among the emergencies for which Cobra has recently been convened were the 2007 foot-and-mouth outbreaks and the terrorist attack on Glasgow Airport—all of which occurred within weeks of Gordon Brown becoming prime minister. When the premier is unavailable, his or her place is taken by the Home Secretary. This happened at the time of the 7 July bombings, because then Prime Minister Tony Blair was at a G8 summit in Gleneagles when the news broke.

▶ Empowering local authorities in the age of the 'Big Society'

While community groups and lower-tier authorities now have enhanced powers to hold higher-tier ones to account—and even to take over running services if dissatisfied with those they are receiving—a 'flip side' of the Coalition's 'Big Society' drive has been to bestow greater freedoms on local government itself. The Localism Act 2011 introduced a 'general power of competence' for all councils—from towns and parishes, through districts, counties, and unitaries, to fire and rescue authorities. To cut 'red tape' and encourage more entrepreneurial thinking by officers and councillors at a time of harsh budget cuts, ministers aimed to move away from what they saw as a 'can't do' culture, in which councils 'can only do what the law says they can', to a 'can do' one that frees them up to 'do anything—provided that they do not break other laws'. As an example, the Act spells out its hope that councils will find increasingly innovative ways of working together to 'drive down costs' and to do 'creative, innovative things to meet local people's needs'.

▌ Local government associations

The Local Government Association (LGA) was established in 1997 to provide a collective voice in Whitehall policymaking for all 353 English local authorities. A self-styled 'voluntary lobbying organization' (rather than a trade union or association), it is based close to Parliament, at Smith Square, in the former Transport House: historic headquarters of the Labour Party. In addition to representing districts and boroughs, counties, metropolitan boroughs, and unitaries, the LGA also speaks on behalf of subscribing police, fire, national park, and passenger transport authorities. Councils in Wales are represented by a Welsh Local Government Association (WLGA), a subset of the LGA, while there is a separate Northern Ireland Local Government Association. Scotland has a Convention of Scottish Local Authorities (COSLA).

In 2007–08, the LGA published strategic objectives summarized in the table entitled 'Local Government Association (LGA) strategic objectives', to be found on the **Online Resource Centre**.

In addition to the central LGA, there are 13 regional **local government associations**, the remits of which broadly follow the boundaries of the government's English regions.

≣ Topical feature idea

Two years after their introduction, police and crime commissioners (PCCs) continue to prove controversial, with media stories repeatedly focusing on their high salaries and ability to take executive decisions about local policing with minimal scrutiny—despite, in many cases, having little experience of working in the police themselves. Who is your local PCC? What is his or her background and qualification for the job? What does a typical 'day in the life' of the PCC entail? What do local people think of his or her track record so far?

✳ Current issues

- **The future of unitary authorities** The Coalition abandoned plans for unitary authorities to be introduced in Norwich and Exeter on entering power. But 22 years after John Major introduced unitaries, individual councils from Huntingdonshire, on the doorstep of his old Commons constituency, and Oxford, in Mr Cameron's backyard, are lobbying for unitary status.
- **New punishments for antisocial behaviour** The Antisocial Behaviour, Crime, and Policing Act 2014 has finally begun replacing the antisocial behaviour orders

(ASBOs) inherited from Labour with various other measures, including crime pre-vention injunctions (CPIs) and tougher criminal behaviour orders (CBOs).

- **Derailing of the 'Big Society' rollout** Encouraged by the Coalition, a growing num-ber of local authorities have outsourced services on a scale never before seen, with councils such as Barnet franchising out almost everything to private companies, the voluntary sector, and community groups keen to run things for themselves. But recent changes of political leadership in some such areas threaten to derail these experiments in direct autonomy.

⸬ Key points

1. Local authorities (councils) first emerged in the nineteenth century to promote public health and build and maintain trade routes. Today, there are 433 local authorities: 353 in England, 22 in Wales, 32 in Scotland, and 26 in Northern Ireland.

2. Outside London and the six metropolitan areas, council structures in England and Wales are either 'two-tier', unitary, or hybrid. In two-tier areas, each citizen is cov-ered by two councils: a county and district or borough. Counties in which unitary and two-tier systems coexist have hybrid structures.

3. In two-tier areas, services are divided between the two different types of council: counties are responsible for schools, waste disposal, highways and transport, social care, and libraries; while districts or boroughs oversee housing, waste collection, planning decisions, and Council Tax collection.

4. Local police forces are led by senior officers called chief constables, but appointed and funded by elected police and crime commissioners (PCCs).

5. Fire services are governed by their own local fire authorities. In two-tier areas, these come under county councils; in unitary and hybrid ones, there are separate 'com-bined' fire authorities.

→ Further reading

Newman, I. (2014) *Reclaiming Local Democracy: A Progressive Future for Local Government, Bristol: Policy Press.* **Up-to-date examination of the challenges and opportunities facing local government in the age of austerity.**

Norman, J. (2010) *The Big Society: The Anatomy of the New British Politics,* Buckingham: University of Buckingham Press. **One-sided, but illuminating, mani-festo for the concept of David Cameron's 'Big Society' written by a loyalist Conservative MP.**

Stallion, M. and Wall, D. S. (2000) *The British Police: Police Forces and Chief Officers 1829–2000,* London: M. R. Stallion. **Exhaustive handbook to the UK police service, from its inception to the new millennium, including profiles of every force past and present, and introductory essays.**

Stevens, A. (2006) *Politico's Guide to Local Government*, 2nd edn, London: Politico's Publishing. **Fully updated second edition of the comprehensive guide to every aspect of local government, including the interplay between local and central administrations.**

Wilson, D., Ashton, J., and Sharpe, D. (2001) *What Everyone in Britain Should Know about the Police*, 2nd edn, London: Blackstone Press. **Fully revised second edition of the informative core text charting developments in the UK police service, from its origins in the early nineteenth century up to the present day, with a focus on recent changes from the idea of the traditional 'Bobby on the beat' to today's target-led—and frequently armed—officers.**

Wilson, D. and Game, C. (2011) *Local Government in the United Kingdom*, 5th edn, Basingstoke: Palgrave Macmillan. **Revised fourth edition of the standard text on contemporary local government in Britain. Covers all of the major recent developments, including the introduction of unitary authorities and elected mayors.**

Online Resource Centre

www.oxfordtextbooks.co.uk/orc/Morrison4e/

Visit the Online Resource Centre that accompanies this book for web links and regular updates.

12

Financing local government

 Some of the most newsworthy local government stories arise from the way in which it is financed—and how this funding is spent. Above-inflation rises in councillor allowances, all-expenses-paid 'fact-finding' junkets for members and officers, hikes in Council Tax bills, and the impact of government cuts on the delivery of grass-roots services are among the bread-and-butter material of headlines.

▌ Revenue versus capital finance

Councils need money for two types of spending: to build infrastructure (offices, roads, traffic crossings, schools, and housing); and to operate and maintain these facilities on a day-to-day basis. The cost of building things falls under **capital expenditure**; that of staffing, lighting, heating, and repairing them, **revenue expenditure**.

▌ Revenue expenditure and how it is financed

Revenue spending is financed through councils' *income*: grants that they receive from central government, taxes that they raise locally, and any up-front fees or penalties that they charge for services (for example parking permits and library fines). The main sources of revenue income today are as follows:

- central government grants;
- Council Tax;

- Uniform Business Rates (UBR); and
- fees, charges, and reserves.

Each of these income streams is examined in detail below.

The reformed government grant system

Around three-quarters of local authority revenue finance derives from government grants. Traditionally, the biggest single grant was the **revenue support grant (RSG)**, or **general block grant**, which individual councils were left to spend at their discretion, focusing on particular local funding needs. Under New Labour, however, the process by which central government grants were allocated to councils became more complex, as ministers increasingly tried to micro-manage their budgets by prescribing precisely where and how they were allowed to spend the money allocated to them. But the Coalition has reversed this trend, with the result that local financial autonomy is gradually being restored, as the percentage of grant money allotted to the RSG steadily rises again by the year.

As of the 2014–15 tax year—the last year of the Parliament—Coalition ministers had yet to banish every 'ring-fenced' grant. However, the system of 'passporting' that Labour ministers used to control precisely how cash was spent had been relaxed, allowing councils more scope to spend money as they wished within the confines of given departmental budgets. The Coalition had also moved closer to ensuring that the majority of revenue income generated in each locality was kept there—from 1 April 2013, allowing councils to keep up to half the proceeds of the UBR raised in their areas, rather than (as previously) having to send them to a central pool, to be reallocated to other authorities according to need.

Types of revenue grant

Central government calculates annually how much money it thinks individual councils need to provide services for their communities, up to a standard 'national level'. Under Labour, grants allocated on this basis were known collectively as 'formula grants'. In addition to RSG, there was also a principal formula police grant (PFPG) and a grant derived from the redistributed UBR (otherwise known as **national non-domestic rates**, or **NNDR**), also calculated according to a formula.

Although the precise ways in which these three different grants were calculated differed, the principle underpinning them all was that a substantial proportion of the government's overall revenue funding pot should be directed to councils on the basis of their comparative 'needs'. In other words, more money would be distributed to councils covering areas with high levels of socio-economic deprivation and/or facing other peculiar demographic challenges, such as disproportionately elderly and/or infirm populations. This approach to funding supplanted the earlier system, which had adopted a more straightforward 'per capita' ('per head') model for funding councils—allocating grants broadly on the basis of the relative *size* (rather than *nature*) of local populations.

In addition to formula grants, Tony Blair's government introduced two types of *non-formula* grants, which had the effect of tying councils' hands by forcing them to spend money on particular services and/or geographical areas that ministers judged high priority. The two main categories were **area-based grants (ABGs)**—payments set aside, as the name suggests, for specific localities within each council's ambit—and **specific grants**. It is the latter to which we will pay closest attention here because, despite the Coalition's rejection of Labour's 'top-down' approach to funding local government, at time of writing £4 out of every £10 in revenue income received by English councils came in the form of specific grants.

Labour divided specific grants into two subcategories: *ring-fenced* and *unfenced* (or 'targeted'). The former—as their name suggested—were 'hived off' for very particular ends. One of the most famous ring-fenced payments (still present today) is the **dedicated schools grant (DSG)**, which councils were forbidden from spending on anything other than staffing and maintaining schools or providing related services such as special needs teaching. Under Labour, as well as being reserved for schools generally, the DSG was at times prescribed further—with ministers stipulating that it must go towards specific running costs, such as buying textbooks or improving extracurricular activities. But such 'micro-passporting' often caused conflict between central and local government—including a row between several councils and then Education Secretary Alan Johnson in 2005 after it emerged that they had used parts of their DSGs to subsidize other services.

By contrast, councils could spend 'unfenced' grants however they saw fit—albeit within certain parameters dictated by ministers. Unlike RSG, they were not calculated on the basis of formulae related to local demographic and socio-economic factors; rather, they were residual pots of money to be spent on services judged equally worthy of central government funding nationwide. An example of a long-standing unfenced specific grant was the Housing and Planning Delivery Grant (HPDG). Although councils could spend it only on services related to housing or planning, in practice they used them in a variety of ways.

By the time Labour left office, the lion's share of local government revenue grants were passported and there was a bewildering array of individual payments—many targeted for highly specific purposes. The lack of manoeuvre councils had to determine for themselves how best to spend the resources at their disposal spurred Coalition Communities Secretary Eric Pickles to introduce a radically simplified system—although he nominally retained the ring-fenced/unfenced distinction. The new breakdown of revenue grants is as follows.

(a) Formula:
  - Revenue support grant (RSG)
  - Principal formula police grant (PFPG)

(b) Non-formula:
  - Local services support grant (LSSG)
  - Specific grants:
  (i) **Ring-fenced grants**—DSG and new **public health grant (PHG)**
  (ii) **Unfenced grants**—including early intervention grant (EIG)

Of the new specific grants, EIG has already proved the most contentious—largely because of the huge expectations placed on it. Former Education Secretary Michael Gove specified that it was to be used to fund multiple costly, complex, and politically sensitive services, ranging from the (previously ring-fenced) Sure Start budget (see Chapter 15, 'Improving access and accountability in preschool education'), through free preschool education for disadvantaged 2-year-olds, to drug and alcohol misuse prevention projects for teenagers. The other most notable new non-formula grant is the **local services support grant (LSSG)**—effectively a replacement for Labour's area-based grant—which councils now receive in 12 monthly instalments a year. To give some idea of the impact of this one reform, LSSG currently draws from seven 'funding streams' (sources), whereas, by the time it ended in 2010–11, ABG drew on 61. But while councils may welcome simplification of their notoriously complex revenue settlements, LSSG does not amount to much as yet: in 2014–15, it totalled just £33 million in England, which barely registered at all as a portion of the overall £98.8 billion revenue budget (see Figure 12.1).

Calculating core grants—how the revenue support grant (RSG) and principal formula police grant (PFPG) are decided

Since 2006–07, levels of both RSG and PFPG awarded to individual authorities have been calculated by subtracting the relative resource amount for each area from its relative needs formula.

- The **relative needs formula (RNF)** is a formula based on detailed information about the population size, social structure, and other characteristics of a council area. By taking into account precise local factors, such as the number of pensioners and school-aged children living in an area and its relative economic prosperity, ministers aim to allocate funds that fairly and accurately reflect the cost of servicing its needs. Within the

RNF, separate formulae determine how much should be allocated to individual councils to cover likely expenses associated with each 'major service area': education, adult social services, children's services, police, fire, highways maintenance, environmental, protective and cultural services (EPCS), and capital financing.

- The **relative resource amount (RRA)**, in contrast to RNF, is a *negative* figure. It is based on the logical assumption that areas with many Council Tax-paying households—particularly those in higher tax bands, indicative of relatively affluent populations—need less financial help from central government than poorer ones. The RRA is subtracted from RNF to give a figure more accurately reflecting what individual areas require in formula grants.

Resulting grants are shared between councils in proportion to their levels of responsibility—with 'upper-tier' counties and unitaries gaining more than 'lower-tier' districts or boroughs, and police and crime commissioners (PCCs) or fire authorities.

Over and above the core chunk of formula grants allocated in this way, a small percentage tends to remain in an overall 'formula pot' to be distributed between council areas on a purely per capita basis. Known as 'central allocation', this is traditionally the same for all councils delivering the same services—that is, all districts or boroughs receive identical per capita amounts. In addition, Labour introduced a procedure known as 'floor-damping' to ensure that every council—no matter how relatively well it fared from a grant settlement—received at least a *minimum* year-on-year increase in formula grant. With real-terms cuts now the order of the day, the days of floor-damping are now a distant memory. The total value of all grants allocated by the government to English councils for 2014–15 was £72.4 billion—down from £77.5 billion the previous year—with those outside London expected to draw on their reserves to the tune of £2.1 billion to compensate for budget shortfalls.

The end of passporting—and return of virement?

Labour's efforts to constrain councils' ability to spend revenue income where they pleased did not end with specific grants. It was once commonplace for those finding themselves facing unexpected shortfalls in one spending department during a financial year to transfer surpluses from another budget, in a process known as **virement**. But under Labour, repeated extensions of the passporting regime rendered all but the most modest shuffling of books impossible. Chancellor George Osborne signalled the return of virement by announcing the abolition of all but two ring-fenced grants in his October 2010 Comprehensive Spending Review (CSR) (see Chapter 7, 'Managing national debt'). But the astute political timing of his gesture (ahead of the announcement of swingeing spending cuts) 'was not lost on the BBC's political editor, Nick Robinson, who evoked the following 'old Whitehall saying' on his blog:

❝Governments with money centralize and claim the credit, those without decentralize and spread the blame.❞

Figure 12.1 gives a full breakdown of the sources of local government revenue finance in England in 2014–15—at which point Mr Pickles' funding overhaul was still a work in progress. Figure 12.2 summarizes the overall percentages of English local authority revenue spending that year in each service area.

Particular aspects of the 2014–15 revenue funding breakdown are worthy of comment. While specific grants still presently comprise the biggest chunk of council income, in keeping with the Coalition's moves towards localizing spending decisions RSG has risen to more than 13 per cent—up from just 0.6 per cent in 2012–13. Council Tax, by contrast, has dropped from 27.1 to 24.3 per cent of the revenue pot in the same period, reflecting the 2 per cent 'cap' imposed by ministers above which it can be raised only with the approval of local electors in referendums. Appropriations from reserves, meanwhile, have risen from 0 to 2.1 per cent, as councils have been required to draw more and more from their own contingency funds to keep services afloat. Figure 12.2 also shows some intriguing patterns—notably the gradual, but steady, decline of education as the dominant area of revenue spending. This fell to £35.8 billion from £38.8 billion a year earlier, as a direct result of more state schools converting to academy status (see Chapter 15, 'The growth of school autonomy—foundation

Figure 12.1 Breakdown of regular local authority revenue income in England for 2014–15

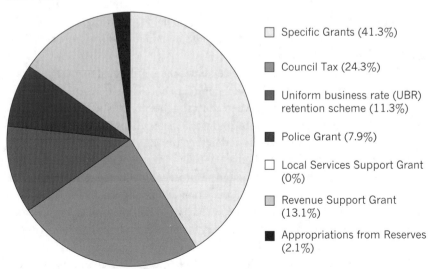

Specific Grants (41.3%)

Council Tax (24.3%)

Uniform business rate (UBR) retention scheme (11.3%)

Police Grant (7.9%)

Local Services Support Grant (0%)

Revenue Support Grant (13.1%)

Appropriations from Reserves (2.1%)

Source: Department of Communities and Local Government (DCLG) © Crown Copyright 2014

Figure 12.2 Breakdown of annual local authority revenue spending patterns for 2014–15

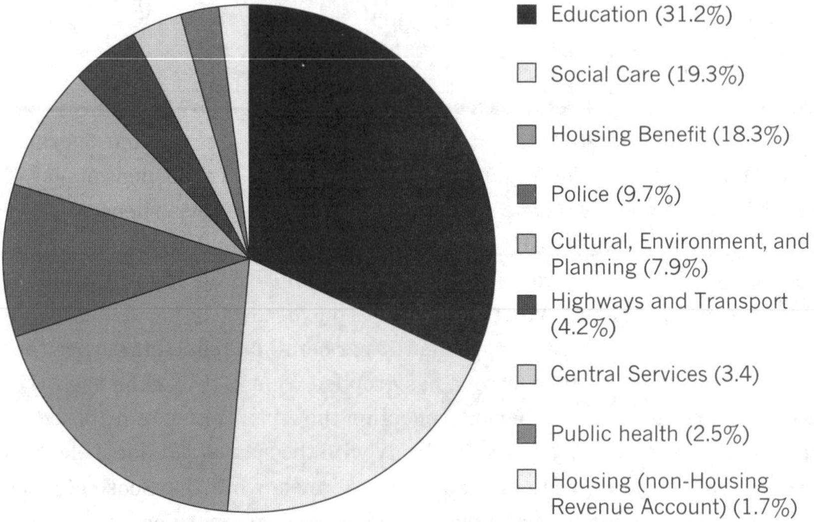

- Education (31.2%)
- Social Care (19.3%)
- Housing Benefit (18.3%)
- Police (9.7%)
- Cultural, Environment, and Planning (7.9%)
- Highways and Transport (4.2%)
- Central Services (3.4)
- Public health (2.5%)
- Housing (non-Housing Revenue Account) (1.7%)

Source: Department of Communities and Local Government (DCLG) © Crown Copyright 2014

schools, free schools, and the rise and rise of academies'), under which they are funded directly by central government. The new category of public health continues to grow (at 2.5 per cent), while, interestingly, the Housing Benefit budget has risen from 17.1 to 18.3 per cent of the total since 2012–13—despite the Coalition's imposition of a £26,000-a-year benefit cap and the 'bedroom tax', among other cuts (see Chapter 17, 'Local authorities, Housing Benefit, and the Local Housing Allowance (LHA)'). This suggests that, while individual households might be receiving less than previously to help them with the cost of rent, the overall number of people whose incomes have fallen to a level at which they are eligible to claim it is increasing.

While the way in which the overall revenue 'cake' is divided to prioritize particular service areas tends to be fairly uniform across Britain, devolution has yielded widening disparities between central government's approach to funding councils in different nations. In 2014–15, 33 per cent of the Welsh local government budget was earmarked for education (exactly the same as in 2012–13), 20 per cent for social services, and 8.4 per cent for policing—broadly on a par with spending allocations in England. However, while the percentages of income Welsh authorities derived from Council Tax and the PFPG (plus floor funding) were comparable to those received by English ones (at 24.4 and 3.8 per cent, respectively), 17 per cent continued to come from business rates (based on redistribution from central government, rather than councils raising and retaining rates locally—see 'Uniform Business Rates (UBR)' in this chapter) and the remaining 54.8 per cent was made up not of passported grants, but an old-style RSG. Although it contrasts with the present picture in England, in relation to RSG at least the funding picture in Wales is likely to be the shape of things to come if Coalition plans to remove ring-fencing come to fruition.

Local taxation and the evolution of the Council Tax

The idea of local taxation dates back to the tithes that medieval parishioners paid their churches for renting their land and the taxes levied on peasant farmers by feudal lords of the manor. But as early as 1601 it began to become more systematic, with the emergence of 'rates'—a property tax based on the 'rateable' (rental) values of individual's homes. This would remain in place (with modifications) for four centuries.

The rates were a tax levied on domestic properties, rather than those occupying them—the broad assumption being that the bigger a property, the wealthier its occupants were likely to be. But, over time, the rating system produced peculiar anomalies that led to growing calls for reform. Before its eventual abolition by Margaret Thatcher's government in 1990 (1989 in Scotland), the most oft-cited illustration of its unfairness was that an elderly pensioner living alone, on a fixed income, in a house for which he or she spent his or her lifetime paying, might be paying exactly the same as several sharing professionals living next door, with much greater individual and combined incomes. Although there was widespread agreement that rates needed reforming, their immediate successor was short-lived. Ushered in by the Local Government Finance Act 1988, the Community Charge—dubbed the 'Poll Tax' by opponents—sought to address the grievances of ratepayers 'punished' for living alone by shifting the onus from property onto people. In future, individual residents would be billed for using local services—forcing everyone to pay their way. But while this may have seemed fairer in theory, in practice the new 'head tax' soon became even more unpopular than rates. While various rebates and exemptions were introduced for certain groups (notably the unemployed), working people living in the same area ended up paying identical sums—regardless of differences in their incomes. A multimillionaire tycoon might be charged exactly the same as his or her cleaner. In addition, some low-income groups previously excluded from local taxation altogether were suddenly included. Full-time students, for example, became liable (albeit with a 75 per cent discount).

Such was the furore over the Community Charge that it is widely viewed as the tipping point that ultimately led to Mrs Thatcher's resignation (see Chapter 3, 'Party'). The tax also proved extremely costly to administer, resulting in part from the fact that many refuseniks seemed prepared to forgo their place on the electoral roll rather than be tracked down by billing authorities. Others openly refused to pay, leading to costly litigation by councils (much of which never bore fruit). In the end, ministers were forced to increase grants temporarily to allow for a gross reduction in Community Charge bills of £140 a person, funded by a 2.5 per cent increase in value added tax (VAT). In 1990–91, the Poll Tax paid for 44 per cent of local expenditure, but this was halved to 22 per cent following the cut (compared to 25 per cent for today's Council Tax).

Following the biggest peacetime protests ever seen in Britain at that time, Mrs Thatcher's successor, John Major, abandoned the charge—replacing it with **Council Tax**. This 'hybrid' tax reinstated the property link, but unlike rates related it to *capital* values, rather than rateable ones. To placate critics of rates, it also retained an element of 'individual' liability introduced by the Community Charge. Each household was billed on the assumption that it comprised two adults (meaning that bills did not increase for three or more). But to avoid returning to a time when households occupying identical properties paid exactly the same—regardless of how many working adults lived in each—a range of reductions and exemptions for single people and low-income groups was introduced to make the system fairer. Those existing today are outlined in Table 12.1.

Although designed to deal with many anomalies and inequities preserved by previous local tax regimes, the new benefits and exemptions system produced its own. Full-time students might have been exempt from Council Tax theoretically, but in practice those renting from private landlords invariably found themselves having to pay it on the homeowner's behalf—or seeing their rent artificially inflated to cover the cost. Students sharing houses with one or more employed adults also lost their exemptions by default, as such households automatically became liable.

Perhaps most controversial has been the 50 per cent reduction traditionally available to households owning two or more properties. In Wales and southwest England, in particular, 'ghost towns' created in picturesque areas favoured

Table 12.1 Council Tax exemptions and reductions

Exemption/reduction	How it works
Single person discount	25 per cent off full Council Tax bill
'Reductions for Disabilities' scheme	Lowers bills for homes in Bands B–H adapted for disabled occupants; ensures that houses are not unfairly overvalued because of expensive modifications
Exemptions	For severely mentally impaired, carers, full-time students, and certain categories of dwelling, such as student halls of residence
Unoccupied dwelling discount	Up to 50 per cent discount—although councils may charge more in 'ghost towns'
Council Tax Reduction	Replaced Council Tax Benefit traditionally used to write off Council Tax bills for unemployed, pensioners receiving Pension Credit (a top-up tax credit designed to offer the poorest pensioners a 'minimum income guarantee'—see Chapter 8, Table 8.2), and other people on low incomes; new 'reduction' scheme costs 10% less than 'benefit' and qualifying criteria are decided by individual councils—although poor pensioners are still protected

by wealthy city-dwellers as holiday home locations have been exacerbated by the relative cheapness of keeping such properties unoccupied for long periods, given the Council Tax discounts that they receive. Under Labour, in certain areas blighted by this trend, councils were given limited discretion to charge more than 50 per cent, to deter property owners from leaving homes unoccupied. A 2003 statutory instrument gave billing authorities power to determine classes of discount in their areas for the first time, in recognition of the risk of such properties being broken into while empty. Unoccupied, but furnished, properties—those most likely to be used as second homes—became liable for reduced discounts of 10 per cent, while some long-term empty homes faced losing their reductions altogether. In April 2008, Newcastle City Council used this new power to scrap discounts for unfurnished and uninhabitable homes.

The Coalition has gone further in some respects to address what it has described as the 'scourge' and 'national scandal' of empty homes. The Local Government Finance Act 2012 dispensed with the long-running 'empty dwelling exemption'—a provision entirely exempting from Council Tax, for up to 12 months, homes undergoing or requiring major repairs to make them habitable—in favour of a locally determined discount. More significantly, from 1 April 2013, it introduced an 'empty homes premium', enabling councils to charge owners of dwellings left empty for two years or more up to one-and-a-half times as much as other homeowners.

For all of these changes, Council Tax is still seen by many as regressive. Newspapers frequently feature stories about financial problems caused to pensioners and others on low or modest fixed incomes, who do not fall into convenient categories making them eligible for reductions—for example people on Employment and Support Allowance (ESA—see Chapter 8, 'Employment and Support Allowance (ESA) and Personal Independence Payments (PIPs)'). Some have even been fined or jailed for 'refusing' to pay. In September 2005, Sylvia Hardy, a 73-year-old retired social worker from Exeter, was imprisoned for refusing to pay £53.71 in Council Tax arrears on time. She told Exeter magistrates' court defiantly that she was following the example of other individuals in history who had fought to change 'unjust laws'.

In Scotland, where the Scottish Parliament has the power to alter local tax regimes, the Scottish Nationalists have long pledged to introduce a local income tax, though this has yet to materialize. In the run-up to the September 2014 independence referendum, then First Minister Alex Salmond confirmed plans to do so in the event of a 'yes' vote, but given Scotland's decision to remain in the UK, it remains to be seen if this will transpire. Table 12.2 outlines arguments for and against a property-based (rather than people-based) local tax.

Council Tax banding

Council Tax bills in England, Scotland, and Wales are based on a system that divides domestic properties into one of eight 'bands' (nine in Wales)—A–H

Table 12.2 Arguments for and against property-based and people-based local taxes

Property-based tax	People-based tax
Cheap to administer and collect, and provides predictable income source.	Boosts local finances because number of bills sent out increases to reflect fact all adults—rather than households—charged.
Difficult for people to avoid paying rates or Council Tax because property, unlike people, is immobile.	Some argue it is fairer, because the burden of paying for services is spread across *all* adults—including those otherwise 'invisible' to taxes based on property values. 'Head tax' does not need to be 'one size fits all': local income tax would reflect ability to pay.
Simple, clearly understood system.	Fosters greater council accountability, because all adults charged and can voice views at elections on how money is spent.
Fair in theory, in that people occupying larger dwellings are likely to be better off.	Because individuals have to complete forms accepting liability for taxes such as the Community Charge, there is a huge disincentive to register. When introduced in Britain, many councils collected barely half what they were owed—and those unable/unwilling to pay lost voting rights by dropping off the electoral roll.
Property taxes can be a disincentive to home improvement, because major refurbishment/extension is likely to hike bills.	Straight head taxes mean that low-income groups such as students, pensioners, and working people on modest wages pay same as vastly richer ones—unless explicit exemptions and reductions are introduced.

(A–I), respectively—according to their notional capital values. In Wales, these bands were revised in 2005, to take account of changes in property prices in the 14 years that had elapsed since the original ones were set on 1 April 1991. Controversially, however, neither England nor Scotland has had its bands changed since they were originally set—meaning that they remain exactly the same as on 1 April 1993 (by which time even original valuations were outdated). Despite pledging in its 2005 election manifesto to revise the bands if re-elected, Labour dropped the policy on returning to power. Cynics saw its reluctance to tackle the issue anywhere but in Wales as an example of political back-pedalling, motivated by a fear that it would lose future votes in marginal constituencies where people whose house prices had significantly risen since the early 1990s might be moved into higher bands. In fact, according to Local Government Association (LGA) research, the number of households likely to lose out in a revaluation was the same as the number that would have benefited (around 4 million).

Whatever the merits of retaining existing bands, it is undeniable that the property values to which they relate are anachronistic today, in light of substantial rises in house prices seen across much of Britain. In England, the highest Council Tax band (H) currently applies to all homes valued at more than

£320,000 in 1991, while in Scotland (where bands are set by Scottish assessors) the top rate starts at just over £212,000. As stated previously, only in Wales has there been any re-banding since 1993: as of 1 April 2005, a top band (I) has applied there for properties worth more than £424,000. Homes built since the dates on which bands were set are given nominal values based on what they would have been worth had they existed on 1 April 1991 (1 April 2003 in Wales). The lowest Council Tax band (A) is set for homes worth £40,000 or less in England, £44,000 in Wales, and £27,000 or less in Scotland, while the 'average band' (D) applies to those worth between £68,000 and £88,000 in England, £91,000 and £123,000 in Wales, and £45,000 and £58,000 in Scotland.

The introduction of revised banding in Wales led to complaints that the country was no longer on an equal footing with the rest of Britain. Moreover, despite the fact that the price ranges covered by each Welsh band were all adjusted upwards to reflect the general surge in property values since 1993, the revaluation was not simply a question of mapping properties in the old Band A into the new one; instead, it produced clear winners and losers. Because values in some areas had risen significantly further than others—with some previously cheaper homes overtaking in value those that were once more expensive—around a third of households found themselves moving into higher bands than before. Most jumped at least one band, while some leapfrogged three or more. Only 8 per cent of homes moved down.

Around one in four homes currently fall into the lowest bands in England and Scotland, although in north-east England this proportion rises to 60 per cent. Current Council Tax bandings in England, Scotland, and Wales are outlined in Table 12.3.

How individual bills are calculated—and who collects the money

So who actually puts properties in bands, and determines the nominal 1991/2003 values of homes built in the years since they were originally set?

Table 12.3 Current Council Tax bands and values in England, Scotland, and Wales

Band	England	Scotland	Wales
A	Up to £40,000	Up to £27,000	Up to £44,000
B	£40,001–£52,000	£27,001–£35,000	£44,001–£65,000
C	£52,001–£68,000	£35,001–£45,000	£65,001–£91,000
D	£68,001–£88,000	£45,001–£58,000	£91,001–£123,000
E	£88,001–£120,000	£58,001–£80,000	£123,001–£162,000
F	£120,001–£160,000	£80,001–£106,000	£162,001–£223,000
G	£160,001–£320,000	£106,001–£212,000	£223,001–£324,000
H	£320,001 and above	£212,001 and above	£324,001–£424,000
I	N/a	N/a	£424,001 and above

Responsibility for valuing homes rests with the Valuation Office Agency (VOA), an executive agency of HM Revenue and Customs (HMRC)—and, ultimately, HM Treasury—but it is for individual billing authorities to maintain lists of valuations. Based in 85 regional offices, the VOA's day-to-day work is undertaken by regional *listing officers*, who compile and update lists of banded properties grouped in their areas. Overall responsibility for running district offices falls to local *valuation officers* (sometimes known as 'district valuers'). It is their job to hear formal appeals initiated by households unhappy with their property valuations.

Although Council Tax banding has never been reset in England and Scotland, homes can still be moved into different bands under certain circumstances. They might go up or down for any of the reasons outlined in the table entitled 'Ways in which properties can change Council Tax bands between revaluations', to be found on the **Online Resource Centre** that accompanies this book.

Over the years, considerable vitriol has been aimed at the VOA, not least by those with homes in higher bands. When valuations were initially set in 1991, an urban myth circulated that its agents 'valued' homes by simply driving past and awarding them notional market values based on their locations and outer appearances—so-called 'second-gear valuations'.

Local authorities fall into two broad categories in relation to their involvement with Council Tax, depending on their degree of involvement in collecting the money, as follows.

- **Billing authorities**, or collection authorities, are councils that send out bills to households, and collect the proceeds to be distributed between themselves and neighbouring authorities. In two-tier areas, billing authorities are districts or boroughs.

- **Precepting authorities** refers to all types of council entitled to issue 'precepts' (instructions or orders) to their billing authorities asking for shares of Council Tax proceeds. In two-tier areas, this applies to billing authorities themselves, counties (in their role as both top-tier councils and fire authorities), and PCCs (see Chapter 11, 'Police force accountability—from authorities to commissioners'). In unitary areas, there are still three precepting authorities: unitary and fire authorities, and PCCs. Council Tax bills received by paying households should include breakdowns of the chunks allocated to each precepting authority. The largest portions go to top-tier councils (unitaries or counties). Parishes also issue precepts for the modest local services that they provide, so precepting authorities are grouped into 'major' (county/district/unitary) and 'minor' (parish/town/community).

When Council Tax bills for the coming tax year have been determined by local precepting authorities, they express their precepts publicly in terms of 'average rates' of Council Tax and 'average rises' in compared to previous years. As indicated earlier, the 'average rate' is that applying to a Band D property. It is determined by the formula:

$$\frac{\text{Total amount the authority intends to spend - Total non-council Tax revenue}}{\text{Council Tax base (number of eligible households)}}$$

How central government 'controls' Council Tax bills

Ministers have powers to prevent excessive Council Tax rises by introducing formal ceilings to stop bills topping specified levels. This process—known as, **capping**—was introduced by the Tories in the Rates Act 1984, and used increasingly in the 1980s and 1990s to restrict bill increases by supposed high-spending councils (often Labour ones in poorer areas, which argued that they faced above-average costs in housing, education, and social care). New Labour was generally reluctant to cap, although it retained reserve powers allowing it to do so and increasingly brandished these towards the end of its 13-year term.

Such examples aside, Labour's approach to holding down Council Tax bills largely remained that of using reserve powers to target specific authorities, rather than favouring across-the-board capping previously used by the Conservatives. Since returning to power, that party has adopted a more indirect way of holding down Council Tax bills—forcing councils wishing to raise them above an annually reviewed threshold set by ministers first to obtain local electors' permission in a referendum. For 2014–15, this applies to any authority hoping to increase Council Tax by 2 per cent or more. One unintended consequence of this 'referendum lock' is that councils are increasingly raising bills to just below the threshold, thereby avoiding referendums—a response condemned by former Housing Minister Grant Shapps as a 'democratic dodge'. In February 2014, Brighton and Hove City Council's minority Green administration proposed raising Council Tax by 4.75 per cent—a policy that, if backed by a vote in full council, would have triggered a referendum. But less than a month later, its plans were blocked by an alliance of Labour and Tory opposition councillors. To avoid negotiations on the city's 2014–15 budget collapsing—an eventuality that would have seen Mr Pickles step in to set a budget involving no Council Tax rise at all—the Greens agreed to a Labour-backed compromise, which saw bills go up instead by 1.99 per cent (just below the trigger threshold).

A similarly rebellious response greeted Mr Osborne's announcement in June 2010 that he would be 'freezing' Council Tax rates across England for two years (a decision prompting immediate calls from the LGA for the projected £625 million loss of revenue to councils to be reimbursed by ministers). Although the Coalition has repeatedly cited the (ongoing at time of writing) 'freeze' as an example of how it is working to ameliorate the impact of financial pressures on hard-pressed households at a time of falling real wages and rising household bills, its claim to have prevented rises across the board is disingenuous. Because the freeze was not imposed as a formal cap, in practice authorities remain at liberty to raise Council Tax if they wish—provided that they respect the referendum lock. Again, a further way in which recent governments have sought to keep Council Tax at reasonable levels is by banning authorities from issuing supplementary precepts—last-minute increases to sums requested from their billing authorities because of previously unforeseen changes to their budgetary predictions for the coming year. This was outlawed in 1982.

The 'gearing' effect

Notwithstanding central government's ability to 'cap' bills, Council Tax has traditionally been the one device available to authorities to generate significant income to finance costly expenditure. Therefore any decision by ministers to *reduce* a council's grant allocation(s) (either by cutting or freezing them) has tended to push them into increasing bills significantly to address resulting shortfalls. Similarly, if councils suddenly face unforeseen revenue demands, but their contributions from government are already set, they will again turn to Council Tax. The disproportionate rise in bills that can result is known as the 'gearing' effect.

Speaking hypothetically, if a council raises a total revenue income for the coming year of £100 million—approximately £25 million from Council Tax—but ends up needing £101 million to meet its final spending demands, it will need to raise Council Tax by significantly more than the 1 per cent shortfall to achieve this, in the absence of other funding streams. In fact, its average Council Tax bills would have to rise by 4 per cent:

$$\text{Projected Council Tax increase} = \frac{\text{£1 million}}{\text{£25 million}} = 4\%$$

Uniform Business Rates (UBR)

In addition to their responsibilities for valuing domestic properties, listing and valuation officers are also charged with administering the 'equivalent' tax for businesses. While this may sound straightforward, **Uniform Business Rates (UBR)** have proved almost as controversial as Council Tax. Introduced alongside the Community Charge in 1990, 'the initial tax bands for UBR were based on a revaluation instigated at the time (aligned to rateable values in 1991), but have since been revalued every five years. The most recent revaluation took place in 2010, based on rateable values at 1 April 2008.

How UBR has traditionally worked—and why it is so unpopular

Like both the long-standing domestic rates system and the preceding local business tax, UBR is based not on a property's capital value, but its **rateable**

value. Listing officers keep rating lists covering all business premises in their area. When first introduced in 1990, UBR caused uproar among many occupants of commercial and industrial land or buildings because of the huge increases in the values of those premises that had occurred since 1973, when the previous business tax—the 'general rate'—had been set.

The UBR has customarily worked as follows. Business premises are valued by local listing officers (in Scotland, assessors), based on how much they could be let for on a relevant date. The amount businesses are actually charged in UBR annually will then depend on a centrally determined calculation made by the Communities Secretary, known as the 'national multiplier' ('poundage' in Scotland). The multiplier is the number of pence in each pound of the rateable value ascribed to a given premises that its owner is liable to pay that year. It is set at two levels: a 'standard' rate for middle-range or bigger companies; and a 'small business' rate for those meeting criteria necessary criteria to be defined as such by the Department for Business, Innovation, and Skills (BIS) and HM Treasury. Whichever category it falls into, the multiplier is normally held below the level of inflation for business properties with 'average' values.

The UBR is therefore determined by the following formula:

$$\text{Rateable value of property} \times \text{National multiplier}$$

For example, a business with premises that have a rateable value of £50,000 would be expected to pay £25,000 in a year when the multiplier was 50 pence.

As of April 2008, empty business premises became liable for UBR—although, as with all bills, companies may appeal against their ratings.

Separate multipliers are currently set for England and Wales. Scotland, in contrast, retains a different system of business rates, which is largely the same as that which first came into existence there in 1854. Although the 1988 Act amended the existing Scottish system as it did elsewhere in Britain, it remains distinct to this day. Until recently, when the Scottish Government began 'pool- ing' business rate revenue and redistributing it from the centre, one of its primary differences from the English and Welsh UBR was the fact it was still a 'local tax'—that is, one both collected and spent in each area.

Indeed, this was long the single most contentious aspect of UBR. Until recently, all money raised by the tax was collected by councils, but then gathered up by central government and redistributed around the country on the basis of perceived need, with poorer areas and/or those facing particular financial challenges for demographic reasons receiving larger slices of the pie than more affluent ones. For decades, this bred resentment among some businesses that the rates they paid were used to subsidize other areas, rather than invested in their own communities. The Local Government Finance Act 2012 put a partial end to this, though, by 'repatriating' up to half the value of UBR generated in each area to be invested in local services. In addition, in an effort to encourage planning authorities to approve hydraulic fracturing (fracking) projects designed to mine shale gas, in 2014 Mr Cameron confirmed that they would be able to keep up to 100 per cent of business rates generated by drilling companies (see Chapter 16, 'From wind farms to "fracking"—the rise of middle-class planning protests'). The Coalition's distaste for 'one of the most centralized' council funding regimes 'in the world' was initially matched by its awareness of an increasingly urgent need to promote growth in Britain's stalling economy—and the pursuit of jobs and industrial expansion is now being used as justification for localizing UBR. By allowing councils to keep 50 per cent of UBR paid in their areas and the same proportion of any increases in UBR takings that they generate over time, the government hopes to incentivize them to proactively push for local business investment-taking advantage of other 'Big Society' changes introduced by ministers to foster partnerships and fast-track planning applications (see Chapter 16, 'Forward planning'). In various consultation and briefing papers issued by Mr Pickles' office prior to the Act, he argued that, if anything, councils previously had a *disincentive* to 'go for growth'—encumbered as they were by planning red tape and having to finance infrastructure to support investment without the necessary means. The proposed changes—which, in theory, will give many authorities short-changed by the previous regime access to extra funds—were introduced in April 2013. To allay the fears of those concerned about authorities with 'weak business rate bases' losing out—many covering relatively deprived areas in need of investment—a new system of central government 'top-ups' was introduced to compensate them for losses. Over time, this short-term safety net is due to be replaced with money redistributed to poorer areas from a new levy on the proceeds of additional UBR income received by more prosperous authorities. But not everyone is convinced that this will be enough to compensate 'losers' for their losses. In January 2012, Neil McInroy, chief executive of the Centre for Local Economic Strategies, explained what he termed 'the Barnsley Question' (an oblique reference to the 'West Lothian Question'—see Chapter 2, 'The West Lothian Question') in an interview with *Public Finance* magazine:

    Barnsley doesn't have a good business rates base, whereas Westminster City Council has the business rates of a medium-sized country.

Moves towards 'localizing' UBR are not all about raising *more* money, however. The Localism Act 2011 empowers councils to offer UBR 'discounts'. This would cut the sums from UBR coming back into localities'—'deficits' that councils would have to make up from other resources. In addition, the Act watered down the generally unpopular Business Rates Supplement Act 2009, introduced by Labour to give counties and unitaries a measure of local determination over income generated from local businesses by allowing them to impose additional levies on companies, provided that the proceeds were directly used to promote economic development. Since 2011, supplements can be levied only if local business communities first approve them in formal ballots (referendums in all but name).

The means used to distribute UBR proceeds is far from the only controversy surrounding it. Another long-standing debate has revolved around how it is calculated—a system that, at time of writing, ministers appeared happy to maintain. The practice of charging businesses according to the rateable values of their premises, rather than their profits, is seen to penalize unfairly companies operating large factories or warehouses, which pay significantly more than businesses based in single offices—irrespective of which generates the most revenue. Many businesses offering IT support or legal and financial advice (the 'service sector') generate huge profits, despite being run from modest premises, with low overheads. By contrast, the decline of the manufacturing sector has seen turnovers plummet for old-style industries producing large consumer goods using expensive plants and machinery.

These examples aside, like Council Tax, UBR offers reductions and exemptions for certain kinds of property. In addition to those left unoccupied for prolonged periods, exemptions include:

- agricultural land and buildings;
- places of public worship—for example churches and mosques;
- properties used by the disabled;
- fish farms;
- sewers;
- public parks;
- road crossings over watercourses—that is, traffic bridges;
- properties built in specified 'enterprise zones'—designations intended to rejuvenate deprived areas; and
- properties occupied by visiting Armed Forces.

Other sources of local authority revenue income

In addition to Council Tax, UBR, and grants, authorities derive income from:

- leisure service use—for example swimming pools, sports centres, library fines, etc.;
- the collection of trade refuse;
- car parking tickets, fines, etc.;
- income from private contractors; and
- European Social Fund (ESF) grants to companies, voluntary groups, and communities in deprived areas to improve training and employment prospects.

The annual budget timetable at local level

As with most other organizations, the financial year for councils runs from 1 April to 31 March. While capital expenditure (see 'The local authority capital budget' in this chapter) has traditionally been planned on three- to five-year cycles, only recently have ministers sought to move revenue expenditure onto the same footing by introducing three-year grant settlements.

The process by which local spending is budgeted for is outlined in Table 12.4.

Stories about councils being forced to slash jobs and budgets for essential services because of real-terms cuts in government grants have long been a staple of British newspapers. But in October 2008, as the full impact of the global banking crisis unfolded (see Chapter 7, 'The global banking crisis and its fallout'), it emerged that at least 100 councils were facing a highly unusual threat to their solvency. The LGA revealed that up to £1 billion of taxpayers' money had been collectively invested by councils and police authorities in collapsed Icelandic banks. Kent County Council had invested £50 milion, while Transport for London (TfL) had deposited £40 million and the Metropolitan Police, £30 million. Although some had been remarkably canny (Brighton and Hove Council decided not to trust the banks' promises), others were named and shamed. For example, Winchester City Council had invested £1 million in Heritable, a subsidiary of Iceland's national bank Landsbanki, barely a fortnight before its parent company's collapse—apparently ignoring early warning signs that Icelandic institutions were on the brink.

In March 2009, the Audit Commission published a report criticizing seven councils for 'negligently' ignoring official warnings by continuing to invest in Icelandic banks even after their credit ratings had been downgraded below acceptable levels. It found that £32.8 million had been deposited between the reclassification of the Landsbanki and Glitnir banks as 'adequate' on 30 September 2008 and their collapse barely a week later, on 7 October. Among the biggest investors were the South Yorkshire Pensions Authority, which deposited £10 million in one go on 2 October, and Kent County Council, which paid in £8.3 million in two chunks on 1 and 2 October. Although not directly related to the issue of investment in banks, the Coalition's wide-ranging review of local finance has led to a loosening of the rules concerning councils' ability to acquire corporate bonds. While the 2003 regulations that introduced prudential borrowing (see Table 12.5) also allowed authorities to invest surplus funds in bonds and shares (albeit at their own risk), it also stipulated that if they were to invest in individual companies, these transactions would be treated as 'capital expenditure' for accounting purposes. This rule—intended to discourage 'speculative' investments—has now been amended explicitly to allow councils to invest in corporate bonds (although not shares). Justifying the change, ministers argued that bonds issued by firms with 'triple-A' credit ratings were often 'a safer investment option than a collective scheme with a lower rating'. The rule change

Table 12.4 Local authority budget-setting timetable

Time	Stage
April	Council holds provisional meeting early in financial year to decide overall 'budget strategy' for next one.
Late April/ early May	Follow-up meeting to decide Council Tax levels needed to finance coming year's expenditure.
Late May/early June	Full council meeting follows earlier meetings of main financial committee (often policy and resources committee) or cabinets (see Chapter 13, 'Local government hierarchies since the LGA 2000'). Council leader/elected mayor must obtain formal endorsement of cabinet for major budgetary decisions.
July– September	Once overall budget strategy determined, broad revenue estimates for following years must be finalized.
October– December	Government announces following year's grant allocations, forcing authorities to adjust budgeting for coming financial year. Usually last stage at which individual departments can increase requests for revenue funding from authority's 'pot'. To do so, they must submit **supplementary estimates**, outlining reasons for higher-than-expected outgoings.
January– February	Council usually confirms and publishes final draft estimates for revenue spending.
February	Full council has 'final say' at special meeting, deciding spending and Council Tax levels for next financial year (approximate budgets normally approved, subject to later modifications).

also altered the definition of *income* generated through the sale or redemption of bonds—specifying that only those acquired before 1 April 2012 would be treated as 'capital receipts' (see next section) on being sold or reaching maturity.

▶ The local authority capital budget

The main sources of local government capital finance are outlined in Table 12.5.

Capital borrowing

Although capital projects are funded in discrete ways significantly different from those used to finance revenue spending, they do incur costs to Council Tax payers. One regular outgoing that councils are compelled to factor into their annual revenue budgets is a 'minimum revenue provision' to cover systematic repayment of outstanding debt. This is usually equivalent to 2 per cent of housing debt and 4 per cent of that incurred for other capital purposes in a given year. In addition to repaying debt itself, councils must also provide for any interest on their long-term capital borrowing—the 'revenue implications of the capital programme'. These repayments of capital interest from the revenue account are known as a **debt charge**.

Table 12.5 Main sources of capital finance available to local authorities

Source	How it works
Prudential borrowing	Introduced in Local Government Act 2003 to replace previous 'credit approvals'—limits agreed by government. Today's prudential borrowing is determined in three ways:
	1. Each council may borrow up to an 'affordable' figure in line with Prudential Code endorsed by Chartered Institute of Public Finance and Accountancy (CIPFA).
	2. Low-interest loans for specific projects from central government, through **Public Works Loan Board (PWLB)**—body operating within UK Debt Management Office (a Treasury executive agency). Councils repay borrowings from own resources without government support. They calculate how much they can afford to borrow according to CIPFA Code.
	3. US-inspired **tax-increment financing (TIF)** introduced in England and Wales in 2013–14—allows councils to borrow money for infrastructural capital investment against future income expected to be generated through UBR from companies benefiting from investment. Also being developed in Scotland.
Supported capital expenditure (supported borrowing in Scotland)	Councils may borrow to finance capital spending with central government support—with funds available to help them to repay loan and interest. Most finance comes from Department of Communities and Local Government (DCLG), but other departments also contribute, including Department for Education (DfE), Department of Health (DoH), and Home Office.
Capital receipts	Money raised through councils' sales of capital (land and buildings). Divided into *usable* and *reserve* parts. Council must set latter aside for specified uses, including repaying existing debts. Former can be used to supplement prudential borrowing for new infrastructure.
	Communities Secretary determines percentage of usable capital receipts at any time. In 1998, agreed percentage was 50 per cent—except receipts from council home sales, only 25 per cent of which could be used for capital spending. 2003 Act revoked stipulation that proportion of housing receipts must be set aside by councils for debt reduction, introducing centralized 'pooling' arrangement under which 75 per cent of capital receipts from council home sales under 'Right to Buy' scheme (see Chapter 17, '"Right to Buy" and the privatization of council housing') and 50 per cent of other housing-related receipts are redistributed from authorities with less housing shortage to needier ones.
	Authorities in 'demonstrable financial difficulty' may apply to DCLG for 'direction' allowing them to use capital receipts for 'specified revenue expenditure'. Items such as redundancy payments, equal pay awards, and pension fund contributions have previously been redefined as capital expenditure.

Table 12.5 (*continued*)

Source	How it works
Capital grants	Traditionally come from government departments, public bodies distributing National Lottery money, or hybrid arrangements combining borrowing with grants (e.g. Transport Supplementary Grant, Single Regeneration Budget, New Deal for Communities, City Challenge, etc.). Coalition moving to 'less bureaucratic' approach, with limited grants drawn from supported capital expenditure budget.
European Union (EU) grants and loans	Money from EU, including: European Regional Development Fund (ERDF—for infrastructure projects and industrial development, usually in deprived areas); European Social Fund (ESF—training/employment initiatives aimed at young people); and structural funds. Currently, EU 'Convergence' funds available to areas, such as Cornwall, where gross domestic product (GDP) less than 75 per cent of Union's average.
Private sector investment	Often 'in kind' offers, such as development land, and/or funding for capital works, such as road access/traffic management, from private company in exchange for ability to recoup investment at later date by running profit-based business related to land concerned (*planning gain*—see Chapter 16, 'Planning obligations (or contribution, or gain)').
	Favourite means of encouraging private capital investment today involves private finance initiative (PFI)/public–private partnership (PPP) deals (see also Chapter 7, 'Private finance initiatives (PFIs) and public–private partnerships (PPPs)'). These see private companies footing much of up-front costs, enabling projects to progress more quickly than if reliant solely on public funds. In return, companies are paid back— with interest—over period of years, in arrangements similar to mortgages. Final costs to taxpayers significantly higher than if projects were funded by councils.
Local lotteries	Councils can run lotteries under conditions outlined in National Lottery Act 1993.
Local strategic partnerships (LSPs)	Labour's £36m Community Empowerment Fund to encourage community/voluntary organizations to cooperate in LSPs to tackle social deprivation supplanted by Coalition's *Total Place*—'Big Society' scheme to boost cooperation between councils and agencies over wider geographical areas, to avoid duplicating services by adopting 'whole area' approach. Councils may invest up to 15% of money that they save to pay employees' pensions in infrastructure projects such as roads and housing (equivalent to £22.5bn of the £150bn collectively held by them in this way). Thirteen councils involved in pilot, with potential future pot of £45bn.

Despite the fact that it incurs interest and can take years to pay off, borrowing money for capital investment is often seen as politically desirable by both central and local government. The rationale is that, by taking out loans, authorities are 'spreading the costs' of their spending over a number of years—meaning that it is not only local taxpayers living in an area at the time that a borrowing decision is taken who shoulder the burden, but anyone benefiting from the resulting investment during its lifetime. In addition, borrowing avoids authorities having to fund expensive projects entirely up front, enabling them to fast-track construction of schools, libraries, and other amenities that they would otherwise take decades to afford.

Similar arguments have been made by recent governments in favour of councils forming co-funding alliances with the private sector—public–private partnerships (PPPs) or private finance initiatives (PFIs)—to enable capital projects that would otherwise take years to realize through public funds alone (see Chapter 7, 'Private finance initiatives (PFIs) and public–private partnerships (PPPs)').

▶ Financial transparency at the local level

For journalists, some of the best (and most accessible) stories can be found in councils' publicly available accounts. Under section 15 of the Audit Commission Act 1998, press and public have the right both to inspect and copy these accounts, and all books, deeds, contracts, bills, vouchers, and receipts relating to them. On completing their audited accounts for the previous tax year (usually by June), all authorities with budgets of £6.5 million or more must open them to public inspection for 20 working days, advertising this in advance both in the local press and on their websites. The publication threshold was raised from £1 million in new regulations issued in 2011, to balance the Coalition's push for greater transparency with its desire to protect smaller bodies, such as parish councils, from punitive publishing costs.

Several notable court judgments have flowed from the 1998 Act, which introduced the 20-day inspection system—most upholding the public's right to disclosure. In December 2009, *Veolia ES Nottinghamshire Ltd v. Nottinghamshire County Council* saw the High Court uphold the council's decision to open the files on confidential documents relating to its signing of a commercial waste management contract. Citing a line in the Act compelling authorities to disclose 'all the financial movements or items of account of the council's funds', it confirmed that the Act did not exempt commercially confidential information (unlike the law governing access to council meetings—see Chapter 14, 'Access to council meetings and business—the "old" system').

However, while the Act has certainly made it easier for Council Tax payers to inspect authorities' balance sheets, the media's attempts to assert similar rights have not always gone unchallenged. In 2004, ITV West narrowly won a High Court judgment forcing Bristol City Council to recognize its status as a 'person interested'—allowing it access to information relating to payments made to a former officer sacked in 1998 for gross misconduct. Justice Elias ruled in the company's favour on a technicality, saying that it only qualified because of its status as a local 'non-domestic-rate taxpayer'.

The Act also redressed the balance in previous legislation towards a particular aspect of local financial transparency: local electors' right to access details of council payrolls under section 17(1) of the Local Government Finance Act 1982. Prompted by the 1985 case *Oliver v. Northampton Borough Council*, the Act precluded public access to accounts or documents containing personal information about authority employees.

The Coalition has embarked on a push to promote more financial transparency by councils—forcing them to publish online everything from senior staff salaries to all items of spending and contracts worth £500-plus (see Chapter 14, 'From "Beacon Councils" to the National Indicator Set—the growth of performance data').

≡ Topical feature idea

The following is an extract from the audited 2012–13 accounts statement of The City of Edinburgh Council. It focuses on the authority's estimates of the likely costs of specified financial 'uncertainties' that it has factored into its budget forecast for the year ahead. How would you use this table as the starting point for generating stories about the financial difficulties facing the council?

Extract from of The City of Edinburgh 'Council, Audited 2012/13 accounts statement

---

Assumptions made about the future and other major sources of estimation uncertainty

The financial statements contain estimated figures that are based on assumptions made by the Council about the future or that are otherwise uncertain. Estimates are made taking into account historical experience, current trends and other relevant factors. However, because balances cannot be determined with certainty, actual results could be materially different from the assumptions and estimates.

The following table details uncertainties on assumptions and estimates, and outlines the potential effect if actual results differ from the assumptions made.

Item	Uncertainty	Effect if actual results differ from assumptions
Property, plant, and equipment	Assets are depreciated over useful lives that are dependent upon assumptions about the level of repairs and maintenance that will be incurred in relation to individual assets. A reduction in spending on repairs and maintenance would bring into doubt the useful lives assigned to the assets.	If the useful life of assets is reduced, depreciation increases and the carrying value of the assets falls.

Item	Uncertainty	Effect if actual results differ from assumptions
		It is estimated that the annual depreciation charge would increase and the carrying value would fall by £13.213m for each year that useful lives were reduced.
Long-term contracts	The Council's approved budgets provides for inflationary uplifts on long-term contracts.	If inflation were to increase by 1%, this would result in an additional cost of £0.433m per annum.
Provisions	The Council has made a provision of £13.152m in respect of the remainder of anticipated equal pay settlements. This is based on the number of potential claimants and assumes similar settlement terms to those achieved previously. There is uncertainty surrounding both of these assumptions.	Should the settlement values increase by 10% this would have the effect of adding £1.315m to the provision required.
Pensions liability	Estimation of the net liability to pay pensions depends on a number of complex judgements relating to the discount rate used, the rate at which salaries are projected to increase, changes in retirement ages, mortality rates and expected returns on pension fund assets. A firm of consulting actuaries is engaged to provide the Council with expert advice about the assumptions to be applied.	The effects on the net pension liability of changes in individual assumptions can be measured.
Arrears	At 31 March, the Council had a balance of sundry debtors of £29.775m. A review of significant balances suggested that an impairment of doubtful debts of £4.631m (16%) was appropriate. In the current economic climate it is not certain that this will be sufficient.	If the Council was unable to recover a further 10% of this amount, it would require to set an additional £2.199m aside as an allowance.
Housing rent arrears	At 31 March, the Council had a balance of housing rent arrears of £2.776m. A review of significant balances suggested that an impairment of doubtful debts of £1.911m (69%) was appropriate. In the current economic climate it is not certain that this will be sufficient.	If collection rates were to deteriorate, an increase of 10% in the amount to be impaired would require an additional £0.278m to be set aside as an allowance.

©The City of Edinburgh Council

✳ Current issues

- **Return of general block grants** After years of revenue grant 'passporting' by Labour, the Coalition is de-ring-fencing many specific grants and increasing the proportion coming from the general revenue support grant (RSG).

- **Holding down Council Tax bills** Council Tax has been 'frozen' in England since 2010, but councils can still raise bills—provided that they first hold successful local referendums, if they propose increases of 2 per cent or more.

- **'Repatriation' of Uniform Business Rates (UBR)** The Local Government Finance Act 2012 allows councils to 'repatriate' up to half of business rates raised locally, to incentivize them to attract more private-sector investment. Those approving 'fracking' applications may keep up to 100 per cent of rates paid by companies involved.

⠿ Key issues

1. Council budgets are divided into revenue and capital accounts. Revenue finances day-to-day spending (staff, maintenance, etc.), and capital is used to build new roads, schools, etc.

2. Around three-quarters of councils' revenue budgets derive from government grants, the biggest being the revenue support grant (RSG), which they may spend as they wish. Specific grants must be spent in particular areas—for example the dedicated schools grant (DSG) for school repairs.

3. Council Tax—a tax on households—makes up about a quarter of councils' revenue incomes. All authorities set precepts and the combined total makes up the bill.

4. Commercial companies also pay a local tax, Uniform Business Rates (UBR), based on a national multiplier set by ministers. Some of this is pooled centrally, but up to half now stays in the area in which it is raised.

5. The main sources of capital finance for councils include public–private partnerships (PPPs), capital receipts from the sale of property, prudential borrowing, and European or government loans.

→ Further reading

Betty, S. (2011) *The PFI: 'Teething Problems or Fundamentally Flawed?' A Critical Analysis of the UK's Private Finance Initiative*, Bury St Edmunds: Lambert Academic Publishing. **Critical overview of the impact, positive and negative, of the PFI revolution in UK capital financing.**

Fischel, W. A. (2005) *The Homevoter Hypothesis: How Home Values Influence Local Government Taxation, School Finance, and Land-Use Policies*, Cambridge, MA: Harvard University Press. **Globe-spanning sociological text examining the impact** of homeowners on the concentration and quality of local services, and the emergence of 'stakeholder-led localism'.

Hollis, G., Davies, H., Plokker, K., and Sutherland, M. (1994) *Local Government Finance: An International Comparative Study*, London: LGC Communications. **Again targeted at local professionals, this offers useful comparisons between Britain's system of local government finance and those applied elsewhere, primarily in mainland Europe.**

Midwinter, A. F. and Monaghan, C. (1993) *From Rates to the Poll Tax: Local Government Finance in the Thatcher Era*, Edinburgh: Edinburgh University Press. **Thoughtful exploration of the turbulent Thatcherite reforms of local government finance, focusing on the replacement of rates by the Community Charge.**

Online Resource Centre

www.oxfordtextbooks.co.uk/orc/Morrison4e/

Visit the Online Resource Centre that accompanies this book for web links and regular updates.

13

Local government decision-making

The previous two chapters examined the nature of councils, how they evolved, and the funding systems underpinning them. But what form do their chains of command take and how do they take decisions?

▶ Councillors and officers—who's who?

Local authorities' work is divided between two sets of individuals: **councillors** and **officers**. Like central government, councils comprise a series of spending departments. These departments—covering areas such as education, housing, and social services—are each administered by paid civil servants who are meant to be politically neutral. Appointed on merit, they are known as officers.

While officers are concerned with process, decisions to put money into one service rather than another—and precise choices about how those services are run—are based on political judgements taken by elected councillors, whose role is to 'govern' authorities in a similar vein to how members of Parliament (MPs) make decisions affecting Britain as a whole. Like MPs, councillors (or 'members') each represent a constituency. And, depending on the arrangements adopted by individual authorities, policymaking is either down to Westminster-style cabinets, led by senior councillors in the ruling group, or committees, comprising members drawn from all parties on the council.

What kind of person becomes a councillor?

The seminal 1972 Bains Report defined councillors' duties as:

- directing and controlling the affairs of the authority;
- taking key policy decisions defining the council's objectives and allocating resources required to attain them; and
- continually reviewing the progress and performance of local services.

This vision of local governance was echoed 14 years later by the 1986 Widdicombe Report, which stressed the importance of the 'complementary relationship' between 'part-time councillors' and 'full-time officers with professional expertise'. It was also tackled by a 1990 Audit Commission discussion paper, *We Can't Go on Meeting Like This*, outlining a threefold role for councillors. Four years later, a report by Robert Gifford, then leader of Milton Keynes District Council, identified four 'typical' councillor profiles. The main conclusions of these seminal papers are listed in the table entitled 'Two models for effective councillors', to be found on the **Online Resource Centre** that accompanies this book.

Although councillors may be likened to MPs in their accountability to voters, there is a fundamental difference between the two: unlike MPs, councillors are unsalaried. Their work is therefore voluntary and, for those trying to juggle it with day jobs or childcare duties, necessarily 'part-time'.

The fact that councillors are unpaid has given rise to considerable controversy, not least because it leads to many councils being dominated by the retired and wealthy—those with time and money to spend on unpaid community work. Because most councils and committees customarily meet for business during normal working days, employed people able to stand as councillors have tended to be in managerial posts or running their own businesses—in other words, free to set their own hours or to negotiate time off for meetings.

This combination of militating factors discriminates against women, fewer of whom have historically held such senior posts. Ethnic minorities have also been under-represented historically—even in areas with large immigrant populations. It is hardly surprising, perhaps, that the media so often portrays town halls (with some justification) as the preserve of pushy pensioners and white, middle-aged, middle-class men. Recent moves to introduce evening sittings—particularly in and around London, where many people work unsocial hours and commute long distances—have done something to address these issues, but not enough to satisfy critics.

In 1986, the Widdicombe Committee found that eight out of 10 councillors were male and 59 per cent hailed from one of three socio-economic groups—professionals, employers and managers, and 'intermediate non-manual' jobs—together representative of only 23 per cent of the overall population. The average councillor at the time was aged 45, with none aged under 24. The oldest was aged 85. The Committee made 88 recommendations—although most concerned moves to democratize the *political* composition of councils and committees. Many were implemented by the Local Government and Housing Act 1989.

A succession of surveys by the Local Government Association (LGA) and Improvement and Development Agency (IDeA) suggest that little has improved since. The 2013 census (the most recent to date) revealed that while the proportion of women councillors had risen by more than half—from 19 per cent in 1986 to 32.7 per cent in 2013—the average age of councillors, far from falling, had continued stubbornly to *increase*—rising marginally to 60.2 from 59.7 in 2010. Ethnic minorities also continued to fare poorly: only 4 per cent were non-white (compared to 8.4 per cent of Britain's population).

Almost as contentious as the question of how to make councillors more representative of multicultural twenty-first-century Britain is the issue of how much work should be expected of them, given their 'unpaid' status. Various attempts have been made to quantify exactly how many hours the average member spends on council duties, both inside and outside 'official hours' (principally meetings). Widdicombe compared his own research with that contained in an earlier (1964) study. At that time, the average number of hours that councillors spent on duties was 52 hours a month; by 1986, this had risen to 74 hours (a finding identical to that of a much more comprehensive survey, carried out by the Joseph Rowntree Foundation in 1994). According to the 2013 findings, this had increased to more than 100 hours (or 25.1 hours per week), if 17 hours a month spent on party or group business was included.

Councillors' allowances and expenses

Introducing 'flexible' working hours is not the only device that councils have used to increase participation by younger working people, women, and minorities. In a radical attempt to widen participation, some are increasingly bending the rules to offer more generous allowances in lieu of formal 'wages'. A recognized system of allowances and expenses has existed for some time. Allowances are designed to give elected members modest payments for attending meetings, while they may also claim reimbursements for the cost of return travel to meetings by car, bicycle, or public transport. Expenses are also available to cover other outgoings arising from their official duties, such as paying for overnight accommodation, subsistence, and subsidizing postal costs and domestic telephone bills for phone calls relating to pastoral work with electors. Councillors aged under 70 are also now eligible to join the generous Local Government Pension Scheme. There are two main types of allowance:

- the **basic allowance**—a flat-rate annual payment, usually paid monthly, for *all* councillors representing a specific authority; and

- the **special responsibility allowance**—an additional payment received by councillors who hold posts of greater responsibility, the size of which varies according to how much responsibility a councillor has (council leaders receive the biggest, while committee or subcommittee members are paid much smaller ones).

Those with dependent children or other relations may also claim separate carers' or dependants' allowances.

Each English council is free to set its own allowance levels, subject to certain restrictions. Since the Local Government Act 2000 (LGA 2000), every council has been required by law to establish an **independent remuneration panel** comprising at least three individuals (none of whom are themselves councillors). It is the panel's task to review and adjudicate on applications by authorities to increase or otherwise amend their allowances—the reverse of the system now adopted at Westminster, under which MPs' salaries are *set* by an independent body (see Chapter 2, 'The Independent Parliamentary Standards Authority (IPSA)'). Intriguingly, though, while councillors can choose to reject remuneration panels' recommendations, MPs are bound by the decisions of IPSA. In Scotland, Wales, and Northern Ireland, the system is administered centrally, with councillors' allowances in each of the devolved countries set by a single independent panel. The powers of the panels are limited, however—for example councillors are not legally obliged to accept panel recommendations to cut or freeze allowances.

Recent surveys point to wide disparities in the generosity of allowances paid by different councils—with some offering payments comparable to full-time salaries. According to figures published in March 2011, a number of council leaders earned £50,000 or more in the 2010–11 tax year, while average annual allowances for other councillors topped £10,000 in many areas and £20,000 in London—defying pay caps and cuts endured by most council employees. The district of Rochford, Essex, had seen the biggest increase in the previous five years—surging by 158 per cent. But such cases tend to be exceptions: as of 2013, the LGA estimated that average basic allowances were around £7,000, while a report published in January that year by the Commons Communities and Local Government Committee, entitled *Councillors on the Front Line*, mooted the idea of introducing a standardized national framework to ensure that they were consistent nationwide—and adequately rewarded councillors for hours they put in. As Robert Gordon, leader of Hertfordshire County Council, put it when addressing the Committee's inquiry:

66 Allowances now for front-line councillors, certainly for leading councillors, are high enough to offend the public but not high enough to encourage any sane person to give up their career and earning capacity to take it on. 🟅🟅

Devolved administrations have proved considerably more generous with allowance settlements: in 2010, the Independent Remuneration Panel for Wales recommended a rise in basic allowances from the £11,000-plus that many councillors had previously received to £13,868, with council leaders (many already 'earning' £40,000 or more) licensed to claim up to £57,785. Alive to public disquiet about the then recent MPs' expenses scandal—not to mention the pay cuts and freezes that many workers had endured under the Coalition's austerity drive—some authorities, including Cardiff City Council, refrained from claiming their full entitlements. Meanwhile, in January 2010, the Convention of Scottish Local Authorities (COSLA) voted to back a one-year freeze on basic allowances (which already averaged £15,000—twice the level in England at the time). In Northern Ireland—where, by August 2010, around two-thirds of members of the Legislative Assembly (MLAs), each earning at least £42,000, also retained seats as local councillors—controversy has focused less on the size of members' allowances, which averaged £9,500 in 2009, than on their (still unresolved) 'double-jobbing' status and the fact that they have been able to continue claiming for council duties while sitting at Stormont.

Meet the experts—the role of local government officers

The number of officers employed by councils varies widely and is ultimately decided by the level of resources that councillors allocate to finance them. Every council is obliged to provide certain statutory services and its administration is therefore split, like Whitehall's, into different departments—each run by an expert professional.

There are two main types of council spending department:

- *service departments* are concerned with delivering housing, education, etc.; and

- *central departments* are those that *administer* the council's functions—principally its legal and financial departments, and those devoted to corporate activities, such as public relations (PR) and marketing.

Officers, like Whitehall civil servants, must be *politically neutral*—whatever their levels of seniority. Those in senior grades are also *politically restricted* (see Chapter 3, 'Political neutrality in practice'). Despite being required to avoid political bias, however, officers are expected to provide councillors with policy advice based on their knowledge and experience. Their roles are to:

- *advise*—defined by the Widdicombe Report as giving 'politically impartial' information and support to aid councillors in their decision-making; and

- *support* the executive, non-executive, and scrutiny arms of the council—helping *all* councillors, not only the most senior ones.

Each department is headed by its own equivalent of a Whitehall permanent secretary. Among the most influential are the leading civil servants in the biggest spending areas: directors of social services and chief planning officers.

Higher up still are three officials whose role is to oversee the workings of the council as a whole, as follows.

- The **chief executive (or 'head of the paid service')** is the council's main policy adviser, manager, and coordinator. Chief executives or their deputies often perform the role of 'acting returning officer' at elections, on behalf of the official returning officer—normally the council chairperson or mayor (see Chapter 4, 'Voting procedure on the day—the role of the returning officer').

- The **monitoring officer** reports to members any acts of maladministration or failures by officers or councillors to uphold the council's **code of conduct**. They are normally also their councils' chief legal officers, should be trained lawyers, and must ensure that councils act within their statutory remits at all times (that is, not ultra vires).

- The chief financial officer (or 'treasurer', or 'director of finance') oversees administration of a council's finances and must be a member of a recognized accountancy body. He or she may also be referred to as 'director of central services' or 'section 151 officer' (referring to the statutory provision from which his or her authority derives).

Under the LGA 2000, chief executives are formally barred from being appointed as monitoring officers. In addition, like any other officer, chief executives, monitoring officers, and chief financial officers are all subject to statutory disciplinary procedures, and ultimate dismissal, for alleged misconduct.

To streamline administration, improve efficiency, and avoid duplication, councils now have 'chief officers' management teams'. These are groups of senior officers, headed by chief executives, which meet weekly or fortnightly to discuss policy ideas to be put forward for councillors' consideration at meetings and/or issues relevant to more than one department.

Despite largely sidestepping the 'politics' of local government, officers are far from immune to controversy. Recent years have witnessed numerous negative news stories about the eye-watering salaries that it is possible for senior council figures to earn—and, like heads of NHS trusts, it is not uncommon for chief executives to be paid more than the prime minister. Partly in response to these furores, Coalition Communities Secretary Eric Pickles introduced a new rule requiring councillors to vote on and publish formal policy statements on pay scales for their officers. In addition to publicizing details of the allowances and expenses claimed by their members, all councils must also now do the same in relation to senior managers and, following a 2011 ruling by the Information Commissioner (see Chapter 20, 'FoI appeals and the Information Commissioner'), it is Mr Pickles' intention that they go further—by publishing the names and salaries of all staff earning £58,200 or more. Following his criticism of some councils for paying salaries that would make

Premiership football managers 'blush', some groups of neighbouring councils now 'share' chief executives to reduce their managerial wage bills and protect front-line services.

New models for service delivery—subcontracting and outsourcing

Until the 1980s, most local services—from refuse collection and street cleaning, to building, equipping, and maintaining schools and care homes—were delivered directly by council employees. But over the past 30 years there has been a fundamental shift in the role of councils from being *providers* to becoming *enablers*. Whereas everyone from local parking attendants to account clerks would once have been council employees, today they are as likely to be on the payroll of a private company, voluntary organization, or agency. Rather than delivering services through their own officers and departments, councils increasingly coordinate and 'commission' them—and the private and voluntary sectors have as much chance of winning contracts as authorities themselves. In the 'Big Society' era, this trend is being accelerated—with local taxpayers now entitled to take over running their services directly, under the Coalition's new 'community rights' to 'bid' and 'challenge', and some councils experimenting with wholesale outsourcing (see 'Cameron's "Big Society"—what role for councillors and officers now?' in this chapter).

The system that originally ushered in this contract-based approach to service delivery was 'compulsory competitive tendering' (CCT). Introduced under the Local Government, Planning, and Land Act 1980, this forced councils to put services out to tender, inviting competing bids from public, voluntary, and/or private organizations. The idea was that the most 'cost-effective' bid would win, cutting waste and bureaucracy, and giving local people better value for money.

The CCT system initially applied largely to 'blue collar' areas of service provision, such as building maintenance and construction work, but was extended by the Local Government Act 1988 to refuse collection, street cleaning, and school catering, and by the Local Government Act 1992 to cover 'professional' and/or 'support services', such as information technology (IT), marketing, and PR. Councils wishing to continue providing services in-house had to form arm's-length 'companies' to compete for contracts with the private and voluntary sectors. When Labour returned to power in 1997, it scrapped CCT, replacing it with a new system of procurement (itself now defunct) called 'Best Value' (BV). A statutory obligation was introduced requiring councils to hire the 'most suitable' provider (whether public, private, or voluntary), choosing those best placed to deliver 'economic, efficient, and effective' services (the 3 Es).

In theory, BV meant that services should be contracted out only if doing so demonstrably offered a better deal. There was a perception that some councils had previously outsourced work purely to cut costs, and the 1998 Green Paper accused the CCT system of 'neglecting' service quality and producing 'uneven and uncertain' efficiency gains, 'antagonism' between rival providers, and 'significant costs for employees', including high staff turnover and demoralization. Yet Labour still expected councils to franchise services out and, although price was no longer the biggest factor in determining successful bids, many argued that 'BV' amounted to CCT in all but name.

Cameron's 'Big Society'—what role for councillors and officers now?

A central plank of the Conservatives' 2010 election campaign was the 'Big Society' concept. Although derided by critics for lacking tangibility, the 'philosophy' underpinning David Cameron's approach to government was an appetite for devolving as much power as possible from Whitehall (and, indeed, councils) to citizens themselves. This delegation of power, and responsibility, to communities manifested itself in several ways in the early days of the new government: the loosening of 'red tape' that Mr Cameron saw as stymieing business investment and the planning process; the 'freeing' of schools and hospitals from direct government control (see Chapter 6, 'New Labour's restructuring of the NHS', and Chapter 15, 'The growth of school autonomy—foundation schools, free schools, and the rise and rise of academies'); and inviting ordinary people, working alone, in groups, or in partnership with charities or private companies, to set up and run their own local services.

The idea of community-run buses or road-sweeping patrols may sound fanciful, but in a speech in July 2010 Mr Cameron signalled his hope of returning to a (to some, imaginary) golden era of active 'volunteerism'. He talked of transforming the 'third sector' (charities and voluntary organizations) into the 'first', and 'turning government upside-down'. While Opposition MPs dismissed this rhetoric as a smokescreen for further cuts and/or a buck-passing exercise enabling ministers to shift the blame for service reduction onto councils, Mr Cameron went on to launch a new Big Society bank (see later in this section), to which people could apply for start-up funding—financed by money held in dormant British bank accounts. He also named four council areas as trailblazing 'Big Society communities': Liverpool, Eden Valley in Cumbria, Windsor and Maidenhead, and Sutton.

Among the (largely Conservative-led) authorities keen to take its 'licence to contract out' to a logical conclusion was the London Borough of Barnet, which, after rebranding itself 'One Barnet', began preparing to shed a swathe of services. This bold experiment—which saw the authority dubbed 'easyCouncil' (a reference to budget airline easyJet)—encountered the first of a series of hurdles when, in June 2011, local bloggers exposed the fact that it had spent £1.3 million buying in services from private security firm MetPro without first conducting basic financial or security tests, or even putting contracts out to tender.

In December 2012, Barnet's plans finally came to fruition, when it agreed a contract worth hundreds of millions of pounds with Capita—outsourcing 70 per cent of its services in one go, including its entire highways, finance, and human resources departments, and those involved in administering benefits. Capita's immediate response was to relocate several of the departments hundreds of miles away from the London borough, to Northern Ireland, and south-west and northern England, with the loss of 200 local jobs. At time of writing, an alliance of activist bloggers and local people affected by the changes was in the process of taking the council to the High Court, while the future of any further outsourcing plans looked doubtful, after Labour overturned the borough's Tory majority in the 2014 local elections. 'Blue-sky Big Society thinking' has caused problems for others, too. In May 2011, Suffolk County Council was forced into a 'period of reflection' over radical plans to outsource virtually all local services, after uncomfortable backbench councillors rebelled. Suffolk's controversial plan, branded a 'new strategic direction' by its most enthusiastic cheerleader, then chief executive Andrea Hill, had prompted criticism from politicians at local and national level—with its own previous leader, Bryony Rudkin, condemning it as 'a circus act with no safety net'.

In future, more typical examples of 'Big Society' localism are likely to come about through the exercise by groups of concerned citizens of the following new 'rights':

- the 'community right to build'—a new right for citizen groups to bypass the normal planning process to construct small-scale, site-specific capital projects, such as community centres, libraries, or pubs;

- neighbourhood planning—a right for communities to decide what developments should be built in their areas, rather than leaving this to councils;

- the 'community right to challenge'—the right for community groups, voluntary organizations, parish councils, or council employees to take over the running of services that they feel they could deliver more effectively than their councils; and

- the 'community right to bid'—the right of such groups to bid to purchase and take over the running of council-owned assets that they judge to be important for their areas.

Of these, community rights to bid and challenge are most relevant here. They are open to everyone—from groups of interested local residents or existing council employees who wish to form their own mutual, to charities, voluntary groups, and parish councils (an echo of enhanced powers previously conferred on 'quality parish councils'—see Chapter 11, 'Parish councils, town councils, and community councils'). The right to challenge allows 'relevant bodies' like these to confront councils proactively at any time about services that the bodies regard as inadequate and ask to take them over. In one sense, the right to bid is a more straightforward extension of the existing process used to outsource services, which allows communities to compete with other organizations for contracts. Where it differs is in allowing 'neighbourhood forums' (that is, citizens themselves) or other community bodies not only to take over responsibility for running services, but also to acquire associated capital assets (for example libraries, children's centres, village shops, or pubs). In considering bids, councils are expected to give such bodies fair, even preferential, hearings. However, if several bids are received from rival groups, the normal procurement process must be followed.

Sceptics argued that, at a time of severe austerity and with many people struggling to find paid work to make ends meet themselves, citizen-run services, manned by volunteers, were unlikely to take off. But by May 2012, so confident was Communities Minister Andrew Stunell that communities up and down the country would be eager to do so that he launched a new 'Communities in Action' map to flag up examples of 'local projects that are making a real difference' for all to see (and, where suitable, to emulate). To buoy such projects, around the same time the government launched **Big Society Capital**—a new, state-sponsored, but independently run, financial institution designed (in its own words) to 'develop and shape a sustainable social investment market', by giving charities, community groups, and other voluntary organizations the funds required to tackle 'major social issues'. By lending money to a range of recognized social investment finance intermediaries (SIFIs)—banks, trusts, and other bodies with track records of financing social enterprises—the fund directs low-interest loans and grants to groups and individuals working at the coal face. Take-up of the various 'community rights' has so far been sluggish. At time of writing, the government's own central website, mycommunityrights.org, could highlight only a handful of projects—including Fresh Horizons, a community-run library 'co-located' alongside a credit union and advice services in a socially deprived, multi-ethnic area of Huddersfield. A larger number were pinpointed on Mr Stunell's map, but it had not been updated since 12 June 2012 and the vast majority were initiatives *launched* by community groups (many of long standing), rather than services that they had taken over from their local authorities.

For now, opinions on the practicability of the 'Big Society' remain deeply divided. In his book, *Faith in the Public Square*, former Archbishop of Canterbury Rowan Williams criticized the concept as 'aspirational waffle designed to conceal a deeply damaging withdrawal of the state from its responsibilities to the most vulnerable'.

The politicization of council officers—the rise of political assistants

While officers are expected to be politically neutral, as early as the Widdicombe Report it was recognized that senior councillors might benefit from access to professional political advice from central government-style special advisers (see Chapter 3, 'Spin doctors and special advisers'). It envisaged 'political assistants' being hired by councils with chief executives who were 'by disposition' managers rather than politicians, or where authorities were 'hung', with three parties sharing the balance of power.

The terms under which such assistants were to be employed are listed in the table entitled 'Conditions of employment for political assistants', to be found on the **Online Resource Centre**.

In addition, elected mayors are entitled to appoint their own political assistants. Successive Mayors of London Ken Livingstone and Boris Johnson hired several 'spin doctors', in addition to policy gurus such as US public transport expert Bob Kiley, the former's adviser on part-privatization of the London Underground. Although many such individuals are effectively independent consultants, journalists should be wary when dealing with councils or their leaderships through advisers, rather than press officers. As political appointees, they are not expected to give objective views of their paymasters' policies and achievements. Indeed, as an active Conservative and former party vice-chairman, Kulveer Ranger, Mr Johnson's director of environment and Digital London, is arguably a political appointee. In an earlier role, as transport adviser, Ranger promoted various green initiatives, including trials of electric cars and the commercially sponsored Barclays Cycle Hire scheme ('Boris bikes'), which allows Londoners to pick up and drop off bicycles at any of 315 'docking stations' scattered around the City of London and eight other boroughs.

▌Local government hierarchies before the LGA 2000 and under 'alternative arrangements'

Before the LGA 2000, one fundamental truth applied to all councillors, irrespective of whether the parties to which they were affiliated held overall power locally: they each had a *direct say* in most policy decisions that their councils took. Proposals were initially referred to specialist subcommittees or committees of councillors covering relevant subject areas, and had to be approved by them before ever being presented for final approval to full council. If rejected at this first hurdle, the full council would never get to discuss them. If reworded, diluted, consolidated, or otherwise amended, the version of the policy voted on by full council had usually been substantially shaped by the committee or subcommittee. Because every councillor (whatever his or her party) sat on at least one committee, he or she had a direct input, however minor, into the policymaking process. Committee decisions were normally

Figure 13.1 The decision-making process in 'old-style' local authorities and district/borough councils operating under 'alternative arrangements'

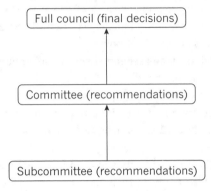

couched as 'recommendations'—that is, subject to final full council approval. Councils also reserved the right to reject their rulings or **refer back** items for further reconsideration. Committees therefore constituted an important part of the day-to-day policymaking function of their councils—a 'bottom-up' approach to policymaking, as illustrated by the flow chart in Figure 13.1.

In addition to giving all councillors a direct (on paper, equal) say in decisions, the set-up pre-LGA 2000 preserved a simple hierarchy not dissimilar to that seen among MPs. A party that won sufficient seats in a local election to secure an 'overall majority' on the council would become 'the government' in all but name and its leader would automatically be appointed **leader of the council**—effectively, local 'prime minister'. Beyond this, there were no visible divisions in 'status' between members of the ruling party (or group) and other councillors. The pre-LGA 2000 model remains relevant to this day, because it still applies to local authorities covering populations of 85,000 or fewer—where it is referred to as 'alternative arrangements'—and is slowly becoming more widespread again, following Mr Pickles' decision to allow councils with cabinets to readopt it if they so wish.

This old-style model includes three types of committee:

- *standing (statutory) permanent committees*, which discharge specific functions (for example taking decisions on education or environmental services);
- *ad hoc committees*—often given briefs directly related to the above, but set up to consider specific issues in greater detail than is possible on standing committees; and
- *area-based committees*—formed to look at policy governing specific geographical areas under a council's control, these sometimes contained members of the local community in addition to councillors, and even had delegated budgets.

As in Parliament, the political composition of committees and subcommittees generally reflects the balance of power on the full council. If the Conservatives are in overall control, most committee chairpersons will be Tories, with overall membership broadly proportionate to the distribution of seats between parties. Where no political group has overall control, standing committees sometimes have no permanent chair; instead, different chairpersons are elected to serve on a meeting-by-meeting basis.

Other conventions governing old-style committees include the following.

- Non-councillors can be 'co-opted' to serve on them, either temporarily or indefinitely. These de facto members do not have voting rights—unless they are church representatives sitting on education-related committees.

- Mayors, council chairpersons, and leaders are *ex officio* members of *all* committees. Significantly, this gives them rights both to attend *and* vote on committees.

- Councils must avoid perceived or real conflicts of interest by ensuring that committees with related functions have different memberships.

- In addition to committees, councils often form working parties comprising both councillors and officers to consider detailed policy options, and their proceedings are not always public.

Despite the influence of committees, like governing parties at Westminster, ruling groups tend to come up with many of the policy ideas debated in full council. Indeed, assuming that they have big enough majorities, they normally muster sufficient votes to drive through their proposals—whatever the relevant committee thinks of them. Leaders also usually appoint chairpersons of the most powerful council subgroup: the **policy and resources committee**. Because this controls the council's purse strings, it has to approve major policy decisions likely to involve significant resources and can veto those that it considers too costly. Many smaller councils have now abolished these committees, but some have retained equivalent 'boards' or 'panels'.

In other ways, ruling groups on 'pre-LGA "2000 councils" have little real executive power, in the sense that the government and prime minister do nationally—a clear contrast to their position in councils with cabinets (see next section). Although leaders can effectively appoint cabinets even under the old model, these have no authority to make executive policy decisions behind closed doors, as commonly occurs both at Westminster and in councils that have adopted post-LGA 2000 executive arrangements. Moreover, in practice, the limited majorities attained by ruling groups in many local elections make coalitions commonplace—forcing largest parties to compromise their policy ideas.

Besides districts or boroughs covering fewer than 85,000 people, the only authorities permitted to retain 'alternative arrangements' until recently were those, like Brighton and Hove City Council, that had held unsuccessful referendums to introduce directly elected mayors. Even then, this was on condition that they adopted committee-based systems with sufficient scrutiny powers to carry out the same functions competently. Under Labour, there was a tacit recognition in these areas that it was only a matter of time before they would be forced to adopt a post-LGA 2000 executive model.

▌ Local government hierarchies since the LGA 2000

The main difference between the 'old-style' system and its principal replacements is that, under post-LGA 2000 structures, the balance of power between 'ordinary' councillors and those in ruling groups has shifted radically towards the latter. Whereas all councillors were once active participants in the local legislative process, today's council leaders—or, where adopted, elected mayors—hold disproportionate power. Their cabinets, too, have moved from being largely nominal entities to become ones that take executive decisions that the rest of the council has little chance of overturning.

The three types of executive management introduced by the LGA 2000 were:

- leader of the council and cabinet/executive;
- directly elected mayor (DEM) and cabinet/executive; and
- DEM and council manager.

The third option was formally scrapped by Labour in the 2007 Act, after the experience of the only council to adopt it—Stoke-on-Trent—became an object lesson for disproportionate powers that could be accrued by some individuals. Under this system, executive decision-making powers were vested in only one person other than the elected mayor: the council manager (an officer). Following repeated claims that this model was leading to a culture of secrecy in Stoke, in October 2008 local electors voted to replace it with a leader-and-cabinet model.

Nonetheless, until the Localism Act 2011, councils continued to be encouraged by ministers to adopt one of the other LGA 2000-style models. Before doing so, authorities must go through the following two-stage consultation process.

1. They must issue an explanation to the public of the three models of executive structure.

2. They must carry out a more detailed formal consultation among local people.

Once a decision has been taken to adopt a particular model, the council must agree the wording of a formal constitution with the Communities Secretary.

Any subsequent attempt to change it requires the constitution to be rewritten in consultation with ministers.

Under both surviving LGA 2000 models, the leader or mayor's position is paramount. All councils adopting either system are further divided hierarchically into the following functions: executive, non-executive, and scrutiny. As is the case nationally, the term 'executive' refers to powers exercised by senior councillors—cabinet members plus the leader or mayor. Like the prime minister and his or her Cabinet, these individuals may initiate policy privately—even taking final decisions on some matters—without needing to consult committees or subcommittees, as happened under the old-style system.

The terms 'scrutiny' and 'non-executive' both apply to committees and subcommittees. Each describes one of the two roles undertaken by committees under the post-LGA 2000 regimes.

Non-executive committees

Committees overseeing regulatory matters such as planning and licensing have delegated powers to take some decisions, rejecting or approving matters brought before them. The range of matters referred to non-executive committees is limited, however, compared to those deliberated over by old-style ones. A planning subcommittee or committee, for example, might decide to reject or approve an application brought before it without the need to refer it to a full council or cabinet for final approval—but this would apply only to *minor* applications (for example those relating to an extension to someone's house). The outcome of such applications will already largely have been dictated by the authority's existing planning rules, as previously agreed by the full council and set by higher tiers of government. Major applications—for example a bid by Tesco to open an out-of-town superstore—must be approved by full council.

Scrutiny committees

'Overview and scrutiny' (or simply 'scrutiny') refers to the function accorded to committees and subcommittees charged with examining specific council policy proposals and the workings of individual spending departments—for example children's services, education, or transport. Their powers, then, are more akin to those of Westminster-style select committees (see Chapter 2, 'Select committees') than old-style council ones: like parliamentary committees, they can propose policy amendments, call witnesses, and publish reports, but have little power to reject or overturn executive decisions. All authorities—including those operating under alternative arrangements—are required to establish an overarching **overview and scrutiny committee** comprising councillors drawn from parties in proportion to the distribution of seats on the council. In practice, most split their scrutiny function among several subject-specific subcommittees or panels, with some even referring to these as 'select committees' in reference to their parliamentary equivalents.

Criticisms of the 'new' systems

One of the Blair government's principal arguments for the new-style hierarchies was a desire to speed up council decision-making, by reducing committees' tendency to delay final policy decisions. But the stark division between the influence on policymaking exerted today by cabinet members, compared to 'ordinary' councillors, has sparked severe criticism of these reforms—not least from veteran councillors who, after years of public service, found themselves with less direct say than previously in running their councils. The new-style models are seen to have introduced two 'tiers' of councillors, as at Westminster: a powerful 'front bench'; and a sometimes vocal, but often toothless, 'back bench'.

Some criticisms of the post-2000 committee changes are arguably justified—not least those levelled by frustrated journalists who yearn for a return to the more knockabout meetings and policy standoffs of old. However, many scrutiny committees have had tangible input into councils' policy initiatives. In July 2009, the London Borough of Hounslow's children and young people scrutiny panel was awarded £90,000 by the Department of Health (DoH) to commission new services to tackle speech and language difficulties among poor children in its area. A month earlier, a credit union was set up to provide low-cost loans to poor households across North Yorkshire after a scrutiny review launched by county councillors brokered a partnership between public, private, and voluntary organizations—following a decade of campaigning by locals.

Table 13.1 gives an overview of arguments for and against the LGA 2000 hierarchical models.

In recognition of the criticisms of the cabinet model, the Coalition's Localism Act 2011 permits councils to bypass it for good—with authorities that previously switched from the old system also allowed to 'move away from an executive form of governance' if they so wish. In order to do so, authorities must first pass majority resolutions favouring such a move, revise their constitutions to incorporate the proposed changes, and publicize the proposals, including in one or more local newspapers. On 23 May 2012, South Gloucestershire Council became one of the first authorities to revert to a committee-led system, after its ruling Conservative group was outvoted by a coalition of Labour and Lib Dem members approving the move. Before losing control of Barnet Council in May 2014, the Tory-led group announced plans to abandon the cabinet system, while Fylde Borough Council in Lancashire has returned to a committee-led set-up after a local referendum prompted by a petition signed by more than 5 per cent of local electors voted 57.8 to 42.2 per cent in favour.

Table 13.1 Arguments for and against the LGA 2000 management models

For	Against
Allowing leaders, elected mayors, and cabinets to take some executive decisions unilaterally makes the local legislative process faster/more efficient than it was when committees had to approve everything.	New models create 'two-tier' councils, with frontbenchers having more influence on policymaking than backbenchers.
Introducing elected mayors engages the public more with local democracy—giving it a direct say in decisions over council leadership. It is more democratic and councils are more accountable than under old system.	By giving small groups of individuals executive powers, 'elective dictatorships' can form, making councils *less* democratically accountable.
The LGA 2000 laid down a process by which local electorates could demand referendums on the introduction of elected mayors—bottom-up local democracy in action.	Introducing three alternative models for council leadership has led to a patchwork landscape of local authority hierarchies. This confuses voters and can lead to inconsistent local representation.

The dominant decision-making set-up in Wales is the leader-and-cabinet model, but in Scotland most councils continue to operate old-style committee systems. Some, however, have adopted more hierarchical, cabinet-style, set-ups (albeit with notably less executive power accruing to their leaders than in England). Meanwhile, under changes proposed by the Draft Local Government (Executive Arrangements) Regulations (Northern Ireland) 2014, it is proposed that future Northern Irish councils will choose either to continue with the long-standing committee-based system, adopting a bespoke 'prescribed arrangement' negotiated with the province's assembly, or switch to a strict executive-style model, which would delegate most operational decisions to one or more committees made of between six and 10 councillors, with no full council involvement.

Types and levels of council decision

Under post-LGA 2000 executive models, the full council (which used to have to approve virtually all policies before they were implemented) is now concerned only with the most significant decisions. Proposals affecting two or more wards or electoral divisions and likely to incur 'significant' expenditure are called **key decisions**. An example might be the approval of a Council Tax rise or a planning application by developers keen to build a new road (which, by definition, will affect several wards). Each month, in the interests of transparency to local electors, every authority must publish a **forward plan** of all key decisions that it intends to take over the coming four weeks, with its cabinet or executive agreeing its own.

Figure 13.2 The decision-making process in post-LGA 2000 councils

Whatever internal decision-making frameworks they favour, certain other terms are common to the proceedings of all councils, as follows.

- The specific roles or powers delegated to them by statute—and by them to committees, subcommittees, and cabinets—are known as **prescribed functions**.

- Whenever final decisions are taken on matters before committees, full councils, or cabinets and executives, these are known as **resolved items**. Scrutiny committees or panels may, however, 'call in' items resolved in cabinet and/or refer them back for rethinks (as with old-style committees).

Figure 13.2 illustrates the top-down chain of command in post-LGA councils.

The 'leader and cabinet' model

Of the three new executive management options introduced by the LGA 2000, that with most similarities to the existing system is the 'leader and cabinet' model. As under the old-style council hierarchy, the leader is normally head of his or her party—usually that with the most councillors. He or she heads a **cabinet** (or 'executive') comprising close confidantes on the council, normally drawn from his or her own party or (where no single party has overall control) a coalition.

But this is where any similarities between pre- and post-LGA 2000 leader-and-cabinet systems end. 'New-style' cabinets or executives are much more like those formed by prime ministers than the earlier, more informal, ones. Until recently, it was left to individual councils' discretion to decide whether they wanted 'weak' or 'strong' leaders. Under the former approach, the council as a whole selects its leader and individual cabinet members, and all executive decisions must be taken *collectively* by cabinet. The 'strong leader' approach, in contrast, allows the leader (once elected by fellow councillors) to choose cabinet members—delegating Westminster-style policy portfolios to each. In December 2010, this variant became mandatory for all councils with leaders and cabinets—with county councils, London boroughs, metropolitan districts, non-metropolitan districts or boroughs, and unitary authorities introducing them successively in a programme of phased reform under the Local Government and Public Involvement in Health Act 2007. This Act also stipulated that executive leaders should serve automatic terms of four years—an approach dubbed 'strong leader-plus'—whereas the 2000 changes had allowed councils to appoint them for a year at a time.

Controversially, although individual cabinet members are generally expected to consult with frontbench colleagues, in some cases they may take executive action on their own. The same applies to leaders. Of still greater concern to some critics is the fact that although most cabinets now meet publicly at least some of the time, they are *obliged* to do so only in relation to policy matters that they have agreed to resolve collectively. In other words, decisions delegated to individual cabinet members (or, in some cases, unelected officers) may be taken in secret. Under the Localism Act 2011, cabinets retain their ability to meet in private.

Committees have therefore gone from being *proactive* agents in policymaking to largely *reactive* ones. Meanwhile, full council meetings—which still nominally have the final say over whether policies are approved—can resemble 'rubber stamps' for decisions already finalized behind closed doors in cabinet. Similar charges are made of the second model.

The 'directly elected mayor and cabinet' model

As explained in Chapter 11 ('The emergence of modern local authorities'), there is a long-standing tradition among districts/boroughs and metropolitan districts of appointing mayors. The office of mayor (known in Scotland as the 'convenor', or 'provost') has customarily been ceremonial—with elected councillors taking turns to spend a year in the role, before passing on their chain of office to a colleague. Incumbent mayors adopt the role of returning officer in the event of local, general, or European elections, officiate over civic duties (opening fetes, visiting schools, etc.), and (usually) chair meetings of full council. Like the Commons Speaker, mayors (temporarily) drop party allegiances and voting rights for the duration of their office. Some authorities, however, choose to divest mayors of their council chairmanship roles by electing separate speakers to perform that duty. In May 2012, Sylvia Gillard was elected speaker of Bedford Borough Council.

Directly elected mayors (DEMs) occupy different positions entirely. First, unlike both council leaders and old-style mayors, they are not themselves councillors; instead, they are voted in by local electorates in separate ballots run *alongside* council elections. When Mr Johnson thwarted Mr Livingstone's bid for a London mayoral comeback in 2012, the separate election for the London Assembly saw Labour increase its grip on City Hall—securing 12 members to the Tories' nine. In this respect, elected mayors bear more similarity to local presidents than prime ministers. While no Labour premier could remain in post long after an election in which the Tories won more seats, the same is not true of presidents: since the second half of his first White House term, Barack Obama has had to horse-trade with a Republican-dominated House of Representatives and (after the recent mid-term elections) Senate.

Before being permitted to introduce elected mayors, councils must first win referendums of their local electorates. Conversely, if 5 per cent of that electorate decides whether it favours a mayoral system, it may *demand* a referendum—whatever the council's view.

Labour's hope was that *all* English councils would have initiated consultations about their proposed executive frameworks within six to nine months of the LGA 2000's passage—with many favouring the mayoral option. In practice, it took until February 2002 for most to publish proposals and, when they did, eight out of 10 opted for the leader-and-cabinet model.

At time of writing, only 16 councils have elected mayors–with a 17th due to be elected shortly in Copeland, Cumbria, following a decisive 'yes' vote in a referendum demanded by a community campaign calling itself 'Time to Change'. The Greater London Authority (GLA) was first to adopt one, while four of the capital's boroughs have since done so: Hackney, Lewisham, Newham, and Tower Hamlets. Other major towns and cities to do so include Middlesbrough, Mansfield, Leicester, and Bedford—with Doncaster voting to retain its DEM in May 2012 despite repeated controversies surrounding holders of the office.

Supporters of DEMs initially blamed the slow take-up on the fact that, under Labour, whenever a referendum was lost, another could not be held by the same council for five years. Of nearly fifty referendums held to date, seven out of 10 failed to secure majorities in favour of elected mayors. In addition, campaigns have been launched in four areas to abolish the post: successfully in Stoke-on-Trent and Hartlepool (where, in 2009, Hartlepool United Football Club mascot 'H'Angus the Monkey'—alias Stuart Drummond—had earlier become the first DEM to win a third term), but also in Doncaster and Lewisham. The 17 councils operating an elected mayoral system as of 2015 are listed in the table entitled 'Local authorities with directly elected mayors', to be found on the **Online** **Resource Centre**. To boost take-up, Labour published new proposals in July 2008 making it easier for local electors to trigger referendums, by enabling those campaigning for 'yes' votes to recruit supporters through online petitions. The plans were announced shortly after the failure of a campaign by the *Birmingham Mail* newspaper to marshal the 36,000 electors required to kick-start a local mayoral contest.

The Coalition mounted its own drive to persuade cities to adopt elected mayors. On 3 May 2012, Liverpool elected its first DEM (former Labour council leader Joe Anderson) and the 10 other biggest cities outside London were forced to hold referendums. In the event, any 'Big Bang' hopes backfired: nine out 10 referendum cities, including Birmingham and Nottingham, rejected the idea, with only Bristol approving it. As an exercise in 'direct democracy', the referendums hardly set electorates on fire either: average turnouts for the polls, held on the same day as English local elections, were below 29 per cent. To date, only one Welsh authority, Ceredigion County Council, has ever held a referendum on whether to adopt a DEM—and it rejected the idea.

☰ Topical feature idea

Two-and-a-half years after the Coalition introduced new 'community rights' for citizens and third-sector groups to take over the running of 'failing' council services or threatened community resources, such as pubs and libraries, the government's map of such 'Big Society' projects suggests that few have taken up the offer. Are there any community-led projects in your area that are examples of the 'Big Society' in action? If so, what are they and who is behind them? What government resources are available to local people, including readers of your paper, who might be interested in starting one?

✳ Current issues

- **The return of committee-based local government** A growing number of councils—including South Gloucestershire Council and Ryld Borough Council in Lancashire—are abandoning cabinet systems to return to old-style committee-led ones, following Communities Secretary Eric Pickles' decision to change the law.

- **Improving the demographic profile of councillors** A 2013 report by the Commons Communities and Local Government Committee found that 'low pay' was a barrier to more working-aged people and women standing for election as councillors. It found that, contrary to media reports, the average basic allowance was £7,000—far too low to persuade people to give up paid jobs to take part in local democracy. The average age of councillors remains stubbornly high, at 60.2, with only 32.7 per cent women and 4 per cent from ethnic minorities.

- **The wholesale outsourcing of council services** With government cuts continuing to bite, many councils are outsourcing more front-line services. In the most extreme example, December 2012 saw the London Borough of Barnet franchise out 70 per cent of services to one company, Capita—with several whole departments relocated to Northern Ireland, and the north and south-west of England.

⬚ Key points

1. Local authorities are run by two groups of people: officers and councillors (members). Officers are civil servants, paid salaries to administer council departments; councillors are elected to decide councils' policies and receive only allowances.

2. The Local Government Act 2000 (LGA 2000) replaced the 'old-style' way in which councillors used to take decisions with one of two new hierarchies: a 'leader and cabinet', or a 'directly elected mayor and cabinet' model. Under these, policies are devised by 'frontbench' councillors in cabinet, then scrutinized by committees and voted on by full council.

3. Before the LGA 2000, all councillors took part in policy decisions. Policies were initially recommended by subcommittees or committees focusing on specific issues (such as education), then approved or rejected by full council. Although smaller councils still use this model, the Coalition is now permitting others to readopt it, too.

4. At present, there are six directly elected mayors—all in England. Prior to adopting or abandoning elected mayors, councils must hold local referendums. If 5 per cent of local people demand a vote, conversely, one must be held.

5. Rather than being directly provided by councils, many local services today are delivered by private companies and voluntary organizations. Citizens may now take over services themselves, or set up their own, under new 'community rights'.

→ Further reading

Cooper, K. and Macfarland, C. (2012) *Clubbing Together: The Hidden Wealth of Communities*, London: ResPublica. **Report by 'Red Tory' think tank ResPublica on how community-based social activities, clubs, and societies can foster Big Society-style projects delivering public benefit.**

Hodge, M., Leach, S., and Stoker, G. (1997) *Local Government Policy: More than the Flower Show—Elected Mayors and Democracy*, London: Fabian Society. **Pamphlet arguing for the merits of directly elected mayors, prior to their introduction by the Blair government and their embrace by the Coalition.**

Leach, S. (2010) *Managing in a Political World: The Life Cycle of Local Authority Chief Executives*, Basingstoke: Palgrave Macmillan. **Thoughtful and up-to-date overview of the role and importance of chief executives, and the levels of scrutiny to which they and their salaries are subjected.**

Norman, J. (2010) *The Big Society: The Anatomy of the New Politics*, Buckingham: University of Buckingham Press. **Fiercely intellectual critique of the ideas, ideology, and historical traditions underpinning David Cameron's 'Big Society' concept.**

Online Resource Centre

14

Local government accountability and elections

Between them, councils are responsible for spending more than £65 billion a year in taxpayers' money. Perhaps understandably, their decisions are subject to increasing scrutiny.

Councils are accountable to local citizens by:

- publishing their own standing orders, codes of conduct, and constitutions;
- submitting their accounts to independent audits and publishing performance data;
- allowing press and public to attend meetings, and to access agendas and reports; and
- giving local people a direct say through elections.

This chapter focuses on the ways in which today's councillors (and officers) are held to account.

▶ Local government post-Nolan—the new era of transparency

As with central government, councils have long been expected to adhere to systems, rules, and procedures in conducting their business. But the extent to which they were required to *demonstrate* their integrity underwent a profound shift following the succession of high-profile parliamentary scandals that led to the findings of the Nolan Inquiry (see Chapter 2, 'MPs, conflicts of interest, abuses of privilege—and how to avoid them').

The immediate effect of Lord Nolan's recommendations, published in 1996, was to compel all public officials—starting with members of Parliament (MPs), but extending to local councillors or officers—to uphold '*Seven Principles of Public Life*': selflessness, integrity, objectivity, accountability, openness, honesty, and leadership. But he and the prime minister who commissioned his inquiry, John Major, wanted to go further—an aspiration shared by the latter's successor, Tony Blair, who consolidated the reforms in the Local Government Act 2000 (LGA 2000). Today, the processes introduced to police MPs' behaviour also underpin accountability in local government.

▌ The emergence of council constitutions

Under the LGA 2000, every council is now obliged to draw up—and agree with the Communities Secretary—its own **council constitution**. Within reason, this constitution can take any number of forms—whether a broad mission statement, or a more detailed breakdown of the council's responsibilities and services. The very fact that individual councils are free, in theory, to devise their own wording reflects an acknowledgement by government that the particular issues different councils face in running their affairs vary. Since 19 December 2000, however, *all* constitutions have had to contain all of the components listed in Table 14.1.

Table 14.1 Compulsory components of a council constitution

	Component
1.	Summary and explanation of purpose and content of constitution
2.	Description of council's composition, scheme of ordinary elections, and terms of office
3.	Breakdown of principal roles and functions of councillors, including rights and duties of individual members
4.	Scheme of allowances for councillors
5.	Description of local inhabitants' rights and responsibilities, including their rights to vote in local elections and access information about local services and council, committee, subcommittee, and cabinet/executive meetings
6.	Description of council's roles
7.	Rules governing conduct and proceedings of council meetings
8.	Description of roles/functions of council chairperson/mayor, leader/directly elected mayor (DEM), cabinet/executive, individual cabinet members, and officers with delegated executive powers
9.	Description of operational arrangements, terms of reference, membership, and rules for overview and scrutiny committees
10.	Provisions in council's executive arrangements with respect to appointment of committees of executive

(*continued*)

Table 14.1 (*continued*)

11.	Membership, terms of reference, and functions of committees and subcommittees, and any rules governing conduct of their meetings
12.	Description of roles and membership of standards committee and any parish council subcommittee of standards committee
13.	Description of roles and membership of any area committees of authority
14.	Description of any joint arrangements made with other councils
15.	Description of officers' roles, including those of senior management
16.	Roles and functions of chief executive, monitoring officer, and chief finance officer
17.	Code of conduct for officers issued under Act, plus any details governing their recruitment, disciplinary procedures, etc.
18.	Any protocol established by authority in respect of relationships between its members and officers
19.	Description of arrangements for public access to members, and officers to meetings of full council, cabinet/executive, committees, subcommittees, and joint committees
20.	Description of arrangements for public access to members, and officers to information about decisions made—or to be made—by any of above meetings
21.	Register of names/addresses of executive members, their wards/divisions, and names of every executive committee member
22.	Description of rules/procedures for management of authority's financial, contractual, and legal affairs, including procedures for auditing
23.	Authority's financial rules and regulations, and those governing procedures regarding contracts and procurement (including authentication of documents)
24.	Rules and procedures for legal proceedings brought by and against authority
25.	Description of register of members' interests of all full and co-opted councillors, and procedures for publicizing, maintaining, and updating it
26.	Description of rules and procedures for reviewing/revising authority's constitution and management structure
27.	Copy of authority's standing orders and code of conduct

Section 37 of the LGA 2000 specifies that copies of councils' constitutions must be available for inspection by the public 'at their principal offices' within 'all reasonable hours'. Personal copies must also be supplied on request—albeit for a 'reasonable fee'.

The foundation stones of council constitutions

What, then, of the various technical terms highlighted in the government's criteria for the content of constitutions? The concept of **'standing' orders** is one familiar to anyone who has worked for an organization of any size, whether in the public, private, or voluntary sectors. It refers to the overall system of rules and guidelines governing the day-to-day conduct of business. Like their constitution as a whole, individual councils set their own standing orders—so they can be as detailed or indicative as they wish. Some incorporate into them rules governing the propriety of councillors and officers—for example the require-ment that those with financial interests in matters due to be discussed by a committee on which they sit must declare this fact and remove themselves from its meetings. Others may confine their standing orders to mundane proce-dural issues (as a bare minimum, most contain breakdowns of the customary order of business at council, committee, and cabinet meetings).

The LGA 2000 also emphasized that constitutions must address the post-Nolan preoccupation with enforcing national standards of ethical conduct by public officials. Most councils have long had agreed codes of conduct specify-ing lists of 'dos' and 'don'ts' by which members must abide. Following the sleaze allegations of the 1990s, however, a new onus was placed on those in public life at all levels to clean up their acts—in particular, to keep 'outside interests' sepa-rate from duties performed on the public's behalf.

Given that councillors are unpaid and many juggle their duties with earning livings elsewhere, the potential conflicts of interest in local government are more multifarious than those faced by MPs. The councillor who sits on a plan-ning committee as well as the board of a company with local development inter-ests poses an all-too-familiar conundrum—and for this reason most councils have long had clear rules compelling members to make a **declaration of interest** in relation to any outside pecuniary interest. There has also been some criti-cism that councillors in this position are relegated to weaker positions than others—particularly those standing for election on 'independent' tickets relat-ed to particular causes, such as defending local services from closure, rather than conventional party-political platforms. It was partly in response to this concern that Coalition Communities Secretary Eric Pickles inserted a clause into the Localism Act 2011 to 'clarify' rules on so-called 'predetermination'—the notion that, whatever their personal interests in particular local matters, individual councillors should come to council discussions demonstrating 'an open mind'. While any councillor henceforth exposed for withholding details of (or otherwise misrepresenting) a financial interest would be liable for criminal prosecution, the rewritten rulebook would generally allow him or her greater freedom to 'play an active part' in local debate, free from the threat of 'legal challenge'. Journalists had previously complained of councillors' reluctance to speak to them ahead of meetings for fear of 'fettering' their discretion—that is, breaching their code of conduct or prejudicing potential future judicial reviews of council decisions.

The Local Government Act 1972 introduced local registers of interests, but because these were voluntary, councils were not obliged to comply. It was the LGA 2000 that standardized the process, requiring *every* council to publish a reworded constitution reflecting Lord Nolan's '*Seven Principles*'. Declarations of interest, meanwhile, must now be made at the point at which someone first stands for election. As with MPs and peers, they are required to enter all interests on registers of members' interests (see Chapter 2, 'MPs, conflicts of interest, abuses of privilege—and how to avoid them') within 28 days of being

elected. The register must be updated within 28 days of any subsequent interests emerging. Councillors must also declare relevant interests at the start of
meetings in which they are participants if they have personal involvement in
any **agenda** item. They should also remove themselves from those meetings for
the duration of any discussion about that item.

The main types of interest defined by law are:

- employment or business interests;
- contributions to election expenses;
- shareholdings of £25,000 or more, or ownership of more than 1 per cent of
  issued share capital, in a company based in the council's area;
- a business interest in contracts between the council and any other;
- land owned, leased, or held under licence for more than 28 days in the
  council's area; and
- membership or management of a public authority, company, charity,
  trade union, or professional association.

Beyond this, it is the precise 'nature and extent' of a councillor's interest that
determines whether it falls into one of two categories that might affect his or
her ability to carry out his or her duties impartially. Where relevant interests
were once defined as either 'pecuniary' or 'non-pecuniary', and the LGA 2000
redefined them as 'personal' (financial) or 'prejudicial' (likely to cloud a councillor's judgement of an issue before him or her), in England the rules changed
with the 2011 Act and 2012 Regulations, which replaced these definitions with:

- 'disclosable pecuniary interest'—any matter, the outcome of which might
  reasonably be seen as affecting the financial position of the councillor or
  his or her civil partner or spouse, which might include any employment,
  trade, profession, or vocation carried out for profit or gain, or involvement in sponsorship, contracts, land interests or licences, or corporate
  tenancies, or the holding of any securities in parties related to matters
  due for decision; and
- 'sensitive interest'—any personal interest (whether or not pecuniary) of
  which the monitoring office feels disclosure could lead to the councillor
  being subject to violence or intimidation.

The LGA 2000 system continues to apply in Wales.

Regulating standards

Who, then, polices these rules? As explained in Chapter 13 ('Meet the experts—
the role of local government officers'), each council has a designated monitoring officer, whose job is to ensure that it acts within the law and does not

overreach its powers. The introduction of codes of conduct and registers of interests—coupled with the onus placed on officers, as well as councillors, to act accountably—was initially accompanied by a greater emphasis on objective scrutiny. To this end, the LGA 2000 required each council to appoint its own Westminster-style **standards committee** to monitor its officials' actions and to raise concerns about unethical conduct. Its independence was theoretically assured by the fact that, in addition to two or more councillors, it must include at least one individual who was neither a member nor an officer of that or 'any other relevant' authority.

Standards committees were expected to:

- promote and maintain high standards of conduct by members and co-opted members;
- assist members and co-opted members of the authority to observe its code of conduct;
- advise the authority on the adoption or revision of a code of conduct;
- monitor the operation of the code of conduct; and
- advise, train, or arrange to train councillors and co-opted members on matters relating to the code of conduct.

On a day-to-day basis, they often devolved functions to subcommittees, but their compositions and precise remits must be formally agreed with the involvement of local parish councils.

For more than a decade, the conduct of councillors was further overseen by a quango, Standards for England (formerly the Standards Board for England), until its abolition in the Localism Act 2011. The Act also removed the statutory requirement for councils to have standards committees, although in practice many continue to do so. Since then, each authority has had to draw up a new code governing members' conduct, using the full force of criminal law to prosecute them for wrongdoing on the rare occasions on which such action becomes necessary. In the absence of a more independently policed standards framework, however, it remains to be seen how future breaches will come to light in the first place.

In Wales, allegations of councillor misconduct continue to be handled by the overarching Public Services Ombudsman for Wales, while errant members of Scottish authorities may be disciplined by the Standards Commission for Scotland. Following prolonged negotiations, a new 'ethical standards framework' for local government in Northern Ireland came into force on 28 May 2014, to coincide with the elections for the province's 11 new 'super-councils'.

While the various standards regulators have only minimal legal powers, they normally disclose the fact that a complaint has been made (helpfully for the media)—issuing full details of their eventual decisions and any sanctions imposed.

From 'Beacon Councils' to the National Indicator Set—the growth of performance data

Renewed emphasis placed on promoting high ethical standards among public officials corresponded with what critics decried as a spiralling government obsession with centrally directed performance targets, league tables, and ratings systems to grade the quality of their work. First up under New Labour were 'Beacon Councils'—authorities singled out as examples of best practice in service delivery. Then came Best Value performance indicators (BVPIs), followed by various other regimes. Overall responsibility for monitoring the effectiveness of English and Welsh authorities—and taking action when necessary—was handed to a central government quango, the Audit Commission, which discharged this role through locally based district auditors. Scottish councils were to be held to account by Audit Scotland, while Northern Irish ones would have their books pored over by officers from the Northern Ireland Audit Office (NIA).

Taxpayers could visit the Commission's website at any time to access their councils' Comprehensive Performance Assessment (CPA) 'scorecards', while annual reports would 'name and shame' the best and worst performers of the previous year, judging them not only on their absolute star ratings, but also against value-added criteria, known as 'direction of travel'. In time, these measures gave way, first, to the Comprehensive Area Assessment (CAA)—a measure of service standards in each geographical locality, rather than of individual councils' performances—and one final stab from Labour at fine-tuning performance data, 'National Indicator Sets' (NIS), which gave everyone instant online access to all of their local performance data via a single website (known as 'oneplace')

The Coalition scrapped these in June 2010, but in a move seen by some as contradictory Mr Pickles made good on another of the Conservatives' stated aims—to make councils more accountable to local taxpayers for their spending decisions—by stipulating that they publish everything from waste disposal and recycling rates, to food hygiene reports and pub licensing decisions, on their own websites. They must also post details of all items of expenditure, contracts, and tenders worth £500 or more, all payments to councillors, and all staff salaries of £58,200 and over (see Chapter 12, 'Financial transparency at the local level'). Mr Pickles and Mr Cameron repeatedly claimed to be ushering in an era of 'armchair auditing'—empowering ordinary citizens to keep tabs on their councils' (and government's) profligacy from their own living-rooms. To this end, they abolished the Commission (ironically, the brainchild of a previous Tory government in 1983) and replaced it with a network of independent providers. When the first tranche of contracts for this work were awarded in March 2012, critics of this 'privatization' of public sector auditing claimed that their warnings had been vindicated: DA Partnership, an employee-owned offshoot of the Commission touted by ministers as an example of the new forms of community-based company that they wanted to promote as part of the 'Big Society', secured only one of ten regional franchises available. The rest were carved up by private consultancy firms Ernst & Young, KPMG, and Grant Thornton. The latter—which won four five-year contracts, with a combined value of £41.3 million—had pledged to take on 300 of the Commission's existing 2,000-strong staff, but even this proved controversial, with 500 employees taking industrial action in February that year over concerns about their pension rights being eroded during the takeover. The Commission's auditing role ended on 1 November 2012, at which point 700 of its auditors were transferred to the new providers. It was formally abolished by the Local Audit and Accountability Act 2014.

In theory, any 'armchair auditing' revolution may sound like a boon to journalists, but in practice it can be difficult to sift through the sea of data routinely 'info-dumped' on councils' websites under ministers' newly enforced 'transparency' policy. Authorities are inconsistent in where they place details of their spending, councillor allowances, and senior officer salaries online—and details are often presented (as if deliberately) in all but impenetrable form, with lengthy spreadsheets in place of user-friendly graphs or tables. Not for nothing did the Commons Public Accounts Committee (PAC) brand councils' early efforts to throw open their books 'not fit for purpose' in a scathing report in July 2012. So how should journalists make sense of the data? A useful tactic is to utilize one of a number of online data visualization programs that can now be downloaded, free of charge, as open-source software, the most well-known being Datawrapper, available online at **www.datawrapper.de**. More proactive councils, such as Poole, Cherwell, and Cumbria, also use the government's favoured program, Spotlightonspend, which allows easy spending comparisons to be made between comparable authorities covering similar-sized populations. Even where councils do not present data in this way on their own sites, journalists and the public can access graphs and charts illustrating their spending on the website **whatis.spotlightonspend.org.uk**. Beyond all of this, the growing availability of open data from public bodies has spawned something of a new cottage industry in 'data journalism'—with *The Guardian* now having a dedicated 'data blog' adjunct to its main website, and collaborative amateur sites such as **www.openlylocal.com** collating and comparing councils' spending statistics with the help of an online 'dashboard'.

The last resort—the role of Local Government Ombudsman

Of course, targets, league tables, and publication of performance data can achieve only so much in the service of accountability. What should people do if they feel that they have suffered an injustice at the hands of their councils—or that they have lost out because of, say, incorrect decisions by officers about their eligibility for services?

In relation to English authorities, for nearly 40 years the answer has been to lodge a formal complaint with the **Local Government Ombudsman**

(LGO)—officially, the **Commission for Local Administration** in England. The remit of the two ombudsmen employed by the service is to investigate allegations of maladministration—negligent or incompetent running of local services. They are not there simply to consider complaints relating to decisions about which people are unhappy, *unless* those decisions show evidence of maladministration. Since 1988, complainants have been able to take their cases direct to the Ombudsman without needing to use councillors as intermediaries (a principle enshrined in the Local Government Act 1974, which first established the service). This change had an immediate impact on the number of complaints made: in the first year alone, they soared by 44 per cent.

England's twin ombudsmen each oversee patchwork spreads of geographical areas and specific authorities, as follows.

- One covers: all London boroughs except Lewisham; Manchester, York, Trafford, and High Peak; unitary authorities in Essex, Kent, East Sussex, Surrey, Buckinghamshire, and Gloucestershire; authorities in Berkshire, Suffolk, the south and west of England; and several councils in central England.

- The other deals with: Lewisham, Birmingham, Coventry and Solihull; county and district authorities in Essex, Kent, East Sussex, Surrey, Buckinghamshire, and Gloucestershire; and 11 councils in West Sussex, Surrey, Hertfordshire, Cheshire, Derbyshire, Nottinghamshire, Lincolnshire, Warwickshire, and the north of England (except for High Peak Borough Council, Trafford Borough Council, and the cities of Manchester and York).

Handily for journalists (and public), 'annual reviews' of individual councils' overall performance in dealing with Ombudsman complaints are published online at **www.lgo.org.uk/CouncilsPerformance**.

In Wales, since 2006 local government maladministration has been policed by the overarching Public Services Ombudsman for Wales; in Scotland, a Scottish Public Services Ombudsman was introduced in 2003. The Northern Ireland Ombudsman, meanwhile, has been in place since 1969.

Complaints processes to these bodies are subject to various conditions. Those applying in England are outlined in the table entitled 'The conditions for filing complaints with the Local Government Commissioner', to be found on the **Online Resource Centre** that accompanies this book.

As more people become aware of the Ombudsman, so the number of complaints investigated each year rises. The powers of the service have also been extended, allowing the ombudsmen to handle two new categories of complaint: those made by adults arranging and/or funding their own social care (see Chapter 18, 'Choice in community care—the rise of direct payments'); and criticisms by pupils and parents about school performance in 14 local education authority areas. Recent years have also seen notable increases in the

number of complaints about local administration of the benefits system—
significantly, at a time of major cuts to housing and Council Tax benefits (see
Chapter 17, 'Local authorities, Housing Benefit, and the Local Housing
Allowance (LHA)'). Understandably, journalists are always keen to learn
about upcoming cases, because they tend to concern major complaints and be
highly newsworthy. At times, however, these stories can be frustrating: while
final adjudications are always publicized, because the identities of those
involved are usually kept anonymous, resulting reports are rarely as revealing as press or public might hope.

Punishing errant councillors and officers

In exceptional circumstances, individual councillors and senior officers
found culpable of major financial or managerial irregularities have been personally *surcharged* by the Audit Commission. The most infamous example of
wilful misconduct of this kind was the 'homes for votes' scandal of July 1987,
which saw then leader of Westminster City Council Dame Shirley Porter and
her colleague, David Weeks, conspire to sell 500 council houses a year to
potential Tory voters living in marginal wards, to engineer Conservative victories in forthcoming elections, in an abuse of the Thatcher government's
'Right to Buy' scheme (see Chapter 17, '"Right to Buy" and the privatization
of council housing'). Eventually, Dame Shirley, a Tesco heiress, was ordered
to repay the council £27 million, plus interest and legal costs—and she finally
settled by reimbursing it £12 million in 2004. Surcharging powers were
repealed by the LGA 2000 but, like MPs, councillors and officers can be prosecuted for fraud.

▶ Access to council meetings and business—the 'old' system

Until recently, the rights of press and public to attend meetings of councils,
committees, and subcommittees were straightforward. Although authorities
often refer to the Local Government Act 1972 in their published papers, it was
the Local Government (Access to Information) Act 1985—arising out of a private member's Bill introduced by Conservative backbencher Robin Squire—
that enshrined their right to attend *all* such meetings, unless information due
for discussion was 'confidential' or 'exempt'. The former category refers to
specified classes of information supplied by government departments or matters disclosure of which is prohibited under statute or by the courts. An

example might be details relating to national security or crime prevention prohibited by either the Official Secrets Act or anti-terror laws. 'Exempt' information includes:

- details judged 'personal' and/or 'commercially sensitive'—for example those relating to terms of contracts, disclosure of which might have a negative impact on the council's future ability to negotiate value for money;

- matters 'in the process of being negotiated'—for example details of contractual negotiations with competing companies that the council is considering hiring to provide services; and

- issues 'protected by legal privilege'—for example when members are discussing confidential legal advice received in relation to litigation by or against the council, or contractual matters that they are seeking to resolve through the courts.

Under these arrangements, councils tended to use one of two methods for excluding press and public from meetings (or *sections* of meetings). Most commonly, councils divided their meetings into 'part ones' and 'part twos'—with all confidential and/or exempt items (known as 'below the line' items) discussed in the second halves. Alternatively, they might hold votes to exclude press and public during single, specified agenda items. Such votes have to be formally proposed, seconded, and carried by members at the meeting—and *reasons* must be given to those excluded (usually citing the Schedule to the 1985 Act under which the exclusion was being sought). If a motion fails, the matter must be heard publicly, and copies of supporting reports must be instantly circulated to members of the press and public present.

In addition to granting press and public automatic access to meetings, councils are also required to provide information *before* proceedings, and after the event to publicize the outcomes of votes or debates. At meetings themselves, clerks have to ensure that they go further, in the interests of accessibility, than simply unlocking the doors to the press and public galleries. Most of these access provisions are listed in Table 14.2.

In the past, councils were frequently accused of going against the spirit (if not letter) of these access requirements. The not uncommon practice of holding meetings on controversial issues in small rooms—or barring entry because of 'overcrowding'—was once famously condemned as 'bad faith' by then Lord Chief Justice Lord Widgery. Admission for press and public to meetings of other bodies, including NHS trusts and non-principal authorities (parish or

town councils), are guaranteed by the Public Bodies (Admissions to Meetings) Act 1960.

Other measures that councils have long been encouraged to take to improve their communication with—and accountability to—press and public include

Table 14.2 Access-to-meetings requirements expected of local authorities

Requirement	What it means
Public registers	Councils must keep lists of councillors' names and addresses, and details of committees on which they serve. Powers delegated to individual officers must be listed.
Copies of agenda papers	Orders of business and all reports prepared by officers—and submitted during open parts of meetings—must be available on the day. No matters must be heard unless listed on agendas three days beforehand—unless urgent issues arise that could not be predicted. These should be mentioned during 'matters arising', towards end of the agenda.
Access to **background papers**	All reports presented for public inspection should list background papers used to draft them. Press and public may also examine these (although they may be charged 'reasonable fee').
Minutes of previous meetings	Copies of minutes of open meetings should be available automatically to press and local electors on request. Minutes are records of proceedings that *actually* take place—including items debated, but not on original agenda—and all decisions taken. They normally resemble detailed 'summing up' of what each person said, rather than a verbatim record. Minutes of council meetings usually sent to journalists, along with agendas for subsequent meetings.
'Reasonable accommodation'	This must be provided for both press and public, and normally means that there should be sufficient numbers of seats and/or press benches. At meetings expected to be unusually popular, 'overflow rooms' should be provided. If oversubscribed, audio/video feeds of proceedings should be available to those forced to sit/stand outside the meeting room, so that they can see/hear proceedings.

appointing public relations (PR) or press officers (a move suggested in the Bains Report). The remit of such paid PR people would be strictly to promote *council* initiatives and policies, rather than to generate positive publicity for specific *political groupings*. Councils were also expected to give journalists access to individual councillors—particularly committee chairmen or cabinet members—to obtain quotes justifying political decisions, and senior officers, where technical explanations were required.

In practice, by the mid-1990s many councils still had no press offices, although today journalists commonly complain that they place *too much* emphasis on proactive media management, to deflect criticism of their actions and promote council policies, and too little on serving news organizations' needs. Controversy has also surrounded the plethora of taxpayer-funded newspapers, magazines, and newsletters published by councils, ostensibly to inform residents about their services. Editors of commercial newspapers have accused some authorities of undercutting them by courting paid external advertising, and professionalizing their publications by recruiting experienced journalists on generous salaries and broadening their coverage to encompass non-council-related stories. By 2010, *East End Life*, a weekly published by the London Borough of Tower Hamlets, was being posted free of charge through the letterboxes of 81,000 homes, while its long-established independent rival, the *East London Advertiser*, was selling just 6,800 copies at a 50 pence cover price.

In their defence, some councils argue that they have no option but to publish their own news sheets because of their local media's reluctance to run positive stories, or ones concerning worthy, but dull, information that they need to relay to local people. However, mounting concern about the use of public money for such purposes prompted successive Communities Secretaries to liken council publications to the Soviet-era state-owned newspaper *Pravda* and 'propaganda sheets'. In 2011, Mr Pickles clamped down on the practice by introducing a new 'publicity code' banning councils from directly competing with the local press, producing papers more often than once a quarter, or including in their pages anything unrelated to services that they provided or commissioned. He later warned that councils flouting the ban—including the London boroughs of Tower Hamlets and Greenwich—could be penalized by judicial review.

▶ Access to local authority business—the 'new' system

The LGA 2000 introduced significant new limitations on the extent to which press and public would be allowed access to meetings of councils adopting one of the 'new-style' executive arrangements (see Chapter 13, 'Local government hierarchies since the LGA 2000'). While full council, committee, and subcommittee meetings remained as public as ever, access to others became restricted. Because many final decisions were now effectively taken by cabinets or related bodies with delegated powers, critics argued that (contrary to their rhetoric) councils had become *less* transparent than previously. Initially, cabinets were not obliged to meet publicly at all, but the LGA 2000 was modified by government guidance issued in 2002 requiring them to convene openly whenever discussing key decisions (see Chapter 13, 'Types and levels of council decision') taken by their members collectively. Controversially, however, key decisions delegated to individual cabinet members, or even officers, could still be taken in private.

Transparency has since been increased, through new regulations introduced in 2012 following passage of the 2011 Act, which now compel councils to hold *all* meetings in public, including those of cabinets or executives, other than in exceptional cases. The main requirements for openness in council decision-making under the LGA 2000 (as modified by the Local Government and Public Involvement in Health Act 2007 and the 2012 Regulations) are listed in Table 14.3.

Table 14.3 Changes to access-to-meetings criteria following recent legislation

	Change
1.	Executives/cabinets, full councils, committees, subcommittees, including overview and scrutiny committees/panels, to meet in public, subject to 'access to information' requirements under 1985 Act.
2.	Executives/cabinets may meet in private only if presence of public 'likely to result in council breaching legal obligation to third parties about keeping of confidential information' or 'lawful power used to exclude public to maintain orderly conduct or prevent misbehaviour at meeting'.
3.	Decisions of mayors/executive politicians and senior officers subject to 1985 Act— but 'written records' of their decisions must be published on council's website and at its offices.

To journalists and engaged local citizens, the need for the recent relaxation of privacy rules were self-evident. Because many significant decisions about policy formulation and implementation have been taken in cabinet in recent years—or even individually, by elected mayors, leaders, or cabinet members (and sometimes officers) with delegated powers—by holding such meetings privately, councils could stop the public finding out about plans until after the event. In February 2010, Woking Borough Council finalized the £68 million purchase of a shopping centre in a closed meeting—only revealing the fact in a statement afterwards on its website. The buyout relied on a loan from the Public Works Loan Board (PWLB) that would take the borough's taxpayers some 50 years to repay. Such practices are occurring, say critics, at a time when meetings that *are* still held in public—those of subcommittees, committees, and even the full councils—are being reduced to talking shops.

Under the revised rules, press and public also have rights to the following:

- three days' notice of open meetings;
- 'at least 28 clear days' notice' of any matter to be heard in private, to be published on the council's website and at its offices and confirmation of this intention at least five days before the meeting;
- agendas, minutes, and 'written statements' outlining key outcomes of meetings;
- registers of planning applications;
- records of payments to councillors;
- the council constitution, code of conduct, and standing orders;
- a statutory register of members' interests;
- copies of any reports into allegations of maladministration by the Local Government Commissioner (Ombudsman);
- the council's annual accounts, annual audit (including the right to inspect certain items), performance indicators, and future performance plans;

- general financial information; and
- the council's full annual report (including comparative data indicating how well it has performed as against 'similar authorities').

The order of business in local authority meetings

All meetings of councillors—whether committee, full council, or executive—follow the same format as the old system, as outlined in Table 14.4.

Several recent innovations have been introduced to make council meetings more transparent and accessible—many by individual authorities. It is now commonplace for councils to stream key meetings live on their websites and to provide archives of previous ones, to be viewed or re-viewed by journalists and the public at leisure. Meanwhile, town halls have been dragged into the social media age (under duress, in some cases) after Mr Pickles published a guide in June 2013 ordering them to allow press and public to tweet and blog from meetings, and to film or record proceedings for their own purposes. His decision to issue the guide followed repeated complaints from news organizations that councils were denying them these freedoms, all of which were formally introduced in the Local Authorities (Executive Arrangements) (Meetings and Access to Information)

Table 14.4 Order of business in council, committee, and subcommittee meetings

Order of business	What happens
Publication of agenda	Agenda—document outlining matters to be discussed and proposed order of business—prepared by council's chief executive, secretary, or director of administration and publicized in advance.
Approval of minutes	Meeting opens with formal approval of record of previous meeting.
Questions	Usually written down in advance by specific councillors, these are put to committee chairpersons. At full meetings of councils that have adopted a post-LGA 2000 constitution, questions are put to elected mayor, leader, or relevant cabinet member.
Public questions	Observers on public benches given chance to question committee chairpersons (optional).
Petitions	Any petitions from electors (e.g. over planning issue) presented to full council by councillors representing relevant ward or electoral division. Actual debates held at relevant later committee meetings.
Consideration of reports	In full council, reports from committees considered, while committees consider those of subcommittees. Debates often arise over 'political' matters: councillors with strong objections to given proposal may ask for it to be amended or 'referred back' to committee/cabinet.
Notices of motion	Individual councillors should table these in advance. They usually cover issues not formally listed on agenda. In LGA 2000-style councils, any notices impinging on executive issues must be referred to executive/cabinet for final decision.

(England) Regulations 2012. Wrexham Borough Council had reportedly banned the local *Daily Post* newspaper and bloggers from using Twitter in meetings, while Wirral Council tried to stop filming of its pensions committee on grounds of 'health and safety'—citing rules that the Health and Safety Executive (see Chapter 7, 'Workplace health and safety') swiftly dismissed as spurious. In the most extreme case, blogger Jacqui Thompson was handcuffed by police for filming a meeting of Carmarthenshire Council on her smartphone.

Local elections

Until 1974, local elections were held throughout the first week in May, but the Local Government Act 1972 stipulated that they occur on the first Thursday in May (unless the Home Secretary fixed another day, for example to avoid a clash with a general election). The Act also clarified that *all* councillors must be directly elected (until this point, archaic offices had remained in certain areas—for example 'aldermen', who were elected only by other councillors).

Each councillor is now elected for four years—except if voted in at by-elections resulting from the death of a sitting member, or his or her resignation or disqualification, in mid-term. Councillors elected in mid-term by-elections sit for the remaining terms of those they replace and stand for re-election at the same time as colleagues. If a councillor dies or otherwise leaves office after the September of a year preceding an election, however, his or her seat remains vacant until polling day (because it is considered too near the general poll to call a by-election).

Local authority constituencies

Councillors, like MPs, have their own constituencies (albeit covering far smaller geographical areas than parliamentary ones). Unlike Commons seats, however, those used in council elections have up to three representatives at a time.

The terms used to refer to these constituencies differ from one council type to another, as follows.

- 'County divisions'—or **electoral divisions**—are constituencies in county council elections in England and Wales. Some unitary authorities also use electoral divisions. They tend to be geographically bigger (and to represent more people) than those for other types of council.
- **Wards** are constituencies in districts or boroughs, metropolitan districts, London boroughs, and most unitaries. All Scottish councils have wards.

Whether wards or electoral divisions are represented by one, two, or three councillors is determined by their populations. Most urban wards contain roughly the same number of electors and, being based in towns, have fairly high populations. They are generally represented by three councillors. In rural electoral divisions and wards in mixed rural/urban areas, population levels can be significantly more varied—meaning that some have only one councillor, while others are designated 'multimember' divisions/wards, with up to three.

Since 31 December 2010, there have been 9,434 wards and electoral divisions in the UK, each covering an average population of 5,500. The table entitled 'The numbers of wards and electoral divisions in the UK', to be found on the **Online Resource Centre**, gives an overview of the number of wards and electoral divisions in each of the four countries of England, Wales, Scotland, and Northern Ireland.

Local authority election cycles

The precise election cycle followed by a council—that is, the years during which it holds its elections—depends on which 'type' it is. Present cycles in England are listed in Table 14.5.

Table 14.5 Electoral cycles for different types of English council

Type of local authority	Electoral cycle
County council	Every four years, with whole council retiring at same time. Elections last held in 2013, and due in 2017, 2021, etc.
London borough councils	Every four years—with whole council retiring simultaneously. To avoid conflicting with county polls, London boroughs hold elections in different years. Last held in 2014.
Metropolitan borough councils	Three out of every four years—one-third of councillors retire each time (usually one per ward). Elections never take place here in same year as county polls. Current cycle began in 2010.
District/borough councils	Choice of elections *either* three out of every four years, in which case, one-third of council retires each time, *or* every four years, for all councillors in one go. If districts/boroughs opt for former, electoral calendar is same as that for metropolitan districts. If they opt for latter, these are held midway between those of counties—in 2015, 2019, etc.
Unitary authorities	Choice of elections *either* three out of every four years *or* all in one go—with special arrangements in hybrid counties (see Chapter 11, 'The 1990s introduction of unitary authorities'). When new unitary authority is created by amalgamating pre-existing district and county, statutory order may be passed stating that new council should initially sit for *less than four years*—to stop elections clashing with future county ones.
Parish, town, and community councils	Every four years—whole council retires at same time, in 2015, 2019, etc. Each parish must have at least five councillors—but actual numbers are fixed by local district. Some follow ward-based system (like their parent authorities).

As illustrated above, local election cycles can confuse electors. This is especially true for those living in two-tier areas, who face them more often than most, given that they are covered by not one, but two councils: a district or borough and a county. In some areas, where district or borough and county elections are occasionally held in the same year, the process can be particularly baffling.

Among its many other innovations, the LGA 2000 envisaged councils' patchwork election cycles gradually being rationalized. It tried to facilitate this by recommending that they all adopt one of three models:

- whole-council elections *every four years*;
- half of councillors to stand *every two years*; or
- a third of the council stands in *three out of four years*.

Because it was left up to individual councils to decide when (and whether) to reform, little has come of these recommendations. In January 2004, following a lengthy consultation, the Electoral Commission warned that public confusion about electoral cycles was contributing to the general malaise afflicting local democracy, by further eroding turnouts already dwindling as a result of widespread political apathy. It cited research conducted in April 2003 by MORI, which found that a quarter of British people did not know whether elections were due to be held in their areas that May. Only one in six could say how often elections occurred locally. The findings prompted the Commission to make the following (as yet unimplemented) recommendations:

- all English councils should hold whole-council elections every four years; and
- counties and the Greater London Authority (GLA) should hold elections in different years from boroughs or districts, unitaries, metropolitan districts, and London boroughs.

Quite apart from their complexity, the present electoral cycles have produced curious quirks. Because individual districts or boroughs can choose whether to follow a whole-council election model or one in which votes are held in three out of four years, there are some counties in which, in any one year, elections may be held for a borough, district, county, and potentially even neighbouring unitary. By the same token, adjacent districts or boroughs may choose different cycles, meaning that (despite having the same responsibilities) they hold elections on the same day as each other only, at most, once every four years.

Happily, local election cycles in Scotland, Wales, and Northern Ireland are much simpler—with whole-council polls generally held for all authorities once every four years.

Table 14.6 Disqualifications for candidacy as a councillor

Category of person	Details of disqualification
Some bankrupts	Prospective candidates are barred if subject to bankruptcy restriction orders made by Insolvency Service—an executive agency of Department of Business, Innovation, and Skills (BIS). This means that they have acted dishonestly or in other 'blameworthy' way. In Northern Ireland, bar extends to anyone bankrupt; in Scotland, to anyone whose estate is sequestered.
Certain recent convicts	Those convicted of criminal offences with minimum three-month prison term during five years before election.
Electoral fraudster	Anyone convicted of corrupt/illegal election practice in previous five years.
Politically restricted officials	Those working for council for which they intend to stand or holding politically restricted post with any other authority (see Chapter 3, 'Political neutrality in practice'). Whitehall civil servants above 'Grade 7' may stand only with permission of employers (most senior ones banned).

Who can stand as a councillor?

As at general elections (see Chapter 4, 'General elections and candidacy—who can stand?'), any UK, Irish, or Commonwealth citizen normally resident in Britain and over the age of 18 on the day on which he or she is nominated may stand—provided that he or she can prove one of a range of verifiable connections with the local area and is not legally disqualified for any of the reasons listed in Table 14.6. There is no requirement for an election deposit.

Unlike at general elections, candidature is also open to European Union (EU) citizens who meet the same criteria. To be nominated, prospective councillors must obtain signatures from both *proposers* and *seconders*—who must be registered to vote in the relevant election. Candidates must also prove *at least one* of the following:

- they are legitimate electors listed on their local electoral registers (see Chapter 4, 'The British franchise today—who can vote?');
- they have lived locally for 12 months before the nomination process;
- their 'principal or only' places of work have been local for the whole preceding year; or
- they have owned property in the area for the whole preceding year.

'The eligibility of EU citizens to stand as councillors and the rather fluid test of 'residency' in a council's area make the qualifications for council candidates seem less stringent than those for prospective MPs. Unlike in general elections, this liberal attitude extends to peers with seats in the Lords, who, although barred from standing for the Commons, may become councillors. Labour peer and former minister Lord Bassam was, for a time in the 1990s, leader of Brighton and Hove Council.

Who can vote in local elections?

Only people whose names are on the local **electoral register** are entitled to vote. To be eligible for inclusion, a person must be:

- aged at least 18 or due to turn 18 during the 12-month period that the register covers (provided that this is by polling day);
- a UK, Commonwealth, Irish, or other EU citizen;
- normally resident in Britain, serving in the Armed Forces or as a merchant seaman, or a declared voluntary mental patient; and
- not barred because he or she:
  - is a foreign national from outside the EU or Commonwealth;
  - is a convict detained in prison or a mental institution; or
  - has been convicted within the previous five years of corrupt or illegal practices.

As with general elections, it is the electoral registration officer's responsibility to ensure that electoral registration forms are completed and, as of summer 2014, each adult has been expected to register individually—replacing the pre-existing household registration system (see Chapter 4, 'The British franchise today—who can vote?'). Anyone moving from one council area to another may have his or her name added to the register at the start of a given month under a 'rolling registration' system introduced in 2000.

The local election process

The procedure governing local elections is summarized in Table 14.7.

Of the various other rules governing conduct of elections, most notable are those limiting the sums that candidates are allowed to spend on campaigning. The spending cap was most recently raised in March 2005, by statutory instrument, at the Electoral Commission's request. Those standing as councillors may now spend £600 on campaign expenses and mayoral candidates, up to £2,000 (both sums are broadly equivalent to 5 pence per elector). The decision to more than double spending limits—council candidates had previously been forced to keep their expenditure below £242—was partly a belated response to the Representation of the People Act 1983, which, for the first time, required candidates to declare the financial value of 'benefits in kind' such as free stationery, offices, or other facilities. To ensure that limits are not exceeded, agents

Table 14.7 Local election procedure in Britain

Stage	Procedure
Notice of election	Must be published *at least 25 days before an election.*
Nomination papers submitted	To be handed in *by noon 19 days before the election.*
Publication of candidates list	Must be published *by noon on the 17th day before the election.*
Candidate withdrawals	This can happen *no later than 16 days before the election.*
Appointment of officials	Each council appoints returning officer to preside over election count (normally mayor/provost/chairperson, but role may be taken on day by 'acting'/"deputy' returning officer, usually chief executive). It is his/her responsibility to appoint presiding officers and poll clerks to attend polling stations during day, to supervise vote-counting, to rule on whether any ballot papers are 'spoiled', and to publish results.
Polling stations open	Usually based at local schools and community centres, these open from 8 a.m. to 9 p.m. at local elections.
Votes cast	When electors (or proxies) arrive at polling stations, their names are checked against register before ballot papers issued. If electors apply for postal votes, they must send them to designated place, not polling station.

must send inventories of their candidates' expenses to their returning officer after the poll.

Moves towards improving local election turnout

Dwindling engagement in local elections has long concerned UK governments. Compared to many EU countries, the turnout in Britain's local polls is extremely poor: in a 2000 survey by the then Office of the Deputy Prime Minister (ODPM), it came bottom of the European league, with an average turnout of just two out of five electors (a drop of 37 per cent since 1987). Between 2 million and 4 million people are estimated to be unregistered at any time—whether intentionally (to avoid Council Tax) or out of apathy.

New Labour, aided by the Commission, mooted several changes to boost turnout, but up to now these have been implemented in only a piecemeal way:

- introducing anonymous registration for those reluctant to have their names listed;
- opening polling stations at supermarkets, workplaces, colleges, doctors' surgeries, etc.;
- allowing voting over a period of days, rather than only one;
- introducing universal postal voting;

- electronic voting—via email, Internet, text messaging, etc.; and/or
- holding annual elections for at least a portion of each council, to make councils more accountable to electors by forcing them to campaign for votes continually.

The most 'successful' local elections—such as the 2008 and 2012 votes for London Mayor—are often viewed through the prism of what is happening on the national and global political stages, rather than as true tests of public opinion about the merits of local candidates and parties. Results of 'mid-term' local elections—those held partway through Parliaments, by which time voters are often disenchanted with serving governments—frequently send 'shots across their bows', and are consequently styled 'protest votes' by political commentators and pollsters. The 2008 local elections were an object lesson in protest voting: a week after Mr Brown's government had meekly pledged to compensate low-earners hit by the abolition of the 10 pence starting rate of income tax (many its own grass-roots voters), Labour polled its worst result for more than 40 years. It scored barely 24 per cent, coming one point behind the Lib Dems and 20 per cent shy of the Tories—a share that would have sent it to a crushing general election defeat. The success of the UK Independence Party (UKIP) in recent town-hall elections also signifies, to many, a generalized 'protest' against more mainstream political parties and mounting disaffection with the democratic process.

The task of reviewing the English councils' electoral arrangements—and overall structures or boundaries—was until recently the responsibility of a committee of the Boundary Committee for England, but in 2010 it was a replaced by a new dedicated **Local Government Boundary Commission for England (LGBCE)**. This carries out electoral reviews of all councils every few years to ensure that the numbers of electors represented by each councillor are broadly the same nationwide. It may also undertake discrete reviews for individual councils, such as newly established unitaries. There are separate local boundary commissions for Scotland and Wales, and a Local Government Boundaries Commissioner for Northern Ireland.

⠿ Topical feature idea

The following is an extract from the executive summary of Grant Thornton's independent audit of Bristol City Council's accounts to year end 31 March 2013. What questions are raised by the list of 'key issues' identified? What are the potential news angles that you might tease out of these brief comments and how would you research the detail needed to back them up? Overall, is this report a 'good' or 'bad news story' for the council?

Extract from Grant Thornton's independent audit of Bristol City Council's accounts, to year end 31 March 2013 (executive summary)

Key issues arising from our audit

Financial statements opinion

We anticipate providing an unqualified opinion on the financial statements. We have identified no adjustments affecting the Council's reported financial position (details are recorded in section 2 of this report). The draft financial statements recorded net expenditure of £465,689; the audited financial statements show net expenditure of the same. We have made a number of adjustments to improve the presentation of the financial statements. The key messages arising from our audit of the Council's financial statements are:

- The information provided by the financial system is not of sufficient detail to allow full reconciliation between the accounts and the general ledger. Excel spreadsheets are therefore used by Corporate Finance to perform this reconciliation.
- Some instances of delay were incurred due to lateness of information being provided which in one case was approximately two months after first being requested
- There continues to be a risk relating to the breadth of knowledge within the organization. A number of individuals are the sole point of contact and should they be unavailable this could potentially cause serious delays in future years. This has been agreed with the Chief Financial Officer to be addressed in future years.

Further details are set out in section 2 of this report.

Value for money conclusion

We are pleased to report that, based on our review of the Council's arrangements to secure economy, efficiency and effectiveness in its use of resources, we propose to give an unqualified VFM [value for money] conclusion. Further detail of our work on Value for Money is set out in section 3 of this report.

Whole of Government Accounts (WGA)

We will complete our work in respect of the Whole of Government Accounts in accordance with the national timetable. The submission deadline for WGA was revised to 14 August 2013 due to a delay in publishing of the template by the DCLG [Department for Communities and Local Government]. This deadline was not met due to software issues and this has been reported to the Audit Commission in line with national guidelines.

Source: **www.bristol.gov.uk**, © Grant Thornton UK LLP, 2013

✳ Current issues

- **Privatization of local government auditing** The Coalition scrapped the Audit Commission, replacing it with independent oversight of councils' accounts by private contractors. Ten regional franchises have since been awarded to four companies.
- **Continuing decline of voting in local elections** Less than a year before the 2015 general election, turnout in the May 2014 local elections was only 36 per cent—even lower than the recent average of 42.3 per cent.

- **Recording, tweeting, and blogging in council meetings** The Department for Communities and Local Government (DCLG) has issued firm new instructions ordering councils to let journalists and public blog and tweet from meetings, and to film or record them.

⸬ Key points

1. Councillors are elected for four-year terms, whatever the type of authority on which they serve, but electoral cycles vary from one to another. Counties hold elections once every four years, but districts or boroughs and unitaries may choose between this system or one in which a third of councillors are replaced in three out of every four years.

2. British, Commonwealth, Irish, or European Union citizens aged over 18 may stand for council elections, provided that they are not disqualified and can prove one of the following 'local connections': residency for the previous 12 months, a main or only place of work, ownership of property in the area, and/or registration on the electoral roll.

3. The media and public must be given 'reasonable accommodation' and allowed into council meetings unless it is dealing with information classed as 'confidential' or 'exempt', or a 'lawful order' is used to maintain order and prevent misbehaviour at the meeting. 'Confidential' covers details supplied by government relating to security and crime prevention, while 'exempt' usually relates to commercially sensitive information.

4. Councils must also routinely make other information public. This includes agendas and background papers for upcoming meetings, minutes of previous ones, information on councillors' allowances and expenses and senior officer pay, and monthly online disclosures of all spending and contracts put out to tender worth £500 or more.

5. Local citizens who believe that they may have a case against their council for maladministration can appeal to the Commissioner for Local Administration (the Local Government Ombudsman).

→ Further reading

Atkinson, H. (2012) *Local Democracy, Civic Engagement and Community: From New Labour to the Big Society*, Manchester: Manchester University Press. **Forward-looking assessment of the potential for improved democratic participation and civic engagement in the new age of localism.**

Bowles, N., Hamilton, J., and Levy, D .A. L. (2013) *Transparency in Politics and the Media: Accountability and Open Government*, London: I. B. Tauris. **Examination of the growing trend towards 'open government' and publication of data online by British and other Western governments.**

Johnston, R. and Pattie, C. (2006) *Putting Voters in Their Place: Geography and Elections in Great Britain*, Oxford: Oxford University Press. **Thoughtful examination of the geographical differences in voting and turnout patterns in local, national, and European elections. Examines the emergence of safe seats, and the roles of marginal wards and constituencies in winning polls.**

Pratchett, L. (2000) *Renewing Local Democracy? The Modernisation Agenda in British Local Government*, London: Frank Cass. **Still relevant assessment of the impact of 'New Labour' reform agenda, focusing on attempts to increase public participation in local democracy through mayoral elections and new forms of voting.**

 ## Online Resource Centre

www.oxfordtextbooks.co.uk/orc/Morrison4e/

Visit the Online Resource Centre that accompanies this book for web links and regular updates.

15

Local authorities and education

The one policy area that can compete for emotions with the National Health Service (NHS) is education. Whether it is local unrest over changes to school catchment areas, anger over disruption caused by striking teachers, reports about soaring undergraduate student debt, or the frantic scramble for university places through the clearing system each summer, the trials and tribulations of parents and pupils are seldom far from the media spotlight.

Although diluted in recent years, the involvement of local education authorities (LEAs) in this huge policy area stretches across all four 'phases' of the education process beyond preschool level: primary, secondary, further (or 'tertiary') education (FE), and higher education (HE). These are explained in Table 15.1.

In addition, LEAs are responsible for ensuring that suitable preschool education is available across their areas, through nurseries, registered childminders, and other recognized early-years childcare providers. This chapter examines each layer of state education in detail, beginning with perhaps the most important—and certainly the most controversial: schools.

▌ The origins of state schools and comprehensive education

For the uninitiated, today's school landscape is a complex and mind-boggling thing. State-funded schools can be run by their local councils, jointly overseen by LEAs and their own governors, or (as is increasingly the case) entirely 'self-governing'. Moreover, each of these categories embraces more than one type of state school. While those run by LEAs tend to be designated county, community, or 'comprehensives', some areas also retain academically selective grammars. Elsewhere, there are foundation and trust schools, which, although largely

Table 15.1 Structure of the British education system

Phase	Structure
Primary	Education in 'primary' subjects (e.g. English language, maths, basic history, science). Takes place in primary schools (ages 5–11) or infant (5–7) and junior schools (7–11). In some areas, children attend first schools (5–8/9), then middle schools (8/9–12/13).
Secondary	Education for 11–16-year-olds (or 13–16-year-olds in some areas) in core subjects such as English and maths, with increasing specialization in other areas after children take 'options' at age 13/14. Compulsory secondary education in England, Wales, and Northern Ireland leads to final assessment between ages of 14 and 16, through GCSEs and/or vocational diplomas. GCSEs awarded through mix of exams and coursework across eight grade bands: A*–G. In England, GCSEs in English, maths, and sciences to be replaced by new English Baccalaureate Certificate (EBac) from 2017.
	Scotland's GCSE equivalent is Standard Grade (levels 1–7). Standard grades take up first half of four-year National Qualification (NQ) programme, encompassing Scottish equivalent of gold standard pre-degree qualification in rest of UK, A levels (Scottish Higher).
	School-age qualifications and most taught in sixth forms/at FE level in England regulated by **Office of the Qualifications and Examinations Regulator (Ofqual)**, which also oversees vocational qualifications in Northern Ireland. These qualifications accorded a 'level' on National Qualifications Framework (NQF)—a form of 'credit transfer' system for accredited UK courses/exams. In Northern Ireland, school-age qualifications regulated by Council for the Curriculum, Examinations, and Assessment (CCEA); in Wales, in-house by Department for Children, Education, Lifelong Learning, and Skills (DCELLS); in Scotland, by Scottish Qualifications Authority (SQA).
Further education (FE)	'Sixth-form' education in chosen subjects to A level in England, Wales, and Northern Ireland, Advanced Subsidiary (AS) level (taken during first year of standard two-year A level course), vocational diploma, or International Baccalaureate (IB) (qualification widely taught outside UK).
	In Scotland, pupils study for intermediate-level certificates, followed by Scottish Highers.
	'Catch-up' tuition for less academic/those retaking GCSEs/Standard Grades also offered. BTEC National Diplomas, foundation degrees, and other practical, trade-based post-GCSE certificates often taught in school sixth forms, and at further education (FE), technical, or tertiary colleges.
Higher education (HE)	University education to degree—Bachelor of Arts (BA) and Bachelor of Science (BSc)—and postgraduate—Master of Arts (MA), Master of Science (MSc), Doctor of Philosophy (PhD)—level for those gaining requisite A levels or equivalent qualifications.

independent, are still partly overseen by councils. As for those fully self-governing schools, these can either be academies, free schools, or city technology colleges (CTCs).

Until Victorian times, things were very much simpler—if wholly inadequate from the point of view of providing an education for Britain's children. While the aristocracy and burgeoning middle class that emerged during the Industrial Revolution fostered a blossoming private education system for those who could afford it, there was little or no formal schooling for the offspring of the poor.

By the late nineteenth century, however, there was a growing clamour for government to provide basic across-the-board schooling for the nation's children. The foundation stone of the modern 'state school' system—or 'maintained sector'—was the Elementary Education Act 1870, which introduced nationwide *elementary schools*. The term 'elementary' is key: even at this stage, poorer children were offered only the most basic level of teaching and only up to the age of 13 (what would later be termed 'secondary school' level). Neither was even this guaranteed to be within the grasp of all families: local school boards charged up to 9d a week per child. While boards had discretion to waive fees for the poorest households, they could do so only for limited periods. It was with the Education Act 1891 that elementary education became free for most pupils, and not until 1918 that every last fee was abolished. This reform was initiated by county councils—which, as of 1901, were designated LEAs.

The path towards introducing secondary schools was even more protracted: not until the Education Act 1944 was there a nationwide system open to all children, regardless of parents' ability to pay. When the 1870 Act had been passed, the compulsory school age ended at 10 (despite the fact that elementary schools were prepared to teach them up to 13). The leaving age was increased incrementally—first to 11, then 13, then 14—by three subsequent Acts, in 1893, 1899, and 1918. But it was only Tory Education Minister Rab Butler's 1944 Act that introduced secondary schooling for all in England and Wales (a provision extended to Northern Ireland in 1947).

Despite the widespread welcome given to the new universal free secondaries, the Butler Act proved contentious. Its most controversial innovation was the introduction of not one, but three types of secondary school:

- **grammar (or selective) schools**—for the most academically gifted;
- secondary modern schools—a more standard alternative for the less able; and
- technical schools—offering a vocational, rather than academic, education.

Whether a child was admitted into one or other would depend on his or her performance in a new exam that he or she would sit at elementary school leaving age—known as the '11-plus'. This system came to be known as 'selection'. A chronology of key Education Acts can be found in the table entitled 'Timeline of major UK school reforms', to be found on the **Online Resource Centre** that accompanies this book.

Despite having introduced selection, Labour became increasingly opposed to it over time. One of its administrations—Harold Wilson's first, elected in 1964—came close to scrapping grammar schools altogether. Under the Conservative governments of the late 1950s and early 1960s, the number of non-selective secondary schools had gradually increased to cater for the post-war 'baby boom' generation. These schools—focusing on a broad-based academic education—eventually came to be known as **comprehensive schools**, high schools, community schools, and, in Scotland, 'academies' (not to be confused with their modern-day namesakes—see 'The growth of school autonomy—foundation schools, free schools, and the rise and rise of academies' in this chapter).

The number of grammars has since fallen dramatically, thanks to a slow attrition that began in the late 1960s. Between then and the late 1970s, successive Labour and Conservative governments engaged in a game of educational ping-pong over the future of grammars—with Labour instructing councils to abolish them and the Tories countermanding these orders—but by the time Mrs Thatcher became prime minister in 1979, a significant number remained.

In their mid-1960s heyday, there had been several hundred grammars, including 179 'direct grant' schools—fee-paying ones that agreed to take between a quarter and half of their pupils from poorer families in return for state subsidies. Today, there are 164 in England, spread over 10 LEA areas, including Devon, Kent, and Lincolnshire, and 68 in Northern Ireland. The Conservatives' traditional support for selection gave grammars a reprieve in the 1980s, although few new ones were established.

Nonetheless, the great selection debate has repeatedly resurfaced. Mrs Thatcher (an ex-grammar school pupil) did more than simply saving the 11-plus. In 1980, she introduced the 'assisted places scheme'—a means by which pupils from lower-income families who passed entrance exams for independent schools were entitled to state financial aid with tuition fees, according to a sliding scale.

Labour scrapped assisted places when it returned to power in 1997. Yet the 11-plus remains in many areas where it survived the 1970s, thanks to the more consensual way in which the party broached the issue of grammar schools under Tony Blair. Rather than abolishing them (and infuriating new-found middle-class supporters), the School Standards and Framework Act 1998 instead gave parents in areas in which they remained a ballot on whether the 166 English grammars then still standing should be kept or scrapped.

Labour's failure to make good on its long-standing pledge to abolish grammars infuriated many of its backbenchers, and rumblings of unease grew louder when it emerged that ministers were planning actually to *introduce* a degree of selection in academies and specialist schools (see 'The growth of school autonomy—foundation schools, free schools, and the rise and rise of academies' in this chapter).

But it was not only Labour's leadership that had trouble containing its back-benchers over the grammar school question. In 2006, then newly elected Tory leader David Cameron provoked a fight with party traditionalists by announcing that a future Conservative government would not found new grammars. He later climbed down, however—reassuring diehard '11-plus' supporters that a Tory government *would* sanction more grammars in areas where they already existed and there was enough demand.

Sure enough, by subtly rewording the School Admissions Code—the rulebook governing the allocation of school places to children in the state sector—then Coalition Education Secretary Michael Gove paved the way for Kent County Council to approve the first expansion of a grammar school in 50 years. The rewritten Code, introduced on 1 February 2012, contains a clause allowing oversubscribed state schools (whatever their category) to expand beyond their existing boundaries, and prompted Kent councillors (backed by parents) to approve a new 'satellite school' in Sevenoaks as an overflow for oversubscribed grammars elsewhere in the area. However, in December 2013, this 'super-grammar' plan hit the buffers, when 'a Department for Education (DfE) agency, the Education Funding Agency, blocked two rival bids to open the new 1,300-place 'annex' on the grounds that it would constitute an entirely new grammar school, rather than an extension of an existing one.

Meanwhile, philosophical and pedagogic debates about the 'grammar school ideal' continue to rage. While advocates of academic selection have long argued that it can be an engine for social mobility—giving 'bright' pupils from poorer families a leg up, when they might otherwise have been held back by second-rate educations in larger, mixed-ability comprehensives—an academic study published in May 2014 found strong evidence that former grammar school pupils consistently earned significantly more than their bright peers from comprehensives and concluded that academic selection contributed to making society less equal. Its findings echoed an outspoken remark the previous year by Chief Inspector of Schools Sir Michael Wilshaw, who advised ministers to resist the temptation to expand grammar schools, which he described as 'stuffed full' with middle-class children and failing to improve social mobility. Inequalities in educational opportunity fostered by the grammar school system are arguably worsened by the fact that grammars no longer exist in inner cities and other deprived areas, with those surviving generally concentrated in more prosperous middle-class locales.

Concern about the potential for schooling to widen social inequality were also aired by education charity the Sutton Trust in a July 2014 report, revealing that, by the age of 42, adults who were privately educated have earned £57,000 more than those taught in the state sector. The Trust proposed an 'open access' system, which would see the brightest children admitted to independent schools, whatever their backgrounds, with parents charged fees on a sliding scale according to their means and the government paying for those whose families cannot afford them. Sir Peter Lampl, the Trust's chairman, estimated that the cost of the scheme to taxpayers would be £215 million.

◗ The 1988 Act—and the birth of 'independent' state schools

Just as it turned its back on 40 years of consensus over health policy by introducing the NHS 'internal market' (see Chapter 6, 'The end of the post-war consensus and the birth of NHS markets'), in 1988 Mrs Thatcher's Conservative government initiated the most profound change in the state education system since the dawn of comprehensives. The Education Reform Act 1988 marked the culmination of the 'Great Debate' of the early Thatcher years—revolutionizing how many primary and secondary schools were managed by liberating them from LEAs, and giving parents and teachers more say in their day-to-day running than ever. It also polarized political opinion between people who viewed the transfer of power from councils to citizens as a triumph of 'localism' over bureaucratic interference, and those who saw in it a recipe for postcode lotteries and fragmentation of the universal ideal. Debate over how far to increase school autonomy continues to dominate the education agenda in England to this day (see 'The growth of school autonomy—foundation schools, free schools, and the rise and rise of academies' in this chapter).

Until 1988, the designation 'independent schools' was used as an umbrella term for private sector fee-paying schools: 'private schools' and older, more exclusive, 'public schools' such as Eton. What the 1988 Act did was introduce the concept of independent *governance* to schools in the *state* sector. Schools would be offered the opportunity to 'opt out' of LEA control—in much the same way as general practitioners (GPs) could become independent fundholders (see Chapter 6, 'The end of the post-war consensus and the birth of NHS markets'). Schools opting out would be 'grant-maintained' (GM)—autonomous in terms of admissions, staffing, and spending, and funded by direct grants from central government. The Tories were handing them de facto independent status (albeit without the freedom to charge fees) in the name of a new form of localism directly aimed at ordinary citizens, rather than councillors elected to discharge it on their behalf. The underpinning philosophy—a foretaste of Mr Cameron's 'Big Society' (see Chapter 13, 'Cameron's "Big Society"—what role for councillors and officers now?')—was that decisions on running vital public services such as education, health, and social care should be placed in the hands of the individuals who *used* or staffed them, rather than politicians or bureaucrats. The main provisions of the 1988 Act are outlined in Table 15.2.

Table 15.2 Main provisions of the Education Reform Act 1988

Reform	Effect
Introduction of grant-maintained (GM) schools	Primary and secondary schools with 300-plus pupils could 'opt out' of LEA control, becoming GM schools. Initially, entitlement was a 'reward' for high-performing schools (those with high numbers of pupils attaining five-plus A–C GCSEs), but aim was to extend to most schools. GM schools could set staff pay/conditions and decide admissions policies. They received direct grants towards running costs, and could apply for capital funding for new equipment/buildings and repairs.
Local Management of Schools (LMS)	Day-to-day financial decisions and full autonomy over staff recruitment delegated to GM heads, working with boards of governors. LEA-run schools also given greater leeway than before, with heads redefined more as managers than educators, and governors given shared autonomy to hire and fire staff (although LEA remained employer).
Introduction of **National Curriculum (NC)**	Dictated not only key subjects that all schoolchildren must be taught/offered, but also core skills/content covered (e.g. basic spelling and punctuation). Curriculum to cover broadly same content throughout England and Wales, up to and including GCSEs, with exams at 'Key Stages' 1, 2, and 3 (ages 7, 11, and 14), through NC assessments or **Standard Attainment Tests (Sats)**. Welsh Assembly has authority to make slight adjustments in Wales—with Welsh language compulsory in all state schools, alongside English.
Launch of Key Stages (KS)	Formal stages introduced by which each pupil expected to attain objectives ('key stages'). Normally established through testing/continuous assessment.
Emergence of parent choice	First signs of 'choice' introduced in school admissions process, with parents allowed to specify which local school they wanted children to attend.
First school league tables	Publication of school exam results—intended to provide 'objective' information on school performance for parents considering where to send children. Attention today focuses on comparative data relating to truancy, exclusions, and performance in external exams—primarily GCSEs, to benchmark how many children achieve five 'good' passes (A*–C). Since 2007, A*–C grades recorded by all schools for league table purposes—excluding academies—have had to include English language and maths, following criticism that many top grades were obtained by children studying 'easier' subjects.
Introduction of city technology colleges (CTCs)	New generation of specialist schools established, geared to needs of industry and technology sector, with private companies invited to sponsor them. Most later became academies.

The Local Management of Schools (LMS) scheme that supported GM schools proved divisive. The element of selection introduced by some popular schools to simplify the admissions procedures and to cherry-pick 'academic' applicants was seen to favour children with educated, professional parents and to discriminate against those from disadvantaged backgrounds, and critics argued that it would worsen existing inequalities between schools. The ability of head teachers and governors to set their own pay scales to headhunt the 'best' staff was seen to compound this problem: by poaching high-performing teachers from LEA-run schools, or ones with poorer results, they would make their own schools yet more 'successful', further impoverishing those already struggling. To top it all, government money followed high-performing schools—rewarding them with bonuses and extra freedoms, and fast-tracking grant allocations for GM head teachers.

Although it would adopt its own version of LMS after regaining power, Labour initially opposed the 1988 reforms. All the more embarrassing for Mr Blair, then, when it emerged in 1995 that his eldest son, Euan, attended the London Oratory, a Roman Catholic GM school—while Harriet Harman, Labour's then health spokesperson, was sending one of her sons to the same school and her other, to a grammar.

To some opponents, the idea of introducing 'parent choice' into the GM schools equation set the final seal on an emerging 'two-tier' state system. If parents could choose between rival local schools, who in their right mind would opt for the one with worse results and fewer resources? As high-performing schools became richer and yet *more* successful, less popular ones were likely to fall further behind and become 'poorer'. Moreover, successful schools had only limited ability to expand to take in growing numbers of applicants and their vested interest in favouring those most likely to succeed might tempt them to become more selective. A summary of arguments for and against schools opting out of LEA control can be found in Table 15.3.

The first school to gain GM status was Skegness Grammar School, in 1988. By the time GM schools were abolished (in name at least) in 1998, there were nearly 1,100 nationwide—three out of five at secondary level.

City technology colleges (CTCs) and the rise of specialist schools

Although pedants might point to post-war technical schools as early examples of secondaries specializing in specific disciplines (in their cases, practical subjects such as carpentry), the birth of **specialist schools** per se came decades later. Reviving the notion that some children are more predisposed towards vocational subjects than academic ones, the 1988 Act saw the Conservatives introduce a new generation of 'technical schools'.

Table 15.3 Arguments for and against state schools being allowed to 'opt out'

For	Against
Parents know what is best for their children. Giving them direct input into running schools enables them to customize teaching to suit individual children's needs, replacing a bureaucratic 'one size fits all' approach.	Allowing schools to become self-governing worsens inequalities in state system. Given budgetary control, schools poach 'best' teachers/pupils from elsewhere—widening gap between 'successful' and 'failing' schools.
Giving head teachers and governors (parents, teachers, and members of community) more power gives them a sense of 'ownership' of the school. Ownership increases determination to drive up standards.	Giving schools control of own disciplinary procedures, staff recruitment, and budget decisions breeds huge inconsistencies in nature/quality of provision across sector. How long before they can select brightest pupils—or use 'social selection' to do so by back door?
LEAs are unwieldy and bureaucratic, and slow to take decisions. Empowering governors and head teachers speeds up decision-making by 'cutting out middleman'.	LEAs are run by elected councillors and therefore accountable to community at ballot box. School governors accountable to no one but parents of children already attending those schools, and 'responsible' only to those families. Who will stop them taking decisions that adversely affect other schools?

From the outset, these secondary schools-cum-sixth-form-colleges—**city technology colleges (CTCs)**—were distinct from anything before them. Inspired by the US experience of involving business and industry sponsors through 'charter schools', CTCs saw private companies become involved not only in funding buildings and equipment, but also, controversially, day-to-day decisions about their governance. Rather than focusing entirely on teaching practical subjects, they still offered children up to the age of 16 all of the usual subjects. *In addition* to this, however, they were equipped with particular specialisms in science, maths, the then emerging field of information technology (IT), and other disciplines.

But the defining characteristic was the extent of private sector involvement. In capital terms, private sponsors financed up front the expansion and refurbishment of existing schools—and the construction of new ones—in return for long-term leaseback agreements that would make their investments profitable over time. This was one of the first tangible manifestations of the Tories' new 'big idea' for funding expensive public projects, the private finance initiative (PFI—see Chapter 7, 'Private finance initiatives (PFIs) and public–private partnerships (PPPs)'). But the sponsorship arrangements went deeper than this: companies investing in CTCs were given seats on their governing boards. To the horror of some, certain schools even incorporated the names of sponsoring companies into their official titles and logos. The first CTCs were set up in Kingshurst, Birmingham, and Nottingham. But the most controversial early opening—and the first to incorporate the name of its sponsor so brazenly—was

Dixons Bradford CTC, funded by the high-street electrical retailer. The college, which opened in 1990, later converted into an academy. At time of writing, only three CTCs remained: BRIT School, Croydon; Emmanuel CTC, Gateshead; and Thomas Telford School, Telford and Wrekin.

The purpose of CTCs was not solely to provide an education geared to the changing demands of industry. By granting them a degree of independence commensurate with that offered to GM schools, ministers were giving head teachers a decisive say in running their schools—with the quid pro quo that underperformance would be questioned by their increasingly influential governors. Governing boards—far from being old-style talking shops, there for LEAs to 'consult', but otherwise ignore—gave parents, teachers, local residents, and business people a direct say in school management for the first time. This model of governance would, in time, become the norm.

In a further echo of the old tripartite system, Mr Gove introduced a new swathe of **university technical colleges (UTCs)** aimed at children aged 14 and over. Again privately sponsored, their aim is to train future generations of plumbers, electricians, and mechanics—ending what Coalition ministers decried as 'dead-end' vocational courses in favour of hard skills better suited to reviving Britain's flagging industrial fortunes. To inculcate a work ethic among students, UTCs generally eschew the customary 9 a.m.–3 p.m. school day in favour of 'business hours', holding classes for an extra two weeks a year beyond the length of the usual school calendar. Each UTC focuses on one or two technical specialisms, and is expected to work alongside local businesses and a local university, dedicating at least 40 per cent of its time to activities related to its specialism(s), involving design and building, teamwork, and problem-solving. By September 2014, there were already 17 UTCs in place, with another 30 expected to open their doors by 2016.

The growth of school autonomy—foundation schools, free schools, and the rise and rise of academies

Mr Blair's election in 1997 owed much to his 'education, education, education' rallying cry—and his pledge to improve school standards and opportunities for children from all backgrounds. Labour had opposed both CTCs and the principle of schools 'opting out' of LEA control in opposition. But, as in the NHS, it was not long before it was converted into championing specialist schools, the PFI—which it renamed public–private partnerships (PPPs)—and the concept of school autonomy.

New Labour left the state school landscape more fragmented than it found it. The School Standards and Framework Act 1998 converted all existing GM schools into **foundation schools**. Its immediate effect was to bring them back under some measure of LEA control—to the extent that, rather than continuing to be funded direct by government, they would receive grants channelled through councils. In practice, however, the sums allocated to each foundation school would largely be determined by Whitehall, and in many respects they retained an independence akin to that wielded by GM schools beforehand. The land and buildings occupied by foundation schools are owned by their governing boards (unless ownership has been handed, or the school has historically belonged, to a charitable foundation), and although banned from selecting, they control their own admissions policies. They can also hire and fire their own staff, rather than relying on councils to recruit on their behalf.

The most controversial extension of autonomy was the second: if schools were to be allowed to decide which pupils to admit and exclude, critics argued, would this not reintroduce selection by the back door? A layer of complication was added to the debate when, in Mr Blair's final months in office, the Education and Inspections Act 2006 introduced **trust schools**. Trust status—a term borrowed, like 'foundation', from the NHS—has since been offered to foundation schools that set up charitable trusts to manage their affairs. These trusts employ their own staff, manage their own assets, and set their own admissions policies. Within a year, 300 foundation schools were in the process of converting into trusts, and a number have since been formed through the merger of two or more schools, or takeovers of 'failing' schools by more successful ones. Trust schools were not generally offered any additional funding as incentives to convert—nor were they allowed to 'opt out' of local authority control to any greater extent than foundation schools—but in December 2007 then Schools Secretary Ed Balls offered 'sweeteners' to encourage high-performing schools to team up with less successful ones, including the promise of £300,000 cash injections to smooth over the process. The idea of multiple schools 'clubbing together' under the same head teacher and board was extended further by Labour in later years, through the introduction of 'federations'—a form of shared governance, like trust status, open to both primary and secondary schools.

Alongside foundation schools, the 1998 Act retained two other principal types of secondary school: community schools and voluntary schools. **Community school** is the umbrella term for all 'ordinary' state primaries and comprehensives; councils continue to own and maintain their infrastructure, to determine admissions policies, and to recruit staff. Before the 1998 Act, standard primary and comprehensive (or 'high') schools had for some time been known as 'county schools'. Some community schools were renamed community *colleges*, reflecting the fact that, in addition to teaching the National Curriculum, they also offered adult education and training (normally through evening classes) like that provided elsewhere by FE and tertiary colleges.

Voluntary schools are (as their name suggests) stalwarts of earlier times, normally linked to either the Church of England or Roman Catholic (RC) Church. They are divided into two types: *voluntary aided schools* and *voluntary controlled schools*. The former operate from premises owned by either a church or charitable foundation, but receive all of their revenue funding and up to 50 per cent of their capital outlay from central government, in return for teaching the National Curriculum and offering free school places. As with foundation schools, however, their governing boards may determine their admissions and staffing policies. The principal difference between aided and controlled schools is that, in the latter case, the LEA controls admissions and staffing procedures in return for providing all of the funding. Although the term 'voluntary school' is not generally used in Scotland, since the Education Act 1918 it has been commonplace for secondary schools to specify a denominational bias, with a number labelling themselves 'RC schools'.

The emergence of academies—and return of specialist schools

The most significant additional change to state school designations under New Labour was its conversion to the twin ideas of specialization and independent management. The Learning and Skills Act 2000 introduced 'city academies'—schools with state-of-the-art buildings and facilities, part-funded by private sponsors, targeted at poorer postcode areas. They were allowed both to specialize in key subjects geared to the demands of their local communities and to manage their own affairs (including admissions). Some traditionalists saw in this policy a direct contradiction of the party's initial opposition to CTCs, and betrayal of the ideals of state schooling being entirely funded and managed both within and *by* the public sector. Pragmatists such as Mr Blair and then Education Secretary David Blunkett saw it as a way of pumping much-needed resources into deprived areas more quickly than if government were to finance the investment single-handedly, while equipping previously disadvantaged youngsters with the skills demanded by modern industry.

In their early years, **academies** (as they were later renamed) strongly resembled CTCs. Buildings and amenities received significant boosts from private capital, in return for complex PFI/PPP leaseback arrangements and often a stake for sponsoring companies in the running of the schools. For some, this was to be an 'arm's-length' arrangement—a presence on the governing board and consultation over expansions or mergers—but, for others, it became more hands on. Towards the end of Labour's tenure, private investors often became directly involved in the day-to-day staffing of ancillary functions such as administration, security, maintenance, and/or catering at academies such as William Hulme's Grammar School in Manchester. Pupils attending academies (as with CTCs) often work longer days than children in other schools and/or between different term dates. Unlike CTCs, however, they have not tended to specialize in scientific, business, or technological subjects: if their local communities lack adequate sports facilities, or there are demands for people with specific skills, these factors have generally determined their specialisms.

Perhaps the most controversial 'privilege' granted to academies under Labour was their qualified exemption from a cornerstone of the party's traditional education policy: its opposition to selection. From the outset, academies were permitted to select one in 10 pupils on the basis of 'aptitude' in their specialist subjects. The choice of this word—tortuously distinguished from 'ability' by ministers—caused considerable controversy (and bemusement). Labour appeared to be walking a tightrope between offering some head teachers the autonomy that they craved to introduce limited selection and distancing itself from the Conservatives' customary support for selective schools. In drawing what many saw as an artificial distinction between a pupil's 'potential' to do well in a subject (his or her 'aptitude') and his or her proven 'ability' in it, however, ministers left many head teachers nursing headaches. In 2003, the House of Commons Education and Skills Select Committee recommended tests be scrapped, arguing that the government had failed to clearly define 'aptitude'. Ministers countered that the aim of introducing limited selection was to identify pupils who 'would benefit from' accessing a specialism.

Arguments about autonomy aside, the rise and fall of CTCs, and their later metamorphosis into academies, was in many ways the latest manifestation of a decades-old debate about the wisdom of dividing pupils into 'academic' and 'practical', and gearing education towards the *needs of industry* as well as the *aspirations of young people* keen to develop their intellects more widely. In earlier times, this debate had led to the schism between Left and Right over grammar schools; more recently, it has been played out in arguments over the introduction of new qualifications covering vocational disciplines. Since September 2008, 14–19-year-olds have had the option of studying for vocational diplomas covering subjects as varied as health and social care, creative media, and engineering, in addition to—or instead of—GCSEs and/or A levels.

Indeed, the specialization reintroduced under the academies programme is far from confined to those schools today. During the second and third Labour terms, it became so prevalent in the state sector that 3,000 secondary schools (nearly nine out of 10) now specialize in one or more subjects—meaning that the oft-used label 'specialist school' is less a separate *category* than an umbrella term embracing all schools with a specialism. A council-run community school is just as likely to specialize as an academy or one managed by a trust. Achieving specialist status under Labour earned schools significant injections of capital and revenue to support the development of their curriculums (up to an extra £100,000-plus each year in capital grants, plus an additional £130 per pupil). In return, specialist schools were expected to make their improved amenities available to neighbouring schools and community groups. Like academies, many specialist schools were permitted to select one in 10 pupils based on their aptitude in a relevant subject, but only if they specialized in languages, performing and visual arts, or sport. Schools that could, over time, demonstrate improvements in academic performance in their specialist subjects were able to apply for 'high-performing specialist school' status. By the time Labour left office, 900-odd schools (or 30 per cent of those with specialisms) had achieved this.

The Coalition has ended the process of recognizing new specialisms, although existing specialist schools continue to operate. Mr Gove removed the need for schools to apply formally to be designated (or redesignated) 'specialist', rerouted funds for specialist schools through the mainstream dedicated schools grant (DSG—see Chapter 11, 'Types of revenue grant'), and abolished the quangos that previously channelled money to them.

Mr Gove's academies 'revolution'

Labour's original academies programme was meant to prioritize 'failing' comprehensives—principally those in deprived areas—using PPPs to funnel capital into rejuvenating their existing facilities or building new schools from scratch. After a sluggish start, the number of academies grew steadily—rising to 203 by 2010. In Labour's third term, academies' greatest advocate, then Education Minister Lord Adonis, invited private schools struggling to meet recruitment targets as a result of growing competition to consider converting into academies. Several, including Belvedere School in Liverpool and Bristol Cathedral School, subsequently did. Meanwhile, applications for academy status were increasingly being granted to less obviously 'struggling' schools and/or those in more affluent areas.

But the arrival of Conservative Education Secretary Mr Gove heralded both a dramatic acceleration in the rollout of academies and a significantly more liberal attitude towards the kinds of school that qualified. Almost immediately, he wrote to the head teachers of every English primary and secondary, inviting them to convert. Under the ensuing Academies Act, rushed through the Commons before the 2010 summer recess, schools rated 'outstanding' by Ofsted could be 'fast-tracked' by that September—although any currently falling under the auspices of a foundation, trust, charity, church, or other faith group would need their consent before converting. In the event, only around 32 new academies were ready to open by the autumn term.

If take-up initially appeared sluggish, this was to change dramatically. In a pincer movement designed to boost massively the number of academies, Mr Gove reiterated that all 'outstanding' schools should consider themselves 'pre-approved' for academy status, while the 2010 Act gave him new powers effectively to *force* 'failing' schools (those placed in 'special measures' by Ofsted—see 'Monitoring school standards—and the great "parent choice" debate' in this chapter) to convert, without consulting their governing LEAs. A further liberty granted to 'outstanding' schools (and 'good' schools with 'outstanding' features) was an exemption from the customary requirement for prospective academies to first secure sponsors. An explicit distinction was thus made between old-style *sponsored academies*—a status that continues to be accorded to 'failing' schools required to adopt academy status—and new 'successful' *converter academies* that proactively opt out of LEA control in pursuit of greater independence.

Mr Gove's reforms had the desired effect. With heads of outstanding schools required to demonstrate only a commitment to work with other ('struggling') providers to raise standards, and those floundering at the bottom left with no option but to find sponsors and convert, the result was an unprecedented surge in academy numbers. By April 2013, the number of pupils taught in academies had topped 2 million, while 3,444 had opened by that November—a 17-fold increase on the number inherited from Labour. And there were signs of a surge in primary school conversions, too—with 400 forced to become academies in 2013 alone for failing to hit government exam performance targets.

The mass rollout of academies has not been without its controversies. As a mark of their new-found financial freedoms, the 2010 Act included a provision enabling academies to boost their revenue budgets by acquiring direct access to the 10 per cent of central government funding for each state school (academies included) currently still spent by LEAs collectively on their behalf. This provoked immediate criticisms from LEAs and teachers' unions, who argued that it would dilute the communal 'pools' of funding reserved for council-wide school services, including help for pupils with special educational needs (SENs) not attending academies.

There has also been resistance from some 'failing' schools that the government has ordered to convert. Downhills Primary School in Haringey, north London, became a media cause célèbre early in 2012 after teachers, parents, and local member of Parliament (MP) David Lammy (a former pupil) united in protest against Mr Gove's instruction for it to become an academy, following a critical 2010 Ofsted report in which it was ordered to make 'significant improvement'. Under pressure from Mr Gove, the school reluctantly agreed to a further Ofsted inspection, but when it was subsequently placed in 'special measures', its head, Leslie Church, resigned and the school relented.

Making good on his promise to allow heads of newly established academies significant additional freedoms, Mr Gove allowed them to partner other public and private sector organizations, and (like those already established) lengthen their school days and terms, and set their own pay and working conditions. Perhaps most contentious, however, has been his decision to 'disapply' the National Curriculum that his own party introduced in the 1980s for these new academies—exempting them from teaching the same core subjects, in broadly the same ways and stages, as all other state schools. Significantly, the academies established under Labour, although allowed some freedom to deliver the Curriculum as they saw fit, still broadly framed their teaching around it.

A further controversy is the fact that, unlike LEA-run schools, academies are automatically designated charities—a status conferring various privileges, including generous tax breaks. More contentious still is the fact that, unlike other charitable organizations, they have 'exempt' charity status, meaning that they are not overseen by the charities regulator, the Charity Commission.

More seriously, nearly 15 years after academies first appeared, evidence that they perform any better academically than other types of schools remains patchy. In September 2009, at the end of his final academic year as Schools Secretary, Mr Balls announced that GCSE results for academies had improved by more than twice the national average rate in the preceding 12 months. But critics pointed to less rosy examples and the fact Labour's academies were exempt from the Freedom of Information Act 2000 until January 2011 (September 2010 in the case of those established by the Coalition), making it impossible to judge how well they had performed compared to other secondary schools, because their pupils might have been achieving top grades in 'easier' subjects (see Chapter 20, 'Academies'). Proof that self-governing status does not necessarily beget improved performance came in November 2013, when the DfE sent 34 academies 'pre-warning' letters, threatening to 'sack' their existing sponsors if they failed to improve the schools' 'stubbornly low' results.

Table 15.4 outlines the main types of state school at time of writing.

Extending self-determination—the arrival of free schools

Creating academies is but one element of the Coalition's mission to reshape the school system. Shortly after inviting all state schools in England and Wales to apply for academy status in 2010, Mr Gove wrote a second letter—this time to LEA chief

Table 15.4 Main types of state school

School type	Description
Community school/ college	Primary and secondary ('comprehensive') schools run directly by LEAs; community colleges offer evening classes for adults, as well as daytime teaching
Foundation	Largely self-governing, but funds directed via LEA
Trust	Foundation schools with independent trusts managing finances/policies at 'arm's length'
Free	Fully self-governing, charitable primary/secondary providers set up by parents/teachers/communities in locations without sufficient 'good quality' schools
Academy	Fully 'independent' state schools, sponsored by business/ charity/other school; can deviate from National Curriculum and are charities; can select up to 10 per cent of pupils based on 'aptitude'
Special	Dedicated to children with 'special educational needs' (SENs)
Voluntary aided/ controlled	Schools operating from church/charity-owned premises; 'aided' schools set own policies and employ own staff, but 'controlled' schools part-run by LEAs
Faith	Overall terms for schools established by faith groups, including non-Christian ones such as Muslim, Hindu, and Jewish

executives and children's services directors—detailing how charities, universities, and other interested parties (including groups of teachers, governors, and/ or parents) could found *their own schools* in areas lacking 'good quality' extant provision. Like academies, these **free schools** would be run independently of LEAs and allowed to decide their own curriculums. They would also have to admit children of all abilities and be non-selective. The resulting programme, a hybrid of a profit-based 'free school' model that originated in Sweden and the US charter school approach that originally inspired academies, aims to:

- respond to parental demand in areas in which 'good quality' schools exist, by making it easier or quicker to establish new ones; and
- promote hands-on involvement by parents, teachers, and local business-people in developing the ethos, teaching methods, and outcomes of their schools, to foster greater community involvement in place of what the Coalition portrayed as intrusive and controlling state intervention.

Mindful of early scepticism about the logistical hurdles that busy parents might face with the nitty-gritty of setting up their own schools, Mr Gove hired project managers to offer professional guidance through the New Schools Network—a charity established to promote social mobility by means of flexible models of state education. The Coalition also relaxed council planning policies to enable school-building programmes to be fast-tracked, with £50 million immediately diverted from Labour's Harnessing Technology Grant fund to provide up-front capital finance for free schools.

While some critics predicted that Mr Gove's offer would be met with silence (he himself forecast that he would be lucky to see 16 launched in the first year), demand quickly picked up, with 24 start-ups opening their doors in September 2011. Within two years, 174 had opened across England—a figure reached after a doubling of numbers in the year to September 2013 alone. With a further 115 already in the pipeline, February 2014 saw Mr Gove controversially relax the rules governing new school start-ups, to allow proposers of free schools up to three attempts a year, rather than only one, to apply for funding successfully.

Among the most high-profile free schools is the West London Free School, Hammersmith—brainchild of a 400-strong consortium of parents headed by journalist Toby Young, whose father, late Labour peer Lord Young, was, ironically, an architect of the comprehensive system critics accused Mr Gove of dismantling. By summer 2012, the school was able to boast of receiving nine applications for each of the 120 places available in that September's intake. Other prominent free school backers have included glamour model Katie Price (although her consortium's bid was rejected) and Oscar-winning actress Dame Helen Mirren, who fronted a successful campaign for a new secondary school in Wapping, east London.

Opponents of the scheme, initially including Labour, have warned that it will create a two-tier system—with 'pushy middle-class parents' exploiting the new freedoms to set up schools dominated by children from similar households, while families in poorer areas (where new and better schools may well be needed) might lack the skills or confidence to mobilize demand for them. Others argued that it is folly to establish free schools in areas in which there is no shortage of 'good' providers already—simply because some people want them—when their introduction might generate surplus places and jeopardize existing providers. In April 2012, the National Union of Teachers (NUT) warned that, contrary to ministerial assurances, in practice free schools were increasingly being approved in areas with no shortage of places—and having a 'negative impact on existing good or outstanding local schools'. Among the towns and cities adversely affected was Bristol, where the opening of a free school had left four head teachers struggling to fill 300 empty places, at a cost to the LEA of £450 a year per place. And in a counterproductive step even by ministers' own standards, academies were also said to be suffering—with one in Beccles, Suffolk, facing a 15 per cent budget cut because of the loss of potential pupils to a neighbouring free school.

Another criticism of free schools concerns the freedom granted them to employ teachers without formal qualifications—a liberty that Mr Gove extended to academies. By April 2014, 6 per cent (or 8,000) of the 141,000-strong teaching staff working in free schools or academies did not have qualified teaching status (QTS), prompting accusations from teaching unions that staff were being hired 'on the cheap'. Mounting opposition to this policy saw both Labour and the Liberal Democrats pledge to ban unqualified staff from working as teachers in state schools if re-elected in 2015.

Thorniest of all, however, is the ongoing question of whether free schools should be allowed to operate *more* 'freely'—in essence, like fully fledged private companies. They are already permitted to employ US-style 'educational management organizations' (EMOs) to oversee their day-to-day management—and these may operate for profit. Concerns that Mr Gove had been nurturing a private desire to move towards profit-making free schools— despite earlier news stories suggesting that the Lib Dems had forced him to drop any such aspiration—were revived when, in his May 2012 evidence to the Leveson Inquiry (see Chapter 3, 'Press'), he let slip that they might be allowed to 'move toward' becoming fully fledged commercial concerns if the Tories were to win the 2015 election. His words—condemned by unions, but backed by Sir David Bell, a former chief schools inspector and permanent secretary at the DfE—came against a growing backdrop of concern about the long-term effectiveness of the free school model, even in Sweden, where free schools were pioneered in the early 1990s. A report by the Organisation for Economic Co-operation and Development (OECD), published in December 2010—just as Mr Gove was inviting the first round of British free school bids—had found that between 2000 and 2009 Swedish schoolchildren had dropped from 9th to 19th for literacy, and 17th to 24th in maths, in a league table of 57 countries. Critics claimed that part of the reason for the decline was cost-cutting at profit-making free schools, which often employed unqualified teachers and trainees.

Reviewing the curriculum—the future of teaching

In June 2012, Mr Gove announced a wide-ranging review of the primary school curriculum, placing renewed emphasis on teaching traditional subjects, primarily the 'three Rs'—'reading, writing, and (a)rithmetic'—and rote-learned facts and figures about British history and culture. His back-to-basics approach brought him into conflict with the Tories' Lib Dem Coalition partners later that month, when the *Daily Mail* leaked plans for GCSEs to be supplanted by old-style exam-based qualifications, modelled loosely on the 'Ordinary Level' (O level) regime that had preceded them (before one of Mr Gove's idols, Mrs Thatcher, abolished them). The paper reported that 16-year-olds could be sitting the 'tough' new exams as soon as 2016, with less academic students offered ones moulded on the much-reviled Certificates of Secondary Education (CSEs) offered to weaker pupils instead of O levels.

In September 2012, Mr Gove and Mr Clegg jointly unveiled firmer Coalition proposals—abandoning any talk of a 'two-tier' system in favour of replacing GCSEs in English, maths, and science with a new, Continental-style English Baccalaureate Certificate (EBac) from 2017. Other 'core' subjects (including geography, history, and languages) will follow later. A single exam board will oversee the new qualifications. In a separate, but related, move, the Coalition raised the school leaving age to 17 in 2013, and from 2015 children are expected to stay in some form of formal education or training until the age of 18.

The Coalition's decision to call time on GCSEs came as ministers were still struggling to extricate themselves from a furore over that summer's exam grades. The perennial media circus surrounding GCSE 'results day' erupted into a full-blown row between schools, Ofqual, and, by extension, government when it emerged that students sitting English language exams that summer had been marked more harshly than those taking exactly the same papers earlier the same year. Some faced the prospect of having to delay going to university for up to a year to resit exams in pursuit of the all-important C grades that others had already received for work of the same standard. The dispute intensified when the *Times Educational Supplement* published a leaked letter sent by Ofqual to one exam board, Edexcel, apparently urging it to mark that summer's papers more harshly than those sat earlier in 2012. And in a twist that deepened the sense of injustice felt by pupils affected in England, the Welsh Government intervened to confirm that it would be using its devolved power to act as exams regulator in Wales to regrade 2,386 papers previously marked down as D and C grades by the Cardiff-based board WJEC. Although he expressed sympathy for English pupils left with Ds where they had been expecting Cs, Mr Gove refused to pressure Ofqual to do likewise.

The rise of faith schools

Another debate that has bubbled consistently in recent years concerns the future of **faith schools**—an umbrella term used to describe those run by particular religious communities. The term 'faith school' has traditionally been used interchangeably with 'voluntary school', as discussed earlier in this chapter. In this context, however, it also denotes schools run by non-Christian faith groups, including Muslim, Sikh, Hindu, and Jewish communities. There are around 7,000 faith schools in England, Wales, and Northern Ireland, and a growing number in Scotland.

Faith schools were championed by Mr Blair, whose eldest son, Euan, attended one. He and other advocates argued that they had above-average attendance rates and high levels of achievement. They were also praised for instilling firm discipline and respect among pupils. Mr Blunkett famously said that he wanted to 'bottle' their essence as a template for reform elsewhere. Yet faith schools have generated vocal opposition. Although most are subsidized by the state, non-fee-charging, and obliged to follow the National Curriculum, critics such as the National Secular Society regard the idea of children being educated at schools with prescriptive underlying world views as a form of brainwashing incompatible with one of state education's primary roles: to foster freedom of thought and expression. Others, including some politicians and unions, argue that maintaining single-faith schools—whether inside or outside the state system—promotes ghettoization and undermines efforts elsewhere to foster multiculturalism. Some also object to their being allowed to exercise limited selection, albeit faith-based rather than academic, unlike most other state schools. In March 2008, the NUT proposed requiring *all* state schools to become 'multifaith' institutions, offering faith-based instruction, a choice of religious holidays, and varied prayer facilities.

Alleged self-segregation is not the only criticism levelled against faith schools: the ability of academies to vary their curriculums has, say some, enabled those sponsored by religious groups to introduce 'unorthodox' approaches to certain subjects. Concern that some Christian schools were minded to teach 'intelligent design' or 'creationism'—the idea that the natural world was created by God, rather than being the product of evolution—as valid theory in science lessons led, in January 2012, to the DfE threatening to withdraw funding from those attempting to do so. Among those who had campaigned for a crackdown on creationist teaching were the biologist Richard Dawkins, naturalist Sir David Attenborough, and the British Humanist Association.

But an even bigger row over the potential risks posed by 'faith-based' teaching erupted in March 2014, particularly in relation to academies. This concerned the so-called 'Operation Trojan Horse' plot, which emerged when a letter, allegedly written by 'Islamist extremists', outlined plans to infiltrate schools across Birmingham and other British towns and cities. Within weeks, it emerged that Birmingham City Council had received 200 or more complaints from parents alleging that their schools were in danger of being hijacked by extremists. Subsequent investigations into 21 schools across the city by Ofsted and the Education Funding Trust identified five (four of them academies) in which insufficient work had been done to protect children from exposure to extremist teachings. As a result, all five were placed in special measures (see 'Monitoring school standards—and the great "parent choice" debate' in this chapter). The ensuing scandal, still ongoing at time of writing, led to a feverish national debate, with Mr Gove at one point embroiled in an unseemly tussle with Home Secretary Theresa May, who accused his department of being too slow to tackle the threat of Islamic radicalization in schools. Meanwhile, critics of academies saw in it a vindication of their long-held concerns about lack of transparency in self-governing schools. Former Labour Education Secretary Mr Blunkett announced that if his party were to be returned to power in 2015 it would introduce a new Independent Director of School Standards with the power to monitor academies and free schools.

Specialist versus special schools—avoiding confusion

Despite the similarity of the terminology, specialist schools are not to be confused with **special schools**, which specialize not in particular *disciplines*, but in teaching children with learning *difficulties*, such as dyslexia or autism, or mental or physical disabilities. Before 1997, these were commonly known as 'special needs schools'.

To be judged eligible to attend a special school, children must be 'statemented'—awarded a 'statement of special education need'—by their LEAs, following diagnosis by a GP or specialist and (in some cases) formal academic tests. Recent years have seen a growing trend towards integrating such pupils in mainstream schools, to avoid segregation from their peers, and to help them attain skills and qualifications that will give them career prospects comparable to those of other children. Some mainstream primaries and secondaries have their own 'special units', while others integrate statemented children into general classes. However, the disparate approach adopted by different LEAs has created a widening postcode lottery.

The question of 'integration versus segregation' remains politically sensitive, with many councils having closed down special schools, often for financial reasons. During the 2010 election campaign, Mr Cameron was barracked in front of television cameras by the father of a boy with spina bifida, who accused the Tories of planning to 'segregate' disabled children by promoting a return to separate schools. Mr Cameron, whose late son, Ivan, had suffered from cerebral palsy and epilepsy, had used his party's manifesto to condemn what he described as Labour's 'ideologically driven closure of special schools' and end the 'bias' towards pushing them into mainstream ones.

▶ The dwindling role of local education authorities (LEAs)

The LEAs have had their powers progressively eroded—caught between the pincer movement of growing school self-determination and direct intervention in cases of underperformance by successive Education Secretaries. But the single most significant recent reform of local schooling occurred in the Children Act 2004, passed in response to the Victoria Climbié child abuse case (see Chapter 18, 'The 2004 Act and the "Every Child Matters" agenda'). The media inquest into this gruesome tragedy led to a sweeping reorganization, under the 'Every Child Matters' agenda. This saw old-style education departments hand oversight of schools to across-the-board 'children's services' departments (see Chapter 18, 'Child protection'), and chief education officers replaced by all-encompassing 'directors of children's services' in each LEA area. The aim was to join up a range of previously fragmented services affecting children, to better safeguard child welfare and to make it less likely that warning signs of abuse would be missed in future.

Although they played an overarching role in implementing the 2004 Act, LEAs have seen significant reductions in their educational powers. Today, they tend to be less the principal state schooling *providers* in their areas than enablers or coordinators, although their influence would likely increase again if Labour were to win the 2015 election—particularly in relation to 'oversight' of (otherwise independent) academies and free schools. Indeed, Mr Gove was seen by some critics not as a 'localizer'—freeing schools from local bureaucrats to run their own affairs unimpeded—but a 'centralizer', happy to micro-manage academies and free schools from Whitehall. At time of writing, the Local Government Association (LGA—see Chapter 11, 'Local government associations') was calling for LEAs to be given greater powers to oversee academies, in light of growing disquiet about their perceived lack of local accountability. A full list of the powers retained and lost by LEAs in recent years is contained in the table entitled 'Powers retained and lost by local education authorities (LEAs)', to be found on the **Online Resource Centre**.

Despite the gradual erosion of their status, LEAs remain responsible for ensuring that each child in their area has access to schooling. In addition, they still have an input into many of the areas examined next—notably, monitoring school admissions policies and drawing up catchment boundaries.

Monitoring school standards—and the great 'parent choice' debate

Besides selection, the other great issue to have dominated debate about state schooling recently is that over 'parent choice'. This is the long-standing notion that families should be free to send their children to whichever local school they choose. Dividing lines were sharpened in the 1980s and 1990s, with the introduction of two key innovations designed to inform parents better about the relative academic merits of different schools: league tables; and a national inspectorate, the Office for Standards in Education—renamed the **Office for Standards in Education, Children's Services, and Skills (Ofsted)** in April 2007.

League tables of school exam results were introduced under the 1988 Act, but took a while to catch on with parents. The more decisive agent of choice was arguably the introduction of systematic school inspections. Until 1992, school standards were enforced by two bodies: Her Majesty's Inspectorate of Education, and LEAs themselves. But the Education (Schools) Act 1992 and School Inspections Act 1996 established Ofsted in England and Estyn (formally Her Majesty's Inspectorate for Education and Training) in Wales, providing more consistent nationwide frameworks. Northern Ireland has an Education and Training Inspectorate, while in Scotland school inspections are undertaken by a Scottish Government executive agency, Education Scotland, which replaced two previous regulators—Her Majesty's Inspectorate of Education and Learning, and Teaching Scotland—on 1 July 2011 (see also Chapter 18, 'Children's homes').

Ofsted is headed by a Chief Inspector of Schools and has traditionally been tasked with conducting regular inspections of all English state schools. Its first visits to each school were carried out within four years of its inception, but thereafter they became six-yearly until Labour made them more frequent, giving shorter notice periods to allow schools less scope to 'clean up their acts' at the last minute.

Today, Ofsted inspects the following providers:

- nursery and primary schools;
- secondary schools;
- special schools;
- service children's education—for offspring of those in the Armed Forces;
- pupil referral units—for children 'who cannot attend' normal schools, such as pregnant teenagers, those with specific medical problems, and pupils excluded from mainstream schools for problematic behaviour; and
- some independent schools, excluding members of the Independent Schools Council (ISC) and Focus Learning Trust, which are inspected by the Independent Schools Inspectorate (ISI) and School Inspection Services (SIS).

Ofsted has traditionally rated schools 'outstanding', 'good', 'satisfactory', or 'inadequate'. After an inspection, a school is expected to act on any recommendations that the report contains, as outlined in the table entitled 'Process for responding to recommendations in an Ofsted report', to be found on the **Online** **Resource Centre**.

Perhaps unsurprisingly, the arrival of league tables and Ofsted intensified competition for places at high-performing schools. By highlighting the 'best'—and 'worst'—they created a thriving, sometimes ruthless, market for places at successful providers and an exodus of middle-class families from those deemed to be 'failing'. There was no starker illustration of this pattern than the East Brighton Centre of Media Arts (COMART)—a struggling comprehensive that went through not one, but two name changes, and a costly PFI building programme, before finally closing in summer 2005. Based in a deprived ward identified as among the 5 per cent poorest by the government's own Indices of Multiple Deprivation, the school consistently had the worst local GCSE and truancy rates. Better-off parents voted with their feet—reducing its social mix and overall pupil numbers, and sending its standards plummeting further.

Critics claim that 'parent choice' has parallels with 'patient choice' in the NHS, which has seen successful hospitals oversubscribed and failing ones avoided. While more and more 'failing' schools are closing, 'successful' ones gain greater financial rewards and freedoms—enabling them to headhunt experienced staff and improve further. Devoid of these privileges, underperforming schools can become locked in downward spirals. For the media, particularly local journalists, Ofsted reports provide 'easy hit', newsworthy stories that can usefully fill space or air time. As inspections have become more frequent and the process better understood, however, the regulator has sent out fewer reports proactively to newspapers and television or radio stations, so it is usually up to vigilant reporters to chase them. They should also be wary about relying on schools' own accounts of their inspections: as with most things, it is best to go straight to the horse's mouth for the full story. Handily, though, all Ofsted reports are available in downloadable PDF form on its website.

Another controversy related to the growing national obsession with league tables concerns testing. Ministers have consistently clashed with head teaching unions over the sheer volume of assessment that schoolchildren now face, and the pressure that this piles on pupils and teachers. Opposition to testing intensified in summer 2008 when ETS Europe, the commercial company contracted to oversee marking of the Key Stage 2 and 3 tests for 11- and 14-year-olds, presided over a marking fiasco. Results for some schools suffered severe delays and there were reports of exam papers lying uncollected (and unmarked) weeks after exams had been sat. Ministers launched an independent inquiry, headed by Lord Sutherland, and in August ETS Europe had its £156 million five-year contract terminated by the now defunct Qualifications and Curriculum Authority (QCA). It had been paid £39.6 million for 2008 alone.

In October 2008, Mr Balls scrapped Standard Attainment Tests (Sats) for 14-year-olds, promising new US-style 'report cards' for each primary and secondary school child from 2011, giving an overall grade A–F covering not only exam results and performance, but also attendance and truancy, behaviour, and health. But in July 2011 Mr Gove confirmed that he was implementing the recommendations of an independent review into Sats by Lord Brew, a professor of politics at Queen's University, Belfast, by introducing more rigorous testing of core skills such as maths, grammar, and spelling, and improving assessments of children's creativity.

Other recent trends to monitor and improve standards have seen direct state intervention to help struggling schools. Before leaving office, Mr Balls offered schools with fewer than 30 per cent of pupils achieving five GCSE A*–C passes extra money to channel into top-up tuition via a National Challenge for Schools programme. He also introduced 'school improvement partners' (SIPs) in many areas of England—individuals or organizations with relevant expertise offering outside consultancy roles to help struggling schools to improve standards.

For Mr Gove, however, the solution to moving towards a situation in which most state schools could be described as 'good' or 'outstanding' was to shake up the Ofsted regime. From January 2012, he introduced a new inspection framework, exempting schools judged outstanding in their most recent reports from regular inspections—a condition that, up to then, had applied to all providers, whatever their ratings. In future, outstanding schools would be inspected only as and when certain 'triggers' took effect—principally, when Ofsted was contacted by teachers or parents concerned about deteriorating standards. But barely a month after this system came into effect, Sir Michael Wilshaw qualified the exemption by stating that up to a quarter of outstanding schools—those that had failed to achieve that rating in the teaching category—would face reinspection, as before, within the next four-year cycle.

Sir Michael has since further cut the amount of advance warning that schools are given about impending visits—introducing 'no notice' inspections, from January 2014, for schools blighted by unruly pupil behaviour. Most controversially, he abandoned the long-standing 'satisfactory' label entirely, in favour of a new threefold rating system: 'outstanding', 'good', and 'requires improvement'. The inference that schools currently rated 'satisfactory' were effectively being redefined as 'unsatisfactory' raised the hackles of many head teachers. Chris Keates, general secretary of Britain's largest teaching union, the National Association of Schoolmasters Union of Women Teachers (NASUWT), condemned these proposals for 'trashing the reputation of Ofsted and removing anything that parents can rely on by which to judge a school'.

▶ The future of school catchment areas

The flip side of 'failing' schools becoming unpopular is that 'successful' ones are oversubscribed. Trends in school applications fostered by extending 'parent choice' have had an inevitable impact on catchment areas—the geographical patches within which families need to live to be eligible to send their children to particular schools. Pressure on popular schools to admit more pupils—potentially at the expense of maintaining high standards—has seen some councils take drastic steps to 'ration' places, to keep their numbers sustainable and improve the social mix and performance of others.

In 2008, Brighton and Hove Council began allocating places for oversubscribed secondary schools in the city's 'Golden Triangle' by lottery ('random allocation'). Many local families had paid premium prices for their homes, expecting to be automatically entitled to send their children to one of these high-performing schools. Under the lottery, the schools' catchments were extended to cover areas until now devoid of comprehensives and children from outlying districts became as likely to be admitted as those living nearby. Once applications to attend one of the affected schools exceeded the number of places available, a lottery was used as a tie-breaker. Brighton's experiment was soon emulated elsewhere and, after Labour introduced a new admissions code allowing town halls and head teachers of oversubscribed schools to determine who should be offered places by drawing names from a hat, lotteries of one kind or other were gradually adopted by one in three English LEAs. The government's guidelines—meant to stamp out 'selection by mortgage'—also banned schools from interviewing parents, considering their backgrounds, or excluding people financially by, for example, stipulating that they buy uniforms from expensive suppliers. However, a report published by the British Educational Research Association in September 2010 found that, contrary to expectations, Brighton's experiment had failed to produce any visible improvement in 'social mix' at the schools concerned. The report did not criticize the lottery system per se, but rather the fact that the council had redrawn catchments in such a way that even the enlarged area from which applications had since been accepted principally embraced middle-class neighbourhoods, with poorer ones in peripheral areas still excluded.

In May 2011, the Coalition announced plans to find alternative ways of giving children from poorer families access to the best schools. A new admissions code announced by Mr Gove banned LEAs from using lotteries—terminating all those currently in place—instead permitting academies and free schools (but not other state providers) to reserve places for children entitled to free school meals and those whose families earned less than £16,190 a year. Schools now also have to prioritize children in care and those whose parents were in the

Armed Forces, and to ensure that twins and triplets were taught in the same class—although, controversially, the new code also allows class sizes to rise above the notional 30-pupil limit that Mr Gove inherited (already too high for some). In practice, many academies have used freedoms to set their own admissions criteria to introduce lotteries, with others adopting a system known as 'banding' to ensure that each intake offers places to children across the range of abilities. By February 2014, according to the Sutton Trust, 121 self-governing schools were using banding and 42, lotteries—a riposte to critics who feared that their independence would encourage them to adopt more conventional forms of academic selection.

▌ Bridging the educational divide—other recent developments

One tactic that Mr Brown favoured for bolstering the state sector (and breaking the perceived state/independent school divide) was to instruct the Charity Commission—the quango responsible for regulating registered charities—to impose new conditions on independent schools seeking to retain their charitable status. Having a charity label entitles organizations to significant tax breaks not enjoyed by companies. The biggest condition was a requirement to earn this privilege by opening up their playing fields and other facilities to state schools and community groups. These moves were criticized by Chris Parry, short-lived head of the Independent Schools Council, as provoking a new 'cold war' between private and state sectors. Undeterred, ministers pointed to other developments, including a recent invitation to independent schools to sponsor academies (accepted by the £18,000-a-year Wellington School, the head teacher of which was Anthony Seldon, biographer of Mr Blair and Mr Cameron), and to share amenities and expertise with the new trusts, as proof of their desire for partnership.

One innovation introduced by the Coalition is the **pupil premium**—a pot of money reserved for one-to-one tuition for disadvantaged children, to intercept potential educational inequalities early in their schooling. Starting in April 2011, £488 was allotted to each pupil receiving free school meals out of an initial £625 million budget (rising to £1.25 billion in year two). The money was distributed to schools to spend on these pupils' behalf as they saw fit, with LEAs controlling the purse strings for those taught in 'non-mainstream' settings. As of the 2012–13 financial year, it was extended to pupils who had received free school meals at any point during the previous six years. Since September 2014, meanwhile, all infant school pupils in England and Wales (children up to the age of eight) have been entitled to free school meals—a new 'universal' initiative introduced at a time when most, including Child Benefit itself, were being cut (see Chapter 8, ' "Universal benefits" versus "means testing"—the future of welfare for parents and older people').

Despite such initiatives, Coalition ministers have been accused of placing several roadblocks in the way of children from lower-income households. Among their most controversial decisions was the abolition of the Education Maintenance Allowance (EMA)—a £30 weekly allowance introduced by Labour for 16- to 18-year-olds in continuing education, which academic studies credited with enhancing the career prospects of those from poorer households by incentivizing them to attain further qualifications or training. More explosive still was the Lib Dems' wholesale abandonment of a pre-election 'pledge' to the National Union of Students (NUS) to move towards scrapping undergraduate tuition fees, in favour of a Conservative-driven policy allowing universities to raise their annual fees from a £3,290 limit to £9,000. By September 2014, nine out of 10 universities were charging the new 'top rate' for some or all of their courses, prompting critics to argue that many talented prospective students from poorer households would either be forced to abandon hope of studying for anything other than strictly vocational courses (that is, those better placed to 'guarantee' them employment) or deterred from applying altogether.

Ensuring fairness—the role of schools adjudicators

Ofsted was not the only body introduced in the 1990s to police the state school system. The 1998 Act saw the establishment of a second: the **Office of the Schools Adjudicator (OSA)**. Like Ofsted, the office has more than one adjudicator (in fact 10, led by a 'chief adjudicator').

There are many misconceptions about OSA—the most common being that it is there to rule on complaints by parents about their children's failure to get into their chosen school. In fact, that role is taken by independent appeals panels. In contrast, OSA has duties to:

- determine objections to admission arrangements and appeals from schools against directions from the LEA to admit a pupil;
- resolve local disputes on statutory proposals for school reorganization, or on the transfer and disposal of non-playing-field land and assets;
- decide on competitions to set up new schools where the LEA has entered the contest with its own proposals; and
- decide on requests to vary already agreed admission arrangements.

In the last resort, deciding individual cases still in dispute after OSA has made its judgment falls to the Education Secretary. It is one of many forms of direct intervention by the Education Secretary, as outlined in Table 15.5.

Table 15.5 Modern-day powers of the Education Secretary

Power	Effect
Intervention 'in default'	Prevents unreasonable uses of power by LEAs and 'acts in default' when they fail
Managing the availability of school places	Directs LEAs to reduce surplus places in schools, by merging/closing unpopular ones, or to increase provision where there is high demand
Intervening in 'failing schools'	Places 'failing' schools under 'special measures' (two-year period during which Education Secretary closely observes their progress) and instigates 'Fresh Start' if they fail to improve—replacing head teacher and other teaching staff
	In 2000, Mr Blunkett introduced 'fresh starts' for schools at which fewer than 15 per cent of pupils achieved five or more A–C GCSE passes. When Labour left office, schools at which fewer than 30 per cent of pupils achieved five A–Cs were judged 'underperforming', but Mr Gove raised bar to 35 per cent.
Tackling inequalities of educational opportunity	Intervenes, if necessary, to improve educational opportunities for poorer children
	In 2007, Alan Johnson ordered LEAs to ensure good social mixes in their schools.

Other issues affecting schools

Besides the customary slew of stories about damning Ofsted reports, catchment areas, and league tables, there has been significant coverage in recent months about public spending cuts in relation to schools.

More contentious still was Mr Gove's abandonment of Labour's £55 billion programme for refurbishing or rebuilding every secondary school in England: 'Building Schools for the Future' (BSF). This initially saw £3 billion devolved directly to LEAs to spend on improving and maintaining their school buildings, with the aim of renewing the school in greatest need in each locality with money from the fund by 2011. Every LEA was told to start work on at least one major building project by 2016. Mr Gove cancelled the bulk of the programme with immediate effect in July 2010, initially stating that 715 schools previously earmarked for redevelopment would no longer undergo work and that 123 prospective academy projects would be reviewed on a case-by-case basis. In an early embarrassment for the Coalition, however, he had to revise the list of schools spared from the chop not once, but five times—eventually admitting that, of those he had earlier led to believe had been saved, at least 30 rebuilds would not now go ahead. However, in May 2012, Mr Gove announced his own (more modest) version of BSF: the Priority School Building Programme. Under this scheme, 261 English schools in urgent need of redevelopment will be awarded grants out of an overall pot of £2 billion over the five years to 2017.

The school system remains such a hotbed of political disagreement that it is impossible to list all of the issues arising out of it here. However, another key aspect of Mr Gove's reforms was a renewed emphasis on school discipline. Among his main innovations were: the introduction of a scheme to fast-track former members of the Armed Forces into teacher training; a change to the rules governing physical contact, enabling teachers to use 'reasonable force' to restrain disruptive pupils; and a call on school heads to reintroduce mandatory uniforms where they have previously adopted more relaxed dress codes. He also asserted that graduates should, in future, be expected to attain at least a 2:1 level degree before being accepted on Postgraduate General Certificate in Education (PGCE) training courses—despite, contradictorily, allowing free schools and academies to continue employing untrained frontline staff.

▌ The role of LEAs in further education

Councils have long had an on–off relationship with the FE sector. Like schools, FE colleges—or 'technical colleges'—were both managed and financed by county councils up to 1988. But the sweeping reforms under the 1988 Act included liberating FE and sixth-form colleges from LEA control, giving them 'semi-independent' status *within* the state sector, analogous to that granted first to GM schools and CTCs, then foundation and trust schools, academies, and free schools.

Labour initially did little to challenge FE colleges' new-found autonomy, but, by way of answering some criticisms about transparency and accountability levelled at FE colleges, in the Learning and Skills Act 2000 it extended Ofsted's scope to cover FE. From September 2001, all FE and sixth-form colleges began being inspected on four-year cycles. This decision was, in part, an attempt to address growing concerns about lack of transparency in the management of some colleges, shorn of direct LEA scrutiny. For example, in 1998, Stoke-on-Trent College received a bottom grade for management from government inspectors following a succession of scandals that led to an £8 million deficit, and the dismissal of a principal accused of bullying staff and running a pub in Wales while on extended sick leave. Under Mr Brown's government, the tone of FE policy began shifting away from college autonomy. By the time Labour left office, ministers had drawn up plans to return the UK's 385 English and Welsh FE colleges to some form of LEA control, but the Coalition has restored autonomy to FE colleges, with their governing bodies—'boards' or 'corporations'—regaining primary autonomy over their day-to-day management and LEAs providing only a *strategic* role, as with a growing number of schools. Similarly, 'outstanding' FE colleges are now exempt from automatic Ofsted inspections in the same way as top-rated schools. In a rare example of a real-terms spending increase at a time of swingeing cutbacks, in May 2010 Chancellor George Osborne announced a modest £50 million boost for investment in FE building projects. Shortly afterwards, Business Secretary Vince Cable used a speech at London South Bank University to call for an end to artificial distinctions between further and higher education—signalling his intention to increase funds for technical, part-time, and adult courses in FE, and to have more HE-level courses taught in tertiary colleges.

▌ The role of LEAs in higher education

The LEAs play an increasingly limited role in higher education (HE). They are, however, still responsible for providing education maintenance grants to eligible students undertaking full-time degree courses at universities or other HE institutions. As of September 2014, full-time English students whose parents had a joint income of £25,000 or less were entitled to 'full' grants of £3,387 a year and to have their tuition fees paid for them. Those with parents earning up to £42,620 (down from £50,000 previously and, before that, £60,000) still received partial grants, but had to take out loans to cover the short-term cost of their tuition fees—repaying these as and when their own incomes rose to £21,000 or higher. In Northern Ireland, eligibility for grants stops at a lower household income level (£41,540), but they are marginally higher for the poorest students—reaching £3,475 for those from families with joint incomes of £19,203 or less. In Wales, arrangements are noticeably more generous, with Welsh students attending the country's universities entitled to non-means-tested grants of £5,315 a year and those from households with incomes of £18,370 or less receiving an extra £5,161. But by far the best deal—a source of resentment for some living elsewhere in Britain—is that offered to Scottish students taking first degrees in Scotland. Their tuition fees are paid by the Scottish Government, with bursaries of up to £1,750 a year available to those from households earning up to £16,999.

Over and above the mandatory undergraduate grants for students from poorer backgrounds, LEAs also retain the power to make discretionary awards to those who follow courses that do not benefit from this system—for example vocational postgraduate degrees.

Funding and monitoring fairness in higher education

Funding for HE in England is the responsibility of the **Higher Education Funding Council for England (HEFCE)**. There is a separate Higher Education

Funding Council for Wales (HEFCW), while both FE and HE in Scotland are the province of a Scottish Funding Council. In Northern Ireland, funding comes direct from the Assembly's Department of Employment and Learning.

The principal roles and purpose of HEFCE are to:

- distribute public money for teaching and research to universities and FE colleges delivering HE courses;
- promote high-quality education and research in a 'financially healthy' sector; and
- play 'a key role' in ensuring accountability and promoting good practice.

To this end, HEFCE has its own board and committees with the following remits:

- quality assessment, learning, and teaching;
- widening participation;
- research;
- business and the community; and
- leadership, governance, and management.

The task of ensuring that HE institutions operate 'fairly'—particularly in relation to admissions policies—falls to the **Office for Fair Access (OFFA)**, led by a 'Director for Fair Access'.

OFFA's primary job is to ensure that institutions that charge tuition fees above the 'standard level' produce 'access agreements' detailing how they are ensuring that they are accessible to people from disadvantaged backgrounds. In practice, many universities have done this voluntarily, by offering bursaries and scholarships targeted at high achievers from low-income households, those with disabilities, and people from under-represented minority groups.

OFFA arose, in part, out of the perceived continuing bias of some 'top' universities towards children from independent school backgrounds. Concern about this issue has been rumbling since Mr Brown publicly condemned Magdalen College, Oxford, in 2000, for failing to offer Laura Spence, a pupil at Monkseaton Community High School in Whitley Bay, North Tyneside, a place to read medicine—despite the fact that she had achieved 10 A* passes at GCSE and was predicted to gain five As at A level. In the event, Ms Spence (who secured straight As) won a £65,000 scholarship to Harvard.

As recently as August 2013, however, it emerged that private school pupils achieving three A* A levels or more were 9 per cent more likely to be offered places at Oxford than those with the same grades from state schools. Two years earlier, it had emerged that five schools were sending more pupils to Oxbridge each year between them than 2,000 others combined. These included just one state provider, Hills Road Sixth Form College, Cambridge, and four top public schools—among them Eton (attended by Mr Cameron), Westminster (where Nick Clegg was educated), and St Paul's (Mr Osborne's alma mater).

▌ The growth of free preschool education

Today, LEAs have limited direct involvement in providing preschool or nursery education. Before 1997, the Conservatives left it up to individual councils whether to fund free nursery education for children from lower-income backgrounds. Given the choice between squeezing more money out of already tight budgets and leaving it to 'the market' to provide where there was sufficient demand, many voted with their feet. A 1986 audit found that free provision ranged from zero to a maximum of 27.5 places per 100 children—hardly a ringing endorsement of council investment. Many LEAs today run at least some nurseries, but most are provided by the private and voluntary sectors. In addition, money directed to enable children from poorer backgrounds to access preschool education tends to come directly from central government, rather than councils.

In the early 1990s, the Conservatives made limited inroads into funding free nursery care for preschool children. 'Nursery vouchers'—virtual money used to 'buy' access for children aged 4 and over to preschool education and/or childcare worth up to £1,100—were introduced in 1996, but abandoned by Labour. Vouchers had baffled many parents: although billed as an extension of 'parent choice', they could not compensate for the fact that—however willingly families shopped around for desirable nurseries—in many areas there simply were not enough places available.

Labour's solution was to launch its first National Childcare Strategy, focusing on two immediate priorities:

- increasing the number of childcare places available; and
- guaranteeing all 4-year-olds a nursery place from April 1998 onwards.

Provision has been gradually extended. From April 2004, LEAs were obliged to guarantee free nursery places to all 3- and 4-year-olds for up to 12.5 hours a week, for 33 weeks a year. Since September 2010, 3- and 4-year-olds have been entitled to up to 15 hours' free nursery provision for 38 weeks a year, while the Coalition extended this to 2-year-olds from families receiving Income Support or income-based Jobseeker's Allowance (JSA) or Employment Support Allowance (ESA), and those claiming child tax credits and earning £16,190 or less. If they remain in power, both Tories and Lib Dems have also pledged to introduce tax breaks worth up to £2,000 from autumn 2015 for each child aged under 12 with two working parents. For its part, Labour has pledged to extend free childcare for 3- and 4-year-olds to 25 hours a week if elected in 2015.

Improving access and accountability in preschool education

While responsibility for 'early years education' rests with the devolved administrations in Scotland, Wales, and Northern Ireland, in England a new programme was established in 1999 to drive through the government's aims of guaranteeing high-quality provision for children from low-income households: **Sure Start**. Although its primary focus is welfare and educational development, Sure Start has extended its support to the whole of a child's family.

The 'Sure Start' concept arose out of New Labour's conviction that early-years education was crucial to a child's social and emotional well-being, and that families prevented from accessing it were missing out on vital development tools. Ministers' decision that preschool teaching should be a core entitlement, rather than an optional 'add-on' accessible only to the middle classes, was based on research into its impact in later life and the outcomes of experiments in similar schemes pioneered in Scandinavian countries.

Sure Start aimed to:

- increase the availability of childcare for all children;
- improve health and emotional development for young children; and
- support parents as parents and in their aspirations towards employment.

Sure Start operates through a network of children's centres, often based in community centres and church halls. Staffed by multidisciplinary teams comprising health visitors, teachers, and social workers, they have become focal points for liaison between families and other support services, such as Jobcentre Plus, and expert antenatal and postnatal advice for new parents.

Where Sure Start ensures that everyone has *access* to preschool education, Ofsted monitors the *standard* of that provision. Its remit was recently increased to cover nurseries, nursery schools, playgroups, and childminders. While the Coalition has nominally retained Sure Start, by de-ring-fencing its funding it has been accused of giving councils struggling to balance their books as a result of Whitehall cuts the option of scrapping it to save money.

☷ Topical feature idea

There is growing controversy over the question of free schools being opened in areas with no shortage of places and the negative impact that this can have on other local schools—including high-performing ones. Are there any free schools in your area, and if not, are any planned? What evidence is there locally of a 'need' for additional school places, and what do their proponents—and opponents—have to say for themselves?

✳ Current issues

- **A lack of accountability in academies and free schools** The Birmingham 'Trojan Horse' scandal cast the spotlight on, among other issues, the risks of allowing schools to govern themselves and deviate from the National Curriculum—leading some (including former academy enthusiasts) to argue that they now need greater oversight by councils.

- **The row over 'spot inspections' of struggling schools** Chief Inspector of Schools Sir Michael Wilshaw has introduced 'no-notice inspections' for schools with persistent behaviour problems, but former Education Secretary Michael Gove was accused of undermining him by suggesting that teachers receive at least a few hours' notice before inspectors arrive.

- **The pre-election battle over childcare policy** As the 2015 election looms, both Coalition parties have promised to give households in which two parents are working tax breaks of up to £2,000 per child if (re-)elected, while Labour is pledging to increase free childcare for 3- and 4-year-olds from 15 to 25 hours a week.

▦ Key points

1. Education in Britain is divided into five key phases: preschool, primary, secondary, further, and higher.

2. State schools in England and Wales can broadly be divided into those run by local education authorities (LEAs)—unitaries, counties, London boroughs, and metropolitan districts—and 'self-governing' ones, run by their head teachers and governors. LEA-run schools are generally known as 'county' or 'community' schools and colleges, while the main self-governing ones are academies. There are also free schools (set up by parents and teachers), and semi-independent foundation and trust schools.

3. The main roles of LEAs (in addition to running county or community schools) is to ensure that all children have places, to decide catchment areas, and to propose new schools or to close existing ones if there are too many or two few places available.

4. All state schools other than fully self-governing academies and free schools must teach the same core subjects, to the same levels, under the National Curriculum.

5. All state schools are inspected by the Office for Standards in Education and Schools (Ofsted), led by the Chief Inspector of Schools. Regular inspections occur only at 'outstanding' schools if requested by teachers or parents, but 'no notice' ones occur at those with persistent behavioural issues.

→ Further reading

Adonis, A. (2012) *Education, Education, Education: Reforming England's Schools*, Kindle edn, London: Biteback Publishing. **Acclaimed analysis by former Labour Education Minister of the challenges and opportunities facing British schooling in the twenty-first century.**

Birbalsingh, K., Gove, M., Hill, S., Hunter, M., Johnson, D., Martin, J., Lewis, O., Womersley, D., Woodhead, C., and Young, T. (2013) *The Gove Revolution: Transforming England's Schools*, Kindle edn, London: Standpoint. **Series of essays written by supporters and standard-bearers of the Coalition's free school and academy revolution. Best read as a companion and partial retort to Adonis.**

Cribb, J., Jesson, D., Sibieta, L., Skipp, A., and Vignoles, A. (2013) *Poor Grammar: Entry into Grammar Schools for Disadvantaged Pupils in England*. Available online at **www.suttontrust.com/researcharchive/poor-grammar-entry-grammar-schools-disad-vantaged-pupils-england/ Evidence-based critique of the negative impact of the grammar school system on children from deprived backgrounds.**

Phillips, R. and Furlong, J. (2001) *Education, Reform, and the State: Twenty-Five Years of Politics, Policy, and Practice*, London: Routledge Falmer. **Critical overview of the major trends and debates in educational reform in the UK over the past quarter-century.**

Online Resource Centre

www.oxfordtextbooks.co.uk/orc/Morrison4e/
Visit the Online Resource Centre that accompanies this book for web links and regular updates.

Planning policy and environmental protection

If there is one subject (besides tax and bill rises) guaranteed to agitate the great British public, it is planning. Newspapers are crammed with stories about planning controversies every day: from rows about retail parks sucking the lifeblood from town centres to protests by 'NIMBY' ('not in my backyard') residents about proposed traveller camps or wind farms.

But away from the placard-waving and alarmist headlines, planning is serious business. Without it, there would be no schools, hospitals, offices, care homes, supermarkets, or village stores. Before developers can start building work, or businesses, schools, or NHS trusts get anywhere near opening new premises or altering existing ones, planning consent must be obtained. And councils' decisions about whether to grant consent are dictated by overarching guidelines—some set by central government, others by themselves—designed to provide infrastructure and promote economic growth, while limiting its impact on the natural environment.

Compared to other council responsibilities—particularly highways, transport, and public health—'town and country planning' has emerged recently. Its three underlying principles are to:

- ensure that all development is supported by appropriate infrastructure— roads, traffic crossings, bus routes, leisure facilities, etc.;
- ensure that any environmental impact is sustainable; and
- steer development towards land unlikely to be affected by factors such as flooding.

For many years, a single Town and Country Planning Code has governed all forms of development in England and Wales. It was established by nine principal Acts:

- the Town and Country Planning Act 1947;
- the Town and Country Planning Act 1968;

- four separate Acts passed in 1990;
- the Planning and Compensation Act 1991;
- the Planning and Compulsory Purchase Act 2004; and
- the Planning Act 2008.

However, in recent years, there have been significant modifications to the Code and how it is applied in practice in the two countries, with the Welsh Government gaining significant devolved powers under the Government of Wales Act 2006, which places an onus on it to promote 'sustainable' development, and a major relaxation of the planning process emerging through the contentious National Planning Policy Framework that the Coalition introduced to cut red tape in 2012.

Nevertheless, the planning process in both England and Wales remains divided into two levels, as follows.

1. *Forward planning*—At this level, strategic development plans are drawn up by planning authorities (districts or boroughs and unitaries), mapping out long-term strategies for each area and guiding councils' day-to-day planning decisions.

2. *Development control*—This level involves councils' decisions whether to approve individual applications to undertake material changes to existing land or buildings, or to carry out physical development (construction, alteration, or demolition).

The Communities Secretary's role in relation to planning is outlined in Table 16.1.

Table 16.1 Role of the Communities Secretary in relation to planning

Role	Responsibilities
Guidance	Publishes 'planning policy statements' (PPSs) telling planning authorities how to discharge their responsibilities. Overarching regional strategies used by Labour replaced by more localized planning under Coalition.
Setting ground rules	Draws up fixed rules about suitable development land.
Arbitration	Acts as final arbiter in disputes between individuals and councils, appointing independent inspectors to conduct inquiries to determine disputed applications.
Ruling in last resort	'Calls in' most controversial planning applications to give final rulings where inquiries fail to resolve issues.

▌ Forward planning

Between 1991 and 2008, there were three varieties of council development plan, the names of which varied according to the types of council that drew them up. All three—structure plans (counties), local plans (districts or boroughs), and unitary plans (metropolitan or unitary areas)—were eventually replaced by a *regional* approach to development planning. As with most issues concerning local government, the system sometimes produced exceptional quirks. In most hybrid counties (see Chapter 11, 'The 1990s introduction of unitary authorities'), countywide development plans, encompassing elements of all three types, tended to be produced by *joint strategic planning authorities*. In London, unitary plans were produced by individual boroughs, but the Greater London Authority (GLA) oversaw a joint strategic planning authority for the whole city.

The Planning and Compulsory Purchase Act 2004 began simplifying the system, to speed up and harmonize development planning, by giving eight (now-defunct) regional assemblies the power to take strategic decisions for swathes of the country by publishing 'regional spatial strategies' (RSSs). This system was further shaken up in 2010, when regional development agencies (RDAs) briefly took over the 'regional planning body' role and began publishing regional plans. As of March 2012, however, regional planning ceased, following the Coalition's Localism Act 2011. Exemptions currently apply to London, which is still covered by an overarching spatial strategy, and the devolved nations, which retain their own single spatial plans.

While regional planning has ended, the Coalition has retained some of Labour's innovations—building on them to give councils and, more particularly, community groups more say in future development decisions. The principal planning strategies produced by individual councils remain *local development documents* (LDDs). When RSSs were still in place, these were effectively watered-down local or unitary plans, because councils could not deviate from 'guidelines' set regionally. In abolishing RSSs—which he dismissed as 'Soviet-style top-down planning targets'—and the unelected RDAs that had long been a bête noire of many councillors, Communities Secretary Eric Pickles confirmed his intention to make councils' strategic plans less 'bureaucratic' and more 'bottom-up', reflecting the Coalition's 'Big Society' agenda.

To this end, November 2010 saw communities empowered to propose their own long-term **neighbourhood plans**, which, if approved by 51 per cent of locals in a referendum, would have to be implemented by their councils in the same way as if councillors had devised them. Theoretically, neighbourhood plans allow small numbers of engaged citizens to decide for themselves where (and whether) they want new homes, shops, and offices built, what resulting developments will look like, and which firms will build them. In the first year of the new policy, four waves of council areas piloted it, including Exmoor in Devon and Milton Keynes. One so-called 'vanguard authority' was the Royal Borough of Windsor and Maidenhead, which by April 2012 had plans under way in six neighbourhoods, including improvements to Windsor and Eton (the location of Mr Cameron's alma mater).

Hand in hand with neighbourhood plans came the new 'community right to build' (see Chapter 13, 'Cameron's "Big Society"—what role for councillors and officers now?'), launched in April 2012. This entitles local citizens and other community groups to build their own amenities—for example shops, housing, community halls, and playground facilities—where a demonstrable 'need for development' exists. Its virtue, theoretically, is that it circumvents the need for communities in desperate need of low-cost homes for key workers to follow the normal planning process (see next section), thereby fast-tracking their applications. As with neighbourhood plans, however, development can take place only subject to the rest of the community approving it in a referendum and the council, too, giving final approval. Money enabling community groups across England to build in this way is being drawn from a new fund administered by the Homes and Communities Agency (see Chapter 17, 'From housing associations (HAs) to social landlords'), worth £175 million over three years, with separate arrangements applying in London.

Nearly three years after their introduction, there are early signs that neighbourhood plans have the potential to provoke conflict over whether local communities' wishes should take precedence over those of elected councils. At the same time as it shifted from regional to hyper-local 'neighbourhood' planning, the Coalition abandoned Labour's centrally determined 'national policy statements' (NPSs). With them went the top-down 'housing quotas' and other targets that ministers had previously used to parachute developments into particular areas (see Chapter 17, 'The rise of owner-occupancy and the "affordable housing" debate').

Abolishing RDAs and NPSs initially left a vacuum in terms of channelling rejuvenation funds to areas facing particular economic challenges. To answer concerns about this, Mr Pickles established **local enterprise partnerships (LEPs)**, which, like the groups responsible for drawing up neighbourhood plans, would be staunchly 'local' alliances of councils and businesses. Despite this, he left open the option for councils and business leaders to form regional alliances if these were justified or necessary.

The future of large-scale developments

Labour's final years saw renewed emphasis on planning for major infrastructural projects—an outcome of the 'fiscal stimulus' that characterized its response to the 2007–08 banking collapse (see Chapter 7, 'The global banking crisis and its fallout'). To this end, a short-lived Infrastructure Planning Commission was established to fast-track major construction projects, including nuclear power stations and wind farms—if necessary overruling regulations preventing building on greenfield and greenbelt sites (see 'Greenfield versus brownfield sites—and the decline of the greenbelt' in this chapter). It was abolished by the Coalition in 2011.

It 'was not long, however, before the new government also stood accused of allowing governments to override local decision-makers by imposing major developments on them. A new National Planning Policy Framework announced in June 2011 introduced a 'presumption in favour of sustainable development'. Billed as a way of boosting economic output by fast-tracking construction of new homes and business premises by means of removing obstructive 'red tape', this sparked immediate outcries from interest groups as varied as *The Daily Telegraph* (a long-time Conservative Party cheerleader) and the National Trust. To placate the environmental lobby, which raised the spectre of large tracts of English countryside being bulldozed, ministers emphasized the word 'sustainable'. However, critics argued that, however green they might be, any 'presumption' that major projects should be approved would severely blunt the ability of councils (let alone community groups) to obstruct developments judged commercially desirable. Examples of such projects include the high-speed rail link planned between London and Birmingham (dubbed 'HS2'), and hotly debated proposals for a third Heathrow Airport runway—both opposed by several of the government's own back-benchers because of the negative environmental impact that they could have on their constituencies.

▌ Development control

Although long-term development plans impact significantly on British families and businesses, it is specific planning applications that typically arouse strongest emotions. This is invariably reflected in the nature of press coverage about planning issues: while most people would struggle to remember details of their council's overall planning strategy, most can recall local disputes about the proposed locations of new sewage works and landfill sites.

The procedure used by councils to determine planning applications is known as 'development control'. The right to build on sites from scratch or to make major structural alterations to existing developments is known as **planning permission**. Minor building alterations require no permission, or only 'one-stop' decisions from councils to give consent; most 'new-build' applications, however minor, require permission in two stages.

1. **Outline planning permission**/planning consent (or consent 'in principle')—Obtaining outline permission is often used by major developers to 'test the water' with proposals that they may not pursue once they have

investigated further to gauge their commercial viability—for example proposed shopping centres. Plots of land are often sold to prospective developers with outline permission already in place. This lasts five years from the date granted, but if developers have not proceeded to the next stage within three, it lapses.

2. *Detailed (full) planning permission/consent*—Once outline permission is obtained and a developer decides to proceed, he or she applies for detailed consent. With major schemes, the outline planning process will usually have highlighted 'gaps' in detail the developer needs to fill—for example detailed proposals for out-of-town retail parks need to address concerns about transport, access, and environmental impact. They must also specify the exact locations, dimensions, and make-up of proposed developments—including how many shops and parking spaces they will include. Like outline permission, detailed permission lapses if not used within five years.

When considering planning permission, authorities have three options:

- *unconditional consent*—approving the application with no alterations;
- *conditional consent*—approving it subject to provisos (for example better site access or improved traffic crossings), in which event developers will often be given outline permission with attached conditions and expected to satisfy these before gaining detailed consent; or
- *refusal*—outright rejection.

Before councils can decide whether to grant a proposed development permission, they are expected to follow a detailed process designed to give every 'interested party'—those most directly affected by its approval—a chance to air their views. This procedure is detailed in Table 16.2.

Small-scale planning applications—and changes of use

While a tight rein is kept on more ambitious plans because of their potential to affect large numbers of people, formal permission is not needed for some minor alterations to land or buildings. Under the Town and Country Planning (Use Classes) Orders 1987 and 1995, land and property are split into 'classes', and material changes of use 'within the same class' normally needs no consent; neither will certain changes between 'related' classes (provided that they do not entail major building work).

For example, a greengrocer's shop may be changed to a newsagent's with no need for permission, because both are class A1 business premises and therefore considered sufficiently similar. Restaurants, meanwhile, can be changed into shops without permission, because both are within the same overall 'class

Table 16.2 Stages of the development control application process

Stage	Process
Completing an application	Official forms obtained from planning authority (district/borough, unitary, or metropolitan district/London borough).
Entering on the register	Application appears in formal register of applicants, is published on councils' websites, and immediate neighbours are notified. Parish/town/community councils are fully consulted.
Advertising application	Major applications advertised in local press to enable others who 'may be affected' to comment.
Public consultation and exhibition stage (major applications only)	Public exhibitions organized for major developments, often involving detailed plans/models, at council offices or local libraries.
Subcommittee, committee, and full council decisions	Detailed reports on plans drawn up by officers, with recommendations to reject or approve (with or without conditions), to be presented to councillors. Routine/small-scale applications (e.g. domestic extensions) normally determined at subcommittee/committee level, on basis of published regulations.
	Major applications affecting two or more wards, or likely to incur 'significant' cost, treated as key decisions (see Chapter 13, 'Types and levels of council decision'), and determined by both cabinet and full council.
Appealing	If application refused, applicant has six months to appeal to Communities Secretary. Each stage of application must be determined within two months (unless granted extension). If not, applicant may apply for central government ruling on 'non-determination' grounds.
'Calling in'	Communities Secretary may 'call in' controversial applications for final decision—normally when bid raises 'unusual issues' or ones of national/regional importance, or arouses 'more than local opposition', or it becomes 'unreasonable' for council to adjudicate alone.

order' (the former A1 and the latter A3). The same is not always true in reverse, however: changing a shop into a restaurant may also involve making further applications, including obtaining a liquor licence. The table entitled 'Changes of use allowed without acquiring planning permission', to be found on the **Online Resource Centre** that accompanies this book, outlines changes currently allowed without formal permission.

In addition to permitted changes of commercial use, the 1995 Order allows home extensions to proceed without planning consent—provided that they comply with specified conditions. Councils have discretion, however, to pass an 'Article 4 direction' removing some of these permitted rights—particularly if the extension will negatively affect the view or quality of light of a neighbouring property. Planning consent is not usually required to lop or cut down a tree—provided that it is not subject to a tree preservation order (TPO) or in a conservation area. If the former is violated, the council may prosecute.

Planning applications are *always* required for material changes of use involving amusement centres, theatres, scrapyards, petrol filling stations, car showrooms, taxi firms, car hire businesses, and youth hostels—all of which are categorized as *sui generis*.

Planning appeals and inquiries

It is possible for either unsuccessful applicants or their executors to appeal to the Planning Inspectorate over councils' rejection of applications—but only within six months of the dates on decision letters. If permissions are refused, or only conditional consent granted, applicants may lodge free appeals. There is one inspectorate each for England and Wales.

Appeals are decided in one of three ways:

- by means of a planning inspector's consideration of written representations by both parties, alongside a brief site visit;

- by formal hearing, with both parties present; or

- after a full **planning inquiry**—by far the lengthiest and most costly option.

Four out of five appeals are determined by the 'written method', 16 per cent by hearings, and 4 per cent after inquiries. Although third-party objectors have no right of appeal against successful applications, they may mount legal challenges—sometimes resulting in inquiries (or even court cases). Plans to build nine wind turbines in west Devon, approved after an initial inquiry in 2006, were later subjected to a second after an alliance of local residents calling itself the 'Den Brook Judicial Review Group' persuaded the Secretary of State to overturn the decision owing to fears about noise pollution.

In Scotland, the Planning (Scotland) Act 2006 altered the previous appeal system—which saw them referred directly to the Scottish Government's Directorate for Environmental and Planning Appeals—to bring decision-making closer to the ground. In Northern Ireland, the planning appeal process remains the responsibility of the Planning Appeals Commission.

The most high-profile planning inquiries are invariably those concerning applications generating the strongest opposition. Stansted Airport was the subject of two recent inquiries, both related to the expansion plans of its owner, BAA (forcibly abandoned after the High Court upheld a Competition Commission ruling in February 2012 that BAA must sell Stansted). The company's plans for a fifth terminal at Heathrow—finally realized in 2008—were subject to an inquiry lasting nearly four years, starting in May 1995.

Even after an inquiry, the Secretary of State occasionally intervenes with final rulings, based on inspectors' recommendations. This was the case in the decade-long debacle over Brighton and Hove Albion Football Club's ultimately successful application to build a new 22,000-seater stadium near the village of Falmer, East Sussex, which prompted two inquiries.

The only way in which the Secretary of State's 'final decision' in these exceptional cases may be challenged is in the High Court, by judicial review based on a point of law. Both appellant and council may apply to the inspector for the other side to pay its costs should the judgment favour them. In the Brighton case, then Secretary of State John Prescott's decision to back the proposal in October 2005 led to a pledge by its main opponents—Lewes District Council, Falmer Parish Council, and the South Downs Joint Committee—to challenge him. But after his successor, Hazel Blears, reaffirmed his verdict in July 2007, they reluctantly dropped their resistance.

The procedure surrounding planning inquiries is outlined in the table entitled 'Procedure for planning inquiries', to be found on the **Online Resource Centre**.

Inquiries can be a fertile source of stories, often providing high drama during hearings and numerous follow-up angles. If reporters attend evidence sessions and register as interested parties, they should automatically receive copies of inspectors' full reports when they are ready—ensuring that they are kept abreast of final decisions.

▌ Other issues affecting major developments

Although notionally rigorous, the convoluted consultation procedure surrounding planning applications has often been dismissed as a paper exercise. Despite its supposed transparency, councils (and developers acting under their instructions) are frequently criticized for doing too little to publicize 'consultations'—sticking poorly photocopied notices to trees and lamp posts, rather than proactively leafleting homes. The planning process was memorably lampooned in the Douglas Adams' book *The Hitchhiker's Guide to the Galaxy*, in which the hero, Arthur Dent, awoke to find a bulldozer demolishing his house to make way for a bypass, about which he had found out only by taking a torch into a disused toilet bearing a sign with the legend: 'Beware of the Leopard!'

In real life, if a proposed development is lawful, the odds are stacked in favour of major projects—especially where likely to generate jobs and other economic benefits—and councillors have frequently been criticized for being won over by grandiose gestures and promises of prestige.

Planning obligations (or contribution, or gain)

Developers have increasingly sought to persuade councils to look kindly on their applications by offering 'sweeteners', such as additional infrastructure that the council would otherwise struggle to afford. For example, a company seeking permission to build a new luxury apartment complex might offer to build social housing elsewhere at a reduced price, to induce councillors to back its principal project. This offer of a 'benefit in kind' is known variously as **planning obligations**, **planning contribution**, and **planning gain**. Gain is also intended to avoid major new developments putting unnecessary strains on existing infrastructure by ensuring that developers make the changes necessary to accommodate them.

Although it had operated informally for some years beforehand, planning gain was legally recognized only in the early 1990s. Until then, it had been the convention for developers to provide only infrastructure—roads, crossings, and community amenities—*within* the precincts of developments that they were building. All external roads, access points, traffic crossings, etc., tended to be financed by councils. Since 1991, it has become commonplace for developers to provide both 'on-site' *and* 'off-site' gain to enable proposed developments to function properly—for example to give people access to the site and/or transport them there. Although this saves councils money and 'penalizes' developers, the quid pro quo is that applicants can use the incentive of off-site planning gain as a 'carrot' to wave before councils more liberally than previously. In this sense, planning contribution is a 'gain' for both developer and council.

In England and Wales, planning gain was formalized by the 1990 and 1991 Acts, in the guise of 'section 106 agreements'. The Scottish equivalent is the 'section 75 agreement' introduced by the Town and Country Planning (Scotland) Act 1997. These rules specify that, having already granted outline permission, councils can subsequently require developers to sign legally binding contracts obliging them to provide community infrastructure, to avoid damaging existing facilities, or even to transfer ownership of development land to the authority or another body for 'safe keeping'. Examples include:

- developers giving an area of woodland to the council, together with a fee to cover future maintenance;
- developers being required to plant specified numbers of trees and to maintain them for stipulated periods—or to use some land for a particular amenity purpose; and
- requirements for developers to build specified quantities of social housing in particular locations, to provide funds for schools or other community facilities local to estates that they have constructed, or to create parks, playgrounds, or nature reserves.

Developers cannot be *forced* to sign section 106 agreements. In practice, however, they often happily do so—especially in relation to controversial developments otherwise likely to become the subject of protracted legal challenges by disgruntled locals—because they offer the developer as much protection as the council.

Planning gain has undeniably helped to finance many worthwhile projects. Recent examples have included the £2.5 million invested by London's Canary Wharf (a privately owned estate) in the Tower Hamlets Further and Higher Education Trust—a grant-giving body designed to provide educational opportunities for people from deprived backgrounds. Indeed, ministers have looked for even more imaginative ways of helping councils to profit from commercial development. In its 2006 White Paper (the first of two that formed the basis of the 2008 Bill), Labour proposed a new 'planning gain supplement'—a tax of up to 20 per cent on profits made by landowners selling off land for development. The idea was that 70 per cent of the proceeds would be reinvested locally to finance schools, roads, and community amenities needed to support the government's huge house-building programme. But, following extensive lobbying by the building industry, which argued that less land would be available for housing as a result, the plan was shelved. The 2008 Bill also promised a new tax on development land—the 'community infrastructure levy'—which never materialized.

Greenfield versus brownfield sites—and the decline of the greenbelt

An enduring conflict facing councils is their struggle to balance the perceived need for certain developments—homes, schools, hospitals, etc.—with their legal and ethical obligations to protect the environment. At a basic level, they must take daily decisions about whether to approve applications to build on **greenfield sites**—locations that have either never been occupied or which have remained 'natural' for long periods. Obvious examples of greenfield land include agricultural fields, parks, and public gardens. The alternative is to build on **brownfield sites**. These are plots of land, normally in town centres or suburbs, which were previously developed. They may be locations of abandoned office blocks or car parks, or largely derelict scraps of land devoid of extant buildings.

Between the 1960s and 1980s, successive governments liberalized planning laws, making it easier for developers to build on 'out-of-town' or 'edge-of-town' greenfield sites, to ease pressure on tightly developed town centres (many originally developed in unplanned, organic ways). By the late 1990s, however, a backlash had begun against such developments, with town centre businesses complaining of losing custom to the then new breed of out-of-town superstores, and growing social and infrastructural problems afflicting housing estates in outlying areas—many the preserve of the poor and unemployed.

In its first few years in office, New Labour sought to redress the balance, introducing guidelines to encourage councils to lure developers into town centres. Its stated aim was twofold: to regenerate eyesore urban sites, while

providing homes and amenities in the hearts of communities (integrating previously marginalized groups and helping them to obtain work or training).

But times (and government priorities) change. Soaring house prices in the
1990s and 'Noughties' boom years saw many British people—including modestly paid 'key workers', such as nurses and teachers—unable to climb onto
even the lowest rung of the property ladder. The limited space offered by
brownfield sites for development on the scale believed necessary to tackle the
national shortage of affordable homes led to sweeping quotas being imposed on
many regions (and councils). This trend saw more developments targeted at
rural areas, including the **greenbelt**—'fallow' land formally preserved around
towns and cities, to prevent urban sprawl and to protect wildlife.

Introduced in 1935 by the then Greater London Regional Planning Committee,
the notion of a ring of land indefinitely protected from urbanization quickly
became fashionable in smaller centres. It was eventually formalized by central government—first, in the Town and Country Planning Act 1947, and then,
Planning Policy Guidance Note 2 (PPG2, introduced in 1995). By 1993, around
13 per cent of the English countryside was designated greenbelt, covering
14 discrete areas.

Planning Policy Guidance Note 2 specifies that greenbelts should:

- check the unrestricted sprawl of large built-up areas;
- prevent neighbouring towns merging;
- assist in safeguarding countryside from encroachment;
- preserve the setting and special character of historic towns; and
- assist in urban regeneration, by 'recycling' derelict and other urban land.

Once an area has been designated greenbelt, that designation is expected to
safeguard:

- opportunities for access to open countryside for the urban population;
- opportunities for outdoor sport or recreation near urban areas;
- attractive landscapes and enhanced landscape near people's homes;
- the improvement of damaged or derelict land around towns;
- secure nature conservation areas; and
- land in agricultural, forestry, and related uses.

For many years, greenbelts were treated as sacrosanct, but under pressure to
meet Labour's targets councils increasingly compromised their long-held
resistance to expansion into these zones.

Between 1996 and 2010, developers proposing to build new supermarkets on
the outskirts of towns, or within easy reach of them, were forced first to satisfy

both 'needs tests' and 'impact tests'. The former required them to prove that new stores were 'needed' in these locations, given lack of choice for consumers elsewhere, while the latter was meant to limit negative impact on trade in nearby town centres. Towards the end of Gordon Brown's premiership, however, a new planning policy statement was issued, scrapping the needs test—a move that, according to the Association of Convenience Stores, had led to a notable rise in the number of out-of-town stores when adopted in Scotland. Instead of the needs test, then Planning Minister John Healey announced a 'tougher' impact test, although his Tory opposite, Caroline Spelman, said that this amounted to 'tying the hands' of councils by preventing them blocking superstores on grounds that there was already sufficient local grocery provision. Once in power, however, the Coalition declined to reintroduce the needs test in its own planning framework.

Greenbelts are not the only designation used to protect land from development. Some rural and coastal areas are regarded as so exceptional that they qualify for designation under the National Parks and Access to the Countryside Act 1949 as:

- an **area of outstanding natural beauty (AONB)**—a locality deserving special protection to conserve and enhance its natural beauty, to meet the public's need for quiet enjoyment of the countryside, and to protect the interests of those living and working there;

- a **national park**—an area with additional statutory protection against development, commercial exploitation, and habitation; or

- a **site of special scientific interest (SSSI)**—an area judged to have special or unique natural features, further subdivided into *biological SSSIs* (those with rare or unusual flora or fauna) and *geological SSSIs* (those of particular physiographic interest).

Until recently, English AONBs, national parks, and SSSIs were designated by the Countryside Agency, but this job now falls to **Natural England**. In Wales, it is the preserve of **Natural Resources Wales** (formerly the Countryside Council for Wales). Both are expected to 'conserve, protect, and manage the natural environment for the benefit of current and future generations', and seek to promote:

- a healthy natural environment;

- enjoyment of the natural environment;

- sustainable use of the natural environment; and

- a secure environmental future.

Despite its remit, Natural England has been prepared to challenge some 'sacred cows' since its inception in October 2006. In 2007, then chairman Sir Martin

Doughty used his speech marking its first anniversary to argue that 'the sanctity of greenbelt land should be questioned' in light of perceived need to find space for 3 million more homes by 2020 (see Chapter 17, 'The rise of owner-occupancy and the "affordable housing" debate').

There are currently 38 English and Welsh AONBs: 33 wholly in England, four entirely in Wales, and one straddling the border. Eight exist in Northern Ireland, all overseen by the Environment and Heritage Service of the province's Department of the Environment. The smallest is the Isles of Scilly (designated in 1976), which is just 16 km², and the largest, the Cotswolds (covering 2,038 km²). Although they notionally qualify for greater protection than mere greenbelts, in practice councils are not required by law to preserve AONBs and have little power to do so, other than by applying standard planning controls more rigorously.

Perhaps because of this, significant development has continued on or alongside AONBs, prompting vociferous protests from countryside pressure groups such as the Campaign to Protect Rural England (CPRE). In 2006, it highlighted the plight of Dorset AONB, threatened by major road plans, and the Kent Downs, which faced the encroachment of thousands of new homes and offices proposed by Imperial College, London. Brighton's stadium debacle (see 'Planning appeals and inquiries' in this chapter), meanwhile, was particularly sensitive because of the scheme's proximity to the Sussex Downs AONB (now a national park).

National parks are a higher form of designation afforded greater statutory protection than AONBs. Protected by their own national park authorities, there are 15 in total—10 in England, three in Wales, and two in Scotland, where AONBs do not exist (the nearest equivalent being national scenic areas, or NSAs). The existing national parks are listed in Table 16.3.

In addition to AONBs, national parks, SSSIs, and greenbelts, successive governments have tried to protect Britain's ancient woodlands from ever-increasing development demands. The quango responsible for preserving woods for public benefit is the Forestry Commission, headed by a chairman and 10 regional commissioners. The freedom that people have long enjoyed to ramble through forests unimpeded is so prized that woe betide any government that interferes with it. The Coalition found this out to its cost when then Environment Secretary Ms Spelman published proposals to sell off 258,000 hectares of woodland to promote a new 'mixed model' of ownership between public, private, charitable, and community sectors. Visions of 'no entry' signs and ticket booths springing up along public footpaths and bridleways achieved the seemingly impossible by uniting in opposition everyone from the Labour Party to *The Daily Telegraph* and moneyed middle-class activists in 'true blue' Tory heartlands. By February 2011, the policy had been dropped—forcing a humiliated Ms Spelman to concede that she had 'got this one wrong'.

Table 16.3 National parks

National park	Year established
Peak District	1951
Lake District	1951
Snowdonia (Welsh: *Eryri*)	1951
Dartmoor	1951
Pembrokeshire Coast (Welsh: *Arfordir Penfro*)	1952
North York Moors	1952
Yorkshire Dales	1954
Exmoor	1954
Northumberland	1956
Brecon Beacons (Welsh: *Bannau Brycheiniog*)	1957
The Broads	1988
Loch Lomond and the Trossachs	2002
Cairngorms	2003
New Forest	2005
South Downs	2008

Land-banks and the great supermarket stranglehold

A planning issue that has come to prominence recently, relating to the wider controversy over out-of-town developments, is the growing trend for some big developers and their clients to accumulate 'land-banks'. This term refers to the practice of purchasing pockets of land—and often obtaining outline planning permission to develop them—without actually commencing building for prolonged periods. Land-banks are viewed as unscrupulous by many: although developers argue that they are merely guaranteeing themselves 'first refusal' to build on sites, the habit of 'sitting on' them without doing so is seen as anticompetitive behaviour designed to stop others doing so. In some cases, land-banks have proved even more controversial, with developers or their clients buying up land only to sell it on to third parties—writing clauses into the sales agreements preventing it being developed by rival companies.

Of all alleged 'land-bankers', the one most often cited is supermarket giant Tesco. Perceived threats to the historic town centre marketplace of St Albans posed by a dormant land-bank purchased by the company prompted the formation of a media-savvy 'St Albans Stop Tesco Group' and captured national headlines in 2007.

Traveller and gypsy sites

During the 1990s, local newspapers were full of disputes between traveller and gypsy communities looking for land on which to camp—often temporarily, but sometimes for longer periods—and sedentary households concerned about mess, noise, and damage to their own property prices allegedly caused by such encampments. Labour responded by introducing clear rules requiring councils to provide adequate land for camps. Over time, they received £150 million in grants to facilitate the construction of designated traveller sites.

In May 2010, the Coalition scrapped the £30 million set aside by Labour for new sites that year, three months later announcing a major revision of the previous government's rules on establishing encampments. However, in describing most travellers as 'law-abiding', Mr Pickles said that councils would be allowed to use some money from the New Homes Bonus scheme introduced to encourage affordable house-building to establish additional authorized traveller sites in suitable locations.

Otherwise, the Coalition's approach to accommodating travellers has been loose—requiring councils only to 'make their own assessment' of need in their areas, to plan for necessary sites 'over a reasonable timescale', and to protect greenbelt from 'inappropriate development'. At the same time, it has urged councils to promote 'private traveller site provision' wherever possible—encouraging travelling communities to buy their own land, instead of 'squatting' on other people's—while increasing their powers of 'enforcement' to block or remove 'unauthorized' encampments. A vivid illustration of this no-nonsense approach to camps was Basildon Council's successful eviction of a 1,000-strong commune from Dale Farm, which made international headlines in late 2011/ early 2012. Although the travellers had purchased the 6 acre plot on which they were camped, it was located within a greenbelt and they had built up their settlement extensively without obtaining prior planning permission (although, to complicate matters, consent *had* been secured for a camp comprising 34 legal pitches at neighbouring Oak Lane). After a decade-long legal battle, culminating in several High Court hearings and interventions by both the United Nations and Council of Europe in defence of the travellers' human rights, the council won its case, and the community was forcibly removed amid scenes of violence on both sides.

From wind farms to 'fracking'—the rise of middle-class planning protests

Back in the 1990s, pressure for development in rural areas led to mounting opposition among previously passive elements of the middle classes, with major protests against the building of new roads, in particular (see Chapter 19, 'The roles of the Secretary of State and the Highways Agency'). Today, middle-class protestors are on the march once again—opposing everything from the proposed North–South high-speed rail link to onshore wind farms (which Mr Cameron has pledged he will no longer subsidize if he wins the 2015 election).

The bête noire of the moment for Britain's rural classes, however, is the government-approved practice of hydraulic fracturing, commonly known as 'fracking'. This involves mining companies injecting high-pressure liquid into rocks through drill-holes in pursuit of shale gas—a fuel recently embraced by HM Treasury as a future source of cheap energy to boost the country's self-sufficiency and temper the UK's increasing reliance on imported gas from volatile overseas markets (see Chapter 7, 'Energy'). Concerns about the safety of shale gas exploration were first aired in Britain after a November 2011 study confirmed that two earth tremors recorded earlier that year in Lancashire were likely to have been caused by the drilling activity of fracking company Cuadrilla. Opposition to fracking has since intensified, with e-petitions and social media campaigns drawing together local communities, international organizations such as 38 Degrees and Avaaz, and single-issue protest groups such as the combatively named Frack Off.

In terms of visible protest, things first came to a head when, in July 2013, an unlikely mix of colourfully dressed environmental campaigners and well-heeled middle-aged locals set up camp to stop Cuadrilla carrying out exploratory drilling operations in the deeply conservative village of Balcombe, West Sussex. The protest became a media circus, but from a public affairs perspective it was interesting in several respects—not least because permission for Cuadrilla to commence its operation was given by Balcombe Parish Council (one of whose members, Simon Greenwood, managed Balcombe Estate, where it was due to take place), although the council would later publish a local poll showing that 82 per cent of village residents opposed the drilling.

Despite Cuadrilla's retreat from Balcombe, fracking continues to be a live issue. Alongside the many relaxations that ministers have introduced to liberalize planning law, they have introduced various incentives to persuade councils to look favourably on applications for shale gas exploration. Committing Britain to 'going all out for shale', in January 2014 Mr Cameron told councils that they could keep 100 per cent of their Uniform Business Rate (UBR) receipts (see Chapter 12, 'How UBR has traditionally worked and why it is so unpopular') from companies involved in fracking (compared to the 50 per cent limit in place up to that point). He had already declared that mining prospectors must pay local communities £100,000 ahead of any test drilling and hand over a further 1 per cent of any revenues they generated on finding shale gas. Critics immediately retorted that such sweeteners placed austerity-hit councils in invidious positions: leaving them duty-bound to act as responsible planning authorities, but tantalizing them with handouts that they could ill afford to turn down. Undeterred, Mr Cameron went even further in championing the fracking cause in his 2014 Queen's Speech—confirming plans to change the laws on trespass to allow firms to drill beneath private land, including people's homes, without first seeking planning permission. Ministers had already abolished regulations requiring prospectors to inform local residents individually of impending fracking activity. On the day of the announcement, Greenpeace campaigners in hard hats and high-visibility jackets responded by sealing off Mr Cameron's cottage in the Oxfordshire hamlet of Dean with security fencing—putting up a sign proclaiming, 'We apologize for any inconvenience we may cause while we frack under your home'.

And still the controversies continue. In May 2014, *The Independent* reported that, in addition to being expected to perform a contortionist act by 'objectively' vetting prospective fracking projects on planning grounds while simultaneously weighing up the potential economic benefits of successful operations, the position of some councils had become even more compromised. Some authorities, it revealed, had vested interests in fracking going ahead, because their pension funds had invested millions of pounds in companies involved in the emerging 'dash for shale gas'. Lincolnshire County Council had £1.9 million invested in Total, the first major oil firm to get involved in UK fracking, while West Sussex County Council (the authority that oversees Balcombe) had indirect holdings in Cuadrilla.

Compulsory purchase orders (CPOs) and planning blight

Sometimes, plans are approved for such mammoth developments—or ones with such a potentially huge impact on surrounding environments—that it is necessary for land or buildings that might otherwise stand in their way to be demolished before work proceeds. Examples of such projects include airport runways, roads, waterways (canals), or harbours. In such cases, councils sometimes seek to 'force' homeowners and businesses to move, so that their premises can be bulldozed. A **compulsory purchase order (CPO)** must therefore be served.

The CPO is not the only means by which councils can incur compensation claims from property owners because of planning decisions. Should a property's value drop because of a controversial application, it might be regarded as 'blighted'. In such cases, owners can effectively force councils to buy their properties—a 'CPO in reverse'.

▌ Other quirks of the planning system

Authorities may decline to consider planning applications on grounds that the Secretary of State has refused a 'similar' one, on appeal, within the preceding two years. In addition, there are various ways of *enforcing* planning controls, as well as monitoring to ensure that developments granted are lawful, as listed in the table entitled 'Other forms of planning notice', to be found on the **Online Resource Centre**.

Building regulations

Even when formal permission is not required for 'new builds' or to adapt existing structures, **building permission** (or compliance with **building regulations**) invariably will be. The reason for such regulations is to ensure that buildings are structurally sound. An inspector (normally from the council) will visit the property during work to ensure that it meets specified safety standards.

Other than in inner London (which has its own system), the standard of regulations is the same across England. It derives from the Public Health Act 1961—which stopped councils making their own building by-laws, returning this power to ministers—and the Health and Safety at Work Act 1974. The process for applying is as follows:

- plans for the building work must be submitted to the council; and
- if they comply with basic regulations and are not defective, prima facie they must be approved—but if not, they must be rejected.

Building regulation cases are usually overseen by trained inspectors, rather than councillors, because of their technical complexity. Councils can order buildings without consent to be demolished or remedial work to be undertaken by owners. Alternatively, they can carry out the work themselves—at the owners' cost.

Listed buildings and conservation areas

Although buildings of historic or architectural interest are not immune to demolition if they fall into severe disrepair, their owners can obtain substantial help with their upkeep by having them 'listed'.

Buildings are listed—on the advice of **English Heritage**, a quango funded by the Department for Culture, Media, and Sport (DCMS)—if they have:

- 'architectural interest'—for example the recently renovated Grade II* Morecambe Bay Hotel in Lancashire, regarded as a classic example of Art Deco;
- 'historical interest'—reflective of a particular period or movement;
- links to nationally important people or events—for example Charleston, the Grade II listed country home of the Bloomsbury Set, near Lewes, East Sussex; or
- 'group value' as an architectural or historical unit, or a fine example of planning—for example the Regency Brunswick Square in Hove.

There are three 'grades' of **listed building**:

- *Grade I*—buildings judged 'exceptional';

- *Grade II**—fractionally lower down the pecking order than Grade I, these include the Shakespeare Memorial Theatre in Stratford-upon-Avon; and
- *Grade II*—buildings judged 'particularly important'.

Decisions to list buildings must be approved by the Culture Secretary under the Listed Buildings Act 1990. Although there was long reluctance to list post-war buildings, in 1988 a rolling '30-year rule' was introduced, stipulating that any qualifying structure that is at least three decades old can be listed.

When buildings are listed, the lists themselves must be published and notified to councils, their owners, and occupiers. Once listing is confirmed, any alteration or addition to a building entails the owner obtaining listed building consent as well as other permissions. New constraints will include limitations on the types of material that they may use—and obligations to keep the property in a good and characteristic state of repair. Unauthorized work on listed buildings may see councils issue enforcement notices, requiring the work to be reversed.

One of many controversies that arose out of Chancellor George Osborne's 2012 Budget was his decision to levy value added tax (VAT) on alterations made to listed buildings. This went down badly with the custodians of such buildings, including English Heritage and the National Trust, at a time when they were already struggling with rising costs (and falling visitor numbers). Vociferous critics of the policy included 23 cathedral deans, who warned that adding this 20 per cent surcharge to the cost of refurbishments 'seriously jeopardizes the sustainability of our great buildings'.

If councils wish to protect 'non-listed' buildings threatened with demolition or serious alteration, they may serve building protection notices—a process referred to as 'spot-listing'. This covers the building for six months, during which time the Culture Secretary must decide whether to list it formally.

One further way of protecting groups of buildings—or whole areas of a village or town deemed of 'special architectural or historic interest'—is to designate **conservation areas**. Introduced by the Civic Amenities Act 1967, these offer particular protection for buildings from unsympathetic or inappropriate cosmetic alterations. Special attention is paid to conservation areas whenever planning applications arise within them. 'Permitted development rights', allowing changes of use of buildings without the need for planning permission, do not apply to those in conservation areas. Planners can also make 'Article 4 directives' to increase their control over the insertion of replacement doors and windows.

Councils must advertise in local papers all applications in conservation areas that might affect their 'character or appearance'—giving the public 21 days in which to object. It is a criminal offence to lop or cut down trees in conservation areas.

⊟ Topical feature idea

The following extract is from a list of planning applications submitted during the week commencing 9 June 2014 to the City of Bradford Metropolitan District Council. How would you go about making sense of this and deciding whether any of the items have news potential for the *Bradford Evening Telegraph*, on the basis of the scant information reproduced here? Which details would you follow up and how?

Extract from a list of planning applications submitted to City of Bradford Metropolitan District Council, w/c 9 June 2014

- **Conversion of existing offices and storage (B1 and B8) to mixed use development of offices, storage and 14 apartments (B1, B8 and C3)**

  12–14 Adelaide Street Bradford West Yorkshire BD5 0EA

  Ref. No: 14/02506/MAF | Received: Sat 14 Jun 2014 | Validated: Sat 14 Jun 2014 | Status: Pending Consideration

- **Submission of details to comply with conditions 1,3,4,8,10,11,12 and 15 of permission 13/02782/MAF dated 11/07/2014: 17 new dwellings and associated access road**

  Land Former Site of Butterfield Industrial Estate Otley Road Baildon West Yorkshire

  Ref. No: 13/02782/SUB01 | Received: Fri 13 Jun 2014 | Validated: Fri 13 Jun 2014 | Status: Partial Grant – Approval of Details

- **Conversion of existing office in Burley House into 4 dwellings, renovation and conversion of The Mews into 5 dwellings and conversion and extension to the North of the existing Coach house to 4 dwellings**

  Burley House Bradford Road Burley in Wharfedale Ilkley West Yorkshire LS29 7DZ

  Ref. No: 14/02495/MAF | Received: Fri 13 Jun 2014 | Validated: Fri 13 Jun 2014 | Status: Pending Consideration

  Change of use from garments shop to * a hot food takeaway

  9–11 Low Street Keighley West Yorkshire BD21 3PJ

  Ref. No: 14/02556/FUL | Received: Fri 13 Jun 2014 | Validated: Fri 13 Jun 2014 | Status: Application Granted

  Single storey extension to form store

  MCC Auto 662 Manchester Road Bradford West Yorkshire BD5 8NF

  Ref. No: 14/02500/FUL | Received: Fri 13 Jun 2014 | Validated: Fri 13 Jun 2014 | Status: Application Granted

- **Retrospective application to re-position footpath and use land to form parking area**

  72 Baildon Road Baildon West Yorkshire BD17 6AG

  Ref. No: 14/02483/FUL | Received: Thu 12 Jun 2014 | Validated: Thu 12 Jun 2014 | Status: Application Granted

- **Construction of single storey rear extension of the following dimensions: Depth of extension from the original eaves: 6m | Maximum height of extension: 4m | Height to eaves of extension: 3m**

  63 St Margarets Road Bradford West Yorkshire BD7 2BY

Ref. No: 14/02493/PNH | Received: Thu 12 Jun 2014 | Validated: Thu 12 Jun 2014 |
Status: Prior Approval Not Required

- **Installation of four illuminated facia signs**
  64 Queens Road Bradford West Yorkshire BD8 7BT

  Ref. No: 14/02532/ADV | Received: Wed 11 Jun 2014 | Validated: Wed 11 Jun 2014 |
  Status: Application Granted

- **Installation of timber gates to driveway/entrance of property**
  Fieldhead House 9 Highfield Close East Morton Keighley West Yorkshire BD20
  5SG

  Ref. No: 14/02465/HOU | Received: Wed 11 Jun 2014 | Validated: Wed 11 Jun 2014 |
  Status: Application Granted

- **Alterations to existing shopfront**
  30 Kirkgate Bradford West Yorkshire BD1 1QL

  Ref. No: 14/02440/FUL | Received: Wed 11 Jun 2014 | Validated: Wed 11 Jun 2014 |
  Status: Application Granted

Source: City of Bradford Metropolitan District Council, **www.planninag4bradford.com**

✳ Current issues

- **The great 'shale rush'** Ministers are offering councils financial incentives to approve fracking projects—and companies no longer need formal permission to explore beneath private land.

- **The end of onshore wind farms in England?** Amid mounting complaints about noise and visual pollution caused by onshore wind farms, Conservative Energy Minister Michael Fallon announced in April 2014 that all government subsidies to the industry would cease if his party were to win the 2015 election, because Britain would already have reached its 2020 wind energy target. English and Welsh councils would also be given a 'decisive say' over whether new wind farms should be approved.

- **Conflicts between planning authority wishes and new neighbourhood plans** Local communities may now propose their own long-term development plans and have these approved through referendums. In some areas, including Littlehampton, West Sussex, 'neighbourhood plans' are starting to conflict with those of planning authorities.

▦ Key points

1. Planning policy is implemented in two ways: long-term strategic planning, involving all types of council; and development control, focusing on whether individual applications should be approved.

2. Planning authorities (districts or boroughs, unitaries, metropolitan districts, and London boroughs) may make one of three decisions when considering applications: approval with conditions, approval without conditions, or refusal.

3. Larger-scale applications, such as major housing or retail developments, require two levels of consent: outline permission and detailed permission.

4. Developers are allowed to offer 'sweeteners' to persuade councils to approve applications—including improvements to local infrastructure or 'off-site' benefits, such as schools and playgrounds. This is known as 'planning contribution' or 'planning gain'.

5. Buildings of historical or architectural interest are often 'listed' by English Heritage. Developing them entails obtaining both planning permission and listed building consent.

→ Further reading

Dillon, D. and Fanning, B. (2012) *Lessons for the Big Society: Planning, Regeneration, and the Politics of Community Participation*, Kindle edn, Farnham: Ashgate. **Intriguing case study of planning and regeneration in the London Borough of Haringey as a litmus test for Coalition neighbourhood plans.**

Gallent, N. and Robinson, S. (2013), *Neighbourhood Planning: Communities, Networks, and Governance*, Bristol: Policy Press. **Illuminating and timely evaluation of the new trend towards 'bottom-up' planning policy introduced by the Coalition's neighbourhood plans.**

Hall, P. and Tewdwr-Jones, M. (2010) *Urban and Regional Planning*, 5th edn, Kindle edn, London: Routledge. **Fifth edition of the classic text charting the history of town and country planning in Britain up to and including the New Labour years.**

Ricketts, S. (2012) *Localism and Planning*, Haywards Heath: Bloomsbury Professional. **Indispensible overview and assessment of recent moves towards localizing town and country planning.**

Online Resource Centre

www.oxfordtextbooks.co.uk/orc/Morrison4e/
Visit the Online Resource Centre that accompanies this book for web links and regular updates.

17

Local authorities and housing policy

Councils have traditionally been responsible for the following aspects of housing policy:

- building and maintaining housing stock;
- liaising with housing associations (see 'Thatcherite housing policy and the decline of the council home' in this chapter), other voluntary bodies, and private companies to bring low-cost or social housing to their local rented sector and affordable homes to the private market;
- granting planning permission for public, private, and voluntary housing schemes in locations best suited to meet demand;
- providing night shelters, temporary accommodation, and, where necessary, longer-term support for the homeless; and
- assessing claims for Housing Benefit or Local Housing Allowance (LHA) and administering it locally.

Until the mid-1980s, councils played a direct role in providing social housing for the poor and unemployed, by building flats and houses, then making them available for rent at subsidized rates. But during Margaret Thatcher's premiership, the council housing stock steadily diminished, as long-term tenants were given the right to buy their homes at discounted prices, and councils' ability to build more to replace them was curbed in favour of an expanded role for the voluntary and private sectors.

Today, 2 million homes remain in council ownership nationwide and about the same number are managed by housing associations. But, perhaps ironically, in September 2009 the National Housing Federation predicted that, by 2011, around 2 million families would be on waiting lists for rented social homes.

'Capacity' available in the social housing sector varies from area to area. In some, the number of surviving 'council homes' is piecemeal; in others, non-existent. Much of the rented accommodation currently available to low-income tenants is today owned by private agencies, professional and semi-professional landlords, and a new generation of amateur 'buy-to-let' developers. Meanwhile, as successive governments have asserted the public's 'right' to aspire to own their homes, the political focus has switched, at least in part, away from 'social', towards 'affordable' housing—making houses and flats on the private property market more accessible to ordinary working people.

▌ From prefab to new town—a potted history of social housing

Providing fit and proper public housing has been one of the prime purposes of local government since embryonic councils first emerged (see Chapter 11, 'The first British local authorities'). Eliminating overcrowding and poorly constructed housing—and introducing proper sanitation and sewerage systems, and improving hygiene—was a vital part of the fight against diseases such as cholera, dysentery, and typhoid fever undertaken by early public health authorities.

Public housing and the prefab

During the interwar period, there was a period of major public housing activity. A campaign dubbed 'Homes Fit for Heroes' arose out of concern about the poor physical health of many young servicemen from lowly backgrounds recruited to bolster the troops and, under the Housing Act 1919, a start was made on clearing the worst slums. Planned estates were constructed in their place, largely in existing urban areas. But it was not until after the Second World War that a proper house-building boom began, as the struggle to provide shelter for people rendered homeless by Hitler's bombing campaigns became a national emergency.

Ironically, the Blitz helped to clear the way for development. The large areas of wasteland created by the bombings of Britain's major cities offered ample scope for extensive housing projects, and it was not long before the new spirit of collectivism channelled into the 'war effort' was being harnessed to build cheap, functional homes for those returning from the battlefront and the many families left dispossessed by air raids.

Displaced families needed housing at a time when materials were in short supply, so 'prefabs' were developed—literally, prefabricated, single-storey compact houses, made not out of conventional bricks and mortar, but out of anything from shipping containers to surplus aluminium aircraft parts. Prefabs could be manufactured off-site and erected quickly. Their lifespan was intended to be limited, but they fared so well that they survived into the 1970s and can be viewed in building museums to this day.

Prefabs were not the only weapon in the post-war Labour government's bid to provide new housing. In October 1945, Lord Reith was appointed chairman of a 'new town housing committee' charged with devising a workable solution to the growing problem of city overspill. His suggested solution was to draw inspiration from the British New Town movement of Victorian philanthropist Ebenezer Howard, who created the Hertfordshire garden cities of Letchworth and Welwyn: government-backed development corporations would acquire land for construction within 'designated areas'. The resulting New Town Act 1946 designated Stevenage (again in Hertfordshire) as Britain's first official 'new town' and, within a decade, there were 10 more.

The rise of high-rise living

The 1950s 'baby boom' inevitably led to increasing demand for housing and, by the end of the decade, ministers had empowered councils to clear away jerry-built prefabs, to demolish remaining inner-city slums, and to commence a mammoth house-building programme.

Under a series of Acts, beginning with the Housing Act 1957, councils embarked on extensive slum-clearance schemes, using compulsory purchase orders (CPOs—see Chapter 16, 'Compulsory purchase orders (CPOs) and planning blight') to obtain enough land sufficiently quickly to facilitate the construction of suitable alternative housing. But no sooner had they done so than they faced an immediate dilemma that echoes to this day in the decision-making of urban planners: how were they to accommodate a rapidly rising population without resorting to similar tactics to their forebears—namely, cramming homes together in high-density Victorian-style terraces or overcrowded estates? Their solution was to build upwards, rather than laterally—creating the first high-rise tower blocks.

Although a number of multi-storey blocks still exist in and around major towns, there has been a growing backlash against them since the 1970s by planners, politicians, and public. Tight terraces and sink estates might have been shoddily built and poorly served by infrastructure, but at least many such homes had their own backyards or small gardens, facilitating neighbourly interaction. Neither were residents forced to share the entrances into their blocks or to take temperamental lifts up 10 or 20 floors before reaching home. Many tower blocks were initially of sturdier construction than social housing that preceded them, but over time their sheer scale led to structural weaknesses. The lack of accessible shared social spaces and amenities—especially for those living on higher levels—contributed to serious social problems such as drug-taking, vandalism, violent crime, and general isolation. Today, like the sprawling slums that they replaced, tower blocks are viewed by many as ghettoes for a forgotten 'underclass', cut off from mainstream society.

Some tower blocks witnessed particularly ugly scenes. Broadwater Farm in Tottenham, north London, was depicted as one of the worst places to live in Britain in Alice Coleman's influential 1985 book *Utopia on Trial*. Later that year, it witnessed one of the most notorious riots of the 1980s and, in an echo of that time, was the starting point for a protest march prompted by the police shooting of local man Mark Duggan, which, in turn, sparked the 2011 'riots'.

The great 'new town' boom

Given the limited capacity of tower blocks to cater for rapidly rising populations and the social deprivation increasingly associated with them, by the 1960s both central and local government were looking for alternative ways in which to provide mass low-cost housing for those unable to buy their own homes.

A consensus quickly emerged that there should be a further new towns roll-out and 10 more were founded in the 1960s. By far the most famous was Milton Keynes in the Midlands—founded from scratch in 1967. In other cases, the term 'new town' proved a misnomer: the ancient Cambridgeshire cathedral city of Peterborough was designated one in 1967, with Northampton acquiring this status a year later. In effect, these designations gave the towns—along with Warrington—a licence to expand on a scale out of step with towns elsewhere.

The advantages of new towns over other housing solutions were manifold. By effectively starting out with blank slates, urban planners could freely design roads, estates, and other infrastructure in an ergonomic, 'human-centred' way—making maximum use of space and integrating vital community facilities to enhance residents' quality of life. Housing itself was built on a more domestic scale, with two- to three-storey homes arranged along clear street patterns, backed and/or fronted by individual gardens and focal spaces.

But new towns had downsides: established urban areas rarely provided enough space for them, so they tended to develop in largely rural locations, becoming satellite or dormitory towns from which residents had to commute—often considerable distances—to established urban centres for work. Efforts were made to ensure that new towns were as self-sufficient as possible, though—with shops, sports and leisure centres, cinemas, and, in time, employment opportunities—to such an extent that some became so populated that new local authorities had to be established to provide their services.

Despite their demonstrable benefits for families on modest incomes previously excluded from the property market, in practice new towns brought limited gains for those at the bottom. During the 1970s and 1980s, a growing divide opened between poorer households fortunate enough to live in new towns, in which there had been sufficient investment in council housing, and the large number of council tenants still confined to tower blocks elsewhere.

Between 1947 and 1970, 21 new towns were established in England and the new town experiment has since been extended to the rest of Britain, with Scotland acquiring six, and Wales and Northern Ireland, two each. The 32 existing new towns to date, in alphabetical order, are as follows: Bracknell, Basildon, Central Lancashire (Preston, Chorley, and Leyland), Corby, Craigavon, Crawley, Cumbernauld, Cwmbran, Dawley, Derry, East Kilbride, Glenrothes, Harlow, Hemel Hempstead, Irvine, Letchworth, Livingston, Milton Keynes, Newton Aycliffe, Newtown, Northampton, Peterborough, Peterlee, Redditch, Runcorn, Skelmersdale, Stevenage, Telford, Warrington, Washington, Welwyn Garden City and Hatfield. All of the major parties have pledged to revive the new town/garden city ideal if elected in 2015, with Labour promising five more (including four around London) as part of a drive to build 200,000 more homes a year to ease Britain's affordable housing crisis.

▌ The Housing Revenue Account (HRA)

Every housing authority is required by law to record all income and expenditure relating to it on a separate balance sheet from that used for its general revenue funds (see Chapter 12, 'Revenue expenditure and how it is financed'). this 'Housing Revenue Account' (HRA) is split into two halves: one covering revenue income and spending; the other, capital. Most income generated by the HRA takes the form of rent, but councils may also charge one-off fees for arrears or property damage, and accounts accrue interest. the primary purpose of the HRA's capital component is to record all income generated from 'Right to Buy' (RTB) sales (see '"Right to Buy" and the privatization of council housing' in this chapter). The way in which HRAs operate is currently under review.

Council tenants' rights and how they qualify

Council tenancies have traditionally boasted significant advantages over standard assured shorthold tenancies available when renting in the private sector, including:

- secure tenure;
- no deposit;
- rent set at levels substantially below market averages; and
- the tenants' right to buy the home at a discount.

Unsurprisingly, social housing is much prized among those on low incomes. To ensure that they allocated their limited housing stock as fairly and equitably as possible, councils traditionally kept 'housing registers' (or 'waiting lists'). Anyone over the age of 16 who met certain eligibility criteria could apply, with certain applicants prioritized—for example minors, the elderly, and those with long-standing local connections. This system was changed by the Homelessness Act 2002, which introduced a 'points system' to prioritize applicants. It stipulated that 'reasonable preference' should be given to anyone falling into a set of specified categories, although other long-standing factors favouring certain households over others must also be considered. These are outlined in the table entitled 'Criteria for prioritizing social housing applicants', to be found on the **Online Resource Centre**. Those granted council homes normally begin with one-year 'introductory tenancies'. Assuming that they 'pass' these probation periods, they are usually then awarded 'secure tenancies', *unless* evicted for:

- not paying rent;
- causing nuisance to neighbours;
- using the property for illegal activities such as drug dealing; or
- leaving or subletting their homes.

The continuation of tenancies 'for life', although for many years seen as a justified perk of council housing, has become increasingly controversial as home shortages have worsened, particularly in oversubscribed areas of the southeast, where private accommodation is disproportionately pricey. Recent governments have faced growing pressure to prioritize Britain's limited social housing stock, if necessary by terminating tenancies for people whose financial positions significantly improve during their occupancy (enabling lower-income households to replace them). In 2010, George Osborne scrapped secure tenancies for new social tenants in favour of fixed-term contracts. This followed David Cameron's earlier pledge to introduce greater 'flexibility' to encourage unemployed tenants to move around in pursuit of work and to move those whose incomes increased over time into private renting—freeing up housing for the neediest. Ministers also launched a 'Freedom Pass' scheme, allowing English social housing tenants to swap homes with those in other areas, to facilitate economic mobility. 'Social rents' are also undergoing a transformation: at the same time as Housing Benefit was being capped, the Coalition introduced a new 'affordable rent' initiative, allowing registered housing providers to charge up to 80 per cent of local market rent levels for accommodation aimed at those on low incomes. By giving suppliers the flexibility to push rents higher than they were under traditional models of social housing, ministers hoped that they would incentivize suppliers to invest more in relatively low-cost homes. In his 2013 Budget, Mr Osborne shifted the emphasis of housing policy further away from 'social' and more towards 'affordable' (see 'The rise of owner-occupancy and the "affordable housing" debate' in this chapter) by launching an 'affordable housing guarantee', with the government agreeing to underwrite money borrowed by private providers and housing associations (HAs—see 'Thatcherite housing policy and the decline of the council home' in this chapter), provided that they used it to build cheaper homes.

Councils can also impose extra conditions to determine which people qualify for social housing. Some use their discretion to explicitly *disqualify* those who have left a previous tenancy owing money. Others introduce harsh sanctions for those judged in breach of their social housing contracts: Burnley Borough Council, Lancashire, has written clauses into tenancy agreements allowing social housing providers to evict tenants for antisocial behaviour (a sanction authorized by the Housing Act 1996). The concept of 'earned' tenancies was embedded by the Coalition, with individual councils given greater licence to distinguish between more and less 'deserving' cases. In December 2011, *The Guardian* reported plans by Westminster City Council to require unemployed people hoping to qualify for social housing and related benefits to sign 'civic contracts' pledging to undertake local voluntary work as a precondition. The idea (since replicated elsewhere) was one of several proposals that the Tory-run council said it was introducing to end the 'something-for-nothing culture' and better reward those who 'play by the rules'—language that could have been lifted from speeches by Coalition ministers. Among the other ways in which Westminster is now rationing the points that it allocates to prospective social tenants is to give more to nurses, volunteer police officers, Territorial Army members, ex-service personnel, and those who foster or adopt children—while deducting them from adults whose children persistently skip school and those penalized for antisocial behaviour.

However brutal these measures may seem, there are signs of an emerging consensus on the need for tougher rationing of social housing. In June 2012, ministers published new guidelines pressing councils to move employed people looking for social homes higher up their housing lists. Recognizing both the increasing appetite of its own core working-class voters to penalize 'undeserving' welfare recipients and the scarcity of social resources amid the Coalition's austerity drive, Labour signalled that it, too, might introduce harsher points-based qualifications if returned to government. Significantly, Westminster Council's Labour opposition abstained in the crucial vote on whether to introduce the Tory-instigated housing qualifications.

Other local authority housing responsibilities

Councils not only have to provide *new* rental homes, but also must maintain and improve *existing* ones—as well as monitoring the state of local private accommodation. Many have now combined their housing and environmental health departments, following several court actions brought against landlords under various Public Health Acts. The 1990 Act outlined councils' duty to inspect existing buildings in their areas to detect and, if necessary, 'eliminate' smoke, dust, fumes, rubbish, noise pollution, and other 'statutory nuisances'.

Councils may also take action over any houses deemed 'unfit for human habitation'. When assessing if somewhere is 'unfit', they consider its state of repair, freedom from damp, natural lighting, ventilation, water supply, drainage, and sanitation. The Housing Act 1985 gave councils powers to serve 'repair notices' on owners of unfit homes. Alternatively, they may carry out specified repairs to bring dwellings up to habitable standards, sending owners the bill. In exceptional circumstances, they can serve 'closure notices' (ordering owners to cease using dwellings for that purpose) or 'demolition notices', or even buy unfit houses outright and absorb them into their own stock. Sometimes, it is necessary to act against an entire 'area', requiring or undertaking improvements or demolition. Demolished areas are known as 'clearance areas'. Before a clearance order can be made, the authority must arrange rehousing for all tenants and finance the work. The Housing, Grants, Construction, and Regeneration Act 1996 enables councils to pay discretionary relocation grants to displaced people to help them to buy at least a part-share in a new home in the same area.

The Local Government and Housing Act 1989 also empowered councils to declare whole districts 'renewal areas' for up to 10 years. These normally encompass at least 300 dwellings, 75 per cent privately owned, and are areas in which a third of inhabitants receive benefits. Once renewal areas are designated, councils may acquire the land by agreement or by CPO, providing new housing, improving existing stock, and disposing of property to suitable third parties.

Private accommodation can also benefit from council help. The Housing Act 1996 introduced means-tested, mostly discretionary, grants to help homeowners unable to afford essential adaptations themselves. More recently, various new 'green' grants—funded by central government—have also been introduced to help tenants and homeowners to improve their energy efficiency, to reduce both their fuel bills and carbon footprints. The Queen notoriously tried to take advantage of this scheme, as revealed by a Freedom of Information request made by *The Independent* in 2010 (see Chapter 20, 'The Queen and Royal Household'). The main types of grant are listed in the table entitled 'Local authority grants available to private homeowners', to be found on the **Online Resource Centre**.

▌ Thatcherite housing policy and the decline of the council home

As with many other areas of policy, the Thatcher government had a profound effect on the availability of social housing in Britain. Less than a year after gaining office, the Conservatives embarked on a radical overhaul of the extant council house framework—giving long-standing tenants the chance to buy their homes at knock-down prices and forcing authorities to sell to them. Within the decade, responsibility for building and maintaining social housing had moved decisively away from councils, towards new not-for-profit organizations independent of direct democratic control, known as **housing associations (HAs),** overseen by a similarly unaccountable national quango, the Housing Corporation. Things would never be the same again.

'Right to Buy' and the privatization of council housing

 One of the defining election-winning policies of the Thatcher era was the 'Right to Buy' (RTB) programme ushered in by the Housing Act 1980 in England and Wales, and the Tenants' Rights (Scotland) Act 1980 north of the border. Under this scheme, some 5 million 'long-term' council tenants were offered the chance to purchase their homes at a discount on the price that the houses were estimated to be worth on the open market.

Eligible tenants could initially claim the following discounts:

- households who had occupied their homes for at least three years could buy at discounts of 33 per cent for houses or 44 per cent for flats; and

- those who had rented from councils for more than 20 years received 50 per cent discounts on either houses or flats.

The Housing Act 1985 increased the value of discounts significantly, as follows.

- Tenants living in houses for more than two years could claim 32 per cent discounts *plus* 1 per cent for each complete year by which the qualifying period exceeded two years (up to 60 per cent).

- Those resident for two years or more in flats could claim 44 per cent *plus* 2 per cent for each complete year by which the qualifying period exceeded two years (up to 70 per cent).

Between 1980 and 1995, 2.1 million homes previously in the council, HA, or new town social sectors were transferred to private ownership. Since then, social housing has continued to be privatized at a rate of 60,000 a year—with the result that some areas, including Leicester and parts of Argyll and Bute in Scotland, now have little or no council-owned stock left.

Right to Buy—lauded by Mrs Thatcher in the Tories' 1983 election manifesto as the 'the biggest single step towards a home-owning democracy ever taken'—was understandably popular with aspirational working-class voters. By the time of the party's 1987 election victory, even Labour had dropped its formal opposition. On the face of it, the policy also provided a welcome boon to hard-pressed councils, liberating them from responsibility for maintaining often aged and creaky accommodation, and raising millions in capital receipts that (theoretically) could be spent in other areas of need. According to social policy think tank the Joseph

Rowntree Foundation, proceeds from council home sales between 1987–88 and 1989–90 generated £33 billion—more than the windfalls from privatizing BP, British Telecom, British Gas, British Airways, and Rolls Royce combined.

But critics believe the RTB has had a devastating impact on the ability of councils and HAs to provide homes for future generations without the financial means to rent privately or buy. Perhaps its most controversial feature was the strict controls that ministers imposed on councils' ability to spend receipts generated by sales on improving or increasing their remaining housing stock. Initially, they were limited to spending only 20 per cent of this income on housing, rising to 25 per cent after the Housing Act 1989. But what the 1989 Act gave with one hand, it took with the other: the three-quarters of receipts remaining had to be spent not on building schools, care homes, or roads, but on paying off debts. Despite later modifications, similar rules continued for many years.

The Coalition has re-embraced RTB—with the nominal guarantee that, this time round, councils will not only be permitted, but also required, to ensure that income generated from selling homes is ploughed directly into building new ones for those who need them. Former Housing Minister Grant Shapps pledged that, for each additional council home sold, a new one must be provided at 'affordable rent'. The 'catch', however, was that councils selling off homes would be allowed to use only 30 per cent of their RTB receipts to fund new homes—forcing them to find the balance from a combination of the 'affordable rent' (of up to 80 per cent of market value) that they were charging on other properties, borrowing, and 'cross-subsidy' from their 'own resources'. Those now eligible are able to buy their homes at £75,000 below the market price—a numerical reduction that effectively trebles the discount cap that applied in most of England (and quadruples that in London) by the end of Labour's tenure.

Nonetheless, the mass sell-off of council homes continues to be blamed by some for reducing picturesque villages and coastal towns to 'ghost towns'. The lack of social housing in such areas has priced many locals out of the property market, with buy-to-let and absentee holiday home buyers pushing up both private rents and sale prices way beyond the means of local people employed in traditional rural and seaside jobs. In Tenby, Pembrokeshire, the average house price had risen to £200,000 by 2010 and four out of 10 were second homes. However, as of July that year, the Welsh Assembly Government was granted devolved powers to ban RTB purchases in situations in which allowing them would have detrimental effects on housing stock. At a wider national level, the Coalition's favoured solution to shortages of affordable housing is for local communities to take it into their own hands to promote development—by allowing them to fast-track applications for small-scale housing projects.

Between 1997 and 2010, Labour took incremental steps towards restoring councils' ability to build new housing stock—for example permitting the construction of 2,000 new council homes across England in September 2009, amid warnings that a further 200,000 families were headed for housing waiting lists. Nevertheless,

Table 17.1 Arguments for and against 'Right to Buy'

For	Against
Offers low-income households chance to buy own homes. It is progressive policy promoting opportunity, aspiration, and ownership among the poor.	Councils historically allowed to spend only fraction of capital receipts from RTB sales on building more. This leaves fewer available for those needing them in future. Also, many of those sold off were homes in best state of repair, leaving councils with less attractive stock, with higher maintenance demands.
Council tenants traditionally had to rely on local authorities for repairs and maintenance—often waiting months or years. Enabling them to buy their homes liberates them from local bureaucracy—giving them flexibility to pay for repairs when needed and motivating them to maintain properties to high standards.	Distribution of council housing has historically been unequal, with some more proactive about promoting RTB than others. Tenants' ability to buy their homes subject to 'postcode lottery'—with those on low incomes forced to rent from private landlords because of lack of rentable social housing.
Raises significant revenue for local government to repay debts. Less debt means healthier finances, because more money left for essential services—and savings may lead to lower Council Tax.	Selling housing enables councils to offload repair costs onto (former) tenants. While initial sale prices may be attractive, disrepair of some homes leaves those purchasing them with high ongoing costs.

with the Office for National Statistics (ONS) predicting that Britain's population is likely to top 65 million by 2020, the country continues to lack the sustained investment in housing that some say is needed. Following a lengthy review of RTB north of the border, the Scottish Parliament voted to scrap the policy in June 2014. Arguments for and against 'Right to Buy' are explored in Table 17.1.

Despite its manifest attractions for aspiring homeowners of limited means, RTB contained caveats designed to deter people from cashing in. If a house was sold within three years of being bought by a tenant, part of the discount had to be repaid—pro rata the time that had elapsed since its purchase. The general thrust of the government's approach, however, was to do everything possible to persuade tenants to purchase housing and councils to part with it. If councils were doing too little to promote the scheme, the Secretary of State could appoint commissioners to investigate and, if necessary, enforce it. Some Labour authorities, such as Norwich City Council, actively sabotaged it and ended up mounting unsuccessful legal fights to preserve their housing stock.

Ministers also introduced 'RTB mortgages', administered by councils—although in time these were replaced by 'rent-to-mortgage' schemes introduced under the Leasehold Reform, Housing, and Urban Development Act 1993. The price fixed for a house or flat comprised two elements:

- an *initial capital payment*—a part-mortgage paid in regular instalments at the same or a similar level to the rent for which they were previously liable; and

- a *deferred financial commitment*—a lump sum that accrued no interest, but was repayable on the property's sale, purchaser's death, or by voluntary payments at any time.

These models were forerunners of the shared ownership schemes commonplace today, under which 'tenants' buy shares in properties from HAs, using normal home loans, and rent the remainder.

From housing associations (HAs) to social landlords

The 1957 Act had formalized councils' responsibilities as primary social housing providers, but when the 1985 Act supplanted it as the 'principal' housing law, this mantle was passed to new not-for-profit HAs. Coming at the same time as Mrs Thatcher's government was confronting the Greater London Council, metropolitan borough councils, and 'loony Left' authorities elsewhere, the decision to dilute the powers of local housing departments was viewed by some as another assault on the autonomy of elected councillors. Councils, it seemed, were caught in a carefully orchestrated pincer movement—between households keen to buy council homes, on the one hand, and newly emancipated HAs (backed by Whitehall), on the other.

Sometimes called the 'third arm of housing', Britain's 1,800 HAs—today known as 'registered providers'—are regulated and funded by the Homes and Communities Agency (HCA). In Scotland, HAs are regulated directly by the Scottish Government; in Wales, by the Welsh Assembly; in Northern Ireland, by the Northern Ireland Housing Executive. Most HAs are registered as industrial and provident societies. All have volunteer management committees elected by their membership. Some have no professional staff, while others are large, with substantial workforces.

Councils may loan money or provide guarantees to registered HAs, in return for interest. They normally have the right to nominate up to half of council tenants in their areas for HA schemes.

The primacy of HAs was cemented by the introduction of 'Tenants' Choice' in the Housing Act 1988, under which councils were pressurized to promote them as alternative social housing providers. But rather than simply giving tenants the right to move into HA properties, the Act sought to transfer housing stock itself into associations' hands. In truth, even some Labour-run authorities (whatever their ideological objections) relished offloading homes, given the high running costs and other complexities associated with repairs and maintenance. By July 1996, 51 councils had transferred their entire stocks to HAs—totalling 220,000 properties.

Further emasculation of councils followed. The 1993 Act and detailed regulations flowing from it introduced the concept of 'tenant management organizations' (TMOs). Groups of council tenants living in designated areas were permitted to set up TMOs to take over day-to-day management of their housing and its finances—effectively *replacing* councils and forming de facto HAs. The National Federation of Tenant Management Organizations had more than 100 member TMOs by September 2010.

Another development came with the Housing Act 1996, which introduced the label 'social landlord'—an umbrella term covering a variety of different models of shared social housing management. Whatever precise form they take, social landlords are overseen, like HAs, by the HCA. They include not-for-profit 'housing companies'—often partnered with, but not directly controlled by, councils and/or tenants themselves—and 'housing co-operatives' (a variation on TMOs).

The outcome of this flurry of reforms was precisely what the Conservatives wanted: 'a more pluralist and more market-oriented system'. A symbolic final seal was set on the logical direction of the party's policies when the Local Government and Housing Act 1989 explicitly freed councils from any obligation to retain their own social housing stock.

The rise of owner-occupancy and the 'affordable housing' debate

Recent surveys—produced separately for England, Scotland, Wales, and Northern Ireland—suggest that, despite years of spiralling house prices and the well-reported financial obstacles faced by first-time buyers, Britain is close to becoming that great 'home-owning democracy' heralded by Mrs Thatcher back in 1983. Figure 17.1 and 17.2 provide a comparison between the breakdown of dwelling types in England in 1961 (the year in which records began) and 2012–13 (the most recent year for which data is available). Information from the 31 March 1961 census revealed that, of the 13.83 million dwellings in which English people then lived, 6.1 million (44 per cent) were owner-occupied houses and flats, with 4.4 million (32 per cent) rented from private landlords or as part of the residents' job or business, and 3.38 million (24 per cent) council housing. Some 50 years later, the United Kingdom Statistics Authority's English Housing Survey 2012–13 found that, of a total of 22 million dwellings, the number of owner-occupied properties had soared to 65 per cent (14.3 million)—although, in light of the ongoing restraints on mortgage lending (see Chapter 7, 'Regulating the financial markets'), this had fallen from 17.5 million four years previously. The proportion renting from councils or other social landlords had dropped by more than a third over the half-century—with the effect that the private rented sector had overtaken it for the first time since the 1960s. While 4 million households (18 per cent) were renting privately, only 3.7 million (17 per cent) were living in social homes.

Despite the growth in home ownership, however, many—particularly those on low incomes and single people in south-east England—found it next to

Figure 17.1 Where English residents were living, 31 March 1961

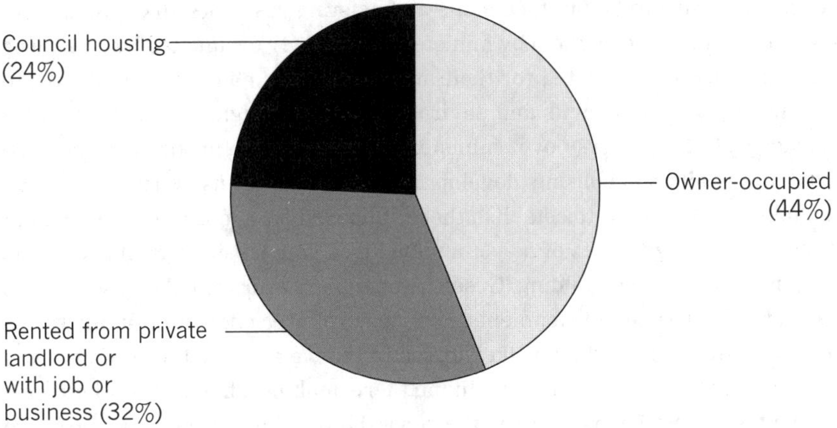

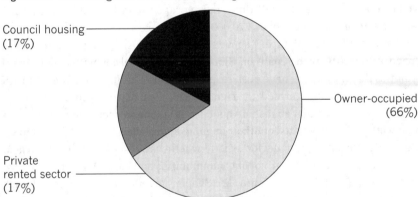

Council housing (24%)

Owner-occupied (44%)

Rented from private landlord or with job or business (32%)

Source: Department for Communities and Local Government (DCLG) © Crown Copyright 2012

Figure 17.2 Where English residents were living, 2012–13

Council housing (17%)

Owner-occupied (66%)

Private rented sector (17%)

Source: Department for Communities and Local Government (DCLG) © Crown Copyright 2014

impossible to enter the property market during the Noughties housing boom. As a consequence, recent years have seen numerous policy initiatives geared towards helping out those who neither qualify for conventional social housing nor can afford their own homes. Particular emphasis has been placed on the plight of 'key workers'—public servants such as teachers and nurses (especially those living in areas such as inner London, where prices are disproportionately high).

To guarantee that the market provided more 'affordable' houses, New Labour aimed to build 3 million new homes by 2020, at a projected cost of £8 billion. In theory, by targeting them at areas with shortages of affordable private sector homes, this would have both provided bricks and mortar up-front and forced prices down across the board. The sheer scale of development proposed for some areas generated fierce opposition. In the south-east, where 200,000 new houses were due to be built, councils and existing residents alike objected to the 'quotas' imposed on them by ministers. The newly designated South Downs National Park was targeted for thousands of homes (many in flood plains), to the fury of parish councils and environmental campaigners. There was also considerable controversy over ministers' pledge to give preferential permission to sustainable housing developments, or 'eco-towns'. Criticisms have included the fact that, to establish these supposed paragons of environmental friendliness, large tracts of as-yet-undeveloped countryside would need to be surrendered to house-building. Green campaigners also argued that some sites earmarked for such developments were in rural areas bereft of public transport infrastructure—a factor likely to lead to above-average levels of car ownership among those who ended up living there, making a mockery of their 'eco' credentials. Campaigns against the mass house-building programme were launched from the south-west to the north-east, although some experts claimed that the government's plans were too modest: in October 2007, the National Housing and Planning Advice Unit predicted that typical UK house prices would spiral to nine-and-a-half times the average salary by 2026 unless ministers were to increase supply by 270,000 homes a year.

Whatever the true picture, Labour's top-down housing targets were abandoned in July 2010 by the Coalition. Since then, individual councils, and the communities that they serve, have been responsible for deciding what Communities Secretary Eric Pickles termed 'the right level of local housing provision in their area'. To allay fears that abolishing quotas might leave a short-term policy vacuum while councils worked out their ongoing approaches to strategic planning, Mr Pickles urged them to decide swiftly whether to abandon or retain targets previously imposed on them, so that 'communities and landowners know where they stand'. The following month, Mr Shapps unveiled a New Homes Bonus scheme, designed to incentivize councils to build affordable housing by offering them extra funding for doing so. For every new home built, the government would match Council Tax raised on the premises for the following six years. But Mr Shapps's Labour opposite, John Healey, quipped that, in practice, existing government grants to councils were likely to be raided to finance it—meaning that ministers would be 'robbing Peterborough to pay Poole'.

Boosting housing supply is, in any case, only one part of the equation. A major obstacle facing many first-time buyers since the financial crash has been the reluctance of banks and building societies to grant them mortgages without demanding hefty deposits. In London and the south-east, even professional earners have been unable to borrow sufficient multiples of their salaries to afford the most modest homes available. The Coalition's response was a 'Help to Buy' scheme designed to enable households to purchase homes worth up to £600,000 with deposits of as little as 5 per cent of their value. By offering mortgage lenders taxpayer-backed guarantees on loans to eligible customers, between the scheme's October 2013 launch and the following May the government enabled 7,313 applicants to each borrow up to 85–90 per cent of their homes' values. At time of writing, there were signs that Britain's volatile housing market was once more in danger of overheating, stoked in part by 'Help to Buy', with Halifax reporting in May 2014 that there had been a year-on-year increase of 8.5 per cent in average property prices over the previous 12 months—putting many homes further beyond the reach of those not benefiting from the various ministerial initiatives.

▶ Housing policy and the homeless

Councils have a statutory duty to house the 'unintentionally homeless' and those threatened with homelessness 'within 28 days of being made aware of their predicament' under the Housing (Homeless Persons) Act 1977 and Homelessness Act 2002. Under the Housing Act 1996, however, the ambit of 'homelessness' was narrowed to allow councils to take into account available accommodation across Britain and even 'elsewhere'. The reform's aim was to help out councils presented with disproportionately high numbers of homeless people (particularly asylum seekers) because it would be unreasonable for them to house all applicants in their own areas. Ensuing regulations also tightened the law regarding asylum seekers' eligibility for housing assistance: anyone who did not claim this status at the port of their arrival was rendered ineligible (barring refugees and those granted 'exceptional or unconditional leave to remain' in Britain). The Act also introduced a two-year limit on provision of accommodation in certain cases and a review of all cases after that.

The types of homeless people treated as priority cases are those:

- with dependent children;
- made homeless by emergencies or disasters (flood, fire, etc.);
- vulnerable because of old age, or mental or physical disability; and
- who are pregnant.

When assessing applications from homeless people for permanent housing and while waiting for flats to become available, councils often use short-stay, hostel, and/or 'bed and breakfast' accommodation (in reality, seldom more than dingy bedsits or studio flats within multi-occupancy dwellings).

The overriding controversy over councils' responsibilities towards the homeless, however, relates to the Act's wide-ranging definition of 'unintentional homelessness'. Under the law, the 'intentionally homeless' include people evicted from private sector accommodation for falling behind with rent and even those fleeing home 'voluntarily' to escape domestic abuse. Nonetheless, if 'intentionally homeless' people fit into priority categories, councils must provide them with advice, assistance, and temporary accommodation.

The Coalition has further diluted councils' responsibility towards the homeless—allowing them to abandon their 'duty of care' once they have successfully steered people into private accommodation for a year.

Tony Blair's government made a high-profile effort to tackle street homelessness during its first term. His bullish 'Homelessness Tsar', Louise Casey, launched the Rough Sleepers Initiative, initially in central London, then several other cities with high levels of homelessness, including Bristol and Brighton. Its stated aim was initially to provide places in short-term hostels and leased spaces in 'move-on' accommodation, before rerouting street-sleepers to permanent homes, high-dependency specialist care homes, and special accommodation for people with drink or drug problems. The initiative officially ended in March 2002, having (according to ministers) largely achieved its aims.

Not everyone was convinced by its figures, however. 'Spot counts' of rough sleepers were periodically carried out on the streets of target towns and cities—but controversy erupted in December 2002 when volunteers working with the homeless in Waterloo and Westminster alleged that they had been moved out of the London boroughs two nights before a count, to gerrymander the figures downwards.

Homelessness has returned to the media agenda again following the Coalition's benefit cuts (see Chapter 8 and the next section). According to the figures from the Department for Communities and Local Government (DCLG) itself, between April and June 2013 3,580 households became homeless because their private tenancies ended—a leap of 32 per cent on the same period in 2012. The number of people in temporary accommodation (an indicator of incipient homelessness) rose by 9 per cent, to 56,210, with most of those affected (41,250) living in London. Interpreting the figures as evidence of a direct correlation between welfare changes and rising homelessness, Leslie Morphy, then chief executive of Crisis, had this blunt message for ministers:

> People who need the support of housing benefit to make ends meet have seen cut after cut in the amount they receive. We have been warning for years that this would drive up homelessness and today's figures could not be clearer.

▶ Local authorities, Housing Benefit, and the Local Housing Allowance (LHA)

Councils are responsible for administering Housing Benefit on behalf of the Department for Work and Pensions (DWP—see Chapter 8, 'The Department for Work and Pensions (DWP)'). Since April 2008, Housing Benefit—a payment equivalent to all or part of the rent charged to low-income tenants living in private, public, or voluntary sector accommodation—has been calculated using a **Local Housing Allowance (LHA)** formula.

For many years, there were two types of Housing Benefit, depending on individuals' circumstances:

- *standard*—for low-earning workers; and
- *certificated*—for those on out-of-work benefits such as Jobseeker's Allowance (JSA), or Incapacity Benefit or Employment and Support Allowance (ESA).

These distinctions have been supplanted by simplified eligibility criteria based purely on individuals' status as tenants, their low incomes, and their lack of more than £16,000 in savings.

The principal difference between the new and old ways of calculating Housing Benefit relates to the method used to assess how much claimants receive. Housing Benefit used to involve individual properties being inspected by housing officers to determine their (notional) rental values, with successful claimants receiving payments commensurate with what their council felt the accommodation was worth. The LHA has simplified this process, by offering claimants blanket rates for different levels of property (from one-bedroom flats to four-bedroom houses) based on 'middle of the range' (median) market rents for each category in their neighbourhoods (known as 'broad market rental areas', or BMRAs).

Anti-poverty campaigners argued that the 'new' calculation method, introduced by Labour, meant that the sums received by even those granted full help with rental costs and living in modest properties often fall well short of what landlords actually charged. Disability groups, meanwhile, complain that the LHA discriminates against severely disabled people who require two-bedroom homes to accommodate live-in carers. In November 2009, a benefits tribunal found against Walsall Council in a case brought by the mother of a severely disabled woman, who argued that the reforms had unfairly left her with a weekly £70–75 rent shortfall on the two-bedroom home that they shared.

Discontent over cutbacks to Housing Benefit and the LHA escalated following passage of the Welfare Reform Act 2012, which paved the way for them to be absorbed into an all-encompassing Universal Credit (UC—see Chapter 8, 'Rationalizing welfare—Universal Credit'), and the introduction of benefit capping. As well as bringing in a £280 weekly limit for a one-bedroom flat and one of £400 a week for a four-bedroom house, the Act formalized an across-the-board annual benefits cap for households of £26,000, including Housing Benefit—putting paid to the type of story, beloved of the *Daily Mail*, about welfare-dependent families receiving tens of thousands of pounds a year to live in palatial London homes that most waged households could never afford.

The way in which the LHA itself is calculated has also become less generous: Labour set payments at 50 per cent of the BMRA, but the Coalition has reduced this ratio to 30 per cent. But most explosive of all was the introduction of the 'spare room subsidy'—dubbed the 'bedroom tax' by critics—which removed £40 a month from social tenants living in properties with additional bedrooms not used for sleeping and £70 from those with two extra rooms. The move was designed to 'free up spare capacity' for those on waiting lists, but led to warnings from housing charities that vulnerable people would be forced out of their homes, and perhaps made homeless. Despite the offer of discretionary payments for the most needy, to be channelled through councils, the 'tax' was heavily opposed by disability campaigners, who argued that it would disproportionately penalize those whose 'spare' rooms were needed to store specialist equipment or to accommodate short-term carers. Within months of the subsidy's introduction, various reports testified to its negative impact: in February 2014, the National Housing Federation revealed that two-thirds of the 523,000 tenants affected had fallen into arrears, many for the first time, with 72,000 HA renters attributing this directly to the new 'tax'. Of these, 15 per cent had already received eviction risk letters from their landlords. So serious were shortfalls in some households' budgets—and so limited their options, in terms of moving to smaller properties—that numerous councils opted to introduce 'no eviction' policies to protect rent-defaulters. Official DWP figures confirmed a similar picture that July, finding that six out of 10 affected households had been unable to meet shortfalls of £14–£22 caused by the introduction of the 'tax', forcing them to borrow from high-interest payday loan companies and to make invidious 'heat or eat' decisions. So stark were the findings that, 10 months before the 2015 election, they prompted Lib Dem Deputy Prime Minister Nick Clegg to call for the policy to be overhauled, arguing that the market's failure to provide smaller homes for those affected meant that it was 'not working'. Meanwhile, the Scottish Government pledged to find money centrally to cover the subsidy's £50 million cost in 2014–15, and Labour vowed to repeal it if it won in 2015.

Criticism of the Coalition's Housing Benefit reforms has come from an even wider range of voices. Before the 2012 Act received royal assent, some London boroughs revealed that they were already seeking 'bed and breakfast' accommodation in cheaper outlying suburbs in anticipation of a rise in evictions—prompting Labour frontbencher Chris Bryant to condemn the government's reforms as 'social cleansing'. Influential backbencher Jon Cruddas likened them to latter-day 'clearances'—a reference to moves to corral paupers and the unemployed in the eighteenth and nineteenth centuries. Even Boris Johnson, Conservative Mayor of London, told a radio presenter that he would not allow poor people to be shunted out of the capital 'on my watch'. Ministers retorted that such claims were scaremongering—arguing that benefit cuts would merely induce claimants to move into more modest rented properties (of which they said there were plenty) and/or landlords to charge less, as the private market corrected itself.

But since the Act came into force, some fears appear to have been borne out. Investigations by *The Guardian* and BBC Radio 4's *Today* programme have demonstrated that, in London and Oxford (the second most competitive rental market in England) respectively, there is a severe shortage of surplus private rented properties priced at or below LHA level, the owners of which will accept benefit claimants. Given these findings, it came as little surprise to critics of the government's reforms when, in April 2012, *The Guardian* reported that Westminster and Hammersmith councils had begun shipping social tenants priced out of their homes elsewhere, while Labour-run Newham Council had approached a Stoke-based HA asking it to accommodate 500 families whom it argued had been forced to leave the London borough as a result of the Housing Benefit cap. Newham's move prompted ministers to accuse Labour of 'playing politics' with social tenants. But, responding to Mr Shapps's insistence that there were more than 1,000 affordable rental properties within a five-mile radius of Newham available on the Rightmove lettings website as of April 2012, *Guardian* journalist Polly Curtis conducted her own experimental search. While she found 339 four-bedroom houses available in the area at or below the new £400 cap level, not one of the half-dozen agents whom she called randomly to enquire about the properties said that they were willing to accommodate claimants.

In June 2012, meanwhile, *The Guardian* reported a warning by England's HAs of a chronic lack of space in social homes for the estimated 100,000 people who had already received letters telling them that they needed to find smaller properties to continue receiving benefits. Iain Sim, chief executive of Coast & Country, one of the largest providers in north-east England, told the paper that while he had 2,500 properties with at least one 'spare' room that could be freed up if 'under-occupiers' were to move out, he had only 16 one-bedroom flats available to house those who did. Around the same time, a government-commissioned study by the Centre for Regional Economic and Social Research at Sheffield Hallam University found that four out of 10 private landlords in London, and a third of those elsewhere in England, were planning to stop accepting claimants within the year.

Others have cast doubt on the entire premise for the Coalition's reforms—principally, the idea that workless benefit claimants are being unfairly subsidized by 'hardworking families' struggling to pay their own way unaided. In a 2010 article in *Inside Housing*, trade journal of the social housing sector, Helen Williams, assistant director of the National Housing Federation, argued that, far from being a mass of feckless, work-shy scroungers, three-quarters of the 4.7 million households claiming Housing Benefit were either retired, disabled, or full-time carers. Of the remaining 24 per cent, half were in work. Figures from homelessness charity Shelter and the DWP itself backed up this assertion, with the former demonstrating that fewer than one in eight Housing Benefit claimants were unemployed.

Although the administration of housing-related benefits is set to change, delays in implementing UC in most areas meant that, at time of writing, it remained with councils. Alongside LHA, they have traditionally administered Council Tax Benefit, which used to equate to full Council Tax rebates for LHA claimants. In April 2013, Council Tax Benefit was scrapped for everyone other than pensioners, to be replaced by a new, more localized, system known as Council Tax Reduction, administered according to criteria determined by each council. Critics condemned the new scheme as a postcode lottery in the making, adding that numerous low-income households who had never previously been charged Council Tax would be billed for the first time, because the budget set aside to implement the new policy was 10 per cent (£414 million) lower than that preceding it. Sure enough, in January 2014, the Institute for Fiscal Studies (IFS) think tank reported that 2.5 million working households had already lost an average of £160 in the 2013–14 financial year. Seven out of ten councils had asked households that previously qualified for Council Tax Benefit for a minimum payment, with only one in five managing to maintain existing levels of support.

▌ Forcing down market rents—the case for 'rent controls'

Controversy about housing shortages and benefit cuts has revived debate about a long-standing policy for protecting low-income tenants, abandoned by the Thatcher government nearly a quarter of a century ago: 'rent controls'. Between 1915 and 1988, council-employed rent officers could intervene directly in their areas to limit rental costs for the unemployed and low-paid. The axing of controls was accompanied by the introduction of six-month 'assured shorthold' tenancies for both landlords and renters. At the time, ministers argued that, however noble the intention behind them, controls had the effect of stifling investment in private rented housing, encouraging 'slum landlords' to let out substandard accommodation at bargain-basement rents to the poor. The reintroduction of rent controls was one of the signature policies to which Labour's Ken Livingstone shackled his ultimately unsuccessful campaign to be reinstated as London Mayor in May 2012. In May 2014, Mr Miliband committed an incoming Labour government to legislate for limited rent controls—capping the levels by which private-sector rents would be allowed to rise in any given year. He also pledged to scrap fees for letting agents and introduce longer, securer, tenancies for those renting.

☰ Topical feature idea

The following is extracted from an article published in the *Yorkshire Evening Post* on 5 January 2014. It focuses on a sharp rise in the cost of providing emergency accommodation for the homeless in Leeds as a result of a lack of local social housing. How would you develop the story into a balanced background feature? Who would you interview and what would you ask them?

Extract from an article published in *Yorkshire Evening Post*, 5 January 2014

Leeds City Council's £1 million housing crisis

By Joanna Wardill

Yorkshire Evening Post

5 January 2014

Web link: **www.yorkshireeveningpost. co.uk/news/latest-news/top-stories/ leeds-city-council-s-1-million-housing-crisis-1-6351593**

Leeds City Council has spent just more than £1m on providing emergency accommodation for the homeless in the last year, the Yorkshire Evening Post can reveal.

Figures obtained under the Freedom of Information Act show the £1m spent by the council in 2012/13 was nearly twice the £540,000 from the previous year.

The cost been [*sic*] rising since 2010/11—when it stood at £209,000—as the housing crisis continues to deepen in the economic downturn.

Residents are put into emergency accommodation when deemed homeless in what is meant to be a temporary move—but figures show people have been going months without a proper home. One stay racked up 46 weeks in 2012/13, costing a total of £36,463.

The cost for placing households in B&B accommodation has also doubled over the past year—from £83,962 in 2011/12 to £169,348 in 2012/13.

The longest B&B stay in 2012/13 lasted 41 weeks, at £45 a night, costing £12,915.

Council bosses told the YEP it recognised the rocketing costs were 'unsustainable' and has now had a radical overhaul of its response to homelessness. Its forecast cost for 2013/14 was expected to fall to £100,000.

Coun John Hardy, lead member for homelessness, said: 'There is a new attitude and new way of working, of moving people on and helping them to get sorted out and their lives back on track. We deal with people on the day.'

He said the new system scrapped B&Bs and places more residents in private rentals, where they can then apply for housing benefit.

As previously reported in the YEP, there remains a huge backlog in Leeds of social housing—with around 15,000 currently on waiting lists. The council recently agreed to spend £40m to boost housing stock—a move charities say is of key importance. Dave Paterson, of Unity in Poverty Action in Leeds, said a concern with private landlords is the emphasis on making money, rather than tenants' welfare. 'To me, social housing is more ethical—the responsibilty [*sic*] underneath is to care for people. Social housing is key and the more we can get of it, the better. I fully support every effort the council's making to get on with what are really difficult situations.'

✳ Current issues

- **The impact of recent benefit changes** According to the National Housing Federation, the 'spare room subsidy' (or 'bedroom tax') has caused 72,000 housing association tenants to fall into rent arrears, many for the first time, while 2.5 million low-income working households have faced their first Council Tax bills since the scrapping of Council Tax Benefit.

- **The switch from 'social' to 'affordable' renting** The Coalition is allowing social housing providers to offer rents at up to 80 per cent of market rates, hoping to encourage them to invest in more low-cost homes. Ministers are also guaranteeing loans to providers who build affordable social housing.

- **The rise of 'Help to Buy'** More than 7,000 mortgage applicants benefited from the government's 'Help to Buy' scheme between October 2013 and May 2014. The scheme allows first-time buyers and others struggling to buy private housing to borrow up to 85–90 per cent of a property's value, with taxpayers guaranteeing their loans.

▦ Key points

1. 'Social housing' is the generic term for houses or flats available at reduced rents to those on low incomes. Traditionally provided by councils, it is now largely managed by housing associations (HAs).

2. 'Affordable housing' is a term applied to houses or flats available to purchase at prices below the market average. It is often targeted at first-time buyers and 'key workers' (essential professionals such as nurses and teachers).

3. The Housing Revenue Account (HRA) is a dedicated budget used to manage and maintain councils' housing stock. It is separate from the general revenue account and its principle income is rent received from tenants.

4. The main welfare support available to low-income tenants is Housing Benefit (HB), now generally known as the Local Housing Allowance (LHA). The maximum that can be claimed in most areas is 30 per cent of median rents in tenants' postcode areas.

5. Councils are legally obliged to house the 'unintentionally homeless'—a category excluding those evicted for rent arrears or leaving home voluntarily. They must also provide emergency accommodation for pregnant women, adults with dependants, elderly people, and those left homeless by fire, flood, or other disaster.

→ Further reading

Hanley, L. (2013) *Estates: An Intimate History*, London: Granta Books. **Critical, but affectionate, first-hand evaluation of the life and culture of post-war housing estates by a former resident, set against the evolving policy landscape of recent decades.**

Jones, C. and Murie, A. (2006) *The Right to Buy: Analysis and Evaluation of a Housing Policy*, London: Wiley-Blackwell. **Thorough and balanced evaluation of the legacy of the Thatcher government's 'Right to Buy' policy, set in the context of later housing reforms.**

Lund, B. (2011) *Understanding Housing Policy*, 2nd edn, Bristol: Policy Press. **Up-to-date appraisal of issues in social and low-cost housing, focusing on the decline of local authority housing, and growth in the involvement of housing associations, cooperatives, and other providers.**

Malpass, P. (2005) *Housing and the Welfare State: The Development of Housing Policy in Britain*, Basingstoke: Palgrave Macmillan. **In-depth historical critique of the evolution of housing policy in Britain since the Second World War.**

Online Resource Centre

www.oxfordtextbooks.co.uk/orc/Morrison4e/
Visit the Online Resource Centre that accompanies this book for web links and regular updates.

18

Children's services and adult social care

One of the most intricate, sensitive, and (occasionally) explosive aspects of local policy delivery is 'social services'—an umbrella term referring to provision of everything from foster care and adoptive parents for vulnerable children, to residential and nursing homes for the elderly and disabled. Today, 1.5 million people in England rely on support from social services, including 400,000 children.

Although the term 'social services' may not appear in the media as often as 'NHS' or 'welfare', stories relating to its work—and failings—are seldom far from the agenda. Controversies have ranged from complaints about errant social workers failing to uncover child abuse until it is too late, to screaming headlines about prematurely discharged mental patients running amok.

Most of these stories, however, have arisen out of atypical circumstances and, excepting specialist sections such as *Society Guardian*, Britain's media is often accused of neglecting the complexities of this 'difficult' policy area in favour of sensationalism. But given some of the UK's current demographic and social trends—the liberalization of the adoption laws, rising diagnoses of mental illness, and a rapidly ageing population—only a foolish editor would ignore the underlying issues that determine policy (and occasionally give rise to the more dramatic situations about which we often hear).

Until the early twentieth century, such social services as existed were provided on an ad hoc basis by charities and voluntary foundations, or in workhouses or infirmaries funded by parishes under the Poor Law. But social reform under the modernizing governments of David Lloyd George and Clement Attlee brought more coordinated social care provision, paralleling the nationwide establishment of the National Health Service (NHS) and welfare state. The main landmarks included a seminal report by the 1968 Inter-Departmental Committee on Local Authority and Allied Personal Services (the 'Seebohm

Report'), leading to the decision, two years later, to form discrete social services departments by merging pre-existing health and welfare and children's departments under the Local Authorities Social Services Act 1970. The new departments, run by county councils, worked closely with district or borough housing departments and the NHS.

Until 2004, when children gained their own dedicated departments following the Climbié case, social services departments were responsible for three broad policy areas:

- child protection;
- domiciliary and residential care for the elderly and disabled; and
- care for those with mental health problems.

▌ Child protection

Historically, child protection has been overseen collaboratively by social (now children's) services departments, in partnership with:

- local education departments (normally within the same authority);
- police child protection units;
- NHS trusts and primary care trusts (PCTs), now clinical commissioning groups (CCGs—see Chapter 6, 'The Health and Social Care Act 2012 and the reinvention of the NHS');
- the National Society for the Prevention of Cruelty to Children (NSPCC); and
- registered adoption agencies.

Until 2004, these various bodies liaised through area review committees (ARCs), which determined the child protection procedures that each should follow and conducted reviews of cases in which those processes failed to prevent 'non-accidental injury' taking place. Information on vulnerable children was shared between them through local child protection registers maintained by the ARC.

The Children Act 2004, a response to the Climbié case, abandoned ARCs in favour of **children's trusts**—all-in-one bodies bringing together representatives of every statutory agency involved in promoting child welfare and comprising multidisciplinary teams of experts, including social workers, health visitors, paediatricians, and child psychologists. Local child protection registers were replaced by individual **child protection plans**, drawn up by professionals following initial conferences to assess a child's degree of risk.

The sweeping changes, ushered in under the 'EVERY Child Matters' banner (see 'The 2004 Act and the "Every Child Matters" agenda' in this chapter), saw all services relating to children—from schooling to social care—combined under new 'children's services' departments, headed by directors of children's services. Adult social care remains within the remit of social services, albeit under discrete directors of adult services.

Children's social services are required to:

- promote children's general welfare;
- encourage children's upbringing by their families (wherever possible);
- pay regard to children's wishes and feelings;
- work in partnership with parents in children's best interests;
- provide accommodation for children for whom no one has 'parental responsibility'—taking on a 'corporate parent' role if a child is lost or abandoned, or if the person responsible is unable to provide care; and
- advise, assist, and befriend children who leave local authority care—and provide financial assistance and support to find accommodation.

The following two sections primarily focus on the web of regulations and guidelines governing child protection policy in England and Wales, as derived from two key Acts:

- the Children Act 1989; and
- the Children Act 2004.

The Children Act 1989 and the definition of 'parental responsibility'

The 1989 Act synthesized existing public and private law on the care, protection, and safe upbringing of children, making it more cohesive. It came into force in England and Wales in 1991, and in Northern Ireland, in 1996.

The Act implicitly presumed that the best place for children to be brought up was at home with their parents or guardians—unless there were serious concerns for their welfare in that environment. Councils were given a 'general duty' to 'keep a child safe and well', and to provide suitable support services to help them to remain with their families. Its definition of 'family' was quite fluid—referring to any adult(s) with legal 'parental responsibility' for a child. It defined 'parental responsibility' as 'all the rights, duties, powers, responsibilities and authority which by law a parent of a child has in relation to the child and his property'.

The Act defined 'children in need' as those who are:

- disabled—that is, blind, deaf, dumb, or with a mental disorder or physical impairment;

- unlikely to have—or to have the opportunity to have—'a reasonable standard of health or development' without the help of services from a local authority; and/or

- unlikely to progress in health or development without the help of local authority services.

Under the Act, parents, guardians, or carers whose children might be eligible for services are entitled to contact councils for 'needs assessments'. Carried out by qualified social workers, these should take into account not only *children's* needs, but also those of their parent(s) or guardian(s). For example, the child might require remedial educational support or therapy, but the adult with parental responsibility might qualify for financial assistance, counselling, or (depending on circumstances) respite care—a short break from caring, perhaps even a holiday, while the child is looked after by professionals. Since 2000, assessments have been conducted in a 'multi-agency' way, under the 'Framework for the Assessment of Children in Need and their Families of the Department of Health (DoH). In addition to providing for a child's immediate physical, mental, and emotional needs, a more holistic plan must be drafted—catering for ongoing specialist social, financial, or educational requirements.

The range of services available under the 1989 Act includes:

- short breaks;
- holiday play schemes;
- care at home—including help with washing, dressing, and mobility;
- some aids and adaptations—for example stair lifts, hoists, and wheelchairs; and
- financial help—for example to pay for fares to hospital visits.

Services can be arranged by councils on behalf of families, with some provided in-house and outside agencies or charities contracted to deliver others. Alternatively, parents or guardians may request *direct payment* schemes. These involve families receiving cash payments, so that they can 'shop around' for services of their choice rather than being offered the 'one size fits all' provision traditionally offered by councils. Direct payments (or 'self-directed support')—based on a similar principle to 'patient choice' in the NHS—were piloted in the context of care packages for the elderly as early as 1996, but have recently been extended, controversially, to severely mentally impaired adults (see 'Choice in community care—the rise of direct payments' in this chapter).

As well as setting out the day-to-day services available for children in need, the 1989 Act addressed the thorny issue of councils' role in wider child welfare. In particular, it defined circumstances in which social (now children's) services should intervene to ask family courts to decide where (and with whom) a child 'at risk' of neglect or abuse by his or her parent(s) or guardian(s) should live. It set out four types of court order—collectively known as 'section 8 orders'— which are explained in the table entitled 'Types of '"section 8 order"' under the Children Act 1989', to be found on the **Online Resource Centre** that accompanies this book.

Sometimes, the level of intervention that councils are permitted is insufficient to deal with children's care needs; at other times, orders may be breached, again putting children at unacceptable risk. In such circumstances, councils will need to consider taking children 'into care'—that is, away from those with parental responsibility. The procedure for doing this and the range of care options available to children once removed from home is discussed in the sections entitled **'Care orders'**, **'Fostering and other forms of local authority care'**, and **'The adoption process'**.

The 1989 Act applies only to England and Wales, although most of its provisions are reflected in the Children (Scotland) Act 1995. The one significant difference is that, under Scottish law, legal proceedings surrounding child welfare follow a distinct 'children's hearings system', established in the early 1970s, which determines any compulsory supervision measures that a minor may need. The one notable strengthening of existing procedures under the 1995 Act was its emphasis on the role of 'safeguarders'—individuals with relevant professional backgrounds (normally lawyers, social workers, or teachers) appointed as the 'voice of the child'.

The Children Act 2004 and the 'Every Child Matters' agenda

The 2004 Act focused less on introducing additional duties of care or legal powers for councils and courts than on radically shaking up child protection 'culture'. Its main emphasis was on improving early intervention and communication between professionals, following the horrific case of Victoria Climbié.

In 2000, 8-year-old Victoria died of hypothermia, with 128 separate injuries to her body, after two years of systematic torture and abuse by her great aunt, Marie Thérèse Kouao, and the latter's boyfriend, Carl Manning, in their London bedsit. Victoria's parents, both living on the Ivory Coast, had sent her to Britain in the hope of a better life. In the months before her death, Victoria was systematically beaten, burnt with cigarettes and scalding water, tied up, and forced to sleep in a bath with only a bin liner over her naked body. Police, social workers, and the NSPCC failed to treat warning signs sufficiently seriously—prematurely ending a child protection investigation based on a paediatrician's mistaken diagnosis that scars on her skin were caused by scabies.

After Victoria's treatment was finally exposed, both Kouao and Manning were jailed for murder at the Old Bailey, several social workers at Haringey Council were sacked, and three major investigations were launched—by the council, the Independent Police Complaints Commission (IPCC), and a public inquiry chaired by former Chief Inspector of Social Services Lord Laming.

Reporting in January 2003, Lord Laming made 17 recommendations for reforming child protection procedures. The most significant are explained in the table entitled 'Main recommendations of the Laming Inquiry', to be found on the **Online Resource Centre**.

The government's response was a famous Green Paper, *Every Child Matters*. It outlined four key aims for improving child protection:

- increasing the focus on supporting families or carers—'the most critical influence on children's lives';
- ensuring that necessary intervention takes place before children reach crisis point and that they are protected from falling through the net;
- addressing underlying problems identified by the report into Victoria Climbié's death—weak accountability and poor integration; and
- ensuring that people working with children are valued, rewarded, and trained.

Following a widespread public consultation and a further paper, *Every Child Matters: The Next Steps*, many of Lord Laming's recommendations came into force under the 2004 Act. They revolved around five 'Every Child Matters' outcomes, which set out to enable all children to

- be healthy;
- stay safe;
- enjoy and achieve;
- make a positive contribution; and
- achieve economic well-being.

To pursue these ends, the government created children's trusts—multidisciplinary teams comprising various professionals involved in child protection. To improve coordination of children's services on the ground, trusts would bring together various professionals at single locations in the local community, such as children's centres or schools. Between them, these agencies would:

- conduct joint needs assessments of children in need;
- reach shared decisions on priorities relating to children's well-being;
- identify all available resources suited to improving children's well-being; and
- collaboratively deploy resources, to avoid duplication or overlap.

Even before trusts were in place everywhere, plans were unveiled in June 2008 for their remit to be widened to encompass aspects of youth justice previously overseen by the Police Service and Prisons Service Agency. Then Children's Secretary Ed Balls increased collaboration over the care of the 2,900 under-18s in young offender institutions, private secure training centres, and council-run secure units between the Youth Justice Board, established earlier by Labour, and children's trusts. His stated aim was to replace the then punitive approach to youth justice with early-intervention strategies designed to 'catch' potential career criminals early and prevent repeat offending. The policy—branded 'Integrated Resettlement Support' (IRS)—evoked the 'tough on crime, tough on the causes of crime' view espoused by Tony Blair in his days as Shadow Home Secretary.

To steer Labour's changes to child protection policy, an independent **Children's Commissioner for England** was appointed in March 2005. The Commissioner, currently Maggie Atkinson, formerly head of children's services at Gateshead Council, is there to:

- promote awareness among all sectors of children's views and interests;
- work closely with organizations that take decisions affecting all aspects of children's lives, including police, schools, hospitals, and voluntary groups; and
- respect the framework of the five 'Every Child Matters' outcomes and children's rights under the 1989 UN Convention on the Rights of the Child.

In the run-up to the Commissioner's appointment, consultation among children found that their main concerns were bullying, personal safety, and pressure in education (especially exams). Difficulties associated with deprived and minority social backgrounds were also raised.

A further significant reform flowing from 'Every Child Matters' was the introduction of discrete children's services departments, and their requirement to develop integrated systems to coordinate needs assessments, planning, early intervention, and periodic reviews of local services. As of April 2006, social care for under-16s was removed from the general social services arena and combined with education provision under this new all-embracing umbrella. The Act also stipulated that every authority—except those with 'excellent' ratings under Comprehensive Area Assessment (CAA—see Chapter 14, 'From "Beacon Councils" to the National Indicator Set—the growth of performance data')—must publish periodic 'children and young people's plans' (CYPPs), to which every agency should contribute. These should detail all local services for children and young people, and the shared objectives of partner organizations for improving them.

The council-run boards demanded by Lord Laming were introduced in the guise of **local safeguarding children's boards (LSCBs)**. These are charged with coordinating the various agencies involved in delivering services and monitoring their collective effectiveness. The Act defined three levels of action to be taken by boards, as outlined in Table 18.1.

Table 18.1 Three levels of responsibility of local safeguarding children's boards

Type of responsibility	Meaning
Activities	Preventing maltreatment—'impairment of health or development'—by introducing better mechanisms to identify abuse/neglect and providing clear, accessible contact points for children to report it.
Proactive work	Offering outreach activities for specific groups—e.g. children 'in need', but not suffering abuse/neglect.
Reactive work	Responding more quickly and effectively where children are suffering neglect/abuse at the hands of family members, other adults known to them, other young people, professional carers, or strangers.

To further facilitate a more joined-up approach to providing care and support to vulnerable children, a short-lived database, ContactPoint, was launched in 2009 enabling communication and expertise to be exchanged between different agencies involved in a child's care. Controversially, its aim was to keep on record basic identifying details for each child in England up to their 18th birthdays—from their names, addresses, genders, dates of birth, and unique identifying numbers, to the contact details of every service or professional to which and whom they were known.

Months before the £224 million database had even been launched, it was already generating controversy. Despite ministerial assurances that only professionals involved in children's care would be able to access it—and then only subject to passing advanced Criminal Records Bureau (CRB) checks to ensure that they had no convictions for child-related offences—the Conservatives and several charities expressed concern about potential security breaches. Perhaps unsurprisingly, the Coalition switched off ContactPoint in August 2010, although, in a sign of their determination to introduce their own changes to better safeguard children, ministers ordered a swift review of child protection by Eileen Munro, a professor of social policy at the London School of Economics. Published in April 2011, this argued for abandoning a top-down, target-driven approach to protecting children in favour of locally driven strategies based on past experiences and professionals' 'expert' judgements. It made the following recommendations, most of which were swiftly accepted by ministers:

- specific legal requirements for assessments of children's needs to be completed within rigid, centrally determined timescales should be scrapped;

- adapting child protection services to specific local needs and liberating them from 'nationally prescribed ways of working', with professionals trusted to redesign services based on informed research and feedback from families;

- dropping the punitive approach to serious case reviews (SCRs), instead placing more emphasis on learning from how mistakes were made and why professionals behaved as they did, rather than simply naming and shaming culprits, with Ofsted's ability to evaluate SCRs removed;

- introducing a new 'duty' for all local services to make an 'early offer of help' to families who may not (yet) meet criteria for intervention under child protection legislation, to prevent situations escalating to the point at which they do meet those criteria;

- improving Ofsted inspections of children's services, to put more weight on feedback from children and families themselves and observing social workers in action;

- encouraging experienced social workers to continue to work part-time on the front line, to ensure that their expertise is passed down directly to junior levels; and

- that each children's services authority should appoint a principal child and family social worker to report regularly the views and experiences of front-line staff to management.

To begin the process of enabling councils to adopt many of Ms Munro's recommendations, ministers confirmed that future council funding settlements would include provision for a (non-ring-fenced) **early intervention grant** (see Chapter 12, 'Types of revenue grant').

Besides abandoning ContactPoint, the Coalition has modified certain other elements of Labour's joined-up approach to children's services. On 31 October 2010, it withdrew statutory guidance on children's trusts, allowing individual authorities more flexibility about precisely how they met the need to coordinate child protection in their areas. Although councils and their partner bodies must still retain collaborative children's trust *boards* to manage their collective caseloads, many areas have now adopted arrangements known as **children's partnerships**—essentially, forms of collaboration that are structured in a less prescriptive, one-size-fits-all way than previously. The idea is to allow councils and their partners to adapt to the specific needs of their areas, harmonizing the configurations of their child protection arrangements with those of their local health and well-being boards (see Chapter 6, 'The Health and Social Care Act 2012 and the reinvention of the NHS'). Additionally, the stipulation that all areas must produce CYPPs was removed, although trusts or partnerships were permitted to maintain them if doing so 'makes sense locally'.

Care orders

The reforms described so far illustrate the extent to which children's services and other child protection agencies have become increasingly interventionist—resulting in part from pressure from media, public, and families themselves.

But sometimes they are required to be more proactive still, in the interests of children whom they fear are at serious risk of abuse or neglect if they remain with their parents or guardians. The Climbié case highlighted what can happen if early warning signs are not noted or acted upon. Similar allegations were levelled at the same council more recently over the death of 17-month-old Peter Connelly (known initially as 'Baby P') after eight months of abuse by his step-father and a family lodger in Haringey—just streets away from where Climbié had perished. The scandal led to the sacking of Haringey's director of chil-dren's services, Sharon Shoesmith, and the resignations of its leader and cabi-net member for children and young people.

While lambasting the system for any failure to identify abuse, the media is equally quick to criticize conscientious social workers who, fearing that children are living in abusive environments, intervene overzealously to remove them.

Perhaps the most infamous example of heavy-handed intervention occurred in Cleveland in 1987, when 121 cases of suspected child abuse were diagnosed by two Middlesbrough-based paediatricians, Marietta Higgs and Geoffrey Wyatt. Several children were removed from their families by social services in the ensuing investigation, using a power introduced under the Children and Young Persons Act 1969: a 'place of safety order'. In the end, 26 children from 12 families were found by judges to have been wrongly diagnosed and cases involving another 96 were dismissed by the courts.

More recently, several newspapers—notably the *Daily Mail*—castigated Portsmouth City Council for being too ready to take children into care follow-ing the drowning of a 17-month-old girl, Anna Hider, in her foster parents' swimming pool, allegedly while they were entertaining guests. But the pendu-lum swung back the other way yet again when news broke in April 2009 of a vicious attack by two brothers, aged 10 and 11, on two other boys in Edlington, south Yorkshire. An SCR concluded that the violent sexual assault might have been prevented had 31 chances to intervene with the families not been missed by nine agencies over a 14-year period. The case review launched by Doncaster Council marked the tipping point in a five-year period during which seven chil-dren had died in and around the town—despite being registered as 'at risk'.

Recent Acts have seen successive governments attempt to walk the tight-rope between guaranteeing high standards of child protection and preventing cavalier intervention by social services and other agencies. Since the 1989 Act, the principal means by which councils have been able to take children into care for indefinite periods—often against their parents' or guardians' wishes—is by applying to family courts for **care orders**. Under these circumstances, parents or guardians must still be allowed 'reasonable access' (unless explicitly prohib-ited by the court), but authorities assume parental responsibility in law and have powers to determine the *degree* of any contact. Occasionally, the need to safeguard a child's welfare is perceived as so urgent that a council can apply to a court for a fast-tracked order to remove him or her from a domestic threat. This is known as an **interim care order**, or **emergency protection order**. Initially granted for up to eight days, but renewable for a further week, these may be granted only if a court judges there to be 'reasonable cause to believe that the child is likely to suffer considerable harm' if left alone. Since the Family Law Act 1996, emphasis has switched to removing 'the source of danger', rather than the child (for example applying for a 'non-molestation order' against another named individual will lead to his or her removal from the situation).

Councils also have the power to apply for a lesser 'supervision order'—a device enabling them to 'supervise' parents or guardians more closely than normal to ensure that children potentially at risk are properly cared for. Under the 1989 Act, a court may make a supervision order only if satisfied that:

- a child is suffering or likely to suffer significant harm; and

- the harm or likelihood of harm is attributable to the care given (or likely to be given) being below what it is 'reasonable to expect a parent to give' or the child's being 'beyond parental control' (persistently truanting from school and/or acting antisocially or criminally).

Under supervision orders, it is councils' duty to 'advise, assist, and befriend' children and approach courts for variations of the orders—converting them into care orders if they prove insufficient in practice. Likewise, councils may apply for court orders to be lifted when no longer necessary. Where requests for orders specifically relate to children's non-attendance at school or their parents' refusal to send them, a local education authority (LEA) may apply for a specific 'education supervision order'.

Fostering and other forms of Local authority care

There are various ways, then, in which children can be removed from their homes, should professionals and courts be sufficiently concerned for their well-being. But where do these 'looked-after children' actually *live* while under protection?

Whether children are subject to emergency protection or full care orders, they will normally be accommodated in one of two ways:

- in registered community children's homes; or

- with foster parents.

Children's homes

As with other forms of residential accommodation for vulnerable groups, today's children's homes may either be run directly by councils or by other 'registered providers', from private companies to specialist charities such as

Barnardo's. Although far removed from the grim Victorian orphanages and homes of yesteryear, many of those operating today still contain shared dormitories, as well as individual rooms. They tend to take both boys and girls, rather than being single-sex, and can house 100 or more children at once (although most limit their intakes to double figures).

Children's homes are designed to:

- keep young people safe;
- give them consistent boundaries and routines;
- give them assistance in accessing education;
- promote their health and well-being; and
- provide quality of life—for example games, leisure activities, and external trips.

Children's homes—like adult care homes—used to be inspected by councils, but this role has shifted to a succession of quangos in recent years. It is currently the responsibility of the Office of Standards in Education, Children's Services, and Skills (Ofsted—see Chapter 15, 'Monitoring school standards and the great "parent choice" debate'). In Scotland, all social care inspections, including those of organizations involved in child protection, have been carried out by the Social Care and Social Work Improvement Scotland (SCSWIS, commonly known as the 'Care Inspectorate') since 2011, when it took on work previously done by three bodies: the Care Commission, the Social Work Inspection Agency, and Her Majesty's Inspectorate of Education. The Scottish Social Services Council (SSSC) is charged with raising standards in both adult and child social care. In Wales, these functions are discharged by the Care and Social Services Inspectorate Wales (CSSIW) and the Care Council for Wales, respectively; in Northern Ireland, all health and social care is regulated by a single body—the Regulation and Quality Improvement Authority (RQIA).

In July 2012, serious questions were raised about both the quality of care in children's homes and the manner in which responsible councils allocated vulnerable juveniles to them, following a highly critical report by deputy children's commissioner Sue Berelowitz, commissioned after nine men were jailed in Rochdale for grooming and sexually abusing young girls, including one in care. This concluded that the high turnover of young people in children's homes provided a 'constant flow of vulnerable children for perpetrators to exploit'. It also highlighted the difficulty of tracking down those who went missing from care because of the absence of clear statistics on the subject.

Ms Berelowitz's report came a month after an all-party parliamentary group investigating the plight of children who vanish from care homes revealed that 46 per cent of juveniles were placed by councils miles (if not hundreds of miles) away from their native communities and support networks, with large concentrations of homes clustered in north-west and south-east coastal resorts.

Condemning the 'very serious weaknesses' exposed in both reports, then Children's Minister Tim Loughton ordered councils to revise placement policies to ensure that juveniles were placed locally whenever possible. Ministers also established an expert group to improve data-gathering and data-sharing to address significant disparities between official council figures for the number of children who go missing from care for 24 hours or more and incidents relating to vulnerable juveniles recorded by police.

In its first ever stand-alone annual report into the social care side of its remit, published in October 2013, Ofsted condemned the standard of child protection offered by 20 English councils as 'unacceptably poor' and said that only one in four councils was doing enough to safeguard children. Its chief inspector, Sir Michael Wilshaw, singled out Birmingham City Council—which failed inspections on seven separate judgements—as 'a national disgrace'. Ofsted has since overhauled its own inspections to ensure that it is picking up on child protection issues, following several recent reports of bullying and abuse by staff in schools and care homes.

Foster parents

Fostering can be arranged on a long-term or short-term basis by children's services, often working with independent foster agencies. Councils tend to view it as preferable to keeping children in community homes because the involvement of designated foster parents places them in familiar, domestic-style settings, rather than impersonal institutions. Children placed in long-term foster care are normally located with 'parents' who have at least one child themselves. They may continue living in this environment for some years, although if they leave home at the age of 16, their foster carers will no longer have legal rights over them. If their stay becomes long-term, however, the foster parents may apply at some stage to adopt them. Assuming that such applications are successful, the foster carers then become the legal parents.

There are various forms of foster arrangement. The main ones are explained in the table entitled 'Different types of fostering arrangement', to be found on the **Online Resource Centre**. The strict vetting procedure for prospective foster parents is outlined in Table 18.2.

As with adoptive parents, there is a national shortage of foster carers. A survey published by the Fostering Network in May 2013 estimated that at least 9,000 more were needed to provide for all of the youngsters waiting to be placed at that time. Eighteen months earlier, it had reported that 59,000 children in care were still waiting for foster placements—up from 49,700 in 2005. Some campaigners have blamed the shortfall on the financial burdens of fostering. In 2007, the same charity called for carers to be paid professional salaries. A survey published at the start of its campaign found that three-quarters of them received less than the minimum wage and four out of 10, nothing at all.

Table 18.2 Vetting procedure for foster parents

Procedure	What happens
Background investigation	Children's services staff provisionally approve prospective foster parents following investigation into their family, medical, and criminal backgrounds. Anyone convicted of causing/permitting bodily harm to children—or anyone living in the same house as such a person—cannot foster. Those who have faced orders to remove children from their care are also barred.
Regular spot checks	Social workers retain the right to see foster children regularly on request and can remove them from care without notice if they believe this to be in the children's interests. Foster parents can apply to courts for residence orders, asserting rights to keep children with them.
Training for foster parents	Prospective foster parents must attend classes on statutory responsibilities of foster carers. Although not yet compulsory, many also study for formal qualifications: in England and Wales, National Vocational Qualification (NVQ) Level 3 in Caring for Children and Young People; in Scotland, a Scottish Vocational Qualification (SVQ) can be pursued.

Despite this, all foster carers qualify for allowances to cover the basic costs of clothing, feeding, and otherwise providing for children. If an arrangement has been negotiated through an agency, it will set the level of this allowance, usually dependent on the child's age, with carers of older children qualifying for more. Since April 2007, guaranteed minimum allowance levels for children in different age groups now exist, as outlined in the table entitled 'The national minimum weekly fostering allowance for England', 2014–15', to be found on the **Online Resource Centre**.

Foster parents have also qualified, since 2003, for income tax allowances, enabling them to 'earn' up to £10,000 a year, tax-free, from foster payments. In addition, they receive tax reliefs of up to £200 a week per child under the age of 11 and £250 a week per child over 11 for every week or part-week for which a minor remains in their care. In addition, there is a National Insurance (NI) backed scheme called 'Home Responsibility Protection', which ensures that long-term foster parents will not retire on less than State Pension—a contributory benefit—even if they have made too few NI contributions to qualify under normal rules.

The adoption process

The distinction between fostering and **adoption** is that while the former is (in theory) a temporary arrangement, the latter is permanent. At any point, up to 4,000 children across Britain are looking for adoptive parents. By law, children can be adopted only through adoption agencies—either councils or government-approved registered adoption societies (voluntary agencies).

Most cover radiuses of around 50 miles from their offices. Not all arrange placements themselves, but they may carry out adoption assessments to ensure that prospective adoptive parents are suitable.

Who, then, is entitled to adopt? Until recently, the right was largely restricted to married heterosexual couples, with those under the age of 40 more likely to be successful than older applicants. But much of this changed with the Adoption and Children Act 2002, which opened adoption up to single people, as well as individual partners in unmarried couples (whether straight or gay). The law was further tweaked in 2005, enabling unmarried couples to apply jointly—effectively giving them the same rights as married ones. For gay couples, the procedure is normally quicker if they are married or in civil partnerships, but provided that they live together they stand as much chance of success as straight couples. Qualifying conditions for adopters are listed in Table 18.3.

Today, anyone wishing to adopt a child faces a two-stage process: 'Stage One' involves a number of preliminary checks on their suitability; 'Stage Two', which follows once they have been provisionally approved, is the serious business of matching them up with a child. The different steps involved in this process are outlined in Table 18.4. In theory, the two stages should take no more than six months to complete, but there is some variation in practice, and the

Table 18.3 Criteria for prospective adopters

Criterion	Meaning
Age	Must be over the age of 21 and able to prove that they will make space in their lives for child, and are patient, flexible, energetic, and determined to make difference to the child's life. No official upper age limit, although agencies can favour younger people.
Criminal background checks	Must not have been convicted of a serious child-related offence. More minor offences must be looked into, but may not preclude adoption.
Relationship status	Couples married or in civil partnerships, single people, or individual partners in unmarried couples (heterosexual, lesbian, or gay) may adopt. Unmarried couples may apply to adopt jointly. Ban on gay and unmarried couples adopting in Northern Ireland overturned by Supreme Court in December 2013.
Good health	Prospective adopters must have medical examinations and health issues (including hereditary conditions) should be explored.
Ethnic/cultural background	People of all ethnic backgrounds may adopt. Preferential treatment often given to prospective parents of same racial/religious identity as child (influenced by research into well-being of minority-adopted adults who grew up with families who did not match their ethnicities).
Disability access	People with disabilities may adopt, subject to case-by-case conditions.

Table 18.4 Adoption process

Procedure	What happens
Initial meeting(s)	Following application through agency, prospective adopter(s) meets social worker, together and individually (if in a couple), on several occasions.
Background investigation	Prospective adoptive parents' personal backgrounds investigated and they are asked reasons for adopting. Confidential enquiries made through local children's services department and police.
Personal references	Supplied by at least two friends of adopter(s), and prospective adopter(s) undergoes GP medical examination.
Independent adoption panel	Hearing by panel (linked to agency through which prospective adopter(s) has applied) considers case and decides if it should progress to final stage: opportunity to meet panel in person.
Provisional care agreed	Once adopters approved in principle, child put into their provisional care (children's services authorities or adoption panels must be notified if done through approved adoption society).
Adoption order confirmed	Decision made by family proceedings court, sitting in private, three months after notification to authority.

procedure has been known to take longer in England than in Wales, Scotland, and Northern Ireland.

Once prospective adopters have negotiated earlier hurdles in the process, they can find themselves facing delays that are beyond their control. If a child's natural parents are willing for them to be adopted—for example if they were conceived during rapes or by mothers below the age of consent (16) who feel unable to take on the responsibility of raising them—adoption orders can be issued fairly simply by the courts. However, if the natural parents *object* to the child being adopted, agencies must apply to the courts for *freeing orders*—removing them from their parents' custody against their wishes.

Growing adoption waiting lists—the number of children placed with adoptive families fell by 15 per cent between March 2009 and 2010—prompted a wide-ranging review by the Coalition of what then Education Secretary Michael Gove decried in February 2011 as 'politically correct' and overly bureaucratic 'edicts' preventing prospective parents from adopting because they were too old or of different ethnic backgrounds from their intended adoptees. Mr Gove, who was adopted himself, issued liberalized guidance for councils to speed up the process—particularly for black children, who take up to twice as long to be placed as those from other groups—while improving scrutiny of the 76 per cent of agencies then recently rated 'good' or 'outstanding'. It was nearly a year before Mr Cameron formally detailed government plans to introduce a 'foster to adopt' system and a 'faster, fairer' vetting process, focusing on measures to make it easier for white parents to adopt black children and forcing social workers to consult the national adoption register to fast-track placements if they failed to find adoptive families locally within three months. The new fast-track system was formally introduced with the issuing of new statutory guidance to authorities and agencies in July 2013.

Childminding

'Childminding' is day care provision for children outside nursery, preschool, or school. Registered childminders look after children in their own homes, normally while their parents or guardians are working. Under the Care Standards Act 2000, regulation of childminding is overseen by Ofsted (and its Scottish, Welsh, and Northern Irish equivalents), rather than councils. Ofsted's role is to:

- provide a register of professionals paid for looking after those under the age of 5 on an area-by-area basis; and
- inspect the homes of anyone applying to be registered as a childminder to ensure that there are adequate facilities, including toilets and play equipment.

Registration is subject to various conditions covering facilities to be provided, number of staff and their qualifications or experience, and the maximum number of children who may be minded at once (particularly those aged under 12 months). If conditions are breached, it can be revoked or modified to reduce the maximum number of children minded.

The Protection of Children Act 1999

Introduced following a series of high-profile scandals about child abuse in residential care homes, the Protection of Children Act 1999 saw the launch of a statutory list of all people considered unsuitable to work with children. The Consultancy Service Index, a list along these lines, had been kept by Secretaries of State since 1993, but the 1999 Act—in Scotland, the Protection of Children (Scotland) Act 2003—formalized the process by enforcing it as a statutory list, to which all existing names were added.

It requires childcare organizations to inform the government if:

- they transferred or dismissed someone who had harmed a child or put one at risk; or
- an individual evaded disciplinary action along these lines by resigning or retiring.

▌ Adult social services and the rise of community-based care

Although children's services account for the bulk of councils' social care budgets—and attract the most media coverage—councils retain significant responsibilities towards the elderly and working-age adults with enduring physical and mental illnesses or disabilities.

Until relatively recently, much of the care provided for people falling into these categories was delivered in institutional environments: long-stay care homes (like adult versions of children's homes) or nursing homes for those who could no longer look after their own basic needs without assistance.

People with mental disorders severe enough to prevent them continuing to live at home were often transferred for prolonged periods into NHS-run mental hospitals or specialist secure asylums managed by councils. The oldest of these facilities had been established in the early 1800s and many continued in more or less uninterrupted use for the best part of 200 years. But under Margaret Thatcher and John Major, a revolution occurred that transformed the culture of social care for both the mentally ill and all other categories of adult 'service user'.

This transformation came in the form of the National Health Service and Community Care Act 1990, which restyled patients as 'clients' and ushered in the now-notorious policy of 'Care in the Community'. In simple terms, it aimed to:

- place greater emphasis on **community care**—providing support for elderly people and those with illnesses or disabilities in their homes, enabling them to remain in 'community' settings for longer, reducing pressure on acute wards and residential facilities; and

- improve cost-effectiveness of social care, and increase choice for 'service users', by means of greater involvement of private and voluntary-sector providers.

Although few opposed the idea of empowering the vulnerable to continue living in community settings in *theory*, many were alarmed by the way in which the NHS and councils began implementing the Act in practice. Long starved of funding for the 'Cinderella service' of mental health, and with many homes and asylums severely under-occupied (and therefore uneconomical), many councils and NHS trusts used freedoms granted by the Act to shut down half-empty units—discharging inpatients to return to 'the community' irrespective of their personal support networks or ability to fend for themselves.

Tabloid newspapers reported a slew of scare stories about assaults, and even killings, by prematurely discharged mental patients. Most infamous was the 1992 murder of musician Jonathan Zito by someone suffering paranoid schizophrenia, who had been released from mental hospital just weeks earlier under 'Care in the Community'. Mr Zito's death prompted the establishment of the Zito Trust by his wife, Jayne, which continues to campaign for changes to mental health policy in the best interests of patients and public. Other high-profile cases included the 1996 murders of Lin Russell and her 6-year-old daughter, Megan, by Michael Stone on a country lane in Kent. Stone, who had a severe personality disorder, had been out of prison, in 'community care', since 1992.

At the time of the murders, it was not only the 1990 Act that attracted media condemnation, but also the Mental Health Act 1983, which, opponents claimed, contained a loophole preventing mental health professionals providing care for people suffering from untreatable conditions, such as Stone's, even when

they asked for help (he had repeatedly pleaded to be admitted to Broadmoor). More recently, in July 2010, it emerged that fugitive gunman Raoul Moat—who led police on a week-long manhunt after murdering his ex-partner's boyfriend, and shooting both her and a police constable—had asked Newcastle City Council social workers to refer him to a psychiatrist months before his rampage.

But not every aspect of the renewed emphasis on community care has proved negative. For many elderly and disabled people, the channelling of social services funding into care packages tailored to their individual needs, and home adaptations to make their domestic environments more comfortable and user-friendly, has proved liberating—enabling them to spend crucial extra years living near friends and family, which would have been 'lost' had they been prematurely admitted to residential care.

The responsibilities with which councils are charged under the 1990 Act in relation to community care are listed in Table 18.5.

Nonetheless, the 'Care in the Community' controversy proved so enduring that, when Labour returned to power, it scrapped it (although in practice the 1990 Act remains the main legal basis underpinning adult social care). Community care is still ministers' preferred option for caring for the elderly and disabled, until such time as they require full-time nursing, although the balance has been redressed somewhat between domiciliary and residential care.

New Labour's biggest reforms included:

- the Health Act 1999, which introduced a new NHS structure and partnerships with the private sector, formally abolishing the joint consultative committees (JCCs) established in 1977; and
- the National Carers' Strategy, which built on the Carers (Recognition and Services) Act 1996, giving statutory recognition to the work of unpaid relatives or friends looking after people receiving community care in their homes and enabling these informal carers to access their own support.

Table 18.5 Main provisions of Community Care Act 1990

Measure	Meaning
Emphasis on 'Care in the Community'	Councils to promote domiciliary (home) care, day care (attendance at day centres and activity groups), and respite services (short breaks for carers and/or cared-for) so that people can live in their own homes.
Emphasis on practical support to promote self-reliance	Ensuring that all agencies/authorities involved prioritize practical support.
Detailed needs assessment	Conducting 'proper assessment' of individuals' needs, followed by good case management by key workers (see 'Community care—the limits of state provision' in this chapter).
Promoting partnerships	Developing flourishing independent/private sector alongside good public services.
Long-term care planning	Preparing strategic plans for community care arrangements, working with NHS; publishing these/keeping them under review in consultation with public and voluntary-sector bodies. Collaboration between NHS and councils to improve non-hospital services previously introduced under National Health Service Act 1977, when joint consultative committees (JCCs) were set up, comprising representatives from all relevant statutory agencies.

Community care—the limits of state provision

Councils are duty-bound to assess the needs of people requiring care as a result of age, infirmity, or disability. If assessments indicate that these people require services, their needs must be determined, along with the extent to which they can be expected to contribute to their own care. Some authorities have been accused of raising the bar with 'eligibility criteria' owing to budgetary concerns, but courts have ruled it appropriate for councils to take their financial resources into account when setting those criteria.

The principal community care services that can be accessed through councils—many means-tested, and most now delivered by charities, voluntary organizations or private agencies, rather than councils themselves—include:

- home help (assistance with washing, dressing, and/or cleaning the home);
- hot meals ('meals on wheels');
- help with shopping and financial management;
- advocacy (advice and support with accessing other services, paying bills, etc.);
- telephone access;
- cheap travel (bus passes and free transport to appointments);
- free and accessible parking by means of the 'disabled badge holder' scheme;

- day care (access to day centres for structured activities, day trips, etc.);

- respite care; and

- home modifications and aids to daily living (stair lifts and hoists are usually provided by housing departments, while wheelchairs and other mobility aids are often accessed through the NHS or charities).

In addition, training and employment can be provided for disabled people in sheltered workshops, while day nurseries and centres are available for their children.

These days, community care 'packages' are arranged by individuals' key workers. Because most social care professionals now work in multidisciplinary teams designed to improve coordination between social services, NHS, and the other agencies, these may be social workers, community psychiatric nurses (CPNs), or occupational therapists (OTs). The OTs' expertise lies in assessing individuals' capacity to perform basic tasks for themselves and providing support in carrying them out where needed.

Key workers have a statutory duty to produce—and regularly update—'care plans' individually tailored to their clients' needs. These should be made available to them or their carers in writing, on request, and should include the following details:

- services to be provided (and by whom), when and where this will happen, and what the services are intended to achieve;

- contact details for dealing with problems about service delivery; and

- information on how to ask for a review of services if circumstances change.

Specific concerns about the plight of people with serious mental health issues led to the introduction, in 1991, of a more rigorous care plan procedure, known as the 'care programme approach' (or 'care plan approach'). This is broken down into four stages, as follows.

1. Initial assessment of the client's needs

2. Consultation with all professionals involved, any informal carer, and (depending on their degree of mental capacity) the client themselves

3. Appointment of a key worker

4. Coordination of services agreed on the basis of the initial assessment by that professional

As with residential care, the quality of domiciliary care (home care) for the elderly has encountered repeated criticism. In March 2012, consumer group *Which?* branded much of the care offered to older people in their homes 'disgraceful', referring to a litany of missed visits by professionals, soiled beds, and food being left out of reach as illustrations of typical complaints detailed in diaries kept by 30 service users and carers that January. Although the organization declined to 'name and shame' errant providers, it highlighted the growing issue of disinterested private care agencies. In a separate survey, half the respondents said that prearranged home visits had been missed in the previous six months—with six out of 10 receiving no prior warning. Four months later, a survey of 739 companies providing domiciliary care by the UK Homecare Association, which represents providers, concluded that three-quarters of councils were 'rationing' home visits for budgetary reasons by demanding that they be completed within half an hour. One in 10 imposed time limits of just 15 minutes. A knock-on effect of shabby homecare provision can be rises in emergency hospital admissions for vulnerable people that might otherwise have been avoided—trends that pile pressure on the NHS (see Chapter 6, 'Hospital closures, deficits, and the perils of market-centred thinking in the NHS'). In its fourth 'State of Care' report, published in November 2013, the Care Quality Commission (CQC—see 'Regulating social care' in this chapter) revealed that more than 1 million over 65-year-olds (and one in 10 over-75s) had been admitted to hospital with potentially avoidable conditions in the previous year.

The role of home carers

Britain's rapidly ageing population, coupled with the growing emphasis on community-based care, has led to a huge rise in the number of carers—people who spend part of their lives looking after elderly or disabled relations in their or the other person's home. According to Carers UK, as of June 2014 there were 6.5 million unpaid carers in Britain. Of these, 175,000 or more were aged 18 or under and 1.5 million were over 60.

Long-running campaigns by carer support groups led to belated recognition of their work, initially through the 1996 Act (entitling them to limited respite care), and the 10-year National Carers' Strategy established by Mr Blair in 1999. Renewed by Gordon Brown in 2008, this made commitments listed in the table entitled '10-year "National Carers' Strategy"', to be found on the **Online** **Resource Centre**.

In practice, although it has improved the situation for some, the strategy was just that. Recent studies suggest that carers still feel isolated, undervalued, and bewildered by the often labyrinthine network of services and providers theoretically available to them, and the bureaucratic processes involved in accessing them. A 2013 report by Carers UK, entitled *Prepared to Care*, found that the burden of caring had led 42 per cent of carers to suffer relationship breakdowns with family members, while six out of 10 struggled to maintain friendships. A similar proportion suffered from depression, while 92 per cent of respondents said that their caring role had left them feeling more 'stressed'.

Choice in community care—the rise of direct payments

As if service users and carers did not already face a sufficiently mind-bog-gling task in navigating the maze of community care options available to them, recent governments have put them more directly in the driving seat as part of their 'choice' agenda (see Chapter 6, 'New Labour's restructuring of the NHS'). The Tories introduced this concept, in the Community Care (Direct Payments) Act 1996. This enabled councils to make cash payments to dependent individuals, enabling them to 'buy' their own services from pro-viders of their choice. The approach was not mandatory, and councils were required to ensure that individuals to whom they paid money had the capac-ity to take informed decisions about their needs and access suitable services. In some cases—when evidence suggested that money had been spent on things other than services related to the their 'needs', such as alcohol or gambling—councils could halt direct payments and even require payments to be refunded.

In January 2006, a Labour White Paper entitled *Our Health, Our Care, Our Say* outlined plans to roll 'choice' out further—taking in groups of clients whose conditions, until then, were judged to have impeded their capacity to make decisions for themselves. These included:

- young disabled people whose parents had managed direct payments on their behalf and whose payments might have had to stop when they reached the age of 18;
- people with dementia, where the use of direct payments was not set out in 'power of attorney' (PoA) agreements—legally binding documents detail-ing individuals authorized to manage their estates; and
- people with more profound learning disabilities.

Variously known as 'individual budgets', 'personal budgets', and now once again 'direct payments', this approach has divided campaigners for the elder-ly and mentally ill. While some have welcomed the flexibility it allows to capa-ble service users to seek out medical and psychological support (not to mention social and leisure opportunities) best suited to them, others argue that vulnerable individuals in dire need of assistance risk losing out on their entitlements because of the complexity of negotiating the system and manag-ing their own accounts. An in-depth 2008 evaluation of the impact of individu-al budgets (as they were then known) in 13 pilot areas found that while working-age people with mental health difficulties had responded positively to them on the whole, they caused 'anxiety and stress' to elderly service users—many concerned that, after lifetimes spent under a top-down, pater-nalistic NHS or social care model, they were suddenly expected to shop around for support.

Care homes, nursing homes, and the rise of the private sector

When a person is no longer well enough to continue living in his or her—or a carer's—home, arrangements are normally made for that person to move into either a long-term residential care home or one with nursing provision (a 'nursing home'). The former are usually 'low dependency' environments, in which residents can enjoy relatively independent lifestyles in the company of other people of similar age or with comparable physical or mental needs. Nursing homes, in contrast, are targeted at individuals with more severe physical or mental impairments—often the very old or those at advanced stages in the progression of their conditions—who require care provided or supervised by registered nurses.

Broadly speaking, the process followed when elderly people reach the point of requiring residential accommodation is as follows.

1. They are assessed by key workers in multidisciplinary teams and placed in homes best suited to their needs (council, voluntary, or private).

2. Where private homes are chosen, their ability to pay 'the full economic cost' of their care is assessed—taking into account the value of any property in their name, which might be sold to contribute to home fees.

Since the late 1980s, there has been a marked increase in the amount of residential care provided by private companies, rather than councils. In many areas, homes are no longer maintained by councils directly; all are owned and managed by the private or charitable sectors.

In tandem with the expansion of private provision and rising fees, Mr Major's government risked infuriating the 'grey vote' with new moves to divide the cost of residential care between state and individual. Under the 1990 Act, anyone with assets of £16,000 or more—including the homes in which they lived until being admitted into residential care—was expected to pay for themselves up to the point at which that money was exhausted (at which stage, the state would take over). In practice, this meant that many people—particularly widows and widowers whose homes were entirely their own—have since been 'forced' to sell houses and flats for which they may have spent much of their working lives paying. The 'capital/assets limit' remains in place, but has been raised incrementally over time to £23,250, although anyone with assets of £14,250 or more must contribute £1 for every £250 that they own above that amount. Devolution has seen the emergence of variations in this system, with the Welsh Assembly introducing a slightly higher upper means test threshold (currently £24,000) and the Scottish Parliament, an even more generous one (£25,750). Since 2002, families of care home residents in Scotland have also benefited from government guidance directing councils to introduce 'deferred payment' schemes, under which the balance of any contribution owed is paid from the beneficiary's estate after his or her death.

So politically combustible had the means test become by 2010—with increasing diagnoses of age-related conditions requiring long-term care, such as Alzheimer's disease and dementia—that then Health Secretary Andy Burnham announced plans for a new 'National Care Service', to improve homecare provision and to stop individuals moving into residential or nursing care having to sell their homes to pay the fees. His unrealized plans—which he touted as a twenty-first-century legacy for Labour, comparable to the NHS that it bequeathed in the twentieth—were lambasted by the Tories, who used a poster campaign to accuse him of planning a 'death tax' on grieving families. They were referring to Mr Burnham's favoured model: a universalized adaptation of the Scottish model, which would have financed the proposed new service from a 10 per cent levy on all estates (payable after their owners' deaths). At the time, the Tories' proposed alternative was to charge people a one-off 'voluntary' payment of £8,000 at the age of 65—a fee that critics pointed out would be beyond the means of many. However, following an independent inquiry headed by Oxford economist Andrew Dilnot, the Coalition moved some way towards restoring a sense of fairness to the system by means of the Care Act 2014. Based on Mr Dilnot's recommendations, the Act will raise the capital threshold above which care home residents are expected to pay their own way to £118,000 from April 2016. No one with capital worth less than £17,000 will be expected to contribute a penny towards care costs. At the same time, a cap of £72,000 (excluding 'living costs', such as utility bills and food) will be introduced on the maximum sum that any individual can be charged for personal care over his or her lifetime—barring an extra £12,000 a year to cover the aforementioned living costs. Moreover, from 2015, all English councils will have to offer individuals contributing to their care costs, and whose personal wealth *excluding* the value of their homes is less than £23,250, the option of deferred payment—in much the same form as this currently applies in Scotland. Although councils have had discretion to introduce such schemes since 2001, the Act described implementation to date as 'patchy'.

Another source of tension that emerged in the 1990s was that between social services departments and the NHS over how to provide for people not yet in need of residential care, but who experienced frequent, sometimes prolonged, bouts of ill health necessitating in-patient treatment. Hard-pressed acute hospitals, already struggling with long waiting lists, increasingly became the subject of news reports about 'bed-blockage' ('bed-blocking')—the need to cater for vulnerable patients too sick to be sent home, but for whom residential care was either unavailable or not yet deemed necessary (see Chapter 6, 'Hospital closures, deficits, and the perils of market-centred thinking in the NHS').

Given that more than half of those over the age of 65 now have a disabling condition requiring long-term care and that Britain's population is ageing fast, it is no wonder that bed-blocking remains a serious issue as councils struggle to find enough care home places to meet demand—particularly for those with unusual or debilitating ailments. Yet critics argue that governments have merely intensified pressure, by getting tough with councils found 'guilty' of contributing to bed-blocking, rather than concentrating on boosting residential care places. Under the Community Care (Delayed Discharges etc.) Act 2003, NHS hospitals may fine councils up to £120 a day for every 'blocked' bed. The Act was motivated, in part, by a 2001 Audit Commission report that found that two out of three patients in English hospitals at any one time were over 65, with around 5,000 people on any given day unnecessarily stuck on acute wards. To discourage hospitals from discharging patients prematurely, then Health Secretary Mr Lansley announced in June 2010 that those having to readmit the same individuals within a month of sending them 'home' would receive no extra funding for additional treatment.

Regulating social care

The regulator charged with ensuring high-quality care standards throughout England is the **Care Quality Commission (CQC)**. In the social care field, it is responsible for inspecting day centres, care homes, domiciliary care agencies, nurses' agencies, children's homes, and residential special schools.

All residential care and nursing homes must be formally registered under the Registered Homes (Amendment) Act 1991 (previously the Registered Homes Act 1984), but since 2004 the 18,500 listed homes have also had to register separately with the CQC. On inspection, all care organizations (including agencies) are rated under a star system. The meanings of these classifications are as follows:

- no stars—poor;
- *—adequate;
- **—good; and
- ***—excellent.

Following an inspection (or subsequent investigation), the CQC may either demand that an organization meets specified 'conditions to improve', bringing it up to agreed minimum standards, or—in extreme cases—order its closure. Since July 2014, homes requiring urgent action short of closure have also been subject to 'special measures', in the same way as ailing hospitals, GP practices, and failing schools (see Chapter 6, 'The Stafford Hospital scandal and the new regulation revolution', and Chapter 15, 'Monitoring school standards and the great "parent choice" debate'). In addition, instances of abuse or neglect may be referred to the police and Crown Prosecution Service (CPS). The Commission is especially vigilant in relation to adults with serious disabilities or impairments that put them at greater risk of abuse—in line with the 'Protection of

Vulnerable Adults' (POVA) scheme introduced in July 2004. As with cared-for children, anyone directly caring for vulnerable adults must undergo periodic CRB checks and there are bans preventing those who have harmed such people previously from working with them again.

Although the CQC has tightened regulation of the increasingly disparate social care 'market', serious concerns have been repeatedly raised about the rigour with which inspections are carried out. In June 2008, an investigation by Radio 4's *Today* programme found that many of the Commission's own inspectors were unhappy with the frequency and quality of its inspections. More than 200 employees of the then Commission for Social Care Inspection (CSCI)—now absorbed into the CQC—participated in an anonymous question-naire, with one commenting: 'I wouldn't leave my dog in 90 per cent of our care homes.'

Criticism of social care regulation has been sharpened following a slew of deeply critical reports published since 2011 exposing the poor quality of residential and inpatient provision for elderly people. The first to attract media attention collated 10 investigations into inadequate care by English NHS trusts and two GP practices carried out by Parliamentary and Health Service Ombudsman Ann Abraham. In October 2011, the CQC concluded that more than half of the 100 hospitals that it had inspected were 'failing' older people, with one in five inadequately catering for their 'dignity' or nutri-tional needs—two benchmarks emphasized in revised standards introduced a year earlier. Its findings prompted Mr Lansley to fast-track inspections for 500 nursing homes, inviting Age UK to recruit past and present service users to participate. Two months later, the first ever 'National Audit of Dementia'—covering 210 hospitals in England and Wales—identified 'problems across practically every aspect of care for patients admitted to hospitals'. It pin-pointed the impersonal manner of staff, poor training and supervision, and patients' feelings of being ignored as key issues—despite the fact that sepa-rate figures suggested one in four hospital beds was occupied by people with dementia.

Long-term care homes have come in for even harsher criticism. In February 2012, a commission set up by Age UK, the NHS Confederation, and the Local Government Association (LGA) published a report, *Delivering Dignity*, in which they issued 'a call to arms to the whole health and social care system'—recommending that residents be directly involved in day-to-day management decisions, that ageist language be stamped out, and that a new rating system be introduced to inform future CQC inspections. The report's overarching emphasis was on improving the quality of the care home experience, by mov-ing beyond a utilitarian approach to running homes—whereby efficiency was measured purely in terms of the speed with which tasks such as washing, dressing, and feeding were performed—toward one in which residents were enabled to lead more active, fulfilling lives. Other recommendations included the establishment of a Care Quality Forum to raise standards of professionalism in older people's care and improved training not only for front-line care workers, but also for managers.

In addition to formal regulation, since the Health and Social Care Act 2012 the social care sector has been subject to the advice and oversight of the recently renamed National Institute of Health and Care Excellence (NICE—see Chapter 6, 'New Labour's restructuring of the NHS'). Its primary role is to develop and publish statutory guidance and quality standards for all aspects of social care, based on an 'evidence-based' model drawing on examples of good (and bad) practice in the field. The first five aspects of social care that it was charged with reviewing (based on concerns arising from then recent scandals) were home care, the care of older adults with long-term conditions, improving the transition from NHS to social care settings for older people, improving the transition from children's to adult services, and handling cases of child abuse and neglect.

'Sectioning' the mentally ill

Since the Mental Health Act 1983, councils have had limited powers to detain mentally infirm adults not in residential care in specialist hospitals or units—a process known as 'sectioning' after the appropriate sections in this and subsequent Acts. The procedures by which they may do so are outlined in Table 18.6.

The Mental Health Act 2007

Before it finally received royal assent in July 2007, Labour's Mental Health Bill endured one of the rockiest rides of any piece of legislation in recent memory. At the heart of the Bill were two key proposals that provoked fury among mental health and human rights campaigners, and a high-profile campaign by *The Independent on Sunday*:

- new powers enabling doctors to detain people with serious mental health conditions who might pose potential risks to themselves or others, primarily for public protection; and
- authority for clinicians (GPs and psychiatrists) to 'impose' treatment on the severely mentally ill, regardless of their wishes and even if they were judged to have mental capacity to make their own decisions.

At various stages, the Bill was opposed by campaign groups—most notably, the Mental Health Alliance, a coalition of 78 organizations, including Mind, the King's Fund, and various bodies representing practitioners. It was eventually watered down, although the ability of doctors to prescribe enforced medication remained in the final version.

Table 18.6 Powers of social services in relation to the mentally infirm

Power	Effect
Application for compulsory observation	Approved mental health practitioners (AMHPs) may apply for person to be admitted to hospital for 72 hours' compulsory observation under s. 136 of Mental Health Act 1983. AMHPs may either be social workers, nurses, occupational therapists (OTs), or psychologists. Application must be supported by two responsible clinicians (RCs). These may be social workers, nurses, OTs, or psychologists—not only GPs and/or psychiatrists, as previously. In 'emergencies', applications may proceed with one RC's endorsement.
Appointment of 'nearest relatives'	Applications for people to be admitted to mental hospital normally subject to consent by nearest relative. If AMHP believes consent is being withheld 'unreasonably', he/she can apply to courts for order appointing someone else as 'nearest relative'.
Application to extend observation	Observation order may be granted for up to 28 days by hospital psychiatrist under s. 2. Six-month renewable treatment period may be agreed under s. 3. RC agreeing to detention under ss 2 or 3 must be a qualified doctor. Detention may be renewed after initial six months, subject to approval by mental health review tribunal (MHRT) and with patient/nearest relative given right to appeal. Further renewal may be made after 12 months and then yearly.
Application for warrants	If AMHP believes patient is being ill-treated/neglected on private property, he/she may apply to a magistrate for a warrant to search premises.
Assumption of the role of 'guardian'	Social services can be appointed 'guardians' to mentally ill people unlikely to respond to hospital treatment, but needing protection. Private individuals can be appointed, too—with council's consent.

The Act's other main features are listed in the table entitled 'Other main provisions of the Mental Health Act 2007', to be found on the **Online Resource Centre**.

Prior to the Act's passage, Labour introduced a marginally less controversial reform in the guise of the Mental Capacity Act 2005, which enshrined the rights of people with severe mental health issues to exercise power over their own care that had previously existed only in common law. The Act covered only England and Wales, but similar provisions had earlier been made under the Adults with Incapacity (Scotland) Act 2000.

The 2005 Act also introduced:

- an Independent Mental Capacity Advocate Service (IMCAS) for England and another for Wales from 2007;
- criminal offences of 'wilful neglect' and 'ill-treatment';
- the ability of service users to nominate 'substitute decision-makers' to their nearest relatives under a new lasting power of attorney (LPA); and
- a Court of Protection with extended powers.

As well as addressing concerns about the financial means tests for those requiring long-term residential care, the Care Act 2014 also introduced several new measures designed to protect adults with mental health issues and/or learning difficulties. Specifically, it required all social services authorities to establish **safeguarding adults boards (SABs)**, to match their existing LSCBs, which will be responsible for 'helping and protecting' adults in need of 'care and support' and/or 'experiencing', or 'at risk' of, 'abuse or neglect'. Those moving from one council area to another also have a right to an immediate needs assessment to ensure that they do not miss out on services to which they are entitled—an innovation known by the buzzword 'portability'.

☰ Topical feature idea

The following is a human interest news story published in the *Oxford Mail* on 13 June 2014, focusing on the response of Britain's biggest private homecare provider, Allied Healthcare, to a report by the Care Quality Commission (CQC) criticizing its lack of safeguards to protect elderly people in its care from suffering 'financial abuse'. Your news editor asks you to explain the background to this story in a feature, 'humanizing' it by finding some of those who receive home care from Allied and finding out more detail about the kinds of 'financial abuse' to which the report refers. How would you go about contacting service users? What other sources would you consult to investigate the story?

Article published in *Oxford Mail*, 13 June 2014

Home care clients 'open to abuse' says damning report

By Oliver Evans

Oxford Mail

13 June 2014

Web link: **www.oxfordmail.co.uk/news/top_news/11274457.Home_care_clients___open_to_abuse___says_damning_report/?ref=mac**

THE county branch of the UK's biggest home care provider said it has improved following a damning report highlighting that users were open to abuse.

The Care Quality Commission (CQC) criticised the Kidlington-based branch of Allied Healthcare for its care of people like OAPs.

The report, which has just been made public, revealed a lack of knowledge by staff of procedures for reporting concerns and preventing clients being open to financial abuse.

The CQC, which inspected Allied in August and again in January, found those who use the service 'were not protected from abuse or the risk of abuse'.

But the service has since been re-inspected and, despite the results not being publically available, the firm said it was confident improvements had been made.

Allied medical director Richard Preece said he was confident the first inspection report reflected a historical view of the branch.

The new report recognised 'significant progress' he said, adding: 'Our improvement has continued. We are now so confident of the progress made since January that we were delighted to be included in CQCs [sic] National Pilot Inspection regime, the results of which are yet to be published.'

Allied Healthcare would not say how many county people it cares for but Oxfordshire County Council said it has 25 clients through Allied, costing £770,000 in 2013/14.

The agency cares for all ages including people with learning and physical disabilities, and mental health problems.

In CQC's August visit, five out of nine staff did not know where to go if they couldn't report concerns to a manager.

One said: 'I don't know, maybe I could call the police?'

And it found a nurse and care worker were not aware a £10 limit had been put on how much a 'vulnerable' client, who had £300 in a drawer, could keep at home.

One relative said management had until recently been a 'shambles'.

✳ Current issues

- **Speeding up of the adoption process** The Coalition has introduced a fast-track, two-stage adoption process, removing barriers to individuals and couples seeking to adopt children—particularly those from ethnic minorities. In Northern Ireland, the Supreme Court has overturned a long-standing ban on gay and unmarried couples adopting.

- **A relaxed means test for the cost of long-term care** From April 2016, people with capital (including property) worth £23,250 will no longer have to pay all of their own residential home costs. The upper means test threshold will be raised to £118,000—although those with assets of £17,000-plus will still have to contribute something. English councils will also have to offer deferred payment schemes to anyone with assets (excluding homes) worth less than £23,250.

- **Improved protection for vulnerable adults** The Care Act 2014 requires all English social services authorities to set up safeguarding adults boards (SABs) to support adults vulnerable to neglect or abuse. Those moving from one council area to another may also request immediate needs assessments by the authority in the location to which they move.

▦ Key points

1. Councils responsible for social care now have two departments overseeing this: children's services and adult social services.

2. Child protection is overseen by children's services departments, collaborating with children's trusts or partnerships, based at centralized locations where families may access professionals from various agencies, and local safeguarding children's boards, which meet regularly to ensure that all 'children in need' are adequately protected.

3. When children are taken into care, family environments are favoured over institutional ones. Short-term care arrangements are known as 'fostering', and long-term ones (in which carers become children's legal parents), 'adoption'.

4. Care of disabled or elderly adults can either be provided at home or in institutional settings. Typical home care involves home help (assistance with washing, dressing, and cooking) and 'meals on wheels', while most residential care is provided in privately owned homes.

5. Regulation of adult social care in England is overseen by the Care Quality Commission (CQC), while Ofsted inspects child protection services. Scotland, Wales, and Northern Ireland have their own CQC counterparts, each overseeing both adults and children.

→ Further reading

Ayre, P. and Preston-Shoot, M. (2010) *Children's Services at a Crossroads: A Critical Evaluation of Contemporary Policy for Practice*, Lyme Regis: Russell House Publishing. **Incisive overview of the tensions between intervention and family-centred policies in contemporary child protection.**

Blackman, T., Brody, S., and Convery, J. (eds) (2001) *Social Care and Social Exclusion: A Comparative Study of Older People's Care in Europe*, Basingstoke: Palgrave Macmillan. **Thoughtful and informative comparisons between different approaches taken by six states—including Britain—to providing social care for the elderly.**

Gray, A. M. and Birrell, D. (2013) *Transforming Adult Social Care: Contemporary Policy and Practice*, Bristol: Policy Press. **Critical evaluation of the current issues and debates in social care for vulnerable adults.**

Philpot, T. (2007) *Adoption: Changing Families, Changing Times*, London: Routledge. **Examination of the British adoption laws, focusing on real-life stories and recent changes to open up the process to same-sex and unmarried couples.**

Online Resource Centre

www.oxfordtextbooks.co.uk/orc/Morrison4e/
Visit the Online Resource Centre that accompanies this book for web links and regular updates.

19

Transport, environment, and 'quality of life' issues

As we have seen from previous chapters, the bulk of local authorities' time and money is spent raising and allocating funds, administering the planning process, and managing (if not always directly delivering) core services such as schools, housing, and social care. But beyond these complex and costly areas, councils are responsible for various other things: maintaining roads; licensing pubs and nightclubs; inspecting hotels and restaurants; and running museums, theatres, and libraries. This broad sweep of service areas—covering everything from public transport to environmental health and trading standards—is where the basic utilitarian needs represented by the core spending areas give way to those that might broadly be described as about 'quality of life'.

▌ Highways and public transport

A prime motivator for the introduction of local government was the promotion of production and trade, and the need to service the rapidly evolving agricultural and manufacturing economy ushered in by the Industrial Revolution. To this end, embryonic nineteenth-century councils became preoccupied with two broad areas of policy designed to facilitate economic expansion:

- *highways and transport*—specifically, the movement of workers and goods from country to town, and between markets, and the maintenance of proper roads; and

- *public health*—the provision of housing and sanitation of sufficient quality to cater for the workers on whose labour the new economy rested. Today, this is split between councils' housing (see Chapter 17), environmental health, and waste management functions, and their recently revived responsibility for overseeing public health and scrutinizing local NHS services.

For hundreds of years, the only highways of navigable standard were the remains of Roman roads and others built from the Tudor era onwards by local parish councils. But the growth of commerce and long-distance trade in the eighteenth century meant that industrialists and merchants soon recognized the need for their goods to be transported speedily and safely. This prompted a dramatic boost in private investment in highways.

The main developments early in the history of highways and public transport are outlined in the table entitled 'Timeline of emergence of road-building in Britain', to be found on the **Online Resource Centre** that accompanies this book.

Types of road and the highways authorities responsible for them

Construction and maintenance of Britain's labyrinthine road network is today divided between multiple authorities. Minor roads and those linking two or more towns together are usually maintained by relevant councils (counties, unitaries, or metropolitan boroughs), but the longest and widest (A-roads and M-roads, or motorways) are normally overseen by the Secretary of State for Transport. Upkeep of these primary roads falls to the Highways Agency, an executive agency of the Department for Transport (DfT). While highway maintenance may sound like a dull subject for news stories, inadequate street lighting, potholes, and general road disrepair are among the most common causes of complaints to councils (which arguably makes them newsworthy). The main road designations and authorities responsible for them are outlined in Table 19.1.

New highways are usually either the result of deliberate local and/or central government road-building schemes—in which case, they are automatically 'adopted' by the relevant authority once built—or incidental outcomes of house-building programmes. In the latter case, a scheme's developer will normally sign a formal agreement with the planning authority to ensure that it can hand over responsibility for the roads when the development is complete. Such agreements are backed with 'bonds' issued by banks or building societies to ensure that if the developer enters receivership or defaults, the roads will be finished without costing local taxpayers.

In some circumstances, however, highways—normally footpaths or bridleways—may be closed or diverted to enable development. There are two main ways in which this is done, as follows.

- If a highway is being closed because it is no longer used, the authority must apply to magistrates for an 'extinguishment order' under the Highways Acts.

Table 19.1 Types of road and authorities responsible for them

Road type	Definition	Authority
Trunk roads (M- and major A-roads)	Major roads linking towns/cities and/or connecting them to ports/airports. Normally divided into at least a dual carriageway, biggest are multilane motorways. M25 will shortly become eight-lane motorway, with one stretch (junctions 12–14) boasting 10 lanes.	Transport Secretary and Highways Agency
County roads (A-roads)	Major arterial roads (almost all A-roads) linking smaller towns, normally within single county.	County councils, unitary authorities, metropolitan borough councils, and London boroughs
Secondary roads (B-roads), and public bridleways and footpaths	B-roads and smaller roads in both rural and urban areas, particularly those linking villages, hamlets, and smaller settlements. Bridleways and footpaths often little more than dirt tracks, following medieval/Roman/ancient routes and paths through fields and woodland.	Councils (as above)
Private roads	Highways contained within boundaries of private estates such as Canary Wharf, east London, or City of London.	Private estates and related businesses (e.g. Canary Wharf)—unless road formally adopted by relevant council under Private Street Works Act 1892

- A highway can sometimes be *realigned* to run around, rather than through, a development, by granting a 'public path diversion order' under various Town and Country Planning Acts.

Developers must conduct detailed research before embarking on their plans, to ensure that they have applied for any necessary extinguishment or diversion orders. This is done by consulting a 'definitive rights of way map' maintained by the council.

The roles of the Secretary of State and Highways Agency

Because of their major infrastructural significance, motorways are designated 'special roads' by government. In relation to both motorways and trunk roads, the Secretary of State is responsible for:

- *overall policy*—whether or where to build new M-/A-roads, the use of tolls and other road-pricing, and the balance between road-building and investment in passenger transport via the rail network and airports;

- *planning, improvement, and maintenance*—the logistics of building, repairing, and maintaining major roads, and implementing policies on the ground; and

- *financing and controlling* the trunk road and motorway programme through taxation.

In practice, many important decisions were traditionally taken in the recently abolished regional government offices, with most maintenance and improvement overseen by the Highways Agency, which, in turn, subcontracts hands-on engineering work to other companies—for example UK Highways. In addition, although county councils have long undertaken road maintenance on behalf of the government, this too is franchised out to private contractors.

There is also an increasingly complex system by which primary, secondary, and unclassified roads can be 'designated' to lower-tier authorities to take control of their day-to-day maintenance, to ensure smooth traffic flows, and to tackle congestion and pollution from noise and petrol fumes. The Transport Secretary can 'designate' responsibility for maintaining motorways and major A-roads to London boroughs, while county councils do likewise to boroughs or districts. When roads are designated downwards, this is known as 'de-trunking'.

The Highways Agency, established in 1994, has its own board and a chief executive earning £180,000 a year. It boasts seven regional control centres and another 28 outstations from which its traffic officers operate. Its official statutory responsibility is to oversee 'operation and stewardship of the strategic road network in England on behalf of the Secretary of State', as well as:

- managing traffic;
- tackling congestion;
- providing information to road users;
- improving journey times, road safety, and reliability; and
- minimizing the impact of the road network on the environment.

The agency, working with the Secretary of State and individual councils, is responsible for organizing wide-ranging consultations when major roads are planned. The main stages in this process are outlined in the table entitled 'Main stages in the consultation process for major road projects', to be found on the **Online Resource Centre**.

In practice, road projects often go far from smoothly. Numerous high-profile protests have occurred in recent years against major projects, the most famous being the campaign against the 'Newbury Bypass'—a 9-mile stretch of dual carriageway built around the market town of Newbury, Berkshire. From January to April 1996, 7,000 protestors—ranging from hardcore environmentalists to middle-aged professionals and pensioners—picketed a 360-acre site in an effort to thwart the building programme, which involved felling 120 acres of ancient woodland. In the end, the work went ahead—but not before the cost of policing the protest (dubbed 'Operation Prospect') topped £5 million, and that of hiring private security firms to erect fences and patrol the perimeter reached £24 million.

Other notable protests include those over the construction of the A30 between Exeter and Honiton in Devon, which saw a network of tunnels and tree houses built at a camp near Fairmile. These protests made a media celebrity out of 'Swampy' (aka self-proclaimed eco-warrior Daniel Hooper), whose later antics included a one-off stint as a panellist on BBC1's current affairs comedy quiz show *Have I Got News for You*.

Recent national reforms of traffic policy

Road-building continues to be a sensitive issue across Britain, not least because there is little evidence that continuing expansion of the network has eased congestion. Studies suggest that funnelling government spending away from public transport and into road-building programmes *increases* traffic jams—by encouraging more people to drive. A review by transport consultant Halliburton published in 2002 predicted an increase in congestion in the M25 corridor of a third by 2016 unless radical steps were taken to persuade people to use public transport, such as charging tolls or introducing a luxury bus service around the motorway.

Concern about road policy is arguably one of the rare issues to unite supporters and opponents, albeit from different perspectives: to environmental campaigners, congestion causes serious pollution and long-term ecological damage, while motorists and long-distance hauliers view traffic jams as a source of discomfort and frustration. Ministers have launched numerous initiatives in recent years to address congestion and pollution, as listed in the table entitled 'Major government traffic and transport initiatives since 1997', to be found on the **Online Resource Centre**.

Despite this, many road and rail users agree that Britain has some way to go before it can boast anything like the 'integrated transport policy' first promised by then Deputy Prime Minister John Prescott in 1999.

Local traffic management, road pricing, and congestion charging

The term 'traffic management' was, for long years, synonymous with little more than road crossings, signs, lights, and 'lollipop ladies'—in short, the bread-and-butter mechanisms used to direct traffic from A to B, to help pedestrians to cross it, and to 'warn' motorists about everything from changes in speed limits to steep slopes, sharp bends, and bumpy road surfaces. To a large extent, councils remain preoccupied with these and other humdrum concerns—many of which continue to excite the attention of local newspapers and television news outlets. The more workaday responsibilities of highways departments include planning, installing, and monitoring everything from traffic lights, roundabouts, and sleeping policemen (speed bumps), to positioning road signage, cycle and bus lanes, and one-way systems, and introducing free 'park and ride' bus services to and from town centres.

In recent years, traffic management has entered a new phase, as pedestrians' and motorists' frustration with mounting congestion has sparked growing calls from both environmentalists and businesses for radical action to address the unsustainable growth in private car ownership. Environmentalists' prime concerns remain pollution caused by carbon monoxide exhaust fumes and noise generated by heavy traffic. Business leaders, meanwhile, are increasingly alarmed by the impact of lengthy traffic delays on the smooth running of the economy. A 2012 survey by the Centre for Economic and Business Research (Cebr) and international traffic analysts INRIX estimated that congestion costs the British economy £4.3 billion a year, in the form of fuel and time wastage, and the impact of businesses passing on consequent price rises for goods and services to households.

Faced with the prospect of roads becoming even more clogged and the associated quality-of-life issues, successive governments have looked to other countries for inspiration as to how to encourage use of public transport. Given the high cost of travelling by rail and severe congestion on many train routes—particularly in south-east England—the 'carrot' of public transport has historically made little impact on car usage, so policymaking has shifted towards adopting a 'stick' approach, focusing on mechanisms such as congestion charging and road-pricing (tolls).

Congestion charging

Introduced in Singapore in 1975, congestion charging is the system by which flat-rate fees are charged to drivers entering specified 'congestion charge zones' (usually in or around urban centres) between specified hours on given days. In Britain, the most famous example—although not the first, which was introduced in Durham—was initiated by former London Mayor Ken Livingstone in February 2003, within a limited central zone defined by the capital's inner ring road. This zone was extended to cover much of west London in February 2007, although in December 2010 Mr Livingstone's successor, Boris Johnson, scrapped the extension as a 'Christmas present' to local people. The charge operates between 7 a.m. and 6 p.m., Monday to Friday, and is currently set at £11.50 a day for all vehicles, although a £1.50 reduction is available to those paying in advance. Drivers may now pay by credit or debit card over the phone, by text message, via a dedicated website, or in shops equipped with PayPoint facilities. Those who fail to pay are fined.

The congestion charge has won praise from both business leaders and green lobbyists, with various reports suggesting that it has cut jams in central London by up to 20 per cent. It has won fans in the medical community, too: according to a 2008 study in *Occupational and Environmental Medicine* magazine, its impact on pollution may have already 'saved' up to 1,888 extra 'years of life' among London's 7 million residents. Perhaps unsurprisingly, however, it has infuriated many motorists—including shift workers required to arrive at (or leave) work in central London at unsocial hours, when little or no public transport is available.

On its launch, the charge became the subject of a high-profile campaign by stage actors, including Tom Conti and Samantha Bond, who cited the plight of low-paid shift workers, but also argued that timings of the daily charge period would adversely affect the size of audiences for West End performances by penalizing theatregoers for entering the zone in early evening.

Nonetheless, its perceived success has seen cities from New York to Stockholm imitating it, and before leaving office Labour (initially sceptical of Mr Livingstone's plans) had committed itself to replicating it elsewhere. In June 2008, then Transport Secretary Ruth Kelly approved what would have been the biggest congestion charge scheme anywhere in the world, in the form of a dual-ring zone around Greater Manchester, covering an area 12 times bigger than the original London zone. However, in December 2008, the plan was thrown into disarray when local residents rejected it by 79 to 21 per cent in a referendum. Advanced plans for other cities, including Bristol, to adopt charges have stalled for now, following then Coalition Transport Secretary Philip Hammond's decision in June 2010 to suspend the Transport Innovation Fund used to co-finance schemes.

In addition to congestion charging, in February 2008 Mr Livingstone introduced a 'low-emission zone' (LEZ) encompassing all 610 square miles (1,580 km²) of Greater London. The worst polluting lorries, buses, and coaches were fined £200 per day for entering the capital between 7 a.m. and 6 p.m. on weekdays, excluding public holidays, with drivers starting journeys late in an evening and ending them early the following morning forced to pay for two days, not one. On entering office, Mr Johnson, who had condemned the charge as 'the most punitive, draconian fining regime in the whole of Europe', moved to suspend it, but in practice it has continued—a fact for which the Mayor has occasionally sought to 'blame' the European Union (see Chapter 9). In January 2012, the LEZ emissions standards were even made stricter, with new classes of vehicle affected, including larger vans, minibuses, motor caravans, motorized horseboxes, and 4 × 4 utility vehicles registered as new before 1 January 2002. Meanwhile, individual councils—including some in London—have experimented with even more novel ways of penalizing 'gas-guzzling' vehicles. In January 2007, Richmond became the first of nine London boroughs to introduce higher-rate residents' parking permits for owners of

'Chelsea tractors' and other cars with larger engines. Although the scheme was replicated elsewhere, after years of protest from residents and motoring organizations such as the Automobile Association (AA), Westminster finally scrapped it in July 2010.

Road-pricing

Congestion charging may be popular among councils seeking to battle traffic problems (and to raise the odd million for investment), but the idea of forcing motorists to pay up-front to use roads is hardly new. In Britain, 'road-pricing' was first mooted by John Major's Conservative government, which proposed introducing a network of privately financed toll roads on major routes, modelled on systems used in France and other mainland European countries. To date, Britain has only one private toll motorway: a 27-mile stretch of the M6 between Coleshill, Warwickshire, and Cannock, Staffordshire, which opened in December 2003. In July 2004, then Transport Secretary Alistair Darling announced plans for two 50-mile 'pay as you go' expressways between Wolverhampton and Manchester. But these remain unrealized, and are likely to remain so in light of figures published by the Campaign for Better Transport in August 2010 revealing that the private company operating the route, Midland Expressway Ltd, had been running it at an annual £25 million loss.

Labour remained ambivalent about private toll roads overall, in light of research into the so-so impact of road-pricing. In January 2005, an answer to a parliamentary question to the DfT revealed that congestion on and around the M6 had *increased* since the opening of the existing toll road. Junctions to the south had seen traffic levels rise by up to 10,000 vehicles daily, with those to the north witnessing 5,000 extra a day. Ministers' focus was also sharpened by the scale of public opposition. In February 2007, 1.7 million people signed an online petition objecting to more tolls—prompting outgoing Prime Minister Tony Blair to reply, stressing that his government's mind had not yet been decided. It never was.

Perhaps the most significant statement of policy direction on roads by a recent British premier occurred in March 2012, when David Cameron risked igniting a row as incendiary as that over the Coalition's short-lived plans to 'privatize' England's forests (see Chapter 16, 'Greenfield versus brownfield sites—and the decline of the greenbelt') by outlining radical proposals to address an 'urgent' need for more private investment in Britain's highways. Among the ideas that he floated were more tolls—beginning with charges to help to fund improvements to the A14 between the Suffolk port of Felixstowe in the M1–M6 interchange—and handing stretches of the road system over to sovereign wealth funds, pension providers, and other commercial companies on long-term leases, to encourage them to invest. Claiming that congestion on Britain's roads cost its economy £7 billion a year, he announced a consultation on proposals to develop 'new ownership and financing models' for improving the network. Following a lengthy process, in April 2014 Transport Secretary Patrick McLoughlin confirmed that, within the year, the Highways Agency would be transformed into a Network-Rail-style government-owned company, the Strategic Highways Company, and handed direct responsibility for 'managing and operating England's motorway and strategic A-road network', with an initial war-chest of £24 billion to invest in new road-building by 2021. The new, semi-autonomous, company would be regulated by two bodies: a consumer body modelled directly on Passenger Focus, and a statutory regulator to be known as the 'Strategic Road Network Monitor'. The latter would take the form of an independent unit within the existing Office of Rail Regulation (see Chapter 7, 'Railways'). The changes were formally introduced in the Infrastructure Bill included in the 2014 Queen's Speech, with details of the government's long-term 'roads investment strategy' due to follow by the end of the year.

'Speed' cameras

The days of roadside safety cameras—used to photograph the number plates of vehicles exceeding official speed limits on roads and to award their drivers fixed penalties for speeding—are fast fading. In July 2010, Oxfordshire County Council became the first major authority to stop funding them. Its decision to end its contributions to the collaborative Thames Valley Safer Roads Partnership, encompassing several counties, saw speed camera enforcement in Oxfordshire cease immediately. Other areas have since followed suit, including Warwickshire and London, where three-quarters of all 754 speed cameras had been switched off by June 2012. Across Britain, 1,522 of the 3,189 cameras were no longer being actively used.

While councils and police forces have decided to dispense with speed cameras for largely pragmatic reasons—regarding their retention as a costly luxury, given the relatively small sums that fines generate—there have been conflicting reports about the 'policy's' impact on road safety. According to figures published in *The Sun* in June 2012, the number of accidents in which speed was a factor in Avon and Somerset actually fell after 69 of the area's cameras were switched off in April the previous year. In contrast, statistics released to *Highways* magazine and the *Salisbury Journal* in February 2012 showed that accidents in which people were injured rose by nearly a quarter in Wiltshire between June and August 2011. This followed the closure a year earlier of the Wiltshire and Swindon Road Safety Partnership and the camera switch-off that accompanied it.

More recently, though, speed cameras have begun slowly to reappear: barely a year after all 305 film-based fixed speed cameras were switched off in the West Midlands, in February 2014 a digital camera pilot scheme was launched at selected sites in Birmingham and Solihull.

Other aspects of highways and transport policy

Lighting, minor road maintenance, and pathways

Street lighting tends primarily to be the preserve of county and unitary councils, except where, as with parking policy (see Chapter 11, Table 11.1), districts
or boroughs have been given delegated responsibility for maintaining and
repairing roads and pathways within towns (along with the budgets required to
contract out the necessary work). Quality parish councils (see Chapter 11,
'Parish councils, town councils, and community councils'), for a time, took over
maintenance of individual roads in smaller towns, villages, and rural settlements, and it is not unusual for parish, town, and community councils to be
delegated budgets by higher-tier authorities to manage the lighting of pathways, public bridleways, and other minor rights of way within the villages and
small towns in which they are based.

Public transport

Since the publicly owned National Bus Company was privatized in the 1980s,
followed by the subsequent deregulation of local routes and introduction of
dedicated passenger transport authorities (PTAs) in metropolitan areas, councils have played a diminishing role in providing public transport. As in many
policy areas, they have largely been reduced to 'enabler' status—monitoring
provision of bus, tram, Underground, and river boat services by the free market, and stepping in as 'providers of last resort' where unacceptable service
gaps or inconsistencies emerge.

Under the Local Government Act 1972, then newly established metropolitan
county councils were charged with providing bus services by means of 'passenger transport executives' (PTEs) designed to promote 'integrated' local
transport. But in 1985, this changed, when Margaret Thatcher's government
replaced metropolitan counties with metropolitan boroughs and scrapped the
Greater London Council (GLC), introducing independent passenger transport
authorities. The most famous was London Transport—now Transport for
London (TfL—see Chapter 11, Table 11.4). At the same time, councils' responsibility for providing transport links to and from airports or docks was transferred to new joint boards. The 1972 Act's one abiding legacy was the transfer
of highways and transport responsibilities from boroughs or districts to counties. While overarching bodies remain in place to coordinate passenger transport in large urban areas, the Local Transport Act 2008 renamed PTAs
'integrated transport authorities' (ITAs).

The effective privatization of local transport was formalized in the Transport
Act 1985, with councils expected to provide only 'socially necessary' services
directly—for example those linking villages and smaller towns—and only then
when the market failed to do so. A year later, the system was formally deregulated, allowing any number of bus companies to compete on 'registered bus

routes'—provided that they first obtained 'public service operator's licences' from the **Traffic Commissioners**. Trams, such as those operating in urban centres from Manchester to Croydon, had to be similarly licensed.

Under the present licensing regime, there are seven regional Commissioners. Their responsibilities are to:

- license operators of delivery lorries or heavy goods vehicles (HGVs), buses and coaches (or 'public service vehicles', or PSVs);
- register local bus services; and
- grant vocational licences, and take action against drivers of HGVs and PSVs if necessary.

The Traffic Commissioner for Scotland has additional powers that, in England and Wales, are exercised individually by officers in council highways departments. These include determining appeals against taxi fares, and removing improperly parked vehicles in Edinburgh and Glasgow.

One side-effect of deregulating local bus services was to undermine councils' ability to subsidize public transport. While, in some areas, introducing competition did improve services by pushing down fares, in others the loss of council-run buses deprived residents of heavily subsidized tickets that found no replacement in the privatized marketplace. Among the most celebrated local services were the cut-price buses ushered in by Mr Livingstone in the days of the GLC and the record-breaking 2 pence fares introduced by future Home Secretary David Blunkett while leader of Sheffield City Council in the 1970s.

Contracting out bus services has also been blamed for the increasing isolation of some communities, particularly those in remote villages and hamlets, because—shorn of state subsidies—private companies have been reluctant to maintain, let alone to initiate, unprofitable routes. On occasion, poorer suburbs have also been left isolated by private operators' refusal to continue running services there—normally in response to outbreaks of vandalism, or verbal and/or physical violence towards drivers. In June 2006, one of Britain's biggest private bus operators, Stagecoach, briefly suspended services to Hull's Orchard Park estate after receiving 16 separate reports of missiles being thrown at buses in four days.

While bus licensing has long since passed to the Commissioners, counties, unitaries, and metropolitan boroughs retain responsibility for issuing licences to taxi operators and minicab firms, including Hackney carriages outside London (where they are licensed by the Commissioner of the Metropolitan Police).

Although bus deregulation may have produced a patchy to non-existent service in many areas, recent years have seen the introduction of generous **concessionary fare schemes** for those who meet certain criteria, such as students, the disabled, and old-age pensioners (OAPs). Councils fund the schemes by subsidizing local bus operators with the equivalent of the full fares that they are

'losing' by implementing them. Since April 2006, all councils have had to provide a bare minimum of free off-peak bus fares for pass-holders, while from
April 2008 registered OAPs and the disabled were entitled to free off-peak (9.30
a.m.–11.00 p.m.) travel anywhere in England and Wales, rather than simply
their local authority areas. Both Scotland and Northern Ireland have equivalent
schemes. Despite speculation that the Coalition might remove subsidies for
better-off pensioners, as part of a wider drive to save money by means-testing
certain benefits that currently apply universally, including the Winter Fuel
Payment (see Chapter 8, '"Universal benefits" versus "means testing"—the
future of welfare for parents and older people'), for now the bus pass remains.

While major transport infrastructure projects have traditionally been overseen by central government, recent years have seen a trend towards devolving
them to local and regional authorities, particularly in metropolitan areas.
However, by June 2010, this short-lived era appeared to be nearing an end following the Coalition's abolition of regional development agencies (RDAs—see
Chapter 16, 'Forward planning') and decision to review individually all transport projects yet to secure planning permission or funding. Among the initiatives axed (together worth £5.2 billion) were phase one of an oft-delayed Tees
Valley Metro system linking Teesside to Darlington, which was later revived on
a smaller scale in the absence of Whitehall funds. In Leeds, a long-awaited network of electric 'trolleybuses' powered by overhead cables was delayed for a
second time by the Coalition, before subsequently being revived—only to end
up bogged down in a public inquiry, which opened in April 2014, after 1,700
objections were received to its proposed 14.8 km route.

Transport for London (TfL)

Transport for London (TfL) is a quango charged with managing (if not directly
running):

- London buses, Croydon Tramlink, and Docklands Light Railway (DLR);
- London Underground (the 'Tube') network;
- Transport for London Road Network (TLRN); and
- London River Services—licensed passenger ferries along and across the
  Thames.

It also:

- regulates taxis and minicabs;
- coordinates Dial-a-Ride and Taxicard schemes, providing door-to-door
  services for people with mobility problems;
- installs and maintains traffic lights across London; and
- promotes safe use of the Thames for passenger and freight movement.

In 1998, a Transport Committee for London was set up by the GLA to replace the four pre-existing bodies responsible for overseeing the Tube, buses, taxis, main roads through the capital, and the DLR (a privately owned company).

While all of this may sound harmonious, at times the process of taking decisions about the future of London's transport network has been anything but. Between 1997 and 2001, Mr Blair's government was locked in a tortuous stalemate with Mr Livingstone and then London Transport Commissioner Bob Kiley over its insistence on 'part-privatization' of the Underground. Despite widespread criticism about the shambolic sell-off of the national rail network, ministers went to huge lengths to persuade the Mayor to accept a public–private partnership (PPP—see Chapter 7, 'Private finance initiatives (PFIs) and public–private partnerhips (PPPs)'), which saw a near-identical model adopted for the Tube, with franchises to run services on individual lines contracted out to competing companies, while tracks, signals, stations, and even rolling stock remained in the hands of a separate authority (in this case, TfL). In the Underground's case, the proposed management/ownership split was three-way, rather than two-way, as with rail—with companies contracted to carry out the £13 billion, 15-year programme of improvements on its infrastructure given a stake in it, too. More recently, TfL was involved in protracted negotiations over Crossrail—the upcoming £16 billion overland train link that, once completed, should connect 37 stations, from Heathrow Airport and Maidenhead in the west to Canary Wharf and Shenfield, Essex, in the east, bringing 24 overland peak-time rail services an hour through the heart of London. Crossrail was finally approved in September 2007, after a decade of deliberation, and work commenced on the biggest engineering project in Europe, with the construction of 21 km twin-bore tunnels stretching under central London in spring 2012. Its central section is due to open in 2018.

Car parking

Responsibility for administering and policing car parking is broadly divided between councils, as outlined in Table 19.2.

Table 19.2 Types of council responsible for car-parking services

Type of parking	Local authority
On-street and residents' parking	Traditionally, county councils and unitary authorities, but now administered by all types of council (subject to local arrangements)
Open-air car parks on public or council-owned land	Traditionally, district/borough councils and unitary authorities, but now depends on local arrangements
Multi-storey car parks	Private firms such as National Car Parks Ltd (NCP)
Car parks at hospitals, colleges, universities, and business premises	Run by organizations themselves, increasingly using private contractors

Parking responsibilities used to be split fairly clearly in two-tier areas between boroughs or districts and counties, with the former managing off-road car parks and the latter on-street parking. In many areas, these distinctions are blurred today, with some districts entering into 'agency agreements' with neighbouring counties, and vice versa, effectively contracting out these functions to the other. To confuse the public further, while fixed-penalty fines tend to be administered by counties or unitaries, placing penalty notices on parked vehicles has traditionally been performed by traffic wardens employed by the police. This recently changed, with council-employed parking attendants (later re-designated 'civil enforcement officers') taking over the role in most areas.

As with traffic management, parking issues have a habit of raising motorists' blood pressure—and consequently provide raw material for endless news stories. A common misconception is that wardens and attendants are paid commissions or 'bonuses' related to the number or value of fixed-penalty notices that they issue. In fact, the government legislated to prevent this happening in the Traffic Wardens and Parking Attendants Act 2005. So combustible has the car-parking issue become in recent years, nonetheless, that ticket recipients may now appeal to a National Parking Adjudication Service (NPAS).

A particular parking management 'scandal' to receive media attention recently was Westminster's highly controversial decision to introduce a blanket charge of up to £4.80 an hour at evenings and on Sundays—a move condemned by an unlikely alliance of local residents and businesses, West End theatres, religious leaders, and London's *Evening Standard* newspaper. A High Court ruling in December 2011 forced the council to put what Mr Johnson described as a 'nightlife tax' on hold until at least after the August 2012 London Olympics. It has yet to be revived.

▌ Waste management and environmental health

Public health has been on the local agenda for longer than almost anything else. A rundown of major Public Health Acts and other relevant legislation is given in the table entitled 'Chronology of public health legislation in the UK', to be found on the **Online Resource Centre**.

The task of ensuring that housing, businesses, and local amenities conform to basic hygiene and safety standards today falls to district or borough and unitary environmental health departments. Of their myriad responsibilities, by far the most costly and complex are those related to the effective organization of waste management—an area so broad that it requires the active involvement of every type of council.

Waste collection, recycling, and waste disposal

There are two overriding aspects to waste management:

- *waste collection*—the responsibility of districts or boroughs, unitaries, and metropolitan or London boroughs; and
- *waste disposal*— the responsibility of counties, unitaries, and metropolitan or London boroughs.

Waste collection

Households and businesses have traditionally benefited from weekly door-to-door waste collections. In recent years, however, a number of councils have introduced fortnightly collections to save money, while the nature of 'rubbish collecting' has changed, with more emphasis on recycling, rather than the simple disposal of refuse at 'tips' (landfill sites).

As with most areas of local service delivery, waste collection is periodically put out to tender (see Chapter 13, 'New models for service delivery—subcontracting and outsourcing'), with the result that many 'bin men' (and women) are now employed not by councils directly, but by private contractors. Having started out with kerbside recycling points at supermarkets, parks, and other public amenities, many English and Welsh collection authorities now operate at least fortnightly door-to-door recycling services. Operators contracted to collect standard 'black bin' household and/or business waste (food waste, plastics, etc.) may not be the same ones picking up the ('green bag') recycling.

Despite dramatically increasing its recycling levels, Britain was slow to embrace 'green waste' compared to most European countries. As a result, Labour ministers considered increasingly fiendish ways of cajoling householders and businesses to recycle more. Most controversial was the mooted introduction of 'pay as you throw' fines for people who chucked away too much, with 'rebates' for those who made most use of their green bins. Then Environment Secretary David Miliband announced plans to give councils powers to charge for excessive black bin waste in May 2007, as part of the government's drive to force councils to recycle at least 40 per cent by 2010 and 50 per cent by 2020. Under the Climate Change Act 2008, trials of bin taxes began in 2009 in five pilot areas, policed by new quangos, known as 'joint waste authorities', which would potentially be able to set new taxes. Not content to wait for the outcome of the pilots, some councils proactively launched pay-as-you-throw schemes: in September 2006, Woking Borough Council was accused of snooping on households after installing electronic chips capable of weighing 'residual' (non-recyclable) waste in wheelie bins. But, on entering office, Coalition Communities Secretary Eric Pickles abandoned the concept— announcing plans to 'incentivize' households to recycle instead, by rewarding the diligent with vouchers to be used in local shops, restaurants, or leisure centres. This idea was based on a popular pilot run by Windsor and Maidenhead Council—earmarked by Mr Cameron as a standard-bearer for his 'Big Society' approach to running local services (see Chapter 14, 'Cameron's "Big Society"— what role for councillors and officers now?').

Whether carrot or stick wins out in the end, British councils face an uphill struggle to meet EU recycling targets over the coming decade: a 1999 directive stipulated that the amount of biodegradable waste dumped in UK landfill (equivalent to 18.1 million tonnes in 2003–04) should be cut to 13.7 million tonnes by 2010, 9.2 million tonnes by 2013, and 6.3 million tonnes by 2020. Failure to meet these targets would see the government fined £180 million a year by the European Commission. Figures released in March 2013 indicated that Britain's recycling rates rose faster than those of any other European country in the 1990s and that 39 per cent of its waste was being recycled by 2010 (putting it ahead of target). It also met its 2013 target and is expected to be recycling half of all its recyclable waste by 2017—two years ahead of the 2020 deadline. Some areas are significantly better than others at recycling, though: in February 2013, Wales recycled 54 per cent of its waste, putting it well ahead of England.

Waste disposal

The Environmental Protection Act 1990 required all waste disposal authorities to form arm's-length local authority waste disposal companies (LAWDCs) to dispose of refuse on their behalf. In turn, these were required to 'hire' waste disposal contractors (in practice, either the company itself or another franchisee) to:

- provide waste transfer and landfill sites to which householders can take large items (for example electrical goods) for landfill or destruction;
- dispose of items collected from local people's homes by collection operators; and
- recycle or sell waste for scrap.

Contractors running waste disposal sites on behalf of councils must obtain waste management licences (WMLs) from the Environment Agency (EA) in England and Wales. In Scotland, applications are made to the Scottish Environmental Protection Agency (SEPA); in Northern Ireland, to the Department of the Environment (Environment and Heritage Service).

Because the European Union has toughened its recycling targets, the issue of straightforward rubbish dumping has become acutely politically sensitive. Faced with rapidly dwindling capacity at Britain's existing landfill sites, successive governments have sought to deter councils from continuing to dump waste in the age-old tradition. The most contentious mechanism that they have used is the Landfill Tax. Introduced in the Finance Act 1996, this was initially levied on councils, waste disposal companies, and other organizations involved in dumping rubbish, at a standard rate of £7 a tonne and a reduced rate of £2 a tonne. In its 1999 Budget, Labour raised the standard rate to £10 a tonne and introduced a 'Landfill Tax accelerator' designed to increase it by a further £1 a tonne each year until 2004, and then Chancellor Gordon Brown announced further planned increases in 2002. For 2014–15, the two rates were:

- *standard rate*—£80 a tonne for household waste that may decay and/or contaminate land; and
- *reduced rate*—£2.50 a tonne for rocks and soils, ceramics and concrete, unused minerals, furnace slag, ash, low-activity inorganic compounds, and water.

To dilute the impact of the tax on site operators, successive governments have introduced discounts for those who demonstrate other forms of 'green' behaviour: Mr Major's government brought in a Landfill Tax credit scheme to reward them with a 90 per cent tax credit against any donations made to environmental bodies registered with the scheme's regulator, Entrust; Labour launched a Landfill Allowance Trading Scheme (LATS), allowing individual waste disposal authorities with surplus landfill space to 'sell' it to those in 'deficit', in the manner of carbon trading.

 Rows over the Landfill Tax and recycling targets are not the only reasons why the issue of waste disposal is constantly in the news. In 2005, an investigation for BBC1's *Real Story* found that 500 tonnes of supposedly recycled waste from UK households had actually been dumped by contractors in Indonesia—raising concerns that British citizens might be salving their consciences over recycling at the expense of developing countries. Around the same time, EA figures revealed that half the 8 million tonnes of green waste generated each year in Britain finished up overseas.

Air quality, noise pollution, fly-tipping, and dog fouling

The council officials charged with inspecting domestic and business premises to ensure that they meet statutory environmental health standards are **environmental health officers**. One of their main duties is to investigate complaints relating to waste collection and disposal—or rather the lack of collection and disposal in cases in which, for example, a property owner or occupier fails to leave his or her rubbish in the correct place for removal by collectors. They also investigate reports of 'fly-tipping'—the practice of dumping rubbish on someone else's doorstep or in fields and country lanes, often used by residents or businesses to offload refuse on neighbours after missing their own collection days or to avoid the cost of disposing of larger items at refuse sites. Complaints typically arise from a neighbour who reports an unpleasant smell or the unsightly presence of overloaded bin bags days before they are (or were) due to be collected. In extreme cases, rotting waste that has been inadequately stored or left out for days between collections may attract vermin, necessitating direct intervention by environmental health 'pest controllers' to remove them. The cost of ridding an area of vermin will normally be passed straight to the offending party—and the council may also choose to prosecute under environmental health legislation. Conviction usually leads to a fine.

Another menace accorded greater priority in recent years is dog fouling. After years of campaigning by environmental groups and others concerned about the potential danger that contact with dog mess poses to young children, so-called 'poop scoops' and dog litter bins have become a common feature of most parks and public rights of way. Yet many areas remained so blighted by it that some councils went so far as to use closed-circuit television (CCTV) cameras to spy on errant dog owners who fail to clean up after their pets until this practice was banned by the Coalition. Councils' ability to do this (using anti-terror measures introduced in the Regulation of Investigatory Powers Act 2000) sparked a media outcry when it emerged in June 2008. In January 2011, Home Secretary Theresa May confirmed that they would no longer be permitted to snoop on residents for 'bin crimes' or other such minor infringements—except in cases in which alleged offences carried custodial sentences. Even then, this would be possible only if councils first obtained formal approval from a magistrate. Reports of such 'spying' have, however, persisted.

Other menaces continue to be the subject of strict statutory powers. In response to growing pressure on Britain to conform to EU directives, the Pollution Prevention and Control Act 1999 made councils responsible for exercising 'local authority pollution prevention and control' (LAPPC) in relation to so-called 'Part B' industrial installations in their areas. These include smaller power plants, glassworks, waste disposal sites, sewerage works, and municipal and hospital incinerators. More major polluting installations—for example oil refineries, nuclear power stations, steelworks, and large chemical plants— were designated as 'Part A1' and placed under 'integrated pollution prevention and control' (IPPC) orders overseen by the EA, SEPA, or Northern Irish Department of the Environment. There is also a third category of process ('Part A2'), which relates to medium-range installations. This, like Part B, is policed by councils in the following way.

- Applications for a process to be carried out must be made to the relevant authority (if refused, appeals can be lodged with the Environment Secretary).

- If an enforcing authority believes that an operator has breached an authorization, it can serve an enforcement notice specifying the nature of the breach, steps that need to be taken to rectify it, and a deadline for their completion.

- If external factors are creating an imminent risk of serious pollution (even if unconnected with the process itself), it can serve a prohibition notice.

Another newsworthy issue recently has been the growing intolerance of 'noise pollution'. In certain circumstances, councils may now seize offending equipment, such as stereos or drills. The Noise Act 1996 empowered them to send officers to investigate sources of excessive noise at night and to 'measure' noise levels. Wherever these exceed statutory limits, warning notices may immediately be served on those responsible. Failure to comply is a criminal offence and officers may subsequently enter properties without warrants to seize offending equipment. Prosecution often also follows.

Noise pollution has also been a notable target of government crackdowns on 'antisocial behaviour' (see Chapter 11, 'The role of chief constables'). In March 2005, Andrew Gordon and his 18-year-old son, Phillip, were banned from their own home in Dunfermline for three months under the Antisocial Behaviour (Scotland) Act 2004 because of noise and disruption caused by drinking, cursing, fighting, and drug-taking at the house when Mr Gordon was away.

Action taken against 'unpleasant' smells has also made numerous headlines. One contentious case involved an award-winning vegetarian cafe in Greenwich, which was ordered to stop serving cooked food in June 2008 after neighbours complained about the smell.

Environmental health officers also oversee various other areas, as listed in Table 19.3.

Environmental health and food safety

A key duty of environmental health officers (or 'inspectors') is the role that they play in promoting food safety by ensuring that restaurants, cafes, pubs, and shops serving food are preparing, cooking, and storing meat and other items of suitable quality and under appropriate conditions. This role—memorably satirized in the classic 'Basil the Rat' episode of BBC1 sitcom *Fawlty Towers*—covers all aspects of food hygiene, including its sale, importation, preparation, transportation, storing, packing, wrapping, displaying, serving, and delivery.

The Food Standards Act 1999 set up a Food Standards Agency (FSA) to oversee hygiene and animal husbandry issues at a national level, while building on existing legislation to introduce two criminal offences for businesses failing to meet minimum standards: rendering food 'injurious to health', or selling produce 'unfit for human consumption'. The Act also introduced new, all-encompassing council environmental services departments, specifying that environmental health officers were responsible for:

- inspecting and seizing suspicious food;
- issuing improvement notices to owners of food businesses;
- serving emergency prohibition notices to close down businesses in the case of perceived serious health risks;

Table 19.3 Additional responsibilities of environmental health officers

Responsibility	Definition
Litter	Councils, 'statutory undertakers' (companies contracted to run local services), and other public landowners legally bound to keep their land free of litter. If council designates a 'litter control area', it is offence to throw, drop, or dispose of litter on land owned by public body in that area.
General health risks	If measures for preserving public health fail and diseases such as dysentery, smallpox, typhoid, or foot-and-mouth break out, authority must inform NHS and local community physician or Director of Public Health.
Maintaining public areas	These range from public parks and playgrounds, to cemeteries.
Vermin control	Tackling infestations of rodents, insects, etc.—if necessary, charging private individuals after an event if infestation relates to private land/property.
Contaminated land	Management of land contaminated by industrial processes or military tests involving radiation is still covered by 1990 Act. Boroughs/districts or unitaries identify and register contaminated land in their areas. If serious problem noted, authority must designate 'special site' and notify EA/SEPA, which takes responsibility for enforcing actions taken. Enforcing authority serves remediation notice on person/business responsible, specifying action needed to remedy problem. In Northern Ireland, contaminated land is overseen by Department of Health under Radioactive Contaminated Land Regulations (Northern Ireland) 2006.
Air quality	Following types of emission prohibited under Clean Air Act 1993 (which built on provisions of Clean Air Act 1956, introduced to eliminate winter smog): • 'dark smoke' issuing from chimneys; • excessive smoke, grit, dust, and fumes from chimneys; • excessively high chimneys; • excessive exhaust emissions; and • smoke emissions in designated 'smoke control areas'. Environment Act 1995 required councils to review present and potential local air quality. Where air not meeting desired standard, councils may designate 'air quality management areas' covered by air quality action plans.
Statutory nuisances	1990 Act empowers councils to serve 'abatement notices' on those responsible for statutory nuisances prejudicial to health. As well as vermin and noise pollution generated by premises, vehicles, machinery, or equipment (e.g. drills), these include smoke, gas, fumes, dust, steam, effluvia, and accumulations of rubbish.
Public lavatories	Providing sufficient public conveniences to hygienic standard, including accessible toilets, baby-changing facilities, etc.

- liaising with the National Health Service (NHS) to address potentially communicable disease risks; and

- issuing additional enforcement notices dictated by central government in instances of sudden crisis—for example the ban on the sale of beef on the bone caused by the late 1980s/early 1990s bovine spongiform encephalopathy (BSE), or 'mad cow disease', crisis.

The 'outbreak' of BSE presented one of the biggest instances in recent memory of environmental health issues affecting the wider public health arena. The alarm generated by early diagnoses of BSE in cattle in November 1986 and subsequent identification of symptoms of Creutzfeldt–Jakob disease (CJD) in several Britons became an international concern—leading to a 10-year ban on the export of UK beef on the bone to EU countries, from 1996 to 2006.

Other examples of recent environmental health scares have included a succession of outbreaks of foot-and-mouth disease in British livestock. The major one occurred in 2001, leading to a mass cull of sheep and cattle—including tens of thousands of healthy animals—in what was widely portrayed in the media as a panicky, unnecessarily costly government reaction. Two localized outbreaks occurred in 2007, attracting more measured responses. Under the law, where landowners suspect outbreaks of communicable (infectious or contagious) diseases among their animals, they must inform police, council, and the Department for Environment, Food & Rural Affairs (Defra). Once outbreaks are confirmed, any movement of animals 'from the land' or 'within and beyond the local area' is prohibited, other than under licence granted by inspectors.

More usually, environmental health officers are called in to individual business premises to remove samples of food for laboratory analysis on receiving public complaints about food poisoning, unpleasant tastes or odours, or outdated food labels. Among the more commonplace—if potentially dangerous—food safety issues arising is the identification of bacteria such as *E. coli* or salmonella. In a notorious example of government overreaction to the latter, in 1988 Junior Health Minister Edwina Currie provoked widespread alarm (and her own resignation) by erroneously telling reporters:

&& Most of the egg production in this country, sadly, is now affected with salmonella. 🔊🔊

Food safety authorities also oversee the regulation of slaughterhouses in accordance with EU rules and inspect the quality of meat bought from them. They are also authorized to provide their own public slaughterhouses, cold stores, and refrigerators.

Environmental health officers are not the only officials involved in policing outbreaks of diseases such as foot-and-mouth, *E. coli*, and salmonella; trading standards officers (employed by unitaries and counties) and other Defra-approved contractors also have duties in such instances, albeit primarily in relation to animal welfare. Trading standards departments (see 'Trading standards and the licensing laws' in this chapter) inspect livestock for signs of illness or poor treatment, and help to enforce UK and EU legislation relating to safe and humane animal transportation. Meanwhile, a 2007 EU directive introduced a requirement for formal 'competence assessments' to be carried out on Defra's instructions on anyone intending to transport livestock, horses, or poultry for more than 65 km.

The future of public health at local level

Amid the wholesale franchising out of most local services promoted by the Coalition, it came as a surprise when ministers announced plans to give councils *additional* powers in relation to one area of policy: public health. The initiative—which revives the tradition that existed prior to the NHS of councils being held responsible for promoting healthy lifestyles and environments—was formalized in a national Public Health Outcomes Framework published in January 2012. Councils are now responsible for everything from encouraging local people to lose weight and give up smoking, through promoting breast-feeding, and cutting tooth decay in children, to reducing rates of heart disease, strokes, cancer, and serious falls among those aged over 65. From April 2013, funding for local initiatives to achieve these ends has been drawn from a new public health grant (see Chapter 11, 'Types of revenue grant')—one of only two ring-fenced payments by central government into their revenue budgets to survive the Coalition's reforms of council finance (initially worth £5.2 billion a year).

▎ Trading standards and the licensing laws

While environmental health officers are responsible for verifying the *safety* of food sold to the public, wider consumer protection duties relating to its sale and presentation fall to **trading standards officers**. Under the Food Safety Act 1990, there are two main criminal offences relating to trading standards:

- selling food 'not of the nature or substance or quality demanded by the purchaser'; and
- 'falsely describing or presenting food'—usually without advertisement or labelling.

Trading standards officers are also responsible for ensuring that businesses comply with government policy in the following areas.

General consumer protection

Consumer protection involves monitoring the accurate description of goods, the use of credit, and product safety for items such as household tools, appliances, and children's toys. Trading standards departments are also responsible for ensuring that local trade is carried out 'fairly', under terms set out by the Competition and Markets Authority (CMA—see Chapter 7, 'The Competition and Markets Authority (CMA)'). So time-consuming and costly can this work be that some authorities have even established dedicated consumer advice departments to pool resources with their local Citizens Advice bureaux and Consumers Association.

The Fair Trading Act 1973 introduced a Director General of Fair Trading, authorized to ask business 'acting in a way detrimental to the interests of consumers' to give assurances about its future conduct. If it fails to do so, the Director General can take individuals to county courts or the Restrictive Practices Court, which has authority to accept an assurance that an offence will not be repeated—or to make an order. Civil claims under the Sale of Goods Act 1979 must be brought by individuals through county courts.

Weights and measures

Each authority must appoint a 'chief inspector of weights and measures' to ensure that all local traders comply with authorized weights and measures (the 'metric system' of metres and litres used throughout the EU, rather than the previous 'imperial system' of yards and ounces).

The history of Britain's reluctant conversion to metric standards is almost as long and tangled as its relationship with the EU itself. It began in earnest with the passage of the Weights and Measures Act 1963, which formally redefined yards and pounds in terms of metres and kilograms, and abolished archaic imperial measurements such as 'scruples', 'rods', and 'minims'. In 1965, under pressure from industry, the then President of the Board of Trade committed Britain to adopting the metric system fully within a decade, and by 1968 a Metrication Board had been established to promote it. The pledge was reaffirmed on its entry into the European Economic Community (EEC) in 1973.

Despite several concrete moves, such as the decimalization of the UK's currency in 1971, subsequent governments further delayed full implementation of metrication, and it was only after two EU directives—in 1995 and 2000, respectively—that Britain was finally ordered to introduce the metric system, first for packaged and then bulk-sold goods (for example fresh fruit and vegetables sold on market stalls).

This diktat did not stop some traditionalists resisting. The first few years after the introduction of metrication in fruit and vegetable markets was marked by high-profile court cases that captured the imagination of the popular press—with so-called 'metric martyrs' continuing to label their goods in pounds and ounces in defiance of EU law. In September 2007, enduring public defiance finally scored a pyrrhic victory when the EU Commissioner responsible for the single market, Gunther Verheugen, announced that they would be permitted to continue labelling their items in imperial measures after all—provided that they also did so in metric measurements. The EU subsequently relaxed its stance even more, allowing most traders to continue using only imperial measures, but some councils still prosecute those who do so. A victory of sorts for the metric martyrs finally came when, in October 2008, the then Department for Innovation, Universities, and Skills (DIUS) issued new guidelines urging councils to take only 'proportionate' action against refuseniks.

In addition to checking that goods are itemized in metric measures, inspectors regularly vet market stalls and shops to ensure that food is not sold in 'short weight'—that is, that scales are used correctly and consumers are sold the correct quantities of goods. Short weight is a criminal offence. Weights of manufactured goods are checked at factories, while those of loose food, fuel, and beer are checked at point of sale.

Sunday trading

The Deregulation and Contracting Out Act 1994 marked the first major liberalization of Britain's retail laws, which up to that point had been among the strictest in Europe—with most shops commonly opening only between 9.30 a.m. and 5.30 p.m., and few allowed to trade on Sundays out of respect for Christian worshippers. The 1994 Act gave individual traders freedom to decide their own opening hours and other employment practices on weekdays and Saturdays. Most remaining restrictions were finally removed in the Sunday Trading Act 1994, which stipulated that:

- 'large shops'—those with internal sales areas of 280 m^2 or more—could open for up to six hours between 10 a.m. and 6 p.m., but must remain closed on Easter Sunday and Christmas Day (if the latter falls on a Sunday);
- smaller shops could open as and when they chose to; and
- shop workers who did not wish to work on a Sunday for religious reasons should have some protection from discipline or dismissal.

In 2012, Sunday trading laws were relaxed even further (albeit only for eight weeks, from 22 July) to enable larger shops across England and Wales to open longer than the traditional six hours during the Olympics and Paralympics.

Trade descriptions

It is a criminal offence under the Trade Descriptions Acts 1968 and 1972 for 'false descriptions' to be ascribed to goods or 'false indications' given of their sale prices—for example for labelling not to include value added tax (VAT) as part of the cover price.

The licensing of pubs and clubs, and drinking by-laws

The Licensing Act 2003, which finally came into force in February 2005, ushered in so-called '24-hour drinking' by allowing pubs and bars to apply to vary their existing liquor licences so that they could open until later than the customary 11.00 p.m. closing time on weekdays and Saturdays, and 10.30 p.m. on Sundays. Nightclubs and restaurants were allowed to apply for 'late licences' allowing them to stay open beyond their usual 2 a.m. shutdown. In liberalizing the drinking laws, Labour's stated aim was to tackle Britain's rising epidemic of 'binge drinking' by ending the frantic 'last orders' culture, which often saw drinkers racing to buy multiple drinks just before closing time to get the most out of the limited time available. The hope was that this more relaxed approach to buying and drinking alcohol would instead foster a Continental-style 'cafe culture', with a steadier stream of drinkers drifting in and out of bars at different times, and fewer explosions of violence and rowdy behaviour at 'chucking out' times.

The 2003 Act also introduced significant changes in the way in which licences were issued and policed. Until 2005, local magistrates' courts were responsible for awarding and varying liquor licences, but the Act transferred this duty to councils, who now work together with police to ensure that the terms of licences are adhered to, and apply to magistrates for formal orders to revoke them if they are breached.

The new licensing laws had a mixed reception from licensees, public, and police alike. A common complaint from landlords and nightclub owners in the early days related to the complexity of the revised system. Rather than simply having to apply for a personal licence to serve alcohol between stated hours on stated days and a single public entertainment licence giving them freedom to stage occasional events, such as concerts or stand-up comedy, they were now required to apply for both the former and a separate premises licence or temporary event notice for each occasion on which they planned to stage any entertainment—whether a live acoustic band or karaoke competition.

Following a high-profile run-in between the Musicians' Union, various other groups representing performers, and the Department of Culture, Media, and Sport (DCMS)—the ministry implementing the reforms—the Act was tweaked to avoid any unintended consequences, such as deterring pubs from putting on shows or plays. In rationalizing this aspect of the law, however, ministers unwittingly made it easier for licensed premises to put on all manner of other performances: lap dancing, for example, was recategorized alongside more innocuous forms of public entertainment, meaning that premises no longer needed to apply for separate 'sexual encounter' licences to stage it. Perhaps unsurprisingly, there has since been a huge increase in the number of clubs and bars offering shows involving at least partial nudity—with the pressure group Object identifying some 300 by the mid-Noughties, compared to a handful 10 years earlier. The Licensing Act has also been criticized by police forces and residents for allegedly turning some town centres into 'no-go areas' for older residents, particularly on Friday and Saturday nights. In its 2008 submission to a government review of the impact of the 2003 Act, the Local Government Association (LGA) described it as 'a mistake', and its then chairman, Sir Simon Milton, told the *Daily Telegraph* that it had 'failed miserably'. The policy has also been openly condemned by everyone from former Archbishop of Canterbury, Rowan Williams, to former Labour Health Secretary Frank Dobson. A Freedom of Information Act 2000 request by the *Daily Telegraph* to all 43 police forces in England and Wales, made just ahead of the publication of the Home Office's official review in February 2008, appeared to support their reservations, by uncovering official statistics confirming that 12 forces had seen a 46 per cent rise in antisocial incidents since the Act was enforced—with 16 reporting an increase of 5 per cent in alcohol-related assaults, harassment, and criminal damage. Nationwide, serious violent offences in the early hours had risen by a quarter.

When it was finally published, in March 2008, the government's review recommended retaining the 'new' licensing regime—but with a new 'two-strikes rule' designed to deter off-licences from selling alcohol to underage drinkers. As for the '24-hour' aspect of the legislation, despite the initial expectation that all-night drinking would become a feature of most town centres, statistics obtained from 86 per cent of licensing authorities in November 2007 found that fewer than 500 English and Welsh pubs and clubs had ever been granted 24-hour licences. Most 'late licences' tended to cover only an additional hour or two of business, and only then at weekends generally. Of the 5,100 venues operating 24-hour licences between April 2006 and March 2007, 3,300 were hotels, 910 were supermarkets, and 460 were pubs and clubs. Nonetheless, concerns about the links between late-night drinking and unruly behaviour remain—prompting the Coalition to signal a 'complete review' in May 2010. At time of writing, however, this had still not materialized, although the LGA published its own review calling for tightening of the licensing regime in February 2014.

On a related note, councils have long had powers under statute to curb public drinking. In the early 1990s, Plymouth and Bristol city councils were among the first to invoke by-laws forbidding public consumption of alcohol in specified locations, and similar measures have since been widely implemented. Additional powers were introduced under the Criminal Justice and Police Act 2001, enabling councils to pass alcohol-free zone orders—or, to use their official title, 'alcohol consumption in designated public places orders'—again related to specified locations. Once a zone is in place, police officers may require individuals spotted drinking there to stop immediately and, where necessary, may confiscate their alcohol. In the last resort, those failing to comply may be prosecuted and, if convicted, fined up to £500. Some authorities have gone still further: within weeks of his election as London Mayor, Mr Johnson banned all drinking from London Underground and other public transport throughout the capital.

Various other initiatives have been used to clamp down on antisocial drinking—from Labour's 'alcohol disorder zones', for which extra policing was funded by licensees, to increased fines introduced by the Coalition for pubs, clubs, and off-licences that sell alcohol to children. Licensing authorities may also now set 'late-night levies' of up to £4,440 a year for pubs and clubs whose decisions to stay open into the night result in more costly policing arrangements. Meanwhile, 'early morning restriction orders' (EMROs) introduced by Labour to limit sales of alcohol between 3 a.m. and 6 a.m. have been toughened up to allow councils to impose them from midnight.

Other measures to curb excessive alcohol consumption have also repeatedly been mooted—most notably, the introduction of 'minimum pricing' to cut down on 'two for one' and/or 'happy hour' promotions in pubs and clubs, and to deter people from bingeing on cheap beer bought in bulk from supermarkets before they even head out for the night. Mr Cameron has twice announced this policy, before placing it indefinitely on hold. By contrast, a Bill to introduce minimum alcohol pricing in Scotland—which has some of the highest rates of alcoholism and related medical conditions in Europe—was introduced in 2012, although in April 2014 it was referred to the European Court of Justice (ECJ—see Chapter 9, 'The European Court of Justice (ECJ)') after the whisky industry appealed against it on commercial grounds.

▌ Leisure and cultural services

Providing for citizens' quality of life arguably means more than managing public transport, clearing up refuse, and maintaining a social environment relatively free of crime and disorder. 'Softer services' traditionally offered by councils include those falling under the broad umbrellas of leisure and/or cultural services. These terms—increasingly fused by some councils—cover everything from maintenance of local swimming pools and sports centres, to provision of theatres, museums, and galleries, and financing of festivals, such as the Edinburgh International Festival or England's largest equivalent, the Brighton Festival.

Swimming pools, leisure centres, parks, and playgrounds

Under the Local Government (Miscellaneous Provisions) Act 1972, councils were given discretion to raise funds for and to provide 'such recreational facilities as they think fit'. These included:

- sports centres;
- pitches for team games and athletic events;

- swimming pools;
- tennis courts;
- stadiums, and premises for athletic and other sporting clubs;
- golf courses and bowling greens;
- riding schools;
- campsites;
- facilities for gliding, boating, and waterskiing; and
- staff (including instructors) for any of the above.

As in most other areas of local service provision, compulsory competitive tendering (see Chapter 13, 'New models for service delivery—subcontracting and outsourcing') was introduced under Mrs Thatcher to force councils to compete with private contractors for franchises to run leisure centres. Wearing another 'hat', however, they still have responsibility for ensuring that *standards* of service meet statutory requirements, not least in health and safety, and disabled access.

Libraries, museums, galleries, and the performing arts

Under the Public Libraries Act 1850, emerging councils were empowered to *provide* libraries, but not actually to stock them with books. This changed under the Public Libraries 1919 Act, which allowed them to 'spend more than a rating limit of one penny in the pound on books'. Today, there is no statutory limit, and councils are obliged to offer 'a comprehensive and efficient library service' covering everything from books, newspapers, and periodicals, to records, CDs, and DVDs. Public libraries have also been required to offer free Internet access to the public since 2002.

There were fears that libraries might become the latest of a long line of 'added value' services to fall prey to the Coalition's public spending squeeze when the DCMS announced plans to shake up local library services in August 2010. With recent figures showing that only 29 per cent of British people now regularly visited their libraries and that many local branches were home to dwindling, outdated stocks of books, Culture Minister Ed Vaizey launched a Future Libraries Programme both to generate cost savings and to attract more users by reorganizing services in ways better suited to the pressures and routines of modern living. Among the ideas that he floated was relocating libraries to premises other than conventional ones, such as shops and pubs. He revealed that he had received 51 submissions for support from the programme, representing 100-plus councils. Ten—involving 36 councils—were being pursued in the initial phase, in counties ranging from Northumberland and Durham in the north-east, to Cornwall and Devon in the south-west.

But libraries remain a sensitive topic. According to a UNISON survey published in March 2013, 205 libraries had been shut for good across England since the Coalition came to power—equivalent to two a week—and 76 in the preceding 12 months alone. Four of these were in Liverpool alone, with others going in Wigan, Portland, and the London Borough of Barnet. While some 41 'Big Society'-style social enterprises had been set up in Leicester, Warwickshire, and elsewhere, anger about the accelerating pace of library closures had led to the formation of a campaign group, 'Speak Up for Libraries', the leading lights of which include the authors Kate Mosse (founder of the Orange Prize for Fiction), Philip Ardagh, and bestselling children's writer Alan Gibbons. In November 2012, meanwhile, the Culture Media and Sport Committee warned that a number of councils were in danger of defaulting on their statutory duty to maintain a comprehensive service.

Although their statutory requirements to do so are less stringent, councils are 'allowed' to provide museums and galleries, and to require neighbouring authorities to contribute to their upkeep. Museum 'activities' beyond collecting, maintaining, and displaying objects—for example public events such as readings or classes—are currently overseen by Arts Council England (ACE). The Local Government Act 1972 also gave councils powers to establish theatres, concert halls, and other entertainment venues, to maintain bands or orchestras, and to foster arts and crafts.

Use of the broad-brush term 'cultural services' to encapsulate these varied 'quality of life' provisions has been increasingly criticized—not least by those directly employed by organizations concerned. Whenever ministers offer councils a less-than-generous financial settlement—as at present— 'non-essential' services such as libraries, museums, and theatres immediately suffer, as authorities protect 'core' areas including education and social services. The museums sector has increasingly dwindled, as long-serving curators have retired without being replaced, while councils have sought to make economies by introducing job-shares and substituting specialist staff with generalists.

Hard-pressed councils are often also 'forced' to withdraw funding from theatres and other venues. In 1990, Derby Playhouse faced closure after its annual £130,000 revenue grant from Derbyshire County Council was withdrawn overnight, following the authority's decision to scrap its entire arts budget. Although thrown a lifeline by ACE, the playhouse again narrowly avoided permanent closure in 2007, after Derby City Council withdrew a £40,000 grant, criticizing the theatre's poor management and what it described as 'unsustainable' losses.

In addition to their overarching role in promoting cultural venues and events for local benefit, councils play a part in encouraging tourism and monitoring its effects on their local economies, in partnership with the national tourist promotion quango Visit Britain.

☰ Topical feature idea

The following is an edited item from the minutes of a meeting of Peterborough City Council's Licensing Act 2003 Sub-Committee, on 17 April 2014, centring on an application by the police for a review of a nightclub's licence terms following a serious public order incident. With an hour until your deadline, your news editor on the *Peterborough Telegraph* has told you to develop this into a bigger story about '24-hour drinking' turning Peterborough city centre into a 'no-go zone' at night. Who would you contact first and how would you expand the angle from this single licensing dispute?

Extract from the minutes of Peterborough City Council's Licensing Act 2003 Sub-Committee, 17 April 2014

Applicant	**Cambridgeshire Constabulary**
Nature of Application	*Application Type*
	Expedited Summary Review of Premises Licence
	Summary of Review Application
	In accordance with section 53A of the Licensing Act 2003, following the submission for a summary review of the premises and the certificate signed by a superintendent from Cambridgeshire Constabulary, the licensing authority was required to hold a hearing.
	A summary of the issues raised within the representations included an incident of serious disorder occurring on the 9th March 2014, involving a member of the public and four Security Industry Authority (SIA) registered door supervisors from the Solstice / Radius.
	The mediated conditions included:
	1. Alcohol sales will cease at 02:30am, and all other Licensable activity will cease at 03:00am. No person will be allowed access into the venue after 02:00am.
	2. The premises licence holder or designated premises licence holder shall ensure that all bar staff, supervisors and managers are trained in the legality and procedure of alcohol sales using a training package approved by the Licensing Authority and Police, prior to undertaking the sale of alcohol. Refresher training should be undertaken every 3 months or whenever licensing legislation changes. Training shall be signed and documented and training records will be kept on the premises either in paper or electronic form. These records should be made available immediately to a Licensing Authority Officer or Police Officer (including PCSO) upon request. The documentation relating to training should extend back to a period of 18 months and should specify the time, date and details of both the person providing the training and receiving the training.
	3. All SIA Registered door supervisors must be employed from a recognised and qualified SIA registered Door Supervisor Security Company that is approved by the Licensing Authority.
	4. A minimum of 8 SIA registered door supervisors, including at least one female door supervisor, will be employed at all

Applicant	Cambridgeshire Constabulary

times a licensable activity takes place from 22:00 hours on each Friday and Saturday night. A minimum of 2 SIA door supervisors will be employed where capacity is expected to exceed 100 on any other night. They will be employed on the main access door and at strategic points around the venue to:

a) Prevent the admission of drunk and disorderly persons.

b) Maintain an orderly queue outside the venue

c) Count those entering and leaving the premises to ensure building capacity is not breached.

d) Assist customers leaving the venue to ensure they leave in a quiet and orderly fashion.

e) To keep out excluded persons circulated via the NightSafe Pub Watch Scheme.

f) Search and exclude those persons suspected of carrying illegal drugs or offensive weapons.

g) Maintain effective communication via City Link Radio, or other means with Peterborough CCTV or the Police when requesting assistance.

5. All door staff shall be trained in the requirements of the Challenge 25 policy, the identification & recognition of drunks and the correct procedures to be followed when refusing service.

6. The premises licence holder and / or the designated premises supervisor shall ensure door supervisors are properly briefed and trained to manage queues in a safe and efficient manner.

7. All door supervisors employed at the entrance / exit of the licensed premises will wear and display their SIA badge in an arm badge holder.

8. All door staff engaged in searching persons (as a condition of entry) shall be fully trained in the use of their powers to do so.

9. The premises licence holder and / or designated premises supervisor shall ensure that the following details for each door supervisor are contemporaneously entered into a bound register kept for that purpose:

Full Name

SIA badge number in full

The time they begun duty

The time they completed their duty

The full details of any agency through which they have been allocated work at the premises.

10. The premises licence holder and/or designated premises supervisor or in their absence another responsible person to keep an 'incident report register' in a bound book, or by electronic means, in which full details of all incidents are recorded. This shall be completed as soon as possible and in any case no later than the close of business on the day of the incident. The time and date when the register was completed, and by whom, is to form part of the entry. The

Applicant	Cambridgeshire Constabulary
	register is to be kept on the premises at all times and shall be produced to an authorised officer of the Licensing Authority or Police Officer (inc any Licensing PCSO) when required. The register should be retained for a minimum of 12 months.
	11. All door supervisors shall be capable of communicating instantly with one another by way of radio or other simultaneous system of communication.
Licensing Objective(s) under which representations were made	The Prevention of Crime and Disorder
Parties/ Representatives and witnesses present	*Applicant* Police Constable Grahame Robinson, Cambridgeshire Constabulary. *Licensee / Representative* Andrew Cave, Solicitor, Licensee Representative Michael Boyle, Premises Owner, Licensee Shaun Boyle, Premises Owner, Licensee Kevin Jeffrey, Designated Premises Supervisor
Pre-hearing considerations and any decisions taken by the Sub-Committee relating to ancillary matters	There were no pre-hearing considerations.
Oral representations	The Regulatory Officer addressed the Sub-Committee and outlined the main points with regards to the application. He explained that mediation had been ongoing and revised hours and conditions had been agreed by all parties. He proposed that the Committee accept the mediated terms. *Applicant* PC Robinson addressed the Sub-Committee and commended Solstice management for working with the police and taking positive steps forward. *Licensee's Representative* Mr Cave recognised the serious nature of the incident in question and explained that the Solstice / Radius wanted to continue to work with the police and licensing authority in the future. In collaboration with the police and licensing authority a new course for bar staff had been devised with the assistance of the new door supervisors to recognise customers who may be causing problems. In response to a question Mr Cave identified that a return to previous licensed hours had not been applied for as a result of the serious nature of the incident. It was anticipated that an application for an extension of licensed hours would be made at some point in the future.

Applicant	Cambridgeshire Constabulary
	PC Robinson commented that ceasing the sale of alcohol at 2:30am was considered appropriate by the police for an interim period to aid a natural dispersion of customers.
	Summing Up
	All parties were given the opportunity to summarise their submissions and each expressed their hope that the mediated terms would be accepted.
3.10 Written representations and supplementary material taken into consideration	None were received.
4. Decision	The Sub-Committee listened to all the evidence put before it and also took into account the contents of the application and all representations and submissions made in relation to it. The Sub-Committee found as follows:
	The interim steps had appeared to alleviate the initial concerns of the relevant authorities and that had been confirmed by further mediation. Given the endorsement of all the relevant authorities for the mediated conditions it was the Committees' decision to agree to the modification of the premises licence in the mediated terms.
	A full decision notice with reasons would be sent to all the relevant parties within five working days.

Source: Copyright © 2014 Peterborough City Council

✳ Current issues

- **Government 'flip-flopping' over minimum alcohol pricing** David Cameron has repeatedly promised to introduce minimum alcohol pricing to curb binge drinking, but plans were shelved in 2013 amid claims that the government was lobbied by the licensing industry. Scotland's minimum pricing has run into trouble after the whisky industry took the Scottish Government to the European Court of Justice complaining about its impact.

- **Britain reaches its recycling targets ahead of schedule** The UK's recycling rate has risen faster than that for any other EU member state in the past decade, hitting 39 per cent of all biodegradable waste by 2010 (well ahead of its 30 per cent target). It looks set to hit the magic 50 per cent by 2017—three years ahead of schedule.

- **Mass library closures** Revenue spending cuts introduced since the start of the Coalition have led to 205 local libraries being permanently closed—four in Liverpool alone. 'Big Society' initiatives have stopped some shutting their doors and revived others, but campaigners argue that a whole generation of young readers and pensioners in some areas are being deprived of what was once considered a vital community resource.

⬚ Key issues

1. Responsibility for building and maintaining many roads through and between towns and villages rests with county councils or unitary authorities and metropolitan or London boroughs. A-roads and M-roads (motorways) are built and maintained by an executive agency of the Department for Transport (DfT), the Highways Agency.

2. Responsibility for waste collection rests with districts or boroughs in two-tier areas, with counties disposing of waste. Waste is either recycled or deposited in landfill sites.

3. Environmental health officers, employed by districts or boroughs in two-tier areas, are responsible for ensuring that shops and restaurants are clean and hygienic in handling food, but trading standards officers (unitary authorities) are charged with making sure that food is labelled (and weighed) accurately.

4. Leisure and cultural services are overseen by counties in two-tier areas. These include everything from swimming pools and sports centres, to theatres and museums.

5. County councils, unitaries, and London or metropolitan boroughs have a statutory duty to provide 'comprehensive' library services.

→ Further reading

Black, G. (2011) *Transforming Museums in the Twenty-First Century*, London: Routledge. **Apposite examination of the challenges and opportunities facing museums and galleries as they adapt to less state funding and a harsher commercial environment.**

Cahill, D. (2010) *Transport, Environment, and Society*, Buckingham: Open University Press. **Acclaimed critique of Britain's overreliance on the car, and the impact of cuts in public transport on social inequality and exclusion.**

Docherty, I. and Shaw, J. (2008) *Traffic Jam: Ten Years of Sustainable Transport in the UK*, Bristol: Policy Press. **Lively critique of the successes and failures of attempts to introduce a more integrated and sustainable transport policy under New Labour.**

Lane, K. (2006) *National Bus Company: The Road to Privatization*, Shepperton: Ian Allen. **Affectionate account of the last years of the National Bus Company monopoly, and the revolution in public passenger transport ushered in by the Thatcher government's privatization and deregulation reforms.**

Morgan, S. (2009) *Waste, Recycling, and Reuse*, London: Evans Brothers. **Practical evaluation of the West's mounting waste management problem, with suggested solutions, focusing on 'three Rs'—reducing, reusing, and recycling.**

Waters, I. and Duffield, B. (1994) *Entertainment, Arts, and Cultural Services*, London: Financial Times/Prentice Hall. **Informative look at changes in the provision and funding of arts, entertainment, and other aspects of cultural services during the 1990s, emphasizing the tensions between different parts of the sector.**

 ## Online Resource Centre

www.oxfordtextbooks.co.uk/orc/Morrison4e/
Visit the Online Resource Centre that accompanies this book for web links and regular updates.

20

Freedom of information

Most of this book is concerned with explaining how Britain is governed—both politically, and through the nuts and bolts of public administration. This final chapter is the exception—focusing as it does not on who wields power, what that power amounts to, or how it is exercised, but on the means by which jour- nalists (and taxpayers) can find out more about decisions taken on their behalf and hold those responsible to account.

What rights, if any, do citizens have to question or challenge the powerful, and how can these be exercised in practice?

▌ The origins of the Freedom of Information Act 2000—what is 'freedom of information' (FoI)?

The 'freedom of information' (FoI) concept rests on the notion that, in a democ- racy, citizens should be entitled to know as much as possible about the actions and decisions of the politicians elected to represent them, and the officials whom they appoint to implement policy. More important still is the principle that participating citizens should be able to find out how public money—largely derived from taxes they pay—is spent on their behalf.

Freedom of information was a long time coming in Britain. At least 70 other states had enshrined their citizens' rights to find out about the inner workings of power long before the Freedom of Information Act 2000—in Scotland, the Freedom of Information (Scotland) Act 2002—received royal assent. It was not until Tony Blair's election in 1997 that a British government committed to implementing such reforms. Even then, it was several years into New Labour's first term before its manifesto pledge was put into action—in watered-down form at that. And not until 1 January 2005, towards the end of its second, did the full force of the new law come into effect, under the then Department of Constitutional Affairs (now the Ministry of Justice).

Freedom of information is a long-cherished concept in the United States, which has a nationwide Freedom of Information Act based on the principle of democratic accountability and numerous state-specific laws governing access to public documentation and records of tax-levying entities—Acts collectively known as 'sunshine laws'. Elsewhere in Europe, where FoI legislation is commonplace, Acts are generally known as 'open records'. The European Union (EU) as a whole is governed by Regulation 1049/2001, passed by the European Parliament and Council of Ministers on 30 May 2001. This sets out a detailed system of rules regarding public access to EU institutions.

Lest blinkered constitutional historians try to convince us that Britain is the seat of democracy, it is worth noting that the earliest known 'open record' was passed in Sweden in the late eighteenth century. And while some might scoff at the idea of openness and accountability operating under dictatorships, it is intriguing to note that, since 1 January 2008, even China has had an FoI law (at least notionally): the Regulations of the People's Republic of China on Open Government Information.

Given the huge number of FoI laws in force globally, perhaps unsurprisingly there is little conformity in their exact provisions. Most share general traits, however—notably, the principle that the 'burden of proof' falls on institutions from which information is being sought, rather than individuals seeking it. In other words, people making requests are not normally required to explain why they want information, whereas organizations questioned must give valid reasons for failing to supply details requested. So what constitutes 'valid' in Britain?

Information that the act covers—and exempts

The UK's FoI legislation applies to more than 100,000 'public authorities', ranging from individual schools and hospitals, to councils, quangos, and entire government departments. If legitimate requests are made under either Act, authorities asked must first tell the questioners whether they hold the relevant information and then, assuming that they do, supply it *within 20 working days*.

Authorities may, however, *refuse* to confirm or deny the existence of information—and/or to provide it—if any of the following conditions apply:

- if information requested is 'exempt';
- if requests are 'vexatious' or similar to previous ones; and/or
- if the costs of compliance exceed 'appropriate limits'.

The term 'exemption' might invite the idea that any authority possessing information can freely refuse to disclose it, but according to the Acts even exempt material should sometimes be made available.

There are two broad classes of exemption: 'absolute' and 'qualified'. While the former may not be disclosed under any circumstances, the latter may be if the 'public interest' in revealing it outweighs that in keeping it secret. For example, authorities involved in security policy might legitimately refuse to disclose exempt information that could compromise public safety by jeopardizing counter-terrorism operations, but would be hard-pressed to do so if the information that they were withholding could *improve* safety—by, for example, revealing the expected time or location of an impending terrorist attack.

In addition to absolute and qualified exemptions, several entire categories of information are exempt. Authorities may also refuse requests that they consider 'likely to prejudice' law enforcement or Britain's interests abroad. The three categories of exemption are listed in Table 20.1.

Even when none of the above exemptions applies, journalists should proceed with caution before reproducing certain 'information' wholesale in the media. Under the Re-use of Public Information Regulations, introduced in July 2005, some details disclosed by authorities under FoI remain subject to their legal copyright. This means that while requesters are entitled to answers, they do not necessarily have 'automatic rights' to reuse the information, other than for

Table 20.1 Exemptions under the Freedom of Information Act 2000

Absolute	Qualified	Categories
Information supplied by/relating to bodies dealing with security matters	Intended for future publication	Information relating to investigations/proceedings conducted by public authorities
Court records and information related to impending prosecution	Related to national security (other than information supplied by/relating to named security organizations)	Court records
Information that would infringe parliamentary privilege	Which might limit defence of British Isles, or 'capability, effectiveness, or security' of Armed Forces	Formulation of government policy
Personal information either: 1. relating to person making request, which could be obtained under Data Protection Act 1998; or 2. about another individual, if it would breach data protection principles	Potentially prejudicial to international relations between UK and another state/international organization/court or its interests abroad	
Information held by Commons or Lords that may be prejudicial to effective conduct of public affairs	Information that might prejudice relations between administrations within UK	

(continued)

Table 20.1 (*continued*)

Absolute	Qualified	Categories
Information provided in confidence	Information likely to prejudice UK's financial and/or economic interests	
Prohibitions on disclosure where prohibited by enactment or would constitute contempt of court	Information relating to investigations and proceedings conducted by public authorities	
	Information likely to prejudice law enforcement—defined as prevention or detection of crime, prosecution of offenders, assessment of taxes, etc.	
	Information relating to public authority with audit functions in relation to another public body (e.g. Audit Commission)	
	Information relating to formulation of government policy, communications between ministers, or operations of ministerial office	
	Information held by public authorities other than Commons or Lords that may be prejudicial to effective conduct of public affairs	
	Information relating to communications between Queen, ministers, and/or other public bodies, including those relating to honours system	
	Information likely to endanger health and/or safety of individuals	
	Environmental information authority is obliged to make public under s. 74 of the Act	
	Personal information believed by institution not to breach data protection principles, but in relation to which individual who is subject of request serves notice that disclosure would cause 'unwarranted substantial damage or distress'	
	Subject to legal professional privilege	
	'Trade secrets' or information liable to prejudice individual's/authority's commercial interests	

the purposes for which it was originally produced by the authorities concerned. Although theoretically these Regulations could be used by disingenuous authorities to delay or prevent journalists disclosing perfectly 'free' information, in practice they tend to be invoked to protect intellectual property rights of third parties whose work is included in disclosed material—for example freelance photographers, architects, or designers.

These, then, are the exempt categories of information, but what of the Acts' definitions of 'public authority'? Are any organizations or individuals that one might expect to fall under this umbrella exempted from FoI requests?

In short, yes.

The Queen and Royal Household

The Royal Family's website defines the status of the Queen and Royal Household thus:

The Royal Household is not a public authority within the meaning of the FOI Acts, and is therefore exempt from their provisions.

It goes on to cite the 'fundamental constitutional principle' that communications between reigning sovereigns and ministers or other public bodies remain confidential—not least to ensure that royals do not compromise their 'political neutrality'. As the site stresses, however, the fact that the Royal Household is not bound by FoI does *not* mean that it is unwilling to make certain information available voluntarily.

To this end, it is happy to 'account openly for all its use of public money'. It does this by posting online every July a consolidated report, including a full annual account and breakdown of the sovereign grant. Additionally, the Prince of Wales voluntarily publishes details of his income from the Duchy of Cornwall—both before and after tax—on his website.

What the sites fail to emphasize is the fact that no information about the Royal Household's funding was made public until 2001, when it was persuaded to agree to greater openness while negotiating with HM Treasury a new 10-year funding settlement. Perhaps even more remarkable is the amount of detail about its dealings that the Royal Family still will *not* disclose. For example, nowhere will British taxpayers access details about other aspects of the royals' personal finances, such as incomes derived by several members of the family from the Armed Forces, the Duchess of York's royalties for her series of *Budgie the Little Helicopter* children's books and numerous television talk show appearances, or the dividends and profits derived from family members' investments. Soon after the 2010 election, the Coalition gave the National Audit Office greater access to the Queen's accounts, but this has yet to yield any major revelations.

The list of specific FoI exemptions for the Queen and the Royal Household are detailed in Table 20.2. The special treatment that the Queen and her immediate family enjoy in relation to FoI became the subject of a public dispute in

Table 20.2 Specific FoI exemptions relating to the Royal Household

Exemption	Details
Financial and other personal matters	Information relating to personal affairs of sovereign/family members—including private finances and personal activities—exempt under s. 40 of FoI Act and s. 38 of Scottish FoI Act (Data Protection Act provisions).
Royal communications	'Absolute' exemption for correspondences sent by/on behalf of/to Queen, heir to throne, or second in line introduced under Constitutional Reform and Governance Act 2010, with same exemption expected to be introduced in Scotland under Freedom of Information (Amendment) Bill. 'Qualified' exemptions apply to communications with other Royal Household/family members under s. 37 of FoI Act 2000. Latter may be disclosed only if 'balance of public interest' deems this necessary. All exemptions apply for whichever longer of 20 years or five years after death of family member concerned.
Correspondences with family members now deceased	Personal information on recently deceased family members relating to communications with Queen, other members of Royal Household/family. If contained in records less than 30 years old, may be exempt under s. 37 of UK FoI Act (s. 41 of Scottish FoI Act).
Other information relating to deceased royals	Information relating to recently deceased family members, disclosure of which would damage 'right to family life' of deceased's relatives, may be exempt under s. 44 of UK FoI Act and s. 26 of Scottish FoI Act, and s. 8 ('Private Life and Family') of Human Rights Act 1998.

January 2012 between the Scottish Government and Scotland's then newly installed Information Commissioner Rosemary Agnew. Interviewed in *Scotland on Sunday*, she criticized Alex Salmond's proposal to turn the 'qualified' exemption covering royal communications north of the border into an 'absolute' one.

The introduction, in 2010, of a similar absolute exemption across the rest of Britain, however, failed to silence *The Guardian* over its then five-year quest to use FoI to force publication of 27 correspondences from Prince Charles to ministers purportedly showing how he had lobbied them to change government priorities. This long-running saga (unresolved at time of writing) led to a showdown between the paper and then Coalition Attorney General Dominic Grieve in 2013, when he refused to disclose the letters' contents on the grounds that they could cast doubt on the Prince's political neutrality—creating constitutional difficulties for him when he acceded to the throne. Mr Grieve had defied a ruling by the Information Tribunal that the public were entitled to see the letters under the FoI Act 2000 and under the Environmental Information Regulations 2004. However, in March 2014, the Master of the Rolls, Lord Dyson, and two other senior judges overruled him—once again, paving the way for the letters' release and forcing ministers to launch a further appeal to suppress them, this time to the Supreme Court. Although the letters themselves have still to be revealed, choice nuggets of information have seeped out via other sources: in interviews for a BBC Radio 4 documentary, *The Royal Activist*, broadcast in June 2014, former Labour Education Secretary David Blunkett claimed that Prince Charles had lobbied him to extend the grammar school system in the 1990s, while ex-Environment Minister Michael Meacher stated that he and Prince Charles 'would consort together quietly' to try to persuade then Prime Minister Tony Blair to introduce more radical policies to combat climate change and abandon investment in genetically modified (GM) crops.

Despite this array of exemptions, placing Britain's Royal Household in a significantly more privileged position than any other, recent annual disclosures of its public accounts have shed light on the huge lengths to which members appear to go to defend FoI applications. According to its 2006–07 accounts, it spent £180,000 of taxpayers' money in that one year shielding itself from FoI requests. Buckingham Palace claimed that the sum was spent 'reminding' government departments of the exemption to prevent them from releasing details of private communications.

Nonetheless, resourceful journalists can find ways of circumventing royals' exemptions. In June 2008, an FoI request to the Ministry of Defence unearthed the cost of Prince William's controversial flight in an RAF Chinook helicopter to an exclusive stag party on the Isle of Wight. The trip—one of five 'familiarization exercises' undertaken by the prince, which saw him stop off en route to pick up his brother, Prince Harry, in London—set taxpayers back £8,716. Embarrassing disclosures teased out of communications with the Royal Household covered only by qualified exemption have included the revelation that, in 2004, the Queen asked ministers for grants worth £60 million to improve the energy efficiency of Buckingham Palace—from a pot of money specifically targeted at low-income households (see Chapter 17, 'Other local authority housing responsibilities'). Among hundreds of other letters obtained by *The Independent* in September 2010 was one exposing a row between the Queen and ministers over who should profit from the sale of land around Kensington Palace.

Utilities, train companies, and other passenger transport operators

Controversially, the privatized utilities—water, electricity, gas, telecommunications, and rail-operating companies—were excluded from automatic coverage by the FoI Acts when they entered their final draft stages. After being included in the remit of the government's 1997 White Paper *Your Right to Know*, hopes were high that they would be subject to scrutiny when the Acts were passed. But after intensive lobbying by the companies concerned—many argued that exposure to FoI could jeopardize commercially sensitive operations—they were omitted.

The decision to exclude companies involved in supplying British taxpayers with such vital 'natural monopolies' as energy and water was enough to infuriate many, but more baffling was the fact that even Network Rail—the not-for-dividend company formed to take over maintenance of the railway infrastructure after the collapse of private firm Railtrack in 2001—was exempted. In a test ruling in January 2007, the **Information Commissioner**—the individual who hears FoI appeals (see '**FoI appeals and the Information Commissioner**')—clarified that Network Rail was a 'private company', not a 'public authority' under the Act's terms. His ruling came in response to an appeal against the company's refusal to answer a May 2005 request, under the Data Protection Act 1998, regarding information about a flood by a railway line.

Although utility companies themselves are immune to FoI, the regulators set up to monitor them—including the Office of Gas and Electricity Markets (Ofgem) and Office of Communications (Ofcom) (see Chapter 7, 'Communications')—are *not*. The fact that it is possible for press and public to access significant amounts of information from utilities *indirectly* has been used as an argument by the Confederation of British Industry (CBI) and other business lobbyists for retaining the 'light touch' approach to the utilities that currently remains.

Academies

Until recently one of the most contentious categories of organization exempt from FoI was academies—'independent' secondary schools operating within the state sector (see Chapter 15, 'The growth of school autonomy—foundation schools, free schools, and the rise and rise of academies'). Their exemption—granted because of the involvement of private sponsors in setting them up and running their ancillary services—was widely viewed as a double standard, because it enabled them to avoid revealing performance data that all other state schools were expected to publish. Some even suggested that the exemption was a convenient way of masking academies' initially sluggish academic progress (when introduced in 2002, they were trumpeted as a way of turning round 'failing' comprehensives by pumping in private capital). Up to January 2011, when the law was amended to bring them within the ambit of FoI by then Coalition Education Secretary Michael Gove, Labour's academies were allowed to publicize their exam results in a different way from other schools—omitting details of the subjects in which GCSE A*–C grades had been obtained, thereby making it hard for parents to take informed decisions about their relative performance.

Some critics also pointed to a clear contradiction between the government's public insistence that, despite being largely privately financed, academies remained in the public sector—as opposed to representing the start of creeping privatization of the state schooling system. In addition to bringing the first wave of academies under the ambit of FoI, in September 2010 Mr Gove extended the Act's remit to cover all those formed under the Coalition.

The British Broadcasting Corporation (BBC)

As a publicly funded organization, the BBC is subject to FoI in relation to much of its activities. However, given that a large part of its remit is to produce, commission, and broadcast programmes and other creative content (on television, radio, and the Internet) for public consumption, there are areas of its operation that are exempt. The scope of the Act as it applies to the Corporation is therefore defined as relating to information 'held for purposes other than those of journalism, art or literature'—in other words, requests for disclosure are not allowed to interfere with the BBC's own editorial decisions and output, which themselves might often involve FoI-related enquiries. Such exempt information will also be excluded from the versions of the BBC's annual report and accounts, which are made publicly available on its website through its own publication scheme.

The Security Service, MI6, and other intelligence agencies

Just as most security-related material is exempt from FoI, there is a blanket exemption for any information relating to the work of the Security Service (MI5), MI6, and other British intelligence agencies. Similar exemptions apply to Special Forces, such as the Special Air Service (SAS) and Special Boat Squadron (SBS).

How to make an FoI request—and how not to

Around 120,000 FoI requests are made each year—six out of 10 by the public, a fifth by businesses, and around one in ten by journalists. That said, the exhaustive nature of some enquiries has taken its toll on authorities' time and resources. The overall cost of complying with media-related FoI requests was estimated at £35.5 million in 2005 alone.

But how does one make one? Although the exact procedure varies from authority to authority, it entails writing either by email or post, detailing specific question(s) to which an answer(s) is requested. Any ambiguity in wording should see authorities enter into dialogue with requesters to clarify the question(s) and supply information as quickly as possible—provided that it is not exempt. Authorities are also expected, where relevant, to supply additional explanatory material if it will clarify complex or confusing information and avoid the need for prolonged correspondence with requesters. As in other states, requesters must give their names and contact details when filing requests, but are not expected to divulge their motivations. In principle, FoI requests are free and it is highly unusual for organizations to charge for answering them.

In addition to the aforementioned exemptions, authorities may refuse to respond to requests for other reasons. If a single request to a government department or body is likely to cost more than £600 in terms of time and/or staffing needed to locate the information (£450, in the case of other authorities), it may be refused. Alternatively, authorities may send requesters notice that they will be charged fees up to the cost of gathering and supplying requested information. If requesters pay, material must then be provided. Authorities may also decline to answer 'vexatious' requests—defined as ones:

- imposing a 'significant burden' on authorities in terms of expense or distraction *and* not having any serious purpose or value;
- being designed to cause disruption or annoyance;
- having the effect of harassing the authority; or
- being otherwise obsessive or manifestly unreasonable.

Examples of 'vexatious' cases have included that of an individual refused information by Birmingham City Council after making more than 70 previous requests. In another case, West Midlands Transport Executive spent 175 hours responding to one person's enquiries. Transport for London (TfL), meanwhile, received so many letters from a single enquirer that it had had to devise a new internal management strategy to cope. But perhaps the most burdensome FoI addict to date was the individual who sent no fewer than 347 requests to police forces, 412 to the Ministry of Defence, and 22 to the Cabinet Office.

Just as authorities are allowed to reject vexatious requests, they may also refuse to answer 'repeated' ones—those identical to others that they have previously answered in full, particularly if they originate from the same individual or organization.

The Environmental Information Regulations 2004

The FoI Act was not the only new legislation designed to promote greater government openness to take effect in 2005. Under EU law, the Environmental Information Regulations (EIR) 2004—in Scotland, the Environmental Information (Scotland) Regulations 2004—came in simultaneously, giving the public access to information about the state of their natural environment, particularly in relation to potential hazards such as pollution.

Unlike FoI, EIR requests—also generally made by post or email and subject to 20-day response times—may be lodged verbally, rather than in writing. They also cover various private sector organizations currently beyond the FoI Acts' remit. For example, EIR requests may be made to privatized utilities, such as water and electricity companies, responsible for activities with direct impact on the environment.

Environmental information covered by the Regulations may relate to:

- the state of 'elements of the environment'—air, water, soil, land, fauna (including human beings);
- emissions and discharges, noise, energy, radiation, waste, and other such substances;

Table 20.3 Exemptions under the Environmental Information Regulations 2004

Absolute	Qualified
Information not held by authority (if so, it has 'duty' to refer request to relevant body)	Release would breach confidentiality of legal proceedings
Request 'manifestly unreasonable'	Might prejudice international relations between Britain and other states/ international bodies, public security, or national defence
Request 'too general' (although authority should still fulfil duty to advise and assist)	Might jeopardize course of justice and right of citizens to fair trial
Requests for unfinished documents or data (in which case, estimated time for completion must be given)	Commercially confidential information
Requests for internal communications	Certain information related to intellectual property rights
Related to personal/voluntary data	Related to environmental protection work

- measures and activities such as policies, plans, and agreements affecting, or likely to affect, the state of the environment;
- reports, cost–benefit, and economic analyses;
- the state of human health and safety, and contamination of the food chain; and
- cultural sites and built structures—to the extent that they may be affected by the state of the elements of the environment.

As with the FoI Acts, there are certain 'absolute' and 'qualified' exemptions to the EIR's provisions, as outlined in Table 20.3.

Enquiries made under EIR tend to incur fees for requesters, provided that these are set at a 'reasonable' level and authorities publish schedule of their charges. Requests may not, however, be refused on cost grounds alone.

FoI versus data protection

The Data Protection Act 1984, as amended by the Data Protection Act 1998, relates to the notion of protecting individuals' privacy, as its name suggests. Superficially, this may appear to conflict with more 'free for all' aspects of information disclosure ushered in by FoI. In practice, however, the two Acts largely consolidate one another—a fact assured by ministers' decision to give the task of policing both of them to the Information Commissioner in 2005.

The 1998 Act relates to 'personal data'. This is 'any data which can be used to identify a living person'—including names, addresses, telephone, fax, and mobile phone numbers, email addresses, and birthdays. It applies, however, only to data that is or is intended to be held on computer or in another 'relevant filing system'. The Act's scope is fairly broad in this latter context: individuals'

Table 20.4 Conditions relating to use of personal data under the Data Protection Act 1998

Condition	Details
Focus	Data may be used only for specific purposes for which collected.
Privacy	Data must not be disclosed to other parties without consent of individual concerned, unless legislation/other overriding legitimate reason requires information to be shared (e.g. crime prevention/detection). It is offence for other parties to obtain data without authorization.
Accessibility	Individuals have right to access information about them, subject to certain exceptions (e.g. crime prevention/detection information).
Time-sensitivity	Data may be kept no longer than necessary.
Protection	Data may not be transmitted outside European Economic Area (EEA) unless individual to whom it relates consents or adequate protection in place (e.g. use of prescribed form of contract). Entities holding personal information required to have adequate security—e.g. technical measures (such as computer firewalls) and organizational ones (such as staff training).
Regulation	Almost all entities that process personal information must register with Information Commissioner.

paper diaries may be considered 'relevant filing systems' if used commercially. The Act is underpinned by seven 'key principles', as outlined in Table 20.4.

The Act gives anyone whose personal data is processed the right to:

- view any data held by an organization, for a small ('subject access') fee;
- request incorrect information be corrected—and if the organization ignores his or her plea, a court may order data to be corrected or destroyed and compensation to be paid;
- require data not be used in a way that causes 'damage or distress'; and
- require that his or her data is not used for direct marketing.

So how do the two Acts—governing 'data protection', on the one hand, and 'freedom of information', on the other—coalesce in practice?

First, many enquiries that individuals might think of making under the FoI Act in relation to information about themselves will be exempt. However, this is only because the correct procedure for accessing such information actually falls under the 1998 Act. That said, if individuals seek to make requests relating to themselves that will disclose information about third parties, the correct law to use is likely to be the FoI Act. Confusingly, though, authorities asked to supply such information must consider 'data protection principles' applicable under FoI before deciding whether to release it.

Because many FoI requests concern what might be termed 'corporate' information—procedural, statistical, and/or constitutional matters—rather than personal data, in practice the number of serious conflicts between the FoI and Data Protection Acts is limited. There have, however, been notable altercations between journalists and councils—particularly in relation to the salaries and perks of senior officers. Councils often try to hide behind data protection legislation when asked for such details under FoI, arguing that, because officers are not elected representatives, they constitute information of a personal nature and should be treated as confidential. The Commissioner has clarified the legal position surrounding this, by distinguishing between information relating to public officials' private lives (exempt) and public duties (covered). Sections 34 and 35 of the 1998 Act exempt individuals from data protection if the data requested consists of information that authorities handling requests are obliged to publicize by law, or if court orders or other 'rules of law' require its disclosure. Either of these can override personal data protections otherwise guaranteed by section 40 of the FoI Act.

A landmark ruling by the Commissioner in June 2011 raised the prospect of a more 'free for all' approach to disclosing information about the public servants' salaries. Defying a Cabinet Office attempt to protect the identities of 24 senior civil servants earning more than £150,000 each, he ordered that their names be publicized—raising the prospect that a strongly resisted request by Communities Secretary Eric Pickles for councils to publish the names and salaries of all officers earning £58,200-plus (see Chapter 14, 'From "Beacon Councils" to the National Indicator Set—the growth of performance data') might return to haunt them. While the Cabinet Office had tried to avoid releasing certain figures, ministers had already taken significant steps towards 'throwing open the books' in relation to mandarins earning more than the prime minister a year before the Commissioner's ruling. In June 2011, the first 'naming and shaming' took place, with disclosure on the **www.direct.gov.uk** web portal about 11 'top earners' in the public sector the previous year, including: John Fingleton, chief executive of the Office of Fair Trading (OFT), who took home between £275,000 and £279,999; NHS head David Nicholson, who took home £255,000–£259,999; and Joe Harley, IT director-general and chief information officer at the Department of Work and Pensions (DWP), who pocketed £245,000–£249,999. A month later, it was the turn of quango bosses, with news that David Higgins, chief executive of the Olympic Delivery Authority, enjoyed a taxpayer-funded salary of £390,000–£394,999—nearly twice that of David Cameron.

FoI appeals and the Information Commissioner

Anyone refused FoI information has a right to appeal, initially through the authorities' own internal review procedures, but ultimately to the Information Commissioner's Office (ICO). In addition to its central London headquarters, the ICO has three offices in the capitals of the devolved nations: Edinburgh, Cardiff, and Belfast.

It is the Information Commissioner's job to ensure that the 23 exemptions are not abused by authorities seeking to keep secret information that they regard as embarrassing, but which is not exempt. In Scotland, complaints are made to the Scottish Information Commissioner. Citizens have a further right to appeal over and above even the Commissioners, via the Information Tribunal.

To aid authorities in complying with the FoI Acts, the ICO has published 'Ten Top Tips'. These are listed in the table entitled 'The Information Commissioner's Office's "Ten Top Tips" for handling requests', to be found on the **Online Resource Centre**.

Complaints may be made to the ICO if authorities fail to:

- provide information requested;
- respond to requests within 20 working days (or explain why longer is needed);
- give proper advice and help;
- give information in forms requested;
- properly explain reasons for refusing requests; or
- correctly apply exemptions.

Complainants must provide the following material:

- a covering letter, detailing the complaint;
- details of the initial request;
- a copy of the authority's initial response '(the 'refusal notice');
- a copy of the complaint made to the authority's internal review or complaints procedure;
- a copy of the authority's response;
- any other information that they think relevant; and
- their contact details.

Stories in which the Commissioner has recently played a prominent role have had more to do with data protection than FoI. In June 2008, he served formal enforcement notices—the toughest sanctions available—against both HM Revenue and Customs (HMRC) and the Ministry of Defence (MoD) over 'deplorable failures' leading to 'serious data breaches'. He was referring to two, then recent, data protection fiascos. In November 2007, HMRC confessed to losing two unencrypted discs containing personal details of 25 million Child Benefit recipients—every British family with a child under the age of 16. The information—including names, addresses, birthdates, National Insurance (NI) numbers, and bank details—had been en route from HMRC's offices at Waterview Park, Sunderland, to the National Audit Office in London.

Table 20.5 Priority types of information covered by the FoI 'public interest test'

Category	Definition
Matters of public debate	Issues about which public debate has been generated and debate cannot properly take place without information disclosure; issue affects many individuals/companies; government has put views on record; issue may affect legislative process
Public participation in political debate	Situations in which local interest groups need sufficient information to represent those interests and requests relate to facts behind major policy decisions
Accountability for public funds	Matters relating to government accountability for sale of public assets or legal aid spending; need for openness relating to tender processes/prices relating to public spending and services; misappropriation of public funds; accountability of elected officials whose propriety called into question; need for public bodies to obtain value for money in spending taxpayers' cash
Public safety	Information relating to air safety, nuclear plant security, and public health, contingency plans in emergencies, and potential environmental damage

The second breach, revealed in January 2008, concerned the theft of an MoD laptop containing confidential details of 600,000 service personnel. In reporting the crime in a Commons statement, then Defence Secretary Des Browne revealed that two further thefts of departmental laptops had also occurred since 2005.

There is a welter of guidance on the ICO's website about the rights of public and media to access information under the Acts that it administers. One of the most useful for journalists is the 'Guidance Notice explaining how authorities should weigh the 'public interest' of a request against potential qualified exemptions' (see Table 20.5).

▶ Freedom of information and the headlines—some case studies

Perhaps unsurprisingly, reporters working on everything from local weekly free sheets to national dailies have embraced FoI as a source of potential stories—not least because they enable a modicum of what might loosely be termed 'investigative journalism' to be carried out within the increasingly restrictive confines of modern newsrooms. Widespread cutbacks—from the offices of regional publishers, to those of major nationals—have seen the size of many papers' reporting staffs dwindle in recent years. Papers face growing competition from the Internet and other forms of new media, and as a result new recruits are expected to 'multitask' as everything from video journalists and photographers, to designers, subeditors, and bloggers. At the same time, ever-tighter economies imposed on newsrooms mean that what conventional reporting is still being done is increasingly carried out over the telephone and/or email, rather than in the face-to-face, hands-on fashion of times past.

Freedom of information therefore offers a means by which journalists with suitably forensic minds can hold authorities accountable 'on the cheap'. Whereas once they might have had to invest significant resources into rooting out information that organizations were keen to keep secret, much of this can now be obtained (at least theoretically) by sending a simple email. FoI legislation has also spawned several 'amateur' journalism websites almost entirely dedicated to using it as an investigative tool (notably **http://helpmeinvestigate. com**, **www.whatdotheyknow.com**, and **www.opendemocracy.net**).

The FoI bonanza did not begin in earnest until January 2005. Within days of the 2000 Act coming into force, *The Observer* ran a story listing a 'who's who' of celebrities and business people who had been wined and dined by then Prime Minister Tony Blair at his country retreat, Chequers, since 2001. The luminaries—whose names it obtained under FoI—included entertainer Des O'Connor, former Spice Girl Geri Halliwell, television presenter Esther Rantzen, Lord Lloyd Webber, Olympic champion rower Sir Steve Redgrave, and then Tesco chief executive Sir Terry Leahy.

That August, BBC2's *Newsnight* used an FoI request to expose the fact that Harold Macmillan's government sold Israel sufficient quantities of uranium 235 and heavy water to enable it to develop its nuclear weapons programme. In a statement to the International Atomic Energy Agency (IAEA), then Foreign Office Minister Kim Howells denied that Britain had been a party to any such sale, but in March 2006 *Newsnight* used a further request to expose sales of plutonium to Israel under Harold Wilson.

Perhaps even more shocking was the disclosure, in December 2005, of a hushed-up report by Scotland Yard detective Tom Hayward into a brutal torture camp operated by British forces in post-war Germany. *The Guardian* used FoI to obtain a copy of the document, detailing the outcome of interrogations of 372 men and 44 women at the Bad Nenndorf camp, near Hanover. Among the grisly details was an account of how two men suspected of being Communists were starved to death, another beaten to a pulp, and numerous others seriously injured. Four months later, the paper published images of emaciated prisoners after winning an appeal against the MoD's refusal to release photographs of the victims contained in the report.

But FoI requests do not always produce such sensational outcomes. In most cases, they 'unearth' humdrum information—much of it unexciting and lacking in any obvious news value. Indeed, there is a feeling in some quarters—not least in the offices of the less well-staffed authorities—that journalists have come to rely on FoI too heavily. Before the concept of 'freedom of information' passed into British law, reporters were forced to rely on those time-worn qualities—guile, ingenuity, and perseverance—to tease out material that organizations wanted to keep away from public view. If they received tip-offs that councillors were fiddling their expenses or public officials taking overseas flights using taxpayers' money, they would often have to confront the authority's press office head on, citing phrases such as 'public interest' and 'public domain' to remind them of their obligations to confirm or deny such activities, and where necessary to supply details. Reluctant though authorities invariably were to expose themselves to criticism by admitting such abuses, more often than not they grudgingly disclosed them. Today, able to hide behind the cloak of having to 'dig out the information' or 'go through the files', the same authorities can cheerfully take far longer to make disclosures—using the cover of the statutory 20-day time limit to craft polished excuses and put off answering questions until any newsworthiness derived from them has dwindled or passed.

Seasoned FoI users—particularly those experienced enough to know the difference between stories requiring the Act and those that can be stood up using more conventional tactics—cite the counterargument that, given the relative ease and effectiveness of the legislation, too few journalists are taking advantage of it. Used in a targeted way, it is certainly true that FoI provides an excellent source of off-diary stories (gold dust for news editors).

▌ The future of FoI—and moves to extend (or restrict) it

New Labour initially made a big noise about its commitment to FoI, but later on it appeared to regret laying itself open to quite so much scrutiny. Ministers' discomfort with outcomes of some FoI requests began emerging in May 2007, when Conservative backbencher David Maclean introduced a private member's Bill (PMB) into the House of Commons—the Freedom of Information (Amendment) Bill—which proposed exempting members of Parliament (MPs) from the 2000 Act (ostensibly to protect details contained in their personal correspondences, including the addresses of private individuals). It would also have incorporated the cost of time that officials spent 'thinking' about whether to disclose information within the £600 limit above which requests become chargeable.

The issue came to a head that June after the Commons provisionally approved the Bill and ministers began seeking a sympathetic peer to 'sponsor' it through the Lords. When none volunteered, and the Bill was condemned by both the Commons Constitutional Affairs Select Committee and Lords Constitution Committee, it finally fell—but not before Leader of the House Jack Straw issued new guidelines urging authorities to ensure that MPs' personal details were not compromised by releasing correspondences with their constituents.

It is not only public authorities that occasionally gripe about FoI. In May 2007, the Commissioner used his address to the annual Freedom of Information Conference to urge people to act with 'restraint' when making requests. He cited an enquiry about how much the Foreign Office spent on Ferrero Rocher chocolates and another asking about the number of eligible bachelors in the Hampshire Police Force as examples of frivolous queries. Significantly, years after these events, Mr Blair confessed in an interview that introducing FoI was one of his biggest regrets.

Beyond measures to *restrict*—or otherwise qualify—FoI in practice, its scope was to have been extended through the inclusion of additional 'transparency' guarantees in a mooted 'Freedom' or 'Great Repeal' Bill beloved of Coalition Deputy Prime Minister Nick Clegg. Such a measure would have superseded an earlier Ministry of Justice (MoJ) Consultation Paper that mooted extending FoI to cover not only bona fide public authorities, but also private companies providing services on the state's behalf and those carrying out 'public' functions (including utility companies and independently run care homes with residents funded by social services), or private providers involved in treating NHS patients or running prisons. The MoJ has, however, extended the scope of FoI to apply to some functions of bodies that are not strictly public authorities, but nonetheless involved in delivering public policy. The Freedom of Information (Designation of Public Authorities) Order 2011 requires the Universities and Colleges Admissions Service (UCAS), a registered charity, to answer FoI requests in relation to its role as a central coordinator of university applications, although not its other areas of responsibility. The same order brought the Association of Chief Police Officers (ACPO) and the Financial Ombudsman Service (FOS) fully within the scope of the Act.

▌ Other sources of information—accessing historical records

For decades, there has been a rule (still present under the FoI Acts) absolving British governments from making public Cabinet papers and other official documents until 30 years after they were written. However, in February 2010, Mr Straw announced that this would be changed to 20 years. The reform—which fell short of a 15-year limit for secrecy proposed by an inquiry headed by *Daily Mail* editor Paul Dacre—is being gradually phased in over 10 years, starting in 2013, allowing 2 million additional documents to be transferred to the National Archives (formerly the Public Records Office) at Kew, west London, at a rate of two years' worth of records per year. There will be some exceptions, though: as under FoI, communications with reigning monarchs and their heirs are absolutely exempt from disclosure, while documents concerning British government policy and activities in Northern Ireland during 'The Troubles' will remain secret for 30 years, as before.

Although, by definition, they will relate to events that took place up to two decades earlier, records released under the new '20-year rule' are likely to provide magnets for journalists—if documents published under the old rules are anything to go by. Previous disclosures have revealed everything from detailed preparations made by Margaret Thatcher's administration in 1981 for the possibility of nuclear war with the Soviet Union, to a private admission by her predecessor, James Callaghan, that his fatal decision to delay an election that he might have won in autumn 1978 was inspired by his 'malicious' delight at confounding the Tories' expectations.

☰ Topical feature idea

Your local newspaper editor has given you three weeks to find an off-diary exclusive using the Freedom of Information (FoI) Act. With plenty of financial and other information already available on your council's website, to which other public authorities could you direct your enquiry? How would you frame your FoI request to dig out the most newsworthy lead?

✳ Current issues

- **Bringing more authorities under the scope of FoI** The Coalition has broadened the definition of 'public authorities' to include some organizations previously excluded from FoI—principally, UCAS, the Association of Chief Police Officers, and the Financial Ombudsman Service. Academies are also now covered.

- **The government's refusal to release lobbying letters from Prince of Wales to government departments** *The Guardian* and Attorney General are battling over the prospective disclosure of 27 letters from Prince Charles to ministers, said to show his attempts to influence government policy. The Court of Appeal ordered their release in March 2014, on public interest grounds, but the government has appealed to the Supreme Court.

- **The 'big data' revolution** Coalition Chancellor George Osborne used his March 2014 Budget Speech to announce a new Alan Turing Institute (named after the Second World War code-breaker) dedicated to researching and analysing 'big data', to keep Britain at the forefront of technological innovation.

▦ Key points

1. The Freedom of Information (FoI) Act 2000 and Freedom of Information (Scotland) Act 2002 allow individuals to make free, written applications for financial and other data to more than 100,000 UK 'public authorities'.

2. FoI requests must be made in writing (usually via post or email) and should be responded to within 20 working days of being received.

3. Certain categories of information held by public authorities are 'exempt', either on an 'absolute' or 'qualified' basis. The former includes information that might be prejudicial to court cases or national security, and letters written to or by the Queen or heir and second in line to the throne.

4. Rules about how FoI should be applied are laid out by the Information Commissioner. People believing that they have been refused information unlawfully may appeal to him or her or, if still dissatisfied, the Information Tribunal.

5. The Commissioner also oversees the Data Protection Act 1998, under which individuals are entitled to access personal information that organizations hold about them—for a small fee—and the Environmental Information Regulations (EIR) 2004, which entitle people to access information on the state of their natural environment.

→ Further reading

Birkinshaw, P. (2010) *Freedom of Information: The Law, the Practice, and the Ideal*, Cambridge: Cambridge University Press. **Excellent overview of the theory and practice of FoI law in Britain, and the conflicts between the need for secrecy in intelligence and crime prevention and open government.**

Brooke, H. (2006) *Your Right to Know: A Citizen's Guide to the Freedom of Information Act*, 2nd edn, London: Pluto Press. **Step-by-step guide to making effective FoI requests by the journalist who exposed the MPs' expenses scandal. Includes an introduction by Ian Hislop, editor of Private Eye, on his magazine's prolific use of the FoI Acts.**

Carey, P. (2009) *Data Protection: A Practical Guide to UK and EU Law*, 3rd edn, Oxford: Oxford University Press. **Handy jargon-busting guide, now in its third edition, offering succinct explanations of the UK's data protection laws and related EU rules—including the Directive on Privacy and Electronic Communication, which came into force in December 2003 and governs the potential for electronic privacy infringement arising from abuse of digital media.**

Wadham, J., Harris, K., and Metcalfe, E. (2013) *Blackstone's Guide to the Freedom of Information Act 2000*, 5th edn, Oxford: Oxford University Press. **Revised fifth edition of popular, user-friendly FoI guide, which contains clear pointers to making worthwhile requests, what not to bother requesting under the Acts, and full explanation of various exemptions.**

Online Resource Centre

www.oxfordtextbooks.co.uk/orc/Morrison4e/
Visit the Online Resource Centre that accompanies this book for web links and regular updates.

Glossary

A

academy Labour's successor to Conservatives' **city technology colleges (CTCs)**, these semi-independent state secondary schools (many funded by private capital) are allowed to specialize and deviate from the **National Curriculum**. Initially targeted at 'failing' comprehensives, academy status is now available to all state schools, including primaries. Up to 10 per cent of pupils may be selected on the basis of aptitude in an academy's specialism(s).

adoption Process by which registered 'children in need' are taken into the permanent care of a family other than their biological one. Adopters become their legal parents, and recent reforms have extended adoption rights to gay and unmarried heterosexual couples, as well as married people. *Cf.* **fostering**

Advisory, Conciliation, and Arbitration Service (ACAS) Quango charged with mediating between employers and employees in industrial disputes. It is often asked to intervene by one of two parties to prevent industrial action, such as strikes, being taken in first place, but can be called in later to bring opposing sides back to the negotiating table in pursuit of a peaceful settlement.

agenda Outline of the items to be considered in a meeting of a subcommittee, committee, full council, **cabinet**/executive, or other body.

alternative vote (AV) Electoral system used in Australia and proposed by the Coalition as a potential replacement for the 'first past the post' (FPTP) procedure presently used to elect British members of Parliament (MPs). Like FPTP, AV returns only one member per **constituency**, but rather than casting a single vote, electors place candidates in order of preference. If no candidate wins half or more of the votes cast on the first count, the lowest-placed contender is struck off the ballot paper and his or her second-preference votes are then distributed among the remainder. The process is repeated until someone finally achieves a simple majority. A form of AV is used in Labour leadership elections.

area of outstanding natural beauty (AONB) Geographical area designated for special legal protection from development and commercial exploitation because of its natural beauty and/or rare or unique flora and fauna.

Assembly member (AM) Elected representative in the **National Assembly for Wales**. There are 60 AMs—40 representing the **constituencies** and four for each of the five larger regions.

B

backbencher Term referring to majority of MPs in the House of Commons, who represent **constituencies**, but have no additional job title or responsibilities in government or Opposition, and therefore sit on the 'back benches' (the seats behind the front row on either side of House).

background paper Document or file produced by a local government **officer** for consideration as support for a policy proposal to be considered at a subcommittee, committee, **cabinet**/executive, or full council meeting.

balance of payments Difference in value between imports to and exports from the UK in given financial year, including *all* types of payment. This encompasses both 'visible' items (such as cars and refrigerators) and 'invisible' ones (such as legal and financial services), as well as the value of financial transfers and debt payments to foreigners. If the value of imports exceeds that of exports, Britain is in 'balance of payments deficit'; if the reverse is true, it is in 'balance of payments surplus'. *Cf.* **balance of trade**

balance of trade Difference in value between imports to and exports from the UK in given year, excluding financial transfers and debt repayments to foreigners. If Britain is importing consumer goods and services worth more than those it is exporting, it is in 'balance of trade deficit'; if the reverse is true, it is in 'balance of trade surplus'.

Bank of England Britain's central bank, based at Threadneedle Street in the City of London. It has its own governor and was given independence from the government by then Chancellor Gordon Brown within days of Tony Blair's 1997 election victory.

basic allowance Standard fee (usually modest) paid to all **councillors** out of their local authorities' revenue budgets. It can vary from area to area.

Big Society Capital New, state-sponsored, but independent financial institution set up by the Coalition to invest in projects launched by charities, community groups, and voluntary organizations aimed at addressing 'major social issues' in their areas.

billing authority Local authority that sends out **Council Tax** bills to households, collects money, and keeps a register of who has or has not paid. This is the responsibility of **district councils** or **borough councils** and unitary authorities. *Cf.* **precepting authority**

borough council Type of local authority with the same powers as a **district council**, but which has the right to call itself a 'borough' because of a historical connection to Crown.

Boundary Commission for England National **quango** responsible for periodically reviewing the sizes and boundaries of English parliamentary **constituencies** to ensure that they cover approximately the same number of voters. Separate boundary commissions also exist for Wales, Scotland, and Northern Ireland—each charged with reviewing boundaries for constituencies for the devolved assemblies, as well as for Parliament. The next boundary reviews are due by 2018.

brownfield site Area of land (usually in a built-up area) previously used for development, which may still have extant buildings on it. *Cf.* **greenfield site**

Budget Annual statement of accounts of 'UK plc', beginning with the Budget Statement made by the Chancellor of Exchequer, in which he or she sets out tax and spending plans for the coming year. This is followed by a Finance Act enshrining the changes in law.

building permission, or building regulations Additional consent required by private individuals or developers on top of **planning permission** in relation to work on extant buildings, normally relating to internal structural alterations. To attain *building permission*, developers must meet a series of *building regulations* relating to health and safety, energy efficiency, etc.

by-law Form of **delegated legislation** that may be invoked by a local authority to combat a specific problem. Many councils have invoked by-laws allowing them to ban the drinking of alcohol in streets to improve public order. *Cf.* **statutory instrument**

C

Cabinet Committee of senior government ministers, which meets at least once a week in Downing Street. *Cf.* **cabinet**

cabinet Form of executive arrangement introduced under the Local Government Act 2000, which mimics the Westminster **Cabinet** system. Most members of local cabinets are drawn from the party with the most seats on the council, with each handed a specific 'portfolio' or brief (such as housing).

Cabinet committees Subsets of **Cabinet**, usually made up of groups of three or more senior ministers whose departmental responsibilities are related. Three types exist: standing (permanent); ad hoc (temporary); and ministerial (permanent, but made up not of ministers, but of senior civil servants from related spending departments).

capital expenditure Share of local authority's annual budget spent on building and repairing infrastructure, such as roads, schools, care homes, and libraries. *Cf.* **revenue expenditure**

capping Process by which central government (particularly under the Conservative Party) has sometimes stopped local authorities from raising **Council Tax** above a certain level. It has also occasionally been used to cap spending in particular areas.

care order Umbrella term for a type of court order for which a local authority must apply in order to remove a child from his or her parents and place him or her into protective care. This can be a temporary arrangement (**fostering**) or a permanent one (**adoption**).

Care Quality Commission (CQC) Regulator established in April 2009 as the amalgamation of the Healthcare Commission and the Commission for Social Care Inspection. It handles complaints about NHS treatment, and conducts regular inspections of social care services in England and Wales, including residential homes and day care facilities.

Chairman of the Conservative Party Title held by an official (often an MP) whose responsibility is to mastermind the public image of the party as a whole and to coordinate its national fundraising operations and membership recruitment.

chief constable Most senior officer in the local police force, responsible for hiring and firing junior officers and ensuring that resources are spread effectively across the area that the force covers. He or she is held accountable by his or her local **police and crime commissioner**.

chief executive, or head of the paid service Most senior **officer** working for a local authority. The chief executive will frequently take the role of 'acting **returning officer**' for his or her area at local, general, and European elections.

child protection plan Formerly known as the 'child protection register', this is list of all recognized 'children in need' in each local authority area, which is shared between various public, private, and voluntary organizations involved in protecting them.

Children's Commissioner for England Government regulator appointed under the 'Every Child Matters' agenda to ensure that all professionals and organizations involved in protecting recognized children in need are discharging their duties effectively.

children's partnerships Collaborative, multi-agency partnerships involved in overseeing child protection in local areas, and generally organized to configure with set-ups of their local **health and well-being boards**.

children's trust All-in-one local body comprising a multidisciplinary team of professionals involved in child protection, including social workers, paediatricians, and child psychologists. Since 31 October 2010, some areas have adopted looser arrangements adapted to their localities, known as **children's partnerships**.

city council Honorary title bestowed on certain **district councils**, **borough councils**, unitary authorities, and metropolitan borough councils granted Royal Charter status.

city technology college (CTC) Type of semi-independent state secondary school, introduced by John Major's Tory government to specialize in maths, sciences, and information technology (IT), often with hands-on involvement from the private sector. *Cf.* **academy**

clinical commissioning groups (CCGs) New consortia of general practioners (GPs) and other health professionals set up to commission NHS services from trusts and other private and third sector providers, in place of Labour's primary care trusts (PCTs).

coalition government Form of Westminster government comprising ministers drawn from two or more parties, formed in the event that no single party wins a working majority at **general election**. Britain's long-standing FPTP electoral system tends to return majority governments, because it produces 'winner takes all' outcomes in each **constituency**, but the May 2010 poll resulted in a Liberal Democrat–Conservative coalition—Britain's first since wartime 'National Government' ended in 1945.

code of conduct System of rules governing the behaviour of **councillors** and **officers** that, since the Local Government Act 2000, each council has had to formally adopt. It must set out details of unacceptable conduct and any penalties incurred.

collective responsibility Principle that all members of a parliamentary party's front bench (especially the government's) should either 'sing from same hymn sheet' publicly, whatever their personal views on some party policies, or be prepared to resign. Late Labour **Leader of the House** Robin Cook resigned in 2003 in protest at the UK's impending invasion of Iraq. *Cf.* **individual ministerial responsibility**

Commission for Local Administration, or Local Government Ombudsmen Three independent officials, each covering a different region, who investigate complaints from public, businesses, and other organizations about alleged incompetence by local government officials.

Commission of the European Union, or European Commission European Union's Civil Service, spread over 33 departments known as 'Directorates-General' (DGs). Unlike the British Civil Service, it *initiates* policy as well as implements it on behalf of elected politicians. Each DG is headed by a Commissioner.

committee stage Third stage of a Bill's passage through Parliament, this gives a committee of **backbenchers** the chance to scrutinize the Bill line by line and to suggest amendments. The type of committee that examines Bills is known as a **public Bill committee** (formerly 'standing committee') and normally sits in the room outside the main Commons chamber. Emergency legislation, however, and committee stages of international treaties due to be incorporated into British law are usually heard on the floor of Commons itself—a so-called 'Committee of the Whole House'. *Cf.* **report stage**

community care Umbrella term for social care provided to the elderly and adults with mental health issues in their homes or those of friends or relatives. Help available under community care includes 'meals on wheels'.

community protection notice (CPN) Order requiring a person to do, or to stop doing, a specified act considered to be antisocial—for example to stop writing graffiti or to stop leaving excess refuse in his or her garden or driveway.

community school Term used for LEA-controlled state secondary schools under 'New Labour'. Some community schools are known as 'community colleges' because they provide adult education and evening classes on top of their primary role as day schools.

Competition and Markets Authority (CMA) New super-regulator formed in April 2014 from a merger of the Competition Commission, which vetted prospective company mergers and acquisitions, and the Office of Fair Trading (OFT), which policed the free and fair day-to-day operation of competitive markets.

comprehensive school Colloquial term referring to all types of LEA-run maintained secondary school other than **grammar (selective) schools**.

Comprehensive Spending Review (CSR) Method used by HM Treasury to encourage individual spending departments to plan strategically for the future by announcing how much money it intends to allocate to them on a three-yearly basis, rather than annually through the **Budget**. Three spending reviews—in 1998, 2007, and 2010—have been dubbed 'comprehensive' because of their more detailed nature.

compulsory purchase order (CPO) Enforceable statutory order used by a local authority to force a homeowner or business to sell up and move out of a property, so that it can be demolished to make way for new development.

concessionary fare schemes Types of discount bus fare scheme, often operated by individual councils and passenger transport authorities, to allow qualifying individuals—such as children, pensioners, or students—to travel at reduced rates. Labour launched a nationwide concessionary fare scheme in April 2008, allowing all pensioners to travel free on local buses anywhere in the UK.

conservation area District of city, town, or village that is characterized by buildings of particular historical and/or architectural vintage, and offered statutory protection from unsympathetic alteration (particularly to exterior appearance).

Conservative Campaign Headquarters (Conservative Central Office) National headquarters of the Conservative Party and the building that it occupies at Victoria Street, Westminster.

constituency Geographical area represented by an MP. There are 650 constituencies in the present Commons and all members (including ministers) must stand for re-election when a **general election** is called.

Consumer Council for Water Consumer watchdog focusing on the water industry.

consumer price index (CPI) Government's preferred measure of **inflation**, this charts movement in the value of a notional 'basket' of goods regularly bought by a typical British household. Unlike the **retail price index (RPI)**, it does not include mortgage payments and its readings therefore tend to be lower than the RPI.

contributory benefits Umbrella term for the more generous social security benefits to which British people are entitled (subject to meeting other criteria) if they have made sufficient **National Insurance (NI)** contributions during previous periods in employment. For example, **Employment and Support Allowance (ESA)** is a contributory benefit related to illness and disability. *Cf*. **non-contributory benefits**

council constitution Each local authority has been obliged to adopt its own constitution since the Local Government Act 2000, outlining its chosen form of executive decision-making arrangements and other procedural matters.

Council of Europe Alliance of 47 European member states formed in 1949, prior to the European Union. It aims to promote common legal and ethical standards in all member states, and its most celebrated achievement is the European Convention on Human Rights (ECHR).

Council of Ministers of the European Union, or Council of the European Union European Union's supreme decision-making body. Composed of senior ministers from each member state, its precise composition varies according to issue being debated. If health policy is on the **agenda**, each state will send its most senior health minister. The Council is chaired by a leading politician from the country holding the EU presidency, which rotates on six-monthly basis.

Council Tax Form of local taxation currently paid by UK residents. It is charged to households and is predominantly property-based (under a system of banding A–H, related to the capital values of homes), but with elements of a 'head tax'. It was introduced in 1993 to replace the unpopular Community Charge (or 'Poll Tax').

councillors Politicians elected at four-year intervals to represent local authority **wards**, or electoral or county divisions. Councillors determine policies to be implemented by **officers**.

county council 'Upper-tier' local authority in parts of England and Wales that retain a two-tier, rather than unitary, structure. Counties are responsible for service areas including children's and adult social services, schools, highways, and waste disposal.

county road Major arterial road—normally an A-road linking one town or city to another—the whole length of which falls within boundaries of single county. *Cf*. **trunk road**

crime prevention injunction (CPI) 'Fast-track' antisocial behaviour order (ASBO) introduced by the Coalition for lower-level antisocial behaviour. These can be imposed more quickly (within days or hours of an 'offence' being committed) and require a lower standard of proof than the ASBO.

criminal behaviour order (CBO) One of two orders introduced to replace antisocial behaviour orders (ASBOs) by the Coalition, these empower police and local authorities to impose 'bans' on antisocial conduct, if necessary forcing miscreants to attend programmes designed to improve their behaviour.

D

debt charge Money that local authorities must set aside each year in revenue budgets to repay interest on outstanding loans taken out for capital projects.

declaration of interest Admission made by a **councillor** on being elected or at the beginning of business in full council, committee, subcommittee, or **cabinet**, that he or she has an outside vested interest in the issue to be discussed or voted on. He or she will be expected to leave the meeting for the duration of said item.

dedicated schools grant (DSG) Ring-fenced grant payment made from central government to local authorities on the condition that it is spent only on school staffing and maintenance.

delegated legislation, or secondary legislation 'Lower-tier law', derived from a parent Act, which may be implemented by ministers without the need to pass further Bills. There are three main types: **statutory instruments, by-laws**, and **Orders in Council**.

devolution Constitutional concept of delegating a degree of power from central parliament to regional and/or local assemblies. In the UK, Scotland, Wales, and Northern Ireland were all granted devolution in 1998—with the Scottish gaining the most powers, including the right to vary income tax by up to 3 pence (later 10 pence) in the pound and almost complete control of its domestic policy following its 2014 **independence** referendum. Devolution is distinct from independence, which is the handover of full sovereignty.

direct taxes Umbrella term for taxes, such as income tax and corporation tax, taken directly from an individual or company, normally at a progressive rate determined by their income levels in given financial year. *Cf.* **indirect taxes**

directly elected mayor (DEM) Most senior and powerful local politician in towns and cities that have voted in a local **referendum** to adopt one of two new forms of executive arrangement retained from the Local Government Act 2000. They run their administrations with the aid of a **cabinet**. Ken Livingstone, the inaugural Mayor of London, was Britain's first DEM.

dissolution Procedure by which Parliament is formally 'dissolved' following the resignation of a government and before a **general election**.

district council Lower-tier local authority in two-tier area, responsible for services including housing, development control, environmental health, and **Council Tax** collection.

E

early intervention grant New specific local authority revenue grant introduced by the Coalition, at the behest of the Liberal Democrats, to fund initiatives designed to improve life chances of children from disadvantaged backgrounds. Although unfenced, it is meant to fund a variety of schemes, including the continuation of **Sure Start**.

elected hereditary peerage Peerages passed from one generation to next. Until 1999, every hereditary peer was entitled by birthright to sit in House of Lords, but all except 92 (90 of whom have since been elected to remain by colleagues) had this privilege removed under the House of Lords Act 1999.

election deposit Deposit of £500 by each candidate who stands in a **general election**. The payment is lost if he or she fails to poll votes from more than 5 per cent of the registered electorate in a **constituency**. It was introduced in 1929 as a deterrent to 'frivolous candidates', but has been criticized recently for being too affordable.

Electoral Commission Quango responsible for ensuring that the correct procedures are followed in parliamentary, local, and European elections, and for enforcing rules on party finance. Its responsibilities include keeping campaign spending by election candidates within agreed statutory limits, and it may refer cases to the Crown Prosecution Service (CPS) if it feels that electoral law has been broken.

electoral division Term used for **constituencies** represented by county **councillors** and some unitary authority councillors. Each has between one and three councillors, depending on the size of its population.

electoral register Official list of all electors registered to vote in local, general, and European elections in a given local authority area. It is compiled by the electoral registration **officer** employed by a **district council** or **borough council**, or unitary authority.

emergency planning officer **Officer** employed by a **county council** or unitary authority to oversee strategic planning for civil emergencies, such as floods.

emergency protection order, or interim care order Type of **care order** allowing a local authority to take a child into care immediately because of a perceived threat to his or her well-being. Initially applies for eight days, but may be renewed for a further week.

Employment and Support Allowance (ESA) Introduced by Labour to replace Incapacity Benefit for individuals judged too sick or disabled to work. From October 2013, ESA will be gradually absorbed into the Coalition's new **Universal Credit**.

English Heritage National **quango** responsible for managing heritage monuments and properties, such as Stonehenge, on the government's behalf. English Heritage also administers the **listed buildings** programme.

enlargement Term referring to the expansion of the European Union. It has been enlarged twice in the past decade, with a number of former Soviet countries joining for first time: ten new states joined in 2004, a

further two—Bulgaria and Romania— in 2007 and Croatia in 2013.

Environment Agency **Executive agency** of Department of Environment, Food, and Rural Affairs (Defra) responsible for regulating the quality and safety of water in rivers and streams, and strategic planning for flood protection.

environmental health officer **Officer** employed by a **district council**, **borough council**, or unitary authority to investigate complaints about environmental health hazards, such as vermin infestation, rotting waste, and noise pollution, and to inspect the hygiene standards of business premises serving food.

Equality and Human Rights Commission (EHRC) **Quango** formed through the amalgamation of the Commission for Racial Equality (CRE) and Equal Opportunities Commission (EOC), to ensure the equal treatment of employees in the workplace, regardless of their gender, race, or age.

euro (€) Single European currency, introduced in all EU member states bar the UK, Denmark, and Sweden on 1 January 2002. Since 2008, the 'eurozone' (the 17 countries using the euro) has been locked in a crisis over the sovereign debts of Greece and several other member states.

European Central Bank (ECB) Based in Frankfurt, the central bank of the European Union, which issues the **euro**.

European Commission *See* **Commission of the European Union**

European Council Newly recognized as one of five EU governing institutions following ratification of the Treaty of Lisbon, this is a periodic gathering of the heads of state or most senior politicians in member states, headed by a permanent president. Charged with charting the future strategic direction of the European Union, it is not to be confused with either the **Council of Ministers** or the **Council of Europe**.

European Court of Human Rights (ECtHR) Based in Strasbourg, the ultimate court of appeal for citizens of states that have signed up to the European

Convention on Human Rights (ECHR) and passed it into their own domestic law. Britain belatedly ratified the Convention by passing the Human Rights Act 1998. The Court was established by the **Council of Europe** and has no link to the European Union.

European Court of Justice (ECJ) Main EU legal body, this ensures that EU law is correctly implemented in member states. Each state contributes one judge—33 in all—although only 13 ever sit in session together. Only major cases go to a full ECJ, with others heard by the General Court. Warring parties have their cases presented to judges by one of 11 advocates-general.

European Parliament (EP) Based primarily in Brussels, but moving to Strasbourg for one week every month, the European Parliament is elected every five years. **Members of European Parliament (MEPs)** sit in political groupings, rather than along national lines—for example the British Labour Party sits with the Socialist Group.

executive agency Subset of large government spending department, staffed by civil servants, charged with delivering particular area or areas of its policy. Examples include the **Health and Safety Executive** within the Department of Health (DoH) and the **Highways Agency** within the Department for Transport (DfT).

F

faith schools Umbrella term for schools run by particular religious communities, including non-Christian groups. There are at least 7,000 faith schools in England, Wales, and Northern Ireland, many of which receive state funding.

federalism Flip side of **subsidiarity**, this is idea promoted by Eurosceptics that further extension of EU powers will lead to individual member states surrendering autonomy for their internal affairs to centralized institutions, turning the Union into a 'United States of Europe'. The 2014 Scottish **independence referendum**

sparked debate about whether Britain should be transformed into a federal democracy, with citizens governed by a hierarchy of national and regional parliaments.

Financial Conduct Authority (FCA) Part of the new, tougher, tripartite regulatory system set up by the Coalition to avert future banking collapses. Established under the Financial Services Act 2012, this polices the overall conduct of every financial company authorized to provide services to public.

Financial Policy Committee (FPC) Modelled on the existing **Monetary Policy Committee (MPC)**, in March 2012 this new committee of the **Bank of England** took over responsibility from the Financial Services Authority (FSA) for identifying risks to the stability of Britain's economy and taking pre-emptive action to combat them.

first reading Formal introduction of a proposed Bill to Commons. The reading usually consists solely of the full title of Bill being read out by a minister. *Cf.* **second reading**; **third reading**

Fiscal Compact Commonly used name for the Treaty on Stability, Coordination, and Governance in the Economic and Monetary Union—agreed by all EU countries apart from Britain and the Czech Republic in December 2011. It requires signatory states to maintain balanced budgets or budget surpluses, or face fines from the **European Central Bank (ECB)**.

forward plan List of upcoming **key decisions** due to be taken by a local authority that must be made public at least a month in advance.

fostering Practice of placing vulnerable children into care with another family, often for a short period of time, while a more permanent situation sought. *Cf.* **adoption**

foundation school Like the Conservative Party's grant-maintained (GM) school, this is a self-governing state secondary school, permitted to spend its budgets as it pleases, within certain conditions set by central government. Money is allocated to it via its local education authority (LEA), but it may hire and fire its own staff, and set its own admissions and disciplinary policies distinct from those of local LEA-run schools.

foundation trust Form of NHS hospital, ambulance service, or mental health trust permitted full autonomy over its own financial and contractual affairs, regulated by **Monitor**. Under the Coalition, all trusts are making the transition to 'foundation status'.

free schools Key plank of Conservative education policy and its 'Big Society' vision of government, and based on a model devised in Sweden, these are a new generation of publicly funded secondary schools that parents, teachers, and other members of their community are setting up and running for themselves.

FT100 Share Index (Footsie) The Financial Times Stock Exchange 100 Share Index (to use its full title) is the most famous of a number of 'indices', or lists, of major companies listed on the London Stock Exchange (LSE). It lists the 100 highest-valued companies at any time in order of share value.

further education (FE) Umbrella term for post-compulsory education and training provided by tertiary colleges and school sixth forms. It can encompass resits of A levels and other qualifications aimed at those of school age, but primarily focuses on vocational courses and diplomas.

G

general block grant Generic term for revenue grants paid by central government to local authorities that may be used for any service area, according to local needs and priorities, enjoying resurgence under Coalition. Often used as a synonym for the **revenue support grant (RSG)**.

general committee Umbrella term for the three types of temporary parliamentary committee formed to scrutinize prospective legislation: a **public Bill committee**, a **private Bill committee**, and a **grand committee**.

general election Name denoting elections for the House of Commons. From May 2015, general elections are to be held at fixed five-year intervals following reform introduced by the Coalition. The electoral system used to elect UK MPs is first past the post (FPTP).

globalization Term describing the gradual convergence of national economies into a bigger international whole. Used increasingly in relation to the ideas of free trade, free movement of labour between countries, and the expansion resulting from the Internet.

grammar (selective) school Type of maintained secondary school, phased out in much of the UK, which admits only pupils who have passed an academic test known as the '11-plus'. Those who fail are admitted to standard **comprehensive schools**.

grand committee One of three types of **general committee** in Parliament, this is convened to debate the impact of prospective legislation on specific UK regions or to scrutinize Bills in the Lords on occasions on which they are not debated on the floor of the House.

Greater London Authority (GLA) London's overarching 'council', which came into being in 2000 at the same time as the capital gained its first **directly elected mayor (DEM)**. Individual London boroughs retain their own councils to run local services at the ground level, but the GLA is responsible for taking strategic decisions for the capital as a whole.

Green Investment Bank New Edinburgh-based financial institution, set up by the Coalition from autumn 2012, backed by a £3 billion capitalization fund, to address private sector market failings by financing environmentally sustainable infrastructure projects.

Green Paper Consultation document on tentative government policy proposal that may, in time, evolve into a **White Paper**, and from there into a proposed Bill. All government Bills (other than emergency legislation) will go through at least one Green Paper stage, although if public and/or interest groups react strongly against proposal, it is unlikely to go much further.

greenbelt Term used for designated zones around towns and cities that have deliberately been kept free of development to prevent urban sprawl and to protect wildlife.

greenfield site Area of land on which there has been little or no prior development. *Cf.* **brownfield site**

gross domestic product (GDP) Total profit from all goods and services generated in Britain in a given financial year, irrespective of which state benefits from them. *Cf.* **gross national product (GNP)**

gross national product (GNP) Total profit from all goods and services generated by British-based companies in a given financial year, irrespective of where they are physically produced—for example Far Eastern call centres owned by UK companies such as BT or Virgin would still contribute to the UK's GNP. *Cf.* **gross domestic product (GDP)**

growth Increase in the **gross domestic product (GDP)** measure from one month, or quarter, or year to another, usually characterized by rises in bank lending and consumer spending, and falling unemployment.

G8 (Group of 8) Loose organization or forum devoted to promoting economic free trade and **globalization**, made up of the world's eight leading industrial nations—currently the United States, Britain, Japan, France, Germany, Italy, Canada, and Russia.

G20 (Group of 20) Loose organization or forum comprising world's 20 leading industrial powers.

H

Hansard Official record of all parliamentary business in both Houses. Protected by legal privilege and now available to read online, it is nonetheless not an entirely verbatim record of proceedings (except for words used by the serving **prime minister**).

head of the paid service *See* **chief executive**

Health and Safety Executive (HSE) **Executive agency** of the Department of Health (DoH), charged with setting and enforcing health and safety legislation in the workplace across the UK.

It recently merged with the Health and Safety Commission (HSC), which had previously drawn up health and safety rules.

health and well-being boards Local bodies formed by all 152 English local authorities to promote integrated approaches to improving health, bringing together all commissioners of health and social care in each area, along with local representatives of **Healthwatch**, and to include local **councillors**.

health service scrutiny committee Statutory body set up by a **county council** or unitary authority, comprising 15 members, including a chairperson, local **councillors**, and representatives from relevant voluntary sector organizations.

Healthwatch New national 'consumer-led' regulator of health services in England, with local branches based on the local involvement networks (LINKs) set-up inherited from Labour.

High Representative for Foreign Affairs and Security Policy Influential new permanent **European Commission** post created under the 2007 Treaty of Lisbon. The first holder of the post, to be backed from 2010 by a diplomatic corps known as the 'European External Action Service' (EEAS), was Britain's former EU Trade Commissioner Baroness Ashton of Upholland.

higher education (HE) Level of education provided by universities for those who have acquired the right qualifications at post-compulsory/tertiary level (such as A levels). Begins with undergraduate ('Bachelor') degrees (of Arts, or BAs, or of Science, BScs, etc.) and progresses to postgraduate degrees (Masters, or MAs, and doctorates, or PhDs) and beyond.

Higher Education Funding Council for England (HEFCE) **Quango** that channels public money for teaching and research into universities.

Highways Agency **Executive agency** of the Department for Transport (DfT) responsible for building and maintaining Britain's major roads.

honours list Generic term used for two annual lists of individuals chosen to be honoured with ceremonial titles by the Queen in recognition of their worldly achievements. Lists are compiled by ministers and shadow ministers, and honours are awarded in the Queen's Birthday Honours List and New Year Honours List.

House of Lords Appointments Commission Quango that vets potential candidates for **life peerages** after they have been nominated by a political party leader. It may have an enhanced role as and when the last hereditary peers are finally removed from the Lords.

housing association (HA) Not-for-profit organization formerly overseen by the Housing Corporation **quango**. Housing associations are principal providers of social housing in Britain today, often working with, or on behalf of, local authorities.

hung parliament Outcome of a **general election** that leaves no single party with an overall majority and the largest one facing the prospect of either ruling as a minority administration or forging a coalition with one or more others. The May 2010 election produced Britain's first hung parliament since 1974.

hybrid structure Type of local government structure that exists in some English and Welsh counties, in which the **two-tier structure** remains in certain areas while others have adopted the newer **unitary structure**. East Sussex is an example of a hybrid county: Lewes is covered by both a **district council** and a **county council**, while neighbouring Brighton and Hove has a **city council**, which is unitary.

I

Income Support Basic level of benefit paid to a range of people who satisfy certain needs-based criteria, but have paid insufficient prior **National Insurance (NI)** contributions to qualify for **contributory benefits**. It is available to certain people between the ages of 16 and 60 who are not in full-time work, such as carers or single parents. As with all other benefits paid to low earners and the unemployed, it is to be subsumed into the **Universal Credit (UC)** between October 2013 and 2017.

independence Constitutional arrangement whereby a constituent part of a state, such as a region or country, is granted full powers of self-government as a sovereign entity. A national **referendum** was held in Scotland on extending the country's devolved powers to full independence on 18 September 2014. Residents voted to remain in the UK.

Independent Parliamentary Standards Authority (IPSA) New regulator created in 2009 to police MPs' and peers' allowance claims and to pay their salaries. This **quango**, which began work in earnest only after the 2010 election, was introduced as a replacement for the in-house Fees Office following the long-running scandal over parliamentary expenses, which led to several resignations and successful prosecutions.

Independent Police Complaints Commission (IPCC) National **quango** responsible for investigating complaints against **chief constables** and/or their forces. Commission automatically launches investigations whenever civilians are killed by police officers.

Independent Press Standards Organization (IPSO) New independent, self-regulatory body responsible for handling complaints from public about newspapers and magazines. It replaced the Press Complaints Commission (PCC) following the Leveson Inquiry into Press Standards, sparked by the *News of the World* phone-hacking scandal.

independent remuneration panel Body comprising at least three non-**councillors**, set up in each local authority area under the Local Government Act 2000 to adjudicate independently on any application by a council to increase its member allowances.

indirect taxes Often referred to as 'hidden' or 'stealth' taxes, these are embedded in the cost of items bought by individuals or companies. Value added tax (VAT) and excise duties on tobacco and alcohol are examples of indirect taxes. Because they are charged at flat rates on relevant items, they are seen as regressive—that is, they do not take account of individuals' or companies' ability to pay. *Cf.* **direct taxes**

individual ministerial responsibility Principle that the **secretary of state** should 'fall on his or her sword' and resign if a major failing is exposed in his or her department. In practice, ministers often have to be pushed by **prime minister** (as happened in case of then Chancellor Norman Lamont after 'Black Wednesday' in 1992). *Cf.* **collective responsibility**

inflation Rises in the prices of goods and services from one month to next. This is calculated using either the **consumer price index (CPI)** or **retail price index (RPI)**, which monitor fluctuations in values of notional 'baskets' of goods containing items regularly bought by typical British households.

Information Commissioner Statutory official appointed to police implementation of the Freedom of Information (FoI) Act 2000, and to adjudicate on complaints from individuals and organizations of public authorities' lack of transparency in response to legitimate FoI requests.

interest rates Instrument of monetary policy used to promote saving and investment, and to reduce consumer spending. Since 1980s, raising interest rates has been the preferred method of controlling **inflation**. The **Bank of England**'s **Monetary Policy Committee (MPC)** meets monthly to decide whether to raise or lower interest rates.

interim care order *See* **emergency protection order**

J

Jobcentre Plus Replaced the Benefits Agency in 2002 as the main body responsible for administering benefits of all kinds, from **Jobseeker's Allowance (JSA)** and **Income Support** to sickness- and disability-related benefits.

Jobseeker's Allowance (JSA) Benefit paid to people over the age of 16 who are registered unemployed and 'actively seeking work'. There are two types of allowance:

contributions-based—related to prior **National Insurance (NI)** payments—and income-based. It is to be replaced by **Universal Credit** between October 2013 and 2017.

K

key decision Policy decision affecting two or more **wards** or **electoral divisions** in a local authority area and likely to involve 'significant expenditure' if approved. These are judged to be so significant that they must be presented for the final say to a full council and cannot be taken solely in **cabinet** unless delegated to the individual portfolio-holder.

L

leader of the council Most senior and powerful local politician in authorities that have either adopted the second new executive arrangement retained from the Local Governments Act 2000 or retained their pre-existing one. Like the **prime minister**, they are normally the leader of the party with the most seats on council.

Leader of the House Government minister responsible for organizing the weekly Commons timetable, and proposing changes to its working hours and order of business.

life peerage Honorary peerages conferred on individuals for life in one of two annual **honours lists**. As their name suggests, these titles die with the recipients and cannot be passed on to their children. *Cf.* **elected hereditary peerage**

listed building Individual building or small group of buildings (such as a Georgian crescent) offered statutory protection against alteration or demolition because of a link to specific historical personalities, events, or architectural movements. There are three levels of listing: grades I, II*, and II.

local enterprise partnership (LEP) Alliance of local council, businesses, and voluntary organizations introduced by the Coalition to boost commercial investment in local areas, this is a more local-level replacement for the recently abolished regional development agency (RDA).

local government association Regional coalition of local authorities that lobby Parliament and central government. There is also the national Local Government Association (LGA).

Local Government Boundary Commission for England (LGBCE) National **quango** tasked with periodically reviewing the boundaries between **wards** and **electoral divisions** to ensure that each is represented by the correct number of **councillors** relative to its population size.

Local Government Ombudsman *See* **Commission for Local Administration**

Local Housing Allowance (LHA) Formula used to determine how much Housing Benefit the unemployed and low earners may claim to help with rental costs. Ultimately paid by **Jobcentre Plus**, it is administered by **district councils** or **borough councils** and unitary authority housing offices. Since April 2008, Housing Benefit payments have been calculated relative to average rental prices in each postcode area (the LHA formula), rather than based on assessments of the value of specific homes rented by claimants.

local safeguarding children's board (LSCB) Committee set up by every **county council** and unitary authority under the Children Act 2004 to coordinate the efforts of all organizations involved in looking after recognized children in need.

local services support grant (LSSG) Replacing Labour's **area-based grant**, local authorities have received this non-formula, unfenced payment to spend as they see fit (within certain parameters) since 31 March 2011.

Lord Speaker Recently introduced post designed to mimic that of the Commons **Speaker**. This title is given to a peer elected by his or her colleagues in the Lords to chair debate in chamber.

Lords Spiritual Collective term for the 26 most senior Church of England bishops, led by the Archbishop of Canterbury, who remain entitled to sit in the Lords.

M

mayor Ceremonial title traditionally rotated between **councillors** on local authorities on a year-by-year basis. The recipient spends 12 months chairing full council meetings on a non-partisan basis and attending civic events.

member of the European Parliament (MEP) Elected representative who sits in the **European Parliament**, of which there are 754, elected every five years. Each state contributes a number of members that reflects its population size.

member of the Legislative Assembly (MLA) Elected representatives to the **Northern Ireland Assembly**. There are currently 108, chosen in four-yearly elections using the **single transferable vote (STV)** system of **proportional representation (PR)**.

member of Parliament (MP) Elected representative to the House of Commons. As of the May 2010 election, there were 650 MPs, each representing average of 65,000 constituents.

member of the Scottish Parliament (MSP) Elected representatives in the **Scottish Parliament**. There are 129 MSPs at any one time, elected every four years using the additional member system (AMS) form of **proportional representation (PR)**.

minister of state Umbrella term for all ministers in government departments, including junior ministers.

Ministerial Code Document outlining 10 key 'principles' of conduct for ministers, including avoiding real or apparent conflicts of interest, and stipulating that the **prime minister** should refer any alleged breach by a minister to the Independent Adviser on Ministerial Interests.

minutes Written record of the proceedings of a meeting of a subcommittee, committee, full council, **cabinet/executive**, or other body.

Monetary Policy Committee (MPC)
Committee of the **Bank of England** that meets once a month to decide whether to raise or lower **interest rates**, on the basis of the previous month's **inflation** figures.

Monitor **Quango** set up as the independent regulator of, and responsible for promoting cooperation and regulating competition between, NHS **foundation trusts**.

monitoring officer Senior local authority **officer** responsible for monitoring **councillors'** and officers' compliance with their council's **code of conduct**, and recording and reporting to members any cases of suspected maladministration.

N

1922 Committee Often referred to as 'the influential 1922 Committee', this is made up of all backbench Conservative MPs at any one time. The 'mood' of the Committee is a crucial test of the likely lifespan of its leadership and it was widely credited with delivering the knockout blow to Margaret Thatcher's premiership after she was challenged by Michael Heseltine in 1990.

National Assembly for Wales Full title of Wales's devolved assembly, based in a purpose-built chamber in Cardiff Bay.

National Curriculum Compulsory content that must be taught in maintained (state) schools in Britain in certain core subjects, such as English language and maths.

National Executive Committee of the Labour Party (NEC) Often referred to as 'Labour's ruling NEC', a senior policy committee composed of representatives of all main branches of Labour Party, including MPs, **constituency** party members, and trade unionists. Major changes to the party's constitution must be approved by this committee.

National Institute for Health and Care Excellence (NICE) **Quango** that vets medication before it is made available on the NHS, carries out its own research into potential cures and treatments, and publishes good practice guidance for social care providers. It is headed by a chief medical officer.

National Insurance (NI) System of contributory payments deducted from employees' wages and topped up by employers to finance entitlement to future benefits should they be needed. The system was originally set up in 1911 to protect workers from poverty should they become unable to work because of sickness or injury.

national minimum wage (NMW) Minimum hourly rate to be paid to all employees in the UK, introduced by Labour in 1998. There are lower NMW rates for 16–18-year-olds and 18–20-year-olds.

national non-domestic rates (NNDR) *See* **uniform business rates (UBR)**

National Offender Management Service (NOMS) **Executive agency** of the Ministry of Justice (MoJ) responsible for recruiting and employing the UK's 48,000 prison staff and overall policy regarding day-to-day running of its 135 jails. The Prisons Service is now part of NOMS and is responsible only for publicly funded jails.

national park One of 14 geographical areas of Britain designated for the highest degree of protection from development or commercial exploitation possible under UK law.

national service framework (NSF) NHS designation for nine clinical conditions considered to be national priorities in terms of prevention and treatment. These include coronary heart disease and cancer.

Natural England **Quango** responsible for conserving, protecting, and managing the natural environment in England for current and future generations.

Natural Resources Wales The Welsh equivalent of **Natural England**.

neighbourhood plan New form of local development plan to be devised by a community itself. The local authority must adopt this in place of its own proposals if it is approved in local

referendum—provided that 51 per cent or more of residents who turn out to vote approve of it.

Network Rail Not-for-dividend company set up by government in 2001 to take over the repairs and maintenance of UK overland rail network (tracks, signals, and stations) from Railtrack—the private monopoly initially given those responsibilities following privatization of British Rail in early 1990s.

NHS England New national **quango** charged with commissioning primary care and specialist health services at regional and nationwide levels.

NHS trust Umbrella term referring to hospitals, ambulance services, and mental health services provided on the NHS. The term 'trust' was coined in the early 1990s and relates to new levels of autonomy given to these bodies to run their own affairs. Each has its own board, like a company, and is designated a service 'provider'—rather than 'commissioner', like primary care trusts (PCTs).

non-contributory benefits Umbrella term for lower-level social security benefits to which British people are entitled (subject to meeting other criteria) irrespective of their previous **National Insurance (NI)** contributions. **Income Support** is an example of a purely 'needs-based', non-contributory benefit paid to people in lieu of higher-level entitlement. *Cf.* **contributory benefits**

North Atlantic Treaty Organization (NATO) Military alliance made up of 26 predominantly Western powers, NATO was formed with signing of North Atlantic Treaty in Washington DC in 1949. It was initially designed to act as a bulwark during the Cold War against the expansion of the Soviet Union and Warsaw Pact.

Northern Ireland Assembly Based at Stormont, this is the devolved chamber for Northern Ireland counties. Since March 2007, when power was restored by the British government to devolved institutions, it has been elected every four years.

O

Office for Budget Responsibility (OBR) **Quango** set up by the Coalition to produce independent economic forecasts, and to comment on the likely impact on jobs and **inflation** of the government's budgetary decisions. For its first three months, it was overseen by Sir Alan Budd, former economic adviser to Margaret Thatcher and founder member of the **Bank of England**'s **Monetary Policy Committee (MPC)**.

Office of Communications (Ofcom) **Quango** dubbed a 'super-regulator' because of its all-embracing responsibilities for overseeing telecommunications, broadcast media industries (radio, television, and the Internet), and now postal services. Ofcom may fine broadcasters, including the British Broadcasting Corporation (BBC), for breaking rules governing taste and decency, and it monitors their public service content (such as current affairs and news output).

Office for Fair Access (OFFA) Regulator charged with ensuring that **higher education (HE)** institutions that charge tuition fees above the 'standard level' produce 'access agreements' detailing practical steps for attracting students from disadvantaged backgrounds.

Office of Gas and Electricity Markets (Ofgem) Regulatory **quango** that oversees Britain's privatized energy market to ensure that there is free and fair competition between suppliers, and that bills are kept within acceptable bounds. It is headed by a Director General of Gas and Electricity Markets.

Office of the Schools Adjudicator (OSA) **Quango** charged with ruling on disputes about local authority plans to change school admissions arrangements and to resolve disputes over school reorganization by councils.

Office for Standards in Education, Children's Services, and Skills (Ofsted) Central government inspectorate, headed by a Chief Inspector of Schools, which visits most maintained schools, preschools, education providers, and

further education (FE) colleges on a rolling basis to monitor standards of teaching and administration, and awards grades from 'unsatisfactory' to 'outstanding'. Schools rated outstanding are now visited only if inspections are triggered by requests to Ofsted from parents or teachers.

Office of the Qualifications and Examinations Regulator (Ofqual) Independent national regulator established in 2008 to monitor standard of qualifications, exams, and tests in England. It is headed by a ruling committee.

Office of Water Regulation (Ofwat) *See* **Water Services Regulatory Authority**

officers Civil servants employed by local authorities to implement policies agreed by elected **councillors**.

Order in Council One of three types of **secondary legislation**, this is a legal instrument enacted by the monarch on the advice of the **Privy Council**.

outline planning permission First stage of obtaining consent to develop a site, during which permission is granted 'in principle', subject to submission of a more detailed plan. *Cf.* **planning permission**

overnight residency requirements Coalition's replacement for night-time curfews of up to 16 hours that Labour used to restrict the movements of terrorist suspects in a community. The new system will limit the duration of overnight curfews to 10 hours.

overview and scrutiny committee Overarching 'super-committee' adopted by some local authorities under the Local Government Act 2000, which scrutinizes the workings of council departments and decisions taken by the **cabinet** and senior **officers**. There will normally be several scrutiny subcommittees—or panels—focusing on specific policy areas.

P

parish meeting Lowest form of local authority, this de facto parish council convenes once a year in small villages to discuss the provision of local services and to make representations to statutory authorities on behalf of local people.

Parliamentary Commissioner for Administration, or Parliamentary and Health Service Ombudsman (PHSO) Also responsible for overseeing administration in the National Health Service (NHS), the Commissioner hears complaints from the public and organizations about alleged maladministration by Parliament, rather than corruption.

Parliamentary Commissioner for Standards Post created on the recommendation of the Nolan Inquiry, which was prompted by series of 'sleaze' scandals involving Conservative MPs in the early 1990s—including the 'cash for questions' affair, when Neil Hamilton was accused of taking payments from Harrods owner Mohamed Al Fayed to ask parliamentary questions on his behalf. The Commissioner polices the rigorous system of disclosure of outside interests introduced after these scandals.

Parliamentary Labour Party (PLP) Labour's equivalent of the Conservative Party's **1922 Committee** and a collective term for all Labour **backbenchers**.

Parliamentary and Health Service Ombudsman (PHSO) *See* **Parliamentary Commissioner for Administration**

parliamentary private secretary (PPS) Very junior government post often offered to an upcoming MP judged to have ministerial potential. The post is a 'link' between senior ministers and ordinary **backbenchers** in a party, and is often used to float potential policy ideas to 'test the water' among parliamentary colleagues.

parliamentary privilege Constitutional convention allowing MPs and peers to speak freely within their respective chambers, even criticizing named individuals without fear of being prosecuted for defamation. Even under parliamentary privilege, however, certain terms are banned in reference to fellow MPs or peers, including the word 'liar'.

parliamentary sovereignty Constitutional principle derived from the 1689 Bill of Rights that elevated Parliament to a position of supremacy over the sovereign in governing England and Wales (and, in due course, the whole UK).

parliamentary under-secretary Lowest form of government minister, a junior minister below the level of **minister of state** and **secretary of state**.

parole Procedure by which prisoners are released early from sentences for 'good behaviour'. Those convicted of more minor offences are usually granted automatic early release after serving half of the total length of their sentences, but serious offenders, including rapists and serial murderers, usually serve at least 20 years.

Passenger Focus, or Rail Passengers' Council Consumer watchdog representing the interests of overland rail commuters and passengers.

permanent secretary Most senior civil servant in government department, he or she offers day-to-day advice to the **secretary of state** and other ministers, and therefore occupies a **politically restricted post**.

Personal Independence Payment (PIP) New, non-means-tested benefit introduced to replace Disability Living Allowance (DLA) for disabled people needing care and/or help with mobility. Recipients are subject to new eligibility tests similar to **work capability assessments (WCAs)**.

planning obligations, or planning contribution, or planning gain Offer by a developer of added value for a local authority in exchange for being granted **planning permission** for a major project—for example a developer may offer to finance a new playground for children in a deprived **ward** as a form of 'sweetener' to help its bid to build a new supermarket.

planning inquiry Public inquiry held into contentious development proposal to which there is strong opposition. It will be chaired by an independent inspector appointed by the **Secretary of State** for Communities and Local Government, and those immediately affected by a proposal will be allowed to speak at it.

planning permission Consent given to an individual, company, or other organization to build new premises, or to extend or adapt existing ones. *Cf.* **outline planning permission**

police and crime commissioners (PCCs) Elected officials who replaced police authorities on 15 November 2012. As with their precursors, they are responsible for overseeing and holding to account their local police forces, with powers to hire and fire chief constables.

police community support officers (PCSOs) Semi-trained officers employed as auxiliary police, with powers to arrest and issue some minor punishments, such as fixed-penalty fines for antisocial behaviour.

policy and resources committee Traditionally, the most powerful local authority committee, because it is in charge of a council's overall budget, this committee must be consulted on major decisions (such as to build new road) because it will have to approve funding.

political sovereignty Constitutional concept of an institution or individual holding political supremacy (or 'sovereignty') over a nation's citizens. In Britain, political sovereignty originally rested with the reigning monarch ('sovereign'), but passed to Parliament after the 1689 Bill of Rights.

politically restricted post Contractual position held by senior public officials (civil servants and local government **officers**) barred from canvassing openly for a political party at elections, or from standing for office, because of their close day-to-day working relationships with politicians.

postal vote Means of casting votes in elections by post, rather than in person. The British government is committed to extending rights to vote by post across the UK, following several recent pilots, but this has provoked criticism from some quarters because of the perceived risk of fraud in multi-occupancy households.

postcode lottery Term denoting the unequal availability around the country of public services theoretically on offer throughout Britain—and most commonly used to refer to NHS treatments.

precepting authority All local authorities that receive some revenue funding through **Council Tax**. The term 'precept' refers to the 'invoice' that such authorities present to the **billing authority**, outlining the sum that they wish to raise through Council Tax in the coming financial year.

prescribed function Role and responsibility formally delegated by a council to its committees, subcommittees, **cabinet**/executive, and individual cabinet members. These will normally be spelt out in the council's constitution.

President of the European Council Recently created permanent post at the helm of the **European Council**, a powerful body comprising most senior politicians from each EU member state. Introduced under the 2007 Treaty of Lisbon, its inaugural holder, former Belgian Prime Minister Herman van Rompuy, was re-elected for further two-and-a-half-year term in March 2012.

prime minister (PM) Commonly used title of the senior minister who chairs the **Cabinet**, officially the 'First Lord of the Treasury'. The 'PM', or 'premier', is constitutionally seen as 'first among equals', in that he or she is an elected **constituency** MP like any other, but with more power than all others.

private Bill Type of primary legislation introduced by government minister(s) for the purpose of conferring specific powers or duties on a particular organization or regional entity. The Act permitting Formula One racing in Birmingham stemmed from a private Bill.

private Bill committee Temporary Commons committee convened to scrutinize a prospective **private Bill** and one of the three types of **general committee**.

private finance initiative (PFI) Main way in which major capital projects are now funded, this is an arrangement between a public authority (such as a council or government department) and a private company, under which the latter foots most of the initial bill and the former pays it back (with interest) over a period of years. *Cf.* **public–private partnership (PPP)**

private member's Bill (PMB) Bill proposed by an individual **backbencher**, normally on an issue near to his or her heart, and/or one that concerns his or her constituents. While they may cast media's spotlight onto an issue, most PMBs are never allotted sufficient parliamentary time to pass into law—but there have been exceptions, including the 1967 Abortion Bill, introduced by future Liberal leader David Steel.

Privy Council Ancient committee of state, originally formed as a group of close confidantes for the reigning monarch to counteract the power of Great Council, or *Magnum Concilium*, composed of the peers of the realm. Today, all serving and past **Cabinet** ministers and leaders of the Opposition are appointed members for life and advise the monarch on matters such as use of the Privy Purse (the monarch's personal pot of money, derived from the Duchy of Lancaster estate) and the issuing of **Orders in Council**.

proportional representation (PR) Umbrella term for electoral systems alternative to the 'first past the post' (FPTP) process used in British **general elections**. Most Western countries use PR, including Ireland, which uses the **single transferable vote (STV)**. Liberal Democrats have been campaigning for STV to be adopted in Britain, arguing that it is fairer than that UK system, because the number of seats won by the party tends to bear stronger relationship to votes cast for them than does FPTP.

prorogation Term denoting the procedure by which Parliament is temporarily suspended (or 'prorogued') at the end of a parliamentary session.

Prudential Regulatory Authority (PRA) Created as subsidiary of the **Bank of England** in 2013 to prevent banks, building societies, or other financial companies taking imprudent risks with their investors' money, the PRA is part of the new tripartite regulatory regime for the finance sector.

public Bill Primary legislation introduced by government minister(s) to change the law of the land. Public Bills usually begin with a **Green Paper**, then a **White Paper**, before going through a series of readings, the **committee stage**, the House of Lords stage, and finally **royal assent**.

public Bill committee Temporary parliamentary committee convened to scrutinize and debate a Bill or another prospective Act of Parliament. Formerly known as a 'standing committee' because, being only temporary, its members were notionally not in post for long enough to warrant permanent seats at committee table, this is one of three types of **general committee**.

Public Health England New national **quango** charged with promoting public health initiatives across England, backed by a £4 billion fighting fund to finance locally run projects.

public health grant (PHG) New ring-fenced revenue grant introduced by the Coalition from April 2013 to help councils to take over the funding of initiatives aimed at improving the well-being of their communities—for example by encouraging people to quit smoking.

public limited company (plc) Type of larger registered company in the UK that issues shares that the general public can buy by 'floating' itself on the London Stock Exchange (LSE). It has legal obligation to maximize profits for its shareholders and to pay them dividends. Most household-name companies in Britain are plcs (for example BP).

public–private partnership (PPP) Financial arrangement used to fund major capital projects, such as roads and prisons, whereby a government department or other public authority will share the cost of initial outlay with a private company or companies. The bulk of the up-front investment is usually made by the private sector and the public sector will pay it off (with interest) over a period of years. The PPP is 'New Labour's' successor to the Conservatives' **private finance initiative (PFI)**.

public sector net cash requirement (PSNCR) Formerly the 'public sector borrowing requirement' (PSBR), this is the sum of money that the British government will need to borrow by means of commercial loans or from the public in a given financial year to meet its public spending commitments—that is, it is the difference between the total taxation that the Exchequer expects to raise in year and actual outgoings.

Public Works Loan Board (PWLB) Body that can lend money to local authorities for major capital projects at a lower rate than those offered by the banking sector. The PWLB is part of the UK Debt Management Office, an HM Treasury **executive agency**.

pupil premium Additional funding allocated annually by the Coalition to schools with high numbers of pupils from disadvantaged backgrounds and/or on free school meals. The aim is to use one-to-one tuition and other strategies to intercept potential education inequalities.

Q

qualified majority voting (QMV) System of voting in the **Council of Ministers of the European Union** that enables certain issues to be decided by majority vote in favour or against, rather than unanimously. Under QMV, each member state is allocated a certain number of votes in proportion to its population, meaning that some have substantially more say in matters than others and that decisions are taken on a 'qualified' majority basis. The UK, for example, has 29 votes, while Malta has just three.

quango, or quasi-autonomous non-government organization Non-departmental body set up by a government department and partly funded by taxpayers, to regulate, monitor, or otherwise oversee a particular area of policy delivery. UK quangos have their own executive boards, like companies, and include Arts Council England and the **Equality and Human Rights Commission (EHRC)**.

quantitative easing (QE) Practice by which central banks—in Britain, the **Bank of England**—purchase bonds or equities from retail banks to increase the prices of those assets and to reduce the **interest rates** payable on them. The aim is to 'free up' finance for businesses and individuals in the wider economy by encouraging banks to lend more and at lower rates.

Queen's Speech Annual address given by the Queen at the State Opening of Parliament in October or November. The speech is actually a list of legislation to be proposed by the government during the coming parliamentary session (year), and is written not by monarch herself, but by the sitting **prime minister** and **Cabinet**.

Question Time Sessions of parliamentary business during which **backbenchers** and/or peers on all sides have the opportunity to question individual departmental ministers on the conduct of their ministerial business. Major spending departments each have a question time session at least once a fortnight, while the most famous is 'Prime Minister's Questions' (PMQs), held every Wednesday lunchtime.

R

rateable value Sum of money that a business premises would be able to earn on the rental market. Both **uniform business rates (UDR)** and rates—the property-based domestic tax that preceded the Community Charge—are (or were) based on rateable values.

recession Economic term used to describe rapid economic slowdown or negative **growth**. Technically, it refers to a period of two successive quarters during which the economy has 'shrunk'—that is, consumers have stopped spending, sales of goods and services have dwindled, and manufacturers have reduced production.

refer back Term used for when a local authority **cabinet**/executive and/or full council meeting asks a committee or subcommittee to rethink its recommendations. It is also used in the context of recommendations

made by **general committees** of the House of Commons.

referendum Public vote on a single issue. In Britain, referendums are rare, but a national referendum was held in 1975 on the question of whether the country should remain in European Community, and the people of Scotland, Wales, and Northern Ireland were consulted in referendums about whether they wanted devolved government. The most recent referendum was held in Scotland on 18 September 2014 to determine whether the country should be granted **independence** from the UK.

register of members' financial interests (formerly register of members' interests) Register of the outside 'interests' (directorships, share holdings, etc.) of MPs and peers introduced to improve transparency in 1974. Local authorities have been required to keep similar registers for their **councillors** since the passage of the Local Government Act 2000.

relative needs formula (RNF) Calculation used by central government to decide how much to allocate each local authority in formula grants for a given financial year. It is based on an assessment of the precise demographic factors in each area, including not only the size of local population, but also its *nature* (for example the number of pensioners).

relative resource amount (RRA) Calculation used by central government to estimate how much money each local authority is able to raise itself for revenue spending in given financial year. The RRA is subtracted from the **relative needs formula (RNF)** to calculate the level of formula grants.

report stage Stage immediately after the **committee stage**, when a **public Bill committee's** chairperson 'reports back' to Commons with its recommendations.

resolved items Matters concluded at the end of a committee, full council, or **cabinet**/executive meeting. A vote will normally be taken to make the final decision.

retail price index (RPI) Measure of **inflation** (changes in prices of goods and services) preferred by most economists to the **consumer price index (CPI)**, this charts movement in the value of a notional 'basket' of goods regularly bought by typical British households. Because it includes mortgage payments, it is usually higher than the CPI.

returning officer Official responsible for overseeing local and **general election** procedures on the day of a poll, ordering recounts where necessary and announcing the result. Officially, this post is held by the chairperson or **mayor** of a neighbouring or coterminous local authority, but a senior council **officer** will usually perform the duties in practice—often the **chief executive** or electoral registration officer.

revenue expenditure Share of local authority's annual budget spent on the day-to-day running costs of schools, libraries, offices, and other local services. *Cf.* **capital expenditure**

revenue support grant (RSG) One of three types of formula grant allocated to local authorities by central government for their revenue spending, this was traditionally biggest single chunk of money that they received. It is calculated on the basis of a formula relating to the demographic make-up of a local area and may be used by councils in any area of revenue spending. Also known as the **general block grant**, the proportion of funding channelled through the RSG is increasing under the Coalition.

ring-fenced grant One of two types of **specific grant** for local authority revenue spending that must be used for the purpose stipulated by central government. All but two ring-fenced grants—the **Dedicated Schools Grant (DSG)** and the new **public health grant**—have been scrapped by the Coalition. *Cf.* **unfenced grants**

royal assent 'Rubber stamp' given to a Bill by the reigning sovereign to make it an Act. In practice, royal assent is a formality today and no monarch has refused to give it since Queen Anne attempted to do so in 1707.

royal prerogative Constitutional term used to refer to the (now largely notional) idea that power in the UK derives from the authority of the reigning sovereign. In practice, today most prerogative powers (such as the ability to declare war and to appoint ministers) rests with the elected **prime minister** of the day.

rule of law Constitutional principle, derived from 1215's Magna Carta, stipulating that no one is 'above the law of the land', including (in theory) the sovereign.

S

safeguarding adults board (SAB) Adult equivalent of **local safeguarding children's board (LSCB)** introduced under the Care Act 2014, English social services authorities must establish these to safeguard vulnerable adults at risk of, or experiencing, neglect or abuse.

Schengen Agreement Collective term for two EU treaties—signed in 1985 and 1990, respectively—which formally abolished systematic border controls between member states.

Scottish Government, or Scottish Executive Title used by the devolved administration in Scotland.

Scottish Parliament Scotland's devolved assembly, based in a purpose-built parliamentary building at Holyrood, at the foot of the Royal Mile in Edinburgh.

second reading First stage at which the main principles of a Bill are formally read out to the House and debated. It normally takes place within a few weeks of the **first reading** and may lead to an early vote on some aspects of Bill. *Cf.* **third reading**

secondary legislation *See* **delegated legislation**

secretary of state Umbrella term for the most senior government minister in a spending department—for example the Secretary of State for Health.

select committee Permanent parliamentary committee charged with scrutinizing the day-to-day workings of a government department and other public authorities related to the responsibilities of that department—for example the Culture, Media, and Sport Select Committee examines the work of the Department for Culture, Media, and Sport (DCMS), as well as that of the BBC.

separation of powers Principle stipulating that the three main seats of constitutional authority in a state—executive, legislature, and judiciary—should be kept separate to avoid concentrating power in too few hands. In practice, in the UK there are overlaps, with the **prime minister** and **Cabinet** (executive) also sitting in Parliament (legislature).

single transferable vote (STV) Form of **proportional representation (PR)** used in **general elections** in the Republic of Ireland and long favoured by Lib Dems for Westminster polls. Candidates are ranked in order of preference and all those who achieve a 'quota' of votes up to a predetermined number are elected to multimember **constituencies**. If not enough candidates achieve the quota, the lowest ranked candidate is struck off the ballot papers and second choices are redistributed among remaining contenders until enough reach the required level.

site of special scientific interest (SSSI) Area judged to have special or unique natural features. There are two types: *biological SSSIs* (those with rare or unusual flora and/or fauna), and *geological SSSIs* (those of particular physiographic interest).

sovereign grant New all-in-one method of financing the Royal Household from taxpayers' money, covering both day-to-day living costs previously funded through the Civil List, and the upkeep of occupied palaces and royal transport traditionally paid as grants-in-aid.

Speaker **Member of Parliament** elected by his or her peers, traditionally on a motion moved by the Father of the House (the member with the longest unbroken service to the chamber) following **general election**, to serve as chairperson of debates and to maintain discipline in the Commons.

special responsibility allowance Top-up fee added to the **basic allowance** for **councillors** in recognition of additional responsibilities, such as sitting on, or chairing, a local authority committee. The allowance can vary according to the level of responsibility.

special school State school dedicated to teaching children with learning difficulties and/or mental or physical disabilities.

specialist school Generic term for all state schools permitted to specialize in one or more subjects over and above teaching the **National Curriculum**. **Academies** are, by nature, specialist schools—but, in practice, most **community schools** also have subject specialisms, enabling them to draw down extra funds to improve facilities.

specific grant One of two different categories of non-formula grant given to local authorities each year to help with revenue spending. Specific grants can either be **ring-fenced grants** or **unfenced grants**. *Cf.* **area-based grants**

spin doctor Layperson's term for the type of special adviser usually employed by a senior figure in a political party to put positive 'spin' on its policies to public and media. Alastair Campbell, former Downing Street director of communications, became one of Britain's most infamous spin doctors during Tony Blair's 10 years in power.

Standard Attainment Tests (Sats) Academic tests taken by state school pupils at three Key Stages in their **National Curriculum** learning. Key Stages 1, 2, and 3 take place at the ages of 7, 11, and 14, respectively.

standards committee Committee set up by each local authority under the Local Government Act 2000 to monitor **councillors'** and **officers'** compliance with the council's **register of members' interests** and **code of conduct**. Committees must have at least one lay member.

standing order System of rules adopted by individual local authorities to govern the day-to-day conduct of business in full council, and its committees, subcommittees, and/or **cabinet**.

statutory instrument Most common form of **secondary legislation**, this refers to the rules and guidelines issued by departmental ministers to implement the changes introduced in a new Bill on the ground.

subsidiarity Loose constitutional principle underpinning the European Union, which holds that member states retain primary sovereignty over their internal affairs, with the Union acting as a 'subsidiary' institution and the last port of call if individual self-determination falters.

supplementary estimate Additional sum for which a local authority department might ask when it has underestimated the level of revenue funding that it will need in the next financial year to fund its projected spending.

Supreme Court of the United Kingdom Britain's final court of appeal for civil cases, and the highest for criminal matters in England, Wales, and Northern Ireland, this was established in October 2009 in an effort to emulate the constitutional **separation of powers** in the United States. It replaced the Appellate Committee of the House of Lords—previously the UK's ultimate court—which had been the seat of the 'Law Lords' for centuries. There are 12 Justices of the Supreme Court, all currently former Law Lords.

Sure Start Government programme launched in 1999 to improve access for low-income families to early-years teaching and other support services.

T

10-minute rule One of three ways in which **private member's Bills (PMBs)** may be introduced into Parliament and the one that most often grabs headlines. The MP must have his or her idea for a Bill proposed and seconded by colleagues, and obtain another eight members' signatures, and will then be given 10 minutes in which to introduce the proposals to the Commons. An MP who opposes the Bill will then have the same amount of time in which to make a speech outlining his or her objections.

tactical voting Type of strategic voting by electors voting in 'first past the post' (FPTP) elections, which sees them vote for a candidate other than their 'sincere preference' in the knowledge that their preferred option would be a 'wasted vote'. Tactical voters instead opt for their 'least worst option'—choosing a 'bearable' third party to stop the candidate whom they most oppose from winning.

tax-increment financing (TIF) Form of capital finance for councils allowing them to borrow money for infrastructural or other capital investment against likely future income generated through business rates from companies likely to be attracted by that investment.

terrorism prevention and investigation measure (TPim) Coalition's replacement for the control orders used by Labour to restrict the movements of those suspected (but not yet convicted) of terrorism plots. Unlike control orders, they will lapse after two years.

third reading Final stage of a Bill's passage through Commons. It is at third reading that MPs are confronted with the final version of Bill's wording, so it is an occasion for any major disagreements to be fought out in a formal vote. *Cf.* **first reading**; **second reading**

trading standards officer **Officer** employed by a **county council** or unitary authority to ensure that local businesses adhere to regulations regarding issues such as product labelling, and weights and measures.

Traffic Commissioner One of seven regional commissioners employed to license public transport routes and operators, and long-distance haulage companies.

Transport for London (TfL) **Quango** responsible for the strategic planning and day-to-day running of London's transport network, including London Underground, Docklands Light Railway, city bus services, and river ferries.

trunk road Major arterial road—A-road or motorway—linking towns and cities, and sometimes crossing the boundaries between counties. *Cf.* **county road**

trust school New form of **foundation school** introduced under the Education and Inspections Act 2006, these are primary and secondary schools supported by charitable trusts, which employ staff, manage assets, and set admissions policies.

trust special administrator Senior Department of Health (DoH) officials appointed to intervene on the Health Secretary's behalf to close or downgrade hospital accident and emergency (A&E) departments, maternity units and other hospital services if they are having a detrimental effect on neighbouring trusts' finances.

two-tier structure Type of local government structure established under the 1974 reorganization of local authorities, in which there are two levels of council operating in the same area: **district councils** and/or **borough councils** responsible for services, such as waste collection, housing, and environmental health; and an overarching **county council** providing countywide services, such as education and highways (roads).

U

unfenced grant One of two types of **specific grant** for local authority revenue spending, it may be spent in whatever way the council sees fit, subject to certain conditions. The Coalition prefers unfenced to **ring-fenced grants** and has unfenced its new **early intervention grant**. *Cf.* **ring-fenced grant**

uniform business rates (UBR) Local taxation paid by companies, the bills of which are calculated according to that **rateable values** of business premises and a national multiplier set each year by government (such as 50 pence in the pound). Money is collected locally, and has traditionally then been funnelled through HM Treasury and redistributed around the country according to need. A growing proportion is now kept by local authorities to be spent in the areas in which it was collected.

UNISON Main local government trade union, it counts among its members many departmental officers, social workers, and health professionals.

unitary structure Type of local government structure that has replaced the **two-tier structure** in many areas, in which a single—unitary—local authority is responsible for all local services, from waste collection to education and social care.

United Nations (UN) Global peace-making body formed in 1945, as successor to the defunct League of Nations established after the First World War. Headquartered in New York, its main constitutional bodies include the UN General Assembly and UN Security Council (which debates international conflict).

Universal Credit (UC) New 'all-in-one' welfare payment for the low-paid and unemployed, due to supplant all other benefits between October 2013 and 2017 as part of the Coalition's efforts to reduce the social security bill and complexity in the system.

university technical colleges (UTCs) New vocational colleges introduced by the Coalition to train 14–19-year-olds in the skills needed to 'rebalance' the British economy towards technology.

V

virement Process allowing councils limited discretion to transfer money from one spending area to another during a given financial year, if the former is in surplus and latter, in deficit. Councils' ability to use virement has been severely curtailed as a result of the rollout of **ring-fenced grants**.

voluntary school Type of school in the state sector, the land and buildings of which are owned by a charity or local church. Voluntary-aided schools receive some local authority funding, but retain significant autonomy (for example employing their own staff and setting their own admissions policies), while voluntary-controlled schools are run directly by local education authorities (LEAs).

W

ward **Constituency** represented by **district council** or **borough council**, and some unitary authority **council- lors**. Each has between one and three councillors, depending on population size.

Water Services Regulatory Authority, or Office of Water Regulation (Ofwat) One of three statutory regulators of the privatized water industry, Ofwat monitors the transparency of individual water companies' accounts and share policies.

Welsh Assembly Government (formerly Welsh Executive) Title adopted by the elected devolved administration in Wales.

whip MPs and peers with the job of 'whipping into line' their parliamen- tary colleagues, making sure that the latter attend important debates and votes, and 'toe the party line'.

White Paper Crystallized version of a **Green Paper**, containing more concrete proposals. If a proposed government Bill has got this far, it will normally proceed further to become a formal draft Bill and may well subsequently become an Act.

work capability assessment (WCA) Periodic medical test, introduced by Labour and continued under the Coalition, to determine whether individuals claiming **Employment and Support Allowance (ESA)** are fit for work.

Bibliography

A

Adonis, A. (2012) *Education, Education, Education: Reforming England's Schools*, Kindle edn, London: Biteback Publishing.

Atkinson,H. (2012) *Local Democracy, Civic Engagement and Community: From New Labour to the Big Society*, Manchester: Manchester University Press.

Ayre, P. and Preston-Shoot, M. (2010) *Children's Services at a Crossroads: A Critical Evaluation of Contemporary Policy for Practice*, Lyme Regis: Russell House Publishing.

B

Bale, T. (2011) *The Conservative Party: From Thatcher to Cameron*, Cambridge: Polity Press.

Bartholomew, J. (2014) *The Welfare State We're In*, London: Biteback Publishing.

Bayliss, J., Smith, S., and Owens, P. (2010) *The Globalization of World Politics: An Introduction to International Relations*, 5th edn, Oxford: Oxford University Press.

Betty, S. (2011) *The PFI; 'Teething Problems or Fundamentally Flawed?' A Critical Analysis of the UK's Private Finance Initiative*, Bury St Edmunds: Lambert Academic Publishing.

Birbalsingh, K., Gove, M., Hill, S., Hunter, M., Johnson, D., Martin, J., Lewis, O., Womersley, D., Woodhead, C., and Young, T. (2013) *The Gove Revolution: Transforming England's Schools*, London: Standpoint.

Birkinshaw, P. (2010) *Freedom of Information: The Law, the Practice, and the Ideal*, Cambridge: Cambridge University Press.

Black, G. (2011) *Transforming Museums in the Twenty-First Century*, London: Routledge.

Blackman, T., Brody, S., and Convery, J. (eds) (2001) *Social Care and Social Exclusion: A Comparative Study of Older People's Care in Europe*, Basingstoke: Palgrave Macmillan.

Blais, A. (ed.) (2008) *To Keep or to Change First Past the Post? The Politics of Electoral Reform*, New York: Oxford University Press.

Bogdanor, V. (2009) *The New British Constitution*, Oxford: Hart Publishing.

Bomberg, E. and Stubb, A. (eds) (2012) *The European Union: How Does it Work?* Oxford: Oxford University Press.

Bowles, N., Hamilton, J., and Levy, D. A. L. (2013) *Transparency in Politics and the Media: Accountability and Open Government*, London: I .B. Tauris.

Brooke, H. (2006) *Your Right to Know: A Citizen's Guide to the Freedom of Information Act*, 2nd edn, London: Pluto Press.

Brown, C. and Ainley, K. (2005) *Understanding International Relations*, 4th edn, Basingstoke: Palgrave Macmillan.

Budge, I., Crewe, I., McKay, D., and Newton, K. (2007) *The New British Politics*, 4th edn, London: Longman.

Burnham, J. and Pyper, R. (2008) *Britain's Modernised Civil Service*, Basingstoke: Palgrave Macmillan.

C

Cahill, D. (2010) *Transport, Environment, and Society*, Buckingham: Open University Press.

Campbell, A. (2012) *The Burden of Power: Countdown to Iraq*, London: Hutchinson.

Carey, P. (2009) *Data Protection: A Practical Guide to UK and EU Law*, 3rd edn, Oxford: Oxford University Press.

Colling, T. and Terry, M. (2010) *Industrial Relations: Theory and Practice (Industrial Revolutions)*, Oxford: Wiley Blackwell.

Cooper, K. and Macfarland, C. (2012) *Clubbing Together: The Hidden Wealth of Communities*, London: ResPublica.

Crewe, I. (ed.) (1998) *Why Labour Won the General Election of 1997*, London: Frank Cass.

Cribb, J., Jesson, D., Sibieta, L., Skipp, A., and Vignoles, A. (2013) *Poor Grammar: Entry into Grammar Schools for*

Disadvantaged Pupils in England.
Available online at: **www.suttontrust.
com/researcharchive/poor-grammar-
entry-grammar-schools-disadvantaged-
pupils-england/**

Crossman, R. (1979) *The Crossman
Diaries: Selections from the Diaries of a
Cabinet Minister, 1964–1970*, London:
Book Club Associates.

D

Denver, D., Carman, C., and Johns, R.
(2012) *Elections and Voters in Britain*,
3rd edn, Basingstoke: Palgrave
Macmillan.

Dillon, D. and Fanning, B. (2012) *Lessons
for the Big Society: Planning,
Regeneration, and the Politics of
Community Participation*, Kindle edn,
Farnham: Ashgate.

Docherty, I. and Shaw, J. (2008) *Traffic
Jam: Ten Years of Sustainable Transport
in the UK*, Bristol: Policy Press.

Driver, S. (2011) *Understanding British
Party Politics*, Cambridge: Polity Press.

F

Farrell, D. (2011) *Electoral Systems:
A Comparative Introduction*, 2nd edn,
Basingstoke: Palgrave Macmillan.

Fischel, W. A. (2005) *The Homevoter
Hypothesis: How Home Values Influence
Local Government Taxation, School
Finance, and Land-Use Policies*,
Cambridge, MA: Harvard University
Press.

G

Gallent, N. and Robinson, S. (2013),
*Neighbourhood Planning: Communities,
Networks, and Governance*, Bristol:
Policy Press.

Geddes, A. (2013) *Britain and the
European Union*, Basingstoke: Palgrave
Macmillan.

Golding, P. and Middleton. S. (1982)
Images of Welfare, Oxford: Mark
Robertson.

Gray, A. M. and Birrell, D. (2013)
*Transforming Adult Social Care:
Contemporary Policy and Practice*,
Bristol: Policy Press.

Grimsey, D. and Lewis, M. (2007) *Public
Private Partnerships: The Worldwide
Revolution in Infrastructure Provision
and Project Finance*, Cheltenham:
Edward Elgar.

Gumbrell-McCormick, R. and Hyman, R.
(2013) *Trade Unions in Western Europe:*

Hard Times, Hard Choices, Oxford:
Oxford University Press.

H

Hall, P. and Tewdwr-Jones, M. (2010) *Urban
and Regional Planning*, 5th edn, Kindle
edn, London: Routledge.

Ham, C. (2009) *Health Policy in Britain:
The Politics and Organisation of
The National Health Service*,
6th edn, Basingstoke: Palgrave
Macmillan.

Hanley, L. (2013) *Estates: An Intimate
History*, London: Granta Books.

Hansen, R. S. (2001) *Citizenship and
Immigration in Post-war Britain: The
Institutional Origins of a Multicultural
Nation*, Oxford: Oxford University
Press.

Hennessey, P. (2001) *The Prime Minister:
The Job and its Holders since 1945*,
London: Penguin.

Hodge, M., Leach, S., and Stoker, G. (1997)
*Local Government Policy: More than the
Flower Show—Elected Mayors and
Democracy*, London: Fabian Society.

Hollis, G., Davies, H., Plokker, K., and
Sutherland, M. (1994) *Local Government
Finance: An International Comparative
Study*, London: LGC Communications.

I

Ishkanian, A. and Szreter, S. (2012) *The
Big Society Debate: A New Agenda for
Social Welfare?*, Cheltenham: Edward
Elgar.

J

Jackson, R. and Sorensen, G. (2012) *An
Introduction to International Relations:
Theories and Approaches*, Oxford:
Oxford University Press.

Johnston, R. and Pattie, C. (2006) *Putting
Voters in Their Place: Geography and
Elections in Great Britain*, Oxford:
Oxford University Press.

Jones, A. (2015) *Britain and the European
Union*, 2nd edn, Edinburgh: Edinburgh
University Press.

Jones, B. (2010) *Dictionary of British
Politics*, 2nd edn, Manchester:
Manchester University Press.

Jones, B. and Norton, P. (2013) *Politics UK*,
8th edn, London: Longman.

Jones, C. and Murie, A. (2006) *The Right to
Buy: Analysis and Evaluation of a
Housing Policy*, London: Wiley-Blackwell.

Jones, N. (2002) *The Control Freaks: How New Labour Gets Its Own Way*, London: Politico's Publishing.

Jowell, J. and Oliver, D. (2011) *The Changing Constitution*, 7th edn, Oxford: Oxford University Press.

K

Klein, R. (2013) *The New Politics of the NHS: From Creation to Reinvention*, 7th edn, Abingdon: Radcliffe Publishing.

L

Lane, K. (2006) *National Bus Company: The Road to Privatisation*, Shepperton: Ian Allen.

Leach, S. (2010) *Managing in a Political World: The Life Cycle of Local Authority Chief Executives*, Basingstoke: Palgrave Macmillan.

Leyland, P. (2013) *Constitution of the United Kingdom: A Contextual Analysis*, 2nd edn, Oxford: Hart Publishing

Leys, C. and Player, S. (2011) *The Plot Against the NHS*, Perth: Merlin Press.

Loughlin, M. (2013) *The British Constitution: A Very Short Introduction*, Oxford: Oxford University Press.

Lund, B. (2011) *Understanding Housing Policy*, 2nd edn, Bristol: Policy Press.

M

Malpass, P. (2005) *Housing and the Welfare State: The Development of Housing Policy in Britain*, Basingstoke: Palgrave Macmillan.

Meisler, S. (2011) *United Nations: A History*, New York: Grove Press/Atlantic Monthly Press.

McCormick, J. (2014) *Understanding the European Union: A Concise Introduction*, 6th edn, Basingstoke: Palgrave Macmillan.

Michie, R. C. (2001) *The London Stock Exchange: A History*, Oxford: Oxford University Press.

Midwinter, A. F. and Monaghan, C. (1993) *From Rates to the Poll Tax: Local Government Finance in the Thatcher Era*, Edinburgh: Edinburgh University Press.

Monbiot, G. (2001) *Captive State: The Corporate Takeover of Britain*, London: Pan Books.

Morgan, S. (2009) *Waste, Recycling, and Reuse*, London: Evans Brothers.

Mullin, C. (2010) *View from the Foothills*, London: Profiles Books.

N

Newman, I. (2014) *Reclaiming Local Democracy: A Progressive Future for Local Government*, Bristol: Policy Press.

Norman, J. (2010) *The Big Society: The Anatomy of the New Politics*, Buckingham: University of Buckingham Press.

Norton, P. (2013) *Parliament in British Politics*, 2nd edn, Basingstoke: Palgrave Macmillan.

O

Olechnowicz, A. (2007) *The Monarchy and the British Nation, 1780 to the Present*, Cambridge: Cambridge University Press.

P

Phillips, R. and Furlong, J. (2001) *Education, Reform and the State: Twenty-Five Years of Politics, Policy, and Practice*, London: Routledge Falmer.

Philpot, T. (2007) *Adoption: Changing Families, Changing Times*, London: Routledge.

Pollock, A. M. (2006) *NHS plc: The Privatisation of Our Health Care*, London: Verso Books.

Pratchett, L. (2000) *Renewing Local Democracy? The Modernisation Agenda in British Local Government*, London: Frank Cass.

Pugh, M. (2011) *Speak for Britain! A New History of the Labour Party*, London: Vintage.

R

Reiner, R. (2010) *The Politics of the Police*, 4th edn, Oxford: Oxford University Press.

Renwick, A. (2011) *A Citizen's Guide to Electoral Reform*, London: Biteback Publishing.

Ricketts, S. (2012) *Localism and Planning*, Haywards Heath: Bloomsbury Professional.

Rogers, R. and Walters, R. (2006) *How Parliament Works*, 6th edn, London: Longman.

Roy, D. (2005) *Liberals: A History of the Liberal and Liberal Democratic Parties*, London: Hambledon Continuum.

S

Sanders, A. (2010) *Criminal Justice*, 4th edn, London: LexisNexis UK.

Stallion, M. and Wall, D. S. (2000) *The British Police: Police Forces and Chief Officers 1829–2000*, London: M. R. Stallion.

Stevens, A. (2006) *Politico's Guide to Local Government*, 2nd edn, London: Politico's Publishing.

Stewart, J. (2003) *Modernising British Local Government: An Assessment of Labour's Reform Programme*, Basingstoke: Palgrave Macmillan.

Stiglitz, J. (2010) *Freefall: Free Markets and the Sinking of the Global Economy*, London: Penguin.

T

Turpin, C. and Tomkins, A. (2011) *British Government and the Constitution: Text and Materials*, 7th edn, Cambridge: Cambridge University Press.

W

Wadham, J., Griffiths J., and Harris, K. (2007) *Blackstone's Guide to the Freedom of Information Act 2000*, 3rd edn, Oxford: Oxford University Press.

Waters, I. and Duffield, B. (1994) *Entertainment, Arts, and Cultural Services*, London: Financial Times/ Prentice Hall.

Wilson, D. and Game, C. (2011) *Local Government in the United Kingdom*, 5th edn, Basingstoke: Palgrave Macmillan.

Wilson, D., Ashton, J., and Sharpe, D. (2001) *What Everyone in Britain Should Know about the Police*, 2nd edn, London: Blackstone Press.

Index

E